HANDBOOK OF REGULATORY AUTHORITIES

Handbook of Regulatory Authorities

Edited by

Martino Maggetti

Associate Professor of Political Science, University of Lausanne, Switzerland

Fabrizio Di Mascio

Professor of Political Science, University of Torino, Italy

Alessandro Natalini

Full Professor of Political Science, Lumsa University of Rome, Italy

EE Edward Elgar
PUBLISHING

Cheltenham, UK • Northampton, MA, USA

Published by
Edward Elgar Publishing Limited
The Lypiatts
15 Lansdown Road
Cheltenham
Glos GL50 2JA
UK

Edward Elgar Publishing, Inc.
William Pratt House
9 Dewey Court
Northampton
Massachusetts 01060
USA

A catalogue record for this book
is available from the British Library

Library of Congress Control Number: 2022938899

This book is available electronically in the **Elgar**online
Political Science and Public Policy subject collection
http://dx.doi.org/10.4337/9781839108990

ISBN 978 1 83910 898 3 (cased)
ISBN 978 1 83910 899 0 (eBook)

Printed and bound by CPI Group (UK) Ltd, Croydon, CR0 4YY

Contents

List of tables   viii
List of contributors   ix
Preface   xii
Acknowledgements   xiii

1   Introduction to the *Handbook of Regulatory Authorities*   1
     Martino Maggetti, Fabrizio Di Mascio and Alessandro Natalini

PART I   REGIONS

2   Tracing the development of U.S. independent regulators   10
     Christopher Carrigan and Mark Febrizio

3   Independent regulators in Europe   27
     David Coen and Andrew Tarrant

4   Independent regulatory agencies in Latin America   43
     Andrés Pavón Mediano and Camilo Ignacio González

5   Independent regulators in the Middle East   60
     Ahmed Badran

6   The age of regulatory agencies: tracking differences and similarities
     over countries and sectors   78
     Xavier Fernández-i-Marín, Jacint Jordana and David Levi-Faur

PART II   SECTORS AND TYPES

7   Central banks   96
     Clément Fontan and Antoine de Cabanes

8   Competition authorities   113
     Mattia Guidi

9   Data protection authorities under the EU General Data Protection
     Regulation – a new global benchmark   128
     Philip Schütz

10   Agencies regulating network services   146
     Matthias Finger

11   Agencies regulating risks   161
     Lorenzo Allio and Nicoletta Rangone

12   Anticorruption authorities   177
      Fabrizio Di Mascio, Martino Maggetti and Alessandro Natalini

PART III   CONCEPTUAL ISSUES

13   Political control of regulatory authorities   193
      Jennifer L. Selin

14   Regulatory independence and the quality of regulation   211
      Christel Koop and Jacint Jordana

15   Independent regulators in the post-delegation stage   227
      Martino Maggetti

PART IV   REPUTATION, PERFORMANCE AND CONTROL

16   Reputation and independent regulatory agencies   241
      Martin Lodge and Kai Wegrich

17   Accountability and regulatory authorities   255
      Sjors Overman, Thomas Schillemans and Machiel van der Heijden

18   Taking stock: strategic communication by regulatory agencies as a form
      of reputation management   273
      Moshe Maor

19   Managing the performance of regulatory agencies   285
      Cary Coglianese

20   Better regulation in the European Union   303
      Claire A. Dunlop and Claudio M. Radaelli

21   Better regulation in the United States   314
      Susan Dudley and Jerry Ellig

22   Judicial review of agency action in Europe   331
      Stéphanie De Somer, Ute Lettanie and Patricia Popelier

23   Judicial review of agency action in the United States   346
      Richard Murphy

PART V   BEYOND REGULATION

24   Agency capture   362
      Justin Rex

25   Regulatory agencies and agenda-setting: state of the art and new ways forward   379
      Edoardo Guaschino

26   Enforcement   394
      Miroslava Scholten

27 EU regulatory agencies   410
    Emmanuelle Mathieu

28 European regulatory networks: foundations and foresights   425
    Machiel van der Heijden and Kutsal Yesilkagit

29 Innovation and regulatory agencies   441
    Cristie Ford

30 Behavioural insights and regulatory authorities   457
    Kai Wegrich and Martin Lodge

31 AI algorithmic oversight: new frontiers in regulation   470
    Madalina Busuioc

32 Expertise and regulatory agencies   487
    Dovilė Rimkutė

Index   503

Tables

2.1	Statutory characteristics of independent regulatory agencies	17
9.1	Top-10 fines worldwide related to data protection violations (September 2021)	141
15.1	The principal–agent model in practice	230
19.1	Regulatory designs	290
24.1	Type and scope of capture	364
27.1	List of ERAs	411
32.1	Summary of organizational reputation dimensions	495

Contributors

Lorenzo Allio is the Owner of allio|rodrigo consulting and an Associate Lecturer at the University of Lausanne, Switzerland.

Ahmed Badran is an Associate Professor of Public Policy, Department Head of International Affairs, Qatar University, Qatar.

Madalina Busuioc is a Full Professor of Governance at Vrije Universiteit, Amsterdam, the Netherlands.

Christopher Carrigan is an Associate Professor of Public Policy and Public Administration at the George Washington University's Trachtenberg School and Co-Director of the GW Regulatory Studies Center, United States.

David Coen is a Professor of Public Policy and Director of the Global Governance Institute at University College London, United Kingdom.

Cary Coglianese is the Edward B. Shils Professor of Law, Professor of Political Science, and the Director of the Penn Program on Regulation at the University of Pennsylvania, United States.

Antoine de Cabanes is a PhD Researcher at UCLouvain, Belgium.

Stéphanie De Somer is an Associate Professor of Administrative Law at the University of Antwerp, Belgium, core member of the Centre of Excellence GOVTRUST, and a part-time Assistant Professor at the Vrije Universiteit Brussel, Belgium.

Fabrizio Di Mascio is a Professor of Political Science at the University of Torino, Italy.

Susan Dudley is Director of the George Washington University Regulatory Studies Center, and Distinguished Professor of Practice in GW's Trachtenberg School of Public Policy and Public Administration, United States.

Claire A. Dunlop is a Professor of Politics and Public Policy at the University of Exeter, United Kingdom.

Jerry Ellig was a Research Professor in the George Washington University Regulatory Studies Center, United States.

Mark Febrizio is a Senior Policy Analyst at the George Washington University Regulatory Studies Center, United States.

Xavier Fernández-i-Marín is a Ramón y Cajal fellow of Political Science at Universitat de Barcelona, Catalonia, Spain.

Matthias Finger is a Full Professor of Economics at Istanbul Technical University, Turkey and a Part-time Professor at the European University Institute, Italy.

Clément Fontan is a Professor of European Political Economy at UCLouvain/USL-B, Belgium and a Co-Director of the journal *Politique Européenne*, Belgium.

Cristie Ford is a Professor at the Peter A. Allard School of Law, University of British Columbia, Canada.

Camilo Ignacio González is an Assistant Professor at the Alberto Lladeras Carmago School of Government at Los Andes University, Colombia.

Edoardo Guaschino is a Postdoctoral Researcher at the Institute of Political Science at the University of Lausanne, Switzerland.

Mattia Guidi is an Assistant Professor of Political Science at the Department of Social, Political and Cognitive Sciences of the University of Siena, Italy.

Jacint Jordana is Professor of Political Science and Public Administration at the Universitat Pompeu Fabra, and Director of the Institut Barcelona d'Estudis Internacionals (IBEI), Spain.

Christel Koop is Reader in Political Economy at King's College London, United Kingdom.

Ute Lettanie is a PhD Researcher at the University of Antwerp, Belgium.

David Levi-Faur is a Professor of Political Science at the Department of Political Science and the School of Public Policy at the Hebrew of Jerusalem, Israel.

Martin Lodge is a Professor of Political Science and Public Policy and Co-Director of the Centre for Analysis of Risk and Regulation, London School of Economics and Political Science, United Kingdom.

Martino Maggetti is an Associate Professor of Political Science at the University of Lausanne, Switzerland.

Moshe Maor is a Professor of Political Science and Wolfson Family Chair Professor of Public Administration at the Hebrew University of Jerusalem, Israel.

Emmanuelle Mathieu is a Lecturer at the University of Lausanne, Switzerland.

Richard Murphy is the AT&T Professor of Law at the Texas Tech University School of Law, United States.

Alessandro Natalini is a Full Professor of Political Science at the Lumsa University of Rome, Italy.

Sjors Overman is an Assistant Professor of Public Administration at Utrecht University School of Governance, the Netherlands.

Andrés Pavón Mediano is a Researcher Fellow at the Faculty of Law at Alberto Hurtado University, Chile.

Patricia Popelier is a Full Professor of Constitutional Law at the University of Antwerp, Belgium, co-promoter of the Centre of Excellence GOVTRUST, and Senior Fellow at the University of Kent, Centre for Federal Studies, United Kingdom.

Claudio M. Radaelli is a Professor of Comparative Public Policy, School of Transnational Governance, European University Institute, Florence, Italy. On leave from School of Public Policy, University College London.

Nicoletta Rangone is a Full Professor of Administrative Law and Jean Monnet Professor on EU approach to better regulation at the LUMSA University, Rome, Italy.

Justin Rex is an Associate Professor of Political Science at Bowling Green State University, Bowling Green, Ohio, USA.

Dovilė Rimkutė is an Assistant Professor at the Institute of Public Administration, Leiden University, the Netherlands.

Thomas Schillemans is a Professor of Public Governance at Utrecht University School of Governance, the Netherlands.

Miroslava Scholten is an Associate Professor of EU Law Enforcement, Utrecht Centre for Regulation and Enforcement in Europe (RENFORCE), Utrecht University, the Netherlands.

Philip Schütz is a Doctoral Researcher at the University of Göttingen and a full-time Data Protection Coordinator at Mercedes-Benz.

Jennifer L. Selin is the Associate Director of the Carl Levin Center for Oversight and Democracy, United States.

Andrew Tarrant is a Director of European Affairs and Public Policy at Whitehouse Communications, United States.

Machiel van der Heijden is an Assistant Professor at the Utrecht School of Governance (USG) at Utrecht University, the Netherlands.

Kai Wegrich is a Professor of Public Administration and Public Policy at the Hertie School, Germany.

Kutsal Yesilkagit is a Professor of Public Administration at the Institute of Public Administration at Leiden University, the Netherlands.

Preface

Regulatory authorities – independent agencies in charge of regulating financial markets, telecom, energy, data protection, food safety, pharmaceuticals, and so forth – come in an impressive variety of shapes and colors, depending on the policy sector, the country of origin, the level of governance, and their evolution over time. Their sheer numerical growth and the continuing quantitative and qualitative expansion of their regulatory reach towards new areas, such as health risks and artificial intelligence applications, epitomizes their crucial role in modern governance. However, writing a handbook on regulatory authorities is not only about mapping independent regulators as the institutional cornerstone of regulatory governance. It also involves thinking more generally about the role of political authority in contemporary societies and the structural transformation of democratic policymaking. Through these at-arm-length institutions, the modern state increases its steering capacity over society, but it does so in a peculiar way, that is, by acting more and more at a distance. The delegation of regulatory powers to these independent bodies provides a functional solution to the need for ensuring the supervision, assessment, refinement, and enforcement of rules, but it also opens up a number of trade-offs, as regulators have to find a balance between their main properties and attributes, such as credibility, expertise, formal and de facto independence, accountability, and performance. How do they operate these balancing processes, and whether they succeed, constitute key empirical questions. We took the challenge to account for this complexity, in a way that is necessarily selective, but, we hope, nonetheless comprehensive and focused on the most pressing issues. Mirroring the regulatory governance studies community, our volume is not only embedded in the political science literature, but it is also explicitly interdisciplinary, including contributions from legal, sociological, and economic perspectives. To take stock, and to look forward, we rely on a coherent mix of leading scholars in the field.

Acknowledgements

At Edward Elgar Publishing, we thank Alex Pettifer for contacting us with the first idea on editing such an ambitious volume and for his assistance with the set-up of the book, and Alexandra O'Connell for her encouragement, support all along the writing process, and patience with the finalization of the project. We also thank Joyce Carraud, whose help with the assembling and polishing of the manuscript has been invaluable. We also gratefully acknowledge the financial support of the Institute of Political Studies (IEP) at the University of Lausanne. This book also benefitted from exchanges of ideas with the scientific and practitioner community around the Osservatorio AIR in Rome. Last but not least, we are deeply grateful to the authors of the chapters of this volume, who embarked in this project with enthusiasm and delivered a vivid, rich, and lively set of contributions, making, we believe, a long-lasting impact on the field.

1. Introduction to the *Handbook of Regulatory Authorities*

Martino Maggetti, Fabrizio Di Mascio and Alessandro Natalini

THE SPREAD OF REGULATORS

Regulatory authorities – that is, independent regulatory agencies – are structurally disaggregated public sector organizations entrusted with specialized regulatory tasks. Their organizational model has risen to prominence and diffused worldwide in the last decades (see Figure 1.1). Examples are the Food and Drug Administration (FDA) in the U.S., the French Autorité de Régulation des Communications Électroniques et des Postes (ARCEP), the Italian Autorità Nazionale Anticorruzione (ANAC), the Telecom Regulatory Authority of India (TRAI), or the Agência Nacional de Energia Elétrica in Brazil. Besides sector-specific regulators, economy-wide competition authorities and central banks are included in this definition, as they also possess the key traits of independent regulatory agencies insofar as they exert regulatory authority while being insulated from direct political control (Thatcher 2002; Gilardi 2007).

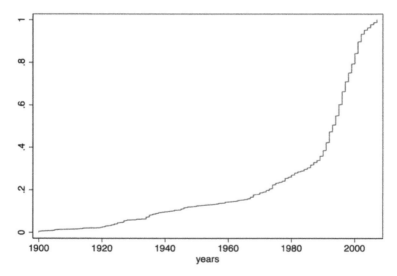

Source: Own calculations based on the dataset compiled by Jordana, Levi-Faur and i Marín (2011), covering 15 sectors in 45 countries (19 Latin American countries and all 30 OECD countries).

Figure 1.1   *The diffusion of independent regulators (cumulative percentages)*

Governments have delegated fundamental regulatory powers to regulators in countless areas, ranging from utilities and finance to food safety, therapeutic products and environmental protection. They are in charge of a wide range of regulatory tasks, such as conformity assessments, licensing, rule refinement, standard setting, monitoring, and eventually sanctioning those being regulated in case of non-compliance. They thereby cumulate executive, legislative, and judicial functions. At the same time, they typically enjoy a certain degree of formal independence from elected politicians, which materializes in statutory prescriptions and organizational features such as those granting policy, managerial, and financial autonomy to these agencies (Maggetti and Verhoest 2014). As such, independent regulatory agencies constitute the institutional cornerstone of the regulatory state (Gilardi 2008), an expression that epitomizes the shift towards increasing reliance on regulation as a mode of governance (Jordana and Levi-Faur 2004). Whilst being considered essential for granting impartial and nonpartisan regulation that is expected to be consistent over the long run, and for providing expert advice to policymakers (Majone 1996), they are not without criticism. In particular, they have been criticized for exerting considerable public authority whereas lacking of direct democratic responsiveness and control, creating thus a democratic deficit in the regulatory state (Vibert 2007).

Research on independent regulatory agencies is entering into a mature stage. Therefore, it is time to take stock and discuss the ways forward. These are the primary goals of this volume, whose content is briefly presented later on in this introductory piece. Each chapter is structured along two parts: foundations and foresight. The first part lays out the fundamental concepts and theoretical and empirical achievements on the topic covered by the chapter, while the second considers the main issues, challenges, and questions that are emerging in each area of research. We approach the study of regulatory governance by following the way paved by previous contributions – namely those collected in the *Oxford Handbook of Regulation* edited by Baldwin, Cave and Lodge (2010) and in the Edward Elgar *Handbook on the Politics of Regulation* edited by Levi-Faur (2011a); however, we do so from a quite different angle. We put regulators themselves at the forefront, as organizations that evolve in relation with their organizational environment, and, at the same time, as institutions that lie at the center of regulatory regimes, shaping regulatory policies and being in turn reshaped by them. Before moving forward, in the next section we outline four main developments pointing to how the reach and the scope of independent regulatory agencies expanded and transformed over time.

THE EVOLUTION OF REGULATORS

The first development concerns the geographical spread of regulators, as anticipated with Figure 1.1. The earliest public sector organization recognized as a regulatory agency has been the U.S. Interstate Commerce Commission (ICC) established by the Congress in 1887 to regulate railroads, and later also in charge of motor carriers, inland waterways, and oil companies (Best, Teske and Mintrom 1997). At the outset, regulatory agencies were considered as a peculiar feature characterizing the U.S. policy system (Moran 2002) – with the partial exception of banking, financial, and competition regulators that were relatively common elsewhere as well. Then, the rise of the regulatory state in Europe since the 1980s has been associated with privatization and liberalization reforms that implied a considerable widening of the scope of regulators to promote competition at the national and European levels (Majone 1994, 1997).

The number of regulatory agencies started to grow considerably in other regions with a small delay, especially in Latin America since the mid-1990s (Jordana and Levi-Faur 2005) and in South and East Asia from the early 2000s (Dubash and Morgan 2012; Ohnesorge 2016). It is also worth noting that, especially after the 2000s, regulatory agencies are also mushrooming at the supranational level, namely in the European Union, where they configure multilevel regulatory regimes (Mathieu et al. 2020). As a result, agencification can be seen as a global macro-trend towards the increasing institutionalization of regulatory governance, which is however displaying considerable cross-country and cross-sectoral variation (Braithwaite 2008; Levi-Faur 2011b).

Second, regulatory agencies extended their reach by colonizing more and more sectors. The first wave of regulatory expansion has been oriented towards market and economic regulation, mainly focusing on re-regulation after the privatization and liberalization of former public utilities, on the enforcement of antitrust and competition law, and on the prudential and systemic risk regulation of the financial and banking sector (Carpenter 2001). The second wave, which started in the U.S. from the 1960s onwards and has been subsequently mainly led by the European Union, was more geared towards social regulation and risk regulation, including in particular environmental protection, public health, and safety at work (Moran 2002). Nowadays, we are in the middle of a third wave, which is characterized by the need for developing a regulatory response to emerging digital technologies and new threats associated with them. This wave started with regulatory efforts for dealing with electronic data protection (Newman 2008) and it is currently deployed to fill in the regulatory void in critical issues for society and democracy such as the use of big data, algorithms in the public sector and in the private sector, cryptocurrencies, blockchains, and artificial intelligence applications (Yeung and Lodge 2019).

Third, and related to the previous point, the rationale for relying on regulatory governance evolved over time. The delegation of public authority to formally independent regulators has been firstly motivated by the functional need of increasing the credibility in the time-consistency of regulatory policies in front of market actors (Gilardi 2002). However, credible commitments became less relevant for regulators whose regulatory activity does not have a primarily economic goal. Social and risk regulation has a wider scope, combining market, technical, societal, and public service aims, producing an entanglement which can result in trade-offs between these competences. Balancing these different goals requires a great deal of sector-specific expertise and the use of knowledge in regulatory policy. In turn, knowledge is a crucial resource that is expected to percolate from regulators into the policy process, whereby policymakers are confronted with increasingly complex policy problems (Bawn 1995; Ossege 2016). Figure 1.2 summarizes these developments, which will be tackled in detail in the chapters of this volume.

Fourth, following a logic of bureaucratic expansion and mission creep, regulatory agencies acquired competences over time that trespass and extend beyond their regulatory tasks in a strict sense. As noted by Carpenter, instead of remaining mere "agents" in charge of implementing rules and regulations, regulatory agencies became players in the "game" of policy creation (Carpenter 2001:116). Evidence from European countries has supported this point by showing that regulatory agencies actively participated in agenda setting and policy formulation in legislative processes that fall into their areas of expertise (Bach 2012; Maggetti 2009). Their unique technical expertise allows them to become a central actor in the regulatory regime and an inescapable participant to policymaking (Littoz-Monnet 2014).

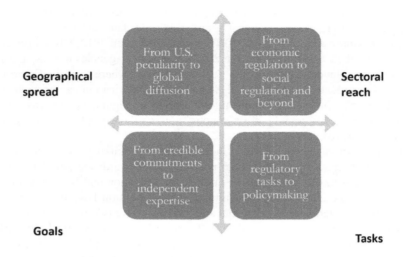

Figure 1.2   The evolution of regulators

THE CONTRIBUTIONS TO THIS VOLUME

The first part of this volume focuses on the development of independent regulators in different regions across the world. Carrigan and Febrizio's contribution (Chapter 2) traces the historical establishment of U.S. independent regulators until the current state of affairs characterized by political polarization. Chapter 3, written by Coen and Tarrant, focuses on regulators in Europe, centering on their multilevelness and on the progressive emergence of new organizational forms. Independent regulators in Latin America are investigated in the fourth chapter by Pavón Mediano and González Becerra, with a particular attention to the regional political context. The case of the Middle-East is dealt with in Badran's chapter, the fifth of this volume, pointing to the issues related to the transplantation of a foreign organizational model into another type of political system. Lastly, Fernández-i-Marín, Jordana and Levi-Faur offer a systematic comparative outlook to regulatory agencies' differences and similarities over countries and sectors in Chapter 6. All in all, it appears that regulators flourish and thrive in a wide range of varieties, some of which configure truly innovative governance arrangements.

Part II comprises contributions on different types of regulators in various sectors. The seventh chapter, written by Fontan and de Cabanes, deals with the specificities of central banks. Competition authorities as economy-wide regulators are treated in Chapter 8 by Guidi. The growing importance and peculiar nature of data protection authorities is outlined in Schütz's contribution in Chapter 9. The tenth contribution by Finger relates to agencies regulating network services, that is, utility regulators. Agencies regulating risks are considered by Allio and Rangone in Chapter 11, while anticorruption regulators are examined by Di Mascio, Maggetti and Natalini in Chapter 12. The main lesson from this section is that regulators differ crucially from sector to sector, and yet a powerful tendency is observed, towards the attribution of more regulatory powers in new areas to regulators, especially those concerned with social regulation.

Part III offers a discussion of three key conceptual issues. The first corresponds to the patterns of agencies' politicization and it is discussed by Selin in Chapter 13. Koop and Jordana investigate regulatory independence and the quality of regulation in Chapter 14. Chapter 15, written by Maggetti, examines the role of agencies in the post-delegation stage. This conceptual overview points to the persisting challenges associated with the raison d'être of independent regulators, that is, their independence. Balancing expertise, political responsiveness, accountability, and insulation from politics requires constant work and reflexivity, like the weaving of Penelope's shroud.

In Part IV, our contributors investigate reputation, performance and control as the key attributes of regulators shaping their relations with other actors. The sixteenth chapter, written by Lodge and Wegrich, outlines what a reputation-based perspective adds to our understanding of regulatory agencies. Overman, Schillemans and van der Heijden present the debates surrounding the accountability of agencies in Chapter 17, with a special focus on relational and perceptual accountability. Maor's chapter, the eighteenth of this volume, considers the issues related to strategic communication by regulatory agencies. A discussion about managing the performance of regulatory agencies is put forward by Coglianese in Chapter 19. Regulatory impact assessment in the European Union and in the United States is described by Dunlop and Radaelli, and, respectively by Dudley and Ellig in their two chapters. Similarly, the judicial review of agency action in Europe is examined by Popelier, De Somer and Lettanie in Chapter 22, while it is analyzed by Murphy in the following chapter as regards the United States. As a result, it appears that multiple factors interact in co-determining the reputation, performance, and control of regulators, creating a complex system which may eventually raise the uncertainty and indeterminacy of the governance arrangement.

Part V presents the most up-to-date academic debates on the role of independent regulators beyond their activity of regulation. Chapter 24 by Rex deals with agency capture. The role of regulators in agenda setting is outlined by Guaschino in Chapter 25. Scholten tackles the issue of enforcement in Chapter 26 with a special focus on the European level. EU agencies and their dynamics are described by Mathieu in Chapter 27, and regulatory networks are presented by van der Heijden and Yesilkagit in Chapter 28. The twenty-ninth chapter by Ford deals with innovation as a priority and at the same time as a challenge for regulators. Behavioral insights are outlined in the thirtieth chapter co-authored by Wegrich and Lodge by focusing on nudges in the field of economic regulation. Busuioc, in Chapter 31, presents algorithmic oversight as the new frontier of regulatory accountability. The question of expertise with reference to regulatory agencies is investigated by Rimkutė in the last chapter of this volume, by connecting it to the reputational approach. To sum up, it can be observed that regulators do not evolve in a void, but they unfold within crowded regulatory spaces, by developing cooperative and conflicting relationships with various types of actors, whereby reputation stands out again as a crucial issue.

WAYS FORWARD

The emerging picture is that we still live in what has been called "the golden age of regulation" (Levi-Faur and Jordana 2005), albeit with some crucial twists. Regulation is the increasingly dominant mode of political governance, embodied by the ubiquitousness of regulatory agencies. In turn, these expert-based public sector organizations entrusted with regulatory tasks and enjoying some degree of formal independence from elected politicians still represent the take-for-granted model for ensuring the implementation of regulatory governance. As a consequence, regulators at different levels of governance are deepening their grip on the regulated sectors and, at the same time, they are extending their regulatory reach towards new directions, such as emerging societal risks and new technologies. In doing so, regulators are generally considered apt in ensuring their day-to-day regulatory activities, namely through regulation by information and regulatory oversight. Nonetheless, while achieving even more central positions in regulatory regimes, regulators also experience growing pressures. The contributions to this volume point to several of the challenges regulatory agencies are facing. Three of them stand out as particularly relevant.

First, regulators appear as particularly sensitive to reputational concerns, and, thereby, potentially vulnerable to reputational threats. Agencies live by their reputation, which is actively cultivated and managed by regulators. Reputation, in turn, is a key attribute that shapes their regulatory power and their independence in practice. However, against the background of mega crises such as the 2007–8 financial crisis, the COVID-19 pandemic, or the climate emergency, regulators are under strain as politico-administrative relations become more politicized and potentially more conflictual, among different public sector organizations and with respect to their political principal. In this context, blame shifting is a risky strategy for policymakers as repeated blame deflection towards regulators may damage their reputation and ultimately imperil their organizational survival. What is more, their reputation is potentially undermined by quick, large-scale technological changes that are also driven and exploited by large corporations. The case of the (non)regulation of Big Tech companies illustrates the difficulty of formulating and applying an appropriate regulatory framework to these areas, because of their highly technical nature, quick evolution, global character, and the asymmetry of information on the data that are collected and the algorithms that are used by these companies.

Second, the independence of regulators is still bearing open questions. Not only formal independence evolves over time, and it may diverge from their independence in practice. It also appears that their statutory insulation from political pressures might not work when it is mostly needed, that is, when a hostile government strives to curtail their regulatory action. In particular, strong populist pressures can be directed towards regulators as expert-based bodies that exert an intermediation function. When compared to other targets of populist pressures such as parliaments or courts, regulators are more at risk as they rely on a limited stock of democratic legitimacy. Being unelected, they cannot benefit from input legitimacy as parliaments do. Respectively, their regulatory powers cover a wider array of features – from advice, rule refinement, monitoring, certification, enforcement, and adjudication – than those attributed to courts, which are clearly delineated and neatly demarcated from other manifestations of public authority. This state of affairs exposes regulators to even more populist criticisms.

Third – and this is an even more transversal issue – regulators appear as ill-equipped when dealing with emerging multilevel issues. Independent regulatory agencies are born in nation states. As a response to the processes of internationalization and supranational (mainly EU) integration, they moved upwards and increased their transnational interactions specifically through regulatory networks. However, regulation is still largely rooted in domestic institutions, whereas those more in need for regulatory responses correspond to global corporations such as large digital platforms. Technological innovation, data protection, and artificial intelligence constitute the big pending issues as they change both the object of regulation (the criteria, the modalities, and the responsibilities of the choices made by those being regulated) and, at the same time, the regulatory style, the information required by regulators, the ways of monitoring behavior, the procedures for risk assessment, and so on.

As a reaction to these challenges, regulators may be able to react and evolve again in unforeseen directions. They could recenter their functioning around their independence as their purpose and mainspring, by withdrawing in the ivory tower at the domestic level. In that way, they would take care of offering expert-based advice and ensuring the technical application of rules, while refraining from taking part in agenda-setting, policy formulation, and direct sanctioning. If they do so, however, they could be at risk of irrelevance and of being sidelined by other actors. Alternatively, they could step into the arena and play the political game more explicitly, for instance with respect to the need for taking action against pressing problems such as the climate emergency. They could also strengthen their international regulatory cooperation and be more proactive in their strategies towards the news media. In this case, however, politicization could backfire, and further undermine their legitimacy. At the end of the day, rather than choosing a strict alternative, it is probably again a question of finding a context-sensitive strategy for balancing the existing trade-offs, so as to provisionally achieve an equilibrium that is necessarily dynamic.

REFERENCES

Bach, Tobias. 2012. "The involvement of agencies in policy formulation: Explaining variation in policy autonomy of federal agencies in Germany." *Policy and Society* 31(3):211–22.

Baldwin, Robert, Martin Cave, and Martin Lodge (Eds.). 2010. *The Oxford handbook of regulation.* Oxford: Oxford University Press.

Bawn, Kathleen. 1995. "Political control versus expertise: Congressional choices about administrative procedures." *American Political Science Review* 89(1):62–73.

Best, Samuel, Paul Teske, and Michael Mintrom. 1997. "Terminating the oldest living regulator: The death of the Interstate Commerce Commission." *International Journal of Public Administration* 20(12):2067–96.

Braithwaite, J. 2008. *Regulatory capitalism: How it works, ideas for making it work better.* Cheltenham, UK and Northampton, MA, USA: Edward Elgar Publishing.

Carpenter, Daniel P. 2001. The forging of bureaucratic autonomy: Reputations, networks, and policy innovation in executive agencies, 1862–1928. Princeton, N.J.: Princeton University Press.

Dubash, Navroz K., and Bronwen Morgan. 2012. "Understanding the rise of the regulatory state of the South." *Regulation & Governance* 6(3):261–81.

Gilardi, Fabrizio. 2002. "Policy credibility and delegation to independent regulatory agencies: A comparative empirical analysis." *Journal of European Public Policy* 9(6):873–93.

Gilardi, Fabrizio. 2007. "The same, but different: Central banks, regulatory agencies, and the politics of delegation to independent authorities." *Comparative European Politics*, 5(3):303–27.

Gilardi, Fabrizio. 2008. *Delegation in the regulatory state: Independent regulatory agencies in Western Europe.* Cheltenham, UK and Northampton, MA, USA: Edward Elgar Publishing.

Jordana, Jacint, and David Levi-Faur. 2004. The politics of regulation: Institutions and regulatory reforms for the age of governance. Cheltenham, UK and Northampton, MA, USA: Edward Elgar Publishing.

Jordana, Jacint, and David Levi-Faur. 2005. "The diffusion of regulatory capitalism in Latin America: Sectoral and national channels in the making of a new order." *The ANNALS of the American Academy of Political and Social Science* 598(1):102.

Jordana, Jacint, David Levi-Faur, and Xavier Fernandes i Marín. 2011. "The global diffusion of regulatory agencies." *Comparative Political Studies* 44(10):1343–69.

Levi-Faur, David (Ed.). 2011a. *Handbook on the politics of regulation.* Cheltenham, UK and Northampton, MA, USA: Edward Elgar Publishing.

Levi-Faur, David. 2011b. "Regulation and regulatory governance," pp. 1–25 in *Handbook on the politics of regulation*, edited by David Levi-Faur. Cheltenham, UK and Northampton, MA, USA: Edward Elgar Publishing.

Levi-Faur, David, and Jacint Jordana. 2005. "The Making of a New Regulatory Order." *Annals, AAPSS* 598:6–9.

Littoz-Monnet, Annabelle. 2014. "The role of independent regulators in policy making: Venue-shopping and framing strategies in the EU regulation of old wives cures." *European Journal of Political Research* 53(1):1–17.

Maggetti, Martino. 2009. "The role of independent regulatory agencies in policy-making: A comparative analysis." *Journal of European Public Policy* 16(3):445–65.

Maggetti, Martino, and Koen Verhoest. 2014. "Unexplored aspects of bureaucratic autonomy: A state of the field and ways forward." *International Review of Administrative Sciences* 88(2):239–256.

Majone, Giandomenico. 1994. "The rise of the regulatory state in Europe." *West European Politics* 17(3):77–101.

Majone, Giandomenico. 1996. "Temporal consistency and policy credibility: Why democracies need non-majoritarian institutions." EUI Working Paper SPS 96(57).

Majone, Giandomenico. 1997. "From the positive to the regulatory state: Causes and consequences of changes in the mode of governance." *Journal of Public Policy* 17(2):139–67.

Mathieu, Emmanuelle, Joery Matthys, Koen Verhoest, and Jan Rommel. 2020. "Multilevel regulatory coordination: The interplay between European Union, federal and regional regulatory agencies." *Public Policy and Administration* 36(3):343–60.

Moran, Michael. 2002. "Review article: Understanding the regulatory state." *British Journal of Political Science* 32:391–413.

Newman, Abraham. 2008. *Protectors of privacy: Regulating personal data in the global economy*. Ithaca, NY: Cornell University Press.

Ohnesorge, John. 2016. "The regulatory state in East Asia," pp. 92–106 in *Comparative Law and Regulation: Understanding the Global Regulatory Process*, edited by Francesca Bignami and David Zaring. Cheltenham, UK and Northampton, MA, USA: Edward Elgar Publishing.

Ossege, Christoph. 2016. *European regulatory agencies in EU decision-making: between expertise and influence*. Dordrecht: Springer.

Thatcher, Mark. 2002. "Regulation after delegation: Independent regulatory agencies in Europe." *Journal of European Public Policy*, 9(6):954–72.

Vibert, Frank. 2007. *The rise of the unelected: Democracy and the new separation of powers*. Cambridge: Cambridge University Press.

Yeung, Karen, and Martin Lodge. 2019. *Algorithmic regulation*. Oxford: Oxford University Press.

PART I

REGIONS

2. Tracing the development of U.S. independent regulators

Christopher Carrigan and Mark Febrizio

INTRODUCTION

Independent regulators have long played a critical role in federal rulemaking in the United States. Moreover, some of the key theories and insights that form the body of scholarship studying regulatory policy and process find their foundations specifically in the study of U.S. independent regulators. Yet perhaps because their development has been more associated with convention than any preconceived plan, the distinction between them and their counterparts in the executive branch remains blurred, even now.

In this chapter, we trace the development of independent regulators in the U.S., examine how independent agencies are commonly distinguished from executive branch agencies, and discuss difficulties with these conventional categorizations. Given their relatively long history in regulating U.S. markets, we further highlight some fundamental themes in regulatory scholarship that have emerged from the study of independent regulatory bodies, such as regulatory capture theory and the deregulation movement.

In so doing, the chapter considers contemporary challenges associated with the study of U.S. independent regulators by exploring research on alternative ways to evaluate independence and the implications of exempting independent regulators from centralized regulatory review requirements. We also highlight areas where additional systematic work is needed to deepen our understanding of U.S. independent regulators. Continued efforts to consider the implications for regulatory performance and accountability of those characteristics that distinguish independent regulators from other agencies provide good reason to believe that their study, just as it did in the past, can provide an impetus for ideas that will propel regulatory scholarship in the future.

DEFINING U.S. INDEPENDENT REGULATORS

The 1995 Paperwork Reduction Act (PRA) presents what is arguably the clearest articulation of which agencies qualify to be called U.S. independent regulators, listing 19 agencies specifically considered "independent regulatory agencies" (44 U.S.C. 3502(5)). That said, the notion of the U.S. independent regulator long predates the PRA, emerging as early as the late nineteenth century. In reality, independent regulators came about less as an intentional category of agencies and more as a group of agencies sharing a common legal status but a varied set of statutory and structural characteristics.

Still, where an agency falls in the categorization has significant implications for how it operates in relation to political entities. The current arrangement creates a functional distinction between independent regulators and agencies within the executive branch. Broadly, the U.S.

federal administrative state is divided into the Executive Office of the President (EOP), the executive departments whose heads are members of the president's cabinet, and independent agencies. The EOP, executive departments like the Department of the Interior, and their subunits such as the Bureau of Land Management are considered to be under presidential control. In contrast, the independent regulatory agencies are seen as "shielded from the control of elected officials" and do not cleanly fall under the purview of any of the three branches of government (Selin & Lewis 2018, p. 10).

U.S. independent regulators differ from regulatory agencies in the executive branch in terms of the extent to which they retain independence from political influence. The application of the title, independent regulatory agency, has propagated a dichotomy in how political oversight is conducted. As one example, whereas executive departments and their subunits submit their rules to the Office of Information and Regulatory Affairs (OIRA) within the Office of Management and Budget (OMB) for centralized clearance, independent regulators do not (Executive Order 12866).

In addition to being distinct from executive branch regulators, independent regulators are also distinguished from another description of independence in the U.S. federal government, that being agencies considered independent because they do not have cabinet representation. The independent agency designation is broader in that it also includes agencies that are not regulators, perhaps because their statutes do not authorize them to promulgate rules (Selin & Lewis 2018). As a result, most independent regulatory agencies also fall within the broader categorization. Still, this is not always true. For example, the Office of the Comptroller of the Currency is defined by the PRA as an independent regulatory agency, but it is not considered an independent agency because it resides in the Department of the Treasury.

The language of the PRA specifically focuses on independent regulatory agencies as a distinct group, rather than independent agencies more generally (44 U.S.C. 3502(5)). The implication is that independent agencies that engage in the rulemaking process play a particular role in the U.S. federal government. Of course, Congress can still delegate new rulemaking authority to those independent agencies currently without it. However, the absence of regulatory authority for certain agencies is an important reminder that independent regulators cannot simply be defined as agencies that do not reside within an executive department.

FOUNDATIONS: HISTORY AND FEATURES OF U.S. INDEPENDENT REGULATORS

Current policies and practices governing independent regulators have emerged through a combination of functional, legal, and political realities. Over multiple decades, contributions to the scholarly literature have demonstrated how understanding the history of U.S. independent regulators is essential to grasp the contingent nature of their independence.

Early History

In the modern U.S. federal government, a variety of agencies possess regulatory authority, including those that reside within cabinet departments like the Department of the Treasury. However, while some of these departments have existed since the late eighteenth century, their rulemaking authority only came later, as regulation was largely conducted by state-level agencies around that time (Bernstein 1955).

Established through the Interstate Commerce Act of 1887, scholars generally consider the Interstate Commerce Commission (ICC) to be the first independent regulator at the federal level in the U.S. (Wilson 1975). Congress established the ICC to regulate common carriers, particularly focusing on railroad rates. Although commissioners were appointed by the president with Senate approval, the president could only remove them "for inefficiency, neglect of duty, or malfeasance in office" (Pub. L. 49–104)—provisions that have come to be associated with "for-cause" removal. Notably, the commission's independence was not discussed during the hearings and debates leading up to the Act (Bernstein 1955). Rather, the purpose of these structural features was to promote expertise and impartial decision-making relative to insulating the ICC from presidential oversight (Datla & Revesz 2013). In fact, the Act itself initially placed the ICC under the control of the Secretary of the Interior, and the decision to move it outside the department two years later was not motivated by any effort to make it independent from the executive branch (Breger & Edles 2000).

Nevertheless, the ICC's structural features served as a template for future independent regulators (Wilson 1975). The Progressive movement of the early twentieth century recognized that there was value in a governmental organization free from politics and so encouraged structural independence for subsequent agencies (Breger & Edles 2000). This approach can be seen quite clearly in the 1914 creation of the Federal Trade Commission (FTC), which was intended to remedy perceived deficiencies in how the Sherman Act was enforced by the Department of Justice (DOJ) and the courts (Massel 1961). Supporters of a new antitrust commission leveraged the Progressive perspective, along with the need to insulate antitrust enforcement from partisanship within the DOJ, to justify creating the FTC as an independent regulator (Breger & Edles 2000). Yet the FTC was certainly not the only agency created with this perspective in mind. The ICC's structure also influenced how the agencies emerging from the New Deal, such as the National Labor Relations Board and the Securities and Exchange Commission (SEC), were designed (Jaffe 1954; Datla & Revesz 2013).

Independent Regulators Become a Distinct Category

While independent regulatory commissions were already the primary instrument for regulating business before the end of the Great Depression, the New Deal fueled the additional growth of administrative agencies through broad delegations of authority from Congress that gave agency officials substantial discretion in the areas they regulated (Kagan 2001). These statutory delegations were paired with structural protections that shielded independent commissions, at least to a degree, from presidential control. Moreover, court decisions supplemented these structural protections with constitutional ones (Breger & Edles 2000). In particular, the 1935 court case *Humphrey's Executor v. United States* solidified the status of independent regulators as distinct from executive branch agencies and positioned for-cause removal as the key element distinguishing them from their departmental counterparts (25 U.S. 602).

In *Humphrey's Executor*, the Supreme Court concluded that William E. Humphrey, who was appointed FTC commissioner by President Hoover to a seven-year term, could not be removed by President Roosevelt except if it were motivated by one of the causes named in the Federal Trade Commission Act. The opinion of the court drew a distinction between "purely executive officers" from a unit of an executive department and an administrative body created by Congress like the FTC (25 U.S. 628 (1935)). The decision supported the notion that the FTC might be more accurately considered a quasi-legislative or quasi-judicial agency, operating independently of executive control. It further established that Congress had a constitutional prerogative to limit presidential authority to remove agency leadership. Thus, both the constitutional status of independence and the classification of regulators as either independent or executive are generally believed to have originated from *Humphrey's Executor* (Datla & Revesz 2013).

Around the same time that agencies, both within the executive branch and outside of it, gained prominence and increasingly engaged in rulemaking during the 1930s and 1940s, academic and policy research began to levy criticisms and propose reforms to administrative regulatory functions. These critiques largely focused on independent regulators. From the 1930s to the 1970s, no fewer than five government reports prescribed reforms for independent regulatory commissions without offering similar recommendations for regulatory programs in executive agencies (Bernstein 1972; McFarland 1961). Similarly, scholarly research on regulation also focused more attention on independent commissions relative to departmental regulatory programs. This asymmetric focus likely deepened the dichotomy between the two categories of regulators, even as scholars acknowledged that independent and executive branch regulators shared similar functions and problems (Massel 1961).

Research Insights Rooted in the Study of Independent Regulators

One consequence of the disproportionate attention paid to independent commissions in the formative scholarship focused on U.S. regulation is that some of the foundational insights from this literature have their roots in the study of independent regulators specifically. Perhaps the most prominent is the theory of regulatory capture, which posits that regulatory bodies may be influenced by and serve the interests of regulated entities or industries, rather than serving the public interest or abiding by statutory mandates (Carpenter & Moss 2014). While broadly rooted in an earlier literature, the development of modern capture literature focused on independent regulators (Novak 2014).

One early study of capture can be found in Samuel Huntington's (1952) account of the ICC, who he argued had become increasingly dependent on the railroad industry for its support. This alienated other interests and caused the ICC to act in ways that were primarily favorable to the railroads themselves. Focusing on a broader set of independent regulators, Bernstein's life cycle of regulatory commissions—from gestation through youth to maturity and, ultimately, old age—contained another expression of the capture phenomenon, delineating how independent regulators could slowly succumb to serving the interests of the industries they regulate (1955).

While these early critiques of independent commissions were characterized by some as a campaign by political scientists (Jaffe 1956), separately economists were also beginning to question the effectiveness of regulation to address monopoly power, particularly in utility industries (Stigler & Friedland 1962; Demsetz 1968). Extending this idea, George Stigler (1971) challenged the public interest view of regulation and theorized that the presence of regulation in various industries could be attributed to interest groups employing government to protect themselves from competition (Carrigan & Coglianese 2015). Although his theory of regulatory capture was not specifically tied to independent commissions, Stigler (1971) predominantly focused on examples of industry-specific regulation managed by these entities and forms of economic regulation that were largely within the purview of the independent regulators. He concluded that the way to avoid capture at an agency like the ICC would be to change its sources of political support and alter the incentives of its commissioners (Stigler 1971). Ultimately, these pioneering studies focusing on the capture of independent regulators spurred an enormous literature examining the application of the concept to a wide array of regulatory contexts.

Interestingly, the emergence of the capture literature, whose roots were in the study of independent regulators, coincided with a shift toward regulating through the executive departments. As regulatory functions proliferated, departments, relative to independent regulators, assumed additional responsibilities (Massel 1961). Specifically, the next wave in the development of the U.S. regulatory state in the latter part of the 1960s included major delegations to executive departments as opposed to independent commissions. The laws achieving these ends included the 1965 Water Quality Act, 1965 Motor Vehicle Air Pollution Control Act, and 1966 National Traffic and Motor Vehicle Safety Act (Wilson 1975).

This regulatory transformation altered the traditional model that used commissions to regulate specific industries to a structure where regulatory responsibilities were assigned to federal agencies with a broader scope of jurisdiction and an emphasis on national objectives (Weidenbaum 1978). In conjunction with this change, the focus on economic regulation, including price controls and entry restrictions, that characterized the responsibilities of independent regulators was supplanted by consideration of different societal problems. These included environmental pollution, unsafe products, hazardous and discriminatory working conditions, and exploitative financial products—a collection now referred to as social regulation (Dudley 2022).

The growth of risk regulation, another regulatory categorization with its own distinct paradigm, also represented a move away from the prior mode of economic regulation. Risk regulation focuses on multiple areas of potential risk (e.g., environmental health, occupational hazards, and vehicle safety) and can take several forms, including prohibitions, reducing risks to the lowest feasible level, eliminating "significant" risks, or balancing the benefits and costs of marginal reductions of risk (Majone 2010). In contrast to traditional forms of economic regulation, risk regulation incorporates a scientific component, risk assessment, in addition to its policy component, risk management (Pollak 1996). Initially, risk regulation was handled by agencies within executive departments that dealt with health, safety, and environmental quality (Breyer 1984). However, independent commissions formed in the 1970s, such as the Consumer Product Safety Commission and the Nuclear Regulatory Commission, were granted authorities to address regulatory challenges distinct from the traditional independent commissions.

Perhaps in response to this shifting landscape, the intellectual and policy debate of the 1970s moved toward greater consideration of deregulation, a debate that was firmly focused on the independent commissions as well (Dudley 2015). In fact, much of the research highlighted by Susan Dudley and Jerry Ellig in Chapter 21 of this volume assessing the effects of deregulation on industry performance has concentrated on areas overseen by independent regulators (Winston 1993). For example, deregulation in contexts like surface freight transportation and airlines centered around creating competition in markets formerly overseen by independent commissions including the ICC and Civil Aeronautics Board. Similarly, railroad regulation was also rolled back, and although the ICC still retained control of rail for a period, the agency was completely disbanded in 1995 and its remaining regulatory responsibilities were shifted to the Surface Transportation Board (Pub. L. 104–88).[1]

Recent History

In contrast to the deregulation movement that focused primarily on disbanding those agencies involved in transportation, the Great Recession beginning in 2007 was the impetus for the creation of as well as expanded authority for certain independent regulators charged with overseeing financial transactions. For example, the Federal Housing Finance Agency (FHFA) was established as an independent regulator with authority over Fannie Mae, Freddie Mac, and the Federal Home Loan Banks through the Housing and Economic Recovery Act (Pub. L. 110–289). Similarly, the passage of the Dodd-Frank Wall Street Reform and Consumer Protection Act of 2010 (Dodd-Frank) spurred the creation of the Consumer Financial Protection Bureau (CFPB) and expanded responsibilities for independent regulators like the Commodity Futures Trading Commission (Pub. L. 111–203).

Still, the expanded role for independent regulators in overseeing financial markets has, in some cases, brought controversy over the unique organizational structures created to accomplish the task. Like the FHFA, the CFPB is an independent regulatory agency with a single director rather than a multi-member commission as well as for-cause removal protections. Likewise, similar to the FHFA which receives funding through Fannie Mae, Freddie Mac, and its member banks, CFPB is supported not through congressional appropriations but rather by the Federal Reserve (Zywicki 2013). In *Seila Law LLC v. Consumer Financial Protection Bureau* (2020), the Supreme Court held that the for-cause removal protections for the agency's single director violated the separation of powers (591 U.S. __). Nevertheless, CFPB continues to operate using its original design.

One significant development for independent regulators over the past decade has been changes to their practices for conducting regulatory analysis in support of their proposed rules. The SEC, for example, has made efforts to improve its economic analysis after the DC Circuit vacated several commission rules for failing to assess adequately important costs and benefits (Revesz 2014). Particularly after *Business Roundtable v. SEC* (2011), the agency took steps to strengthen its capabilities for economic analysis, including hiring additional economists and issuing guidance for conducting this analysis building on principles of Executive Order 12866, which requires executive branch agencies but not independent agencies to conduct benefit-cost analysis to support significant rules (Kraus & Raso 2013). In a similar way, the FCC has also bolstered its regulatory review capabilities, primarily through reorganizing its staff economists and altering its economic analysis requirements (Ellig et al. 2018; Ellig 2019).

Traditional Characteristics of Independent Regulators

Notwithstanding the legal division between independent and executive branch regulatory agencies, the concrete differences between the two types of entities remain somewhat unclear. As described, independent agencies emerged more through evolution than doctrine or theory—tradition turned into precedent and then into law (Breger & Edles 2000). Regardless, the academic literature has identified several characteristics that help distinguish these agencies from their executive branch counterparts.

Despite listing 19 specific U.S. government entities as independent regulatory agencies, the PRA does not include an accompanying definition. It further ends by noting that independent regulators include "any other similar agency designated by statute as a Federal independent regulatory agency or commission" (44 U.S.C. 3502(5)). Similarly, the Administrative Procedure Act (APA) of 1946 defines an "independent establishment" as excluding the U.S. Postal Service, the Postal Regulatory Commission, executive departments, military departments, government corporations, and their subparts (5 U.S.C. 104; Selin 2015). Notably however, the APA definition of executive agency in the section that follows includes independent establishments, along with the executive departments and government corporations (5 U.S.C. 105).

To differentiate independent regulators from others, federal courts most commonly cite the definition applied in *Humphrey's Executor*. The definition emphasizes that an independent commission includes appointed officers who have for-cause removal protections, are part of a multi-member body of experts, and have fixed terms (295 U.S. 602 (1935)). Although there may be other characteristics, the three highlighted in *Humphrey's Executor* are fundamental to how many identify independent regulators.

For-cause removal protections refer to a limitation on a president's ability to remove an agency head or commissioner. In general, statutory language conveying such protection typically provides a list of conditions justifying the removal of an officer serving in the agency. For example, the Interstate Commerce Act provided that ICC commissioners "may be removed by the President for inefficiency, neglect of duty, or malfeasance in office" (Pub. L. 49–104, Sec. 11). The Supreme Court opinion in *Humphrey's Executor* pointed to statutory language like this as a limitation on the president's power of removal for appointed officers in the FTC and other similar bodies (295 U.S. 602 (1935)).

The consensus view in the literature is that limitation on the president's removal power, particularly a for-cause removal provision, represents the line of demarcation between independent and executive agencies (Verkuil 1989; Dooling 2020). Still, as Table 2.1 describing the characteristics of the 19 independent regulatory agencies identified by the PRA illustrates, only 13 have explicit statutory protections against removal except for cause.[2] Nevertheless, even in the absence of explicit statutory language, some agency heads like the SEC commissioner have been granted de facto removal protections by courts (Selin & Lewis 2018). Yet this missing element for some regulatory agencies considered independent raises questions about whether a for-cause removal provision is an appropriate metric to use in deciding whether an agency is an independent regulator (Datla & Revesz 2013).

A multi-member structure is viewed as another indicator of regulatory independence, one also focused on the agency's leadership (Selin & Lewis 2018). The early independent regulators, including the ICC, FTC, Federal Reserve, and those established during the New Deal were primarily created as multi-member bodies. In fact, evidence suggests that Congress gave the Federal Reserve its multi-member board structure to insulate it from political pressure (Selin & Lewis 2018).

As Table 2.1 reveals, among the 19 agencies identified as independent regulatory agencies in the PRA, 15 have a multi-member structure. Exceptions include CFPB and FHFA, two of the newest independent agencies, which are each headed by a single director. The others, namely the Office of Financial Research and the Comptroller of the Currency, are both located within the Department of the Treasury. Still, it is true that many agencies that are not traditionally

Table 2.1   *Statutory characteristics of independent regulatory agencies*

Name	Dates Operational	For-cause Removal	Multi-member	Fixed Terms
Board of Governors of the Federal Reserve System	1913 – Present	Yes	Yes	Yes
Consumer Financial Protection Bureau	2010 – Present	Yes	No	Yes
Commodity Futures Trading Commission	1974 – Present	No	Yes	Yes
Consumer Product Safety Commission	1972 – Present	Yes	Yes	Yes
Federal Communications Commission	1934 – Present	No	Yes	Yes
Federal Deposit Insurance Corporation	1933 – Present	No	Yes	Yes
Federal Energy Regulatory Commission	1977 – Present	Yes	Yes	Yes
Federal Housing Finance Agency	2008 – Present	Yes	No	Yes
Federal Maritime Commission	1961 – Present	Yes	Yes	Yes
Federal Trade Commission	1914 – Present	Yes	Yes	Yes
Interstate Commerce Commission	1887 – 1995	Yes	Yes	Yes
Federal Mine Safety and Health Review Commission	1977 – Present	Yes	Yes	Yes
National Labor Relations Board	1935 – Present	Yes	Yes	Yes
Nuclear Regulatory Commission	1974 – Present	Yes	Yes	Yes
Occupational Safety and Health Review Commission	1970 – Present	Yes	Yes	Yes
Postal Regulatory Commission	1970 – Present	Yes	Yes	Yes
Securities and Exchange Commission	1934 – Present	No	Yes	Yes
Office of Financial Research	2010 – Present	No	No	Yes
Comptroller of the Currency	1863 – Present	No	No	Yes
Total Count		13	15	19

Note: The Federal Mine Safety and Health Review Commission is incorrectly referred to as the Mine Enforcement Safety and Health Review Commission in 44 U.S.C. 3502(5). This error in the U.S. Code was confirmed by an officer of the Commission. Sources for the table include Selin and Lewis (2018); Interstate Commerce Act, Pub. L. 49–104, Sec. 11; and Dodd-Frank Wall Street Reform and Consumer Protection Act, Pub. L. 111–203, Sec. 152.

considered independent also share multi-member structures, including the Board of Veterans Appeals, Federal Crop Insurance Corporation, and National Indian Gaming Commission.

The final defining feature of independent regulatory agencies, fixed terms, represents another limitation on removal that can be applied in tandem with for-cause removal protections. Table 2.1 illustrates that the agency heads or commissioners in all 19 independent regulatory agencies have fixed terms. However, fixed terms also exist for officials in a variety of other agencies, including many executive departments. Of agencies led by a single individual, 19 serve fixed terms but are not protected by for-cause removal provisions (Selin & Lewis 2018).

Put simply, while for-cause removal protections, a multi-member structure, and fixed terms may be present in the majority of U.S. independent regulators, the data suggest that none are reliable indicators of whether a regulatory agency is independent. This reality suggests that independence, rather than being defined by a specific feature, is better thought of as a property stemming from different mixtures of a set of common traits. The difficulty with cleanly distinguishing the characteristics of independent agencies has challenged scholars for decades. However, recent research has made strides by emphasizing that agency independence exists in degrees rather than as a dichotomy, a point we emphasize in the next section.

FORESIGHT: CONTEMPORARY CHALLENGES FOR THE STUDY OF U.S. INDEPENDENT REGULATORS

This chapter opened by examining the historical development of U.S. independent regulators, emphasizing its implications for how they operate today in practice as well as the role that studying them has played in the development of regulatory scholarship. Building from this foundation, the second half of the chapter contemplates the future of independent regulators, considering contemporary challenges for related research, particularly focusing on alternative methods for evaluating independence and the possibilities for extending regulatory analysis requirements to independent agencies. The section also emphasizes research areas that have remained underdeveloped and perhaps deserve more systematic attention.

Alternative Methods for Evaluating Independence

A relatively extensive scholarship has challenged the simplistic conception of regulatory independence, finding the distinction between executive branch and independent regulatory agencies opaque (Massel 1961; Moreno 1994). Still, over the last decade, scholars have begun to rethink how to categorize agencies by advancing alternative ways to evaluate U.S. regulatory independence that break from a binary distinction based on for-cause removal protections. To provide a flavor for this work, we highlight three key contributions that offer alternative approaches to defining independence.

In one such contribution, Barkow (2010) expands the discussion of how to evaluate independence by moving beyond traditional metrics to focus on "overlooked" design elements that mitigate capture by interest groups and insulate them from partisan pressure (p. 17). Because conventional features are insufficient to protect diffuse public interests against organized interest groups, the discussion examines additional agency characteristics that have largely been ignored but can nevertheless be used to assess that agency's independence, including its sources of funding and the extent to which it shares enforcement responsibilities with other entities. Barkow (2010) argues for a contextual approach examining how additional potential insulators interact with other structural features and regulatory environments, suggesting the combined effects offer more evidence than simply considering whether the agency is structured to exhibit the traditional features that signal independence.

Extending Barkow (2010), Datla and Revesz (2013) evaluate patterns among agencies for seven widely accepted indicators of independence to show that both traditional independent agencies and non-independent agencies possess different combinations of these characteristics. Suggesting a strict binary categorization is inaccurate, they further challenge the constitutional status of independent regulators dictated by *Humphrey's Executor*, advocating instead for a statute-centric perspective that avoids making assumptions around implied protections. The article contributes an explicit argument for considering independence as a spectrum, ranks agencies from more to less insulated using a number of indicia, and promotes a perspective of agency authority based on statute rather than implied status.

Finally, Selin (2015) expands upon more qualitative analyses by providing a robust empirical assessment of relative independence using an extensive list of structural features and examining 321 federal agencies. Agencies' current structural independence is evaluated along two dimensions: (1) limitations or qualifications placed on the appointment or removal of agency decision-makers; and (2) restrictions on political review of or interference in agency policy decisions. A key implication from the research is that the traditional emphasis on multi-member bodies with fixed terms and for-cause removal protections may obscure key differences among agencies, specifically statutory provisions that insulate them from political review.

As a whole, these highlighted articles point to an emerging research area that is shifting away from a traditional view of independence, which typically points to a single factor like for-cause removal protections, and toward a more nuanced understanding of independence as a continuum, influenced by a variety of factors and design choices. Still, this new paradigm has yet to translate to the political sphere, where the legal treatment of independence has remained relatively unaffected. While the independence of leadership in most agencies has not significantly changed over time, some agencies have seen noticeable increases in the independence of their policy decisions, including financial regulators like the Federal Reserve and SEC (Selin 2015), which underscores the importance of considering independence more broadly. These differing definitions also have implications for the oversight independent regulators face, especially from the executive branch.

Evolving Requirements for Regulatory Review

Ever since the introduction of regulatory review in the U.S. several decades ago, a stark line has been drawn between independent and executive agencies, where independent regulators face weaker requirements than their executive branch counterparts with respect to analyzing their regulations. In fact, while independent regulators have remained outside of the president's purview, numerous executive orders from multiple presidents have established standards for regulatory analysis, promoted benefit-cost analysis as central to regulatory decision-making, and directed executive agencies to submit certain proposed rules to OIRA for review (Dudley 2022). The result is that independent regulators largely operate without having to adhere to specific standards for analysis (Fraas & Lutter 2011).

The scholarly debate over the usefulness of this distinction has spurred three competing perspectives. The first argues that executive agencies themselves should not be bound by regulatory review requirements, particularly those mandating regulatory impact analyses and the associated benefit-cost analyses (Ackerman & Heinzerling 2002). Such arguments primarily center on issues with implementation of benefit-cost analysis and its impact on regulatory decision-making. A second view regards benefit-cost analysis as being useful when the underlying factors are suitable for its application but expresses skepticism about expanding OIRA review to independent agencies or extending analysis requirements to specific agencies (Rose-Ackerman 2011). For example, some argue that mandating analytical requirements for financial regulation—especially quantitative benefit-cost analysis—would itself not pass a benefit-cost test (Coates 2015). Finally, perhaps not surprisingly, a third perspective argues that exempting independent agencies has artificially limited the scope of OIRA review and simultaneously stunted the development of independent agencies' abilities to conduct analysis (Pildes & Sunstein 1995; Revesz 2017). These realities have prompted some to suggest approaches for how regulatory analysis could be improved within independent agencies (Dudley 2015; Coglianese 2018).

Even in the absence of centralized review by OIRA, independent regulators, at least in some contexts, have undergone a transformation to raise their internal standards for conducting regulatory analysis. Kraus and Raso (2013) highlight some of the positive features of the SEC's 2012 internal guidance, which followed the previously described court decision in *Business Roundtable*. Similarly, FCC's recent process reforms and initiatives demonstrate the increasing role of economic analysis in commission decisions (Ellig et al. 2018). These changes to regulatory analysis requirements, whether within or outside the scope of OIRA review, underscore the importance of monitoring how regulatory review in independent agencies continues to evolve.

Research Areas Deserving More Systematic Work

Notwithstanding the extensive research outlined in this chapter focused on the activities of U.S. independent regulators, numerous topics still deserve more attention. In some areas, systematic work is needed to test theoretical contributions whereas other topics deal with questions that merit empirical exploration while nevertheless lacking solid theoretical foundations. We highlight four maturing topics focused on independent regulators that may warrant more investigation.

First, additional empirical research could systematically consider the connection between independent regulators and the executive branch. One early discussion of the extent to which independent agencies, in practice, operate unencumbered by presidential oversight focused on six executive branch tools, including centralized clearance of budgets and legislative proposals by OMB and presidential designation of commission chairs (Brigman 1981). Subsequently, scholars have empirically evaluated presidential influence over independent commissions, sometimes reaching opposing conclusions (Moe 1982; Cohen 1985). Such research suggests that while presidents exercise a degree of control over independent commissions, the overall direction and magnitude of influence likely depends on which specific mechanism is being considered. Further, many of these studies examine a time period before OIRA's review of proposed rules was widely institutionalized, indicating both that presidents may have had the ability to influence regulatory policy before centralized regulatory review but also that additional research is needed to gauge the effect of OIRA review on independence.

More recently, Livermore (2014) has challenged the notion that benefit-cost analysis is a tool for the White House to facilitate control of agency decisions, arguing rather that such analyses may also be a vehicle for agencies to retain autonomy through their ability to influence how that analysis is conducted. By implication, extending OIRA review to independent regulatory agencies might not necessarily sacrifice their autonomy. Nevertheless, further inquiry might help clarify the extent and conditions where regulatory review might hinder or enhance independent agencies' autonomy. In addition, such investigation could reveal whether this relationship differs depending on a president's political party or regulatory philosophy.

A related topic that deserves continued attention is the extent to which regulatory analysis affects agency decisions. In an article generally supportive of the practice of benefit-cost analysis, Hahn and Tetlock (2008) nevertheless find little systematic evidence to demonstrate that it has improved regulatory decision-making overall. Others have examined the quality of regulatory analyses (Ellig et al. 2013; Bull & Ellig 2018), whether review requirements slow the regulatory process (Yackee & Yackee 2010), and whether net-beneficial regulations are associated with analytical quality (Shapiro & Morrall 2012). Still, much of the existing evidence focuses on the effect on executive agencies. More comparative research on the effects of regulatory analysis would reveal the practical impacts of the different procedural requirements for executive branch and independent regulators. For example, one study surveyed rules from select independent regulatory commissions, finding that their analyses generally fell short of best practices and achieved only the statutorily minimum requirements (Fraas & Lutter 2011). Still, conducting more systematic comparisons of regulatory analyses by executive and independent agencies would help inform the question of whether expanding OIRA oversight to independent agencies is likely to improve regulatory outcomes.

A third area where further work could be useful is in integrating studies of independent agencies with research on different regulatory instruments utilized by those regulators (Pérez, Prasad, & Xie 2019). Sometimes referred to as "new governance" scholarship, the literature studying regulation has focused more attention in recent years on how regulators might employ alternative strategies to affect the behavior of regulated entities (Gilad 2010; Carrigan & Coglianese 2011). These alternative approaches regulators employ, including management-based regulation, information disclosure requirements, and voluntary programs, can in certain circumstances substitute for more traditional and less flexible "command-and-control" vehicles (Carrigan & Coglianese 2011). Still, because independent commissions are generally tasked with economic relative to social regulatory responsibilities, it is not clear whether independent regulators use different approaches to regulating relative to other agencies. And, if they do adopt diverging mechanisms, one might consider whether this justifies treating them differently from other regulatory agencies. Synthesizing the existing research on independent regulators with results produced by the new governance approach could provide substantial insight.

Lastly, scholarly research could further investigate the implications for regulatory independence of political polarization in the U.S., including considering the degree to which the independent status of certain regulatory agencies might insulate them from the effects of such polarization. Given that administrative agencies are never completely independent from politics, partisanship—and thus polarization—could plausibly affect agency decision-making

(Balla 2012). Of course, the extent to which this is true is an empirical question that has not been definitively answered.

In a review of the limited scholarly output assessing the effects of political polarization on agency decision-making, Spence (2019) concluded that policy decisions did not seem to be shifting away from the center in response. Nevertheless, some scholars argue that polarization has reduced regulatory output and altered the composition of agency commissioners and personnel. Potter and Shipan (2019) find that a polarized Congress may hinder the regulatory output of an agency when its congressional opponents are strong, results that apply both to executive and independent agencies alike. Further, Devins and Lewis (2008) show that the amount of time it takes for presidents to appoint majorities to independent regulatory commissions has grown as polarization has intensified. Sustained research in these areas might allow us to appreciate more clearly how the nature of regulatory independence is likely to change with an increasingly polarized U.S. political context.

CONCLUSION

Spanning from the practice of regulation to the development of the regulatory scholarship, U.S. independent regulators have long played a key role for regulation in both a practical and theoretical sense. Yet, despite their importance, the history of independent regulators demonstrates that they evolved into a distinct category over time through convention and tradition, rather than any preconceived plan. For decades, independent regulators received a disproportionate share of attention from researchers, further distinguishing their unique status and providing a rich trove of scholarly insights, including the development of regulatory capture theory and evidence on the effects of deregulation.

Even as scholarly focus has shifted toward executive agencies over time, independent regulators remain a rich area for study. Recent research on alternative methods to evaluate independence has emphasized the interactive effects of various insulating features while recognizing that independence is better considered a continuum relative to a binary categorization. Given their differing treatment from executive branch agencies with respect to analysis requirements, a focus on independent regulators has brought to the fore the question of whether regulatory review requirements should apply universally.

Despites these advances, additional systematic research is needed to better understand the differences between independent and executive branch agencies. Our chapter highlights four areas that deserve attention. First, more empirical work could clarify the extent to which independent regulators are insulated from presidential control in practice. Developments in this area would illuminate for policymakers how changing regulatory review requirements might affect agency independence. Second, comparative work contrasting regulatory analyses conducted by executive and independent agencies would provide more definitive evidence regarding the extent to which analysis requirements affect actual agency decision-making. Third, systematic research connecting independent agencies to the expanding literature on regulatory approaches would help answer the question of whether treating them differently from executive branch agencies is justified and sensible. Finally, examining the role that independent regulators' autonomy may have in an age of growing U.S. political polarization is likely to offer important insights into the long-term effects of this contemporary development.

Considering the breadth of knowledge that has emerged from the study of U.S. independent regulators, continued scholarly focus on the relationship between regulatory performance and independence is bound to produce important insights in the future as well. Deepening our understanding of agency independence could also improve accountability and transparency in rulemaking without sacrificing important benefits produced by political insulation. Undoubtedly, the trajectory of contemporary regulatory scholarship will be influenced by the study of independent regulators, as developments in this research area will continue to fuel improvements in regulatory theory and practice (for more information on regulatory agencies in the U.S. context also see Chapter 21).

NOTES

1. Some have argued that, in contrast to a view of deregulation where markets are the driving force behind regulatory reform, the shifts that began in the 1970s are better characterized as reregulation. From this perspective, combining reregulation with liberalization, regulatory reform—often led by state actors—has ultimately not resulted in fewer rules or less government control (Vogel 1996).
2. To populate Table 2.1, we employed data derived from Selin and Lewis (2018) to assign characteristics for 17 of 19 agencies. The authorizing statutes of the other two agencies provided the relevant information for the remaining two agencies.

REFERENCES

Ackerman, Frank, and Lisa Heinzerling. 2002. "Pricing the Priceless: Cost-Benefit Analysis of Environmental Protection." *University of Pennsylvania Law Review* 150(5): 1553–1584.

Balla, Steven J. 2012. "The Politicization of Administration." *Georgetown Journal of Law and Public Policy* 10(2): 357–359.

Barkow, Rachel E. 2010. "Insulating Agencies: Avoiding Capture through Institutional Design." *Texas Law Review* 89(1): 15–80.

Bernstein, Marver H. 1955. *Regulating Business by Independent Commission*. Princeton, NJ: Princeton University Press.

Bernstein, Marver H. 1972. "Independent Regulatory Agencies: A Perspective on Their Reform." *The Annals of the American Academy of Political and Social Science* 400: 14–26.

Breger, Marshall J., and Gary J. Edles. 2000. "Established by Practice: The Theory and Operation of Independent Federal Agencies." *Administrative Law Review* 52(4): 1111–1294.

Breyer, Stephen G. 1984. *Regulation and Its Reform*. Cambridge, MA: Harvard University Press.

Brigman, William E. 1981. "The Executive Branch and the Independent Regulatory Agencies." *Presidential Studies Quarterly* 11(2): 244–261.

Bull, Reeve T., and Jerry Ellig. 2018. "Statutory Rulemaking Considerations and Judicial Review of Regulatory Impact Analysis." *Administrative Law Review* 70(4): 873–959.

Carpenter, Daniel, and David A. Moss. 2014. "Introduction." In *Preventing Regulatory Capture: Special Interest Influence and How to Limit It*, edited by Daniel Carpenter, and David A. Moss, 1–22. New York, NY: Cambridge University Press.

Carrigan, Christopher, and Cary Coglianese. 2011. "The Politics of Regulation: From New Institutionalism to New Governance." *Annual Review of Political Science* 14: 107–129.

Carrigan, Christopher, and Cary Coglianese. 2015. "George J. Stigler, 'The Theory of Economic Regulation.'" In *The Oxford Handbook of Classics in Public Policy and Administration*, edited by Steven J. Balla, Martin Lodge, and Edward C. Page, 287–299. Oxford, UK: Oxford University Press.

Coates, John C., IV. 2015. "Cost-Benefit Analysis of Financial Regulation: Case Studies and Implications." *Yale Law Journal* 124(4): 882–1011.

Coglianese, Cary. 2018. "Improving Regulatory Analysis at Independent Agencies." *American University Law Review* 67(3): 733–767.

Cohen, Jeffrey E. 1985. "Presidential Control of Independent Regulatory Commissions through Appointment: The Case of the ICC." *Administration & Society* 17(1): 61–70.

Datla, Kirti, and Richard L. Revesz. 2013. "Deconstructing Independent Agencies (and Executive Agencies)." *Cornell Law Review* 98(4): 769–844.

Demsetz, Harold. 1968. "Why Regulate Utilities?" *Journal of Law & Economics* 11(1): 55–65.

Devins, Neal, and David E. Lewis. 2008. "Not-So Independent Agencies: Party Polarization and the Limits of Institutional Design." *Boston University Law Review* 88(2): 459–498.

Dooling, Bridget C.E. 2020. "Bespoke Regulatory Review." *Ohio State Law Journal* 81(4): 673–721.

Dudley, Susan E. 2015. "Improving Regulatory Accountability: Lessons from the Past and Prospects for the Future." *Case Western Reserve Law Review* 65(4): 1027–1057.

Dudley, Susan E. 2022. "The Office of Information and Regulatory Affairs and the Durability of Regulatory Oversight in the United States." *Regulation & Governance*, 16(1): 243–260.

Ellig, Jerry. 2019. "Restoring Internet Freedom as an Example of How to Regulate." *Business, Entrepreneurship & Tax Law Review* 3(2): 236–248.

Ellig, Jerry, Paul LaFontaine, Wayne Leighton, Eric Ralph, and Sean Sullivan. 2018. "Economics at the FCC, 2017–2018: Internet Freedom, International Broadband Pricing Comparisons, and a New Office of Economics and Analytics." *Review of Industrial Organization* 53: 681–707.

Ellig, Jerry, Patrick A. McLaughlin, and John F. Morrall III. 2013. "Continuity, Change, and Priorities: The Quality and Use of Regulatory Analysis Across U.S. Administrations." *Regulation & Governance* 7(2): 153–173.

Fraas, Arthur, and Randall Lutter. 2011. "On the Economic Analysis of Regulations at Independent Regulatory Commissions." *Administrative Law Review* 63, Special Edition: OIRA Thirtieth Anniversary Conference: 213–241.

Gilad, Sharon. 2010. "It Runs in the Family: Meta-Regulation and Its Siblings." *Regulation & Governance* 4(4): 485–506.

Hahn, Robert W., and Paul C. Tetlock. 2008. "Has Economic Analysis Improved Regulatory Decisions?" *Journal of Economic Perspectives* 22(1): 67–84.

Huntington, Samuel P. 1952. "The Marasmus of the ICC: The Commission, the Railroads, and the Public Interest." *Yale Law Journal* 61(4): 467–509.

Jaffe, Louis L. 1954. "The Effective Limits of the Administrative Process: A Reevaluation." *Harvard Law Review* 67(7): 1105–1135.

Jaffe, Louis L. 1956. "The Independent Agency: A New Scapegoat." *Yale Law Journal* 65(7): 1068–1075.

Kagan, Elena. 2001. "Presidential Administration." *Harvard Law Review* 114(8): 2245–2385.

Kraus, Bruce, and Connor Raso. 2013. "Rational Boundaries for SEC Cost-Benefit Analysis." *Yale Journal on Regulation* 30(2): 289–342.

Livermore, Michael A. 2014. "Cost-Benefit Analysis and Agency Independence." *The University of Chicago Law Review* 81(2): 609–688.

Majone, Giandomenico. 2010. "Foundations of Risk Regulation: Science, Decision-Making, Policy Learning and Institutional Reform." *European Journal of Risk Regulation* 1(1): 5–19.

Massel, Mark S. 1961. "The Regulatory Process." *Law and Contemporary Problems* 26(2): 181–202.

McFarland, Carl. 1961. "Landis' Report: The Voice of One Crying in the Wilderness." *Virginia Law Review* 47(3): 373–438.

Moe, Terry M. 1982. "Regulatory Performance and Presidential Administration." *American Journal of Political Science* 26(2): 197–224.

Moreno, Angel Manuel. 1994. "Presidential Coordination of the Independent Regulatory Process." *Administrative Law Journal of the American University* 8(3): 461–516.

Novak, William J. 2014. "A Revisionist History of Regulatory Capture." In *Preventing Regulatory Capture: Special Interest Influence and How to Limit It*, edited by Daniel Carpenter, and David A. Moss, 25–48. New York, NY: Cambridge University Press.

Pérez, Daniel R., Aryamala Prasad, and Zhoudan Xie. 2019. "A Taxonomy of Regulatory Forms." Ch. 2 in *The Relationship Between Regulatory Form and Productivity: An Empirical Application to Agriculture*, George Washington Regulatory Studies Center report.

Pildes, Richard H., and Cass R. Sunstein. 1995. "Reinventing the Regulatory State." *University of Chicago Law Review* 62(1): 1–129.

Pollak, Robert A. 1996. "Government Risk Regulation." *The Annals of the American Academy of Political and Social Science* 545: 25–34.

Potter, Rachel Augustine, and Charles R. Shipan. 2019. "Agency Rulemaking in a Separation of Powers System." *Journal of Public Policy* 39(1): 89–113.

Revesz, Richard L. 2014. "Quantifying Regulatory Benefits." *California Law Review* 102(6): 1423–1456.

Revesz, Richard L. 2017. "Cost-Benefit Analysis and the Structure of the Administrative State: The Case of Financial Services Regulation." *Yale Journal on Regulation* 34(2): 545–600.

Rose-Ackerman, Susan. 2011. "Putting Cost-Benefit Analysis in its Place: Rethinking Regulatory Review." *University of Miami Law Review* 65(2): 335–356.

Selin, Jennifer L. 2015. "What Makes an Agency Independent?" *American Journal of Political Science* 59(4): 971–987.

Selin, Jennifer L., and David E. Lewis. 2018. *Sourcebook of United States Executive Agencies.* Administrative Conference of the United States, Second Edition, October 2018.

Shapiro, Stuart, and John F. Morrall III. 2012. "The Triumph of Regulatory Politics: Benefit-Cost Analysis and Political Salience." *Regulation & Governance* 6(2): 189–206.

Spence, David B. 2019. "The Effects of Partisan Polarization on the Bureaucracy." In *Can America Govern Itself?*, edited by Frances E. Lee, and Nolan McCarty, 271–300. Cambridge: Cambridge University Press.

Stigler, George J. 1971. "The Theory of Economic Regulation." *The Bell Journal of Economics and Management Science* 2(1): 3–21.

Stigler, George J., and Claire Friedland. 1962. "What Can Regulators Regulate? The Case of Electricity." *Journal of Law & Economics* 5: 1–16.

Verkuil, Paul R. 1989. "Separation of Powers, the Rule of Law and the Idea of Independence." *William & Mary Law Review* 30(2): 301–341.

Vogel, Steven K. 1996. *Freer Markets, More Rules: Regulatory Reform in Advanced Industrial Countries.* Ithaca, NY: Cornell University Press.

Weidenbaum, Murray L. 1978. "The Costs of Government Regulation of Business: A Study." Prepared for the Joint Economic Committee, April 1978.

Wilson, James Q. 1975. "The Rise of the Bureaucratic State." *The Public Interest* 41: 77–103.

Winston, Clifford. 1993. "Economic Deregulation: Days of Reckoning for Microeconomists." *Journal of Economic Literature* 31(3): 1263–1289.

Yackee, Jason Webb, and Susan Webb Yackee. 2010. "Administrative Procedures and Bureaucratic Performance: Is Federal Rule-making 'Ossified'?" *Journal of Public Administration Research and Theory* 20(2): 261–282.

Zywicki, Todd. 2013. "The Consumer Financial Protection Bureau: Savior or Menace?" *George Washington Law Review* 81(3): 856–928.

Cases Cited

Business Roundtable v. Securities and Exchange Commission, 10-1305 (D.C. Cir. 2011)
Humphrey's Executor v. United States, 25 U.S. 602 (1935)
Seila Law LLC v. Consumer Financial Protection Bureau, 591 U.S. __ (2020)

Laws Cited

Administrative Procedure Act of 1946, Pub. L. 79–404
Dodd-Frank Wall Street Reform and Consumer Protection Act of 2010, Pub. L. 111–203
Housing and Economic Recovery Act of 2008, Pub. L. 110–289
ICC Termination Act of 1995, Pub. L. 104–88
Interstate Commerce Act of 1887, Pub. L. 49–104
Paperwork Reduction Act of 1980, Pub. L. 96–511

Presidential Documents Cited

Executive Order 12866, "Regulatory Planning and Review," 58 FR 51735 (October 4, 1993)

3. Independent regulators in Europe

David Coen and Andrew Tarrant

INTRODUCTION

Over the last 30 years, the creation of the single market and the liberalisation of the EU markets has resulted in a rapid expansion of EU regulation. This has formed part of a wider process of regulatory reform at both the national and international level (Majone 1994, Levi and Spiller 1996, Levi-Faur 2005, Gilardi 2004). Significantly, there have been radical changes in regulation in EU member states with downwards delegation to new independent regulatory agencies (IRAs) and upwards delegation to EU institutions (Coen and Thatcher 2008, Coen and Héritier 2005, Pollack 1997). However, such delegation has often resulted in either an EU regulatory implementation deficit or raised questions of legitimacy and accountability of EU policymaking (Busuioc and Lodge 2017, Kelemen and Tarrant 2011). Recognising that co-coordinating the single market and EU regulation is a complex task, in recent years the European Commission (EC), member state governments and National Regulatory Agencies (NRA) have encouraged mechanisms for enhancing collaboration or decision-making at the European level, including European Regulatory Networks (ERNs) and European Agencies (EA) (Thatcher and Coen 2008, Thatcher 2011). The ERNs composed of national regulators have taken greater or lesser coordination roles, and EAs have had a variety of mandates and powers, and a range of resources allocated to them over time and across sectors. In this chapter we set out the potential models of EU regulatory institutions and seek to explain their emergence from both a functional and political choice perspective (Kelemen and Tarrant 2011, Mastenbroek and Martinsen 2018, Hanretty and Koop 2012). In so doing the chapter seeks to explore how tensions between centralised rule-making and decentralised implementation have given rise to significant debates about the creation of either new ERNs or EU agencies when seeking to ensure effective implementation of EU regulation (or not) and which modes of integration and varieties of regulatory governance ought to apply to them.

EVOLUTION AND VARIETY OF EU REGULATORY GOVERNANCE

Economic growth and development of the EU internal market relies on coordination of member states, potentially pursuing very different economic strategies rooted in different varieties of capitalism, marrying up to the rival agendas of the different EU institutions and the varied interests of disparate sets of businesses and consumers. In balancing all these demands, the EU must manage not just the formulation of legislation and regulations within the EU institutional policymaking process, but also evaluate and supervise the implementation of EU policies at the national level (Maggetti and Gilardi 2011, Maggetti 2009, Danielsen and Yesilkagit 2014). Recognising this need for multilevel market governance, the EC has sought to establish partnerships between itself and national administrations, national regulators (Majone 1997,

Dehousse 1997), and economic interests (Coen, Guidi, Héritier and Yordanova 2020, Coen, Katsaitis and Vannoni 2021). However, with the liberalisation of the single market, and with it the concurrent rise of the regulatory state, including the widespread adoption of so-called independent regulators (Majone 1994) we have also seen the development in the 2000s of both EU regulatory agencies and ERN coordination (Busuioc 2013, Coen and Thatcher 2008, Kelemen and Tarrant 2011). In this section we set out different institutional models for implementation of EU regulations that have emerged over the last 20 years.

Institutional Choices for Structuring European Regulatory Space

When a choice is made to regulate a sector at EU-level, the legislators have a choice between a range of bodies that can be tasked to implement it. They can leave it entirely to member state discretion, where it is typically handed to a Ministry, or they can choose to delegate to a body defined in European legislation. In that latter case, they have three basic options: the Commission alone, EU agencies in combination with the Commission or so-called independent NRAs which may be organised into ERNs. More than one of these institutions can be selected to regulate in the same sector. The legislators can also organise the hierarchy of relationships between them differently and they can impose varying levels of ongoing control over their activity. This section therefore sets out different institutional choices by looking at models that have been given serious attention for implementation of EU regulation.

An important approach for an understanding of the relation between institutions is principal and agent theory. Principal and agent analyses seeks to understand the hierarchic relationship between institutions which delegate power, for example, in a legislative act, and those which receive it (Pollack 1997; Stone-Sweet and Thatcher 2003). The intent is to examine where discretion to act is granted and to what extent it is constrained. The principals in the EU vary. When it is a question of treaty change, they comprise the member states only. When it is a question of EU legislation, the principals are the member states in the Council, the Commission due to its quasi-legislative role and the Parliament. The agents can be national ministries, NRAs, the EU agencies, and the Commission in its role as an executive actor.

It has been suggested that a weakness of principal and agent-based analyses is that by focusing on powers and control, it artificially assumes that principals and agents possess incompatible goals (Blauberger and Rittberger 2015). However, it is the principals themselves that may indicate to us a potential concern as to incompatible goals or the absence of agreement by the degree and nature of the delegation, including whether they add controls (Pollack 1997). A principal's true preferences may be expressed during negotiations over delegation or where obscured may be inferred from systematic preferences in certain circumstances for specific forms of delegation over others. A criticism that has been made of those who could be considered "functionalists" is that they only entertain a sub-set of potential positive technocratic functions related to efficient European regulation. But function and efficiency for a national political principal may also relate to other factors such as preserving national electoral coalitions which effective implementation may imperil.

NRAs and ministries
Here EU monitoring and supervision involves the classic EU method whereby the EU delegates responsibility for implementing EU regulation to member states. Normally EU legislators make no choices about the nature of the national bodies which implement EU legislation

at the national level. It is left to the member state's discretion. Typically, implementation is accorded to a ministry. However, the European Commission and ECJ are responsible for ensuring that member states correctly implement EU regulation through monitoring and supervision; ultimately this can mean infringement proceedings against member states for failure to comply with EU law.

The EU legislators also sometimes decide that there is a conflict of interest between the objective of regulation and the interests held by member states. In this situation, EU legislation may require member states to set up and empower "independent" national regulators to implement EU law. Almost all the cases where this has occurred have taken place in utility sectors where the member states have ownership stakes in major national companies (Kelemen and Tarrant 2011). The independence requirements have gradually become stricter during successive waves of EU sectoral legislation (Hoynck 2012), However it remains the case that member state governments retain formal powers, in particular the power of appointment of the Heads of NRAs (Ennser-Jedenastik 2016), and informal powers as regards "independent" national regulators.

The European Commission
The EU Commission is sometimes accorded implementation powers in regulatory fields. This is when the member states wish to prioritise harmonised outcomes. Typically, when the Commission is given implementing powers, its draft decisions are reviewed by a committee of member state representatives. Pre-Lisbon, the variety and design of regulatory committees became rather baroque (Blom-Hansen 2011). Nonetheless, the underlying rationale was that as the Commission's discretionary power increased in substance and in salience, the ability of a committee of representatives of national ministries to supervise and ultimately veto draft Commission decisions also increased (Pollack 2003). Comitology was rationalised in the TFEU (Jacqué 2018). There are now two types of committees only, advisory committees and examination committees. A qualified majority on an examination committee can veto a Commission decision, subject to it being backed by an Appeal Committee if the Commission appeals.

European Regulatory Networks (ERNs)
ERNs are not bodies which implement regulation. They are information sharing meetings between sectoral NRAs and they may issue best practice advice. They may also involve the European Commission. They have no formal powers and typically if they have any dedicated staff at all, it consists of a very small secretariat (Thatcher and Coen 2008). Although ERNs have largely been studied in the context of informal coordination between NRAs and the Commission in the utility sectors (Eberlein and Grande 2005, Coen and Thatcher 2008), it should be noted that ERNs also exist where implementation powers are accorded to either European agencies or to ministries (Tarrant 2021). The functional need to collectively discuss implementation practice arises regardless of the type of authority empowered. As such ERNs are a complement not a substitute for the bodies which are selected as the primary decision-makers in any sectoral legislation.

The ERNs relating to "independent" NRAs evolved in the late 1990s as the EU attempted to improve the coordination and implementation of the liberalisation directives in the utilities and financial sectors. Bodies such as the Independent Regulatory Group (IRG) in telecoms, followed by European Regulator group for Electricity and Gras (ERGEG) and CESR in finance emerged (Coen and Doyle 2000, Coen and Thatcher 2008, Eberlein and Newman 2008). However, in many of these cases these bodies were partially replaced by EAs in the late 2000 such as BEREC in Telecoms (Mathieu and Rongoni 2019) and the European Banking Agency (Coen and Salter 2020).

The existence, of an ERN therefore does not in itself tell us about the degree to which member states are interested in substantive regulatory cooperation. Effective cooperation instead may be better correlated with the empowerment of a European institution, agency, or agency plus Commission. The evidence from competition law suggests that an ERN is more active where the EU has substantive decision-making capability while the evidence from the implementation of remedies in telecoms is that a network is less active where the EU does not have this capability (Coen and Thatcher 2008, Kassim and Wright 2010, Kelemen and Tarrant 2011).

European Regulatory Agencies (ERAs)
There are a wide variety of EU agencies. EU agencies are defined as bodies governed by European laws, and equipped with their own legal personality, clearly defined tasks, administrative capacity, and financial autonomy (Kelemen 2005, Busuioc 2013). As of 2020, there are six executive Commission agencies and 37 decentralised agencies with a combined budget of 4.0 billion euros (European Court of Auditors 2020). Examples of ERAs include the European Food Safety Authority (ESFA), the European Agency for the Evaluation of Medicinal Products (EMEA), the European Aviation Safety Authority (EASA) and the Trademark and Designs Office. In economic regulation of the liberalised utilities and financial markets, new agencies have recently been created, such as European Banking Authority (EBA), European Securities and Market authority (ESMA), Agency for the Cooperation of Energy Regulators (ACER) and most recently BEREC in telecoms to supplant ineffective ERNs. (Although note in the case of BEREC that member states have kept it from obtaining jurisdiction over the key powers which continue to be wielded only by individual NRAs acting alone, despite the urging of the Commission and the European parliament to give BEREC a more powerful constraining role vis-à-vis the individual NRAs.)

The majority of EAs are executive agencies which pursue discrete tasks allocated to them by policymakers. Others are information and coordination bodies. A sub-set are in practice European-level regulatory bodies. Technically, these are mostly pre-decision-making bodies (Griller and Orator 2010). This sub-set of agencies prepare draft decisions in a regulatory field, which is then adopted by the Commission, subject to approval in comitology. In the areas where independent NRAs are adopted, the alternative choices legislators face are usually between empowering one of this latter type of agency or the European Commission alone. The creation of the ERA in practice involves a double delegation from the Commission and national governments. Unlike the executive agencies, these pre-decision agencies are not bodies which are separate from the member states. The Heads of NRAs collectively comprise the decision-making instance in these bodies and the draft decisions adopted by them as the Agency, pass to the Commission. The downside from the perspective of a member state that wants the option to defect from single market rules is that this cannot be obtained surreptitiously, and it requires the agreement of the Heads of other NRAs and ultimately the Commission and the comitology committee. If individual NRAs alone are empowered, then the member state only has to persuade its own NRA.

INSTITUTIONAL VARIATION

It can be seen from the discussion above that European legislators have a range of potential institutional variations available to them when they wish to select a body or bodies to set detailed rules and to police the implementation of those rules, in other words to regulate. Very broadly, it might be reasonable to suggest that researchers currently seeking to explain the choice of institutions fall into two schools of thought. For ease of convenience, these schools of thought could perhaps be labelled as functionalists and as exponents of political choice.

Functionalists

The academic pioneer of the regulatory state in the European Union was Giandacome Majone (Majone 1994) and his work has dominated the field of regulatory governance in the EU. A regulatory state is one where the state changes from a producer of goods and services to one which seeks to act as an umpire ensuring that economic actors play by the agreed rules of the game. The incentive for the state to act as an umpire was that it could obtain efficiencies through encouraging competition and it could, if investors believed it was neutral, obtain external investment to fund that competition. Privatisation is identified as a causal mechanism that permits and requires the rise of the regulatory state and independent agencies are the mechanism by which the regulatory state perpetuates itself. Majone expected that regulatory powers would be transferred to the European Commission because of the low implementation credibility of traditional inter-state agreements but that member states would seek to control this delegation using limited budgets and comitology. Nonetheless, Majone expected the Commission to escape these constraints by co-opting relevant national officials (Majone 1994:90). One way of reading functionalist accounts of institutional development is as an attempt to maintain a modified version of the Majone thesis: the accounts recognise that the functionalist pressures he identified to regulate the new privatised actors have not led to the Commission being vested with new regulatory powers in key sectors but have instead led to the Commission attempting to exercise such powers indirectly via ERNs. Functionalists argue that the Commission can induce effective regulation from NRAs through the use of deliberative processes and in the absence of any hierarchical power (Eberlein and Grande 2005; Blauberger and Rittberger 2015).

Appreciating how this school of thought has developed over time, leads us to suggest that there are currently two main variants of the functionalist argument. One argues that member states recognise the need for Europeanised governance to deliver the single market in sectors where they have privatised former state-owned operators but remain attached to the formal exercise of national sovereignty. This means that they insist on the empowerment of national regulators via European legislation rather than any supranational body such as the Commission or an EU agency but accept coordination via ERNs to prevent the development of any "functional gaps" which could otherwise develop (Eberlein and Grande 2005). Implicitly, national ministries are assumed to be unconcerned by NRAs or the Commission using ERNs to informally harmonise the actual content of regulation because they privilege form over content.

Alternatively, European institutions are held to have been empowered to act up to the point at which they would cease to be efficient promoters of the single market. Where complex European regulatory rules require case-by-case national implementation, the legislators prefer to empower national regulators. The latter are necessarily more efficient; they enjoy easier access to the regulated entities, greater knowledge about them and they have more resources to police them than the budgetarily constrained EU Commission (Blauberger and Rittberger 2015). In other words, design of the appropriate institutions is set in conformity with the requirements of subsidiarity; institutions are empowered where they will be the most efficient.

Both explanations envisage ERNs as the mechanism by which tensions between the policy views of the European Commission and the NRAs are resolved in order to ensure appropriate levels of commonality in their regulatory decisions and so to close the "functional gap" which might otherwise arise as a consequence of having 27 decision-makers attempting to deliver a coherent set of rules for the single market. A necessary but implicit assumption for both these approaches is that that NRAs have sufficient de facto independence from other national actors to undertake the appropriate levels of regulatory harmonisation to deliver the single market.

Functionalists' hypotheses regarding the effect of participation in ERNs draw from wider discussions regarding the effectiveness of deliberative forms of "New governance" (Abbot and Snidal 2009, Sabel and Zeitlin 2008, Mathieu and Rongoni 2019). It has been argued that participation in ERNs has a socialising effect on participants, leading them to move away from a narrow consideration of national interests and to adopt a more European perspective when making decisions. Eberlein and Grande suggest a set of conditions which would have to be met to close the "functional gap" created by the necessity for single market regulation to be sepa-rately by NRAs. These conditions are: (i) networks achieve regulatory transparency and give their members informational advantages over purely national officials; (ii) regulatory officials participating in networks are socialised into networks and this causes them to prioritise their obligations to other participants over their relations with other domestic civil servants; (iii) participation in networks requires credible commitments and partly as a function of this and partly as a function of (ii) above, participants feel morally compelled to implement decisions of the network; and (iv) failure to observe credible commitments can lead to exclusion from the network (ibid.).

There is a debate in political science over whether comitology committees are dominated by a collaborative culture which overturns narrow self-interest (Joerges and Neyer 1997) or whether a calculating rationalist approach dominates (Pollack 2003). More recent research has found that different committees exhibit different cultures (Hansen and Bradsma 2009). Unfortunately, this research did not test for the effects of different types of committees. One might suspect that advisory committees, where the member states effectively have to persuade the Commission to change course, might have a different culture from examination commit-tees, where the member states can more easily exercise a veto. What Hansen and Bradsma did find was that distributive effects and business interests were strongly predictive of a culture of intergovernmental bargaining (ibid.). The preconditions which Eberlein and Grande's deem necessary for ERNs of "independent" NRAs to achieve deliberative supranationalism are drawn from the research on cooperative work in comitology. But the assumption of coop-eration in ERNs sits uneasily with Hansen and Bradsma's findings that distributive conflicts produce a different culture, since it is normally only in sectors where there is distributive conflict that EU legislation requires the creation of independent NRAs (Kelemen and Tarrant 2011).

Political Choice

The political choice approach to institutional selection is rooted in rational choice analysis. Member state preferences align with the interest of dominant domestic interest groups, the European Parliament favours more diffuse consumer interests and an increase in its power and relevance, and the European Commission seeks to extend its powers to pursue European integration (Kelemen and Tarrant 2011). Where engaged, the CJEU also has a quasi-legislative role (Hix and Boyland 2011). National courts, where empowered by the legislative norm, act as independent bodies, constraining national bodies to abide by the terms of legislation. The institutions selected to regulate are those which fit the preferences of those decision-makers which are relevant. Relevance in this context is a function of the decision-making structure which varies between treaty making, ordinary legislation, delegated legislation, and the court room and how important a decision-maker is to creating a majority (when that is required). A focus on the formation of winning coalitions can induce sensitivity to the formation of preferences at the national level and sensitivity to the nuances of the agreed rules in which the selected institution operates. Those researching the formation of political choice in the regulatory sphere have, for example, noted that privatisation and the retreat to the role of an umpire by the state has been an Anglo-Saxon rather than a continental European model (Cliften, Comin and Diaz Fuentes 2006). They have noted that NRAs have been subject to interference from national ministries (Tarrant, Coen and Cadman 2014) and that choice of legislative norms has excluded European courts from reviewing national regulatory decisions (ibid.). They have also shown that rules in European directives regulating liberalised markets have neither been detailed nor comprehensive and have instead left discretion over substantive outcome determining content to NRAs (Kelemen and Tarrant 2011, Tarrant, Coen and Cadman 2014, Tarrant and Kelemen 2017).

One theoretical approach of political choice theorists has been to adopt principal–agent analyses (Coen and Thatcher 2008; Kelemen and Tarrant 2011). This was a heuristic device that required classifying the precise nature of the principals and the agents, the regulatory institutions, which were selected and the rules that bound them. One of the insights of principal–agent theory is that agents may be deliberately designed to not be able to deliver some or all the objectives with which they have ostensibly been tasked. From a principal's point of view, attributes can include technical inefficiency as well as efficiency (McCubbins 1985). In the EU context, a desirable function of a regulatory rule or institution from the perspective of some member state principals could be that it permits defection from the ostensibly agreed single market principles.

Once the nature of the principals, agents, and the relationship between them was established, the research agenda has moved to explaining the variation in the selection of regulatory institutions. While this always formed part of the analysis, it was tied to the explanation of variation in specific regulatory sectors (Kelemen and Tarrant 2011). The attempt is now to systematise this by examining whether we can tie institutional variation in the design of economic regulators and regulation to the impact on legislative outcomes of the interaction between systematically different national varieties of capitalism (Tarrant, Coen and Cadman 2014; Guidi, Guardiancich and Levi-Faur 2019). This nonetheless requires researchers to carefully investigate national political economies. As Hancké et al. point out sectoral political economies in a member state may have a different pattern of relationships and institutions than the dominant national pattern (Hancké et al. 2008). To give an example, a society which generally exhibits the characteristics of a coordinated market economy may have very different institutions in a sector which includes a dominant state-owned company.

Principal–agent theory
Principal and agent analyses seek to understand the hierarchic relationship between institutions which delegate power, for example, in a legislative act, and those which receive it (Pollack 1997; Stone-Sweet and Thatcher 2003). The tracing of legislative agreement (and disagreement) over controls and empowerments tells us about much more than solely the relationship between the Commission and NRAs and brings other potential principals and intermediate agents into focus. It may allow us to determine which principals are more important in the legislative process than others. It may inform us as to who gets to influence the ostensibly empowered "independent" national regulator: it may be the case that independence is not defined in the legislation as independence from national ministries. The Commission may be permitted to be an ongoing principal with regards to some sectoral regulatory issues but expressly excluded from involvement others. The dominant principals may agree that NRAs are authorised to regulate certain actors in certain circumstances but exclude them from regulating in others. It may also be that courts can review some types of NRA decision but are excluded from ruling on others. Engaging in this kind of analysis is more demanding than it may seem at first sight. A precise understanding of the legislation and its interaction with an evolving jurisprudence is a necessary but insufficient step. Accurate analysis also requires a deep understanding of the economics and law of a regulated sector to appreciate which powers and controls are relevant and whether they are complete or not. To give one example, political science commentators have sometimes talk of the requirements relating to regulatory rules in the European directives relating to telecommunications as being both comprehensive and detailed (Levi-Faur 1999; Thatcher 2001). Reading commentary from other academic disciplines is likely to be of assistance. Economists have pointed out the absence of detail in directives meant that NRAs enjoy the discretion to set the costs of access at levels that at one extreme could prevent competition altogether and at the other could encourage the entry of less efficient rivals (Cave and Crandall 2001) and lawyers have identified that courts have stated that there is insufficient detail in the directives for them to create direct effect (Tarrant, Coen and Cadman 2014; Larouche and Taton 2011). Such appreciation on the part of the researcher is of course rendered more difficult because the necessity of different types of institution, powers and controls are often highly contested issues in the politics of a regulated sector. Many NRAs and ministries will not readily admit that national institutional choices in legislative discussions are driven by considerations of national advantage.

Varieties of capitalism and regulatory design
The varieties of capitalism literature argues that different types of capitalism operate in different European countries, and they have different configurations of supporting institutions (Hall and Soskice 2001). Most authors would now identify three main strains of capitalism; coordinated market economies, liberal market economies and state-led economies and the three European countries which are typically considered to be the closest to the ideal types are Germany, the UK and France (Schmidt 2002). The effects of comparative advantage are held to apply to institutional configurations just as they do to products so member states will seek to perpetuate existing institutions rather than converge on a particular variety.

A set of the key institutional features which determine the nature of regulatory regimes in networked utility industries, which comprise almost all the sectors in which the EU has required the creation of independent NRAs, has been developed by Thatcher (2007). He notes that it is "perhaps surprising" that national governments largely accepted EU directives in sectors that were traditionally state led in several major member states given that EU framework directives privilege a liberal market economy model (ibid.). However, this puzzle is likely to be solved by detailed parsing of EU legislation in regulated network sectors. While the directives encourage a regulated liberal market in principle, they do not require its adoption in practice at the national level. It was perfectly feasible for countries which wished to preserve other varieties of capitalism to sign up to these frameworks. It could even be positively advantageous, allowing their companies easier access to adjacent liberal markets whilst the configuration of their national institutions operated to inhibit reciprocal cross-border competition (Eberlein 2003). This is not a surprising outcome. EU regulatory frameworks required majority support from member states to be adopted. In all the regulated network sectors in the EU there has always been at least a blocking minority of countries with institutions closer to the characteristics that Thatcher identified as state-led rather than those issuing from the regulated competitive model - similar to what other authors would call the liberal market model.[1]

The advantage of a varieties of capitalism based approach is that it allows us to bring together regulatory studies and comparative political economy (Guidi, Guardiancich and Levi-Faur 2019). EU rules are endogenous to the collective preferences of decision-makers in the Council, so we are likely to be able to better explain the nature of EU legislation and the institutions it creates, if we understand the potential interactions between these institutions and the national systems. Put starkly, in a sector with a blocking minority of countries with state led institutions which make decisions regarding national champions is there likely to be a vote in favour of an EU Agency where legally the Commission necessarily takes the final regulatory decision? Equally, in such a situation, would it be a surprise if there was likely to be a preference instead for a regulatory network, where NRAs can choose to discuss topics of general interest, but the network cannot take binding decisions? Analysis by Wassum and De Francesco has found that at national level, member states grant less regulatory autonomy to utility regulators, the more coordinated an economy is and the more veto players are present (Wassum and De Francesco 2020). If agencies are empowered at the EU-level, they potentially create greater NRA autonomy by making them part of joint decision-making at the EU-level, playing in a nested game.

HOW DO WE TEST THEORIES WHICH SEEK TO EXPLAIN THE CHOICE OF REGULATORY BODY?

The regulatory body or bodies which are adopted are part of the regulatory process. There is always an intended or ostensible logic of consequentiality. The purpose of the body is to make regulatory decisions. The purpose of these decisions is to change the behaviour of regulated entities. The change in behaviour is intended to deliver certain market outcomes as opposed to others (Guidi, Guardiancich and Levi-Faur 2019). Theories can therefore be tested by looking at the effects of changes in the variables that make up this logical chain. If for example, a European directive is ostensibly intended to open up competition in a sector and the institutions adopted to achieve this are NRAs organised into a network, but there is systematic variation in the regulatory output of the NRAs, and this gives rise to systematic variation in market outcomes in the member states, then it may be that the ostensible overarching legislative goal was not actually a shared objective. Further investigation of the negotiating preferences of the decision-makers may reveal differences between member states with different political economies and between the collective Council position and the Commission and the Parliament. Testing the theory is likely to be facilitated by the fact that in most regulated sectors there are now multiple iterations of negotiation over institutional questions. The European Commission returning time and again to push for either itself or European agencies to be given the power to review NRA decisions over market-determining regulatory questions. We may also simultaneously observe on issues in the same sector or in other sectors that member states do agree to European agencies. The interesting question is explaining the cause of this variation.

The Structures Influencing European Legislators

If the focus of the research is EU legislative decision-making, it is important to be cognisant of the specific constraints faced by the legislators. In the regulated network sectors, the status quo ante favours the countries with state-led political economies. The European Commission was able to force them,[2] using innovative own initiative competition law directives, to formally open monopolised sectors with a single state-owned monopoly (Sandholtz 1998; Schmidt 1999). However, competition law was not a sufficient legal norm for then regulating access to the network – a necessity for actual rather than theoretical competition (Ungerer 1996; Tarrant, Coen and Cadman 2014). Regulatory rules or the creation of substantive new institutions require a qualified majority of member states to be in favour. The Commission and Parliament both have some leverage. Either can effectively veto new legislation. This, however, is potentially only a weak power if these institutions are in favour of a liberal market model but the status quo ante favours the state-led model. This endows member states with sectors with this characteristic a great deal of power in circumscribing the contours of legislation.

The legislative conditions operative in the regulated network sectors are not of course applicable across every single sector in which the EU has competence. Competition law is the notable and sui generic exception where the member states gave the Commission power major implementation powers in an important area but did not endow themselves with any substantive review powers (Allen 1996). They had instead attempted to circumscribe the Commission's powers by limiting its scope to cross-border trade and by giving it no control over mergers (Pollack 2003). However, over the decades, the CJEU worked to widen the Commission and EU's scope until solely national jurisdiction became a narrow field and the EU's competence dominated (Kelemen 2011). Legislating in ways which constrained these kind of developments was something which the member states learned from this process (Tuerk, Rowe and Hofmann 2012). Although some have described the form of governance in European competition law as comprising of network governance (Kassim and Wright 2010) this is not a full description, if the definition of network governance remains one where supranational influence is purely deliberative (Blauberger and Rittberger 2015; Abbot and Snidal 2009). There is a network which provides a valuable forum for discussion and requires NCAs to inform the Commission if the former open a case. However, what really constrains national competition authorities to stay within the general competition policy are two forms of hard hierarchical authority. First, national courts are obliged to follow Commission precedents when reviewing the decisions of NCAs and private parties can require national courts to undertake such review. Second, the Commission can and does override National Competition Authorities. This is not by taking cases away from NCAs which it is empowered to do under Article 11(6) regulation 1/2003. Instead, it opens its own case in the same area after the national competition authorities and regulators have concluded, which is far more public and arguably as a consequence more humiliating (Tarrant 2021). The CJEU has ruled that the normal legal principle of not being arraigned twice on the same facts does not apply. The prior decision of a national competition authority cannot prevent the Commission undertaking its own competition law review on the same facts because otherwise "[this] would undermine the power of the Commission".[3] Due to the structuring of the rules in legislation, neither of these powers are available in the rules in the sectors where independent NRAs dominate decision-making.

The Outputs

The essential outputs of regulatory institutions will generally consist of two types: rules and enforcement of rules. Researchers do need to be clear as to what comprise the necessary rules in a sector in order to meet the ostensible regulatory objective. It is not unusual in sector regulation for agencies to be empowered to review NRA decisions on issues which do not determine market outcomes in domestic economies and for NRAs alone to be empowered in areas that are determinative of competition. For example, in telecoms, the Commission and an Agency, BEREC, can review NRA decisions regarding who is regulated but they cannot review decisions about how they are regulated. In rail, safety regulations are determined by an Agency/the Commission but questions regarding economic access to the network are restricted to NRAs.

When examining regulatory output, there needs to be some sophistication regarding its content. Tarrant, Coen and Cadman (2014) looked at wholesale broadband regulation in nine member states in 2009 and found that almost all regulators had mandated that in principle a wholesale product ought to be made available to competitors. However, they also found that almost none had at that time ensured effective implementation in line with the general principles of the directive: which required that a non-discriminatory wholesale product be made available. Most NRAs had set up systems which meant that they could not know whether this was the case and this in a situation where the regulated national entity had an economic interest in making sure that it discriminated against cross-border competitors (Tarrant, Coen and Cadman 2014).

Research on the effectiveness of ERNs has primarily consisted of case studies looking at one sector (Vantaggiato, Kassim and Wright 2021). These have typically involved asking the NRA/NCA participants as to their perception of effectiveness. This is certainly one measure. However, it may not provide a metric which permits comparison between ERNs as the component elements of "effectiveness" may be defined differently or left vague. There is also a risk of bias. The consequence of NRAs disavowing the effectiveness of an ERN would be ammunition for Commission and Parliament advocates for European agencies. It might be advisable to engage in triangulation and ask the companies and consumer groups which interact with the regulation whether they consider that an ERN is effective. This kind of approach has been adopted when analysing the effectiveness of EU agencies (Hauray 2006; Coen and Salter 2020). While perceptions of effectiveness are one source of information as to what happens inside an informal network, if the argument is that ERNs are an effective functional mechanism for closing the "implementation gap", we are not restricted to oral testimony as a source. It should be seen in the degree to which there is a convergence on best practice regulatory output by the NRAs or whether there are divergences which correlate with distinct patterns of political economy. Kudrna has, for example, found that harmonised banking regulation permits a series of national exceptions and that there is a distinct pattern of exceptions exercised depend on the type of banking capitalism in the member state (Kudrna 2020).

The Consequences of Regulation

The ultimate ambition behind EU single market directives which create regulatory institutions is a competitive single market. Regulation is often adopted, particularly in the network sectors, because the single market is still partitioned into distinct national markets.

If regulatory output is effective, then we should see changes in market structure and activity which reflect a Europeanisation of national markets. If we do not see this happening over a period of time in a particular sector, then we should be investigating whether the institutions have been designed in a way which permits the maintenance of separate national markets which are in practice regulated differently and whether different types of institutions in other sectors have given rise to different market outcomes.

Investigation by political scientists of the consequences of sector specific regulation is in its infancy (Mastenbroek and Martinsen 2018, Guidi, Guardiancich and Levi-Faur 2019). Nonetheless, some work on the consequences of national application of EU regulatory rules has already been undertaken. Guidi hypotheses that the more formal independence that a country's NCA enjoys, the more foreign investment it will receive and the lower its general price level will be. Guidi finds that formal independence has no effect on market activity (Guidi 2015). One possible explanation he suggests for this finding is that the formal independence of NCAs is no measure of their actual independence and that inward investors might take a wider view of whether the competition regime is effective in practice or not. If we take a specific sectoral example, telecoms, the de facto rather than the de jure effectiveness of national competition law regimes were a material factor in decisions for British Telecommunications to invest in European countries. Their local legal experts concluded that a majority of national competition authorities would decline to take cases against the local national champion (Tarrant, Coen and Cadman 2014). More generally empirical research has found that there is both significant correlations between state ownership in the utility sector and higher market and between state ownership and less effective implementation of regulation (ibid.).

CONCLUSION AND FUTURE RESEARCH INTO EU INDEPENDENT REGULATION

Forms of European Independent economic regulation has evolved dramatically in the last 20 years. However, what drives this economic integration, and the forms and functions of the European Regulation is still contested. To whom the NRAs, ERNs and EA are accountable, who has delegated authority and what impact have these new bodies had on member states regulatory autonomy are still being explored in economics, law and political science.

Functionalist accounts stress professionalisation and creation of professional norms in networks which have given rise to supernatural deliberation without explaining of what these norms consist or what effect they have had in practice. Nor if these effects do occur, has a robust identification of variation and its causes been undertaken. Evidence from the emergence of ERNs would tend to indicate that national interests and market regulatory goals are what drive regulatory practice and policymaking at the EU rather than networks and best practice (Coen and Héritier 2005, Coen and Thatcher 2008, and Kelemen and Tarrant 2011). Research into the politics of regulatory design at EU-level has tended to focus on the final agreement between the EU institutions without undertaking comprehensive and detailed research into the positions of either the different EU legislators or the different positions held within the institutions. This is of course difficult to do as it requires a detailed knowledge of the sector in order to understand: (i) what the difference is between a detailed regulatory policy proscription and what is a policy principle capable of permitting highly varied national implementing measures; and (ii) the economic ramifications of highly technical policy, permitting an understanding of which policy preferences eventually dominated in the legislative process.

Research into policies adopted by NRAs as part of EU frameworks is similarly difficult because it requires a detailed knowledge of the range of possibilities and the economic consequences of the selection of a particular option. The rarity of such analysis and the need for it is widely acknowledged (Guidi, Guardiancich and Levi-Faur 2020). In agencies with their multiple principals (NRAs, members states, Commission) and control by the ECJ, similar questions arise regarding who dominates the decision-making process, how and why? And what explains variation between the regulatory performance of different agencies? Rather than chasing the chimera of abstract independence, comparing sectors with regulators which are not Europeanised with sectors which are institutionally Europeanised may allow us to identify whether Europeanisation gives rise or not to superior regulation? Here of course the warning continues to apply that accurately identifying "Europeanisation" requires a sharp eye for spotting Potemkin villages (for more information on regulatory agencies in the European context see also Chapters 9 and 20).

NOTES

1.   At the height of privatisation in 2008, it was found that at least ten member states had ownership in economic actors in each of the utility sectors regulated by the EU (Tarrant, Coen, and Cadman: 2014). Since the global financial crisis, state ownership has increased again in Europe with several countries reversing previous privatisations at the national or regional level.
2.   This was very much against the will of several countries which appealed to the CJEU and lost.
3.   Prezes Urzędu Ochrony Konkurencji i Konsumentów v Tele2 Polska sp. z o.o., devenue Netia SA, c-375/09 at para 26.

REFERENCES

Abbot, K. and Snidal, D. (2009) Strengthening International Regulation through Transnational New Governance: Overcoming the Orchestration Deficit. *Vanderbildt Journal of Transnational Law* 42:2.

Allen, D. (1996) Competition Policy, in Wallace, H. and Wallace, W. (eds) *Policy-making in the European Union*. Oxford: Oxford University Press, 157–183.

Blauberger, M. and Rittberger, B (2015) Conceptualizing and Theorizing EU Regulatory Networks. *Regulation & Governance* 9, 367–376.

Blom-Hansen, J. (2011) *The EU Comitology System in Theory and Practice: Keeping an Eye on the Commission?* Basingstoke: Palgrave Macmillan.

Busuioc, M. (2013) *European Agencies: Law and Practice of Accountability*. Oxford: Oxford University Press.

Busuioc, M. and Lodge, M. (2017) Reputation and Accountability relationships: Managing accountability expectations through reputation. *Public Administration Review* 77:1, 91–100.

Cave, M. and Crandall, R.W. (2001) *Telecommunications Liberalisation on Two Sides of the Atlantic*. Washington: AEI-Brookings Joint Center for Regulatory Studies.

Cliften, J., Comin, F. and Diaz Fuentes, D. (2006) Privatizing Public Enterprises in the European Union, 1960–2002: Ideological, pragmatic, inevitable? *Journal of European Public Policy* 13:5, 736–756.

Coen, D. and Doyle C. (2000) Designing Economic Regulatory Institutions for the European Network Industries. *Current Politics and Economics of Europe* 9:4, 455–476.

Coen, D. and Thatcher, M. (2008) Network Governance and Multi-level Delegation. European Networks of Regulatory Agencies. *Journal of Public Policy* 28:1, 42–71.

Coen, D., Guidi, M., Héritier, A. and Yordanova, N. (2020) The Logic of Business Regulatory Venue Shopping. *Public Policy and Administration* 36:3, 323–342.

Coen, D. and Héritier A. (eds) (2005) *Redefining Regulatory Regimes: Utilities in Europe*. Cheltenham, UK and Northampton, MA, USA: Edward Elgar Publishing.

Coen, D. and Salter, J.P. (2020) Multi-level Regulatory Governance: Establishing bank-regulator relationships at the European Banking Authority. *Business and Politics* 22:1, 86–113.

Coen, D., Katsaitis, A. and Vannoni, M. (2021) *Business Lobbying in the European Union*. Oxford: Oxford University Press.

Danielsen, A. and Yesilkagit, K. (2014) The Effects of European Regulatory Networks on the Bureaucratic Autonomy of National Regulatory Authorities. *Public Organization Review* 14, 353–371.

Dehousse, R. (1997) Regulation by Networks in the European Community. *Journal of European Public Policy* 4:2, 246–261.

Eberlein, B. (2003) Formal and Informal Governance in Single Market Regulation, in Tomas, C. and Piattoni, S. (eds) *Informal Governance in the EU*. Cheltenham, UK and Northampton, MA, USA: Edward Elgar Publishing, 150–172.

Eberlein, B. and Grande, E. (2005) Beyond Delegation: Transnational Regulatory Regimes and the EU Regulatory State. *Journal of European Public Policy* 12:1, 89–112.

Eberlein, B. and Newman, A. (2008) Escaping the International Governance Dilemma? Incorporated Transgovernmental Networks in the European Union. *Governance: An International Journal of Policy, Administration, and Institutions* 21:1, 25–52.

Ennser-Jedenastik, L. (2016) The Politicization of Regulatory Agencies: Between partisan influence and formal independence. *Journal of Public Administration Research and Theory*, 26:3, 507–518.

European Court of Auditors (2020) Future of EU Agencies – Potential for More Flexibility and Cooperation Special Report 22 Brussels: Office of Publications of the European Union.

Gilardi, F. (2004) Institutional Change in Regulatory Policies: Regulation through independent agencies and the three new institutionalisms, in Jordana, J. and Levi-Faur, D. (eds) *The Politics of Regulation, Institutions and Regulatory Reform for the Age of Governance*. Cheltenham, UK and Northampton, MA, USA: Edward Elgar Publishing, 67–89.

Griller, S. and Orater, A. (2010) Everything Under Control? The "Way Forward" for European Agencies in the Footsteps of the Meroni Doctrine. *European Law Review* 3:5, 3–35.

Guidi, M. (2015) The Impact of Independence on Regulatory Outcomes: The case of the EU competition policy. *Journal of Common Market Studies* 53:6, 1195–1213.

Guidi, M., Guardiancich, I. and Levi-Faur, D. (2020) Modes of Regulatory Governance: A political economy perspective, *Governance* 33:1, 5–19.

Hall, P.A. and Soskice, D. (2001) *Varieties of Capitalism. The Institutional Foundations of Comparative Advantage*. Oxford: Oxford University Press.

Hancké et al. (eds) (2008) *Beyond Varieties of Capitalism: Conflict, Contradictions, and Complementarities in the European Economy*. Oxford: Oxford University Press.

Hanretty, C. and Koop, C. (2012) Measuring the Formal Independence of Regulatory Agencies. *Journal of European Public Policy*, 19, 198–216.

Hansen, B. and Bradsma, G. (2009) The EU Comitology System: Intergovernmental bargaining and deliberative supranationalism? *Journal of Common Market Studies* 47:4, 719–740.

Hauray, B. (2006) *L'Europe du Medicament*. Paris: Presses de Science Po.

Hix, S. and Boyland, H. (2011) *The Political System of the European Union*. Basingstoke and New York: Palgrave Macmillan.

Hoynck, S. (2012) Indépéndant de qui ? Les trois âges de l'indépendance des régulateurs des télécommunications en Europe revue. *Francaise d'Administration Publique* 143:3, 791–801.

Jacqué, J-P. (2018) *Droit institutionnel de l'Union Européenne*, 9th edition. Paris: Dalloz.

Joerges, C. and Neyer, J. (1997) From Intergovernmental Bargaining to Deliberative Political Process: The Constitutionalisation of Comitology. *European Law Journal*, 3, 273–299.

Kassim, H. and Wright, K. (2010) The European Competition Network: A European regulatory network with a difference, Paper presented at ECPR Standing Group on regulatory governance, Third Biennial Conference, Dublin, 17–19 June 2010.

Kelemen, R.D. (2005) The Politics of Eurocracy: Building a New European State. *The State of the European Union* 7, 173–189.

Kelemen, R.D. (2011) *Eurolegalism*. Cambridge, MA: Harvard University Press.

Kelemen, R.D. and Tarrant. A.D. (2011) The Political Foundations of the Eurocracy. *West European Politics*, 34:5, 922–947.

Kudrna, Z. (2020) The Varieties of Banking Regulation in the EU: An empirical analysis. *Governance* 33:1, 79–92.

Larouche, P. and Taton, X. (2011) *Enforcement and Judicial Review of Decisions of National Regulatory Authorities*. Brussels: Centre on Regulation in Europe.

Levi, B. and Spiller, P. (1996) The Institutional Foundations of Regulatory Commitment: A comparative analysis of telecommunications regulation. *Journal of Law, Economics and Organisation* 10, 201–246.

Levi-Faur, D. (1999) The Governance of Competition: The interplay of technology, economics and politics in European Union electricity and telecommunications regimes. *Journal of Public Policy* 19, 175–207.

Levi-Faur, D. (2005) The Global Diffusion of Regulatory Capitalism. *The Annals of the American Academy of Political and Social Science* 598, 12–32.

Maggetti, M. (2009) The Role of Independent Regulatory Agencies in Policymaking: A comparative analysis. *Journal of European Public Policy*, 16, 445–465.

Maggetti, M. and Gilardi, F. (2011) The Policy-making Structure of European Regulatory Networks and the Domestic Adoption of Standards. *Journal of European Public Policy* 18:6, 830–847.

Majone, G. (1994) The Rise of the Regulatory State in Europe. *West European Politics* 17:3, 77–102.

Majone, G. (1997) The New European Agencies: Regulation by information. *Journal of European Public Policy* 4:2, 262–275.

Mastenbroek, E. and Martinsen, D.S. (2018) Filling the Gap in the European Administrative Space: The role of administrative networks in EU implementation and enforcement. *Journal of European Public Policy* 25:3, 422–435.

Mathieu, G. and Rongoni, B. (2019) Balancing Experimentalist and Hierarchical Governance in European Union Electricity and Telecommunications Regulation: A matter of degrees. *Regulation and Governance* 13:4, 577–592.

McCubbins, M.D. (1985) The Legislative Design of Regulatory Structure. *American Journal of Political Science* 29:4, 721–748.

Pollack, M.A. (1997) Delegation, Agency and Agenda Setting in the European Community. *International Organization* 51:1, 99–134.

Pollack, M.A. (2003) *The Engines of European Integration: Delegation, Agency and Agenda Setting in the EU*. Oxford: Oxford University Press.

Sabel, C. and Zeitlin, J. (2008) Learning from Difference: The new architecture of experimentalist governance in the EU. *European Law Journal*, 14:3, 271–327.

Sandholz, W. (1998) The Emergence of a Supranational Telecommunications Regime, in Sandholz, W. and Stone-Sweet, A. (eds) *European Integration and Supranational Governance*. Oxford: Oxford University Press, 134–163.

Schmidt, S. (1999) Sterile Debates and Dubious Generalisations: European integration theory tested in telecommunications and electricity. *Journal of European Public Policy* 16:2, 233–271.

Schmidt, V.A. (2002) *The Futures of European Capitalism*. Oxford: Oxford University Press.

Stone-Sweet, A. and Thatcher, M. (eds) (2003) *The Politics of Delegation*. London: Frank Cass.

Tarrant, A. (2021) Is "orchestration" likely to deliver harmony? Assessing the motivation for the selection of European Regulatory Networks and supranational agencies in European competition law and European telecommunications regulation and their relative effectiveness in delivering the Single Market. Mastere specialise, Ecole Nationale d'Administration.

Tarrant, A. and Kelemen, R.D. (2017) Reconceptualizing EU Regulatory Networks: A response to Blauberger and Rittberger. *Regulation & Governance*, 11:2, 213–222.

Tarrant, A., Coen, D. and Cadman, R. (2014) EU Regulatory Frameworks in Network Industries: Defining national varieties of capitalism? *European Networks Law & Regulation Quarterly* 1:1, 43–64.

Thatcher, M. (2001) The Commission and National Governments as Partners: EC regulatory expansion in telecommunications, 1979–2000. *Journal of European Public Policy*, 8:4, 558–584.

Thatcher, M. (2007) *Internationalisation and Economic Institutions: Comparing the European Experience*. Oxford: Oxford University Press.

Thatcher, M. (2011) The Creation of European Regulatory Agencies and its Limits: A comparative analysis of European Delegation. *Journal of European Public Policy* 18:6, 790–809.

Thatcher, M. and Coen, D. (2008) Delegation to Independent Regulatory Agencies: Pressures, functions and contextual mediation. *West European Politics* 25:1, 125–147.

Tuerk, A., Rowe, G. and Hofmann, H. (2012) *Administrative Law and Policy of the European Union*. Oxford: Oxford University Press.

Ungerer, H. (1996) Liberalisation of Information Infrastructure and Services. The perspective of EU Competition Policy. Speech to the International Pricing and Facilities Conference, 3 October 1996.

Vantaggiato, F., Kassim, H. and Wright, K. (2021) Internal Network Structures as Opportunity Structures: Control and effectiveness in the European competition network. *Journal of European Public Policy*, 28:4, 571–590.

Wassum, M. and De Francesco, F. (2020) Explaining Regulatory Autonomy in EU Network Sectors: Varieties of utility regulation? *Governance* 33:1, 41–60.

4.   Independent regulatory agencies in Latin America

Andrés Pavón Mediano and Camilo Ignacio González[1]

INTRODUCTION

Neither a country nor a policy sector has remained untouched by the adoption of Independent Regulatory Agencies (IRAs) in Latin America and the Caribbean, including state-controlled economies such as Venezuela and long-standing open economies such as Chile. Indeed, a recent study on IRAs covering 17 regulatory sectors across the world registered 217 IRAs in 20 countries of Latin America and the Caribbean (Jordana et al. 2018), confirming that the agencification of regulatory policy is a hallmark of the region's institutional landscape. The delegation of supervisory and regulatory powers to non-majoritarian administrative agencies managed by non-elected officials and structurally detached from ministries (IRAs) was labeled early in Europe as the "rise of the regulatory state" (Majone 1994), and its worldwide adoption across countries has been identified as a sign of the global diffusion of regulatory capitalism (Braithwaite 2008). In Latin America, the agencification of the regulatory institutional land-scape since the late 1980s has been well documented, and it demonstrates a clear trend of government innovation (Manzetti 2000; Jordana and Levi-Faur 2005, 2006; Lodge and Stirton 2006). Alongside the privatization and liberalization of economic sectors and the democratiza-tion of Latin America, most countries in the region moved away from the direct provision of public services toward their private delivery under agency supervision. Since these large-scale economic and political changes arose simultaneously, it was expected that the administrative reconfiguration of the region's states as regulators had received little attention in the literature at that time. However, a growing body of literature has studied the development, form, and challenges of agencies in the region.

Studies on the regulatory state in developing countries have emphasized that the regulatory agency model interacted with national political processes and, to some extent, it was incorpo-rated without a common understanding of its purpose. As a result, "regulatory agencies in the South are more likely to begin as relatively hollow institutional shells, which are populated by expectations, norms of institutional practice, and operational rules and cultures over time" (Dubash and Morgan 2012, p.267). Therefore, when studying regulatory agencies in Latin America, one must pay particular attention to the region's specific context.

Regulatory institutions in Latin America are characterized by three main contextual factors. First, IRAs have the necessity to combine pro-competition measures with redistributive and developmental policy goals. This diversity in policy goals increases the interaction between regulatory authorities and other public organizations in a context where, in some cases, the concern for redistribution conflicts with the mission of the regulatory authority. Second, regulatory authorities are a part of public administration systems that are often subject to high levels of politicization beyond what can be found in the United States and Western Europe, and which are characterized by low capacity and low professionalization. Finally, regulatory authorities must frequently deal with underdeveloped markets with limited actors and limited competition. These contextual factors suggest that the general conclusions about regulatory agencies in Europe and the United States might not hold in Latin America. Consequently, this chapter presents the rise and evolution of regulatory agencies in the region, discussing their interaction with specific countries' contextual features.

The chapter is structured as follows. The next section summarizes the literature on the rise of IRAs in Latin America and provides insight into the shape of regulatory agencies regarding their formal independence and regulatory capabilities. Moreover, research findings regarding the political economy of delegation to IRAs in the region are presented, discussing the drivers of agencies' institutional design and the role of credible commitment, ideas, and national institutions in the process. The third section stresses the relevance of four research agendas that must be addressed in order to increase our knowledge of how regulatory agencies interact with the regional political context, their functions, and the outputs they generate. We suggest that it is first necessary to extend the research focus beyond the utilities sectors and formal independence. Second, a relevant inquiry is the study of de facto independence, especially, concerning the interaction of agencies with populist governments and market players. Third, we argue that the research on agencies' capacities and tools is still underdeveloped and needs further emphasis. Finally, a key research focus in the regional context regards the interplay of regulatory agencies with development goals and redistributive policies. Conclusions are presented in the final section.

THE RISE OF THE LATIN-AMERICAN REGULATORY STATE

From a comparative historical perspective, the institutional development of IRAs in Latin America has been characterized by two stages of diffusion (Jordana and Levi-Faur 2006). The first stage spanning from the 1920s to 1979 shows a clear sector-centered pattern of diffusion across central banking and financial regulation sectors in the region. The second stage of diffusion is distinguished by the privatization and liberalization of utilities and the extraordinary expansion of IRAs across sectors and countries. This expansion was not only in economic areas but also in social regulatory sectors, and distinct national features shaped IRAs design (idem).

Jordana's (2011) review of the historical roots of IRAs in Latin America has highlighted their institutional origins in the colonial 'superintendencias' – a single-headed public body in charge of managing specific areas of public administration separated from the rest of the administration. This legacy indeed explains why IRAs in the region were commonly called superintendencias and many were designed as single-headed bodies rather than boards as is the case in the U.S. Nonetheless, there is consensus that, as in other regions, the key basis of the institutional development of IRAs was the adoption of mixed public–private central banks during the 1920s and 1930s by more than ten countries in the region, among them Colombia (1923), Chile (1925), Mexico (1925), Ecuador (1927), and Peru (1931), as well as new banking laws and semi-autonomous financial supervisory authorities in these countries. Here, the influence of the U.S. Kemmerer Mission on the institutional development of these agencies across the Andes region must be noted (Jordana and Levi-Faur 2006).

In a post-First-World-War context of growing debt owed to the United States and a higher dependence on U.S. imports, the mission headed by Princeton economist E.W. Kemmerer was highly successful in advising countries on the adoption of a U.S. model of agency configuration (Drake 1989). Although the creation of supervisory agencies modestly continued during the era of the developmental state and import substitutions in Latin America – most notably with the creation of competition law enforcement agencies – it was not until the 1980s and 1990s that IRAs arose in the region, as elsewhere, as a clear sign of institutional reconfiguration (Gilardi et al. 2007).

The rapid emergence of the regulatory state in Latin America has largely been explained by the privatization and liberalization of utilities resulting from fiscal crises alongside a neoliberal economic model of governance that occurred with the spread of globalization and re-democratization in the region (Chong and Lopez-de-Silanes 2005; Dubash and Morgan 2013). The champion of the privatization process in the early 1980s was Chile, which was led by technocrats during Pinochet's dictatorship (Muñoz 1992) who opened the path to reform for the whole region (Gutiérrez 2003). From this point forward, many sectors and countries began to adopt privatization and regulatory reforms, where new legal structures and IRAs were embraced as signals of credible commitment to investors (Levy and Spiller 1997). Following Chile, Argentina, Venezuela, and Mexico experimented a fast process of privatization and agencification (Jordana and Levi-Faur 2006). For instance, in just three years (1990–1992), reforms in Argentina were made in seven regulatory authorities. Brazil began privatizing its steel and petrochemicals industries, and since 1994, the country embraced accelerated privatization in the utilities sectors through the granting of concessions monitored by IRAs rather than asset transference (Amann and Baer 2005). Countries such as Bolivia, Colombia, and Peru started their reforms in the first half of the 1990s and reached a stable regulatory framework rather quickly. Although Central American countries were latecomers to this new model of governance, El Salvador, Guatemala, Honduras, Nicaragua, and Panama passed legislative reforms adopting a similar model of privatization, agencification, and regulation.

Beside reforms in the utilities sectors, privatization and agencification also occurred in the health and pension sectors of many countries, and since the late 1990s, IRAs were increasingly created in social and risk regulatory areas. In parallel, many financial and insurance IRAs were largely redesigned with respect to their autonomy and powers during the same period (Pavón Mediano 2020). As will be shown in the next section, rather than following a similar pattern of institutional design, the institutional shape of IRAs in Latin America has been rather heterogeneous.

The Formal Independence of Latin-American Regulatory Authorities

Although agencification is a clear phenomenon in the institutional landscape of Latin America, many regulatory authorities remain ministries under political control (particularly in social regulation sectors). Furthermore, some agencies are only nominally autonomous, since they are largely dependent from ministries, while others were granted independence at a constitutional level. Using Gilardi's formal independence index (Gilardi 2008), data collected on independence of 104 regulatory authorities across 8 countries and 13 sectors in the region (Figures 4.1 and 4.2) shows high heterogeneity across countries and sectors (Pavón Mediano 2020).

As Gilardi's index registers ministries in charge of regulation as regulatory authorities with zero independence and agencies with full independence equals one, the measure provides a full picture of the administrative structure of each country and sector in the region. To simplify differences among regulatory areas, regulators in Figure 4.1 were clustered by

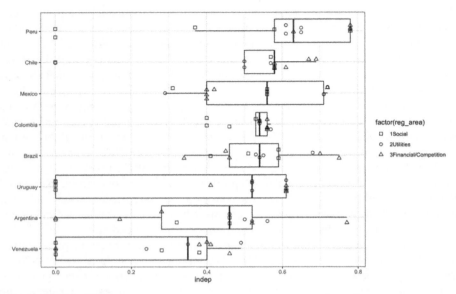

Source: Pavón Mediano (2020).

*Figure 4.1   Formal independence by country and regulatory area based on Gilardi's
index*

social (food safety, pharmaceuticals, environment, and health services), utilities (telecommunications, electricity, gas, and water), and economic sectors other than utilities (competition,
finance, securities and exchange, pensions, and insurance) – the latter hereafter referred to as
'financial/competition regulators'.

At a country level, Figure 4.1 shows that some countries have granted formal independence
in a rather homogeneous way across regulatory areas. This is the case for Colombia, Chile, and
Brazil. In the case of Chile, this can be explained by the common configuration of many IRAs
as *superintendencias*, where agency heads are appointed by the president from a list created
by a committee in charge of high-level civil servant selection, dismissal is generally possible
at the president's discretion, and terms are usually under four years or at the appointer's
discretion.

In the case of Colombia, differences between social and economic IRAs are mainly
explained by the low level of independence concerning the appointment and dismissal of
agency heads in social sectors, while uniformity among economic regulators is explained
by the concentration of financial, insurance, pension, and securities and exchange regulation in one agency, while utilities are regulated by regulatory boards (called *Comisiones de
Regulación*) within a common administrative structure. The adoption of regulatory boards also
explains the uniformity in the institutional design of Brazilian IRAs in the utilities sectors.

Figure 4.1 also indicates that other countries have rather consistently differentiated the independence of their social, utilities, and other economic regulators. In the case of Uruguay, this
diversity is largely explained by the concentration of most non-utilities economic regulators
in its central bank, whose autonomy is established at the constitutional level, allocating in one
agency the oversight of water, gas, and electricity markets, and keeping under ministry super-

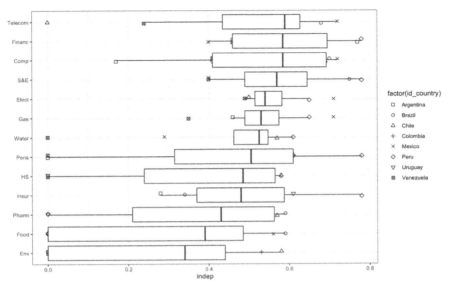

Source: Pavón Mediano (2020).

Figure 4.2   *Formal independence by sector based on Gilardi's index*

vision social regulatory domains. Similarly, Peru's financial, insurance, and pension sectors are under the supervision of the same agency whose autonomy is guaranteed by the country's constitution, while most of its utility regulators were reformed, and given autonomy by law in 2000. On the other hand, agencies in Venezuela have an independence level well-below the median in the region, indicating that ministerial control of supervisory and regulatory agencies is strongly embedded in the Venezuelan administrative structure.

A cross-sectoral examination of the same data is shown in Figure 4.2, highlighting extreme values by country. First, the data unexpectedly indicate that regulators in social sectors, particularly in the environmental and food-safety sectors, are less independent than economic regulators. Second, while independence among social regulators is largely heterogeneous, most utilities regulators present similar levels of formal independence despite the outliers of the Venezuelan gas and water regulators and the Mexican water regulator. The latter is an interesting case study given that it presents the lowest level of independence among Mexican IRAs. Third, the telecommunications sector presents the highest heterogeneity among utilities in the sample. This heterogeneity is illustrated by the contrast between the Mexican *Instituto Federal de Telecomunicaciones*, an agency whose autonomy is granted at the constitutional level, and the Venezuelan and Chilean regulators. The Chilean regulator is also exceptional within Chile's institutional landscape, as it is the only utility regulator in Chile configured as a deputy ministry and not an agency.

Finally and most interestingly, agencies with the highest levels of independence are found among economic regulators in sectors other than utilities. This is a particular feature of the Latin-American regulatory state (Pavón Mediano 2020) since it contradicts expectations based on the literature on credible commitment and evidence from European IRAs, where higher independence among utility regulators is predicted because of the long-term capital expenditures, high degree of asset specificity and the risk of administrative expropriation (Gilardi 2008). Here, it is worth noting the role played by constitution law with respect to the institutional design of some financial regulators presented in Figures 4.1 and 4.2, as many have been granted autonomy at the constitutional level or their competences have been concentrated in central banks. The most notable cases are that of Peru, Argentina and Brazil.

IRAs' Capabilities in Latin America

Besides the emergence of independent agencies, a key feature of the regulatory state is the configuration of agencies as arm's-length bodies capable of overseeing sectors through supervisory powers and the use of norms. Although formally independent, some agencies in Latin America focus only on market supervision and lack either sanctioning powers (reserved to the judiciary) or regulatory powers. In some cases, agencies' decisions can be reversed by other non-independent administrative bodies who are the gatekeepers of regulation, or IRAs competences might cover a small regulatory perimeter, with competences beyond this perimeter remaining under ministerial control. In such context, the study of variations on regulatory capabilities among and within sectors remain relevant to assess the particular form of the regulatory state in the region. In doing so, it is possible to assess the extent to which IRAs in the region are hollow institutional shells defined more by expectations than powers (Dubash and Morgan 2013).

Figures 4.3 and 4.4 provide a glance of the interplay of IRAs' political independence and regulatory capabilities in the region based on a recent major dataset developed by Jordana et al. (2018) that covers the institutional features of IRAs worldwide. The dataset includes 217 agencies in 17 sectors across 20 countries in Latin America and the Caribbean.[2]

Jordana et al.'s (2018) regulatory capabilities dimension considers 14 variables on agencies' supervisory, sanctioning, and regulatory powers and whether agencies' decisions are reviewed by the judiciary or a minister. The political independence dimension comprises variables regarding the appointment, removal, and dismissal of agency heads.[3] The correlation between the two dimensions is 0.40.

Interestingly, Figure 4.3 shows that most IRAs in the utilities sectors score above the mean (zero) in both political independence and regulatory capabilities. Agencies in economic sectors other than utilities are more heterogeneous in terms of regulatory powers, although most of them present values over the mean, both in terms of political independence (73/107) and regulatory capabilities (71/107). Moreover, in these two regulatory areas, the correlation between these two dimensions is rather weak (0.23 and 0.29, respectively), suggesting that other variables might better explain the particular institutional features of these agencies. By contrast, most social regulators have a political independence below the mean (33/49), while regulatory capabilities are distributed evenly above and below this threshold.

The cross-sectoral view of IRA capabilities in Figure 4.4 confirms that utility regulators, particularly electricity and water regulators, have been granted more powers relative to other sectors in the region. Despite outliers mainly found in Cuba, economic regulators in non-utilities sectors show a rather consistent distribution of capabilities within each sector, particularly central banks. This consistency might be partially explained by their original common configuration in the first stage of IRA diffusion in the region, as well as by the fact that many central banks in the region also have competences over other economic regulatory sectors. Regarding social IRAs, most have been granted regulatory capabilities below the

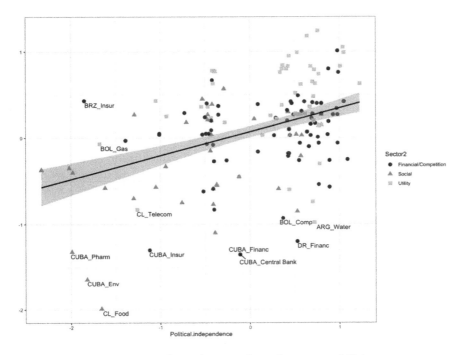

Figure 4.3   IRAs' political independence and regulatory capabilities

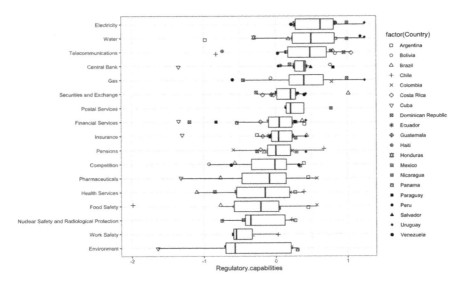

Figure 4.4   IRAs' regulatory capabilities by sector

world mean and present a weak distribution of capabilities relative to economic regulators, especially in the environmental sector, which shows the lowest median value across sectors and the highest dispersion.

Extreme values in terms of low IRA capabilities and political independence in Figure 4.3 are mainly from Cuban regulatory agencies. By contrast, the Bolivian gas agency and the Brazilian insurance regulator are two salient cases of agencies with strong regulatory powers and low political independence. The latter is particularly interesting since most Brazilian regulators in economic sectors other than utilities have been granted considerably greater political independence.

The data presented above confirm that delegating competences to regulatory agencies is a common phenomenon in Latin America. Although the institutional shape of IRAs in the utilities sectors has been more consistent in terms of formal independence and regulatory capabilities, there are considerable differences regarding both dimensions in other sectors and within countries, particularly with respect to social regulation. Whereas exploring the causes and consequences of the institutional design of utility regulators in the region has received considerable attention in the literature, less consideration has been given to cross-sectoral studies and the drivers of the institutional shape of social regulators. The next section provides an overview of this literature.

The Political Economy of Delegation to IRAs in Latin America

First accounts explaining the delegation of competences to IRAs in Latin-American regulatory states emphasized the role of rational choice in the design of regulatory authorities (Levy and Spiller 1997; Montoya and Trillas 2011). Attracting investors by showing credible commitment to a predetermined course of action (e.g., liberalizing markets) and tying politicians' hands despite the rise of new majority coalitions is considered a key explanation for delegation to IRAs that occurred with the rise of the Latin-American regulatory state.

Given Latin-American countries' high degree of administrative discretion and their fear of administrative expropriation of investments (e.g., via renationalization or arbitrary price-setting), creating regulatory agencies with high levels of independence – as well as other institutional reforms – was a way to guarantee trust for market agents (Laffont 2005). Supporting the trust argument, Jordana and Levi-Faur's (2005) cross-sectoral study shows a strong positive effect of privatization on the creation of nominally autonomous IRAs in the region. However, Pavón Mediano's (2020) research indicates that neither privatization nor liberalization significantly impacted IRAs' formal independence levels and that utility regulators were not granted greater independence than other economic regulators. Both findings contradict previous evidence from the study of IRAs in Europe (Gilardi 2008) and cast doubt on ability of the credible commitment hypothesis to fully explain IRAs institutional design.

The role of countries' institutional arrangements and policy ideas have also been studied as possible explanations for shape of IRAs in the region. In studying the proportion of nominally autonomous agencies in a given sector or across country sectors, Jordana et al. (2011) revealed the sectoral and national patterns of diffusion in the region, showing that decisions to create IRAs have been strongly influenced by within-sector channels of diffusion and also by prior decisions to establish IRAs in other sectors in the same country. However, as noted by Dubash (2013), diffusion is unable to explain microdetails of regulatory diffusion that shape regulators. Therefore, testing the role of the diffusion of ideas regarding the 'appropriate' structure for IRAs remains an area of inquiry.

Transnational political interactions within the region through intergovernmental organizations, which facilitate learning and the dissemination of policy ideas, have also been pointed out as a driver of IRAs' diffusion in the region (Fernández-i-Marín and Jordana 2015). Studies have also suggested that IRAs (as with privatization) have been the result of pressure from international organizations (i.e., coercive isomorphism). In this regard, qualitative studies have highlighted how the IMF and the World Bank strongly advocated the development of IRAs in exchange for aid, grants, or loans as part of the 'Washington consensus' (Dubash and Morgan 2013), although there is contradictory qualitative evidence (Lodge and Stirton 2002). On the other hand, quantitative studies measuring the impact of aid assistance on IRA creation and their level of formal independence have found no significant impact (Pavón Mediano 2020; Jordana and Levi-Faur 2005).

Regarding the role of politics on the design of IRAs in the region, Martinez-Gallardo and Murillo (2011) have shown that political biases have affected the policymaking of electric regulators by shaping agencies' regulatory discretion for setting prices and solving conflicts. Moreover, based on Chile's history of regulatory delegation, Pardow (2019) argues that, while Kemmererian reforms were the product of political polarization and technical divergence jointly pushed toward agencies high independence levels, regulatory delegation during Pinochet's dictatorship was implemented with the knowledge that a large political turnover was in the making, impacting in the agencies' insulation mechanisms. More broadly, Murillo (2009) has shown how electoral competition, that is, the risk of electoral replacement by a challenger who could credibly resist market-oriented reforms, weakened the effect of the fiscal pressures that incentivized incumbents to adopt privatization and regulatory agencies in the utility sectors.

The role of veto players as an institutional arrangement mediating the functional forces of regulatory delegation has also been studied in the region. In contrast to empirical findings on IRAs in developed countries (Gilardi 2008), studies in Latin America have shown a positive correlation between veto players and the creation of IRAs (Jordana and Levi-Faur 2005), as well as with the agencies' formal independence levels (Pavón Mediano 2020). This finding suggests that delegating competences to IRAs and veto players operated together as credibility enhancing mechanisms in Latin America rather than as functional equivalents.

PROBLEMATIZING THE REGULATORY GOVERNANCE MODEL IN LATIN AMERICA

Besides delegation to formally independent regulatory agencies, studies in the region have started to explore other problems already highlighted by the regulatory literature of advanced industrialized countries, such as de facto independence, as well as research problems particularly associated with the regional context. In this section, we discuss how the regulatory governance model has evolved and interacted with specific regional characteristics and what research agendas need to be pursued due to this interaction. As a general comment, we found that there is a large concentration of research on utilities sectors using data from the 1990s and early 2000s. Therefore, there is an important need to diversify the studied sectors, particularly by further including social regulators, and to reinvestigate utilities sectors using updated data.

The Evolution of the Regulatory Design Model

Many research findings have shown that the creation of an IRA and its institutional charac-teristics had a positive effect on some sector outputs. For instance, Gutiérrez and Berg (2000) found a positive relationship between some characteristics of telecommunications regulators (independence, enforcement power, neutrality, and the mechanism for resolving conflicts) and increases in telephone lines per capita in Latin America. Similarly, Andres et al. (2008) found that, in the energy sector, the existence of an independent regulator and its institutional design better explain the performance of utility providers. For this, they used data up to 2005. Although these studies were relevant, many years have passed, and the debate around regu-latory agencies has since evolved. Most of these studies considered indicators that aimed to capture the extent of delegation to regulatory agencies (i.e., independence and enforcement power; an exception is Andres et al. 2008). This focus reflects one of the main concerns of the late 1990s and early 2000s regarding the establishment of regulatory frameworks after liberalization: ensuring credible commitment and the independence of regulators from polit-ical interference. However, many other characteristics beyond independence are key to how regulatory agencies should be governed. Furthermore, in terms of institutional design, Estache and Wren-Lewis (2010) found that, in developing countries, there is a great deal of variation in terms of independence and responsibilities of regulatory agencies across countries, sectors, and institutional contexts. Therefore, focusing on independence alone could be misleading.

Indeed, a recent paper by González and Gómez-Álvarez (2021) studied the evolution of reg-ulatory agencies in 17 Latin American countries in three sectors. They encountered diffusion patterns that show that countries have introduced measures to increase control over regulatory agencies, rather than strengthen their delegation. Interestingly, other variables of IRAs insti-tutional design have played a predominant role in the design and functioning of regulatory agencies, such as accountability provision and its interaction with the facto independence, the mandate to use better regulatory practices and its dependence on IRAs capabilities, and regulatory coordination obligations and practice.

Regarding the latter, there are few studies on regulatory coordination in Latin America. González (2017) found that regulatory decision-making processes in the telecommunication sectors of Colombia, Peru, Ecuador, and Venezuela was rather fragmented – actors with reg-ulatory functions do not formally interact with each other when making regulatory decisions. However, there are a significant number of de facto interactions among IRAs and other organ-izations with regulatory functions and market operators when making regulatory decisions in the sector (González 2018; González and Verhoest 2020). More broadly, regarding interna-tional regulatory coordination, using the cases of Turkey and Mexico, Aydin (2019) studied the relationship between middle and established powers of the global economy, showing that Mexico gained more regional relevance to promote rules by increasing regulatory capacity and by aligning its regulatory preferences with the ones of the established powers. Nonetheless, there is a strong need for more research on how regulatory agencies strategically interact with other actors, at both national and international level.

De Facto Independence in the Context of Latin America

Few studies have used de facto measures to study IRAs independence in the region, although there are several reasons why studying de facto independence is a key route of inquiry in

Latin America. Following Maggetti (2007), the facto independence has two components: "the self-determination of agencies' preferences, and their autonomy throughout the use of regulatory competencies, that is, during the activity of regulation" (p.272). Regarding self-determination, Trillas and Montoya (2011) studied de facto independence in the telecommunications sector of 23 Latin-American countries in the 1990–2004 period, measuring the political vulnerability of agency heads after government changes, and the turnover rate of agencies head before their legal period. They found that in 61% of occasions there was a change in the head of the agency within one month after a government changes, and an 88% chance by the end of one year.

Considering the particular presidential nature of state systems in the region, extending the study of the interplay of IRAs' de facto independence and some specific provisions of IRAs formal independence, that is, agency heads dismissal, is of particular importance.[4] For instance, among those IRAs in Pavón Mediano's (2020) sample (supra), almost half of the agency heads were appointed directly by a minister and had no fixed term, and in 71 of 86 cases, either dismissal was possible at the appointer's discretion or there were no specific provisions for dismissal. Testing the impact of this interplay on regulatory performance, Trillas and Montoya (2011) found that formal and de facto measures of independence were positively, albeit modestly, related with network penetration in the telecommunications sector.

The interaction between the regulator, other public bodies and the sector operators has also been explored in the region, albeit mostly regarding utilities. Studying 30 processes of concession contract renegotiations in the Argentinian water and electricity sectors after the early 2000 economic crisis, Post and Murillo (2013) found that mainly ministries conducted negotiations rather than regulatory agencies, limiting the exercise of the agencies' regulatory mandate and negotiations dealt mainly with redistributive aspects. In the same line, analyzing the regulatory decision-making process in the Colombian telecommunication sector, González and Verhoest (2018) showed the strong influence of the sector ministry, as well as the relatively large influence on it of the operator with the highest market share. Regarding the latter, surprisingly, a review of the literature indicates that the influence of industrial interest groups on IRAs' decision-making, that is, regulatory capture, has been barely explored empirically.

Studying agencies' de facto independence from political ministries has become even more relevant in the current political context of Latin America, where several populist governments have come to power. For instance, Venezuela has experienced a dismantling of its long-standing administrative capacity since the Chavist regime started to rule the country. Another relevant route of inquiry. Indeed, populist regimes have had complicated interactions with the existing administrative apparatus.

Capacities

Different studies have explored the capacity of IRAs in the region. Here by capacity we refer to the technical expertise that regulatory agencies have, the sophistication of agency regulatory tools, and the routines and strategies that agencies develop to increase their capacity. Technical expertise among agency personnel have been usually associated with meritocratic practices in their recruitment. A broad study analyzing the meritocratic practices in recruitment and civil service careers of 72 regulatory agencies in 18 Latin-American countries found that such practices have not been institutionalized in the region (Parrado and Salvador 2011). This occurs even in countries with professional civil services, although there is significant variation across sectors. Indeed, while financial, telecommunications, and pension-delivery sectors are more meritocratic, social sectors tend to be less meritocratic (idem). National surveys on the technical expertise of personnel in regulatory sectors in the region have also been conducted, confirming heterogeneity among sectors (Cunha et al. 2017). Looking into the expertise of agency heads and its interplay with their appointment mechanisms, Pardow's (2018) study on 25 years of appointment in 21 Chilean agencies found that IRA heads appointed by Congress have higher technical expertise and lower partisan affiliation than those appointed by the Executive, highlighting the impact of agencies institutional design on their capacities.

In terms of the sophistication of regulatory tools, many Latin American countries have started implementing what has been labeled by international organization as good regulatory practices. However, there are significant gaps in their implementation in the region (Querbach and Arndt 2017) and the literature shows few studies about the implementation and impact of tools such as impact analysis or *ex post* regulatory assessment (Rocha and Peci 2011). For instance, Peci and Sobral (2011) found that many regulatory agencies in Brazil were unfamiliar with the process and methodology of regulatory impact analysis and found difficulties in implementing it. Furthermore, even in agencies with high technical capacities, political factors related to organizational fragmentation, resistance to political control, and weak ministerial oversight impeded the implementation of regulatory impact analysis. As a result, the interaction of these tools with administrative policies and practices already in place, as well as their effectiveness in improving regulatory quality, should be further explored.

Besides new tools for regulatory improvement, studying the strategies to build regulatory capacity through case studies should be a policy priority in a context of administrative bureaucracies with low technical capabilities in the region. For instance, a case study on the Mexican Agency for Security, Energy, and Environment (Dussage-Laguna et al. 2018) provides insights on how studying capacity building among recently created agencies. This research approach shed light on how regulators create their organizations' capacity and routines, and how they develop and strategize, while dealing with thousands of case files and interacting with demands from other public organizations and sector operators.

IRAs' Policy Role and its Interaction with Development

Finally, the tensions between the regulatory independence agency model and the persisting development agenda of many Latin-American countries is another key feature of the region. Indeed, many regulatory institutions in the region are often involved in redistributive policy and, consequently, they are not exclusively focused on promoting competitive markets (Peci et al. 2018). This is expected since the regulatory framework in which regulatory authorities are embedded is affected by the specific regional context and its broader policies. In the case of Latin America, research that considers this interaction becomes especially relevant, as most states have a large redistributive function (Draibe and Riesco 2007). This situation challenges Majone's (2001) regulatory model, where the democratic legitimacy deficit of regulatory agencies is compensated by technical expertise and where agencies are concerned mainly with production efficiency and competition, while politicians deal with redistribution.

Dubash and Morgan (2013) suggest that, in developing countries, including those in Latin America, the distinction between efficiency and redistribution blurs because there are low levels of access to public services, high poverty levels, and in many cases deficient service delivery. This diversity on policy goals implies that the effects of regulations in terms of cost allocations can generate extensive losses to a population's overall welfare. Additionally, the lack of coverage of some services makes granting greater access a crucial regulatory target.

The relation between regulatory agencies, efficiency gains, and redistribution policies is complex. Many studies have shown that desirable features of regulatory agencies during the 1990s and early 2000 were related to efficiency gains and also with increases in service penetration. Andres et al. (2008) found a positive relation between governance characteristics of regulatory agencies, such as autonomy, transparency, accountability, and efficiency gains in electricity companies. However, Estache et al. (2003) found that efficiency gains were captured by industries and not shared with users in their analysis of the use of price caps in concession contracts. They also found that there was a decrease in sector investment.

Other studies such as Ros (2003), Gutiérrez and Berg (2000), and Gutiérrez (2003) found that the existence of regulatory agencies in telecommunications, when possessing certain desirable characteristics, were positively related with the expansion of telephone lines. However, Parker et al. (2008) studied the relationship between infrastructure regulation and poverty reduction, and their findings suggest that regulation in developing countries should have a clear pro-poor policy. The authors showed how Chile had a subsidy policy to assure that water and sanitation services did not surpass 5% of household incomes. A similar case is in Peru, where pay phones in rural areas receive subsides.

The previous examples demonstrate that the relation between regulation and development in Latin America is not settled and that much more research is needed. The majority of previous research has been done on utilities sectors and during the privatization phase of the 1990s. This fact is problematic for several reasons. First, the relation between agencies' concerns of efficiency and redistribution might vary depending on the sector. In utilities and economic sectors, low prices, more competition, more investment, and service quality are crucial; however, in social sectors, the most important element is managing risk (Gilardi 2008). Second, the Latin-American region has evolved drastically with respect to its governmental policy preferences since the 1990s. Many countries have had left-wing presidents in office, and many have dealt with populist regimes. Finally, there are few studies that consider the interaction between regulatory policy and the preferences of other public institutions. Government coalitions, judiciary and legislative institution have their specific policy preference, and they could try to adapt the regulatory structure to such preferences. For instance, Urueña (2012) found that, in the case of the Colombian water sector, although government economists pushed for a depoliticized independent water regulator with the main goal of achieving efficiency gains in the provision of water, the constitutional court pushed for redistributive measures that resulted in mixing the regulatory and neo-constitutional state.

In this regard, at least two broad questions remain to be addressed by the regulatory-agency research agenda in Latin America. Firstly, to what extent is there a relation between regulatory-agency design and governance model and sectors outputs, especially in non-utilities sectors. Second, to what extent do regulatory agencies consider redistribution in their decision-making.

CONCLUSION

This chapter has explored the literature on the evolution of regulatory agencies in Latin America, their main features, and their interactions with historical legacies and the current context of the region. First, this literature review indicates that the evolution of regulatory agencies in Latin America has been a historically and politically dependent phenomenon. Despite the relevance of the diffusion of IRAs in the late 1980s and early 1990s, the configuration of IRAs institutional landscape is much more complex. Colonial legacies, administrative developments, and policy preferences of Latin-American countries have shaped the manner in which IRAs have been configured.

Second, studying these interactions and legacies helps explaining the heterogeneity of the institutional configurations of agencies in the region. Although there are some clear sectoral patterns, which are related to the diffusion of the regulatory agency model in the utilities sectors (Levi-Faur and Jordana 2006), there is also a great deal of variation across sectors and countries that is largely unexplained. In sectors where Majone's regulatory agency model was not established during the 1990s reform wave, many countries have used existing administrative structures, such as the *superentintencias*, which differ from the independent regulatory agency model. Furthermore, research has shown that, even where independent regulatory agencies were created, their capabilities and their interactions with other institutions and government priorities and ideologies tend to affect how these regulatory institutions actually function. Particularly, agencies in the region seem to be involved in larger policy goals beyond promoting policy competition, that is, redistribution.

Third, the research revised reveals that, although initial studies highlighted how creating regulatory agencies improved the utilities sectors' efficiency, there is evidence that formal independence and regulatory delegation have not been the main reform concerns regarding regulatory agencies since the 1990s wave of agencification (at least for telecommunications, gas, and electricity sectors). Moreover, the relation between independence and credible commitment is no longer so evident (González and Verhoest 2018; Pavón Mediano 2020). This point suggests further research should explore other regulatory design indicators, such as accountability and coordination and their relation to agency performance and sector development. Furthermore, there is a large research gap concerning how the evolution of regulatory design since the 1990s has affected regulatory practices and sector outputs.

Finally, de facto independence seem to be a policy priority in the region. Research has shown that the independence of regulatory agencies varies at the de facto level in comparison with the formal level. Although this has been found elsewhere, the issue is especially relevant in Latin America because of the recent rise of populist and authoritarian governments.

NOTES

1. Part of the research that is presented in this chapter was funded by los Andes university assistant professors research fund of the Research Vice rectory.
2. In this dataset, IRAs' institutional features were measured as latent dimensions inferred from different observable formal variables of the agency institutional design, by applying an IRT model. The dataset only includes regulatory agencies (not ministries), and values equal to zero must be interpreted as an agency having a value equal to the mean in the dimension in the whole dataset.
3. Besides political independence, a measure of managerial autonomy is also available at Jordana et al. (2018), based on variables regarding on autonomy for budget, personnel and organization management. The two dimensions correlates 0.55 in the region. It is worth to point out that while these two dimensions – albeit measured differently – are unified in the Gilardi's index (2008) applied by Pavón Mediano (2020), they are divided in Jordana et al. (2018).

4. De jure independence indexes might be criticized for overestimating the weights of accessory stat-
    utory provisions, by assigning the same weight to each provision under study and combining areas
    such as appointment, dismissal, personnel policy or budget autonomy (Hanretty & Koop, 2012;
    Jordana et al. 2018).

REFERENCES

Amann, E., & Baer, W. (2005). From the developmental to the regulatory state: The transformation of
    the government's impact on the Brazilian economy. *The Quarterly Review of Economics and Finance*,
    45(2), 421–431.
Andres, L., Guasch, J. L., & Azumendi, S. L. (2008). Regulatory governance and sector performance:
    Methodology and evaluation for electricity distribution in Latin America. The World Bank.
Aydin, U. (2019). Rule-takers, rule-makers, or rule-promoters? Turkey and Mexico's role as rising
    middle powers in global economic governance. *Regulation & Governance* (early view). https://doi
    .org/10.1111/rego.12269
Braithwaite, J. (2008). *Regulatory capitalism: How it Works, Ideas for Making it Work Better*.
    Cheltenham, UK and Northampton, MA, USA: Edward Elgar Publishing.
Chong, A., & Lopez-de-Silanes, F. (Eds.) (2005). Privatization in Latin America: Myths and reality. The
    World Bank.
Cunha, B. Q., Pereira, A. K., & de Ávila Gomide, A. (2017). State capacity and utilities regulation in
    Brazil: Exploring bureaucracy. *Utilities Policy*, 49, 116–126.
Draibe, S. M., & Riesco, M. (2007). Latin America: A new developmental welfare state in the making?.
    In M. Riesco (Ed.), *Latin America. Social Policy in a Development Context* (pp. 21–113), Palgrave
    Macmillan. https://doi.org/10.1057/9780230625259_2.
Drake, P. (1989). *The Money Doctor in the Andes: The Kemmerer Mission, 1923–1933*. Duke University
    Press.
Dubash, N. K. (2013). Regulating through the back door: Understanding the implications of institu-
    tional transfer. In N. K. Dubash & B. Morgan (Eds.), *The Rise of the Regulatory State of the South*
    (pp. 98–114). Oxford University Press.
Dubash, N. K., & Morgan, B. (2012). Understanding the rise of the regulatory state of the South. *Regulation
    & Governance*, 6(3), 261–281.
Dubash, N. K., & Morgan, B. (Eds.) (2013). *The Rise of the Regulatory State of the South*. Oxford
    University Press.
Dussage-Laguna, M., Lodge, M., Heredia, J., & Casas, A. (2018). Construyendo las capacidades reg-
    ulatorias de la ASEA. In A. Elizondo, & M. Dussauge-Laguna (Eds.), *ASEA. Un Nuevo Modelo de
    Institución del Estado Mexicano* (pp. 127–147). CIDE.
Estache, A., & Wren-Lewis, L. (2010). Regulation and development. In M. Cave, R. Baldwin, & M.
    Lodge (Eds.), *The Oxford Handbook of Regulation* (pp. 371–406). Oxford University Press.
Estache, A., Guasch, J. L., & Trujillo, L. (2003). Price caps, efficiency payoffs and infrastructure contract
    renegotiation in Latin America. The World Bank.
Fernández-i-Marín, X., & Jordana, J. (2015). The emergence of regulatory regionalism: Transnational
    networks and the diffusion of regulatory agencies within regions. *Contemporary Politics*, 21(4),
    417–434.
Gilardi, F. (2008). *Delegation in the Regulatory State*. Cheltenham, UK and Northampton, MA, USA:
    Edward Elgar Publishing.
Gilardi, F., Jordana, J., & Levi-Faur, D. (2007). Regulation in the age of globalization: The diffusion
    of regulatory agencies across Europe and Latin America. In G. Hodge (Ed.), *Privatization and
    Market Development* (pp. 127–147). Cheltenham, UK and Northampton, MA, USA: Edward Elgar
    Publishing.
González, C. I. (2017). Measuring and comparing the distribution of decision-making power in regula-
    tory arrangements of the telecommunication sector in Latin America. *Utilities Policy*, 49, 145–155.

González, C. I. (2018). How regulatory decisions are made at the de facto level: Conceptualizing and measuring regulatory decision making in the Colombian telecommunications sector. *Latin American Policy*, 9(1), 55–76.

González, C. I., & Gómez Álvarez, S. (2021). Delegation versus control: A comparison of reform patterns and diffusion channels in Latin American regulatory agencies. *Journal of Comparative Policy Analysis: Research and Practice*, 1–24.

González, C. I., & Verhoest, K. (2018). The formal delegation of regulatory decisions in the telecommunication sector: An explanation using classification trees. *Review of Policy Research*, 35(4), 617–641.

González, C. I., & Verhoest, K. (2020). De facto regulatory decision-making processes in telecommunications regulation: explaining influence relationships with exponential random graph models. *Journal of Public Policy*, 40(1), 144–170.

Gutiérrez, L. H. (2003). Regulatory governance in the Latin American telecommunications sector. *Utilities Policy*, 11(4), 225–240.

Gutiérrez, L. H., & Berg, S. (2000). Telecommunications liberalization and regulatory governance: Lessons from Latin America. *Telecommunications Policy*, 24(10–11), 865–884.

Hanretty, C., & Koop, C. (2012). Measuring the formal independence of regulatory agencies. *Journal of European Public Policy*, 19(2), 198–216.

Jordana, J. (2011). The institutional development of the Latin American regulatory state. In D. Levi-Faur (Ed.), *Handbook on the Politics of Regulation* (pp. 156–168). Cheltenham, UK and Northampton, MA, USA: Edward Elgar Publishing.

Jordana, J., & Levi-Faur, D. (2005). The diffusion of regulatory capitalism in Latin America: Sectoral and national channels in the making of a new order. *The ANNALS of the American Academy of Political and Social Science*, 598(1), 102–124.

Jordana, J., & Levi-Faur, D. (2006). Toward a Latin American regulatory state? The diffusion of autonomous regulatory agencies across countries and sectors. *International Journal of Public Administration*, 29(4–6), 335–366.

Jordana, J., Fernández-i-Marín, X., & Bianculli, A. C. (2018). Agency proliferation and the globalization of the regulatory state: Introducing a data set on the institutional features of regulatory agencies. *Regulation & Governance*, 12(4), 524-540. https://doi.org/10.1111/rego.12189

Jordana, J., Levi-Faur, D., & Marín, X. F. i. (2011). The global diffusion of regulatory agencies channels of transfer and stages of diffusion. *Comparative Political Studies*, 44(10), 1343–1369.

Laffont, J. (2005). *Regulation and Development*. Cambridge University Press.

Levi-Faur, D., & Jordana, J. (2006) Toward a Latin American regulatory state? The diffusion of autonomous regulatory agencies across countries and sectors. *International Journal of Public Administration*, 29 (4–6), 335–366.

Levy, B., & Spiller, P. (1997). *Regulations, Institutions, and Commitment*. Cambridge University Press.

Lodge, M., & Stirton, L. (2002). Regulatory reform in small developing states: Globalisation, regulatory autonomy and Jamaican telecommunications. *New Political Economy*, 7(3), 415–433.

Lodge, M., & Stirton, L. (2006). Withering in the heat? In search of the regulatory state in the Commonwealth Caribbean. *Governance*, 19(3), 465–495.

Maggetti, M. (2007). De facto independence after delegation: A fuzzy-set analysis. *Regulation & Governance*, 1. 271–294.

Majone, G. (1994). The rise of the regulatory state in Europe. *West European Politics*, 17(3), 77–101.

Majone, G. (2001). Two logics of delegation: Agency and fiduciary relations in EU governance. *European Union Politics*, 2(1), 103–122.

Manzetti, L. (2000). *Regulatory Policy in Latin America: Post-privatization Realities*. North-South Center Press, University of Miami.

Martinez-Gallardo, C., & Murillo, M. (2011). Agency under constraint: Ideological preferences and the politics of electricity regulation in Latin America. *Regulation & Governance*, 5(3), 350–367.

Montoya, M. A., & Trillas, F. (2011). Commitment and regulatory independence in practice in Latin American and Caribbean countries. *Competition and Regulation in Network Industries*, 12, 27–56.

Muñoz, O. (Ed.) (1992). *Después de las Privatizaciones. Hacia el Estado Regulador*. CIEPLAN.

Murillo, M. (2009). *Political Competition, Partisanship, and Policy Making in Latin American Public Utilities*. Cambridge University Press.

Pardow, D. (2018). ¿Técnicos o políticos? Radiografía del sistema de nombramiento de directivos de agencias regulatorias independientes. *Revista Chilena de Derecho*, 45(3), 745–769.

Pardow, D. G. (2019). Political insulation, technical expertise and the technocrat's paradox. *Review of Law & Economics*, 16(1), 102–120.

Parker, D., Kirkpatrick, C., & Figueira-Theodorakopoulou, C. (2008). Infrastructure regulation and poverty reduction in developing countries: A review of the evidence and a research agenda. *The Quarterly Review of Economics and Finance*, 48(2), 177–188.

Parrado, S., & Salvador, M. (2011). The institutionalization of meritocracy in Latin American regulatory agencies. *International Review of Administrative Sciences*, 77(4), 687–712.

Pavón Mediano, A. (2020). Agencies' formal independence and credible commitment in the Latin American regulatory state: A comparative analysis of eight countries and 13 sectors. *Regulation & Governance*, 14(1), 102–120. https://doi.org/10.1111/rego.12187

Peci, A. & Sobral, F. (2011). Regulatory impact assessment: How political and organizational forces influence its diffusion in a developing country. *Regulation & Governance*, 5(2), 204–220.

Peci, A., Souza, R., & Dutra, J. C. (2018). Agenda regulatória na prática: uma análise das políticas adotadas por agências reguladoras nos últimos 20 anos. Escola Brasileira de Administração Pública e de Empresas, EBAPE/FGV. http://hdl.handle.net/10438/25958

Post, A., & Murillo, M. V. (2013). The regulatory state under stress: Economic shocks and regulatory bargaining in the Argentine electricity and water sectors. In N. K. Dubash & B. Morgan (Eds.), *The Rise of the Regulatory State of the South* (pp. 115–134). Oxford University Press.

Querbach, T. & Arndt C. (2017). Regulatory policy in Latin America: An analysis of the state of play (OECD Regulatory Policy Working Papers, No. 7). OECD Publishing. https://doi.org/10.1787/2cb29d8c-en

Rocha, F. & Peci, A. (2011). Regulatory impact analysis: A new tool for better regulation at ANVISA. *Rev Saúde Pública*, 45(4), 802–805. https://doi.org/10.1590/S0034-89102011000400023

Ros, A. J. (2003). The impact of the regulatory process and price cap regulation in Latin American telecommunications markets. *Review of Network Economics*, 2(3). https://doi.org/10.2202/1446-9022.1029

Trillas, F., & Montoya, M. A. (2011). Commitment and regulatory independence in practice in Latin American and Caribbean countries. *Competition and Regulation in Network Industries*, 12(1), 27–56.

Urueña, R. (2012). The rise of the constitutional regulatory state in Colombia: The case of water governance. *Regulation & Governance*, 6(3), 282–299.

5. Independent regulators in the Middle East

Ahmed Badran

INTRODUCTION

The political and social transformations in the Middle East have resulted in a period of transition aimed at building more democratic government systems. Various reform processes have taken place to address the economic, social and political priorities of the countries of the region. Regulatory reform can be seen as one of the pivotal building blocks of transforming and creating new state apparatus. In this context, the proliferation of Independent Regulatory Agencies (IRAs) in different social and economic sectors raises fundamental questions about the main characteristics of this regulatory model and the driving forces behind its widespread diffusion in the Middle East. The topic of regulation and the regulatory state model has attracted much attention from scholars in the western world and developed countries; nonetheless, little attention was devoted to investigating the rise of such a phenomenon in the context of the Middle East. Therefore, in this chapter, regulatory reforms and the rise of the IRAs in the Middle East will be examined by focusing on the experiences of selected countries. The liberalization of the economic sectors have made regulation a necessity. Consequently, independent sector regulators were created in different countries in the Middle East for protecting the public interest and attracting new private investments.

Despite the various regulatory options available for policymakers in the region, the reformers have chosen the IRA model. Such an observation begs the question about the way(s) in which the notion of regulatory "independence" is perceived in the context of the Middle Eastern countries.[1] Another important area of study when considering the spread of IRAs in the Middle East is the diffusion mechanisms. In this context, it would be helpful to discuss and explain the mechanisms via which IRAs have been instituted in the studied countries and the rationale for creating such agencies as means to regulate economic sectors.[2]

The chapter is organized in five sections including the introduction and the conclusion. In section two, the state of the established knowledge about the regulatory reforms in the Middle East will be discussed in an attempt to contextualize the debate about the role of IRAs in regulatory reforms in the region. The primary focus will be on the regulatory policies, tools, and institutions that were developed in the region as parts or the regulatory reforms processes. Section three is devoted to identifying and investigating the contextual factors affecting regulatory reforms in the region. The future venues for research in the area of regulatory reforms in the Middle East alongside the emerging regulatory challenges will be discussed in section four in order to underline and guide future research in this area. The discussion in this chapter will be inspired by the theoretical and conceptual insights derived from the literature on regulatory governance and IRAs. The observations provided are based on a holistic approach. That means a more detailed analysis founded on a single case study approach for each country might be needed in order to address specific regulatory issues in some countries of the region.

REGULATORY REFORMS IN THE MIDDLE EAST: AN OVERVIEW

Over the past few years, developing regulatory policies and institutions have become an increasingly important issue for regulatory reforms in the Middle East. The aim in many countries was to improve national economies and strengthening their ability to adapt to change. Governments realized that they cannot provide a favourable regulatory environment alone. In other words, the challenges posed by the interdependence of sectors and economies call for a comprehensive government approach to support regulatory reforms.

The current debate about the regulatory reforms in the Middle East represents one facet of the overall discussions about governance and more particularly about regulatory governance in the region. Given the relative novelty of the regulatory policies and institutions, many countries are focusing on developing the fundamental elements of regulatory regimes. In other words, the focus of regulatory policymakers is on the approaches by which they can foster the current regulatory reforms in a transitional environment that might lack many of the institutional guarantees for successful reforms.[3]

Regulatory Policies in Middle East

Regulatory policies are emerging across the region, and paths of regulatory reforms are converging. Different purposive courses of action have been developed in order to reform diverse social and economic sectors.

By examining the regulatory policies in the Middle East, it can be noticed that different countries have developed regulatory policies using various approaches (Badran 2020). In Lebanon for instance, the Lebanese government have promoted regulatory frameworks addressing different regulatory issues including illicit wealth, public procurement law, access to information, and public–private partnership (OECD 2014). Added to this, several countries in the region are developing regulatory policies and promoting initiatives in pursuit of greater regulatory transparency. Open government policies besides introducing consultation processes into regulation making using information and communication technology tools are among the most common approaches.[4] In Egypt, the Egyptian initiative to reform the business climate known shortly as (ERRADA) has made it possible for the public to access an inventory of more than 30 business-related regulations including laws, presidential decrees, prime ministerial decrees, ministerial decrees, and subordinate authorities' decisions (Abdel Gawad 2013, p.71).

In the context of open government regulatory policies, participatory decision-making mechanisms have been emphasized by many centuries in the region. The aim was to enhance regulatory decision-making transparency by engaging the stakeholders. To this end, governments have used different forms and levels of public consultations.[5] The spread of public consultations in the Middle East region does not necessarily mean it is an effective tool to influence regulatory decision-making processes. As noted by Badran (2013a) the use of public consultations could be instrumental in the sense that they are merely used to legitimize new regulations and regulatory policies without a real impact of the participated regulatory actors on final decisions. Added to this, in other countries such as Morocco, public consultations are not being conducted in a systematic manner to include all regulatory issues. In Lebanon, consultations processes are dominated primarily by government institutions and the scope of public participation is considerably limited to hearing sessions if needed. As such, accessing regulatory decision-making centres by the affected stakeholders is entirely at the discretion of the regulators and government entities (OECD 2014).

Regulatory Tools in Middle East

Salamon (2002, p.19) defines regulatory tools as "an identifiable method through which collective action is structured to address a public problem". Such methods and tools are employed by institutions including regulators to do what they wish to do (Gunningham and Grabosky 1998). As such, regulatory tools can be regarded as the different forms of interventions by governments in pursuit of specific socio-economic outcomes. Such outcomes cannot be achieved through other coordination mechanisms such as economic markets. A glance at the literature on regulation and regulatory tools reveals that there is not an agreed upon taxonomy of regulatory tools (Freiberg 2010). Nonetheless, Eisner et al. (2006) notes that the most common regulatory policy tools: prohibitions; licensing; price, rate, and quantity restrictions; product standards; technical production standards; performance standards; subsidies; information provision; and assigning property rights and liability.

In the context of the Middle East, different countries have designed diverse regulatory interventions using numerous regulatory tools. In this regard, several countries in the region including Egypt, Jordan, Lebanon, and Morocco have embarked on regulatory reform initiatives aiming at simplifying administrative procedures and reducing administrative burdens. The design and implementation of such tools have been regarded as a means for enhancing and insuring regulatory quality.[6] From this angle, the simplification of administrative procedures can be regarded as an effective tool for reducing the complexity of the regulatory environment and updating the inventory of regulations by identifying and removing outdated and ineffective laws and regulations. A good practice in this respect is provided by ERRADA in Egypt.[7]

In the process of reviewing and streamlining regulations, the Regulatory Impact Assessment (RIA) has been introduced as a major policy tool for gathering information on the potential impacts of regulatory measures at the start of the regulatory policy cycle. In this respect, RIA had been regarded as a tool that helps regulatory bodies assessing the effects of regulations and measure potential benefits, costs, and impacts before adopting any new regulatory rule. RIA can also be conducted following the implementation of certain regulations to find out their impact(s) on the regulated bodies (Megacom 2005). In the words of Abdel Gawad (2013, p.72), RIA can be perceived as "an evidence-based decision-making tool that explores different options to government policies and programmes". In that sense, a good RIA should enable policy solutions to be created in a way that minimizes undesirable burdens whilst maximizing the positive impacts and effectively achieving the intended regulatory policy goals (Megacom 2005, p.245). Hence, the RIA not only contributes to justifying regulatory actions, but also promotes transparency in the regulatory process. It supports the credibility of regulatory processes and increases public confidence in regulatory institutions and policymakers.

Despite the fact that RIA is seen by many countries in the Middle East region as an important regulatory tool to assist regulators and policymakers in developing effective regulations, different countries exhibit different status in terms of the utilization of such a tool. At a general level, RIA is still a new regulatory tool in the Middle East region. In fact, RIA has not been fully accepted and implemented at the regulatory policymaking levels, as many regulatory agencies and government institutions have not yet fully understood the value and rationale behind putting such an important policy tool in place as an integrated part of their daily routine. Countries such as Mauritania for instance do not use RIA in a systematic fashion to evaluate the impacts of regulatory rules. In Morocco, RIA is implemented sporadically in relation to certain types of regulatory rules in specific regulatory areas including commerce in services and commodities. Other countries like Jordan reflect in their regulatory practices a higher level of commitment to the implementation of RIA.[8]

Regulatory Institutions in Middle East

Regulatory institutions can be broadly conceived as all forms of rules, norms and codes designed to control the behaviour and govern interactions among regulatory stakeholders participating in regulatory processes. This conception of regulatory institutions can be extended to include the regulatory bodies themselves through which interactions among stakeholders take place. In this section, we will focus on the second notion of regulatory institutions that refers to regulatory organizations as key institutional mechanisms for regulatory reforms. In this respect, Dusk et al. (2020) note that, developing such institutional mechanisms is a key to create a supportive regulatory environment.

At the regulatory institutions level, the creation of Independent Regulatory Agencies (IRAs) has been a defining feature of regulatory reforms in the Middle East region. In the process of reforming their regulatory regimes, many countries in the Middle East have chosen to adopt the IRAs model (e.g. Egypt, Jordan, and Lebanon). IRAs have been regarded in this context as a catalyst for a number of positive effects generated by the quality of political institutions (Abrardi et al. 2016). As such, the notion of IRAs has been perceived as creating regulatory agencies that are independent making and taking their own decisions without undue interventions from political and economic interests (Badran 2013b). That includes government agencies, consumer groups, and the private regulated industries. In that sense, and based on the legal mandate granted to them, the IRAs are supposed to work at arm's-length from their parent organizations as well as other private interests. Hence, IRAs operate under the authority of laws. They are created and can be revised by legislators, based on annual budgets. IRAs operate under the leadership of regulators who should be appointed to work within the policy framework established by the government. The construction of these relationships will define the nature of regulatory independence (Badran 2017). Such an institutional composition that includes governmentally designed public policies, which are implemented by an autonomous and financially independent public authority, has been regarded as a cornerstone for improving economic efficiency (Estache et al. 2006).

Different types of independent regulatory authorities have been created in diverse economic and social sectors. The newly established IRAs have been intrusted with different regulatory functions including inspection, referral, licensing, accreditation, enforcement and advice to a third party. From a social regulation perspective, many countries in the region are paying more attention to regulating some areas including health and safety and the environment. The UAE for instance have developed the legislative and regulatory framework required for protecting the environment. The federal Law No. 24 of 1999 for the protection and development of the environment has been issued alongside other relevant laws and legislations. At the institutional level, the key regulatory authorities for supervising environmental issues have been established and assigned environmental protection duties. These regulatory authorities include the federal environment agency, the federal ministry of climate change and environment, the air quality department of the ministry of environment and water, the ministry of agriculture and fisheries (Thacker 2020).

With regard to occupational safety and health regulations, countries such as Qatar were active in developing and enforcing regulations aiming at promoting the provision of quality occupational health and safety services at the national level by eliminating or minimizing the causes of hazards inherent in the working environment. Such regulations extend to cover all employers and workers in all sectors of the economy and all forms of the employment relationship. The guiding regulatory principles developed in this regard are consistent with Qatar National Vision 2030 as well as the Second National Development Strategy (2018–2022), The National Health Strategy (2018–2022), and The National Policy on Labour Inspection, adopted in April 2019. Among the key institutional players responsible for monitoring the enforcement of the developed regulatory rules come the Ministry of Administrative Development, Labour and Social Affairs (MADLSA) and the Ministry of Public Health (2020) of the State of Qatar (https://www.moph.gov.qa).

From an economic regulation perspective, regulatory reforms in telecommunications sectors in the region is a case in point. As noted by Wavre (2018) the regulatory reform model has emphasized the shift from state-owned monopolies to the delegation of core state functions to independent regulatory authorities. In Egypt for instance, the main elements of the new regulatory system were embodied in Law 19/1998 and the presidential decree 101/1998 that created an independent regulatory authority named Telecommunications Regulatory Authority (TRA), and a joint stock company named Telecom Egypt (TE), as a service provider controlled by the state.[9] In practice, such division of roles was not as clear as stated above (Badran 2011). As noted by El-Nawawy and Ismail (1999) many market players at that time found it hard to distinguish between TE and TRA. For such actors, TE was acting as regulator and regulatee at the same time.

In Jordan, the story was not so much different. The deterioration in the quality of telecoms services as well as the need to attract private investments were among the main driving forces behind the regulatory reforms in this sector. Jordan's Telecommunications Corporation (TCC) was privatized, and the private sector companies were given the green light to enter into this previously monopolized market. Added to this an independent regulatory agency named as Telecommunications Regulatory Commission (TRC) was created in 1995 (Gentzoglanis 2001).[10]

The experience of the Maghreb countries (Algeria, Morocco, and Tunisia) have many similarities with the abovementioned examples. The regulatory reform in their telecoms sectors have been heavily influenced by the French model especially in are of the competition regulatory framework (Mezouaghi 2008). Focusing on the Moroccan case the same pattern of regulatory reforms described above can be notices. The sate-owned telecoms incumbent Itissalat Al Maghrib (IAM) has been privatized and the Agence Nationale de Réglementation des Télécommunications (ANRT) was instituted in 1997 as the sector's independent regulatory agency.

Other economic sectors have also witnessed regulatory reforms modelled on what happened in the telecoms sector. The water sector in Egypt for example has gone through a similar regulatory reform. As noted by Lasheen (2019) the Open Door Policy, known locally as Infitah, was introduced under the regime of Anwar Sadat, the successor of Nasser, in an attempt to attract foreign investment from the Gulf and from international donors. As a result of this policy, international development agencies, including the United States Agency for International

Development (USAID), started operating in Egypt and initiated several water projects during the 1970s and the 1980s. These projects aimed at providing technical assistance to water and sanitation organizations in big cities including Greater Cairo, Alexandria, and the Suez Canal cities. Rural and provincial cities wherein almost three quarters of the population live did not receive as much attention from international agencies. The lion's share of the projects went to the big urban cities and communities with almost half of the aid directed to assist water and sanitation organizations in these areas (The World Bank 1995).

The Egyptian Water/Wastewater Regulatory Agency (EWRA) was instituted in 2006 in accordance with the Presidential Decree No 136/2004. The establishment of EWRA was part of an overall reform plan in the water sector in order to rely less on government organizations and to put in place a sector that is driven primarily by the needs of its customers and which encourages more participation of the private sector. To this end, a new model for service delivery and regulation has emerged in which the state is no longer the owner and the operator of water utilities but the rule maker and the regulator of the sector. From this angle, instituting EWRA was an important move in order to regulate and manage water utilities on a competitive and commercial basis as well as protecting the rights of the consumers and the public interest in general. To fulfil its role as the sector regulator, the founding legislation has granted EWRA a broad mandate.[11] In this respect, the EWRA, as a supreme authority, is exercising its powers in accordance with governmental laws and regulations at both national and local levels. The scope of the mandate covers not only the operations of governmental utilities but the tasks assigned to private actors as well (Lasheen 2019).

REGULATORY REFORMS IN THE MIDDLE EAST: DOES THE CONTEXT MATTER?

The body of literature on policy transfer in general and the diffusion of IRAs in particular has provided ample evidence that context matters (Rose 1991, 1993; James and Lodge 2003; Levi-Faur 2005; Braun and Gilardi 2006; Marsh and Sharman 2009). Contextual factors including political, economic, social and legal systems either hinder or facilitate diffusion and transfer processes. Added to this, similarities between exporting and importing countries at the level of contextual factors may guarantee the success of the imported models such as IRAs. Having said that, and given the differences in contexts between Europe (where the model was originated) and the Middle East (where the model is imported) it is important to understand why and how such regulatory model was transferred into the context of the Middle East. Equally important is to know how the IRA model was adapted to suite the region's institutional legacies.

At the outset, a distinction can be made between exogenous and endogenous drivers of regulatory reforms in the region. At the internal level, the regulatory reform processes were driven in many countries by the need to modernize different economic and social sectors by simplifying administrative procedures and attracting new private investments. To this end, different policies and regulatory initiatives have been developed in an instrumental fashion in order to signal credible commitments from the governments of the region to private investors. At the exogenous level, the role of the international monetary agencies in shaping regulatory reforms in the region was evident in many cases including Egypt. In this context, different types of isomorphic pressures were exerted by such institutions and conditionality was imposed on the countries of the region that favoured the adoption of certain regulatory models.

The creation of IRAs in many Middle Eastern countries can be seen as a progress for those countries where political and economic decision-making processes are traditionally conducted in a central fashion. Nonetheless, the adoption of the IRA model in the Middle East region raises a fundamental question about the rationale behind delegating regulatory powers to such independent agencies. As noted from the aforementioned discussions, IRAs have become an institutional characteristic of the regulatory state in the Middle East. Nonetheless, a valid question would be why governments in the Middle East are willing to delegate regulatory competencies to specialized institutions that they can only partially control. It seems somehow surprising that politicians are willing to delegate to IRAs, since in principle the same regulatory functions could be accomplished by government ministries that are easier to control. The literature on delegation theory provides some explanatory factors to this phenomenon including, expertise, policy credibility, and political uncertainty (Majone 2001; Gilardi 2003, 2005).

Initially, the creation of IRAs as expert authorities in social and economic sectors is seen to be able to achieve many advantages. At the one hand, independent regulators are meant to regulate more efficiently and build confidence among key regulatory stakeholders. Additionally, IRAs are supposed to be shielding newly liberalized markets from political interference and providing market incentives. IRAs are also regarded as the protectors of public interests and the promoters of consumer welfare via fostering competition among services providers. From a governance perspective, IRAs are expected to encourage good regulatory governance practices by enhancing accountability, transparency, integrity and rule of law (see Jacobs 2001).

This argument of expertise does not fully explain the adoption of IRAs in the context of the Middle East. On the contrary, lack of expertise in the newly established regulatory agencies in addition to the weak governance systems in the region have been identified by the World Bank as main reasons behind the regulatory institutional failures in terms of anticompetitive practices and market opacity. In Algeria, Morocco, and Tunisia for example, despite following the same path of competition regulatory frameworks that have been adopted in Europe namely France, the competition regulatory rules in these countries were weakly enforced. The main reason for this is that regulatory agencies in those countries lack expertise. Added to this, the judicial system does not help in enforcing competition rules especially with professionals and consumer associations play a marginal and considerably weak role. Insufficient access to economic information adds to the aforementioned complications and stifles competition in regulated markets (Mezouaghi 2008).

The desirability of governments making credible long-term policy commitments can also be seen as a possible explanation for the phenomenon of delegation to IRAs. As noted by Majone (2001), credibility is a valuable asset for politicians when they carry out regulatory policies. For the success of any regulatory policy, the response of the targeted group(s), namely the investors, should be considered. To guarantee a positive response from private parties, governments should send them signals of credibility via delegating their own competencies to IRAs. IRAs will be responsible in such cases for applying the policy and monitoring the regulated sectors instead of governmental units, which may be subject to the influence of politics. Therefore, as Spiller (1993) noted, delegation to IRAs works as a means to improve the credibility of regulatory commitments, and therefore to ameliorate the prospects of successful regulatory reforms.

The credibility argument though was quite evident in the case the Egyptian regulatory state. Examining regulatory reforms in Egypt shows that the creation of the IRAs in Egypt represents a rational response to the external isomorphic pressures. The response of the Egyptian policymakers to those pressures can be explained on functional and practical grounds rather than any other factors of democratic governance or political uncertainties. Focusing on the telecommunications sector as an illustrative example, opening up this sector to the participation of the private sector after a long history of state monopoly was not an easy decision for policymakers. The predicament was that the government wanted to encourage that participation of the private sector in service provision but without harming the interests of the incumbent, which acted for years as the service provider, and the regulator of the sector at the same time. In this context, a gradual approach to market liberalization appeared to be the best option as it allows a limited number of private actors to enter the market while giving a transitional period to the previous incumbent to adjust its position to be able to compete on an equal footing with the private sector (Badran 2012).

While policy credibility is one of the most popular explanations justifying the delegation to IRAs, the neglected side of the story as Moe (1990) describes is political uncertainty. The core of the political uncertainty hypothesis is that governments delegate to IRAs in order to prevent future majorities from undoing their policy choices (Gilardi 2003). Because political property rights in the political arena are not guaranteed forever, and because politicians come to the office for a specific term, they always tend to try to insulate their policies from the possibility of being changed by the successors. In this sense, delegation to the IRAs is regarded as an institutional instrument that can secure some sort of continuity to the regulatory policy, which on the one hand benefits politicians currently in power, and on the other hand gives stakeholders in the regulatory arena a sign of credibility for the commitments.

While it seems attractive at first sight and valid to justify and explain the delegation to IRAs in the context of many western and European democratic countries, the hypothesis of political uncertainty is not the same in the case of many countries in the Middle East, including Egypt. Given the political context and recalling the experience of the Egyptian regulatory state, Badran (2012) has concluded that the hypothesis of political uncertainty does not seem very plausible to explain why the Egyptian government in regulated sectors such as telecommunications has chosen to delegate some of its powers to IRAs. Regulatory reforms in Egypt affirm that the liberalization and regulation decisions in sectors such as telecoms were strategic policy choices made by the government on practical and professional bases with no place for the notion of political uncertainty. The major concern was how to attract and encourage private investors to invest in this sector. The answer was by creating a regulatory system that assures them that they can invest and perform in an environment which will enable them to get a return on their investment without any discrimination between private and incumbent parties. In other words, the notion of policy credibility and the desire of the government for making credible policy commitments makes a great deal of sense in explaining regulatory reforms in Egypt (Badran 2012).

Since the regulatory reforms recently introduced into the Middle Eastern countries are broadly modelled on developed country experience, a valid question in this regard would be *how regulatory initiatives and models have been diffused in the regulatory state of the Middle East*. A glance at the diffusion literature shows that different mechanisms including policy transfer and lessons learning, the role of globalization as a facilitating factor, and institutional isomorphism may come into play when we try to explain the spread of IRAs in the Middle

East. From a policy transfer and lessons learning perspective, contextual economic and political factors are paramount in determining the success or failure of regulatory reforms (Massey 2009). However, examining the regulatory initiatives in different Middle Eastern countries it can be noticed that there are some fundamental differences in the political and economic structures, which may render an assumption about policy transfer and policy learning inaccurate. Considering the role played by the conditionality imposed by the international agencies on countries such as Lebanon, Jordan and Egypt gives a good example of how free the policy agents are in these countries when deciding upon the selection of regulatory reforms and associated models. Their ability to decide on policy options is greatly limited by the conditions imposed upon them by the international agencies (Badran 2012).

Regarding globalization and its possible impact on regulatory reforms in the Middle East region, one can notice that, at the outset, questions about the real impact of globalization on the diffusion of policy instruments including IRAs are highly debatable. No conclusive answers can be provided to whether or not globalization has facilitated the transfer of regulatory models in the region. To put it another way, the extent to which globalization alone facilitates or obstructs the process of IRA diffusion among the Middle Eastern countries remains an empirical question. That means a reflexive research agenda that closely analyses and demonstrates the effects of increased globalization on policy diffusion in general, and in certain policy areas such as the diffusions of regulatory reforms and models in particular, is needed to guide the research in these areas (Gilardi and Levi-Faur 2006).

The notion of isomorphism particularly 'coercive isomorphism' as presented by DiMaggio and Powell (1983, 1991) appears more plausible for explaining the diffusion of IRAs. Accordingly, "Once an organizational field becomes well established [...] there is an inexorable push toward homogenization" (DiMaggio and Powell 1983, p.148). Both formal and informal isomorphic pressures are exerted on organizations by other institutions in the surrounding environment on which they are dependent (DiMaggio and Powell 1991). Such isomorphic pressures can be exerted to force other organizations to adopt certain models or ideas in so-called '*direct coercion*'. Conditionality for provision of loans applied by international financial institutions including the International Monetary Fund and the World Bank is a case in point. In their race for development, many countries in the Middle East compete for loans and grants. This makes the competing Middle Eastern countries vulnerable to whatever conditions that could be forced upon them by the donors.

At the same time, Henisz et al. (2005, p.12) mentioned another form of isomorphic pressures '*indirect coercion*' wherein outsider institutions try to intervene and to change the balance of power between domestic groups to support those who favour their ideas or reform programmes. This can be done by providing the targeted groups with resources, legitimacy, or rhetorical arguments, or through prompting various groups to join in the pro-reform coalition. Developing countries might also find themselves compelled to adopt certain organizational models such as the IRAs out of the necessity that they do not want to be left behind and their willingness to remain members of the international society. In this regard, these countries may '*symbolically imitate*' certain models in order to maintain and enhance their credibility and competitiveness as well as to legitimatize other policy decisions, such as liberalization and privatization, and regulatory reforms (see Gilardi 2005). In this context, the adoption of IRAs is purely instrumental, either to satisfy the donors or to attract private investors.

A detailed investigation of such diffusion mechanisms goes beyond the limits and the scope of this chapter and requires rigorous research projects aiming at unpacking the different ways in which regulatory reforms have spread in the Middle East region. Nonetheless, several features of coercive isomorphism can be seen in the Egyptian case. The reform process has been associated from the very beginning with the deteriorated economic conditions and the intervention of the international financial institutions in the Egyptian economy. Because of the huge debt of the Egyptian government at the end of the 1980s, Egypt had to adapt a Structural Adjustment Plan in 1991 following negotiations with the IMF and the WB. At the top of their recommendations, these two international financial institutions have emphasized the primacy of market forces and privatization and ordered the retreat of the state from many economic and social fields. Hence, from the very beginning the choice of the economic reform model has been dictated by the WB and the IMF, which indicates the role of coercive isomorphic pressures. These pressures have been consolidated by the need for economic development, which made the successive Egyptian governments prone to the conditionality of the donors. The same applies to other countries in the region including Lebanon, Jordan, and Morocco.

REGULATORY REFORMS IN THE MIDDLE EAST: A FUTURE RESEARCH AGENDA

This section intends to shed light on some limitations of the regulatory governance research in the Middle East region and to suggest directions for future research. Starting with the limitations related to the research ideals, it is worth mentioning that regulatory governance research could be enriched with detailed comparative case studies among the countries of the region analysing the emerging regulatory regimes/policies and their role in addressing policy problems in social and economic sectors (Wiedemann and Ingold 2021). Such cross-country and cross-sectoral comparative perspectives could enable more in-depth investigations of regulatory initiatives and frameworks in the Middle East. By doing so, regulation scholars will be able to identify similarities and differences related to the newly established regulatory regimes and the ways in which regulatory processes are being conducted. Identifying such similarities and differences via comparisons provides a good starting point for figuring out the general patterns of regulatory reforms and modelling regulatory processes by focusing on interactions between regulatory stakeholders involved in making and enforcing regulations in each country.

Focusing on formal regulatory regimes and the major players in regulatory processes including the government institutions and the private regulated industries have led some scholars to neglect the role played by consumers and end-users. According to the public interests perspective on regulation, regulatory authorities are established to protect the interests of the public (Croley 2008). Therefore, the general public including consumers and end-users should be present in regulatory debates and should play a role in shaping the very regulations, which control their behaviours and limit their choices. Different participatory governance methodologies/techniques can be used to shed light on the role of the public in regulatory processes in the Middle East (see Fischer 2012). In this regrade, holding public consultations and conducting systematic surveys of end users will reflect their opinions on how effective the regulatory regimes and independent regulators are in handling regulatory issues and harnessing the activities of private service providers (see OECD 2011). In other words, researchers and regulatory policymakers need to discuss and agree upon participation mechanisms via which the public can echo their voices regarding the different regulatory issues at stake. It is equally important to make sure that the participation channels such as public consultations are effectively used on shaping regulations and are not utilized just as a legitimization tool for regulatory decisions (Badran 2013a).

Regarding the limitations related to the availability of resources, the lack of funding for research projects on regulation is one of the main constraints, which restricts the expansion of regulatory research. Furthermore, the process of data collection provides one of the challenges that are facing regulation scholars the Middle East. The overall environment in many of the Middle East countries is not conducive for conducting research in general and research on regulation in particular. The scientific research budgets are significantly small which limits the ability of universities and research centres to conduct rigorous research and to finance serious research projects. Added to this, the lack of cooperation from studied governmental and private sector institutions in addition to the culture of information hording inside such organizations makes it difficult for researchers to examine in-depth the established regulatory regimes and to evaluate their effectiveness in managing and regulating the different social and economic sectors.

The abovementioned limitations of regulatory research in the Middle East together with the relative novelty of the notion of regulation and regulatory governance have resulted in limited contributions from the Middle Eastern regulatory scholars. Compared to the advanced field of regulatory governance studies in the western countries, the countries of the Middle East still have long way to go to catch up with the recent developments in this area. Avenues for future research are quite open to examine several regulatory issues. At the macro level, cross-national institutional analysis of regulatory reforms in the Middle East and the western countries can be an interesting topic for further investigation. The experience of regulation in social and economic sectors in the Middle East indicates that a universal model of regulatory reforms, where markets are opened to the participation of the private sector under a regulatory framework executed via IRAs, is in place in many countries including Egypt, Lebanon, Saudi Arabia, and Jordan. Considering the essential political, legal, economic and institutional differences between these countries, the question that springs to mind is whether the fundamental functional elements of the IRAs model can be found in the context of the Middle East countries. In other words, the rise of the regulatory state model of the south in general and in the Middle East in particular with its distinctive features requires more attention and focus from the scholars in this region (Dubash and Morgan 2013). The aim is to figure out why the Middle East countries follow the same models of regulatory reforms that was originated in the west despite the fundamental differences at the level of the contextual social, economic, and political factors. Is it just imitation, fashion, superficial change or there is an underlying policy learning processes? How can the new institutionally constructed IRAs be accommodated within the existing regulatory environment? (Dunlop and Radaelli 2018).

Another important area for future research at the macro level is to conduct cross-sectoral institutional analysis of regulatory reforms in the Middle East countries. It would be interesting in this regard to find out whether IRAs in these sectors follow the same regulatory patterns in terms of the way in which they steer regulatory processes towards the achievement of the intended regulatory goals. Such an analysis would enlighten regulatory scholars about different aspects of regulation in social and economic sectors. It would also shed some light on how different regulatory approaches might lead to different outcomes. In addition to this, by conducting cross-sectoral institutional analysis of regulatory reforms scholars would also be able to understand whether the particularities of specific sectors interfere with the ability of regulators to steer them in a specific way.

At the micro level, the relationship between regulatory structures and regulatory outcomes represents another direction for future research (OECD 2018). The investigation of this topic raises many questions about how the structure of specific regulatory institutions affects their functions and in turn their outcomes. In other words, are there regulatory structures that perform better than others do? What are the determinants of regulatory institutions' effectiveness? How are institutional boundaries formed? What are the rules for inclusion and exclusion in regulatory processes? How is institutional complexity reflected in the ability of the sector regulators to pursue certain types of management strategies? What are the limitations of regulatory management in the light of market compositions?

Added to the abovementioned micro-level investigation points, the way in which certain regulations impact on the performance of the regulated companies can also be an interesting topic on the agenda for future research. Examining this issue comes at the heart of regulator–regulatee relationships (Etienne 2013). Regulatory burdens can be among the most important obstacles that hinder the progress of the regulated companies and in turn the developments in social and economic sectors. In this context, it would be important to figure out how regulatory agencies calculate the potential burdens of their decisions on the regulated companies. In what way they construct the delicate balance between public and private interests. Moreover, in case they have passed a regulation that carries burdens for the regulates, how the latter respond to this regulation. Would the regulatees shift these burdens to consumers by charging higher prices for their services?

An interesting question, however, which has been left unanswered is how can we explain the success of the transferred regulatory models in some of the developing countries despite the contextual differences between these countries and the exporting ones? The regulatory reform of the telecommunications market in Egypt is a case in point. Different criteria and indicators reflect the success of the IRA model including the level of investments, the trust of the regulated companies, and the economic performance of the whole sector. Considering the contextual differences mentioned before, one should not expect this level of success, which requires a search for the determining factors of success outside the box of traditional socio-economic and political justifications (Dunlop and Radaelli 2018).

Regarding regulatory tools, RIA is still an underdeveloped area of investigation in many countries in the region. As noted above, RIA carries great potential for making regulations and regulatory processes more efficient. Nonetheless, this important regulatory tool is not used in a systematic fashion by the countries of the Middle East region. This observation begs the question on how to integrate RIA in the process of regulation making and enforcement (Dunlop et al. 2012).

In addressing the aforementioned questions, the regulators in the region are facing some additional challenges: chief among them are the cost of regulation, the possibility of regulatory capture, the need for coordination and accountability mechanisms. Regulation is not a cost-free activity (Anderson and Sallee 2011). Government interventions via regulation normally result in new economic costs for both public and private organizations. For government organizations, design, development, administration and enforcement activities related to new regulatory rules add to costs incurred by such organizations. For private regulated companies, new regulations means additional costs to comply with the new rules. This may in turn result in an increase in administrative, capital, and indirect costs of those businesses. Some of the cost might be transferred to the end user by increasing the price of the provided services. Hence, any regulatory intervention should be deigned to strike the balance between the expected benefits and the required costs. In other words, IRAs have to grapple with their assigned tasks of modernizing the respective sectors by attracting new investments and the costs of regulations imposed on the regulated industries.

Given the novelty of the notion of regulation in the Middle East, many of the newly established regulators are prone to the risk of capture. In theory, IRAs are supposed to protect the public the interests and the consumers. In practice, the more experienced regulated industry with all the information they may have about the markets they operate in can make the inexperienced IRAs more inclined to serve the interests of the private companies at the expense of the public interests. Added to this, the principal–agent dilemma and the associated information asymmetries between principals (parent organizations) and agents (e.g. regulators) on the one hand, and between the regulator and the regulated industries on the other has to be addressed. The key question in this regard is how to control agents to work for the benefits of their principals. In other words, how to move beyond capture in regulatory theory and practice (Croley 2011).

The creation of IRAs in different economic and social sectors in the Middle East has also raised some fundamental concerns about accountability and coordination mechanisms. As is the case with other countries in the west, many of the Middle Eastern countries have witnessed the phenomenon of agencification (see Christensen et al. 2008). Many IRAs have been created outside the traditional bureaucratic hierarchical control. As such, the question has become who regulates the regulators. How can we hold IRAs accountable for their actions? Additionally, coordinating regulatory activities and incivilities have become a problematic issue given the intersection and the overlap among the regulated economic and social sectors. For IRAs in the region, regulation is still a learning curve. That means they still have a lot to learn about this subject. They also have to muddle through the emerging regulatory issues in their respective sectors.

CONCLUSION

There have been arduous efforts at regulatory reform in the Middle East region for several years. Despite continuing regional turmoil, many governments have demonstrated an explicit commitment to regulatory reforms and acknowledged its vital role in achieving economic development. Since 2005, 90% of the region's economies have implemented business regulatory reforms to make it easier for private companies to do business. Nonetheless, regulation and regulatory reforms are still representing a relatively new area of public governance the Middle East, as regulatory reforms are still slow and are concentrated mainly in the area of trade. Algeria and Jordan, for instance, improved the infrastructure of their ports, which led to a reduction in the time required to carry out shipping operations, while Morocco reduced the number of documents required for export. Tunisia has also made paying taxes less expensive for companies by lowering the corporate tax rate. Despite the efforts to improve the business regulatory environment in the region, the World Bank (2014) has reported that, business regulatory reform has remained narrow, as only 55% of the countries in the Middle East region have implemented reforms, compared to 60% in East Asia and the Pacific and 74% in sub-Saharan Africa.

This observation means the regulatory reforms in the Middle East regions need to be continued on a larger scale. Added to this, the issue of regulatory reforms needs to be regarded as an integrated part of the overall governance reform processes. For IRAs to function independently in an accountable fashion the overall political structures in the Middle East are required to be reformed to reflect more democratic, participative institutions and processes. Furthermore, one of the most important tools to assist policymakers in developing effective regulations is RIA. RIA should be supported at the highest institutional levels. This could be the responsibility of the central agencies such as the supervisory authority or various regulatory institutions and ministries. There is no doubt that this is necessary to ensure the support of all institutions concerned with preparing legislation and rules. To sum up, the journey of regulatory reforms has started in the Middle East, nonetheless, the Middle Eastern countries still have a long way to go.

NOTES

1. While regulatory independence is perceived as one of the main institutional guarantees for effective regulation in the west, the close relationships between the relatively newly established regulatory agencies in the liberalized sectors in many Middle Eastern countries and their parent organizations (government ministries) calls for more investigation and reconsideration of the notion of regulatory independence. Such an examination of the notion of independence in the Middle East is imperative in order to understand the relationship between the de facto and de jour independence of such agencies. The underlying assumption here is that the way in which those agencies translate their formal independence into actual practices will interfere with their ability to fulfil their duties and to achieve their policy goals.
2. The core question in this regard is why governments in the Middle East delegate part(s) of their powers to independent agencies that are supposed to work at arm's-length from the government organizations.
3. As such, it is worth noting that given the diverse economic, social, legal, and political contexts in the region, it would be over-simplistic to assume that a one-size-fits-all regulatory approach would automatically apply to all countries. Furthermore, providing an exhaustive list of regulatory reforms in the Middle East goes beyond the scope of this chapter. Therefore, to organize the discussion in this section, the focus will be on three main areas of regulatory reforms: regulatory policies, regulatory tools, and regulatory institutions.
4. The Palestinian legal and judicial database run by the Institute of Law at Bir Zeit University provides a good example for the efforts to enhance regulatory transparency and public access to regulations and legislations (http://muqtafi.birzeit.edu/en/index.aspx).
5. That includes informal consultation with selected groups, sending regulatory proposals for comment by stakeholders, publishing regulatory proposals on the official websites, and inviting regulatory stakeholders to hearing sessions.
6. In this regard, actions were taken in order to reducing red tape imposed by excessive administrative procedures and requirements that might involve unnecessary paperwork. Regulatory costs associated with obtaining permits, filling out forms, preparing reports and notification requirements for the government have been targeted by the reform initiatives. The aim was to minimize such unnecessary costs for the regulated companies.
7. In the context of the Egyptian regulatory reform initiative, ERRADA has worked collaboratively with different ministries in various sectors including agriculture, investment, tourism, local development, housing, finance, transport, petroleum, electricity, administrative development, trade and industry, and health and population in order to streamline and simplify their laws, regulations and procedures. In each of the participating ministries, an inventory of all laws and subordinate regulations and decrees was created and reviewed in order to create an electronic registry of all laws and regulations affecting citizens and businesses. The inventories of regulations were filtered using

three main criteria: Is the regulation needed? Is it legal? Is it business friendly? The answers to these questions determine if a regulation will be kept or will be eliminated (ERRADA 2008).

8. As reported by the OECD (2014), Jordan adopted RIA as a regulatory tool in 2009. In 2012, Jordan established an Impact Assessment Unit to assess formulating, programming, implementing, and evaluating the national developmental plans. In this context, the Impact Assessment Unit has provided specific assessments of government policies and programmes using three forms of RIA: planning, standard and full RIA (Jacobs 2010, p.5). The planning RIA is used during the preparatory stage of making regulations and focuses on regulations that are included in the annual legislative agenda proposed by the ministries or the government as a whole. The standard RIA is conducted for new and amended regulations with potential impact on citizens and businesses. This form of RIA is done during the process of drafting new regulations or amending existing ones. It can also be used during the consolation processes. The final form of RIA is conducted for certain types of regulations where the standard RIA indicates potential significant impacts. This form of regulatory assessment applies also when consulted stakeholders or political authorities identify a regulatory issue(s) as important.

9. The responsibilities for managing and developing the sector were divided between TRA and TE (Hassanin 2003). The duties of TRA were extended to cover several regulatory functions including the following: overseeing various technical aspects including frequencies and their spectrums; issuing service licenses; approving tariffs; increasing private investment; encouraging competition; ensuring transparency; and balancing the relationship between service providers and consumers. As the sole operator, at that time, TE was responsible for establishing, maintaining, and operating the local telecommunications networks and international links.

10. The vision of TRC is to excel in making the ICT and postal sector the pillars for growth at the national level and the highly distinguished regulatory environment regionally. In this context, the TRC is acting as an independent governmental commission aiming at regulating the performance of the ICT and postal sector. Added to this and as is the case with the NTRA in Egypt, TRC is aiming at stimulating competition, protecting the interests of the beneficiaries, and monitoring the implementation of quality of service indicators (KPIs). The TRC also guarantee telecoms services provision at affordable prices in order to achieve sustainable growth in all relevant sectors (https://trc.gov.jo).

11. The mandate of EWRA not only covers technical and financial issues but it also extends to include economic and social aspects. Accordingly, the founding decree has assigned EWRA a comprehensive responsibility for regulating and managing the quality, cost, and price of water services in Egypt.

REFERENCES

Abdel Gawad, S. (2013). The Egyptian Experience in "Better Regulation" Reform. *Law in Transition*, 68–72.

Abrardi, L., Cambini, C., & Rondi, L. (2016). Investment and Regulation in MENA Countries: The Impact of Regulatory Independence. In A. Rubino, M. Campi, V. Lenzi, & I. Ozturk (eds), *Regulation and Investments in Energy Markets*. Cambridge, MA: Academic Press, pp.243–273.

Anderson, S., & Sallee, J. (2011). Using Loopholes to Reveal the Marginal Cost of Regulation: The Case of Fuel-Economy Standards. *American Economic Review*, 1375–1409.

Badran, A. (2011). The Regulatory Management of Privatised Public Utilities: A Network Perspective on the Regulatory Process in the Egyptian Telecommunications Market. VDM Verlag Dr. Müller. ISBN-13: 978-3639367959.

Badran, A. (2012). Steering the Regulatory State: The Rationale behind the Creation and Diffusion of Independent Regulatory Agencies in Liberalised Utility Sectors in the Developing Countries: Thoughts and Reflections on the Egyptian Case. *International Journal of Public Administration*, 204–213.

Badran, A. (2013a). The Role of Public Consultations in Regulatory Decision-Making: Thoughts and Reflections Based on Regulatory Decision-Making Mechanisms in the Egyptian Telecoms Market.

The Observatory on Independent Regulators. http://www.osservatorioair.it/pages-in-english/about -the-observatory-on-independent-regulatorsria/: RIA.

Badran, A. (2013b). Understanding the Egyptian Regulatory State: Independent Regulators in Theory and Practice. In N. Dubash, & B. Morgan (eds), *The Rise of the Regulatory State of The South: The Infrastructure of Development*. Oxford: Oxford University Press, pp.53–74.

Badran, A. (2017). Revisiting Independence of Regulatory Agencies: Thoughts and Reflections from Egypt's Telecoms Sector. *Public Policy and Administration*, 66–84.

Badran, A. (2020). The Regulatory Policies of Telecommunication Sectors in the Arab Region: Selected Case Studies. *Siyasat Arabia (Arab Politics) Journal*, 2, 79–93.

Braun, D., & Gilardi, F. (2006). Taking "Galton's Problem" Seriously: Towards a Theory of Policy Diffusion. *Journal of Theoretical Politics*, 298–322.

Christensen, T., Lie, A., & Lægreid, P. (2008). Beyond New Public Management: Agencification and Regulatory Reform in Norway. *Financial Accountability and Management*, 15–30.

Croley, S. (2008). *Regulation and Public Interests: The Possibility of Good Regulatory Government*. Princeton: Princeton University Press.

Croley, S. (2011). Beyond Capture: Towards a New Theory of Regulation. In D. Levi-Faur (ed.), *Handbook on the Politics of Regulation*. Cheltenham, UK and Northampton, MA, USA: Edward Elgar Publishing, pp.50–69.

DiMaggio, P., & Powell, W. (1983). The Iron Cage Revisited: Institutional Isomorphism and Collective Rationality in Organizational Fields. *American Sociological Review*, 48, 147–160.

DiMaggio, P., & Powell, W. (1991). The Iron Cage Revisited: Institutional Isomorphism and Collective Rationality. In W. Powell, & P. DiMaggio, *The New Institutionalism in Organizational Analysis*. Chicago: University of Chicago Press, pp.34–56.

Dubash, N., & Morgan, B. (2013). *The Rise of the Regulatory State of The South: The Infrastructure of Development*. Oxford: Oxford: Oxford University Press.

Dunlop, C., & Radaelli, C. (2018). Does Policy Learning Meet the Standards of an Analytical Framework of the Policy Process? *The Policy Studies Journal*, 46 (S1).

Dunlop, C., Maggetti, M., Radaelli, C., & Russel, D. (2012). The Many Uses of Regulatory Impact Assessment: A Meta-Analysis of EU and UK Cases. *Regulation and Governance*, 23–45.

Dusk, M., Pegani, A., & Al-Mashat, R. (2020). Reshaping the Economic and Social Systems of the Middle East and North Africa. Asharq Al-Awsat Newspaper; https://aawsat.com.

Eisner, A., Worsham, J. , & Ringquist, J. (2006). *Contemporary Regulatory Policy*. Boulder, CO: Lynne Rienner Publishers.

El-Nawawy, M., & Ismail, M. (1999). Overcoming Deterrents and Impediments to Electronic Commerce in Light of Globalisation: The Case of Egypt. the 9th Annual Conference of the Internet Society, INET 99. San Jose, USA.

ERRADA. (2008). Regulatory Reform: Building Egypt's Competitive Advantage. Amman: OECD/GfD.

Estache, A., Goicoechea, A., & Manacorda, M. (2006). Telecommunications Performance, Reforms, and Governance. World Bank.

Etienne, J. (2013). Ambiguity and Relational Signals in Regulator–Regulatee Relationships. *Regulation and Governance*, 7, 30–47.

Fischer, F. (2012). Participatory Governance: From Theory To Practice. In D. Levi-Faur (ed.), *The Oxford Handbook of Governance*. Oxford: Oxford: Oxford University Press, pp.50–74.

Freiberg, A. (2010). Re-Stocking the Regulatory Tool-Kit. The Conference on Regulation in an Age of Crisis. Dublin: http://www.regulation.upf.edu/dublin-10-papers/1I1.pdf.

Gentzoglanis, A. (2001). Reforms and Optimal Regulatory Design in MENA Countries: Lessons from the Telecommunications Industry. *Journal of Development and Economic Policies*, 7–41.

Gilardi, F. (2003). Explaining Delegation to Independent Regulatory Agencies: The Role of Political Uncertainty. Institut d'Etudes Politiques et Internationales Université de Lausanne.

Gilardi, F. (2005). The Same but Different: Central Banks, Regulatory Agencies and Politics of Delegation to Independent Authority. The conference "Credibility through Delegation? Independent Agencies in Comparative Perspective", Centre of Competition Policy. East Anglia, Norwich.

Gilardi, F. J., & Levi-Faur, D. (2006). Regulation in the Age of Globalisation: The Diffusion of Regulatory Agencies across Europe and Latin America. Barcelona: IBEI Working Papers.

Gunningham, N., & Grabosky, P. (1998). *Smart Regulation: Designing Environmental Policy*. Oxford: Oxford University Press.

Hassanin, L. (2003). Africa ICT Policy Monitor Project: Egypt ICT Country Report. http://africa.rights.apc.org/research_reports/egypt.pdf, accessed 4 February 2007.

Henisz, W., Zelner, B., & Guillén, M. (2005). The Worldwide Diffusion of Market-Oriented Infrastructure Reform, 1977–1999. http://knowledge.wharton.upenn.edu/papers/download/HZG_ASR_Paper_Final.pdf.

Jacobs, S. (2001). Building Credible Regulators for Liberalized Utility Sectors. The First Workshop of the APEC–OECD Co-operative Initiative on Regulatory Reform. Beijing, China.

Jacobs, S. (2010). A Manual for Regulatory Impact Assessment (RIA): Jordan. http://regulatoryreform.com/wp-content/uploads/2015/02/Jordan-RIA-Manual-2010.pdf. USAID/Economic Growth Office (EG).

James, O., & Lodge M. (2003). The Limitations of "Policy Transfer" and "Lesson Drawing" for Public Policy Research. *Political Studies Review*, 1, 179–193.

Lasheen, W. (2019). Explaining Water Governance in Egypt: Actors, Mechanisms and Challenges. Exeter: Unpublished Phd, University of Exeter.

Levi-Faur, D. (2005). The Global Diffusion of Regulatory Capitalism. *Annals of the American Academy of Political and Social Science*, 12–32.

Majone, G. (2001). Non-Majoritarian Institutions and the Limits of Democratic Governance: A Political Transaction-Cost Approach. *Journal of Institutional and Theoretical Economics*, 57–78.

Marsh, D., & Sharman, C. (2009). Policy Diffusion and Policy Transfer. *Policy Studies*, 269–288.

Massey, A. (2009). Policy Mimesis in the Context of Global Government. *Policy Studies*, 383–397.

Megacom. (2005). Research Study on Streamlining the Egyptian Laws, Regulations and Procedures Governing SMEs Establishment, Growth, Export and Exit. International Comparative Study and Recommendations Report. http://www.mof.gov.eg/MOFGallerySource/English/SME/Research_studies/21/21-1.pdf. Ministry of Finance.

Mezouaghi, M. (2008). Privatisation and Regulatory Reform in the Middle East and North Africa (MEDA) Area – Telecom Case Study. Agence Française de Développement.

Moe, M. (1990). Political Institutions: The Neglected Side of the Story. *Journal of Law, Economics, & Organization*, Vol. 6, Special Issue: [Papers from the Organization of Political Institutions Conference, April 1990], pp.213–253.

OECD. (2011). Regulatory Consultation: A Mena-OECD Practitioners' Guide for Engaging Stakeholders in the Rule-Making Process. https://www.oecd.org/mena/governance/MENA-Practitioners-Guide-%20EN.pdf: OECD.

OECD. (2014). Regulatory Reform in the Middle East and North Africa. www.oecd.org/publishing: OECD Publishing.

OECD. (2018). OECD Regulatory Policy Outlook 2018. https://www.oecd-ilibrary.org: OECD.

Rose, R. (1991). What is Lesson Drawing? *Journal of Public Policy*, 3–30.

Rose, R. (1993). *Lesson-Drawing in Public Policy*. Chatham NJ: Chatham House.

Salamon, L. M. (ed.) (2002). *The Tools of Government: A Guide to the New Governance*. New York, NY: Oxford University Press.

Spiller, T. (1993). Institutions and Regulatory Commitment in Utilities' Privatisation. *Industrial and Corporate Change*, 387–450.

Thacker, S. (2020). Environmental Law and Practice in the United Arab Emirates: Overview Environmental Regulatory Framework. https://uk.practicallaw.thomsonreuters.com/w-008 3980?transitionType=Default&contextData=(sc.Default)&firstPage=true.

The Ministry of Public Health. (2020). Occupational safety and health policy in the state of Qatar. Doha: https://www.moph.gov.qa.

The World Bank. (1995). Project Completion Report: Arab Republic of Egypt. http://www-wds.worldbank.org.

The World Bank (2014). Doing Business 2014: Understanding Regulations for Small and Medium-Size Enterprises. DOI: 10.1596/978-0-8213-9984-2.

Wavre, V. (2018). Regulatory Trends in MENA Telecommunications. In V. Wavre, *Policy Diffusion and Telecommunications Regulation*. London: Palgrave Macmillan.

Wiedemann, R., & Ingold, K. (2021). Solving Cross-Sectoral Policy Problems: Adding a Cross-Sectoral Dimension to Assess Policy Performance. *Journal of Environmental Policy & Planning.* https://doi .org/10.1080/1523908X.2021.1960809.

6. The age of regulatory agencies: tracking differences and similarities over countries and sectors

Xavier Fernández-i-Marín, Jacint Jordana and David Levi-Faur

INTRODUCTION

Regulatory agencies started to be created already during the first decades of the twentieth century, and it is also possible to identify some proto-examples in the last decades of the nineteenth century. However, it wasn't until the late 1980s and particularly during the 1990s that a combination of extensive economic restructuring, public sector transformations, and new political leadership created a wave of regulatory reforms which spread over the world (Jordana et al. 2011). This wave of regulatory innovations involved also the establishment of regulatory agencies in multiple countries and sectors, which coincided with and contributed to the global expansion of regulatory capitalism (Braithwaite 2008, Levi-Faur and Jordana 2005).

Early creations of regulatory agencies were strictly limited to a few countries and sectors, particularly in the United States and the Anglo-Saxon world in banking, insurance and pensions. These institutional creations at that time were much diverse and had varied characteristics, but most shared as a common trait a strong professionalism and concentration of their task on supervising existing regulations. They also used to have some separate identity from the ministerial branches, although agencies' political independence was not at stake at that time. In any case, during most of the twentieth century, this administrative group remained quite marginal, and only from time to time were new ones created, to address some very specific needs, for example the case of nuclear safety commissions or securities commissions since the 1960s. Only in North-America were they quite common, as they had been expanding quite significantly over the century.

Maybe because of the iconic transformations of the United Kingdom in the 1980s, with major privatizations and market-making experiences, or Carter's and Regan's regulatory reforms in the United States, or maybe because of more functional needs related to the growing process of globalization at that time (Henisz et al. 2005, Gilardi et al. 2007, Shapiro 1997), the number of regulatory agencies created started to grow smoothly in the decade of the 1980s, gaining momentum and accelerating intensively in the 1990s, reaching almost all countries and many sectors over the world (Fernández-i-Marín and Jordana 2015). This was an impressive transformation, where institutional diffusion mechanisms took a very relevant role, but the strength of weak ties across different sectors and countries in a very particular moment of intense globalization and no major geopolitical confrontations worldwide was also important (Jordana et al. 2011).

In this chapter, and making use of updated data from our previous research, we provide a detailed examination of the expansion of regulatory agencies in recent decades, and the differences and similarities they show over countries and sectors. The next section introduces the datasets we plan to employ, providing also details on their scope and selection criteria. A third section provides a general overview from this data on the expansion and diffusion of regulatory agencies, both from sector and territorial perspectives. The subsequent section focuses on examining a crucial variable that has not been considered in detail in most studies of regulatory agencies diffusion: the democratic rule of a country as a determinant of agencification in regulatory governance, but also of agencies' variations. This analysis is continued by a discussion of similarities and differences of regulatory agencies, to assess to what extent they show some differences, often not very visible. A final section on the prospects of regulatory agencies amid professionalism, globalization and democracy concludes.

TWO DATASETS ON REGULATORY AGENCIES

This chapter combines two different datasets that we have been assembling and revising through time for different purposes. The first dataset is called *RA-creation*, and contains data of the creation dates of actual regulatory agencies. It started as a dataset for a regional case study, to examine the expansion of the regulatory state in Latin America (Jordana and Levi-Faur 2005), and a few years later we expanded it to include all OECD countries, aiming to analyze the global diffusion of regulatory agencies (Jordana et al. 2011). A further step was done to include ASEAN countries to study patterns of regulatory regionalism (Fernández-i-Marín and Jordana 2015), and more recently has reached 85 countries and 17 sectors, including new OECDs, most African and the remaining Asian countries. Moreover, the original dataset had a time span between 1966 and 2007, and this one extends it to regulatory agencies' creations between 1920 and 2017. So this book chapter extends the creation dates one century back, ten years forward, while almost doubling the number of countries and adding two sectors of recent increasing importance.

The 17 sectors in which we examine the presence of regulatory agency activity are competition, electricity, environmental, financial services, food safety, gas, health services, insurance, pensions, pharmaceuticals, postal services, securities and exchange, telecommunications, water, work safety, data protection and central banking. In our approximation to the creation of regulatory agencies, what we measure in this dataset is when an agency started to be active in a particular sector, not when the administrative organization was created. In other words, if a country created an agency to regulate electricity in 1994, for example, and in 1999 this agency was also entitled to regulate the gas sector, we consider that in 1999 a new country-sector case was activated by the establishment of a regulatory agency in that sector.

The second dataset is called *RA-2010* and contains institutional features of regulatory agencies as administrative entities. This database was introduced by Jordana, Fernández-i-Marín and Bianculli (2018) and partially used by Fernández-i-Marín, Jordana and Bianculli (2015), aimed to examine the diversity of institutional configurations regulatory agencies might present. The dataset is a snapshot of the formal characteristics of regulatory agencies at the end of 2010, covering 115 countries (>10M inhabitants and/or >100 billion US$ GDP, plus member countries of EU, ASEAN and DR-CAFTA) and 17 sectors (it includes nuclear safety but not data protection). This dataset contains 43 original variables related to different institutional and organizational aspects of the agencies. With these more than forty variables, a collection of four different latent dimensions was generated: regulatory capabilities, managerial autonomy, political independence and public accountability. The combination of the original variables into the final dimensions was performed using a full Bayesian measurement model with a loss function penalizing missing data. The units of analysis in this dataset were the regulatory agencies identified across the sectors and countries considered. There are a total of 799 of them, for which the four different dimensions are gathered.

However, how can we be sure that we are talking about the same type of public agencies when referring to these public specialized bodies' expansion? One thing is clear: the political independence trait of regulatory agencies shall not be taken for granted. Although politicians in many countries included such characteristics in the institutional design of regulatory agencies when creating them – basically since the late 1980s – this was not always the case, and also, such characters were introduced with dissimilar intensity across countries and sectors. Actually, our definition of regulatory agencies is based on some particular characteristics, but not on the nature of its autonomy, to the extent that political delegation to the agency responsible created an independent status within the public sector or not. To be included in our datasets, agencies should meet four key criteria: First, they must show their own identity rather than being part of a ministerial department (regardless of hierarchical links between the agency and the executive). Second, agencies should concentrate only on regulatory tasks and activities (rule supervision, rule enhancement, rule definition, etc.). Third, agencies are public entities capable of holding public authority. Finally, they should be a stable institution regulated by public legal acts and ordinances. We use the legal date of creation or the date of issuance of the law or ordinance, not the initial operations date, to define the creation of a regulatory agency.

The two datasets, *RA-creation* and *RA-2010* are related in the sense that they adopt the same definition of regulatory agency to be included in, but they are very different in their conception. While *RA-creation* focuses on the temporal dimension of *spaces* defined by the combination between Country and Sector, the *RA-2010* focuses on specific public organizations, on the characteristics of concrete *agencies*, and only for a single point in time (end 2010). This difference in the units of analysis implies that the potential for exploring different topics is multiplied, as the two approaches enable researchers to apply different strategies and assess complementary hypotheses and research challenges.

A REGULATORY AGENCIFICATION OVERVIEW

A first finding is the impressive popularization that the regulatory agency model has reached over the world across many sectors. Figure 6.1 presents an ideographic map of the agencies' coverage of regulatory spaces at the end of the period considered (2017). Black squares represent a space (country / sector) covered by the activity of a regulatory agency. The horizontal axis presents the countries in the database sorted by the amount of their sectors covered. Equivalently, the vertical axis presents the sectors sorted by the amount of countries that have an agency in that specific sector. Regulatory spaces are all possible combinations of country and sector where it is possible that an agency has regulatory attributions. In our case, it is defined by 85 countries and 17 sectors, or a total of 1,445 potential spaces. In the last year from our dataset (2017) 67% of the spaces (970) were occupied by regulatory agencies (see also Figure 6.2). These figures do not show the *number* of regulatory agencies, but rather whether one agency, or even more than one, covers a specific potential regulatory space.

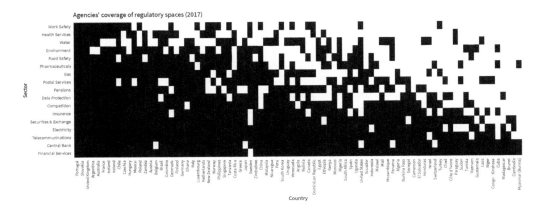

Source: Own elaboration, *RA-creation*.

Figure 6.1   *Coverage of regulatory agencies over countries and sectors (2017)*

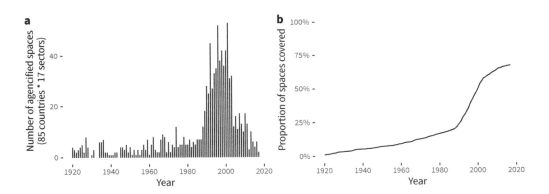

Note: a) describes the number of spaces (defined by a country and a sector) where a new regulatory agency is established every year; b) describes the cumulative proportion of the whole set of spaces that is already covered by a regulatory agency.
Source: Own elaboration, *RA-creation*.

Figure 6.2   *Sector–country spaces covered by regulatory agencies (1920–2017)*

To facilitate visualization, the data is organized in Figure 6.1 from more agency-intensive countries and sectors to less-intensive. The highest density of agency coverage happens in three countries, namely Portugal, Slovakia and the United Kingdom, and in two sectors, namely financial services and central banks. From this area of high density of regulatory agen-cification its intensity fades away until the less intensive countries (Myanmar and Cambodia), and sectors (work safety and health services) are reached. Obviously, the 17 sectors selected are all selected considering that cases where regulatory governance has been increasing in recent decades, and does not pretend to be a sample of all possible policy sectors, but still, the intensity in institutional creation and expansion we observe for a few decades is more than impressive.

Figure 6.2 illustrates this expansion very clearly. From our sample of countries and sectors, we can observe that between 1989 and 2001, the number of sector–country cases covered by regulatory agencies almost tripled, and after this period, its growth continued, but at a more reduced pace. It is worth noting that such expansion, in particular since late 1990s, has not been related mainly to the creation of new regulatory agencies – meaning the establishment of new organizations – but to the expansion of existing regulatory agencies to new adjacent sectors (Jordana and Levi-Faur 2010). In addition, there is another relevant observation: very few cases of agency termination appeared, and only a negligible number of agencies were dismantled or placed back into the ministry. All in all, it appears that the regulatory agency model has reached some stability and probable consolidation as a core public institution for the domestic governance of a quite large number of policy sectors in the age of globalization.

The process of agencification has shown some particular patterns in different time periods, as any process of diffusion of innovations does. From Figure 6.2, we can observe its evolution: there seems to be a long period of early adoption that went from the beginning of the twentieth century until the mid-1980s. Then the early majority exploded during the 1990s, peaking in the 2000s. From there, the late majority continued expanding agencification until recent years, where adoptions have become really scarce, by the country and sector laggards. A classical S-shaped diffusion curve has arrived to two thirds of the space occupied by regulatory agencies in 2017. From the 1920s to the 1980s the process was steady and sustained, with an average occupation of space of about two to three spaces per year in our sample. During the 1990s the explosion of regulatory agencies adoption leaves adoptions at a rate above 20 occupied spaces per year, peaking around the year 2000 with over 40 spaces occupied by a regulatory agency in a year. And as equally quickly as the process boomed in the maximum expansion period, in the last decade (2010s) it has faded away to go back to a rate of two to three agency occupations per year.

When we break down this data by the different world regions (Figure 6.3) we observe that the agency coverage differs as to its intensity, but also regarding the period in which its expansion accelerated. On the one hand, we see that Latin America and Europe have a quite similar progression, that only deviates since the 1990s, when European countries continued creating regulatory agencies – basically expanding this institutional model to more sectors – while Latin America largely stopped creating more agencies or expanding existing ones to other sectors. To some extent, the dynamics of European integration and the support of EU institutions to expand this regulatory model to more sectors were probably very influential for this move (Jordana et al. 2011 observed a significant influence of EU membership in the continued diffusion of agencies in the 2000s). On the other hand, African and Asian countries show a different pattern, with less intense creation of regulatory agencies during all the periods considered, but also having a different pace of acceleration, that extends until the first decade of the 2000s, at least. Finally, the North America and Australasia line shows a completely different dynamic, with constant growth since the 1960s, without an acceleration of momentum, contrary to all other regions. To the extent that the regulatory agency institutional design originated from the world of Anglo-Saxon public administration, this is not a surprise, as far as its development followed a more intense endogenous process compared to the other parts of the world, where diffusion dynamics came largely from outside.

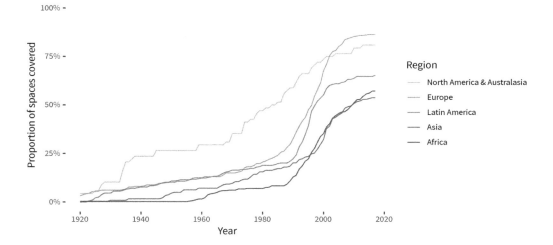

Source: Own elaboration, *RA-creation*.

Figure 6.3   Regulatory agency coverage by regions (1920–2017)

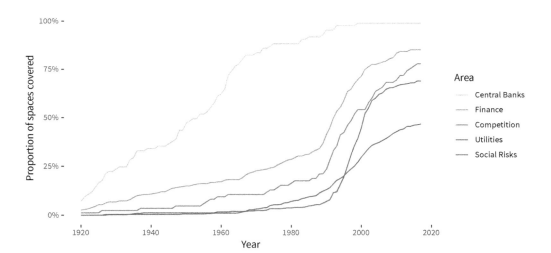

Source: Own elaboration, *RA-creation*.

Figure 6.4   Regulatory agency coverage by areas (1920–2017)

Figure 6.4 presents the same data from the point of view of areas of regulation. There are three areas grouping all regulatory sectors included in the dataset, plus two sectors considered in isolation: competition and central banks, both representing a particular category of agencies substantially different from the other areas of regulation. The first group covers all financial regulation, and includes four sectors: banking, pensions, insurance, and securities. The second group concentrates all utility sectors, from telecoms and electricity to gas, postal services and water. The last group, named social risks regulation, includes food safety, pharmaceutical, health services, data protection, environment and work safety. In this figure, we can easily observe the different patterns of central bank creation, completely different from the rest of the sectors. Most central banks were created much earlier than regulatory agencies and in the 1990s all countries selected in our sample already had established their central bank. Comparing the different groups of sectors (finance, utilities, social risks), it is clear that financial regulatory agencies emerged before, and expanded progressively over the century, while utilities agencies were almost nonexistent until the 1980s, and then boomed during the 1990s to expand to multiple countries in a few years. The case of agencies in charge of regulating social risks shows slower expansion, reaching less than 50% coverage at the end of our period. However, its growth during the 1980s and 1990s was quite significant.

A step further to better understand how the expansion of regulatory agencies occurred can be pursued focusing on how the distribution of sectors covered by agencies across countries evolved over time: whether all existing sectors covered by agencies are concentrated in a few countries, or whether they are distributed more evenly across all countries in the sample. During most of the twentieth century, only a few countries in the world created agencies, concentrated in a few sectors. However, since the 1960s, more and more countries have been moving in the direction to cover their regulatory spaces with regulatory agencies. This process of agency expansion across countries peaked in the 1990s, when more sectors incorporated the rule of regulatory agencification. Agencies multiplied also in other sectors. From the 2000s onwards, sectors with very small coverage did not expand substantially in the following years. Differences in the number of sectors covered by agencies in countries continued to reduce.

DEMOCRACY AND REGULATORY AGENCIES

Regulatory agencification can be understood also as a process of the expansion of delegation and the growing power fragmentation within modern States. In this sense they are one of the most important signifiers of the age of governance. Besides the classical horizontal separation of powers (legislative, executive and judicial) and vertical separation (federalism and decentralization), regulatory governance fragments power from an administrative point of view. With the establishment of regulatory agencies, the traditional Weberian view of the administration is challenged by an institutional organization having a less-hierarchical structure. Given this trend to disseminate power, it is logical to ask whether democracies, as regimes where power is inherently less concentrated than in non-democracies, are more likely to engage in such a substantial administrative transformation.

However, to the best of our knowledge, the literature so far has not explored regulatory agencification as a democratic phenomenon. Much attention has been concentrated on the legitimation and accountability problems of regulatory agencies (Majone 1999, Maggetti 2010, Jordana et al. 2015), and much less to the question of why democracies seem to be the natural environment in which independent regulatory agencies proliferate. Democracies are political systems where power is dispersed and fragmented by design, and checks and balances abound. To a certain extent, any single official cannot escape from other's supervision, and everyone can maintain a different opinion. Creating more decentralization and fragmentation

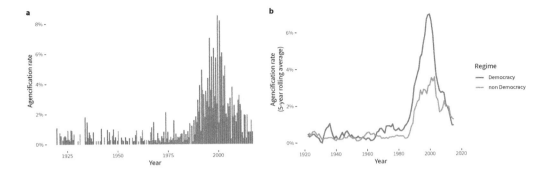

Note: a) shows absolute number; b) shows the five-year rolling average.
Source: Own elaboration, *RA-creation*.

Figure 6.5   *Annual agencification rate (proportion of spaces covered by a regulatory agency, out of the total possible spaces available for agencification), by regime*

to the political system, meaning the establishment of regulatory agencies with an effective power parcel, is not a major challenge, but something that often can be logically absorbed without major stress by a democratic regime. We show that democracy matters for the establishment of agencies, and particularly for its political independence. Democracies tend to create agencies earlier and when they create them, they grant them higher political autonomy.

In order to assess whether the political regime is more or less likely to engage in an agencification process, we have assigned to each possible space whether the country at that year is actually a democracy or not (Boix et al. 2013). Then, we use all the possible spaces that are under risk of being covered by a regulatory agency (hence discarding all spaces already covered by a regulatory agency) and define the agencification rate as the proportion of regulatory spaces newly covered by an agency divided out of the total possible regulatory agencies at risk, at that specific time. Then, when divided by regime type, the agencification rate allows us to compare the capacity of agency diffusion between democracies and non-democracies. Figure 6.5 shows the temporal dynamic of the agencification rate, by regime. In the left hand side the bars indicate the annual rates. For instance, during the late 1990s the agencification rate reached 7% in democracies, which means that at that specific moment, agencies were established or enlarged in 7% of the regulatory spaces that weren't agencified before. The rate for non-democracies at that same moment was a maximum of 3% of the spaces.

In the 1970s the agencification rate for democracies was kept at twice the rate of non-democracies, even if the absolute rate was less than 1%. During the agencification boom in the 1990s and 2000s the agencification rate for democracies kept being twice that of non-democracies (up to 7% in democracies and almost 4% in non-democracies). Actually, the agencification rate has been almost always higher for democracies than for non-democracies. Only a brief period during the decolonization in the 1960s, where many central banks were created in newly independent countries is when the agencification rate for non-democracies has overpassed that of the democracies. Also briefly during the 1920s, but very slightly over, and it seems that in the 2010s this may also be the case.

So for the last 50 years it seems clear that the logic of agencification as a matter of sharing the administrative power really does compel democracies to create agencies or expand existing ones in their political spaces at twice the rate of non-democracies. The drivers of such a differential can be found in the nature of democratic institutions, that allow to isolate areas of public policy making from the uncertainties of majoritarian politics. We cannot argue about a causal force, but an enabling political configuration that makes it more probable that some relevant actors successfully promote the establishment of these peculiar institutions.

Two different mechanisms can account for this differential effect. First, the aim for isolation by professional bureaucracy in the context of democratic disputes and political demands (DeCanio 2015), and second, the expectation of elected politicians to safeguard some policy issues/areas form the majority will, either in the short or in the long term, providing stability and autonomy to regulatory institutions (Tucker 2018). Thus, over the years, democracies have introduced institutional designs in which more responsibilities are granted to regulatory agencies. In this way, we also can perceive regulatory agencies as a democratic singularity that have expanded to different policy areas and sectors over the years (Fernández-i-Marín et al. 2021).

INSTITUTIONAL CHARACTERISTICS OF AGENCIFICATION

The next logical step once the process of agencification is understood is to turn from the creation and diffusion to their institutional characteristics. The unit of analysis is no more date of creation and coverage of potential space. Instead we analyze characteristics such as the rules for appointing agency head and board members, or how the agency budget is approved, among many other formal established norms defined by national laws and ordinances referring to the agencies.

Methodology and Analytical Approach

The source of data for this section is the *RA-2010* dataset, which covers 115 countries for the year 2010. Here we also identify the regulatory space (Country and Sector) as the unit of analysis, instead of the specific agencies, and examine how these concrete institutions can cover more or less of such space. This gives us more versatility in how to summarize scores assigned to agencies to averages for countries and sectors. Also, it brings *RA-2010* closer to *RA-creation*, as now in both cases we use the regulatory space unit. However, we need to solve a theoretical problem about how to aggregate results when we aim to summarize them for countries and sectors, in particular regarding the value of institutional variables that we collect for each single agency.

There are several strategies to this purpose. We have opted for an approach that is a compromise between the two extreme options: on one hand, to dismiss spaces not covered by a regulatory agency and simply average by country/sector.[1] On the other extreme, to perform an extraction of the scores for countries and sectors, at the same time, using a proper latent measurement model.[2] A plausible compromise is to assign the agency's scores to the regulatory spaces that this agency is covering, repeating their value if the agency covers more than one sector. And for the sectors that are not agencified, we assign them a value of zero. In fact, it makes sense since in the case of no agency, all scores can be interpreted as being

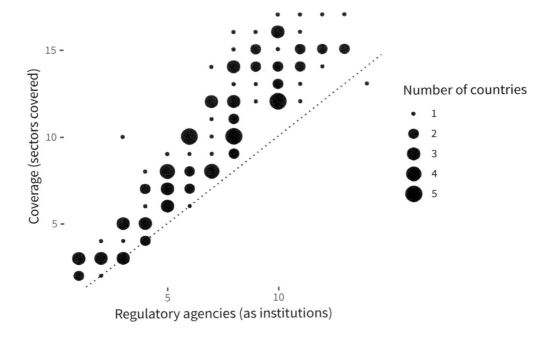

Note: The dot size indicates the number of countries in such a position.
Source: Own elaboration, *RA-2010*.

Figure 6.6   *Scatterplot that compares the number of regulatory agencies (institutions)
existing in a country, in the horizontal axis, against the coverage that such
agencies provide, in the vertical axis*

at their minimum level. In that case, an absolute minimum, which is precisely what a lack of
agency means in the dimensions (at least clearly in the managerial autonomy and political
independence).

Actually, we move forward with the third option. However, before discussing the results,
Figure 6.6 presents how the shift from regulatory agencies (as institutions, in the horizontal
axis) translates into agency coverage (country-sector spaces covered). The dots represent
countries, and their size is mapped to the number of countries actually in that position. This
also means that the existence of multi-sector regulatory agencies has become quite common,
and in some countries, they cover many different sectors (Jordana and Levi-Faur 2010). So in
this case we see that in general countries have more sectors covered than agencies. Only India
has more agencies (14) that cover fewer spaces (13 sectors). Conversely, Uruguay covers up
to 10 sectors with a very modest number of agencies (3).

Also from Figure 6.6 it is important to notice that the higher the number of agencies in
a country, the higher the number of sectors covered, which indicates that the process of
country agencification (covering sectors with a regulatory agency) is stronger than the process
of agency creation (adding another institution to the administrative branch of the state). If

countries were equally likely to cover more spaces than agencies needed, we would observe a dot cloud parallel to the 1:1 dotted line. But we indeed find that the slope of the dot cloud is higher than the line. In other words: countries that create many agencies are more likely to cover *even more* sectors than countries with fewer agencies.

The *RA-2010* database includes more than 40 variables measuring different institutional aspects of regulatory agencies, that are classified in four different groups aiming at facilitating the analysis. Each group of variables refers to a particular aspect defining the nature of regulatory agencies: regulatory capabilities, political independence, managerial autonomy, and public accountability. In a second step, once we sorted out four groups of variables, we employed factor analysis techniques to define latent dimensions for each group. A latent dimension is an indicator of a concept that is inferred using manifestations of several variables (Treier and Jackman (2008) for a latent measure of democracy). Once having calculated a value of each latent dimension for each agency, we can use this data to assess and compare the nature of each agency. For example, there are cases in which independence is strong, but managerial autonomy is weak; in other cases, agencies rely on strong accountability but enjoy few regulatory powers, so much so that their organizational autonomy becomes irrelevant (for details on the estimation of these latent dimensions and their analysis, see Jordana et al. 2018).

Identifying the Four Dimensions of the Analysis

Employing the criteria to aggregate values previously discussed for the four latent dimensions estimated for each regulatory agency, we can calculate average points of each dimension for each country and sector, allowing different types of comparisons as to the characteristics of regulatory agencies in different settings. In Figure 6.7 we present how the four dimensions distribute across each sector. This allows us to clearly observe the average intensity of each institutional trait (independence, autonomy, accountability, regulatory powers) in each sector, and also to classify sectors according to these latent dimensions. The original data in *RA-2010* is reported in a standard normal scale. We use here the logit transformation to facilitate its interpretation in a bounded scale that goes between 0 and 1. Results are quite puzzling, as their order differs within each of the sectors included (for example, in some sectors independence is stronger than accountability, while in others, this is the other way round), but also the intensity differs across sectors. Average agencies operating in the utilities and some sectors of finances show more intense levels than those agencies active in risk regulation.

Figure 6.8 shows the distribution of average scores of countries, by regime type. This is an example of how we can combine a relevant variable, as for example the existence (or not) of democracy in a country (here referring to the year 2010) with the different latent dimensions referring to the main institutional characteristics of regulatory agencies. Results are quite clear: agencies in democracies have more autonomy, more independence and are more accountable than agencies in non-democratic regimes. Even for regulatory capabilities, it appears that democracies delegate more responsibilities to agencies, compared to dictatorships. To some extent, it emerges that agencies in non-democratic agencies tend to be very weak institutions on all fronts. Actually, a large number of them are probably empty institutional boxes that were created in a context of a very powerful international diffusion process, mostly driven by emulation dynamics during the peak period of agency creation, in the 1990s. Some exceptions probably exist, as we can observe the extended tails for the four latent dimensions moving towards increasing levels (and the contrary as well).

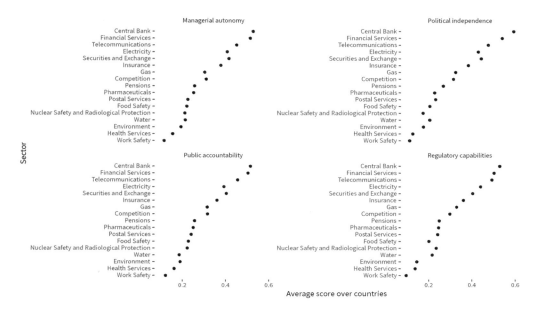

Source: Own elaboration, *RA-2010.*

Figure 6.7   *Average score over countries, for each sector and by each latent dimension*

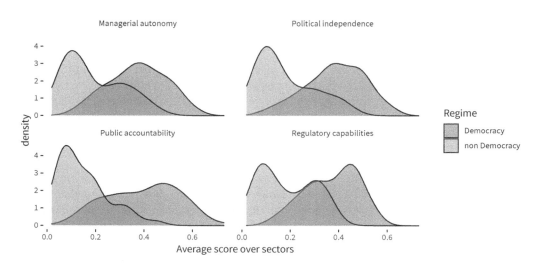

Figure 6.8   *Average score over countries for each latent dimension of agencies'
institutional characteristics, by regime type*

Beyond such type of analysis, we also can focus on existing similarities among counties as to the characteristics of the agencies they have created. However, how can countries be classified using their average scores? Recall that for every country we are able to identify four different institutional characteristics: namely regulatory capabilities, managerial autonomy, political independence and public accountability. Here we apply an unsupervised machine learning algorithm to classify countries according to their similarities. Countries are classified taking their agencies' score averaged over sectors, for each of the four dimensions. Distances between units are calculated using Euclidean measure, and clustering is performed using an agglomerative hierarchical algorithm (Everitt et al. 2011).

Similarities and Differences Across Countries and Sectors

Figure 6.9 shows the results using a dendrogram, that is, a diagram representing a tree of relationship between different objects of features. This dendrogram of countries is classified according to the similarities of the institutional form of their regulatory governance, considering these four institutional dimensions, to identify their *regulatory governance institutionalization* (RGI). The algorithm divides the set of 115 countries in three different main groups. The main distinction is between the top-left group (Haiti to Niger) that contains countries that we identify with a low RGI and the remaining two groups: the middle RGI (Russia to Brazil); and the high RGI (UK to Colombia). The low RGI countries include mostly non-democratic regimes and developing countries, but also relatively advanced economies like Israel, South Korea or Turkey. The group of middle RGI is a mixture of regimes and economic development (ranging between Uganda, China, or Japan and the Netherlands). Finally, the group of high RGI contains democracies that are mostly highly economically developed (and some Latin American countries).

Besides the identification of big groups of countries, Figure 6.9 also allows us to identify close associations in the extremes of the trees. For instance, the relatively short leaves shared between Haiti and Yemen (blue, low RGI) indicate that all these countries are very similar between them, and quite different from the adjacent closer group (that goes from Myanmar (Burma) to Congo - Kinshasa). Similarly, there are countries that are quite unique in their features, like Russia, Ethiopia or Brazil (all of them in the middle RGI, orange group). Therefore, the dendrograms allow us to identify cases based on their similarities/differences and on their uniqueness/commonness. This is indeed a useful tool for researchers when it is necessary to provide context to case studies, or when a selection of countries for case studies is needed, in the sense that similar/different countries can be easily recognized.

We can also classify the average sector scores and assess which ones are closer to others, and where are the biggest differences between them. Sectors are classified taking their agencies' score averaged over countries, for each of the four dimensions. Distances between units are calculated using Euclidean measure, and clustering is performed using an agglomerative hierarchical algorithm. Figure 6.10 shows the dendrogram with the classification (following the same procedure described above). In the cases of sectors, the algorithm divides the sectors into four groups, instead of three for countries. The results show that the closest sectors are Postal Services and Pharmaceuticals (because they have the shortest leaf size connecting any pair of sectors). Conversely, the sector that shows the most differentiated regulatory governance institutionalization is Telecommunications. Recall from the dendrogram before that such a tool is very useful to give contextual information to analysis of one or few sectors, as well

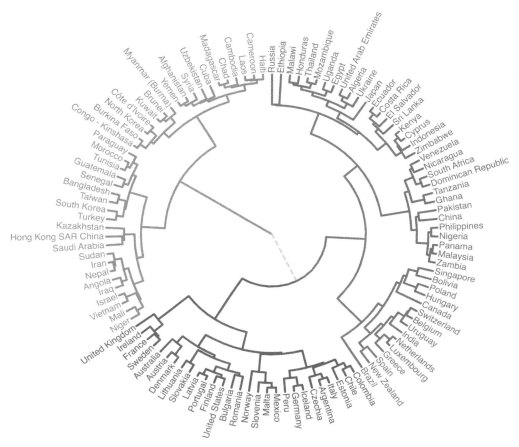

Source: Own elaboration, *RA-2010.*

*Figure 6.9   Dendogram with the classification of countries in three Regulatory
            Governance Institutionalization (RGI) groups*

as to provide help choosing similar/different sectors for case studies. In this sense, it is worth
noting that the classical choices for studying regulation and regulatory agencies all are very
much alike regarding their institutional design: agencification in Financial Services, Central
Banks and Telecommunications has produced similar institutional arrangements. Therefore,
studies that compare one of these sectors with another one are very narrow. In this sense,
to select sectors that offer more variability will very likely provide more returns in terms of
performing detailed comparisons.

FORESIGHTING AGENCY DIFFUSION

The regulatory agency model has reached stability and shows signs of being a consolidated
trait as a core public institution for the domestic governance of a quite large number of policy

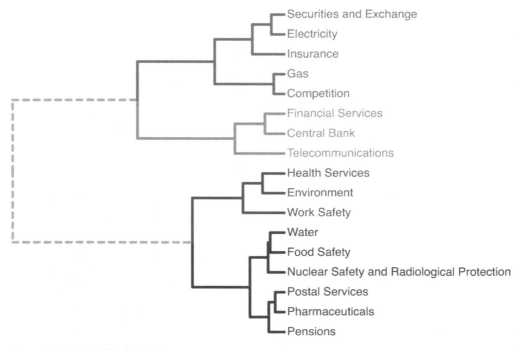

Source: Own elaboration, *RA-2010*.

Figure 6.10   Dendogram with the classification of sectors in four groups

sectors in the age of globalization. However, during the 2010s the creation of regulatory agencies almost stopped in most parts of the world, even in those sectors having a few agencies created, and only in the case of Africa some new creations were identified. In this sense, it was evident that in the 2010s the trends towards agency creation reached a plateau, after several decades of intense creation. To foresight future developments as to agency creation is not an easy task. We can observe that some regulatory agencies are still created in areas without tradition of agencification, such as infrastructures or transportation, or new topics of concern, such as data protection or quality assurance in higher education. So, regulatory agencification can still expand to more sectors and policy areas, if the social and political environment allows it – as for example if democratic backsliding does not make more progress worldwide.

Agency restructuration and agency termination may also be more frequent in the next few years than we have observed until now, during the strong diffusion period we have referred to before. While restructuring can involve a devolution of some regulatory powers to ministries, termination means a radical option to dismantle the agency. Some governments may decide that regulatory agencies have embedded some institutional preferences on particular policy goals that do not fit well with their purposes, and take advantage of critical conjunctions to terminate or restructure agencies. This can be highly dependent on many factors in each country, from veto players to bureaucrats, but also it is related to how agencies reached a relevant consolidation with the administrative state.

CONCLUDING REMARKS

Our mapping of the diffusion and the spread of regulatory agencies provides a broad longitudinal picture of the rise of the regulatory state. This, in turn, should be understood as part of
the ever-expansion of the administrative state. Think about the regulatory state as part of the
rise of the administrative state. And think about the rise of neoliberal policies and the decline
of the direct and ever-expanding welfare program (of the postwar period) not so much as the
decline of the state and the rise of markets but instead as the rise of regulation as a mode of
governance. The growth of taxing and spending by the state had indeed slowed considerably
since the 1970s and at least until the COVID-19 pandemic. Still the expansion went on and on
– using regulatory means – and this despite the rhetoric of deregulation and some significant
efforts to curtail regulation. The various agencies as studied here reflect different functions
and indeed morphs of the state: developmental, risk, welfare, security. Together they represent
the growing capacity of the state, some states more than others. Their internationalization
and the formation of regulatory networks across sectors and regions promise some degree of
global governance in their sectors. What remains an open question is the degree that these
agencies can form legal, legitimate, and effective centers of governance for regional and global
governance.

NOTES

1. For instance, we may consider that the value for some characteristics related to political independ-
    ence in Senegal is equal to the average of the values of agencies currently observed in Senegal.
    Although it is certainly a simple approach, it does not take into account the fact that some countries
    have agencies in sectors that are more likely to have agencies scoring higher/lower. So what if,
    for instance, Senegal has only one agency in a sector where political independence variables are
    generally granted very high? So not taking into account all the sectors is highly problematic.
2. This also has the advantage of being able to quantify the uncertainty inherent in moving from agen-
    cies (as institutions) towards countries. The problem is that it is computationally intensive and not
    obvious to implement, which makes it adequate only when inference-based outcomes and technical
    complexity are needed.

REFERENCES

Boix, C., Miller, M., & Rosato, S. (2013). A complete data set of political regimes, 1800–2007.
    Comparative Political Studies, 46(12), 1523–1554.
Braithwaite, J. (2008). *Regulatory Capitalism: How it works, ideas for making it work better.*
    Cheltenham, UK and Northampton, MA, USA: Edward Elgar Publishing.
DeCanio, S. (2015). *Democracy and the Origins of the American Regulatory State.* New Haven, CT:
    Yale University Press.
Everitt, B. S., Landau, S., Leese, M., & Stahl, D. (2011). Hierarchical clustering. *Cluster Analysis*, 5,
    71–110.
Fernández-i-Marín, X., & Jordana, J. (2015). The emergence of regulatory regionalism: transnational
    networks and the diffusion of regulatory agencies within regions. *Contemporary Politics*, 21(4),
    417–434.
Fernández-i-Marín, X., Jordana, J., & Bianculli, A. (2015). Varieties of accountability mechanisms in
    regulatory agencies. In Bianculli, A.C., Fernández-i-Marín, X., & Jordana, J. (eds) *Accountability and
    Regulatory Governance.* London: Palgrave Macmillan, pp. 23–50.

Fernández-i-Marín, X., Jordana, J., & Levi-Faur, D. (2021). Where does regulatory autonomy come from? The democratic origins of regulatory agencification. Paper presented to 8th Biennial Regulatory Conference, Exeter.

Gilardi, F., Jordana, J., & Levi-Faur, D. (2007). Regulation in the age of globalization: the diffusion of regulatory agencies across Europe and Latin America. In Godge, G. (ed.), *Privatization and Market Development: Global Movements in Public Policy Ideas*. Cheltenham, UK and Northampton, MA, USA: Edward Elgar Publishing, pp. 127–147.

Henisz, W. J., Zelner, B. A., & Guillén, M. F. (2005). The worldwide diffusion of market-oriented infrastructure reform, 1977–1999. *American Sociological Review*, 70(6), 871–897.

Jordana, J., Bianculli, A. and Fernández-i-Marín, X. (2015) When accountability meets regulation. In Bianculli, A.C., Fernández-i-Marín, X., & Jordana, J. (eds) *Accountability and Regulatory Governance*. London: Palgrave Macmillan, pp. 1–22.

Jordana, J., Fernández-i-Marín, X., & Bianculli, A. C. (2018). Agency proliferation and the globalization of the regulatory state: Introducing a data set on the institutional features of regulatory agencies. *Regulation & Governance*, 12(4), 524–540.

Jordana, J., & Levi-Faur, D. (2005). The diffusion of regulatory capitalism in Latin America: Sectoral and national channels in the making of a new order. *The Annals of the American Academy of Political and Social Science*, 598(1), 102–124.

Jordana, J., & Levi-Faur, D. (2010). Exploring trends and variations in agency scope. *Competition and Regulation in Network Industries*, 11(4), 342–360.

Jordana, J., Levi-Faur, D., & Fernández-i-Marín, X. (2011). The global diffusion of regulatory agencies: channels of transfer and stages of diffusion. *Comparative Political Studies*, 44(10), 1343–1369.

Levi-Faur, D., & Jordana, J. (2005). The rise of regulatory capitalism: the global diffusion of a new order. *The Annals of the American Academy of Political and Social Science*, 598(1), 200–217.

Maggetti, Martino (2010). Legitimacy and accountability of independent regulatory agencies: a critical review. *Living Reviews in Democracy*, 2, 1–9.

Majone, Giandomenico (1999). The regulatory state and its legitimacy problems. *West European Politics*, 22, 1–24.

Shapiro, M. (1997). The problems of independent agencies in the United States and the European Union. *Journal of European Public Policy*, 4(2): 276–277.

Treier, S., & Jackman, S. (2008). Democracy as a latent variable. *American Journal of Political Science*, 52(1), 201–217.

Tucker, P. (2018). *Unelected Power: The quest for legitimacy in central banking and the regulatory state*. Princeton, NJ: Princeton University Press.

PART II

SECTORS AND TYPES

7. Central banks

Clément Fontan and Antoine de Cabanes

INTRODUCTION

Do central banks have a place in a handbook on regulatory agencies? While this question might sound provocative given the presence of our chapter in this volume, a quick look back at past academic debates reminds us that there is no easy answer. Before the early 1990s, the vast majority of central banks were deeply embedded within the state apparatus and could hardly be categorized as "agencies" (Singleton 2011). While this situation changed with the isolation of central banks from political pressures and the rise of the "regulatory state", the academic literature on the topic often excluded central banks from their analysis (Majone 1994, Moran 2001). More precisely, Majone (2001, p.105) argued that agency theories were ill equipped to grasp the relationships between central banks and political authorities. In line with this argument, recent handbooks on regulatory agencies do not include chapters on central banks (Baldwin et al. 2010, Levi-Faur 2011).

This lack of consideration contrasts with the specialized literature on central banking, which underlined that the diffusion of the central bank independence (CBI) template since the early 1990s was one of the most spectacular recent examples of the delegation of core sovereign authority to independent agencies (McNamara 1998, Elgie 2002, Quaglia 2008). Rebutting Majone's argument, Pollack (2003) argued that even if central banks enjoy a higher degree of autonomy than other agencies, agency theories are still useful because the delegation of authority creates similar risks (policy drift, agency slack). In the same vein, Forder (2002, p.62) underlined that: "statutes do not free central banks of all concerns for their status; they do not leave them in a happy state, seeing no advantage in anything but the public interest. On the contrary, the existence of independence promotes the maintenance of independence as a policy goal."

This paradoxical place of central banks within agency theories echoes a core ambiguity in the role and place of central banks in modern political systems: they wield regulatory powers of a sovereign nature while operating at arm's length from political authorities. On the one hand, while the realm of competence of independent regulatory agencies is often limited to a specific sectoral policy, central banks have been historically tasked to maintain price and financial stability thanks to their monopoly over the issuance of the legal tender. When trying to reach these objectives, central bankers face complicated policy trade-offs that have deep distributional implications for all the economic players of their currency area (Forder 2005). From this perspective, central banks are similar to other macroeconomic sovereign entities, such as national treasuries. On the other hand, since the early 1990s, a vast majority of central banks have been insulated from political pressures and electoral logics and enjoy an unprecedented degree of autonomy (McNamara 2002). In turn, independent central bankers are confronted with challenges that are very similar to the ones faced by other independent regulatory agencies: their regulatory power is tied to their organizational reputation and their political legitimacy (McPhilemy and Moschella 2019).

In this chapter, we present how central banks can be analysed as independent regulatory agencies in light of this institutional ambiguity. Beyond the realm of economics and early agency debates, central banks have triggered an academic interest only recently and, at this stage, it would be imprudent to extrapolate distinct schools of thought from this literature. Moreover, central bankers are both judge and party as they influence academic debates on their own roles and operations. Against this background, we first present how different academic streams, including agency theories, have analysed the inception and developments pertaining to the CBI template. Then, we show how the reactions of central banks to the 2007–2009 Global Financial Crisis (GFC) induced new academic debates and research agendas.

APPROACHES: EXPLAINING AND ANALYSING THE INDEPENDENCE OF CENTRAL BANKS

The diffusion of the CBI template prompted questions that are familiar to scholars studying independent agencies. Why did elected officials delegate core sovereign powers to independent technocrats? How do governments ensure that central banks respect the terms of the delegation contract? Are central bankers captured by the industry they are supposed to regulate?

Why Independence? Public Choice, Temporal Inconsistency and Blame Avoidance

Modern central banks emerged at the end of the nineteenth century, when they were granted the monopoly to emit the legal tender in their currency area. This monopoly allows central banks to reach two objectives that remained constant through their history: price and financial stability (Singleton 2011). Throughout their history, central banks were tasked with additional goals, according to the evolution of the dominant economic paradigms and the balance of power between states and markets (Goodhart 2011). The scope of their missions usually determined their degree of autonomy: the smaller their set of goals, the higher their autonomy, and conversely. For example, in the aftermath of the Second World War, the Banque de France played a central role in the allocation of credit to specific sectors of the economy but it had to coordinate tightly with the State and multiple other economic agents (Monnet 2018).

Today, central banks from Western industrialized countries are organized along the principles set up by the Central Banking Independence (CBI) template, which swept the world in the early 1990s (McNamara 2002). This template promotes a "narrow" model of central banking, in which central bankers enjoy a high level of independence from elected authorities to attain the overarching objective of price stability. More precisely, adding other competences than price stability was perceived as suboptimal as it would create difficult policy trade-offs that could undermine central bank's anti-inflationary commitment (Issing et al. 2001). For example, when central banks supervise financial institutions, they could realize that tightening their monetary policy would endanger the financial position of a systematically important bank and they might refrain from doing so. This is why, in the late 1990s, both the European Central Bank (ECB) and the Bank of England (BoE) were deprived from supervisory competences. In sum, under the CBI template, the division of labour between central banks and other institutions was strict: the former should only care about price stability while the latter should take monetary policy as a given and fix their own regulatory policies accordingly. There was no, or little, coordination between monetary policy and other levers (Dietsch et al. 2018).

The success of the diffusion of the CBI template was caused by three factors: an ideational convergence between policymakers on new Keynesian macroeconomic theories, strategies of blame-avoidance and depoliticization as well as coercive pressures from international organizations.

First, the CBI template emerged from academic debates about inflation control in the 1970s and 1980s. Economists found out that monetary policy suffered from two potential sources of inflationary bias. The first source is related to the public choice argument: elected policymakers face different temptations to manipulate the money supply (for example, to boost the economic output on the eve of elections), which could spur inflation on the middle and long term (Friedman 1968). Central bankers should thus enjoy a certain degree of protection from such interferences (Buchanan and Wagner 1977). The second inflationary source stems from the policy trade-offs faced by central banks when they follow multiple objectives (such as pursuing growth and price stability). New Keynesian macroeconomists argued that multiple monetary objectives are "time-inconsistent" because they diminish the anti-inflationist credibility of central banks in the eyes of market operators (Kydland and Prescott 1977, Barro and Gordon 1983, Rogoff 1985). For these economists, the policy upshot related to this dilemma was to implement monetary rules (Kydland and Prescott) or appoint a central banker whose preferences are more inflation-averse than the government (Rogoff). Finally, these theories assumed that, under the CBI template, monetary policy did not generate significant distributive effects in the middle and long term (Issing et al. 2001). In this context, monetary policy was broadly perceived as a "purely technical matter where the goal is both narrow and consensual and the means to attain it benign" (Dietsch et al. 2018, p.13). Taking these macroeconomic theories at face value, the first generation of CBI scholars claimed that the delegation of monetary policy to independent central banks was mainly motivated by the anti-inflationary preferences of policymakers and voters (Alesina and Grilli 1991, Grilli et al. 1991, Alesina and Summers 1993).

Second, political economy scholars nuanced the importance of policymakers' beliefs in the time inconsistency argument to explain the spread of the CBI. They argued that the CBI template was never consensual since the functional link between CBI and low inflation was contested both empirically and theoretically, even in the early 1990s (Forder 2005, Klomp and de Haan 2010). Then, they point out that the delegation of monetary policy to central bankers was motivated by other strategic considerations: governments were looking to reap the political benefits of low inflation without taking the blame for the societal damages induced by this stabilization regime (Burnham 2001, Krippner 2011). In other words, by delegating monetary policy to independent central banks, governments pursued a depoliticization strategy in that they removed a contentious policy from the partisan realm and reduced the potential for choice, collective agency and deliberation (Hay 2007). Third, McNamara (2002) claimed that the spread of the CBI template was also fuelled by the coercive role of international organizations. Indeed, central bank independence was a compulsory requirement for countries receiving IMF financial assistance or participating in the European Union (EU) integration process.

In sum, the delegation of monetary policy to independent central banks was caused by multiple self-enforcing factors. From this perspective, the creation of the ECB in 1999 is ideal-typical (Dyson and Featherstone 1999, Verdun 1999, McNamara 1998, Howarth and Loedel 2005). First, there was a unanimous intellectual agreement between European central bankers on the fact that the ECB needed to follow the CBI template to solve inflation issues (Verdun 1999). Second, some elected officials, such as Italian or French representatives, saw the ECB creation as an opportunity to deflect the blame associated with anti-inflationary policies onto the EU level (Dyson and Featherstone 1996). Third, central bank independence at the national level was a legal obligation to be part of the Eurosystem in particular, and the EU, in general (Johnson 2016).

The Obvious Side of Independence: Central Banks and Political Authorities

The high degree of independence enjoyed by central bankers under the CBI template generates a tension over delegation: how can elected policymakers ensure that central banks' policies remain in line with their mandate?

According to the Principal Agent (PA) framework, agency slack occurs when the agent does not purposely fully attain the objectives set by the principal (shirking) or follows its own interests instead of the principal's preferences (slippage) (Delreux and Adriaensen 2017). The principal has tools to control these risks: the appointment of central bankers and the definition of the mandate form *ex ante* controls, while *ex post* controls include political scrutiny over monetary policy as well as the eventual dismissal of central bankers and veto over monetary policy decisions (Elgie 2002, Chang 2020).

However, as we hinted in the introduction, academics disagree on the usefulness of the Principal Agent framework for analysing the independence of central banks. Indeed, the logic of delegation to central banks differs from those of other agencies because it is related to a commitment problem of the principal (time inconsistency) rather than an efficiency problem linked to information asymmetries between the principal and the agent (Majone 2001). From that perspective, the relationship between central banks and governments reminds more of the role of a trustee than the hierarchical relationship between principal and agents in standard theories of delegation. Moreover, the role played by veto players in the delegation process differs between central banks and other regulatory agencies (Gilardi 2007). In the case of central banks, a high number of veto players are a precondition for credible delegation while it might reduce the efficiency of the delegation for other agencies.

These theoretical limitations have practical implications that undermine the use of PA frameworks for analysing central banks. For example, in his seminal article, Elgie (2002) recognized that the application of the PA framework to the ECB could lead to two opposite conclusions: that the ECB suffers from democratic deficit or not. This paradox is caused by divergent perspectives on how to interpret ECB objectives, which were left deliberately vague in the Maastricht Treaty. If this vagueness is interpreted as a commitment to ensure a high level of autonomy to the ECB, risks of agency shirking or slippage are highly unlikely since central bankers define their objectives by themselves. By contrast, if this vagueness is interpreted as a way to allow principals' preferences to evolve, agency shirking or slippage can occur, but the time inconsistency problem remains.

A second stream of literature started to analyse the relations between independent central banks and political institutions with the concept of accountability. Central bankers introduced this concept to justify the CBI model, as they presented accountability as "the reverse side of the coin of independence" (Issing 1999). This framing led to intense debates between central bankers about the optimal balance between the degrees of accountability and independence from political actors (Buiter 1999). In the same vein, the first generation of CBI scholars discussed how to measure the degree and different dimensions of central bank independence and accountability and applied these metrics on a global scale (de Haan and Eijffinger 2000).

In latter stages, the literature took a critical turn on the relationship between accountability and independence. First, Goodhart and Meade (2004) argued that the configuration of central banks' independence and accountability does not derive from functionalist implications of this dyadic relationship but, rather, depends on the more general political structures they are embedded in. For example, the institutional framework defining the interactions between the European Central Bank and other authorities is more similar to the European Court of Justice than to the Federal Reserve (Fed) or the Bank of England. Moreover, scholars underlined that accountability mechanisms are not suited to control the discretionary power of central banks (Dawson et al. 2019). For example, additional transparency and disclosure requirements increased central banks' procedural reporting but it did not affect the quality of political oversight (Curtin 2017). Similarly, when courts were asked to control the legality of monetary instruments, they only focused on the procedural dimensions of the cases and did not attempt to develop a substantial analysis on the legality of monetary policy decisions (Baroncelli 2016). In other words, the lack of substance of accountability channels weakens the logic of checks and balances between central banks and other authorities.

Finally, a last stream of literature focused on monetary politics, which analysed partisan preferences about monetary policy and how they impact the interactions between central bankers and political actors, notably through institutional channels (Woolley 1983, 1984, Scharpf 1991). This approach was mostly applied to the US in order to account for the impact of political dynamics and electoral competition on monetary policy, with a specific focus on the partisan patterns underpinning the appointment to the Fed's Board of Governors (Chang 2003). Indeed, the White House's selection of nominees depends on the partisan configuration of the Senate (in charge of confirming the nominees) and the alignment of preferences between the executive and the legislative (Chang 2001). Research also found out that when appointments occur at the end of the term, the profile of the nominee is more likely to be less inflation-focused (Waller 1992). Adolph (2013) systematized this research agenda with a seminal quantitative analysis of central bankers' trajectories from 20 developed countries from 1950 to 2005. He showed that partisan orientation of governments determines the selection of specific profiles of central bankers. Left-wing governments tend to favour economic growth to price stability in monetary policy trade-offs, while right-wing governments have opposite preferences. Hence, the former are more prone to appoint central bankers whose previous professional experiences indicate a relative tolerance of inflation for achieving full employment and growth, while the latter tend to select profiles whose careers signal a more conservative approach to inflation.

The Other Side of Independence: Central Banks and Financial Markets

To paraphrase Janet Yellen (quoted in Braun 2018), central banks "work through financial markets" to "help Main Street", and, thus, achieve their regulatory goals. Indeed, central banks do not control directly the level of prices in their economy. Rather, they expect to have a significant impact on the economic output through various channels of transmission, which are formed by financial institutions (Braun 2018). Under certain conditions, this ambivalent position allows a certain degree of leverage from market operators, which constrains central banks' regulatory powers (Dyson 2009). The financialization of Western economies since the 1970s amplified constraints for the conduct of monetary policy because the development of deeply interconnected, systemic financial institutions modified the environment in which central banks operate (Hardie and Howarth 2013, Gabor 2016).

Central banks have an ambiguous relationship with financialization (Dyson 2009). On the one hand, central banks supported financialization for two reasons. First, their initial expertise on financial markets became more valuable within decision-making circles as the political importance of financial logics grew (Fontan 2018). Second, central bankers believed that financialization would help them to better steer the economy at distance and reach their policy goals (Turner 2015, Dietsch et al. 2018, Walter and Wansleben 2019). For example, the Federal Reserve realized that buoyant markets were helpful to reach its dual mandate since rising asset prices were lifting growth prospects without upward pressure on consumer prices (Krippner 2011). On the other side of the Atlantic, the ECB supported financialization to compensate for the lack of fiscal tools, which was problematic for the smooth functioning of the Eurozone. In particular, central bankers hoped that deeper financial integration would trigger capital flows from the core to the periphery of the Eurozone and, in turn, would boost economic integration (Gabor and Ban 2016).

On the other hand, financialization increased the risks of capture and regulatory challenges for central banks. To start with, financialization generated new regulatory challenges as the central role played by financial institutions created new risks to financial stability and the conduct of monetary policy (Dyson 2009). Because financial institutions control the system of payments and provide credit to the real economy, modern economies became dependent on well-functioning financial markets to thrive. In turn, when financial institutions acquired a systemic role within this system, they became "too big to fail" (TBTF), that is, their collapse would undermine financial stability and, thus, economic activity as a whole. In face of this situation, central bankers faced a dilemma (Goodhart et al. 2014). On the one hand, preventing financial collapse increased the risks of "moral hazard", to the extent that financial institutions would not suffer the consequences of their past risky behaviour. On the other hand, not bailing out a TBTF institution generated side effects that are hardly manageable, as exemplified by the collapse of Lehman Brothers. Therefore, the rise of TBTF institutions collided with the financial stability objective of central banks and constrained their room of manoeuvre.

Moreover, financialization increased the "infrastructural entanglements" between central banks and financial operators, thereby limiting policy space for the former (Braun 2018, Braun et al. 2018, Gabor 2020). In fact, the financialization of banking systems made the transmission of credit in the economy more complex. In order to steer the economy at distance, through markets, central bankers had to take these changes into account in the implementation of their monetary decisions. For example, the rise and the spread of asset-backed securities within the financial sector forced the Federal Reserve to intervene on these market segments in order to avoid a financial meltdown in 2008–2009 (Jacobs and King 2016).

Central bankers also face the traditional regulator dilemma (Stigler 1971): they must have impartial attitudes towards the regulated industry but they need expert input from the latter to keep up with its latest developments. Financialization intensified this dilemma and increased the porosity of central bankers' careers trajectories with financial markets (Adolph 2013, Lebaron 2008, Lebaron and Dogan 2016, 2020). In turn, this porosity increased the risks of regulatory capture, which can occur in two different ways. *Ex ante* capture refers to the influence of previous professional experiences on central bankers' preferences when they are in office. For example, past careers in the banking and financial sector or in the IMF are correlated with stronger support for financial deregulation (Mishra and Reshef 2019). *Ex post* capture includes the "revolving doors" phenomena, which refers to the incentives that central bankers have to conceive and implement regulations in line with the interests of the financial industry, which might employ them after their term. Kalaitzake (2019) highlighted that, since the early 2000's, an increasing number of members of the ECB's Executive Board were recruited into senior positions in major financial firms after their term, while others joined private financial lobbies.

In sum, in the aftermath of the GFC, the academic literature started to analyse critically the relationship between central banks and markets. Scholars showed that the benign neglect of central banks towards buoyant financial markets was caused by both ideational and strategic factors: central bankers believed that financialization would make financial markets more resilient and help them to better steer the economy at distance. Yet, this support constrained their room of manoeuvre vis-à-vis market operations and it was ultimately conducive to the financial imbalances that morphed into a full financial and economic crisis from 2007 onwards.

FUTURE PERSPECTIVES: WHITHER POST-CRISIS CENTRAL BANKING?

The Global Financial Crisis (GFC) changed the role played by central banks in our economic systems in two different ways. First, because of the increased complexity and interconnectedness of global financial markets, central banks moved far beyond their traditional role of lender of last resort, which consisted in providing loans at a punitive rate to individual financial institutions suffering from liquidity troubles (Bagehot [1892] 2011). In fact, with the provision of ample liquidity at negative interest rates and large purchases of financial securities, central banks intervened directly to stabilize problematic market segments and, thus, acted as "market-makers" of last resort (Mehrling 2011). Second, central banks regained or expanded financial supervisory competences they were deprived from when they became independent (Ertürk and Gabor 2017, Howarth and Quaglia 2016). However, while this new monetary framework and the gain of prudential competences were successful in stabilizing financial markets, they also undermined central justifications for the CBI template, such as the optimality of narrow monetary objectives and economic neutrality (Dietsch et al. 2018, Högenauer and Howarth 2019). In this section, we introduce the research on the strategies implemented by central banks to manage this tension as well as the debates on the democratic challenges triggered by their new role.

Managing Reputation in Times of Financial Crisis

Before the GFC, the topic of central bank reputation was narrowed down to its anti-inflationary understanding in new Keynesian macroeconomics (see above). Since the GFC, the changing role of central banks and the rising salience of monetary issues in the public sphere have shifted scholars' attention towards a wider understanding of reputation that is similar to other studies on regulatory agencies (Carpenter 2010).

Central banks' reputation mainly relies of the fact that they are perceived by their audiences as expert institutions focused on their regulatory goals. Indeed, when central banks became independent, they started to follow a strategy of "scientization", which framed the policy challenges pertaining to monetary policy as technical questions to be resolved by experts

(Marcussen 2009). By doing so, central bankers attempted to "apoliticise" monetary policy, in order to circumvent outsider criticism and increase their autonomy. For example, the ECB invested intensively into the build-up of its scientific prestige in order to build itself an autonomous policy space, beyond the logics of intergovernmentalism that shape Eurozone politics (Mudge and Vauchez 2016, 2018). In a similar vein, after the collapse of the USSR, central bankers from Central and East Europe were trained in Western economic departments in order to obtain the social recognition attached to central bankers' scientific prestige and strengthen their independence at home (Johnson 2016). Finally, the Federal Reserve invested heavily into the production of an academic form of knowledge in order to build its scientific reputation, a pattern that other central banks adopted increasingly. In turn, today, central banks dominate the monetary and financial academic fields: more than half of the articles published in the top financial and monetary journals today include at least one central banker, whereas the mark was at 20% in the 1970s (Claveau and Dion 2018). However, the GFC challenged these apolitical and scientized perceptions of central banking in three ways: the economic narratives and models used by central bankers failed to anticipate the crisis and the distributive implications of post-crisis monetary instruments are more pronounced. Furthermore, the gain of supervisory competences expose central banks to additional controversies. In turn, central bankers adopted strategies to contain these challenges and adapt their reputation.

First, in the early steps of the GFC, central bankers struggled to make sense of the crisis, in part because the economic models and stories underlying their decision-making process did not consider the possibility of severe financial imbalances (Fligstein et al. 2017). For example, the Federal Reserve policymakers relied on intuitions as well as simple economic stories to help them to make sense of the crisis (Abolafia 2020, Golub et al. 2015). Yet, a complete overhaul of these belief systems would have been detrimental to central bankers since these ideas form the intellectual bedrock of the CBI template. Hence, in order to protect this template, central bankers adapted the New Keynesian economic framework to this new economic environment (Levingston 2020). For example, they forged new alliances with academic economists to legitimize the macroprudential agenda without threatening the statute of independence and expertise associated with central bankers (Thiemann et al. 2020). In the Eurozone area, central bankers were also instrumental to frame the Eurozone crisis as caused by states' budgetary and fiscal profligacy rather than by the financial imbalances that were partly caused by their own policies in the previous decade (Fontan 2014, Ban and Patenaude 2019).

Second, central banks extended their set of competences well beyond their traditional narrow mandate as they acquired new financial supervision powers. In the aftermath of the GFC, governments decided to reform their supervisory systems, whose flaws were exposed by the crisis. Central bankers acted strategically and used this window of opportunity for gaining both micro and macro supervisory competences, albeit to a varying extent (McPhilemy 2016, Fontan 2016). For example, the Fed acquired new macroprudential powers in addition of their preexisting microprudential powers, but they only got one seat out of ten in the governing committee of the new body (the Financial Stability Oversight Council) (Goodhart 2015). By contrast, the ECB dominates the European Systemic Risk Board, the EU body in charge of macro-prudential supervision created in 2011, and the Single Supervisory Mechanism (SSM), the EU body in charge of microprudential supervision created in 2014 (Howarth and Quaglia 2016). These new competences also brought additional risks for central banks' reputation. Indeed, when both monetary and prudential competences are concentrated in a single institution, the regulated industry has more incentives to capture the regulator (Boyer and Ponce

2012). Moreover, supervisory failures could affect the regulatory reputation of the central bank. Finally, these new powers could create turf wars or make other institutions redundant. For example, with the creation of the SSM, the European Banking Authority faced an "existential search" for a "value added contribution" in the constellation of EU supervisory institutions (Ferran 2016).

Third, the implementation of unconventional monetary policy was also a risk for central banks since new monetary tools contradict many key tenets of the CBI paradigm. In particular, contrary to the assumption of economic neutrality associated with the CBI paradigm, large-scale asset purchases on secondary markets generate significant distributive consequences among economic players and households (Colciago et al. 2019). According to central bankers themselves, this constitutes a threat to central bank independence since the political implications of monetary policy become more salient and open the door to political backlash (Goodhart and Lastra 2018). Against this background, central bankers set-up their monetary instruments and their communication strategies accordingly to decrease the political, reputational and legal risks associated with this new role (McPhilemy and Moschella 2019). For example, Lombardi and Moschella (2016) argued that the evolution and the features of the ECB bond purchasing programmes were influenced by concerns about the protection of its independence from national governments. In the same vein, central bankers downplayed the novelty of their corporate asset purchase programmes by subsuming them under the pre-crisis justification of CBI. In fact, today, a vast array of central banks that purchase corporate securities, including the ECB, the BoE, the Fed and the Swiss National Bank, try to obfuscate the distributive consequences of their purchases by claiming that they are "market neutral" (van 't Klooster and Fontan 2020). Yet, this market neutrality strategy carries its own reputational risks because central banks end up replicating the different bias of corporate securities markets in their own portfolio (Naef 2020). For example, members of the European Parliament criticized the ECB because its purchase portfolio is skewed towards large multinational firms with a heavy carbon footprint (Matikainen et al. 2017, Dafermos et al. 2020).

Moreover, central bankers implemented rhetorical strategies to deflect the blame associated with their new role. For example, in their speeches, central bankers tended to minimize their responsibility associated with the distributive consequences of their asset purchases and claimed that such concerns lie outside their mandate and should be tackled by fiscal authorities (Fontan et al. 2016). More generally, the ECB responded to an increase in public contestation over its monetary policies by an expansion of its participation to policy debates on wider legitimacy and macroeconomic issues (Diessner and Lisi 2020, Moschella et al. 2020). Finally, in order to address the post crisis extension of their competences, central bankers added new layers to their paradigmatic discourse on the centrality of price stability and central bank independence (Johnson et al. 2019).

Weak Political Controls, Strong Central Banks?

The extension of central banks' competences and macroeconomic role since the GFC affected the relations between states and central banks in two ways. On the one hand, while their new role went well beyond the mandates initially assigned to them, central banks did not suffer from significant losses of independence (de Haan and Eijfinger 2016). This disequilibrium raised legitimacy issues and risks of political backlash. On the other hand, this new macroeconomic role of central banks questioned the separation of monetary and fiscal policy, which is a key component of the CBI template, and raised the issue of macroeconomic coordination.

In the wake of the GFC, the political controls over central banks' activities changed in a very limited way. In the US, the 2010 Dodd–Frank Act modified, among other provisions, the section 13(3) of the Federal Reserve Act, imposed transparency requirements and limits to the uses of the central bank's emergency lending programmes (Binder and Spindel 2017). In the Eurozone, elected officials developed non-binding accountability channels, on top of existing control mechanisms. For example, the president of the ECB started to visit national parliaments on a regular basis to explain and justify the central bank's crisis measures and new policies, particularly its asset purchases programmes (Tesche 2018). In addition, members of the European Parliament intensified their scrutiny of ECB measures by increasing the number of central bankers' hearings (Torres 2013). However, these hearings were mostly "ceremonial", that is, they were designed to satisfy audiences without revelling relevant information, and they did not affect ECB policies and its management of the Eurozone crisis (Collignon and Diessner 2016, Tesche 2018). The most significant changes in the political controls over central banks were related to the prudential competences obtained by the latter. For example, when the ECB gained supervisory powers, the European Parliament obtained binding powers over the appointment of members of the supervisory board (Fromage and Ibrido 2018). Similarly, the Dodd–Frank Act gave new supervisory powers to the Fed in order to better regulate systemic financial institutions, but the Fed has to share some of these powers with the Treasury and other agencies such as in the Financial Stability Oversight Council (see above and Conti-Brown 2016). Overall, the political controls over central banks' activities did not evolve in line with the extension of their competences and the economic impact of their policies.

These very limited changes are surprising from an historical point of view. Indeed, in the US, Congress' attitude towards the Fed is usually countercyclical: when a crisis occurs, parliamentarians are prone to scapegoat the Fed for deteriorating economic conditions and thus amend the Federal Reserve Act (Binder and Spindel 2016). Yet, in the GFC context, partisan polarization precluded significant amendments. On the one hand, Democrats wanted stronger financial regulation and greater limits on the Fed's emergency powers. On the other hand, Republicans' criticism focused on the inflationary risk of the Fed unconventional policies and asked for an audit of the Fed in order to increase transparency on the conduct of monetary policy. Against this background, Democrats managed to pass the Dodd–Frank Act, which was their main legislative attempt to reform the financial system, but the most ambitious reforms on the Fed did not make it into law because of the impossibility to reach a bipartisan consensus (Binder and Spindel 2017).

The Eurozone political fragmentation also precluded substantial institutional changes in the ECB framework. Indeed, even when they belong to the same European political party, members of the European Parliament have divergent views over monetary policy because their economic beliefs formed within different national spaces (Jabko 2009). In the European Council, member states have divergent preferences on monetary policy according to the configurations of their economic systems and dominant economic beliefs in their countries (Henning 2015). In turn, the combination of weak political controls over central banks and the distributive consequences of their policies led to extra-parliamentary contestations of post-GFC monetary policies (Macchiarelli et al. 2020). For example, German proponents of conservative monetary policies systematically challenged the legality of the ECB's purchases of sovereign debt in front of courts (de Boer and van't Klooster 2020, de Cabanes and Fontan 2019). However, these contestations had more impact on the German constitutional order than on the ECB monetary policy since the CJUE refrained to second-guess the ECB justifications for its unconventional monetary policy (van der Sluis 2019).

Finally, the post-crisis role of central banks raised new challenges for the macroeconomic coordination between monetary and fiscal authorities. The CBI template prevented a close cooperation between the central bank and the State. Rather, the optimal policy mix would consist in the adaptation of fiscal policy to the interest rates set by the central bank for achieving its price stability mandate (see above and Issing et al. 2001). This changed in the early stages of the crisis because the stabilisation of deep and interconnected financial systems required a close cooperation between central banks and governments (Mabbett and Schelkle 2019). Yet, in latter stages of the crisis, when governments started to implement fiscal tightening measures, central banks were the "only game in town" to counter deflationary tendencies (van Riet 2018). Despite an unprecedented expansion of monetary policy in the last decade, central banks still undershot their inflation targets and economic performances remained weak. Van Doorslaer and Vermeiren (2020) explain this paradox by the persistence of a "self-defeating macroeconomic policy mix" whereby central bank additional liquidity fail to trickle down from financial markets to the economy and fiscal policies remain too tight to significantly raise wages. Finally, Green and Lavery (2015) underline the inequalitarian consequences of this policy mix: both fiscal austerity and monetary expansion tend to favour the well-off households. In turn, these inequalitarian dynamics contribute to the weakness of the post-crisis economic recovery and exacerbate social tensions. The policy upshot of this debate is that actual forms of coordination between central banks and fiscal authorities are likely to be increasingly debated and contested, as long as weak economic growth persists.

CONCLUSION

Central banks appeared on the regulatory agencies' research agenda when the CBI template swept the world in the early 1990s. The first generation of CBI studies took the economic justifications for CBI at face value and argued that delegation of monetary competences was motivated by policymakers' concerns about inflation. This perspective was quickly challenged by political economy scholars who underlined the role played by institutional factors and blame avoidance strategies in the diffusion of the template. In parallel, central bankers introduced the concept of accountability as a suitable framework to analyse the relationships between central banks and political authorities.

The GCF challenged this first generation of studies on multiple fronts. First, scholars realized they had not paid enough attention to the other side of central bank independence, that is, the relationship with financial markets. A new research agenda successfully demonstrated how and why central banks played an instrumental role in the promotion of financialization, which was conducive to the GFC. Second, scholars found out that, since the GFC, central bankers engaged large efforts to protect and promote their apolitical reputation, in a bid to maintain their high level of independence despite their extended role. Third, persisting lacklustre growth gave birth to new macroeconomic debates that might lead to a reconfiguration of the interactions between central banks and fiscal authorities.

The evolution of the role of central banks since the COVID-19 pandemic strengthen the relevance of these new research agendas. As central banks are going further in unchartered waters to stabilize the economy in a context of weak fiscal capacities of the states, the challenges they have been facing since this new crisis also increased. For example, policymakers start to acknowledge that a better coordination between monetary and fiscal policies is warranted to meet these challenges as rising debt levels and low productivity gains associated to pandemic economics increasingly constrain their room of manoeuvre (Schnabel 2020). In parallel, under the pressure of civil society, central banks are starting to take into account global warming and other environmental challenges in their operations, which make them stray even further from the CBI template (Campiglio et al. 2018). In other words, more than ten years after the GFC, the COVID-19 pandemic has confirmed that central banks are pivotal institutions to stabilize financial systems and the main support for economic growth today. Yet it remains to be seen if and how political authorities redefine their interactions with these independent agencies. Buoyant research agendas are very likely to emerge on this topic in the near future.

REFERENCES

Abolafia, M. (2020). *Stewards of the Market: How the Federal Reserve made Sense of the Financial Crisis* (1st ed.). Harvard University Press.

Adolph, C. (2013). *Bankers, Bureaucrats, and Central Bank Politics: The Myth of Neutrality*. Cambridge University Press. http://public.eblib.com/choice/publicfullrecord.aspx?p=1099952

Alesina, A., & Grilli, V. (1991). *The European Central Bank: Reshaping Monetary Politics in Europe* (No. w3860; p. w3860). National Bureau of Economic Research. https://doi.org/10.3386/w3860

Alesina, A., & Summers, L. H. (1993). Central Bank Independence and Macroeconomic Performance: Some Comparative Evidence. *Journal of Money, Credit and Banking, 25*(2), 151–162.

Bagehot, W. ([1892] 2011). *Lombard Street: A Description of the Money Market*. Cambridge University Press. https://doi.org/10.1017/CBO9781139093620

Baldwin, R., Cave, M., & Lodge, M. (Eds.) (2010). *The Oxford Handbook of Regulation* (1st ed.). Oxford University Press. https://doi.org/10.1093/oxfordhb/9780199560219.001.0001

Ban, C., & Patenaude, B. (2019). The Professional Politics of the Austerity Debate: A Comparative Field Analysis of the European Central Bank and the International Monetary Fund. *Public Administration, 97*(3), 530–545. https://doi.org/10.1111/padm.12561

Baroncelli, S. (2016). The Gauweiler Judgment in View of the Case Law of the European Court of Justice on European Central Bank Independence: Between Substance and Form. *Maastricht Journal of European and Comparative Law, 23*(1), 79–98. https://doi.org/10.1177/1023263X1602300105

Barro, R. J., & Gordon, D. B. (1983). A Positive Theory of Monetary Policy in a Natural Rate Model. *Journal of Political Economy, 91*(4), 589–610.

Binder, S., & Spindel, M. (2016). Congress and the Federal Reserve: Independence and Accountability. In J. A. Jenkins, & E. M. Patashnik (Eds.), *Congress and Policy Making in the 21st Century* (pp.187–208). Cambridge University Press. https://doi.org/10.1017/CBO9781316411117.008

Binder, S., & Spindel, M. (2017). *The Myth of Independence: How Congress Governs the Federal Reserve*. Princeton University Press.

Boyer, P. C., & Ponce, J. (2012). Regulatory Capture and Banking Supervision Reform. *Journal of Financial Stability, 8*(3), 206–217. https://doi.org/10.1016/j.jfs.2011.07.002

Braun, B. (2018). Central Banking and the Infrastructural Power of Finance: The Case of ECB Support for Repo and Securitization Markets. *Socio-Economic Review*. https://doi.org/10.1093/ser/mwy008

Braun, B., Gabor, D., & Hübner, M. (2018). Governing through Financial Markets: Towards a Critical Political Economy of Capital Markets Union. *Competition & Change, 22*(2), 101–116. https://doi.org/10.1177/1024529418759476

Buchanan, J. M., & Wagner, R. E. (1977). *Democracy in Deficit: The Political Legacy of Lord Keynes*. Liberty Fund.

Buiter, W. H. (1999). Alice in Euroland. *Journal of Common Market Studies*, *37*(2), 181–209. https://doi.org/10.1111/1468-5965.00159

Burnham, P. (2001). New Labour and the Politics of Depoliticisation. *The British Journal of Politics and International Relations*, *3*(2), 127–149. https://doi.org/10.1111/1467-856X.00054

Campiglio, E., Dafermos, Y., Monnin, P., Ryan-Collins, J., Schotten, G., & Tanaka, M. (2018). Climate Change Challenges for Central Banks and Financial Regulators. *Nature Climate Change*, *8*(6), 462.

Carpenter, D. P. (2010). *Reputation and Power: Organizational Image and Pharmaceutical Regulation at the FDA*. Princeton University Press.

Chang, K. H. (2001). The President versus the Senate: Appointments in the American System of Separated Powers and the Federal Reserve. *Journal of Law, Economics, & Organization*, *17*(2), 319–355.

Chang, K. H. (2003). *Appointing Central Bankers: The Politics of Monetary Policy in the United States and the European Monetary Union*. Cambridge University Press.

Chang, M. (2020). "Sui generis" no More? The ECB's Second Decade. *Journal of European Integration*, *42*(3), 311–325. https://doi.org/10.1080/07036337.2020.1730349

Claveau, F., & Dion, J. (2018). Quantifying Central Banks' Scientization: Why and How to do a Quantified Organizational History of Economics. *Journal of Economic Methodology*, *25*(4), 349–366. https://doi.org/10.1080/1350178X.2018.1529216

Colciago, A., Samarina, A., & Haan, J. de. (2019). Central Bank Policies and Income and Wealth Inequality: A Survey. *Journal of Economic Surveys*, 1–33. https://doi.org/10.1111/joes.12314

Collignon, S., & Diessner, S. (2016). The ECB's Monetary Dialogue with the European Parliament: Efficiency and Accountability during the Euro Crisis?: The ECB's Monetary Dialogue with the EP. *Journal of Common Market Studies*, *54*(6), 1296–1312. https://doi.org/10.1111/jcms.12426

Conti-Brown, P. (2016). *The Power and Independence of the Federal Reserve* (Paperback edition). Princeton University Press.

Curtin, D. (2017). "Accountable Independence" of the European Central Bank: Seeing the Logics of Transparency. *European Law Journal*, *23*(1–2), 28–44. https://doi.org/10.1111/eulj.12211

Dafermos, Y., Gabor, D., Nikolaidi, M., Pawloff, A., & van Lerven, F. (2020, October 20). *Decarbonising is easy: Beyond market neutrality in the ECB's corporate QE* [Monographs and Working Papers]. New Economics Foundation. https://neweconomics.org/2020/10/decarbonising-is-easy

Dawson, M., Bobić, A., & Maricut-Akbik, A. (2019). Reconciling Independence and Accountability at the European Central Bank: The False Promise of Proceduralism. *European Law Journal*, *25*(1), 75–93. https://doi.org/10.1111/eulj.12305

de Boer, N., & van 't Klooster, J. (2020). The ECB, the Courts and the Issue of Democratic Legitimacy after Weiss. *Common Market Law Review*, *57*(6), 1689–1724.

de Cabanes, A., & Fontan, C. (2019). La Cour de Justice face à Gauweiler: La mise en récit de l'indépendance de la BCE. In A. Bailleux, E. Bernard, & S. Jacquot (Eds.), *Les récits judiciaires de l'Europe* (pp.169–191). Bruylant. https://dial.uclouvain.be/pr/boreal/object/boreal:222654

de Haan, J., & Eijffinger, S. C. W. (2000). The Democratic Accountability of the European Central Bank: A Comment on Two Fairy-tales. *Journal of Common Market Studies*, *38*(3), 393–407. https://doi.org/10.1111/1468-5965.00227

de Haan, J., & Eijffinger, S. C. W. (2016). The Politics of Central Bank Independence. *SSRN Electronic Journal*. https://doi.org/10.2139/ssrn.2887931

Delreux, T., & Adriaensen, J. (Eds.) (2017). *The Principal Agent Model and the European Union* (1st ed.). Springer International Publishing: Imprint: Palgrave Macmillan. https://doi.org/10.1007/978-3-319-55137-1

Diessner, S., & Lisi, G. (2020). Masters of the "Masters of the Universe"? Monetary, Fiscal and Financial Dominance in the Eurozone. *Socio-Economic Review*, *18*(2), 315–335.

Dietsch, P., Claveau, F., & Fontan, C. (2018). *Do Central Banks Serve The People?* Polity Press.

Dyson, K. H. F. (2009). The Age of the Euro: A Structural Break? Europeanization, Power and Convergence in Central Banking. In K. H. F. Dyson, & M. Marcussen (Eds.), *Central Banks in the Age of the Euro: Europeanization, Convergence and Power* (pp.1–52). Oxford University Press. http://orca.cf.ac.uk/27042/

Dyson, K. H. F., & Featherstone, K. (1996). Italy and EMU as a "Vincolo Esterno": Empowering the Technocrats, Transforming the State. *South European Society and Politics*, *1*(2), 272–299.

Dyson, K. H. F., & Featherstone, K. (1999). *The Road to Maastricht: Negotiating Economic and Monetary Union.* Oxford University Press.

Elgie, R. (2002). The Politics of the European Central Bank: Principal–Agent Theory and the Democratic Deficit. *Journal of European Public Policy, 9*(2), 186–200. https://doi.org/10.1080/13501760110120219

Ertürk, I., & Gabor, D. (Eds.) (2017). *The Routledge Companion to Banking Regulation and Reform.* Routledge.

Ferran, E. (2016). The Existential Search of the European Banking Authority. *European Business Organization Law Review, 17*(3), 285–317. https://doi.org/10.1007/s40804-016-0048-9

Fligstein, N., Stuart Brundage, J., & Schultz, M. (2017). Seeing Like the Fed: Culture, Cognition, and Framing in the Failure to Anticipate the Financial Crisis of 2008. *American Sociological Review, 82*(5), 879–909. https://doi.org/10.1177/0003122417728240

Fontan, C. (2014). L'art du grand écart: La Banque centrale européenne face aux dilemmes provoqués par la crise de la zone euro. *Gouvernement et action publique, 2*(2), 103. https://doi.org/10.3917/gap.142.0103

Fontan, C. (2016). The New Behemoth? The ECB and the Financial Supervision Reforms During the Eurozone Crisis. In I. Ertürk & D. Gabor (Eds.), *The Routledge Companion to Banking Regulation and Reform* (pp.175–191). Routledge.

Fontan, C. (2018). Frankfurt's Double Standard: The Politics of the European Central Bank during the Eurozone Crisis. *Cambridge Review of International Affairs,* 1–21. https://doi.org/10.1080/09557571.2018.1495692

Fontan, C., Claveau, F., & Dietsch, P. (2016). Central banking and inequalities: Taking off the blinders. *Politics, Philosophy & Economics, 15*(4), 319–357. https://doi.org/10.1177/1470594X16651056

Forder, J. (2002). Interests and "Independence": The European Central Bank and the Theory of Bureaucracy. *International Review of Applied Economics, 16*(1), 51–69. https://doi.org/10.1080/02692170110109335

Forder, J. (2005). Why is Central Bank Independence so Widely Approved? *Journal of Economic Issues, 39*(4), 843–865. https://doi.org/10.1080/00213624.2005.11506857

Friedman, M. (1968). The Role of Monetary Policy. *The American Economic Review, 58*(1), 1–17.

Fromage, D., & Ibrido, R. (2018). The "Banking Dialogue" as a Model to Improve Parliamentary Involvement in the Monetary Dialogue? *Journal of European Integration, 40*(3), 295–308. https://doi.org/10.1080/07036337.2018.1450406

Gabor, D. (2016). The (Impossible) Repo Trinity: The Political Economy of Repo Markets. *Review of International Political Economy, 23*(6), 967–1000.

Gabor, D. (2020). Critical Macro-finance: A Theoretical Lens. *Finance and Society, 6*(1), 45–55. https://doi.org/10.2218/finsoc.v6i1.4408

Gabor, D., & Ban, C. (2016). Banking on Bonds: The New Links Between States and Markets: Banking on bonds. *Journal of Common Market Studies, 54*(3), 617–635. https://doi.org/10.1111/jcms.12309

Gilardi, F. (2007). The Same, But Different: Central Banks, Regulatory Agencies, and the Politics of Delegation to Independent Authorities. *Comparative European Politics, 5*(3), 303–327. https://doi.org/10.1057/palgrave.cep.6110098

Golub, S., Kaya, A., & Reay, M. (2015). What Were They Thinking? The Federal Reserve in the Run-up to the 2008 Financial Crisis. *Review of International Political Economy, 22*(4), 657–692. https://doi.org/10.1080/09692290.2014.932829

Goodhart, C. (2011). The Changing Role of Central Banks. *Financial History Review, 18*(2), 135–154.

Goodhart, C., Gabor, D., Vestergaard, J., & Ertürk, I. (Eds.) (2014). *Central Banking at a Crossroads: Europe and Beyond.* Anthem Press.

Goodhart, C., & Lastra, R. (2018). Populism and Central Bank Independence. *Open Economies Review, 29*(1), 49–68. https://doi.org/10.1007/s11079-017-9447-y

Goodhart, C., & Meade, E. (2004). Central Banks and Supreme Courts. *Moneda y Crédito, 218*, 11–42.

Goodhart, L. M. (2015). Brave New World? Macro-prudential Policy and the New Political Economy of the Federal Reserve. *Review of International Political Economy, 22*(2), 280–310. https://doi.org/10.1080/09692290.2014.915578

Green, J., & Lavery, S. (2015). The Regressive Recovery: Distribution, Inequality and State Power in Britain's Post-Crisis Political Economy. *New Political Economy*, *20*(6), 894–923. https://doi.org/10.1080/13563467.2015.1041478

Grilli, V., Masciandaro, D., Tabellini, G., Malinvaud, E., & Pagano, M. (1991). Political and Monetary Institutions and Public Financial Policies in the Industrial Countries. *Economic Policy*, *6*(13), 341. https://doi.org/10.2307/1344630

Hardie, I., & Howarth, D. J. (Eds.) (2013). *Market-based Banking and The International Financial Crisis* (1st ed.). Oxford University Press.

Hay, C. (2007). *Why We Hate Politics*. Polity Press.

Henning, C. R. (2015). *The ECB as a Strategic Actor: Central Banking in a Politically Fragmented Monetary Union* (SSRN Scholarly Paper ID 2548333). Social Science Research Network. https://papers.ssrn.com/abstract=2548333

Högenauer, A.-L., & Howarth, D. (2019). The Democratic Deficit and European Central Bank Crisis Monetary Policies. *Maastricht Journal of European and Comparative Law*, *26*(1), 81–93. https://doi.org/10.1177/1023263X18824776

Howarth, D. J., & Loedel, P. H. (2005). *The European Central Bank: The New European Leviathan?* Palgrave Macmillan. http://site.ebrary.com/lib/alltitles/docDetail.action?docID=10263275

Howarth, D. J., & Quaglia, L. (2016). *The Political Economy of European Banking Union* (1st ed.). Oxford University Press.

Issing, O. (1999). The Eurosystem: Transparent and Accountable or "Willem in Euroland". *Journal of Common Market Studies*, *37*(3), 503–519. https://doi.org/10.1111/1468-5965.00175

Issing, O., Gaspar, V., Angeloni, I., & Tristani, O. (2001). *Monetary Policy in the Euro Area: Strategy and Decision-Making at the European Central Bank* (1st ed.). Cambridge University Press. https://doi.org/10.1017/CBO9780511492457

Jabko, N. (2009). Transparency and Accountability. In K. Dyson, & M. Marcussen (Eds.), *Central Banks in the Age of the Euro: Europeanization, Convergence and Power* (pp.391–406). Oxford University Press.

Jacobs, L. R., & King, D. S. (2016). *Fed Power: How Finance Wins*. Oxford University Press.

Johnson, J. (2016). *Priests of Prosperity: How Central Bankers Transformed the Postcommunist World*. http://www.vlebooks.com/vleweb/product/openreader?id=none&isbn=9781501703751

Johnson, J., Arel-Bundock, V., & Portniaguine, V. (2019). Adding Rooms onto A House We Love: Central Banking after the Global Financial Crisis. *Public Administration*, *97*(3), 546–560. https://doi.org/10.1111/padm.12567

Kalaitzake, M. (2019). Central Banking and Financial Political Power: An Investigation into the European Central Bank. *Competition & Change*, *23*(3), 221–244.

Klomp, J., & de Haan, J. (2010). Inflation and Central Bank Independence: A Meta-Regression Analysis. *Journal of Economic Surveys*, *24*(4), 593–621. https://doi.org/10.1111/j.1467-6419.2009.00597.x

Krippner, G. R. (2011). *Capitalizing on Crisis: The Political Origins of the Rise of Finance*. Harvard University Press.

Kydland, F. E., & Prescott, E. C. (1977). Rules Rather than Discretion: The Inconsistency of Optimal Plans. *Journal of Political Economy*, *85*(3), 473–491.

Lebaron, F. (2008). Central Bankers in the Contemporary Global Field of Power: A "Social Space" Approach. *The Sociological Review*, *56*(1_suppl), 121–144. https://doi.org/10.1111/j.1467-954X.2008.00765.x

Lebaron, F., & Dogan, A. (2016). Do Central Bankers' Biographies Matter? *Sociologica*, *2*, 0–0. https://doi.org/10.2383/85290

Lebaron, F., & Dogan, A. (2020). Central Bankers as a Sociological Object: Stakes, Problems and Possible Solutions. In F. Denord, M. Palme, & B. Réau (Eds.), *Researching Elites and Power: Theory, Methods, Analyses* (pp.95–111). Springer International Publishing. https://doi.org/10.1007/978-3-030-45175-2_8

Levi-Faur, D. (Ed.) (2011). *Handbook on the Politics of Regulation*. Cheltenham, UK and Northampton, MA, USA: Edward Elgar Publishing.

Levingston, O. (2020). Minsky's Moment? The Rise of Depoliticised Keynesianism and Ideational Change at the Federal Reserve after the Financial Crisis of 2007/08. *Review of International Political Economy*, 1–28. https://doi.org/10.1080/09692290.2020.1772848

Lombardi, D., & Moschella, M. (2016). The Government Bond Buying Programmes of the European Central Bank: An Analysis of their Policy Settings. *Journal of European Public Policy*, *23*(6), 851–870. https://doi.org/10.1080/13501763.2015.1069374

Mabbett, D., & Schelkle, W. (2019). Independent or Lonely? Central Banking in Crisis. *Review of International Political Economy*, 1–25. https://doi.org/10.1080/09692290.2018.1554539

Macchiarelli, C., Monti, M., Wiesner, C., & Diessner, S. (2020). *The European Central Bank between the Financial Crisis and Populisms*. Palgrave Macmillan. https://doi.org/10.1007/978-3-030-44348-1

Majone, G. (1994). The Rise of the Regulatory State in Europe. *West European Politics*, *17*(3), 77–101. https://doi.org/10.1080/01402389408425031

Majone, G. (2001). Two Logics of Delegation: Agency and Fiduciary Relations in EU Governance. *European Union Politics*, *2*(1), 103–122. https://doi.org/10.1177/1465116501002001005

Marcussen, M. (2009). Scientization of Central Banking: The Politics of A-Politicization. In K. Dyson, & M. Marcussen (Eds.), *Central Banks in the Age of the Euro: Europeanization, Convergence, and Power* (pp 373–390). Oxford University Press.

Matikainen, S., Campiglio, E., & Zenghelis, D. (2017). The Climate Impact of Quantitative Easing. https://doi.org/10.13140/RG.2.2.24108.05763

McNamara, K. (2002). Rational Fictions: Central Bank Independence and the Social Logic of Delegation. *West European Politics*, *25*(1), 47–76. https://doi.org/10.1080/713601585

McNamara, K. R. (1998). *The Currency of Ideas: Monetary Politics in the European Union*. Cornell University Press.

McPhilemy, S. (2016). Integrating Macro-prudential Policy: Central Banks as the "Third Force" in EU Financial Reform. *West European Politics*, *39*(3), 526–544. https://doi.org/10.1080/01402382.2016.1143243

McPhilemy, S., & Moschella, M. (2019). Central Banks under Stress Reputation, Accountability and Regulatory Coherence. *Public Administration*, *97*(3), 489–498. https://doi.org/10.1111/padm.12606

Mehrling, P. (2011). *The New Lombard Street: How the Fed became the Dealer of Last Resort*. Princeton University Press.

Mishra, P., & Reshef, A. (2019). How do Central Bank Governors Matter? Regulation and the Financial Sector. *Journal of Money, Credit and Banking*, *51*(2–3), 369–402. https://doi.org/10.1111/jmcb.12578

Monnet, E. (2018). *Controlling Credit: Central Banking and the Planned Economy in Postwar France, 1948–1973*. https://doi.org/10.1017/9781108227322

Moran, M. (2001). The Rise of the Regulatory State in Britain. *Parliamentary Affairs*, *54*(1), 19–34. https://doi.org/10.1093/pa/54.1.19

Moschella, M., Pinto, L., & Martocchia Diodati, N. (2020). Let's Speak More? How the ECB Responds to Public Contestation. *Journal of European Public Policy*, *27*(3), 400–418.

Mudge, S. L., & Vauchez, A. (2016). Fielding Supranationalism: The European Central Bank as a Field Effect. *The Sociological Review*, *64*(2_suppl), 146–169. https://doi.org/10.1111/2059-7932.12006

Mudge, S. L., & Vauchez, A. (2018). Too Embedded to Fail: The ECB and the Necessity of Calculating Europe. *Historical Social Research / Historische Sozialforschung*, *43* (Special Issue: Economists, Politics, and Society. New Insights from Mapping Economic Practices Using Field-Analysis)(3), 248–273. https://doi.org/10.12759/hsr.43.2018.3.248-273

Naef, A. (2020). The Investment Portfolio of the Swiss National Bank and its Carbon Footprint. *Applied Economics Letters*, 1–6. https://doi.org/10.1080/13504851.2020.1854436

Pollack, M. A. (2003). *The Engines of European Integration: Delegation, Agency, and Agenda Setting in the EU*. Oxford University Press.

Quaglia, L. (2008). *Central Banking Governance in the European Union: A Comparative Analysis*. Routledge.

Rogoff, K. (1985). The Optimal Degree of Commitment to an Intermediate Monetary Target. *The Quarterly Journal of Economics*, *100*(4), 1169. https://doi.org/10.2307/1885679

Scharpf, F. W. (1991). *Crisis and Choice in European Social Democracy* (R. Crowley, & F. Thompson, Trans.). Cornell University Press.

Schnabel, I. (2020). Pulling Together: Fiscal and Monetary Policies in a Low Interest Rate Environment. Speech at the Interparliamentary Conference on Stability, Economic Coordination and Governance in the European Union, Frankfurt am Main, 12 October 2020, https://www.ecb.europa.eu/press/key/date/2020/html/ecb.sp201012~167b6b14de.en.html

Singleton, J. (2011). *Central Banking in the Twentieth Century*. Cambridge University Press.

Stigler, G. J. (1971). The Theory of Economic Regulation. *The Bell Journal of Economics and Management Science*, 2(1), 3–21. https://doi.org/10.2307/3003160

Tesche, T. (2018). Instrumentalizing EMU's Democratic Deficit: The ECB's Unconventional Accountability Measures during the Eurozone Crisis. *Journal of European Integration*, 1–17. https://doi.org/10.1080/07036337.2018.1513498

Thiemann, M., Melches, C. R., & Ibrocevic, E. (2020). Measuring and Mitigating Systemic Risks: How the Forging of New Alliances Between Central Bank and Academic Economists Legitimize the Transnational Macroprudential Agenda. *Review of International Political Economy*, 1–26. https://doi.org/10.1080/09692290.2020.1779780

Torres, F. (2013). The EMU's Legitimacy and the ECB as a Strategic Political Player in the Crisis Context. *Journal of European Integration*, 35(3), 287–300. https://doi.org/10.1080/07036337.2013.774784

Turner, A. (2015). *Between Debt and the Devil: Money, Credit, and Fixing Global Finance*. Princeton University Press. https://press.princeton.edu/books/hardcover/9780691169644/between-debt-and-the-devil

van der Sluis, M. (2019). Similar, Therefore Different: Judicial Review of Another Unconventional Monetary Policy in Weiss (C-493/17). *Legal Issues of Economic Integration*, 46(3), 263–284.

Van Doorslaer, H., & Vermeiren, M. (2020). Pushing on a String: Monetary Policy, Growth Models and the Persistence of Low Inflation in Advanced Capitalism. *New Political Economy*, 1–20. https://doi.org/10.1080/13563467.2020.1858774

van Riet, A. (2018). The European Central Bank as the Only Game in Town: How Could Fiscal Policy Makers Play Along? *Credit and Capital Markets*, 51(1), 93–111.

van 't Klooster, J., & Fontan, C. (2020). The Myth of Market Neutrality: A Comparative Study of the European Central Bank's and the Swiss National Bank's Corporate Security Purchases. *New Political Economy*, 25(6), 865–879. https://doi.org/10.1080/13563467.2019.1657077

Verdun, A. (1999). The Role of the Delors Committee in the Creation of EMU: An Epistemic Community? *Journal of European Public Policy*, 6(2), 308–328. https://doi.org/10.1080/135017699343739

Waller, C. J. (1992). A Bargaining Model of Partisan Appointments to the Central Bank. *Journal of Monetary Economics*, 29(3), 411–428. https://doi.org/10.1016/0304-3932(92)90034-Y

Walter, T., & Wansleben, L. (2019). How Central Bankers Learned to Love Financialization: The Fed, the Bank, and the Enlisting of Unfettered Markets in the Conduct of Monetary Policy. *Socio-Economic Review*. https://doi.org/10.1093/ser/mwz011

Woolley, J. T. (1983). Political Factors in Monetary Policy. In D. R. Hodgman (Ed.), *The Political Economy of Monetary Policy: National and International Aspects*. Proceedings of a Conference Held at Perugia, Italy, July 1983 (pp.177–203). https://www.bostonfed.org/-/media/Documents/conference/26/conf26.pdf

Woolley, J. T. (1984). *Monetary Politics: The Federal Reserve and the Politics of Monetary Policy* (1st ed.). Cambridge University Press. https://doi.org/10.1017/CBO9780511571510

8. Competition authorities
Mattia Guidi

INTRODUCTION

Among the policies whose enforcement has been delegated to regulatory agencies in the last decades, competition (antitrust) policy is certainly prominent. Its origins date back to the Sherman Act, passed by the US Congress in 1890, which prohibited anti-competitive agreements and monopolies. Already in 1914, the US delegated antitrust enforcement to a public agency (the Federal Trade Commission) separated from the Congress and the Government. In Europe, competition policy arrived in the aftermath of the Second World War, first in the UK in 1948 (with the establishment of the Monopolies and Restrictive Practices Commission), then in West Germany in 1958 (where the Bundeskartellamt was established). In the same years, competition policy came to be one of the building blocks of the European Coal and Steel Community (1951; see Karagiannis 2013), and of the European Economic Community (1957), and its enforcement was delegated to the European Commission.

The three decades following the end of the Second World War – the era of "embedded liberalism" (Ruggie 1982) – were not characterized, even in the "liberal" world, by a strict adherence to the principles of competition policy. First the need to rebuild countries devastated by the war and to expand the welfare state, then the economic turmoil of the 1970s (caused by the collapse of the Bretton Woods system in 1971 and by the 1973 oil crisis) elicited government intervention and tolerance towards anti-competitive agreements, especially in Europe (Guidi 2016). It was only by the end of the 1970s that competition gained momentum as a principle guiding policy-makers across the globe. These years were indeed characterized by an acceleration in the establishment of competition legislation and competition authorities in many countries (Jordana, Levi-Faur, and Fernández i Marín 2011). This process culminated in a "golden age of competition" (Monti 2014, p.19), namely the years going from 1990 to the Great Crisis, in which competition policy expanded worldwide, being embraced by most countries in the Global South as well (Koop and Kessler 2020).

In this context, NCAs have proliferated, gained autonomy from national governments, and created supranational networks that strengthened their position and influence, such as the International Competition Network (ICN). At the same time, the Great Crisis and the COVID-19 crisis have created an environment that is potentially hostile to competition policy – at least to the way in which it was interpreted and enforced in the 1980–2008 period. This has inevitably led competition authorities to redefine their priorities. Also, cost-saving and efficiency considerations have led some countries to merge their competition authorities with sector regulators.

The standard handbooks on regulation and regulatory policies (Levi-Faur 2011; Baldwin, Cave, and Lodge 2010b) do not treat competition policy and competition authorities, under the assumption that regulation is something distinct from competition enforcement. However, the promotion of competition has been the fundamental force behind the rise of regulation, which was characterized by "markets [that] were liberalised, state-owned enterprises transferred into private ownership, and regulatory agencies [which] became prominent features of the policy landscape" (Baldwin, Cave, and Lodge 2010a, p.7). If competition policy could in theory exist without regulation and regulatory agencies, there is little chance that current economic regulation could exist without applying the principles of competition policy. Although a distinction between competition and regulation certainly exists theoretically, it hardly exists in practice, as competition authorities have been created together with other regulatory agencies worldwide (Jordana, Levi-Faur, and Fernández i Marín 2011).

This chapter will begin by defining competition policy and summarizing why specialized agencies in charge of enforcing it have been created. It will then proceed by analysing the most prominent feature of competition authorities: independence. To this end, it will review the most important contributions concerning two research questions: first, why are competition authorities made more or less independent? Second, does independence improve the way they perform their functions? The chapter will then explore how competition authorities have established supranational networks, and what are their consequences. Finally, it will recall how the Great Crisis and the COVID-19 crisis have put into question competition policy, pushing it to learn from past mistakes and adapt to a new political and economic environment.

COMPETITION POLICY AND THE ESTABLISHMENT OF COMPETITION AUTHORITIES

Although the *theoretical* definition of competition policy and its boundaries are debated (see Guidi 2016, pp.14–15, for an overview), there is a general *empirical* agreement on the basic tasks that all competition authorities are meant to perform. These consist in preventing the following conducts or situations:

- *horizontal agreements*, occurring between firms at the same level of the supply chain;
- *vertical agreements*, occurring between firms at different levels of the supply chain;
- dominant positions or monopoly positions;
- horizontal and vertical mergers;

insofar as they (to borrow the wording of the 1914 US Clayton Act) "substantially lessen competition." This qualification is important, because none of the conducts or situations listed above is forbidden *per se* under competition law: it is not illegal to have (explicit or tacit) agreements with other firms; it is not illegal to have a dominant position in a market; it is not illegal to consolidate a firm's position with mergers or acquisitions. A merger could allow a firm to benefit from economies of scale and therefore increase its efficiency. A dominant position in a market for a company could simply be the result of the quality and innovation of its products, and not of discriminatory or predatory practices.

In one of the most relevant competition policy jurisdictions in the world, the European Union, the policy also includes control on *state aid*. The European Commission is required to assess whether fiscal or regulatory policies adopted by EU member states constitute a discriminatory advantage for particular firms or groups of firms in their jurisdiction. The rationale for including state aid in EU competition policy was similar to that for anti-cartel and anti-monopoly policy: once trade restrictions are abolished between EU member states, subsidizing national companies (in the case of state aid) or allowing cartelization or dominant positions at domestic level would distort the functioning of the common market.

Given the nature of competition policy (very general rules that must be applied to many different concrete cases),[1] competition authorities constantly carry out a delicate exercise that involves a considerable amount of discretion – not only assessing what firms have done in the past (as is the case of cartels or abuses of dominant position), but also envisaging what could be the future consequences of certain operations (in the case of merger authorizations or dominant positions). While the methodologies to carry out these assessments have been to a great extent standardized across jurisdictions, important differences remain, especially between the US and EU approaches (see e.g. Accardo 2013). These differences are evident by looking at how the two systems have dealt with US tech giants, Microsoft in the early 2000s (Jennings 2006) and, more recently, Google and Apple. On top of that, the enforcement of competition policy is likely to reverberate on other crucial policy fields, like international trade (Damro 2006) and corporate taxation (see for instance the recent European Commission's investigations on Apple and Amazon).

Generally speaking, competition policy is a field in which the creation of an independent regulator is common. Jordana, Levi-Faur, and Fernández i Marín (2011) find that competition authorities are the second most common type of regulatory agency worldwide, after financial regulators. Having a national competition authority (NCA) is the norm in the most advanced economies (members of the Organisation for Economic Co-operation and Development, OECD, and EU member states). The influence of the US, the first country to establish a competition policy regime and a competition authority, is certainly a factor accounting for this diffusion – Japan, for example, established its competition authority during the American occupation, in 1949 (Thurston 1993). Moreover, the fact that the policy was one of the cornerstones of European integration made the establishment of a NCA a de facto prerequisite for countries that wanted to join the EU since the 1990s.

As shown by Koop and Kessler (2020), competition authorities have become very common also among countries of the Global South. The authors find that the establishment of a NCA is less common in authoritarian countries and in countries whose economy relies strongly on petroleum. Moreover, countries with larger economies and higher standards of living are more likely to have an earlier start of the operations once the NCA is established.

If we look at the institutional structure of competition authorities in different countries, we observe a considerable variation along three dimensions: the number of competition authorities, the number of functions attributed to them, their degree of independence from politics. Let us see them in more detail.

The Number of Competition Authorities

Most countries have a single authority that both carries out investigations on suspected violations of competition policy and issues sanctions. Some countries, however, have opted for a "dual model" in which one agency investigates (acting as a sort of public prosecutor) and another decides on cases (as a sort of jury). In Europe, Austria, Belgium, Luxembourg and Ireland have adopted the second model (Trillas and Xifré 2016).

The Number of Functions Attributed to Competition Authorities

Some authorities are responsible only for investigating (and usually sanctioning) violations of competition policy (as defined at the beginning of this section), while others have been assigned additional tasks, like consumer protection (many competition authorities in Europe, including the French, British and Italian ones have both competition and consumer protection among their tasks). A relevant number of authorities in Europe are also responsible for regulating specific sectors. For instance, the Spanish competition authority was merged in 2013 with the energy, telecom, postal, media, railway and air services regulators. In the same year, the Dutch competition authority was merged with the consumer and the post and telecommunications authorities (besides, energy regulation was already comprised in the tasks of the authority). European countries like Austria, Denmark, Czechia and others have followed a similar strategy. The rationale for unifying multiple regulators in one single authority is centralizing the collection of information, increasing efficiency and making regulatory capture less likely (Trillas and Xifré 2016), but whether merging regulators constitutes a successful strategy is still something open for debate.[2]

The Degree of Independence from Politics of the Competition Authority

As we have already mentioned, it is nowadays common that competition enforcement is carried out by an agency that enjoys some independence from politics. But not all authorities are equally independent from the government or from the parliament. The literature has shown how there can be a great variation among competition authorities with respect to their *degree* of independence from politics. Independence can be achieved through many different instruments, whose combination can yield agencies with very little independence and others with considerable autonomy. In the next section, we will see why independence is a crucial feature for NCAs, what explains the degree of independence enjoyed by different NCAs, and whether independence does or does not have an impact on the quality of regulation and on the competition agencies' performance.

INDEPENDENCE OF COMPETITION AUTHORITIES: CAUSES AND CONSEQUENCES

Explaining the Independence of Competition Authorities

Starting from the observation that independence[3] varies significantly among regulatory agencies, a considerable body of political science literature (Gilardi 2002, 2005, 2008; Elgie and McMenamin 2005; Guidi 2014; Guardiancich and Guidi 2016; Hanretty and Koop 2013; Wonka and Rittberger 2010) has focused on identifying the factors that can explain these differences. The main hypothesis that has been tested was drawn from earlier studies on the independence of central banks, which found that independence, detaching monetary policy from the influence of elected politicians, made the commitment to a certain inflation target *credible* (Cukierman, Webb, and Neyapti 1992). Whereas elected politicians may renege on their promises because of short-term electoral incentives, unelected bureaucrats would implement the policy consistently, following the mandate they received (Majone 1996). All democratic systems have in principle this *time inconsistency* problem, and regulatory independence appeared as the main tool to solve it. Another concept that has received attention is that of *political uncertainty*. It has been hypothesized that the need to reassure economic actors could be stronger for countries that experience frequent alternation of governments and higher polarization (see e.g. Franzese 2002).

The findings of this literature have shown that independence is higher in economic regulation (and especially in utilities regulation), where politicians need to attract investors with long-term commitments, and after sector liberalizations (Gilardi 2008; Elgie and McMenamin 2005). The impact of political uncertainty has also been confirmed (Gilardi 2008; Wonka and Rittberger 2010), as well as that of veto players, which act as moderators of the previous pressures.

As regards competition authorities, Gilardi (2008, 2005) has found that they enjoy, on average, more independence than agencies involved in the so-called "social regulation" (environment, food safety, health) but less independence than agencies regulating utilities. Gilardi's hypothesis is that the main goal of independence is to increase "the credibility of [the politicians'] regulatory commitments when investments are more likely to be discouraged by fears of adverse changes in the regulatory environment" (Gilardi 2005, p.151). Investors (international investors in particular) want stable regulatory frameworks. Governments might not credibly grant stability, but independent experts can. Simplifying, what Gilardi argues is that the more stability you want to grant, the more independence you will give to the regulator. This need for credibility is present in economic regulation in general, but more acutely so "in utilities regulation[,] since investments are relatively more irreversible and, therefore[, the negative effects of regulatory changes are more severe" (Gilardi 2005, p.152). For this reason, the author tests the impact of the type of regulator on independence separately for utilities regulators and for "other economic regulators," namely financial markets regulators and competition authorities. His results confirm that, even if utilities regulators are more independent on average than financial markets and competition authorities, the latter's independence is still affected by some "need for credibility." Using Gilardi's data, Guardiancich and Guidi (2016) also show that competition authorities are characterized by an intermediate degree of independence.

What independent competition authorities "grant" to investors and market actors in general is still debatable. That state-led firms will not abuse their market power? That domestic and foreign investors will be treated equally? That collusions between domestic actors will not be treated with indulgence? The contributions of Guidi (2014, 2016), focused specifically on the independence of competition authorities in EU member states, allow us to say something more about the reasons that lead politicians to delegate in this specific policy field.

According to the author, a key factor explaining why some countries give more independence to their NCA is the degree of *economic coordination* of a certain political system. The literature on "varieties of capitalism" (Hall and Soskice 2001; Hancké, Rhodes, and Thatcher 2007) finds that nations cluster into identifiable groups based on the extent to which firms and other economic actors rely on market (liberal market economies, LMEs), strategic (coordinated market economies, CMEs) or intermediate, often state-led modes of coordination to pursue their political economy goals.

Guidi (2016) finds that, since both LMEs and CMEs provide an economic environment that is more coherent and more efficient as regards its performance, politicians in these countries are less in need of reassuring economic actors (abroad and at home) by giving independence to their NCAs. Legislators in economies with intermediate levels of coordination, instead, face a higher cost for not sending a strong signal of commitment to preserving competition to the market. For this reason, they tend to give more independence to NCAs. In addition to this factor, the author also finds that political uncertainty and length of EU membership affect positively the independence of NCAs. These findings, obviously, cannot easily be generalized outside of the European context, but they offer valuable additional insights to the general findings of the literature on regulatory agencies seen above.[4]

CONSEQUENCES OF COMPETITION AUTHORITIES' INDEPENDENCE

A question that is inevitably related to the explanation of NCAs' institutional features is the impact of these features on competition enforcement. Even though we may all agree on the fact that policy-makers create a very independent competition authority because they need to credibly commit to enforce competition policy, this tells us nothing about whether this effect is actually achieved. Do institutional features make a difference in how the policy is enforced?

A relevant number of studies has tried to assess competition enforcement in general (see Ilzkovitz and Dierx 2015, for an overview). As is normal to expect, scholars have addressed a great variety of competition regimes' features, and focused both on the micro and macro impact of competition policy enforcement. Contributions investigating the micro-economic impact of competition policy seek to analyse how different regimes (with a particular focus on legal aspects of national competition law and rules of procedures of the authorities) influence enforcement. These studies analyse the impact of decisions taken by competition authorities (merger authorizations, breaking of cartels, etc.) on the behaviour of firms, on the prices charged on consumers, or on the market(s) affected (Werden and Froeb 1994; Clougherty and Duso 2009; Kwoka 2013; Aguzzoni et al. 2014; Carletti, Hartmann, and Ongena 2015).

Other scholars have focused instead on the macro-economic impact of competition policy, generally adopting a quantitative methodology. These studies aim at detecting whether particular aspects of competition enforcement are reflected in how a country's economy performs compared to others. The assumption of these contributions is that, if competition allows for the most efficient allocation of resources, better competition enforcement should result in better economic performance (see for example Kee and Hoekman 2007; Clougherty 2010; Petersen 2013). Ilzkovitz and Dierx (2015) identify three channels through which competition enforcement can improve a country's economic performance: a) by improving its allocating efficiency, favouring business dynamism; b) by improving the performance of management, giving managers better incentives; and c) by fostering economic innovation and thus long-term growth sustainability.

Very few of these studies have considered independence as an explanatory factor. This is partly due to the inherent difficulty in measuring independence (see Hanretty and Koop 2012), and partly to the fact that independence is usually *assumed* to have a positive impact (Koop and Hanretty 2018). In a study on the drivers of antitrust effectiveness, Borrell and Jiménez (2008) include independence among the possible explanatory factors, considering it as a binary variable, taking value 1 if an independent competition authority exists and 0 otherwise. Their results do not indicate a significant impact of independence on the effectiveness of antitrust enforcement. Voigt (2006, 2009) develops a series of indicators for formal and de facto (actual) independence in an analysis that aims to measure the effect of competition policy on total factor productivity. His evidence is mixed: both types of independence seem to affect factor productivity, but their impact is not consistently significant across all models.

Ma (2010) tests the effect of (among others) de jure and de facto independence on antitrust effectiveness (measured as perceived effectiveness from a survey of experts) using Voigt's index of formal independence for the former. He does not find any impact of formal independence, while de facto independence appears to matter. Buccirossi et al. (2011, 2012) develop an index of independence that takes into account six institutional features, focused on procedural independence in decision-making – ignoring for example appointment rules or accountability relationships with parliament and government (Buccirossi et al. 2011). They conclude that independence of the NCA, together with other institutional variables, has a positive impact on sectoral factor productivity growth.

More recent attempts to measure the impact of NCA independence on regulatory performance and regulatory quality have been carried out by Guidi (2015, 2016) and Koop and Hanretty (2018). Guidi estimates the impact of NCA formal independence[5] on foreign direct investment and consumer price index, finding no impact of formal independence on either. Koop and Hanretty (2018), instead, use the expert ratings published by the *Global Competition Review* as a proxy for regulatory quality, finding that more independent authorities tend to have a higher perceived regulatory quality, while authorities that are more accountable to politics tend to have a lower perceived quality of enforcement.

From this short review, we can conclude that there is not yet a method for measuring the independence or the performance of NCAs that is accepted by all scholars: independence is measured in many different ways, the items included vary considerably, features of democratic accountability are sometimes comprised and sometimes excluded by indices of independence. Similarly, impact, performance, quality of regulation can be measured with different approaches (decisions, impact of decisions, impact on macro-economic variables, expert surveys). In this context, although no study has found that NCA independence has *negative* consequences on enforcement (however measured), we do not have conclusive evidence that it is beneficial either.

REGIONAL AND GLOBAL COOPERATION AMONG COMPETITION AUTHORITIES

Like other institutions in other policy fields, competition authorities have intensified their participation and collaboration in supranational networks. Even though competition-related matters are also discussed in intergovernmental forums like the United Nations Conference on Trade and Development (UNCTAD) and the OECD, we will focus in this section on networks in which competition authorities participate without the involvement of national governments. The two most relevant examples of such networks are the European Competition Network (ECN) and the ICN.

The ECN has been created in the context of the 2003–2004 reform of EU competition policy. Regulation 1/2003 has marked a relevant change compared to the previous regime (established in 1962), which saw the Commission as the only enforcer when it came to violations of EU competition policy. With Regulation 1/2003, the NCAs of the member states have been empowered to enforce not only national, but also EU competition policy. At the same time, to guarantee the consistent enforcement of EU competition policy in all member states, the ECN was set up. The participants in the ECN are the Commission (represented in practice by staff from the Directorate-General for Competition) and the NCAs of the member states.

The ECN is defined by the Commission itself as "a forum for discussion and cooperation in the application and enforcement of [EU] competition policy," which "should ensure both an efficient division of work and an effective and consistent application of [EU] competition rules" (European Commission 2004). Its main tasks are debating the allocation of cases (in situations in which it is not self-evident which NCA should have competence), coordinating approaches and measures (in situations in which more than one NCA is dealing with the same case), and discussing strategies and sanctions. Although there is no formal hierarchy in the ECN (and neither are formal decisions taken), there is a general consensus on the fact that the DG COMP is the most influential member of the ECN. This is due both to the fact that the European Commission has been the first, and continues to be the most important competition enforcer in the EU, and to the fact that the Commission has the power to advocate a case from a national agency even when this has already started an investigation (Art. 11.6 of Regulation 1/2003). The circumstance that this power has never been used so far indicates that the Commission has always been able, through the ECN, to retain for itself some cases when it considered it appropriate, or to influence the strategy of NCAs when they were investigating.

Scholars generally agree that the 2003 reform and the creation of the ECN have made the Commission more powerful vis-à-vis the member states in competition enforcement (Wilks 2005; Blauberger and Rittberger 2015). Lehmkuhl (2008) argues that, behind the facade of an apparent decentralization, the Commission has become able to exert its influence directly on bureaucratic agencies of the member states, escaping any control of the Council. Sabel and Zeitlin (2008) note that, although the enforcement of EU competition policy resembles the features of multi-level experimentalist governance, its unified legal framework makes it a rather top-down example compared to other policy fields.[6]

Turning to the International Competition Network, we must begin by noting that, differently from networks like the ECN, created within an established legal framework, the ICN has been a real bottom-up project, created in 2001 by some influential competition authorities (with the decisive input of the US Federal Trade Commission and Department of Justice and of EU's DG Competition), without the direct involvement of national governments, and aimed at fostering cooperation (and supporting the activities of) competition authorities. Its main objective is to promote convergence across competition regimes worldwide (Hollman and Kovacic 2011). A key feature of the ICN is that, besides the involvement of NCAs, it encourages the participation of non-governmental advisors (NGAs) in its meetings. NGAs are competition lawyers, academics, representatives of multinational corporations (Townley, Guidi and Tavares forthcoming). The ICN's objective is achieved through an organization and a decision-making process that make it a quintessential example of "international soft law" (Newman and Posner 2018): all members have "the same rights and privileges" (International Competition Network 2012, p.2), decisions are taken without formal votes (so by consensus), and the ICN only issues recommendations (recommended practices and guidelines) that its members are free to implement or not.

However, beyond this apparently open and inclusive organization, the ICN functions, in practice, in a rather hierarchical way. For instance, the organization's Steering Group, which has substantive powers (International Competition Network 2012), has been rotationally composed by only 21 NCAs out of more than 120 members. This is facilitated by the fact that outgoing members select the incoming ones (Townley, Tavares, and Guidi 2019). Moreover, the most influential competition authorities (which include the US Federal Trade Commission, the European Commission, and some NCAs of OECD countries) are the only ones possessing the resources and the expertise to effectively shape the content of the ICN work products. This clearly divides ICN members between "rule-makers" and "rule-takers" (Townley, Guidi, and Tavares 2020): the standards and "best practices" that end up being recommended are those of the most influential jurisdictions. Even though more research is needed to assess to what extent ICN recommendations are adopted by NCAs, the fact that these recommendations might be adopted by autonomous agencies after having been drafted by an organization composed of autonomous agencies, with no democratic checks in the process, is an issue that requires attention. Does the ICN care only about the advancement of competition policy? Or do its members also pursue their own agendas? Also, can the advancement of competition policy (especially in developing or recently democratized countries) be considered as neutral or inherently beneficial?

COMPETITION POLICY AND COMPETITION AUTHORITIES IN THE CONTEXT OF THE GREAT CRISIS: WHAT WAYS FORWARD?

Like in many other policy domains, there is a pre- and a post-Great Crisis in competition policy. The Great Crisis has forced the epistemic community of competition scholars and enforcers to re-think the way competition policy had been theorized and applied in the previous decades. On the one hand, the financial crisis of 2008 (whose consequences have not yet been absorbed as of today), bringing many banks on the verge of bankruptcy, has forced competition enforcers to prioritize safeguarding the stability of the financial sector over classical competition concerns (Adler, Kavanagh, and Ugryumov 2010; Cejnar 2011). State aid to banks, and mergers and acquisitions, have become standard tools to prevent financial institutions from failing, and they have been assessed with considerable leniency, given the severity of the economic crisis.

In the EU, the Commission has shown a great deal of flexibility (Doleys 2012; Baudenbacher and Bremer 2010), and it is doing so even more decisively with the COVID-19 crisis. Its powers of intervention against state aid have probably been altered permanently (Sanchez-Graells 2016). In this context, it cannot go unnoticed how the Commission has attempted to re-interpret with some creativity its competences on state aid. In the practical impossibility to block interventions of financial support to private firms due to the economic crisis, the Commission has turned its attention to how some countries have granted undue fiscal privileges to big tech giants. The cases against Ireland[7] (for the tax benefits granted to Apple) and against Luxembourg[8] (for the treatment granted to Amazon) signal a more general change in the Commission's approach, as they challenge one of the cornerstones of European integration: competition between member states in corporate taxation (Genschel, Kemmerling, and Seils 2011). At the same time, the Commission has targeted several alleged abuses of dominant positions by Google and, more recently, Apple. The position towards the big tech giants has shown once again a clear divergence between the US and the EU approach: in their home countries, Google, Apple and Amazon have faced considerably less scrutiny. To what extent this reflects a different approach to antitrust or simply economic nationalism is a matter of debate.

Even in the US there is, however, an ongoing reflection on whether the "Chicago School" (Posner 1979) approach to antitrust policy (that has been prominent in the US since the 1970s), which advocated for a focus on consumer welfare and on protecting "competition rather than individual competitors,"[9] could be responsible for excessive tolerance towards big companies (Stucke 2012; Steinbaum and Stucke 2019; Horton 2015). The Chicago School approach has warned against the risk of sanctioning firms with large market shares: an apparently dominant position might just be the result of efficiency and of goods and services appreciated by consumers; antitrust enforcement should not punish innovation by sanctioning these firms in favour of less efficient and less innovative competitors. Critics of this approach argue instead that excessive consolidation of big companies is responsible for making markets less competitive in the long run and for increasing inequality (Steinbaum and Stucke 2019). Also, big companies can easily become too-big-to-fail companies when a crisis hits. Thus, an apparently "hands-off" approach can paradoxically lead to inevitable state intervention in case of crisis, making big private companies and the state reliant on each other's support.

CONCLUSIONS

This necessarily brief overview has served to highlight that competition policy keeps evolving. Although the rules that form its basis have remained fairly stable through time, their practical interpretation has adapted, taking stock of historical contingencies and of the academic debate. Moreover, competition authorities continue to differ in their approaches and practices.

The advent of an economic approach to competition policy advocated for by the Chicago School, begun in the 1970s, has coincided with the diffusion of economic policies like liberalization of financial markets and labour markets, sector liberalizations, privatizations. Competition has become a fundamental component of the "economic constitution" in liberal democracies. The parallel advent of the "regulatory state" (Majone 1999) has favoured the diffusion of independent competition authorities as the appropriate enforcer of this policy.

Today, both principles (competition and regulatory independence) are increasingly questioned. The intensification of economic and financial crises, culminated with the Great Crisis (and now further exacerbated by the COVID-19 crisis) has put into question the capacity of markets to self-regulate. The power acquired by big digital platforms (especially US ones) is likely to receive increasing attention, and redefine the boundaries between industrial policy and competition policy. States have had to intervene to save the markets from their own self-destructive tendencies. Increasing inequality, among firms and among citizens, calls for a stronger intervention of the state to correct injustices. The appeal to technical expertise as a way to make societies better off, which was popular in the 1980s and in the 1990s, is increasingly problematic.

In spite of this (or, better said, exactly because of this), competition policy and competition authorities remain a field with many potential avenues for future research. First, from an institutional point of view, many aspects relating to organization, structure, and independence deserve further scrutiny. Future studies might seek to explain under which conditions countries decide to set up a competition authority with particular characteristics or functions: why do some states separate different regulatory tasks among various regulators while others decide to merge existing agencies? Second, there is certainly a lot to explore as regards the relationship between institutional features and performance: are stand-alone competition authorities more efficient than competition authorities that also act as sector regulators? Do they adopt different priorities and strategies in their investigations and decisions? Third, more attention should be devoted to developments over time. Given the complexity of studying regulators, most studies avoid to take into account the time dimension, but it is of utmost importance to assess how changes in the political economy and in the economic strategies of governments and supranational actors affect the establishment, reforms and regulatory output of competition authorities.

These research questions relate more broadly to the issue of measuring the effectiveness, efficiency and quality of regulation. As we have seen, we are still far from a unified framework. But if we cannot properly and reliably assess the performance of regulators, how can we decide if they should do more or less, focus more on some issues or on others, be made more independent or more accountable to democratic bodies?

The principle of independence, which is more easily defensible when the mandate is straightforward (like in the case of central banking, at least before the Great Crisis), becomes problematic if an agency is expected to supervise many different activities, at many levels, with many degrees of discretion that can be employed at various stages (Vickers 2010). At the same time, bodies like the European Commission remain convinced that independence is crucial for proper competition enforcement (Alves, Capiau, and Sinclair 2015), and it is difficult to imagine that a policy requiring such a complex appreciation of economic trade-offs is not dealt with by specialized agencies. As Kovacic and Hyman (2012) show, many arrangements are possible with regard to the institutional design of competition authorities. While it is unlikely that policy-makers will focus their effort in reforming competition authorities in the near future, it is important that the debate concerning which competition policy is needed in the interest of society and how it ought to be enforced does not remain confined to experts.

NOTES

1. Let us consider, just as an example, that the formulation of the articles of the European treaties identifying violations of competition (current Articles 101, 102 and 107 of the Treaty on the Function of the European Union) has never changed since 1957, while competition enforcement has undergone profound changes since then (Cini and McGowan 2008).
2. Studies that compare the performance of different competition authorities based on this institutional feature are still missing, although there are some case studies – see e.g. Besselink and Yesilkagit (2020).
3. An important distinction to be made is between formal (or "institutional," or "legal" or "de jure") independence and actual (or "de facto") independence (Cukierman, Webb, and Neyapti 1992; Gilardi and Maggetti 2011; Maggetti 2012). The former indicates whatever is explicitly mentioned in laws and statutes that establish regulatory agencies, dictate their rules of procedure and confer specific tasks on them. The latter refers to how the rules are translated into practice in the agencies' day-to-day activity: frequency of "revolving doors" phenomena, partisanship of nominations, internal organization and so on (see Maggetti 2007, 2012; Hanretty and Koop 2013).
4. The interplay between varieties of capitalism and regulatory institutions has been further explored by some recent contributions (Fink 2019; Guidi, Guardiancich, and Levi-Faur 2020; Wassum and De Francesco 2020; Kudrna and Wasserfallen 2020; Mizrahi-Borohovich and Levi-Faur 2020).
5. The sample includes all EU member states as of 2009 from 1993 to 2009.
6. Brook (2019) argues, in contrast, that great divergences between NCAs and Commission, and between NCAs, persist in the application of EU competition policy.
7. See https://ec.europa.eu/commission/presscorner/detail/en/IP_16_2923.
8. See https://ec.europa.eu/commission/presscorner/detail/en/IP_17_3701.
9. See https://www.law.uchicago.edu/news/reassessing-chicago-school-antitrust-law.

REFERENCES

Accardo, Gabriele. 2013. "Vertical Antitrust Enforcement: Transatlantic Perspectives on Restrictions of Online Distribution Under EU and US Competition Laws." *European Competition Journal* 9 (2): 225–340. https://doi.org/10.5235/17441056.9.2.225.

Adler, Emily, James Kavanagh, and Alexander Ugryumov. 2010. "State Aid to Banks in the Financial Crisis: The Past and the Future." *Journal of European Competition Law & Practice* 1 (1): 66–71. https://doi.org/10.1093/jeclap/lpp006.

Aguzzoni, Luca, Elena Argentesi, Paolo Buccirossi, Lorenzo Ciari, Tomaso Duso, Massimo Tognoni, and Cristiana Vitale. 2014. "A Retrospective Merger Analysis in the U.K. Videogame Market." *Journal of Competition Law and Economics* 10 (4): 933–58. https://doi.org/10.1093/joclec/nhu011.

Alves, Sofia, Jeroen Capiau, and Ailsa Sinclair. 2015. "Principles for the Independence of Competition Authorities." *Competition Law International* 11: 13–27.

Baldwin, Robert, Martin Cave, and Martin Lodge. 2010a. "Introduction: Regulation in the Field and the Developing Agenda." In *The Oxford Handbook of Regulation*, edited by Robert Baldwin, Martin Cave, and Martin Lodge, 3–16. Oxford, UK: Oxford University Press.

Baldwin, Robert, Martin Cave, and Martin Lodge, eds. 2010b. *The Oxford Handbook of Regulation*. Oxford, UK: Oxford University Press.

Baudenbacher, Carl, and Frank Bremer. 2010. "European State Aid and Merger Control in the Financial Crisis: From Negative to Positive Integration." *Journal of European Competition Law & Practice* 1 (4): 267–85. https://doi.org/10.1093/jeclap/lpq028.

Besselink, Tobias, and Kutsal Yesilkagit. 2020. "Market Regulation Between Economic and Ecological Values: Regulatory Authorities and Dilemmas of Responsiveness." *Public Policy and Administration*, July, 095207671982763. https://doi.org/10.1177/0952076719827630.

Blauberger, Michael, and Berthold Rittberger. 2015. "Conceptualizing and Theorizing EU Regulatory Networks: Conceptualizing and Theorizing ERNs." *Regulation & Governance* 9 (4): 367–76. https://doi.org/10.1111/rego.12064.

Borrell, Joan-Ramon, and Juan Luis Jiménez. 2008. "The Drivers of Antitrust Effectiveness." *Hacienda Pública Española/Revista de Economía Pública* 185 (2): 69–88.

Brook, Or. 2019. "Struggling with Article 101(3) TFEU: Diverging Approaches of the Commission, EU Courts, and Five Competition Authorities." *Common Market Law Review* 56 (1): 121–56.

Buccirossi, Paolo, Lorenzo Ciari, Tomaso Duso, Giancarlo Spagnolo, and Cristiana Vitale. 2011. "Measuring the Deterrence Properties of Competition Policy: The Competition Policy Indexes." *Journal of Competition Law and Economics* 7 (1): 165–204. https://doi.org/10.1093/joclec/nhq021.

Buccirossi, Paolo, Lorenzo Ciari, Tomaso Duso, Giancarlo Spagnolo, and Cristiana Vitale. 2012. "Competition Policy and Productivity Growth: An Empirical Assessment." *Review of Economics and Statistics* 95 (4): 1324–36. https://doi.org/10.1162/REST_a_00304.

Carletti, Elena, Philipp Hartmann, and Steven Ongena. 2015. "The Economic Impact of Merger Control Legislation." *International Review of Law and Economics* 42 (June): 88–104. https://doi.org/10.1016/j.irle.2015.01.004.

Cejnar, Leela. 2011. "After the Global Financial Crisis: Key Competition Law Developments in Australia, the United States, the EU and the UK." *Law and Financial Markets Review* 5 (3): 201–12. https://doi.org/10.1080/17521440.2011.11428181.

Cini, Michelle, and Lee McGowan. 2008. *Competition Policy in the European Union* (2nd ed.). European Union Series. New York: Palgrave Macmillan.

Clougherty, Joseph A. 2010. "Competition Policy Trends and Economic Growth: Cross-National Empirical Evidence." *International Journal of the Economics of Business* 17 (1): 111–27. https://doi.org/10.1080/13571510903516995.

Clougherty, Joseph A., and Tomaso Duso. 2009. "The Impact of Horizontal Mergers on Rivals: Gains to Being Left Outside a Merger." *Journal of Management Studies* 46 (8): 1365–95. https://doi.org/10.1111/j.1467-6486.2009.00852.x.

Cukierman, Alex, Steven B. Webb, and Bilin Neyapti. 1992. "Measuring the Independence of Central Banks and Its Effect on Policy Outcomes." *The World Bank Economic Review* 6 (3): 353–98.

Damro, Chad. 2006. "The New Trade Politics and EU Competition Policy: Shopping for Convergence and Co-Operation." *Journal of European Public Policy* 13 (6): 867–86. https://doi.org/10.1080/13501760600838565.

Doleys, Thomas. 2012. "Managing State Aid in a Time of Crisis: Commission Crisis Communications and the Financial Sector Bailout." *Journal of European Integration* 34 (6): 549–65. https://doi.org/10.1080/07036337.2012.707360.

Elgie, Robert, and Iain McMenamin. 2005. "Credible Commitment, Political Uncertainty or Policy Complexity? Explaining Variations in the Independence of Non-Majoritarian Institutions in France." *British Journal of Political Science* 35 (3): 531–48.

European Commission. 2004. "Commission Notice on Cooperation Within the Network of Competition Authorities (Text with EEA Relevance)." *Official Journal C* 101, April, 43–53.

Fink, Simon. 2019. "Varieties of Capitalism and Privatization in a Globalized World: How Trade Integration Shapes the Relation Between Type of Capitalism and Privatization." *Comparative European Politics* 17 (3): 338–60. https://doi.org/10.1057/s41295-017-0096-8.

Franzese, Robert J. 2002. *Macroeconomic Policies of Developed Democracies*. Cambridge Studies in Comparative Politics. Cambridge, UK: Cambridge University Press.

Genschel, Philipp, Achim Kemmerling, and Eric Seils. 2011. "Accelerating Downhill: How the EU Shapes Corporate Tax Competition in the Single Market." *Journal of Common Market Studies* 49 (3): 585–606. https://doi.org/10.1111/j.1468-5965.2010.02136.x.

Gilardi, Fabrizio. 2002. "Policy Credibility and Delegation to Independent Regulatory Agencies: A Comparative Empirical Analysis." *Journal of European Public Policy* 9 (6): 873–93. https://doi.org/10.1080/1350176022000046409.

Gilardi, Fabrizio. 2005. "The Formal Independence of Regulators: A Comparison of 17 Countries and 7 Sectors." *Swiss Political Science Review* 11 (4): 139–67.

Gilardi, Fabrizio. 2008. *Delegation in the Regulatory State: Independent Regulatory Agencies in Western Europe*. Cheltenham, UK and Northampton, MA, USA: Edward Elgar Publishing.

Gilardi, Fabrizio, and Martino Maggetti. 2011. "The Independence of Regulatory Authorities." In *Handbook on the Politics of Regulation*, edited by David Levi-Faur, 201–14. Cheltenham, UK and Northampton, MA, USA: Edward Elgar Publishing.

Guardiancich, Igor, and Mattia Guidi. 2016. "Formal Independence of Regulatory Agencies and Varieties of Capitalism: A Case of Institutional Complementarity?" *Regulation & Governance* 10 (3): 211–29. https://doi.org/10.1111/rego.12080.

Guidi, Mattia. 2014. "Delegation and Varieties of Capitalism: Explaining the Independence of National Competition Agencies in the European Union." *Comparative European Politics* 12 (3): 343–65. https://doi.org/10.1057/cep.2013.6.

Guidi, Mattia. 2015. "The Impact of Independence on Regulatory Outcomes: The Case of EU Competition Policy." *Journal of Common Market Studies* 53 (6): 1195–1213. https://doi.org/10.1111/jcms.12280.

Guidi, Mattia. 2016. *Competition Policy Enforcement in EU Member States: What Is Independence for?* Basingstoke, UK: Palgrave Macmillan.

Guidi, Mattia, Igor Guardiancich, and David Levi-Faur. 2020. "Modes of Regulatory Governance: A Political Economy Perspective." *Governance* 33 (1): 5–19. https://doi.org/10.1111/gove.12479.

Hall, Peter A., and David Soskice, eds. 2001. *Varieties of Capitalism: The Institutional Foundations of Comparative Advantage*. Oxford; New York: Oxford University Press.

Hancké, Bob, Martin Rhodes, and Mark Thatcher, eds. 2007. *Beyond Varieties of Capitalism: Conflict, Contradiction, and Complementarities in the European Economy*. Oxford; New York: Oxford University Press.

Hanretty, Chris, and Christel Koop. 2012. "Measuring the Formal Independence of Regulatory Agencies." *Journal of European Public Policy* 19 (2): 198–216. https://doi.org/10.1080/13501763.2011.607357.

Hanretty, Chris, and Christel Koop. 2013. "Shall the Law Set Them Free? The Formal and Actual Independence of Regulatory Agencies." *Regulation & Governance* 7 (2): 195–214. https://doi.org/10.1111/j.1748-5991.2012.01156.x.

Hollman, Hugh M., and William E. Kovacic. 2011. "The International Competition Network: its past, present and future role." In *The International Competition Network at Ten: Origins, Accomplishments and Aspirations*, edited by Paul Lugard, 51–92. Cambridge, UK and Portland, OR: Intersentia.

Horton, Thomas J. 2015. "Efficiencies and Antitrust Reconsidered: An Evolutionary Perspective." *The Antitrust Bulletin* 60 (2): 168–87. https://doi.org/10.1177/0003603X15584941.

Ilzkovitz, Fabienne, and Adriaan Dierx. 2015. "Ex-Post Economic Evaluation of Competition Policy Enforcement: A Review of the Literature." European Commission, Directorate-General for Competition, June. https://doi.org/10.2763/83196.

International Competition Network. 2012. International Competition Network Operational Framework.

Jennings, John P. 2006. "Comparing the US and EU Microsoft Antitrust Prosecutions: How Level Is the Playing Field?" *Erasmus Law and Economics Review* 2 (1): 71–85.

Jordana, Jacint, David Levi-Faur, and Xavier Fernández i Marín. 2011. "The Global Diffusion of Regulatory Agencies: Channels of Transfer and Stages of Diffusion." *Comparative Political Studies* 44 (10): 1343–69. https://doi.org/10.1177/0010414011407466.

Karagiannis, Yannis. 2013. "The Origins of European Competition Policy: Redistributive Versus Ideational Explanations." *Journal of European Public Policy* 20 (5): 777–94. https://doi.org/10.1080/13501763.2012.736726.

Kee, Hiau Looi, and Bernard Hoekman. 2007. "Imports, Entry and Competition Law as Market Disciplines." *European Economic Review* 51 (4): 831–58. https://doi.org/10.1016/j.euroecorev.2006.06.006.

Koop, Christel, and Chris Hanretty. 2018. "Political Independence, Accountability, and the Quality of Regulatory Decision-Making." *Comparative Political Studies* 51 (1): 38–75.

Koop, Christel, and Philip Kessler. 2020. "Keeping Control of Regulation? Domestic Constraints on the Creation of Independent Authorities in Emerging and Developing Economies." *Governance*. https://doi.org/10.1111/gove.12523.

Kovacic, William E., and David A. Hyman. 2012. "Competition Agency Design: What's on the Menu?" *European Competition Journal* 8 (3): 527–38. https://doi.org/10.5235/ECJ.8.3.527.

Kudrna, Zdenek, and Fabio Wasserfallen. 2020. "Conflict Among Member States and the Influence of the Commission in EMU Politics." *Journal of European Public Policy*, May, 1–12. https://doi.org/10.1080/13501763.2020.1751681.

Kwoka, John E. 2013. "Does Merger Control Work? A Retrospective on US Enforcement Actions and Merger Outcomes." *Antitrust Law Journal* 78 (3): 619–50.

Lehmkuhl, Dirk. 2008. "On Government, Governance and Judicial Review: The Case of European Competition Policy." *Journal of Public Policy* 28 (1): 139–59. https://doi.org/10.1017/S0143814X08000810.

Levi-Faur, David, ed. 2011. *Handbook on the Politics of Regulation*. Cheltenham, UK and Northampton, MA, USA: Edward Elgar Publishing.

Ma, Tay-Cheng. 2010. "Competition Authority Independence, Antitrust Effectiveness, and Institutions." *International Review of Law and Economics* 30 (3): 226–35. https://doi.org/10.1016/j.irle.2010.04.001.

Maggetti, Martino. 2007. "De Facto Independence After Delegation: A Fuzzy-Set Analysis." *Regulation & Governance* 1 (4): 271–94.

Maggetti, Martino. 2012. *Regulation in Practice: The de Facto Independence of Regulatory Agencies*. Colchester, UK: ECPR press.

Majone, Giandomenico. 1996. "Temporal Consistency and Policy Credibility: Why Democracies Need Non-Majoritarian Institutions." EUI Working Papers RSCAS 1996/57.

Majone, Giandomenico. 1999. "The Regulatory State and Its Legitimacy Problems." *West European Politics* 22 (1): 1–24. https://doi.org/10.1080/01402389908425284.

Mizrahi-Borohovich, Inbar, and David Levi-Faur. 2020. "Varieties of Consumer Credit Data Regimes: A Regulatory Governance Approach." *Governance* 33 (1): 109–34. https://doi.org/10.1111/gove.12473.

Monti, Giorgio. 2014. "Independence, Interdependence and Legitimacy: The EU Commission, National Competition Authorities, and the European Competition Network." SSRN Scholarly Paper ID 2379320. Rochester, NY: Social Science Research Network.

Newman, Abraham L., and Elliot Posner. 2018. *Voluntary Disruptions: International Soft Law, Finance, and Power. Transformations in Governance*. Oxford and New York: Oxford University Press.

Petersen, Niels. 2013. "Antitrust Law and the Promotion of Democracy and Economic Growth." *Journal of Competition Law and Economics* 9 (3): 593–636. https://doi.org/10.1093/joclec/nht003.

Posner, Richard A. 1979. "The Chicago School of Antitrust Analysis." *University of Pennsylvania Law Review* 127 (4): 925–48. https://doi.org/10.2307/3311787.

Ruggie, John Gerard. 1982. "International Regimes, Transactions, and Change: Embedded Liberalism in the Postwar Economic Order." *International Organization* 36 (2): 379–415. https://doi.org/10.1017/S0020818300018993.

Sabel, Charles F., and Jonathan Zeitlin. 2008. "Learning from Difference: The New Architecture of Experimentalist Governance in the EU." *European Law Journal* 14 (3): 271–327. https://doi.org/10.1111/j.1468-0386.2008.00415.x.

Sanchez-Graells, Albert. 2016. "Digging Itself Out of the Hole? A Critical Assessment of the European Commission's Attempt to Revitalize State Aid Enforcement After the Crisis." *Journal of Antitrust Enforcement* 4 (1): 157–87. https://doi.org/10.1093/jaenfo/jnv036.

Steinbaum, Marshall, and Maurice E. Stucke. 2019. "The Effective Competition Standard: A New Standard for Antitrust." *The University of Chicago Law Review* 86: 595–623.

Stucke, Maurice E. 2012. "Reconsidering Antitrust's Goals." *Boston College Law Review* 53: 551.

Thurston, Richard L. 1993. "Japan: The Antimonopoly Act and Japanese Fair Trade Commission Enforcement." *The International Lawyer* 27 (2): 533–40.

Townley, Christopher, Mattia Guidi, and Mariana Tavares. 2020. *The Law and Politics of Global Competition: Influence and Legitimacy in the International Competition Network*. Oxford, UK: Oxford University Press.

Townley, Christopher, Mariana Tavares, and Mattia Guidi. 2019. "Influence in the International Competition Network (ICN): Who Seeks It, How Do They Do This and Why?" SSRN Scholarly Paper ID 3415067. Rochester, NY: Social Science Research Network. https://doi.org/10.2139/ssrn.3415067**Error! Hyperlink reference not valid.**

Trillas, Francesc, and Ramon Xifré. 2016. "Institutional Reforms to Integrate Regulation and Competition Policy: Economic Analysis, International Perspectives, and the Case of the CNMC in Spain." *Utilities Policy* 40 (June): 75–87. https://doi.org/10.1016/j.jup.2016.04.009.

Vickers, John. 2010. "Central Banks and Competition Authorities: Institutional Comparisions and New Concerns." SSRN Scholarly Paper ID 1717809. Rochester, NY: Social Science Research Network. https://doi.org/10.2139/ssrn.1717809.

Voigt, Stefan. 2006. "The Economic Effects of Competition Policy: Cross-Country Evidence Using Four New Indicators." SSRN Scholarly Paper. Rochester, NY: Social Science Research Network.

Voigt, Stefan. 2009. "The Effects of Competition Policy on Development: Cross-Country Evidence Using Four New Indicators." *Journal of Development Studies* 45 (8): 1225–48. https://doi.org/10.1080/00220380902866862.

Wassum, Moritz, and Fabrizio De Francesco. 2020. "Explaining Regulatory Autonomy in EU Network Sectors: Varieties of Utility Regulation?" *Governance* 33 (1): 41–60. https://doi.org/10.1111/gove.12437.

Werden, Gregory J., and Luke M. Froeb. 1994. "The Effects of Mergers in Differentiated Products Industries: Logit Demand and Merger Policy." *Journal of Law, Economics, & Organization* 10 (2): 407–26.

Wilks, Stephen. 2005. "Agency Escape: Decentralization or Dominance of the European Commission in the Modernization of Competition Policy?" *Governance* 18 (3): 431–52. https://doi.org/10.1111/j.1468-0491.2005.00283.x.

Wonka, Arndt, and Berthold Rittberger. 2010. "Credibility, Complexity and Uncertainty: Explaining the Institutional Independence of 29 EU Agencies." *West European Politics* 33 (4): 730–52.

9. Data protection authorities under the EU General Data Protection Regulation – a new global benchmark

Philip Schütz

THE IMPORTANCE AND PECULIARITY OF DATA PROTECTION REGULATION AND ASSOCIATED SUPERVISORY AUTHORITIES

While most of the classical regulatory authorities analysed in this book operate in the realm of correcting market failures, supervisory authorities in the regulatory field of data protection, so-called data protection authorities (DPAs), are above all supposed to act as guardians of the fundamental right to data protection (data privacy) (cf. ECJ 2010: recital 23), monitoring not only corporations, but also the state itself in their insatiable hunger for more data, information, power and control.

As noted frequently, data has become the new oil of the twenty-first-century information and knowledge societies, spawning ever larger and mightier growing IT companies, so-called Big Tech (mostly referring to the US-American Big Five Apple, Microsoft, Amazon, Alphabet (Google) and Facebook). The market capitalisation of these monopolists is moving from one record to another, even accelerated by the COVID-19 pandemic, while at the same time entire state economies as well as certain economic sectors are in danger of collapsing.

In the meantime, the Snowden revelations of 2013 have impressively shown the increasing convergence of commercially collected data and state-run surveillance, whereas the *Cambridge Analytica* scandal exemplified the detrimental effect the unregulated access to massive collections of personal data by IT companies either willingly breaking or ignoring data protection laws can have on sensible points of democratically organised societies, such as their electoral processes. Both cases highlight the great significance of and the associated strategic interest in (personal) data.

Accordingly, the need for an effective regulation in that area is evident. With the General Data Protection Regulation (GDPR 2016) the European Union set a new global benchmark *inter alia* with regards to important legal requirements for an effective working supervisory authority. That is why the main focus of this contribution lies on DPAs in the EU (including – despite its withdrawal – the United Kingdom), however also taking data protection regulation in the United States of America, the most dominating data controlling nation worldwide, into account. This contribution furthermore pursues a comparative perspective on DPAs, drawing on key results of the author's doctoral research study, including theoretically developed variables trying to explain regulatory effectiveness of DPAs, such as their independence, resources, regulatory powers and practices (cf. Schütz forthcoming).

After a state-of-the-art analysis summarises the most significant research and literature on DPAs, theoretical and methodological challenges in doing research on DPAs are outlined and a brief history of the development of data protection legislation is presented in order to get a better understanding of the current national and international data protection regimes. The empirical part of this work then focuses on a comparative analysis of DPAs' independence, resources, regulatory powers and practices, eventually concluding with prospects on future data protection research.

STATE OF THE ART

The media coverage on surveillance, privacy and data protection violations these days is enormous. However, the huge popularity of the topic should not hide the fact that this is an often shallow and non-scientific debate lacking systematic empirical research and long-term studies in the field. Not surprisingly, legal scholars from a more theoretical perspective and computer scientists with a more application-oriented approach have been dominating debates and research on data protection so far.

On the contrary, social sciences, and in particular political science have long neglected the policy field of data protection. That is why classical social science methods, such as quantitative and qualitative analyses, as well as comparative approaches have only slowly made their way into research on data protection.

Only a few authors (particularly Flaherty 1989 and Bennett 1992) have early on conducted comparative policy research in the field of data protection, contributing over the years to a better understanding of the differences in and mechanisms behind data protection legislations.

While the contribution of Flaherty (1989) is extremely rich in detailed empirical research on data protection regimes in West Germany, Sweden, France, Canada and the US with practical recommendations for the improvement of privacy regulations in the end, the work of Bennett (1992) has a much more analytical character, trying to answer the question as to how and why different countries with divergent institutional settings and cultural traditions choose certain regulatory approaches to data protection.

With the emergence of the EU Data Protection Directive there seems to be a break in comparative research on data protection legislation, rather shifting to analyses at the international level (e.g. Mayer-Schönberger 1998; Bennett & Raab 2006, 2020) and investigating the creation of the Directive itself (e.g. Newman 2008), associated agreements (e.g. Busch 2013) or networks of DPAs (e.g. Raab 2011).

One of the rare comparative social science research projects in data protection (Busch 2010) devotes itself to the analysis of the different national regulatory answers towards potentially privacy-invasive technologies. The project found not only different modes of regulation, but also varying degrees of politicisation often caused by citizens trust or distrust of the state (ibid.: 20).

Important comparative works on DPAs in the following years involve particularly Righettini (2011), who focuses in her analysis on different regulatory activities and styles of the French and Italian data protection authority, Bignami (2011), dedicating her work to an empirical analysis of data protection regulatory styles in France, Britain, Germany and Italy, as well as Greenleaf (2012) and Schütz 2012b, both dealing with the issue of DPAs' independence from a comparative perspective.

In 2013, the PHAEDRA (and later PHAEDRA II) project chose a more practical-oriented research subject, dealing with possible solutions in the light of GDPR's new challenging cooperation and coordination mechanisms (cf. section on International cooperation and coordination mechanisms as well as networks of DPAs). During the project series, several pieces of research that comprise helpful empirical data on DPAs were published (see for example Barnard-Wills 2017, De Hert et al. 2015 and Wright & De Hert 2016).

Further comparative works on DPAs and their different regulatory handling include for example Vranaki (2016). With the advent of the GDPR, not only the European Data Protection Board (EDPB) (2020) saw the need for a thorough evaluation of the status and role of DPA in EU Member States, but there was also an increased scientific interest in DPAs and, for example, associated case law (Bieker 2017), their IT know how (Raab & Szekely 2017) and enforcement practices (Daigle & Khan 2020; Sivan-Sevilla forthcoming).

Moreover, there are a variety of legal commentaries on the GDPR, national data protection legislation and associated supervisory authorities written by local data protection experts in their respective language. These commentaries range from works merely reciting the existing law to oeuvres conducting veritable, in-depth interpretation and far-reaching analyses of data protection policies, including as in the case of one of the most influential German commentary by Simitis et al. (2019: 158ff.) – unfortunately only in German – highly elaborate historical and comparative analyses of data protection laws, DPAs and their regulatory practices.

THEORETICAL AND METHODOLOGICAL CHALLENGES

There have been, in particular, little theoretical frameworks and/or methodological approaches to the analysis of DPAs. Though theoretical foundations of and empirical findings on other independent regulatory authorities (IRAs) can help to serve as a framework for the analysis of DPAs (cf. Schütz 2012a, 2012b), existing research on IRAs very much focuses on the *de jure* and *de facto* configuration of independence (including the autonomy of IRA decision-makers, financial and organisational autonomy) (cf. e.g. Gilardi & Maggetti 2011) and associated good governance principles (*inter alia* accountability, transparency and integrity), largely ignoring further elements that determine regulatory effectiveness, for example overall institutional settings at the national and supranational level, regulatory powers as well as individual leadership skills, regulatory styles and traditions (cf. Schütz forthcoming).

Since – as we will learn later – data protection legislation and surrounding *de jure* features of DPAs are more and more converging (at least within the EU), analysing differences in the *de facto* regulatory handling of supervisory authorities should come to the fore. In that respect, there are above all two important works focusing on regulatory practices of DPAs.

Making use of Richardson et al.'s (1982) national policy style concept, the first is Righettini (2011: 145), who identifies two major archetypes of regulatory styles that shape different approaches to the regulation of data protection: "the *active* type, focused on a *command and sanction* approach and the *reactive* type, focused on a *soft and self-regulation* approach". These styles differ most of all in their degree of intrusiveness of the public independent authority. She identifies DPAs' resources, independence, certain overall institutional settings (such as the role of the state or the landscape of other IRAs), but above all institutional leadership as key explanatory variables for the differences in regulatory outcomes (ibid.: 162).

The second is Bignami (2011) who observed a convergence not only in European data protection laws, but also in DPAs' regulatory practices. Opposed to the US-American adversarial litigation style in regulating data protection, she has coined the term *cooperative legalism* for the regulatory style of European DPAs, describing a mix of deterrence-oriented approaches (e.g. the threat of inspections or sanctions) and self-regulatory mechanisms (such as appointments of data protection officers or the usage of privacy seals) (ibid.: 460). Above all, she sees systemic variables, such as "regulatory realities of the new digital marketplace, [...] the credible commitments logic [of policy-makers] and the diffusion process triggered by Europeanization" responsible for that development.

Both of these works are extremely valuable to the comparative analysis of DPAs, but will only be briefly touched upon in this work that otherwise concentrates on the empirical analysis of differences in independence, resources, regulatory powers and practices.

THE FOUR STAGES OF DEVELOPMENT IN DATA PROTECTION LEGISLATION IN EUROPE AND THE USA

According to Simitis et al. (2019: 179ff.) data protection legislation in the Western hemisphere – including the establishment of competent supervisory authorities – mainly followed four stages of development.

The first laws in the 1970s were directed towards restrictions of huge centralised data banks and storage facilities mostly operated by governments. The pioneering Hessian Data Protection Act (1970), the Swedish Data Act of 1973 as the first national data protection law worldwide, the US Privacy Act of 1974, the Data Protection Act of the German state Rhineland-Palatinate in the same year and the German Federal Data Protection Act (1977) can all be regarded as direct attempts to tackle the challenges arising from publicly run mainframe computers and national data banks (Mayer-Schönberger 1998: 221). As part of that development, by and large three distinct regulatory models emerged: on the one hand, the German Federal Data Protection Act focused on a more general, all-encompassing, yet also rather flexible legal framework with DPAs fulfilling a rather consultative and advisory function, whereas Sweden took the opposite direction, introducing a licensing approach that made the automated processing of personal data subject to prior authorisation by the competent supervisory authority (Simitis et al. 2019: 179f.). The United States, on the other hand, neither established a general data protection framework (the Privacy Act only applies to the Federal Government) nor an independent DPA (today as one of a few OECD countries left), but opted instead for a patchwork of different sector-specific regulations (ibid.: 180) that have been revealing large gaps in effectively regulating the processing of personal data (Bennett & Raab 2006: 131). Entrusted with the enforcement of the Fair Credit Reporting Act of 1970, the Federal Trade Commission (FTC) represents the central regulatory authority with regards to the processing of personal data by US companies, which are not at all subject to the afore-mentioned Privacy Act.

Next to the numerous national data protection provisions, also international regimes, such as the OECD Privacy Guidelines (1980), started to play an influential role in the proliferation of data protection legislation in Europe. Opposed to the non-binding OECD Guidelines, the Data Protection Convention 108 of the Council of Europe (CoE) in 1981 was the first international data protection agreement comprising legally binding rules for all signing Member States. However, it was not until 2001 that the CoE adopted an additional protocol (ETS No.181) to Convention 108, requiring Member States to set up an independent national supervisory authority that monitors compliance with data protection legislation.

For Simitis et al. (2019: 181), the Convention marks the advent of the second development stage of data protection legislation, heralding the internationalisation and beginning of data protection convergence in Europe. In that context, the authors (ibid.: 181) particularly refer to the UK as a textbook example of the major influence the Data Protection Convention had in resolving the gridlock situation that dominated the national data protection policy-making process for over a decade, resulting in the first UK Data Protection Act of 1984.

The third development stage is characterised by a period of revision, dominated by the question how to enable individuals to exercise control over their personal data in practice. In 1983, the landmark decision of the German Federal Constitutional Court (*Bundesverfassungsgericht* – BVerfG 1983) to overturn the national census law and establish the fundamental right to informational self-determination provided a legal answer to this question. In that so-called *census decision*, the BVerfG (1983: 49) emphasised the involvement of independent data protection authorities as of significant importance for the effective protection of the right to informational self-determination.

During that period of revision policy-makers also started to realise that none of the afore-mentioned different regulatory models, that is, licensing, flexible arrangements or sectoral approaches, worked as effective and efficient as originally envisaged (Simitis et al. 2019: 181f.). On the one hand, the licensing approach in Sweden and France resulted in excessively bureaucratic and hence highly burdensome registration procedures, hindering competent supervisory authorities to adequately fulfil their other, equally or even more important regulatory tasks (Flaherty 1989: 394). On the other hand, the rather vague and fuzzy data protection provisions in Germany let data controllers profit from the different and sometimes even contradictory interpretations of the law, while sectoral regulations in the US without any DPA whatsoever led to huge regulatory gaps and different standards in rules on how to handle the processing of personal data (Simitis et al. 2019: 182).

With the end of the Cold War the drafting of data protection legislation received a significant boost throughout the whole of Europe. Most ex-communist countries in Central and Eastern Europe, including the new federal states of Germany, not only quickly passed data protection acts, but also incorporated data protection as a fundamental right into their newly created constitutions. While that development highlights the great priority attributed to data protection as a fundamental right in the democratisation processes and emergence of constitutional states in Central and Eastern Europe, data protection in most of the Western European states had already begun throughout the 1980s to "cease to be merely a human rights issue; it was also intrinsically linked to the operation of international trade" (Bennett & Raab 2006: 93).

Due to the complicated patchwork of different data protection acts and standards in Europe the international transfer of personal data particularly among transnational corporations became increasingly difficult. National data protection rules had become above all a veritable trade barrier. The imminent risk of a serious obstacle in the completion of the internal market was in the following used as the main argument for the European Commission to start drafting the proposal for a Data Protection Directive in 1990 (cf. Gutwirth 2002: 91).

Regarding the emergence of a common EU data protection framework in 1995, Simitis et al. (2019: 183ff.) speak eventually of a fourth development stage characterised by a significant decrease of national regulatory competences (supranationalisation). Opposed to Convention 108, this time EU Member States did not have a choice in transposing the Directive into national law. That way, even EU nations which had not yet succeeded in passing their own data protection legislation were forced to draft their first data protection acts. In contrast, EU Member States that could look back at a long tradition of data protection, such as France and

Germany, particularly struggled – even under the threat of EU infringement procedures – to bring their data protection laws in line with the Directive (Simitis 2019 et al.: 183).

Part of that fourth development stage is the fact that data protection became a fundamental right in the *EU Charter of Fundamental Rights* (2010: Art. 8), which only came into force in 2009 when the Treaty of Lisbon was enacted. Additionally, DPAs were granted constitutional status in Article 8 (3) of the Charter, clarifying that compliance with data protection rules "shall be subject to control by an independent authority."

With the enactment of the GDPR in 2016 the period of supranationalisation preliminary finds its end (Simitis et al. 2019: 183), resulting in an even more assertive generation of data protection legislation that not only continues the process of decreasing national regulatory competence in data protection (relevant for all EU Member States and candidate countries, as well as transnational actors processing personal data of EU residents (cf. *Lex loci solutionis*)), but also significantly enhances the enforceability of already existing data protection principles by strengthening above all DPAs' intervention powers, such as the opportunity to issue monetary penalties of up to 4 per cent of the annual turnover of non-compliant data controllers. That way, the GDPR has become a new global benchmark for rules governing the processing of personal data.

The following empirical part will analyse the *de jure* and *de facto* role of DPAs under the GDPR, including important elements of their effective functioning, such as their independence, resources, regulatory powers and practices.

THE ROLE OF DPAS UNDER THE GDPR

At the international level, the EU General Data Protection Regulation represents the most comprehensive and influential legislative framework of data protection worldwide. As an EU Regulation immediately enforceable as law in all Member States at the same time, the GDPR (Article 56) foresees that a single national supervisory authority (i.e. the *lead authority*) shall be responsible for the data controller that is located with its main establishment (including European headquarters of international corporations) in the authority's jurisdiction. That approach is called the *one-stop shop principle*.

International Cooperation and Coordination Mechanisms under the GDPR

In order to ensure its consistent application, the GDPR foresees several cooperation (Article 60–62) and coordination (Article 63–67) mechanisms. For example, to counter the risk of a lead authority failing to carry out its regulatory duties, Article 63 provides for a so-called *consistency mechanism*, which enables the European Data Protection Board (EDPB), that is, the EU supranational data protection body composed of representatives of the EU Member States' DPAs, to issue legally binding decisions by a two-thirds majority that would overrule previous decisions made by a lead authority or enforce otherwise omitted regulatory actions. Though the consistency mechanism has often failed to fulfil its function so far (since necessary majorities in the EDPB are difficult to organise) the latest monetary penalty against WhatsApp shows that the mechanism can indeed work in practice (cf. section on Regulatory practices).[1]

Inner-organisational Structures

The most widespread organisational principle of DPAs in the EU (but also worldwide) is the so-called *Commissioner model*, which 18 out of 28 Member States chose to follow, while 10 DPAs in the EU are organised in form of a commission with varying numbers of appointed officials (from 2 to 17). Despite the rather balanced result on pros and cons of the two models (cf. Stewart 2004), there is a trend towards the *Commissioner model* (see for example the latest shift from Data Protection Commission to Data Protection Commissioner in Austria in 2014), strengthening the view of Flaherty (1989: 15) that "individualistic direction of data protection has been more effective than collective efforts".

The Complete Independence Requirement

Contrary to IRAs for example monitoring (financial) markets or the utilities sector, it is a distinctive feature of DPAs that they are not only assigned to watch over private-sector organisations, but also to check on the compliance of the public sector, including political actors, such as ministries. Since these political actors can become subject to harsh criticism and potentially strict regulations by supervisory authorities themselves, they have an increased interest in being able to influence and at worst controlling the output of DPAs' actions (cf. Schütz 2012a: 125f./136). Thus, DPAs administratively linked and accountable to the political executive are particularly at risk of being held in check by governments.

That is why Article 52 (1) of the GDPR – as equally stipulated already by the Directive – explicitly foresees that a DPA "shall act with complete independence in performing its tasks and exercising its powers [...]." Opposed to the Directive and as a learning effect from a set of later discussed judgements of the European Court of Justice (ECJ) (cf. Bieker 2017: 127), the GDPR (Art. 52 (2–6)) specifies in much more detail concrete conditions for that independence:

2. The DPA "shall [...] remain **free from external influence**, whether direct or indirect, and shall neither seek nor take instructions from anybody." (Decisional independence)
3. DPA officials "shall **refrain from any action incompatible with their duties** and shall not, during their term of office, engage in any incompatible occupation, whether gainful or not." (Autonomy of decision-makers/Incompatibility arrangement)
4. The DPA shall be "**provided with the human, technical and financial resources, premises and infrastructure** necessary for the effective performance of its tasks and exercise of its powers [...]." (Adequate resources)
5. The DPA shall choose and have "its **own staff** which shall be subject to the exclusive direction of the [DPA] [...]." (Organisational independence)
6. The DPA shall be "subject to **financial control which does not affect its independence** and that it has separate, public annual budgets, which may be part of the overall state or national budget." (Financial autonomy)

Moreover, Articles 53 and 54 provide for additional safeguards with regards to the necessary competence and the autonomy of DPA decision-makers, stipulating that "[e]ach member shall have the qualification, experience and skills, in particular in the area of the protection of personal data [...]" (Art. 53 (2)), "shall be dismissed only in cases of serious misconduct or if the member no longer fulfils the conditions required for the performance of the duties" (Art. 53 (4)), and have a term of office of no less than four years (Art. 54 (b)).

In the past, the legal and political reality of applying the complete independence requirement of the Directive has been difficult, reflecting extremely different interpretations and notions of the term "complete independence". The legal set up and status of DPAs, the appointment and dismissal procedures of data protection commissioners (or members of data protection commissions), as well as the degree of organisational and financial autonomy of DPAs have varied from country to country or in a federal state like Germany even from Land to Land sometimes enormously (cf. Schütz 2012b).

In that context, it is worthwhile to briefly discuss three seminal ECJ rulings. In the first judgment, the ECJ (2010) found some of the German Länder had violated the Directive's complete independence requirement by incorporating supervisory authorities responsible for monitoring non-public data controllers into the ministerial bureaucracy (mostly ministries of the interior) and thereby subjecting them to State scrutiny, that is, legal and administrative supervision. The court (ECJ 2010: rec. 30) was of the opinion that complete independence "precludes not only any influence exercised by the supervised bodies, but also any directions or any other external influence, whether direct or indirect, which could call into question the performance by those authorities of their task[s] [...]", serving as a blueprint for Article 52 (2) GDPR.

The second ruling of the ECJ (2012) addressed the lack of organisational independence of the Austrian Data Protection Commission (at that time). The court particularly saw a violation of the Directive in the fact that not only the managing member of the Commission, but also the staff (mostly civil servants) of the DPA were directly employed by the Federal Chancellery. This finding led to the discussed formulation of Article 52 (4) GDPR.

Eventually, the third decision by the ECJ (2014) denounced the dismissal of then Hungarian Data Protection Commissioner András Jóri by his government in 2011, clarifying that the premature dismissal of data protection commissioners must be subject to stringent restrictions with regards to the occasion and reasons for that dismissal – even in cases of passing or amending superior (e.g. constitutional) law. This ruling found reflection in Article 53 (4) GDPR.

Beyond the clear influence that these ECJ decisions had on GDPR stipulations, there are a variety of aspects influencing DPAs' independence that were not (or only partially) touched upon in the Regulation. One of the most important is open, fair and transparent nomination and appointment procedures of DPA decision-makers. While the GDPR provides for more transparency in appointment procedures (Art. 53 (1)) and explicitly requires qualifications and eligibility conditions for the appointment of DPA decision-makers to be integrated into the respective national data protection law (Art. 54 (b)), the Regulation refrains from addressing the highly significant selection processes of DPA decision-makers prior to the actual appointment as well as the obligatory involvement of a branch of government (other than the executive), such as parliament, in nomination and appointment procedures. And indeed, reality shows that the government is very often the agenda-setter in not at all open and transparent nomination and appointment procedures of DPA decision-makers (see e.g. FRA 2010: 19ff.), with the absurd effect that also in times of the GDPR the executive, as an important regulatee itself, often chooses its own regulator.

With GDPR's harmonisation and improvement of crucial elements in DPA independence (above all organisational and financial autonomy) and – as we will see later – regulatory powers, other variables determining regulatory effectiveness that can not necessarily be dealt with in legal terms become more and more important, such as the actual funding and staffing, individual leadership skills, regulatory styles and practices.

Financial and Human Resources

Since the legally most independent DPA can only fulfil its tasks properly with an adequate budget and number of staff, the material dimension of DPAs' independence is closely linked to the question as to what financial and human resources supervisory authorities can draw on in their regulatory day-to-day work.

In practice, a variety of studies and reports came repeatedly to the conclusion that many DPAs in Europe suffer from an insufficient level of financial and personnel resources, limiting them in their *de facto* independence and fulfilment of their tasks (e.g. FRA 2010: 20). In order to check on these findings and provide in-depth empirical data on the subject, this section presents a comparative analysis of the levels of budget as well as numbers of staff of DPAs in the EU, based on latest figures by the EDPB (2020). Figure 9.1 shows the total annual budget and number of staff of DPAs in the EU as of 2019, sorted by total number of staff in ascending order.

In terms of the absolute amount of financial (76.6 million euros) and human resources (888 FTEs) made available to DPAs, Germany is by far the leading nation not only in the EU but also worldwide. However, since Germany as a federal state has currently eighteen different DPAs, all German figures presented in the following comprise sums of numbers on the federal and state DPAs, hence not necessarily giving evidence of, for example, the financial and staff situation of each single German DPA.

In contrast, clearly the best-financed (52 million euros) and -staffed (680 FTEs) single DPA in Europe is the Information Commissioner in the UK, followed at some distance with approximately only a third (or even less) of the staff and budget by DPAs in Poland, France,

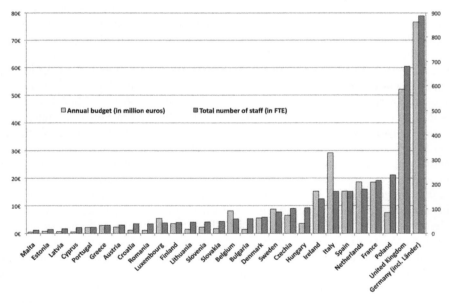

Source: EDPB (2020).

Figure 9.1   *Financial and human resources of DPAs in the EU (2019)*

the Netherlands, Spain, Italy and Ireland. Poland and Italy represent special cases insofar as the Polish DPA (as supervisory authorities of other East European Member States) shows a huge gap between a relatively small budget (7.5 million euros) and a high number of staff (238 FTEs) probably due to the low level of wages, whereas the opposite is true for the Italian DPA that is apparently confronted with relatively high fixed costs. It also comes as no surprise that the smallest EU Member States Malta, Estonia, Latvia and Cyprus (with the exception of Luxembourg) mark the end of that ranking.

However, if DPAs' level of funding is put in relation to the population of the respective country, the new adjusted ranking looks quite different (cf. Figure 9.2).

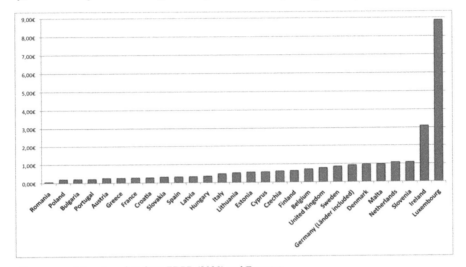

Source: Own research based on data from EDPB (2020) and Eurostat.

Figure 9.2   *Euros spent by EU Member States on DPAs per capita (2019)*

Particularly Luxembourg (8.87 euros) and Ireland (3.10 euros) stand out by only recently providing their DPAs with a disproportionally high level of budget in relation to their overall population. This is probably due to the fact that a significant number of the world's leading IT companies (such as the afore-mentioned Big Five) have chosen to locate their European head-quarters in one of these two countries, making it necessary to invest additional sums in order to be able to present a credible commitment for an effective supervision of data protection. Slovenia and the Netherlands (both 1,08 euros) as well as Malta and Denmark (0.97 euros) follow the two outliers with respect to the amount of euros spent on their supervisory author-ity per capita. On the other end, by far Romania (0.06 euros), but also Poland (0.20 euros), Bulgaria and Portugal (both 0.20 euros) spend rather little financial resources per capita on its DPA (keeping in mind the afore-mentioned bias probably due to low labour costs).

In order to get an even more accurate picture of what EU Member States are indeed willing and able to invest in their supervisory authorities it is worthwhile to take a look at DPA budgets in relation to the overall general government expenditures of the respective country (cf. Figure 9.3).

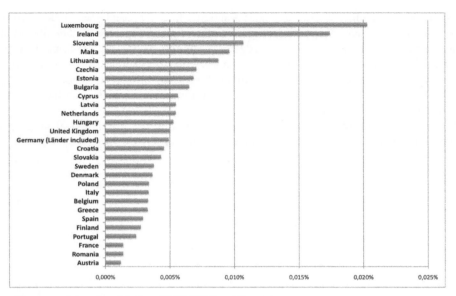

Source: Own research based on data from EDPB (2020) and Eurostat.

Figure 9.3   *DPA budgets in per cent of total general government expenditures of EU Member States*

Thus, Luxembourg and Ireland – as before – take top positions when it comes to financial resources spent on their DPAs in relation to the overall government expenditures, followed at some distance by Slovenia and Malta. On the contrary, supervisory authorities in Austria, Romania and France seem to receive a much smaller share of what is in general publicly spend by their governments.

To sum up, the analytic results of this section show that there are a variety of EU Member States that score way below average with regards to DPAs' level of budget per capita (Romania, Poland, Bulgaria, Portugal, Austria, Greece, France and Croatia), indicating in some cases that they do not provide their DPAs with adequate financial resources. However, whereas to some extent Bulgaria seems to push their financial limits in the attempt to provide adequate resources, especially Austria, Romania and France appear to rather ignore DPAs in the allocation of public funds, probably lacking the political will to do so (cf. Figure 9.3). In general, there is a clear trend towards a more solid funding and staffing of DPAs under the GDPR.

All of this is, however, particularly relevant in the light of Article 52 (4) GDPR. Adequate financial and personnel resources of DPAs have thus become a legally mandatory requirement that could – with a view to the understaffing and -resourcing of some DPAs in the EU – become subject to judicial review of the ECJ in the near future.

Tasks, Powers and Regulatory Practices

Legally stipulated tasks and powers

Undoubtedly, the most significant harmonisation effect the GDPR has had was on the specification of tasks and powers of DPAs in the EU. While supervisory authorities in times of the Data Protection Directive particularly differed in their advisory, investigative and enforcement powers (see e.g. FRA 2010: 20ff.), the GDPR foresees a very detailed and extended set of tasks (Article 57) and powers (Article 58) that each DPA in the Member States is assigned and provided with.

On the one hand, there are the rather soft regulatory assignments and powers, such as complaint handling, educating and raising awareness with the general public, consulting and influencing the private and public sector (including the power to directly address the public, parliament or government, and give advice in legislative processes) as well as new authorisation powers to, for example, adopt standard data protection clauses, approve codes of conduct or accredit certification bodies. On the other hand, hard regulatory instruments involve investigative powers, such as the ability to conduct audits and investigations, as well as corrective powers, including the ability to issue monetary penalties and order a data controller to inform about, publish, erase, correct or cease the processing or transfer of certain personal data.

With the *de jure* harmonisation of most tasks and powers of DPAs in the EU differences in regulatory practices including the *de facto* application of these powers (analysed to some extent in the following section) come to the fore as important explanatory variables for regulatory outcomes.

Regulatory practices

Unfortunately, there is still very little comparative empirical research on *de facto* regulatory activities and practices of supervisory authorities before and after the GDPR, except for data collected by Righettini (2011) and Bignami (2011) as well as attempts to get a quantitative grasp on monetary penalties under the GDPR (cf. e.g. Daigle and Khan 2020), such as provided by the international law firm CMS with its enforcement tracker website. Figures 9.4 and 9.5 diagrams are based on that data, kindly provided by CMS.[2]

Figure 9.4 shows the accumulated amount of fines as well as the highest single fine under the GDPR (both in million euros) issued by DPAs in EU Member States from the beginning of the GDPR's implementation in May 2018 to mid September 2021 and sorted by the accumulated amount of issued fines in ascending order.

With respect to the highest overall amount of issued fines, only recently Luxembourg (€746.1M) and Ireland (€225.9M) have taken over the lead, outpacing the Italian DPA (86.2 €M), France (€57.3M), Germany (€49.3M) – the German states are included – and the UK (€44.3M). Particularly in Luxembourg (€746M against Amazon) and Ireland (€225M against WhatsApp – though forced by the EDPB), but also in the rest of these countries a record-braking single fine (France: €50M against Google Inc.; Germany (Hamburg): €35.3M against H&M; Italy: €27.8M against Telcom Italia (TIM); UK: €22.1M against British Airways) makes up a significant part of the overall accumulated amount. DPAs in Spain (€32.6M) and Sweden (€15.3M) have so far issued monetary penalties in the low double-digit million range, whereas the Netherlands, Bulgaria, Poland, Austria and Belgium comprise a group that fined data controllers only an overall amount from a few to one million euros. Supervisory authorities in the rest of the EU Member States did not make use of significant monetary penalties, so far.

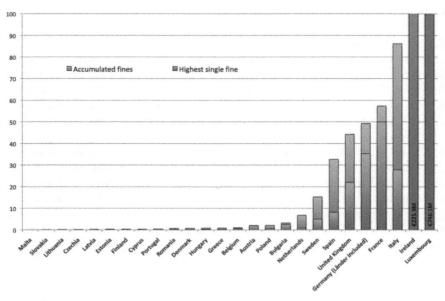

Note: The sample does not include the EU Member States Croatia and Slovenia.
Source: Own research based on data from CMS (2021).

Figure 9.4   *DPA fines (in €M) under the GDPR in the EU and UK from 2018 to 2021
(17 September)*

In terms of the total number of fines issued (cf. Figure 9.5), Spain (286) leads by far the ranking, followed by Italy (92), Romania (62), Hungary (44) and Germany (30) – again Länder included.

Taking a look at the average of monetary penalties issued, it becomes apparent that a large group of predominantly Eastern European countries (see also Daigle and Khan 2020: 10), that is, Malta, Czechia, Romania, Cyprus, Slovakia, Hungary, Lithuania, Greece, Finland, Belgium, Slovakia, Latvia, Denmark, Estonia and Poland, does not yet make use of deterrent monetary penalties (average fine below €100k). In all other EU Member States average fines have significantly increased in comparison to the pre-GDPR period, ranging from €106k in Portugal and €114k in Spain to €1.8M in Germany (Länder included), €3.2M in France, €8.9M in the UK, €25.1M in Ireland and €67.8M in Luxembourg, of course sometimes biased by a very high single fine.

However, it is worthwhile to look at the global level (see Table 9.1), where the United States have pushed financial punishments for data protection violations to yet another level in the post GDPR era. That way, Facebook had to pay a record-braking fine of $5bn for its severe data protection infringements surrounding the initially mentioned *Cambridge Analytica* scandal. And also Equifax, a US-American consumer credit reporting agency, was forced to pay around $650M due to a massive data breach. With latest monetary penalties from DPAs in Luxembourg and Ireland more rigorous fining practices in the EU gain momentum, beginning to match those in the US. And even more important, the development process of the latest fine against WhatsApp, in which the EDPB was able to force the responsible lead authority

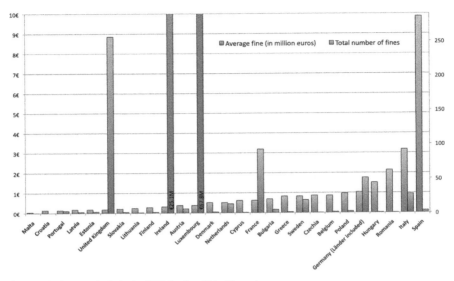

Note: The sample does not include the EU Member State Slovenia.
Source: Own research based on data from CMS (2021).

Figure 9.5   *Total number and average of DPA fines under the GDPR in the EU and UK from 2018 to 2021 (17 September)*

Table 9.1   *Top-10 fines worldwide related to data protection violations (September 2021)*

Rank	Fined entity	Amount of fines and penalties	Year	Country	Status
1	Facebook, Inc.	$5bn	2019	US	settled
2	Amazon Europe Core S.à r.l.	€746M	2021	Luxembourg	issued
3	Equifax Inc.	$650M	2019	US	settled
4	WhatsApp Ireland Limited	€225M	2021	Ireland	issued
5	Google LLC, YouTube LLC	$170M	2019	US	settled
6	Uber Technologies, Inc.	$148M	2018	US	settled
7	Google LLC, Google Ireland Limited	€100M	2020	France*	issued
8	Blue Global Media	$104M	2017	US	suspended due to bankruptcy
9	Facebook, Inc.	$100M	2019	US**	settled
10	Google LLC	€50M	2019	France	settled after judicial review

Note: * Not issued on the basis of the GDPR, but under national French cookie rules; ** not issued by the Federal Trade Commission, but by the Securities and Exchange Commission (SEC), the US-American supervisory authority for the financial service industry.
Source: Own research.

in Ireland to substantially increase the fine from initially €30–50 to €225 million, has clearly shown that GDPR's consistency mechanism is starting to work in practice, mitigating the risk of single national supervisory authorities undermining EU data protection standards.

It is crucial to note here that most of the US-American monetary penalties are part of a directly applicable settlement with the infringing party, whereas fines issued by DPAs in Europe are normally not part of a deal and thus become increasingly subject to judicial review or DPAs' anticipatory obedience in expecting judicial review. For example, while the Highest Administrative Court in France upheld the €50M-fine against Google in 2020, German courts substantially slashed the monetary penalty against 1&1 (a German telecommunications provider) by 90 per cent (from €9.6M to just €900,000) or even annulled the fine of €14.5M of the Berlin DPA against German property company Deutsche Wohnen. In Austria, the record-braking fine of €18M against the Austrian Post was also overturned by the Federal Administrative Court because of infringements of procedural requirements, and other more peculiar cases involve the significant reduction of fines against British Airways (from £184M to £20M) and Marriot International (from £99M to £14.4M) by the ICO, apparently due to the COVID-19 pandemic and associated economic crisis of these companies.

Briefly summarised, comparative data on regulatory actions by DPAs in the EU and globally are largely missing. With respect to one out of many enforcement tools, namely issuing monetary penalties, there is more and more systematically aggregated, quantitative data. In the US, supervisory authorities clearly make use of *de facto* deterring financial sanctions. Whereas a small group of DPAs (especially in Luxembourg, France and Ireland, but also Germany, Italy and the UK) is trying to impose more rigorous monetary penalties (yet often still on a different scale as in the US), supervisory authorities of most of the other Member States have not yet exercised their newly acquired fining powers for significant monetary penalties.

One of the key problems is, however, that some EU Member States seem to have adopted the role to function as data protection (as well as tax) havens, attracting most of the leading IT industry players. Despite recent efforts in massively increasing resources (cf. section on Financial and human resources) as well as establishing more rigorous fining practices, these DPAs are overrun by cross-border complaints not being able to react in a timely manner. This is particularly the case for Ireland, where – even after the enormous fine against WhatsApp – 98 per cent of major cross-border complaints remain unresolved (Irish Council for Civil Liberties 2021: 3).

CONCLUDING REMARKS

What we have learned so far is that the topic of data protection authorities – despite its regulatory and societal relevance – is still massively under-researched, particularly from a social science perspective, lacking systematically aggregated qualitative as well as quantitative data.

There are more than 130 privacy and data protection authorities worldwide with a very large part of them (about 60) located in Europe. With the enactment of the GDPR in 2018 the EU set new standards in data protection worldwide. The GDPR perpetuates the process of policy convergence as well as significant improvements in the legal set up of supervisory authorities for an effective regulation, such as DPAs' independence, resources, tasks and powers.

With respect to the complete independence requirement, particularly the absence of rules addressing the highly significant selection processes of DPA decision-makers prior to the actual appointment as well as the obligatory involvement of a branch of government (other than the executive), such as parliament, in nomination and appointment procedures remains problematic.

While the GDPR clearly foresees DPAs to be provided with adequate human, technical and financial resources (including appropriate premises and infrastructure), the reality of many DPAs in the EU is quite different, posing enormous challenges in the attempt to fulfil the wide range of different functions. Regarding regulatory tasks and powers of DPAs, the GDPR heralds indeed a new era of *de facto* enforceability of data protection law. However, with a view to regulatory and particularly fining practices, the majority of supervisory authorities in the EU acts so far rather reserved, while other struggle with the sheer number of cases to be assessed or the actual execution of their monetary penalties in court.

In that respect, it is crucial to bear in mind that the debate on effective means of enforcement must not be restricted to easily quantifiable and publicly presentable monetary penalties, which only comprise one tool out of many and are often exclusively directed towards private-sector data controllers. Instead, a mixture of soft and hard regulatory tools seems to be most promising, including educating and raising awareness with the general public as well as organisations (e.g. through mandatory full-time data protection officers), but also ordering the immediate cessation of the processing or transfer of personal data, and as a last resort ensuring personal liability and/or criminal prosecutions against relevant decision-makers (e.g. single chief executive officers). Eventually, it is worthwhile to take a closer look in that context at the interplay of data protection and competition law. New and more aggressive regulatory approaches in antitrust politics in the EU but also in the US (cf. e.g. Khan 2017), including discussions on forced break-ups, could help to put additional pressure on Big Tech to really change business practices also with regards to data protection.

Drawing on theoretical and methodological approaches of research on IRAs has proven to be quite helpful, though the analytical scope has to be broaden in order to be able to explain regulatory outputs of DPAs. Due to the increasing convergence of data protection legislation (at least with regards to liberal democracies worldwide), also spawned by GDPR's external effects to function as the new gold standard, future research on DPAs should not so much concentrate on *de jure* features but rather *de facto* practices. The presented empirical findings show considerable differences in regulatory practices of DPAs in Europe (at least with regards to fining practices), contradicting to a certain extent Bignami's (2011) observation of converging regulatory styles for the time being. Also litigation plays an increasingly relevant role mostly due to more significant fines and associated incentives to challenge them in court. But GDPR's establishment of the right to compensation and liability (Article 82) in cases of data protection violations, coupled with new opportunities, for example for NGOs to file class action suits will also result in more judicial decisions on claims of compensation.

The lowest common denominator in the understanding of DPAs' regulatory role in society is certainly the clarification of the ECJ (2010) that DPAs shall act as "the guardian of those fundamental rights and freedoms" with respect to the processing of personal data (ibid.: recital 23), striving for a fair balance between observance of the fundamental right to private life and the interests requiring free movement of personal data (ibid.: recital 24). The GDPR provides an adequate legal framework for the fulfilment of these tasks. However, it is up to DPA decision-makers to live up to that role with all necessary means the GDPR provides them with, not only individually at the national, but also together at the European or even worldwide level. Further research on DPAs should critically scrutinise and accompany those developments (for more information on regulatory agencies in the European context see also Chapters 2 and 20).

NOTES

1. There are furthermore numerous international networks of DPAs inside and outside the EU, such as the Consultative Committee of Convention 108 of the Council of Europe, the European Conference of Data Protection Authorities, the Global Privacy Assembly or the Global Privacy Enforcement Network.
2. It is important to keep in mind that the CMS data only comprise monetary penalties issued under the GDPR and if necessary upheld in court, not including fines for violations of data protection rules exclusively stipulated under national legislation, e.g. with regards to cookies (cf. France* Table 9.1) or employee data, as well as annulled by the judiciary.

REFERENCES

Barnard-Wills, D. (2017): "The technology foresight activities of European Union data protection authorities". *Technological Forecasting and Social Change* 116: 142–150.
Bennett, C. (1992): *Regulating Privacy: Data Protection and Public Policy in Europe and the United States*. Ithaca: Cornell University Press.
Bennett, C. & Raab, C. (2006): *The Governance of Privacy: Policy Instruments in Global Perspective* (2nd edn). Cambridge, MA and London: MIT Press.
Bennett, C. & Raab, C. (2020): "Revisiting the Governance of Privacy: Contemporary Policy Instruments in a Global Perspective." *Regulation & Governance* 14 (3): 447–464.
Bignami, F. (2011): "Cooperative Legalism and the Non-Americanization of European Regulatory Styles: The Case of Data Privacy." *American Journal of Comparative Law* 59 (2): 411–461.
Bieker, F. (2017): "Enforcing Data Protection Law – The Role of the Supervisory Authorities in Theory and Practice" in *Privacy and Identity Management: Facing Up to Next Steps*, edited by A. Lehmann et al. (eds). Karlstad, Sweden, 21–26 August 2016, Revised Selected Papers, Springer, pp. 125–139.
Busch, A. (2010): Coping with Innovation: The Political Regulation of Personal Information in Comparative Perspective: Full Research Report ESRC End of Award Report. RES-062-23-0536-A. Swindon: ESRC.
Busch, A. (2013): "The Regulation of Transborder Data Traffic: Disputes Across the Atlantic". *Security and Human Rights* 23 (4): 313–330.
BVerfG (1983): Volkszählungsurteil (Census decision). Urteil des Ersten Senats vom 15. Dezember 1983 auf die mündliche Verhandlung vom 18. und 19. Oktober 1983.
Daigle, B. & Khan, M. (2020): "The EU General Data Protection Regulation: An Analysis of Enforcement Trends by EU Data Protection Authorities." *Journal of International Commerce and Economics*, May 2020: 1–38.
De Hert, P., Kloza, D. and Makowski, P. (eds) (2015): *Enforcing Privacy: Lessons from Current Implementations and Perspectives for the Future*. Warsaw: Wydawnictwo Sejmowe.
ECJ (2010): Judgment of the Court (Grand Chamber) of 9 March 2010. European Commission v Federal Republic of Germany.
ECJ (2012): Judgment of the Court (Grand Chamber) of 16 October 2012. European Commission v Republic of Austria.
ECJ (2014): Judgment of the Court (Grand Chamber) of 8 April 2014. European Commission v Hungary.
EDPB (2020): Contribution of the EDPB to the Evaluation of the GDPR under Article 97. European Data Protection Board.
Flaherty, D. (1989): *Protecting Privacy in Surveillance Societies: The Federal Republic of Germany, Sweden, France, Canada, and United States*. Chapel Hill, NC and London: University of North Carolina Press.

FRA (2010): Data Protection in the European Union: The Role of National Data Protection Authorities. Strengthening the fundamental rights architecture in the EU II. Luxembourg: European Union Agency for Fundamental Rights (FRA).

Gilardi, F. & Maggetti, M. (2011): The Independence of Regulatory Authorities. In: *Handbook on the Politics of Regulation*, edited by D. Levi-Faur. Cheltenham, UK and Northampton, MA, USA: Edward Elgar Publishing, pp. 201–214.

Greenleaf, G. (2012): "Independence of Data Privacy Authorities (Part II): Asia-Pacific Experience". *Computer Law & Security Review* 28 (2): 121–129.

Gutwirth, S. (2002): *Privacy and the Information Age*. Lanham/Boulder/New York/Oxford: Rowman & Littlefield Publishers.

Irish Council for Civil Liberties (2021): Europe's Enforcement Paralysis. ICCL's 2021 report on the enforcement capacity of data protection authorities.

Khan, Lina M. (2017): "Amazon's Antitrust Paradox". *Yale Law Journal* 126 (3): 564–907.

Mayer-Schönberger, V. (1998): "Generational Development of Data Protection in Europe". In: *Technology and Privacy: The New Landscape*, edited by P. E. Agre & M. Rotenberg. Cambridge, MA, USA: MIT Press, pp. 219–241.

Newman, A. (2008): "Building Transnational Civil Liberties: Transgovernmental Entrepreneurs and the European Data Privacy Directive". *International Organization* 62 (1): 103–130.

Raab, C. (2011): "Networks for Regulation: Privacy Commissioners in a Changing World". *Journal of Comparative Policy Analysis: Research and Practice* 13 (2): 195–213.

Raab, C. & Szekely, I. (2017): "Data Protection Authorities and Information Technology". *Computer Law & Security Review* 33: 421–433.

Richardson, J., Gustafsson, G. & Jordan, G. (1982): "The Concept of Policy Style". In: *Policy Styles in Western Europe*, edited by J. Richardson. New York: Allen & Unwin, pp. 1–16.

Righettini, M. S. (2011): "Institutionalization, Leadership, and Regulative Policy Style: A France/Italy Comparison of Data Protection Authorities". *Journal of Comparative Policy Analysis: Research and Practice* 13 (2): 143–164.

Schütz, P. (2012a): "The Set Up of Data Protection Authorities as a New Regulatory Approach". In: *European Data Protection: In Good Health?* edited by S. Gutwirth et al. Dordrecht: Springer, pp. 125–142.

Schütz, P. (2012b): "Comparing Formal Independence of Data Protection Authorities in Selected EU Member States". Conference Paper presented at the 4th Biennial ECPR Standing Group for Regulatory Governance Conference 2012, Exeter, UK.

Schütz, P. (forthcoming): Data Protection Authorities in Comparative Perspective. The Cases of the United Kingdom and the Federal Republic of Germany (working title).

Simitis, S. et al. (2019): Einleitung. In: *Datenschutzrecht. DSGVO mit BDSG (Nomos Kommentar)*, edited by Simitis, S. et al. (1st edn). Baden-Baden: Nomos, pp. 158–240.

Sivan-Sevilla, I. (forthcoming): "Europeanization of Policy Implementation? A Qualitative Comparative Analysis (QCA) of Data Protection Authorities' Enforcement Styles Post-GDPR". *Journal of European Public Policy*.

Stewart, B. (2004): "A Comparative Survey of Data Protection Authorities Part 1: Form and Structure". *Privacy Law and Policy Reporter 46*, 11 (2).

Vranaki, A. (2016): "Cloud Investigations by European Data Protection Authorities: An Empirical Account". In: *Research Handbook on Electronic Commerce Law*, edited by J. Rothchild. Cheltenham, UK and Northampton, MA, USA: Edward Elgar Publishing, pp. 518–541.

Wright, D. & De Hert, P. (eds) (2016): *Enforcing Privacy*. Law, Governance and Technology Series 25. Cham ZG (Switzerland): Springer International Publishing.

10. Agencies regulating network services
Matthias Finger

INTRODUCTION

The focus of this chapter are the authorities that regulate network industries or utilities.[1] These typically cover energy (electricity and gas), transport (rail, air, but sometimes also road and maritime transport), communications (telecommunications and postal services) and water (drinking water and wastewater). Recently, it has been argued, the newly emerging digital platforms could also be seen as a new type of network industries and be regulated accordingly.

The approach to this chapter is both historical and cultural; more precisely, I will show how the agencies regulating utilities or network industries have evolved, or not, in the United States and Europe. The focus of the chapter will, however, be more on Europe, as the European approach to then regulation and to the regulators of the network industries is more mature, but also more in line with today's challenges network industries face. This is not to say that the European approach does not have problems, especially when it comes to the more recent challenges of digitalization and climate change, as we will see.

The chapter is structured as follows: in a first section I will recall the evolution of the infrastructures in both the US and Europe, as well as how they have been "regulated" up to approximately the 1990s, the age of globalization. In a second section I will then focus on the European approach to sector-specific network industry regulation, by contrasting it with the US approach of regulating utilities. This European approach has indeed become the dominant approach worldwide. However, in order to assess its relevance beyond Europe, it is necessary to understand the reasons why it came into existence in the first place. The third section will look into the future of network industry regulation and regulatory authorities, as these industries have become highly dynamic as a result of competition, permeated by digital technologies and have increasingly become the concern of policy makers because of their impact on climate and the environment. As I will show, these new challenges lead to sector convergence, "platformization" and multi-modal or even multi-sectoral approaches, for which the currently existing regulatory authorities are ill equipped.

INFRASTRUCTURES BEFORE GLOBALIZATION

Before their liberalization during the 1990s, we did not really speak of network industries. Rather, the term "infrastructure" was used in Europe and replaced, as a result of their liberalization, by the term "network industries". In the United States the term "utilities" was and still is prevalent. This cultural difference is also reflected in different ways to "regulate" infrastructures, utilities and network industries (see Finger, 2020).

Europe and its Colonies

In Europe and its colonies – mostly the French, but also the British, the German, the Spanish, the Portuguese, the Dutch and the Italian colonies – "infrastructures" must be seen as an integral part of the nation-building process during the late nineteenth and the early twentieth century. The relevant concept here is the concept of "infrastructures" (and not "utilities"), which are, just like in the US, essentially local in nature (e.g., water utilities). As significant contributors to nation-building, infrastructures are thus primarily the object of public policies aimed at economic and social development at the national scale (e.g., postal services, telecoms, railways, electrification, air transport later on), aimed at national security and defense (e.g., air traffic control, railways, electricity), at employment creation (e.g., postal services, railways), at diplomacy and international connectivity (e.g., airlines), at public health (e.g., water and sanitation), and sometimes at other public policies.

The basic tool to implement these public policies aimed at nation-building are the so-called "State-Owned Enterprises" (SOEs). These are typically the result of their nationalization during the late nineteenth century. As of the 1920s, most of the infrastructures considered to be essential for nation-building in Europe and its colonies in Africa and Asia (to a much lesser extent in Latin America) were fully owned by the respective nation-states. Needless to say that, in the case of the communist countries (e.g., Russia, China), this model reached beyond the network industries into the entire economy.

SOEs are also typically granted a monopoly so as to be best equipped to carry out their public policy missions. Sometimes the monopoly was granted on national security grounds (e.g., air traffic control), but most often the reasoning was more economic, namely to take full advantage of both economies of scale and the direct network effects, which are so typical of the network industries. In other words, state-owned monopolies were simply considered to be the most efficient way to implement such nation-building policies. Cross-subsidies were a typical way of financing these public policy missions as implemented by the SOEs: let me mention, for example, cross-subsidies between densely (thus lucrative) and less densely populated areas (thus loss-making), between customers able to pay (for example industry in the case of electricity, long-distance phone calling customers) and customers whose services need to be (cross-)subsidized, between different regions of a country, as well as others more. There is a variation to this model in the federalist countries (e.g., Germany, India), where some of these infrastructure SOEs were regionally owned, and the monopoly was thus a regional monopoly.

It is important to understand that these SOEs were not "regulated", at least not in the sense regulation is currently understood. As a matter of fact, SOEs were in essence considered to be an extension of the core public administration: their governance was typically as political as (still) is the governance of the public administration, where administrators (we would call them managers today) are politically appointed. At that time, SOEs were not yet corporatized – corporatization of SOEs only emerged during the 1980s – and so there was no board overseeing them. Most often, they were directly steered and controlled by the respective ministries (e.g., ministry of PTT, ministry of energy, ministry of railways, etc.). One may say that SOEs were "regulated by virtue of their public ownership" (political and administrative appointments of the managers), as well as on the basis of sometimes very detailed legal specifications. Typically, each SOE had one (or sometimes several) specific legal acts, which more or less clearly defined their mandate, but also their remit, that is, the activities the SOE was to perform, but most often what they were not allowed to do. All this was enshrined in the legal "principle of specificity".

Despite the lack of their regulation, the SOEs were – and actually still are – in essence "hybrid" organizations, that is, neither public administrative entities, nor commercial businesses: were they commercial businesses (with a monopoly), they would (have to) be regulated, as we will see in the case of the US below; were they purely administrative entities, they would have to be treated like the rest of the public administration. Instead, they enjoy some managerial and financial autonomy from the state (financed mainly by the sale of their services), while at the same time having to fulfill their respective public policy (sometimes called public service) missions, as defined in the law (see: Finger & Rentsch, 2015). As we will see in section 2, with liberalization SOEs became corporatized and sometimes even privatized, but often also unbundled, that is, split-up into a monopolistic infrastructure and a (in theory) competitive services part. This led to the necessity to regulate, but such regulation and corresponding regulatory authorities will be equally "hybrid" as are the SOEs, their off-springs and their competitors, torn as they are between economic efficiency and public policy/service objectives. I will come back to this in the next section.

The US Model[2]

Of course, the United States also have infrastructures, albeit less developed and generally of lesser quality than in Europe, as well as the challenge of nation building. However, and this is the big difference with Europe, infrastructures in the US are not really seen and even less so used as a public policy tool for nation-building. In addition, the US is an extreme version of a federalist country and as such only comparable to Switzerland, from the which the US took inspiration. It is significant that the only substantive federal infrastructure (with the exception of the US Postal Service) is Inter-State Highway System, legally enacted only in 1956 and mostly with a Cold War perspective in mind. No coherent and comparable federal electricity or railway infrastructure, for example, exists in the US to this day.

As a matter of fact, and in total contradistinction to Europe, infrastructures in the US are local and private; they were never consolidated, nor integrated at the national level. This is why they are rather called utilities in the US context. But, like all infrastructures, they are essentially monopolies, owing to economic efficiency considerations (economies of scale and direct network effects). The only exception is the United States Postal Service (USPS): the USPS was created as a federal agency at the creation of the US federal government in the late eighteenth century. Like in all other countries of the world, the postal service served as a country's core communication network and was thus of strategic importance for any government. But unlike all other countries in the world, telecommunications in the US, later on, was never nationalized and even less so integrated into what became called the PTT (Post, Telegraph, Telephone) in every single country of the world (except the US). Whereas all other infrastructures in the US were local or state monopolies, telecom (i.e., AT&T for American Telephone and Telegraph) was a private national monopoly, to be broken up only in 1982 by US Anti-Trust law.

Given the predominantly private nature of the American utilities, regulation and regulatory agencies of these so-called utilities developed as early as the 1920s, that is, 70 years earlier than in Europe, where regulation and regulatory agencies of infrastructures, now called network industries, are the result of their liberalization during the late 1980s and mostly the

1990s. But if the US was early in terms of regulation and regulatory agencies, it has hardly evolved since and remains limited to the US. Let us thus briefly look at the unique features of this US regulatory model.

Given the decentralized nature of the US utilities at local and sometimes state levels, regulation was also set up at the state and not at the federal level. Consequently, regulatory agencies – the so-called "public utilities regulatory commissions" or sometimes called "public services regulatory commissions" – are set up at the state level, with the consequence that each of the 50 US states has built up its own utilities' regulators, which has led to considerable diversity. Also, these utilities regulatory agencies typically are multi- or cross-sectoral, as they cover all the utilities, namely electricity, gas, public transport, water, and even cable TV and others. The main concern of these regulators is the different utilities monopolistic nature, more specifically the tendency of monopolies to abuse their dominant position.

The task of US utility regulators is at the same time simple and complex: it is simple because it is mainly about one thing, namely "rate-making", that is, about determining whether the rates utilities charge to their consumers are "correct". But it is also complex because, on a theoretical level, such utilities' regulation is based on the theory of public goods: utilities are considered to be delivering toll or club goods and, as such, are regulated as monopolies. In other words, the utility enjoys an exclusive franchise over a given territory, typically the entire state or a city. As part of that franchise, utilities are protected from competition and antitrust law. The utility also enjoys the right of eminent domain, the recovery of approved costs, a reasonable opportunity to earn a fair return, and the right to charge for the cost of service. In exchange, the utility "has the obligation to provide all paying customers with access to safe, adequate, reliable, convenient and non-discriminatory service on just and reasonable terms, while assuming certain business and market risks and subjecting itself to regulatory reporting, reviews and oversight" (Beecher, quoted in Finger, 2020, p.31).

In other words, the utilities commit to some sort of "*regulatory compact.*" The main dimensions of this regulatory compact are the commitment to a universal service, a given service portfolio, service efficiency, operational standards, service reliability and quality, as well as capacity utilization. This compact further includes much broader commitments to consumer education, public and worker safety, and economic development. The regulator, in turn, makes sure that the compact is adhered to. This relative lack of precision is first due to the cross-sectoral nature of these utilities regulators. But it is also due to the underlying quite fuzzy theory of toll goods. In addition, regulatory authorities in the US are quite political, at least more political than in the case of Europe. And finally this lack of precision is due to the federalist nature of the US utilities regulatory system, where each state develops its own regulatory practice, to be counter-balanced only by the US legal system. Indeed, regulators and utilities typically end up before courts, first at the state and ultimately at the federal level.

So, who are these regulators, or public utilities regulatory commissions? First, they are as diverse as the 50 US states. Each state has its own regulatory commission, with little standardization, and especially no federal rules, as to the structure and powers of these regulators. As we will see below, this is totally different in the case of Europe. Typically, these regulators are structured into a set of commissioners who ultimately make the decisions, and a staff which does the work. The commissioners are either appointed by the governor of the state or directly elected by the population of the state. Commissioners therefore have a political color. Yet, their political inclinations are again checked by the courts (which are also political). In this way and over time, some regulatory stability nevertheless emerges.

Indeed, over the past 80 or so years, some jurisprudence has been established by the US Supreme Court as to what constitutes good regulatory practice or a "good regulatory compact". Beecher has summarized the key jurisprudence as follows, which however makes things hardly more precise, as can be seen from the below list:

- Returns are authorized but not guaranteed
- Regulation involves the "fair interpretation of a bargain"
- Returns should reflect "corresponding risk"
- Regulators should not substitute their judgment for "board discretion"
- Prudence is presumed but "wasteful" expenditures should be disallowed
- Rate base property must be "used and useful" to ratepayers
- Regulation does not ensure that businesses will produce "net revenues"
- Regulators are not bound by formulas and are free to make "pragmatic" adjustments
- Due process does not insure or protect utilities from losses due to "economic forces"
- A contract rate is not "'unjust' or 'unreasonable' simply because it is unprofitable"
- Utilities must "operate with all reasonable economies"
- Regulators should not usurp management or judge prudence based on "20/20" hindsight
- Courts allow regulators to decide within a "zone of reasonableness"
- Rate methodologies should not arbitrarily shift risks to and from investors.

Looking at this jurisprudence, one can see that regulators have substantial freedom of interpretation, and the same is true for the regulated utilities. In the US, the ultimate "regulator," however, are the courts, and in the end, the Supreme Court. Such is the US model of regulation, a model that is difficult to replicate outside of the US federalist and highly legalistic system. Not astonishingly, then, the US approach has not been copied anywhere else, and this despite aggressive efforts by the National Association of Regulatory Utilities Commissioners (NARUC), the US government and the World Bank to export this model worldwide.

Yet, state utility regulators do have serious limitations: indeed, over time, utilities – especially electricity, gas, and telecommunications – have come to cover several states and even the entire US territory. Electricity and gas, for example, may be produced in one state and sold in another. Telecommunications operators, after the breakup of AT&T in 1982, started to compete nationwide. Aviation and railways cover the entire US territory. The state level is no longer the only, and perhaps no longer the most appropriate level, at which utilities should be regulated. Consequently, over time some national regulators have emerged, such as the FCC – the Federal Communications Commission – and FERC – the Federal Energy Regulatory Commission. Yet, the United States remains a federalist system, that is, a subsidiary and bottom-up system, and these federal regulatory commissions are only competent when it comes to interstate matters. It is thus fair to say that the US regulatory system urgently needs to be reformed; in particular it needs a much more federal or centralized and top-down approach to regulation. And this is where the much more recent EU model comes in.

Conclusion: Two Very Different Approaches to the Same Challenges

When it comes to its institutional dimensions, the European model could not be more different from the US one, as I will show in the next section. However, at this point, let me already highlight the main differences between the US and the European model of infrastructure regulation:

- If the US model is a bottom-up and a subsidiary model, the EU model is just the opposite. In the United States, the utilities' regulators make decisions at the state level. These decisions, over time and thanks to jurisprudence, achieve some sort of federal legitimacy. Federal regulators can only act where interstate matters are concerned. In contradistinction, the European model is a top-down model, where all the rules are decided at the supra-national level, including the way national regulators should be structured, staffed and should operate.
- If the US utilities' regulators are mainly concerned with local private (or sometimes public) monopolies and regulate these as toll or club goods, the EU model is concerned with Europe-wide competition, with the public goods or public service dimension being treated totally separately, typically as a problem of market distortion.
- If the US model is quite political, the European model is basically technocratic. Indeed, since the US model deals with public goods and since regulators are politically appointed or even elected, US regulators are in fact political actors. In the EU, instead, regulation is seen as a technocratic matter, with regulators focusing mostly on the technicalities of imperfect competition. Consequently, and as we will see below, the independence of the regulators from politics is much more important.
- Finally, if the US utilities' regulators are cross-sectoral, the EU regulatory model is sector-specific. Indeed, in the EU, there are no "utilities" regulators; instead there are energy regulators, telecommunication regulators, rail regulators, air transport regulators, postal regulators, and others.

THE EU APPROACH: SECTOR-SPECIFIC REGULATORS

In this section let me therefore explain this totally different European approach to regulation and regulators. Again we have to start with history, more precisely the project of Europe's political integration in reaction to globalization. In a first section, I will therefore explain what has become called "regulatory Europe" (Majone, 1996), that is, the technocratic idea of building an EU-wide infrastructure as a means of "Europe-building", very similar to the early twentieth-century idea of nation-building. In a second section, I will focus on the particular role independent regulatory authorities play when implementing "regulatory Europe".

Liberalization of the National Infrastructures as a Means Towards Political Integration (EU)

Whereas the Treaty of Rome (1958) triggered the process of European integration, the Treaty of Maastricht (1992) can be considered a new and probably decisive step in the process of European integration. Indeed, the Treaty of Maastricht comes after a decade of economic globalization, as well three years after the end of the Cold War, as a result of which the different European nation-states became acutely aware that some form of political integration was a necessity in order to be able to compete with the US and rising China. Within this ideological context of free markets, it was only logical to use market opening between the different

European nation-states as a means for political integration. This approach was implement in the different infrastructure sectors in a very systematic way (see: Finger & Künneke, 2011; Finger & Jaag, 2015).

To recall, infrastructures in Europe (and in the European colonies) were since the late nineteenth and early twentieth century public monopolies, and as such mostly owned by national and sometimes regional governments. Infrastructures were thus (and still are) a particularly sensitive issue when it comes to their liberalization, but also to their Europeanization. On the other hand, if it became possible to transform these different national infrastructures into truly European network industries, a significant step forward in European integration could be taken. This all coincided, as said above, with a period of neo-liberal ideology, the ideology underpinning economic globalization. Neo-liberalism considers SOEs as being particularly anachronistic and in need of reform, if not to be privatized as a rapidly as possible. The European Union, more precisely the European Commission, astutely used this particular ideological moment to further its political integration.

What did the trick was the economistic idea that efficiency could be furthered, that is, welfare increased, if state-owned infrastructure monopolies were broken up – "unbundled" in EU parlance – and exposed to competition. So-to-speak as a side-effect, political integration could be facilitated as well, not speak about the additional benefit for the EU resulting from weakened nation-states. Of course this could not be done in one stroke, given the opposition from SOEs, unions, national governments, and others more. It had to be done sector by sector and step by step. Also, economies of scale and direct network effects which had led to infrastructure monopolies in the first place should not be lost artificial competition. A true challenge, which the European Commission (mostly) started tackle as early as the beginning of the 1990s in all the infrastructure sectors, but in particular in telecommunications, postal services, railways, aviation, electricity and gas.

The ultimate vision at that time was, and actually still is twofold: on the one hand the creation of a EU-wide infrastructure, called "copper-plate-Europe" in electricity or "single European sky" in aviation, for example. This infrastructure would still be monopolistic, and monopolies could still be national and owned by governments, but the infrastructure would be harmonized thanks to technical regulations (standards) to the point that electrons, data or airplanes, for that matter, would no longer encounter any physical obstacles when travelling across Europe. In this way, direct network effects could even be increased. In other words, an EU-wide infrastructure is not only a more efficient and welfare-enhancing, it is also a foundation for Europe-building, just as a national infrastructure was a foundation for nation-building in the early twentieth century. On the other hand, competition among services providers could take place on the basis of such an EU-wide infrastructure. Just like in aviation, where airlines can use (monopolistic) air traffic control and airport infrastructures and by doing so make consumers benefit from competition, the same could happen – and has to a certain degree happened – in telecommunications, postal services, electricity, gas and rail freight.

In order to make this happen, a sophisticated regulatory system has to be put into place. This regulatory system has three essential dimensions:

● The first regulatory dimension is the monopoly: just like in the case of US utilities, regulation has to determine what the correct price for using the monopoly (e.g., the railtrack, the airport, the electricity grid, the telephone cable, etc.) is. But unlike US utilities' regulation, the monopoly is not considered a toll or club good, but simply a monopoly which should operate as efficiently as possible and be regulated accordingly. Also, the customer of this monopoly is not the final consumer (as is the case in the US), but the companies offering services on the basis of this monopoly. In addition, there is also technical regulation so as to interconnect the different historical monopolies and monopolists at national and state level, another dimension that US utilities regulation does not address, as monopolies are (considered to be) self-contained. There, interconnection is the task of the federal regulators and not of the utilities regulatory commissions, if it is regulated at all.

- The second regulatory dimension pertains to access, that is, to the relationship between the monopolistic infrastructure on the one hand and its users, in other words the companies offering services on the basis of this infrastructure. This is not only a question of charges (see price of the monopoly above), but also of priorities to use them (given that infrastructures have congestions), as well as a technical question of interoperability. Furthermore, many infrastructure companies (SOEs) are still not properly unbundled, leading to self-preferencing and discrimination, which also need to be regulated. This dimension does not exist in the case of US utilities regulation.
- The third regulatory dimension pertains to systems integrity: indeed, despite unbundling and competition between companies using the same infrastructure, infrastructures, network industries or utilities are complex systems which can only function as systems. For example, an airplane is useless without an airport and so is an electricity grid without generators of electricity. Because of unbundling, these systems have been artificially fragmented and the role of the regulator now is to make them work again as systems. This is a very tricky task of technical (systems management), economic and even political nature for a regulator. But it is essential for network industries to deliver infrastructure services. It also another task that US utilities regulators do not perform.

To conclude, it appears clearly that all these regulatory dimensions and functions cannot be performed by a general, multi-sectoral utilities regulator as this is the case in the US. Rather, the technicalities which are different in each of the network industries' sectors require a sector-specific regulator, who is capable of understanding the inner workings of each of these industries and industry-specific technologies. Furthermore, the technological dynamics in each of these sectors are different, and therefore the different network industries evolve at very different pace, something that, again, argues in favor of a sector-specific approach. Finally, many of these sectors have safety (and sometimes security) issues, which are highly sector specific, thinking, for example, of safety in air transport (accidents) or electricity (blackouts). It is therefore only logical that the European Commission opted for the creation of sector-specific regulatory authorities. As a result, regulators are typically mandated by EU legislation for each country in the following sectors: postal services, telecommunications, railways, air transport, electricity often combined with gas, sometimes road transport and water.

Independence of Regulators

The preoccupation with the independence of the sector-specific regulators is not European. We find the same preoccupation in the US when it comes to utilities' regulators. Indeed, a significant portion of the literature especially in the US about regulators has been devoted to so-called "regulatory capture," although this concept only focuses on the question of the independence of the regulators from the regulated firms. And regulatory capture is indeed a problem, especially in the network industries, which require technical expertise. Generally, such expertise can only be acquired while working in the industry itself. Competent sector-specific regulators, especially commissioners, have thus typically previously worked in the industry, where they have acquired their competence and knowledge.

But there is a second dimension to the independence of regulators, namely the independence from politics. Of course, at an abstract level, regulatory independence from day-to-day politics is equally important in Europe and the United States. But in the United States, the utility regulator has a much more political role. Rates should strike a balance between the firms' investment and operational needs, consumer protection, and the broader public interest. In the case of the European approach, however, regulators are first of all technocrats, whose role it is to apply the rules set by politicians, more precisely the European Commission, often approved by Council and sometimes even the European Parliament. Their leeway is thus quite limited. Courts of course also play a role, but are much less important than in the United States; they basically decide whether regulators have respected due process and the law set by the European Commission and transposed it into national legislation. There are two reasons why regulatory authorities need to be independent from politics, both unique to Europe. The first and most obvious reason is because in Europe many operators, especially the infrastructure operators, are state-owned. Sometimes, they are not even unbundled. The second reason is the logical consequence of the EU approach: as we have seen, the ultimate goal of EU network industries' de- and re-regulation is political integration, in particular the creation of an EU-wide infrastructure in all the sectors as a means for Europe-nation-building as well as for building a single European infrastructure services market, also in all the sectors. Corresponding regulation is decided at the top, that is, in Brussels, and must be implemented – the technical word is "transposed" – by each member state. Regulatory authorities (in each member state) thus have the function to make sure that EU regulation is applied as originally designed. And this is why they have to be independent from (national) politics. Their independence from politics is thus the guarantee that a harmonized European infrastructure and a harmonized European infrastructure services market will prevail; in short, regulatory independence is a matter of credibility of the entire European approach to the network industries. And this is precisely why EU legislation in the matter of network industries does not only cover rules about how to regulate monopolies, access, interconnection, interoperability, congestion, system management and others, but also, and equally importantly, rules about regulatory authorities, in particular their independence, their powers, their resources and even their staffing.

But, sometimes, this is not sufficient. Indeed, over time, significant differences emerge among these national regulators: some grow rapidly, become very powerful and act independently, while others remain invisible and toothless. As a first step, therefore, the European Commission encourages regulators to self-organize along sectoral lines, so as to exchange experiences, harmonize their practices, the more advanced ones being encouraged to teach the less advanced ones. As a result, regulators' associations are formed; to my knowledge, this has occurred in all the infrastructure sectors.

But then the European Commission becomes frustrated with these associations of regulators, which are generally too slow and do not really have the powers to bring the laggards along. Thus, in a second step, the European Commission creates its own sector-specific European regulator in addition to the regulators' associations and the national regulators. Again, this has happened in all sectors except in the postal sectors. As this is an important step where power is removed from national regulators and given to European regulators, the

European Commission proceeds with caution, first transferring powers to the European regulators in the least controversial areas, such as safety and other technical issues. But gradually, and this is the third step, even some economic regulatory powers are transferred to these European regulators. At the very end of this process, the national regulators will be merely the executing agents of the European regulators, who in turn are the executing agents of the European Commission. Note that no equivalent evolution has occurred in the United States, where, because of the bottom-up approach, the few federal regulators that exist are not a substitute of the state regulators, but rather are competitors, thus adding to the already important institutional incoherence.

Conclusion: A Preliminary Assessment

Both, the US and the EU approaches, address the same issues: on a technological level it is the highly complex nature of these infrastructures, each having their own specific technologies. On an economic level, it is the monopolistic nature of mostly privately owned utilities in the US and the same monopolistic but rather state-owned infrastructure companies in Europe. Politically, it is the fact that the services provided by these monopolies have public interest or public service functions.

The US model of utilities regulation has a much longer history and is rooted in decentralized (state-level) regulatory commissions, stemming back to the 1920s; from there it has to work its way so-to-speak from the bottom up: federal regulators have to step in where infrastructures extend beyond state borders, as this is now typically the case in electricity and transport, where the entire US Northeast has grown into one single infrastructure system. It is also the case in the road, the rail, the air, the telecommunications and the postal sectors. The underlying reason is of course the fact that the US population has grown from 100 million in 1920 to 330 million in 2020, leading to urbanization and ensuing infrastructure developments and needs. The question is whether this US institutional approach to the regulation of an increasingly urbanized country is still up to the task, and whether a EU-type approach would not be more effective.

The situation is no different in Europe, where population has grown from about 250 million in 1920 and about 450 million in 2020. The European continent is much more densely populated and much more urbanized than the US, and has grown at least in the Western part of Europe into one single urban area reaching from the UK to Northern Italy, the so-called Liverpool–Milan corridor or "Blue Banana". Consequently, the need for a harmonized approach to infrastructure development, management and governance (including regulation) is much more pressing than in the US, even though the US Northeast is by now comparable to the blue banana when it comes to infrastructure challenges. In my view, the European approach to infrastructures must therefore not only be seen as a reaction vis-à-vis globalization and as an attempt towards Europe-building, but also as a logical response to addressing the infrastructure needs of "Metropolis-Europe". And as such, the EU top-down approach is without doubt more effective than the US bottom-up approach. And this precisely why other major emerging countries facing the same challenges of metropolitanization – for example China, India, Brazil, Turkey – are copying the European and not the American approach to governing their infrastructures.

CHALLENGES TO THE REGULATION OF THE INFRASTRUCTURE SECTORS

But the challenges to infrastructure development, management and governance do not stop at population growth, densification, urbanization and metropolitanization, a challenge that the US approach does not address. At least three new challenges have emerged since the European institutional approach to regulating infrastructures has emerged during the 1990s. These are recent technological developments, the challenge to decarbonize at least some of the infrastructures and, most recently, digitalization, all leading ultimately to various forms of infrastructure "convergence". Let me briefly explore, in this section, how each of these three developments challenge the institutional regulatory regime as it is currently becoming institutionalized in Europe and beyond.

Recent Technological Developments

Technological developments challenge the current European approach to regulatory governance in two important ways, namely in terms of vertical integration and in terms of sectoral boundaries. These technological developments in the different infrastructures are the direct result of the dynamics that has been created because of infrastructure liberalization in the first place. Indeed, unbundling and access to competition has triggered substantive technological innovation, precisely at the interface between the infrastructure monopoly and the competitors using this infrastructure. This is because unbundling has led to efficiency losses (as a result of vertical disintegration) and therefore engendered research and development efforts in the so-called "interface technologies", where efficiency and therefore commercial gains appeared to be most promising. Such interface technologies are, for example, smart meters offering a more efficient utilization of the existing infrastructure thanks to a better control over supply and demand in electricity. Similarly, ERTMS (the European Railway Traffic Management System) offers to more efficiently manage the interface between high-speed trains and the underlying rail infrastructure. Another such interface technological development are batteries, which, again, allow for a more efficient articulation of supply and demand on the one hand and grid availability on the other. Of course, these interface technologies could also have emerged in vertically integrated companies, but their unbundling, thanks to European legislation, has clearly triggered and accelerated the process.

As a matter of fact, the emergence of such interface technologies challenges the supposedly clear separation between monopolistic infrastructures on the one hand and competition on the basis of this monopolistic infrastructure on the other, a separation upon which an entire European regulatory apparatus, both in energy and transport has been built. While such interface technologies and ensuing vertical integration does not really challenge the sectoral approach to infrastructure regulation, and therefore not the existence of sector-specific regulatory authorities per se, it nevertheless significantly complexifies their tasks, thus leading to a danger of overregulation, especially in technological matters where innovation is key and most likely jeopardized by overregulation.

But there are of course many other technological developments that have been triggered by the liberalization of the infrastructures, in particular in the areas of automatization, decentralization and sectoral blurring. Many of these developments have furthermore been facilitated by digitalization and decarbonization policies (see below). For a start, automatization has triggered drones, self-driving cars and unmanned trains, but this is only the beginning. While sector-specific regulatory authorities are not challenged in their existence when it comes to regulating automatization in the network industries, their current regulatory tools must nevertheless be profoundly adapted to this new reality. Decentralization is another area where both the EU top-down regulatory approach and European and national regulators are challenged: for example, electricity is increasingly generated and consumed decentrally, leading to new local vertically integrated monopolies, for which the current regulatory framework is ill equipped. Similarly, decentralized technological solutions, such as in the case of city logistics or urban mobility hubs, trigger regulatory actions by equally decentralized public authorities, namely cities or metropolitan governments, thus bypassing existing regulatory authorities and undermining the current EU top-down regulatory approach. Still other technological developments, such as electric vehicles or combined heat and power technologies (CHP), blur the originally clear sectoral approach to regulation, thus either triggering conflicts between (energy and transport) regulators, or leaving these new activities unregulated. The question that arises here is whether such sectoral convergence between transport and energy for example, should not lead to more integrated regulators. But can the already highly institutionalized European regulatory approach be reformed so as to take into account all these technological developments, which, paradoxically, have been triggered by this very approach?

Decarbonization, Climate Change

The second big and perhaps even bigger challenge to EU regulatory governance are decarbonization policies and, more generally, public policies affecting the infrastructures, such as policies about security of supply, pollution, social justice, support to particular industries (be it for employment or strategic reasons), and others more. Indeed, the European approach to infrastructure regulation was built on the assumption that competition could dynamize the SOEs and create European infrastructure markets in the different sectors and by doing so further European political integration. Public policy objectives were not excluded nor neglected, but the idea was that they would be subsidiary and minor, and could be handled by way of precisely defined and sometimes remunerated public service contracts given to specific operators without distorting the different infrastructure markets. Newly emerging broad and fundamental public policy concerns, such as climate change or European energy independence or simply industrial policy objectives, challenge this very idea.

Let us take the example of climate change and corresponding decarbonization policies – to recall Europe aims to be carbon-neutral by 2050 – which affect both the energy and the transportation sectors. The massiveness and ambition of this general policy can no longer be handled sector by sector separately, where it was treated up to today as a (simple) problem of market distortion. To recall, mitigating market distortion was the traditional way by which sector-specific regulators, sometimes together with competition regulators, handled such public policy concerns in their respective sectors.

Let me take one example to illustrate this challenge: modal shift. If Europe is to totally decarbonize, it will not be sufficient to decarbonize each sector separately, something which the European Commission fully recognizes. Transport will have to be moved from the road to the already much more decarbonized, rail, as well as to more energy efficient public transport. Currently, each transport is regulated separately, each time by a separate regulatory authority. There is no such thing as a mobility or transport regulator (see: van Baal & Finger, forthcoming). While there are of course substantive efforts to internalize climate (and other) externalities, a coherent internalization of these externalities can only be achieved within a single regulatory framework and probably by a single integrated mobility regulator. Otherwise decarbonization will simply end up becoming a massive market distortion mitigation exercise, if not an open conflict between the different transport modes and their respective regulatory authorities.

Without an institutional reform of transport regulation and even more so of transport regulatory governance, modal shift as a core instrument for the decarbonization of transport will never happen. Or, the other way round, such a cross-cutting and massive public policy objective as is decarbonization has the potential to jeopardize the entire EU approach to governing and regulating the different network industries. Indeed, this is not just a challenge for the regulation of the transport sector, it is also a challenge for the energy sector, as electricity generation has to be equally decarbonized, thus leading to similar issues of market distortion and conflicts between sectoral policies and corresponding sectoral regulatory authorities.

Digitalization

Digitalization of the network industries poses a similar, if not more radical challenge to the current approach to regulating the network industries. Digitalization is a much more pervasive technological transformation, than are sector-specific technological innovations, such as drones or solar panels for that matter, both of which can still be handled by the existing regulatory approach and the existing sector-specific regulators.

For a start, digitalization leads to more efficient infrastructure operators and infrastructure sectors, as digitalization facilitates and smoothens the coordination of formerly inefficiently coordinated infrastructure assets. But this of course also favors vertical integration between the monopolistic infrastructure on the one hand and the services provided on the basis of this infrastructure on the other, thus going against one of the key pillars and regulatory instruments of EU sector-specific de- and re-regulation.

Preventing such digitally enabled vertical re-integration will only accelerate the entry of so-called digital platforms into the different network industries, even though such platforms will probably enter the infrastructure sectors anyway sooner or later. We already know how telecommunication services have been "platformed" by so-called Over-The-Top (OTT) platforms such as Skype, WhatsApp and others more (Montero & Finger, 2017). Similarly, we have already witnessed the platformization of the traditional media by GoogleAlerts and Facebook, for example. Similar platforms are currently entering the transport and the energy sectors, which will end up being platformed in the same way (Montero & Finger, forthcoming).

Such platformization of the traditional infrastructures challenges current regulatory governance in multiple ways. For a start, the current sector-specific regulatory framework and regulatory authorities are not equipped to deal with such out-of-industry digital platforms, which can be seen as a new (infrastructure) layer (layer 3), on top of the traditional monopolistic infrastructure (layer 1) and competitive network industry services layer (layer 2). As a result, the monopolistic – for example, "winner-takes-it-all" – nature of these platforms goes typically unaddressed until it is too late. And similarly, the two main consequences that these platforms have on the existing infrastructures has hardly been recognized by the different sector-specific regulators and even less so addressed.

The focus of the current regulatory framework and one of the main activities of infrastructure regulators pertains to access pricing. The goal here is to make sure that the users of the infrastructure remunerate the infrastructure in a balanced way, neither too much (avoiding monopoly rents), neither too little (avoiding underinvestments). Digital platforms, however, platformize both the monopolistic infrastructure and the providers of the services, meaning that the value-added occurs now in the platform and the profits are no longer reinvested into the network industries. This missing money problem will either lead to lower investments or require public subsidies. Regulators are powerless in light of this reality, as digital platforms are private and global and in any case are too powerful to be regulated at the national level.

Digital platforms not only platformize infrastructures and infrastructure services providers, they also put them into competition with one another, while at the same time not offering them a level playing field. On a mobility platform, for example, public transport now competes against taxis or even against Uber. At the same time, the platform decides, in the most untransparent way, which operator gets which treatment. This can be even better illustrated in the case of media platforms, such as GoogleAlerts, where the (Google) platform, that is, the underlying algorithm, decides which news from which newspaper is fed to which customer, not to speak about the fact that all the newspapers are now put into competition with one another for the attention of readers. Again, neither the currently existing regulatory framework, nor the existing regulatory authorities are equipped to deal with these challenges. As a matter of fact, it is not even clear whether sector-specific regulators should be addressing this issue, which is by nature cross-cutting, or whether there should be a new specific regulator regulating platforms in general.

CONCLUSION: PLATFORMS AS THE NEW NETWORK INDUSTRIES?

The above challenge points to a much more profound challenge caused by digitalization, namely the challenge of how to make public policy when algorithms controlled by global platforms decide which services users get (and at which price) and which infrastructure services provider gets to offer its services on the platform (and at which price). And this regardless of which public policy governments, or the EU for that matter, want to implement: competition, decarbonization, equity, safety, and so on. As we have seen all along this chapter, infrastructures are there to serve public policy objectives, originally nation-building, in the case of the EU Europe-building and increasingly also other much more pressing objectives such as decarbonization, poverty reduction and others more.

Network industry regulation and regulators EU-style were created so as to contribute to building a single European market in the different infrastructures separately; in the case of the US, the goal is much less ambitious, namely to prevent monopolies from abusing their power. Both objectives are of course still valid and therefore the current regulatory authorities still have a "raison d'être", but they are now permeated, if not overridden, by other, more urgent, public policy objectives. This leads to the question whether the current market-oriented regulatory governance approach is still valid or at least effective in order to also reach these other more pressing public policy objectives.

Also, digital platforms have now entered the infrastructures, leading to their platformization. Infrastructures are not replaced, rather they become commodities at the service of global platforms, commodities over which governments now lose control, yet have to pay for. How to regulate such platforms which are, in our mind (Montero & Finger, forthcoming), best conceptualize as yet a new, additional infrastructure layer (layer 3), which comes on top of the monopolistic infrastructure (roads, railtracks, electricity grids, etc.), but also on top of the infrastructure services typically provided on the basis of these monopolistic infrastructures (e.g., electricity, trains, public transport, water)? Clearly, the current sector-specific regulatory authorities are not equipped to take on this task; worse, thanks to the way they regulate today, they are probably actively helping the digital platforms to establish themselves ... as the new network industries.

NOTES

1. I use the word "infrastructure" as the overarching concept; the word "utilities" is used for local infrastructures, whereas the phrase "network industries" characterizes infrastructures once subjected to liberalization (e.g., infrastructure markets).
2. I am thankful to Prof. Janice Beecher, Director, Institute of Public Utilities Policy Research & Education (IPU), Michigan State University, for her profound insights into US-style utility regulation and regulators.

REFERENCES

Finger, M. (2020). *Network Industries. A Research Overview*. London: Routledge.
Finger, M. & C. Jaag (eds.) (2015). *The Routledge Companion on Network Industries*. London: Routledge.
Finger, M. & R. Künneke (eds.) (2011). *International Handbook of Network Industries. The Liberalization of Infrastructure*. Cheltenham, UK and Northampton, MA, USA: Edward Elgar Publishing.
Finger, M. & C. Rentsch (2015). Yes, no, maybe: the ambiguous relationship between state-owned enterprises and the state. *Annals of Public and Cooperative Economics*, Vol.86, No.4, pp. 617–640.
Majone, G. (1996). *Regulating Europe*. London: Routledge.
Montero, J. & M. Finger (2017). Platformed! Network industries and the new digital paradigm. *Competition and Regulation in Network Industries*, Vol.18, Nos.3&4, pp. 217–239.
Montero, J. & M. Finger (forthcoming). *The Rise of the New Network Industries: Regulating Digital Platforms*. London: Routledge.
van Baal, P. & M. Finger (forthcoming). Regulating the interdependencies of the mobility and electricity sectors. In: Probst, O., Castellanos, R. & Palacios, R. (eds.) *Transforming the Grid Towards Fully Renewable Energies*. London: Institute of Engineering and Technology, pp. 307–326.

11. Agencies regulating risks

Lorenzo Allio and Nicoletta Rangone[1]

INTRODUCTION

Each of us is exposed to multiple sources of risk, both individually and collectively. It is not realistic to expect that such risks be fully and permanently eliminated. Any mitigating intervention engenders positive as well as negative consequences. These three statements are logical but not often are they taken for granted. We are aiming at a "toxic-free environment" and seek a "zero-risk society". We expect our governments to master this ambition, while our levels of trust and confidence for government action are on the decline.

Yet, the gulf is widening between the sophistication of contemporary challenges and the ability of regulators to organise and deploy methodologies to handle that sophistication. "Getting the risk governance right" has become topical for today's government because of the salience of systemic problems and ambition of societal goals. COVID-19 crisis management and post-pandemic recovery; the Fourth Industrial Revolution; and the Agenda 2030 (and associated various "Green Deals" sustainable development objectives) – all these call on regulators to ensure that their risk management decisions maintain both high levels of protection and level-playing fields for innovation. Regulatory agencies must strike a balance between risk aversion and precaution on the one hand and framing acceptable (yet necessary) risk-taking in society on the other, and risk regulation features centrally in these dynamics (Allio, 2015).

This chapter briefly takes stock of the fundamentals of risk regulation literature and proposes six among the most topical themes that affect the future position of regulatory agencies. Such prospective themes are:

1. Risk regulation after COVID-19: Insights and lessons from a global crisis.
2. Reaping the potential of innovation: What is there for risk regulation?
3. The governance of risk regulation: What is at stake?
4. The essential input to effective risk regulation: Scientific integrity.
5. Risk regulation 2.0: The role of Big Data in risk management.
6. "Humanising" risk regulation: Leveraging behavioural research.

The conclusions present ideas on how to shape "Better Risk Regulation", which will allow governments to adequately address the challenges and meet the opportunities of contemporary society.

THE FUNDAMENTALS OF RISK REGULATION – A PRIMER

Conceptual Considerations

Broadly speaking, "risk" is defined as the uncertain (and negative) consequence of an event or activity on something to which we attribute value (for instance, our health or our savings).[2] Importantly, classic risk analysis differentiates between the intrinsic property of a substance, activity or process to cause harm or adverse effect – the *hazard*; and the combination of the likelihood and the severity of such a substance, activity or process to cause *harm* (UK Royal Society, 1992). A wild hungry lion constitutes a concrete danger for me in the savanna, but I am not exposed to any risk if the same lion (the hazard) is behind a glass wall in a zoo: I am not exposed to the risk. While the risk assessment phase should primarily be science-based, the management of risk typically pertains to the political domain, where the overall levels of acceptance and proportionality criteria are determined (OECD, 2010).

On the hazard-risk paradigm rest the three pillars of "classic" risk analysis, as consolidated in the authoritative US National Research Council "Red Book" (US NRC, 1983) – that is, *risk assessment* (which starts off by hazard characterisation and then appraises and quantifies doses, types and probabilities of exposure and their effects); *risk management* (which subsequently conducts ancillary risk–risk trade-offs, cost-effectiveness and cost–benefit analyses on options to accept, avoid, reduce or transfer the risk); and *risk communication* (which ensures an informed dialogue among experts, regulators and the public).

The conceptualisation of what constitutes a risk is nonetheless neither mechanistic nor static. Moving away from a rationalistic, scientific perspective to risk, strands of literature have framed risk as a social construct resulting from our collective individual values, beliefs and competing narratives and knowledge (Beck, 1999; Jasanoff, 2004), as well as from heuristics and bias (Tversky / Kahneman, 1974; 1983). Being context-specific by definition, it is argued, risk cannot be demonstrated (and hence managed) scientifically. This is the basis of the post-modernist approach to risk analysis (Foucault, 1982; Douglas / Wildavsky, 1982; Funtowicz / Ravetz, 1995). Arguably, this approach blurs the conceptual and consequently also the organisational divides between risk assessment and management – see Demortain (2020) for a comprehensive review of the "Red Book" conceptualisation, its application to administrative governance models and the controversies embedding regulatory agencies.

The Public Management of Risk

Public decision makers cannot be arbitrary nor capricious. A number of core good governance principles appear thus critical for the correct and legitimate unfolding of the assessment, management, and communication phases. Data collection, appraisals and decision-making processes must be transparent, and the system must be supported by arrangements for enforcing and scrutinising quality standards, while checks and balances mechanisms ensure accountability and redress. Participatory channels must be in place to not only enrich the evidence underpinning decisions but also to facilitate compliance and strengthen legitimacy and trust in public action. Ongoing updates to reflect progress in scientific knowledge and post-implementation reviews are also integral parts of good risk governance, for they contribute to keep risk management decisions fit-for-purpose.

From the mid-twentieth century onwards, governments have largely built their risk regulatory systems to reflect this design, thereby accompanying and further contributing to the emergence of a "regulatory State" (Majone, 1994). Societal policy goals are pursued through extensive primary legislation that is implemented by complex regulatory and administrative processes (Fisher, 2010).

From a macro-perspective, risk is a major organising factor for national polities to determine governance choices and trends in the strategies for evaluating and responding to negative outcomes. In France and Germany specifically and unlike the United Kingdom, for instance, the acceptance of possible adverse outcomes is shaped by the constitutional philosophies and the role attributed to the State to provide *security* to *all* citizens and to work for the general good (Rothstein et al., 2013). This may help interpret shifts from responsive, evidence-based risk management to more pro-active and preventive approaches (Ansell / Baur, 2018). On continental Europe at least, a hazard-based, precautionary regulatory paradigm has taken root that stretches the idea that technologies should be prohibited unless proven *safe* to the one that they should prohibit, unless proven essential and *necessary* (Garnett / van Calster, 2021; Monfort, 2021).

Institutionally, there is allegedly a tension between de-centring risk regulation across sectoral agencies by also involving private actors on the one hand and elevating it to a governing meta-concept on the other. Risk plays different roles. Regulators typically act on addressing potential harm to society but are also subject to the risk of failing to do so. Ensuring the agency's effectiveness and efficiency is at the basis of the modern, tailored, and targeted approach to inspecting and enforcing actual and potential risks. Risk is therefore the *object* of regulatory agencies but also their *organisational and procedural* pivotal element, serving as the source of *accountability* and *legitimacy* (Black, 2007; Baldwin / Black, 2016).

SHADING LIGHT TO AN ADAPTIVE AGENDA

Against this backdrop, this section proposes some consideration on areas where regulatory agencies might need re-calibrate their role, organisation, and function.

Risk Regulation after COVID-19: Insights and Lessons from a Global Crisis

It is not uncommon to hear that there will be a pre- and a post-coronavirus world.[3] Risk regulators have been in the eye of this systemic storm but can also benefit greatly from the lessons from the crisis. Not only have decision-makers been caught by surprise by an essentially foreseeable threat (Alemanno, 2020; Bar-Siman-Tov, 2020).[4] They then also failed to organise the involvement and contribution of the risk and behavioural science community, giving rise to superficial risk–benefit considerations – if at all (Chakraborty 2020). Reaction to the pandemic took the form of command-and-control regulations (such as lock-downs, quarantine, physical distancing, or mask-wearing obligations); more cognitive-based approaches (e.g., recommendations and visual messages); and forms of "RegTech" (e.g., apps that provide information on physical distancing in public transport). While working on multiple fronts through policy mixes reflects good practice, coordination was not ensured (Coglianese / Mahboubi, 2021).

Admittedly, the task is herculean and no universally accepted methodology for the evaluation of the impacts from pandemics is used (Madhav et al., 2017). The COVID-19 crisis epitomised situations where knowledge is fast evolving; evidence is preliminary and limited; harm is severe, and risks are systemic. Global inter-connectedness has worked as a multiplying factor. Exactly under such conditions, recourse to science-based approaches and trust in science are key (Aksoy et al., 2020; Aven / Bouder, 2020; OECD, 2020a). The pandemic made "risk–risk trade-offs" (Graham / Wiener, 1995; Wiener, 2002) become visible to the public for what they are: pervasive and ubiquitous. Let us just consider the choice between imposing stringent lock-downs to avoid infections and the increase in other risks due to foregone medical treatments, inequalities in home-schooling, or longer-term social costs because of the economic crisis. Related to that, the pandemic has also re-opened the debate about the appropriateness and reliability of epidemiological modelling and cost–benefit analysis applied to risk regulation.[5] Continuously evolving knowledge has proved the ineffectiveness of initial measures, such as Plexiglas separations requirements which do not protect from aerosol, or regular surface disinfection obligations in the light of unlikely surface contact transmission. This reaffirms the central role of careful post-implementation reviews, especially for "emergency" regulations adopted through a fast-track procedure (OECD, 2020b).

The pandemic also highlighted the effects of regulatory and administrative rigidity. The swift placing on the market of vaccines strikes with the normally lengthy approval procedures (DiMasi et al., 2016). Cumbersome authorisation procedures for laboratories have delayed the deployment of adequate capacities for testing in France and Italy, for instance. The rigid European biocide regulation, to take another example, has made it more difficult to produce hand disinfectants (Blanc et al., 2020). Emergency ("fast-track") procedures and derogations have been introduced in most countries to allow governments to face the crisis. While this has allowed more agile contingent responses, more fundamentally it questions the boundaries of discretionary powers exercised by the executive in modern decision-making – including through delegated, administrative action (Meads / Allio, 2019). An important lesson from the pandemic is, therefore, certainly the necessity for government to temporarily revert to extraordinary procedures or derogations in exceptional and crisis conditions – but to do so with a strong attention to ensure coordination and cohesiveness among all regulatory and communication actors and across all levels of government (Rangone, 2020). As soon as the emergency regime comes to an end, the risk regulatory frameworks will have to be made more resilient and embedded principles of good regulation and administration as well as checks and balances to enforce them systemically.

The pandemic has also shown how inter-connected today's economies and societies are. Product and supply chains are intricated and spread across continents (OECD, 2020c). COVID-19 contagions were exacerbated also by blockages that stopped the supply of protective clothing and face masks, 80% of which are manufactured in China. Risk regulators must account for the need to more resilience in the future – not only in crises but when designing policies (OECD, 2021). As an example, the EU Chemicals Sustainability Strategy,[6] which is grounded on the doctrine of a "toxic-free environment", seems to clash with the need for Europe to ensure supply security of critical raw materials, metals, and chemicals (EC, 2019; 2020a; ESIR Group, 2020).

The COVID-19 crisis has put risk regulators – and governments in general – at a crossroads on these and several other issues. The next sections of the chapter are an attempt at mapping the most prominent areas for consideration.

Reaping the Potential of Innovation: What is there for Risk Regulation?

Innovation is the single most important driver in mature economies to ensuring prosperity. The economic[7] notion of innovation typically refers to the creation, introduction, and provision of new or enhanced technologies, operating methods and processes, products (goods and services), or new business models altogether, that innovators make available to economic operators and consumers.

Risk regulation closely relates to innovation because the latter is the result of entrepreneurship and risk-taking. Innovation flourishes when societies create conditions in which investors and entrepreneurs are encouraged to take risks. The main task for governments is therefore to stimulate innovation by regulating the risk–reward nexus. In financial terms, this refers to setting the adequate risk-adjusted return on investment; in societal terms it is about balancing out the socialisation of risks (or the distribution of externality costs) and the privatisation of profits.

Governments can take an "entrepreneurial" stance and shape their research and industrial policies to directly influence innovation (Bonvillian / Van Atta, 2011; Mazzucato, 2014);[8] or they can facilitate networking and serve as a catalyst of dynamic comparative advantage and institution builder, leveraging enabling framework conditions for innovation such as access to risk capital and availability of critical infrastructure (Porter, 1990; Ambec, 2011).

Regulatory frameworks count among such conditions, but claiming that regulation stimulates or stifles innovation a priori is misleading. By altering the incentives of economic operators, consumers and citizens, individual regulatory measures trigger various types of impacts. One key step in determining whether and how regulation is affecting innovation is thus to get the full "intervention logic" right. This is an empirical, case-by-case exercise, typically carried out in Regulatory Impact Analyses, and depends on the balance between "innovation-inducing" and "innovation-constraining" factors (Blind, 2012). Besides appraising benefits from reduced exposure to harm, therefore, regulating risk also implies understanding how the regulatory measure alters the attractiveness of engaging in R&D for innovation (Steward, 2010). Risk regulatory agencies rarely possess guidance and expertise to investigate these dynamics.

The Governance of Risk Regulation: What is at Stake?

Regulatory agencies face three pressing *governance* challenges. They pertain to managing innovation; to organising scientific advice and risk communication; and to mitigating institutional fragmentation.

Digitalisation poses a series of challenges to risk regulators (OECD, 2019) in as much as they are confronted with *pacing* and *disruption* problems. The sheer pace of technological changes and the blurring of usual markets and sectors (e.g., by platform technologies) make the regulatory and social structures governing innovation rapidly obsolete. Traditional *enforcement* mechanisms are challenged because of the reconsideration of liability on the one hand, and of territorial jurisdiction on the other. Technologies such as 3D-printing or driverless vehicles are points in case. Similarly, the obligation to preserve freedom of speech against abuses requires a new conceptualisation of social media. There is, moreover, a *normative* problem: appraising a priori the social desirability of innovation is a key yet very challenging step that each society must learn to make (or accept not to make). While some innovations are obviously "good" (e.g., penicillin) and others manifestly "bad" (such as nerve gas), most technologies are ambiguous, and the focus should be on their applications. "Responsible Research and Innovation" (RRI)[9] and the concept of "essential use" (Garnett / van Calster, 2021) seek to steer narratives and investments towards certain technologies or innovations rather than others, on the basis also of ethical and normative considerations. The capacity of such approaches to anticipate possible future technological developments and exclude others has not been tested, yet. Deliberations in this regard must rest on participatory and weight-of-evidence inputs from the public and the experts to be legitimate (Mulgan, 2016; von Schomberg, 2019; Wittrock et al., 2021).

A second set of challenges posed to risk governance refers to shaping and credibly informing decision-makers and the public through institutionalised scientific advice. The effectiveness and relevance of scientific advice to policy-making rests on several pre-conditions – the expertise and credibility of the advisers themselves; the capacity to consolidate and convey multi-disciplinary perspectives on reality; and the ability to get scientific evidence across to different audiences (Wilsdon / Doubleday, 2015; CSA-SAM, 2019). Again, the COVID-19 crisis has catalysed those key features. Social distancing measures, for instance, are central to counter the spread of the virus and the socio-economic consequences of such measures are complex and long lasting. For this reason, multi-disciplinarity in scientific advice is required not only from the biological, epidemiological, and medical fields but also from the social, economic, and behavioural sciences to consider moral acceptability, ethics, socio-psychological impact, culture, and communication. Scientific advice depends on the trust among all the actors involved. This is particularly important when it comes to establishing authoritative, trustworthy courses of action in (crisis) risk management as well as when facing fake news, manipulation, and capture. Social media can act as spring-boards and multipliers of activist science or "post-normal" relativism. It is the task of scientific advisors to resist such misinformation and champion science within the decision-making process (Šucha / Sienkiewicz, 2020).

The two sets of challenges mentioned above confirm the need to address the fragmentation of risk regulators in contemporary government. Analyses have shown that countervailing risks and regulatory failures are far less the "fault" or malpractice of negligent regulators than the result of siloed organisational design and uncoordinated mandates and incentive schemes. The proliferation of multiple autonomous, specialised sectoral risk agencies has hindered the flow of information and led to regulating each individual risk in isolation at the cost of a more synergetic approach (Wiener, 1998; Vecchione, 2017). The mismatch between the transboundary nature of emerging technologies such as digitalisation or the spread of a virus on the one hand, and the fragmentation of regulatory frameworks across jurisdictions on the other undermines the effectiveness of action, increase systemic risks, and therefore potentially also people's trust in government.

The Essential Input to Effective Risk Regulation: Scientific Integrity

Unlike scientific advice, *regulatory science* refers to the knowledge used to assess the safety (and sometimes the quality and efficacy as well) of regulated products. We distinguish, therefore, between "scientific experts" and "science advisors". While the first provide evidence, the latter mediate between the processes designed to generate scientific evidence, the politicians and regulators, and the public.

To credibly guide risk management, regulatory science must meet two criteria – it must be both *excellent* and *impartial* (OECD, 2010). Governments are responsible for setting out quality and integrity criteria for regulatory science, and developing structures, processes, and policies for ensuring that the best available science guides and informs risk management decision-making. It is not about the production of scientific knowledge. The design, organisation, management, and execution of scientific *research* has indeed received extensive attention. Several principles and codes of conduct for "research integrity" have been developed and are now embraced by scientific academies, government institutes and private researchers worldwide. Eminent scientific journals have also drawn up policies to timely detect and manage "questionable research practices".[10]

When it comes to ensuring that the best available science is used in public decision-making, however, risk regulators are yet to formalise dedicated organisational and procedural arrangements. While the imperative for scientific excellence is largely unchallenged in principle, practice has often deviated from it. Uniform, government-wide guidance, and instruments are seldom available, embedded or systematically applied in risk assessment agencies. Only a relatively small number of governments have set up equivalent systemic mechanisms, mostly Anglo-Saxon countries.[11] Similarly, steps undertaken by government to test the impartiality of regulatory science have traditionally focused on identifying and addressing material factors such as financial linkages of scientists and experts to the private sector. International research nonetheless indicates that conflict of interests may be based also on personal factors (such as academic or professional ambitions and family relationships) as well as on values, for instance beliefs, ideals, ideologies, or political affiliations (US NASEM, 2003; Young, 2009; Moore et al., 2010; KNAW et al., 2017). These latter sources of bias are at least as pernicious to the excellence and impartiality of scientific expertise as the challenges posed by material conflicts. Adequately managing conflict of interests through tiered approaches, openness and independent systematic peer-review processes can help retain high-quality expertise.

Oftentimes, therefore, tensions arise between regulators, policy-makers and the public about the trustworthiness of regulatory action. An example is the call for a clarification between political agendas and regulatory science governance launched by the Executive Director of the European Food Safety Authority in the glyphosate dossier (Url, 2018).[12] The situation is not unique to specific industrial sectors (in that case: crop-protection products), nor to the EU, as the "Appeal" subscribed by dozens of leading scientists testifies (Gori, 2016; Ashner et al., 2016). Contributions to the various scientific disciplines can help improve risk regulation frameworks across agencies. The natural sciences have elaborated codified principles of toxicology and epidemiology, which explicitly rest on the *scientific method* (Berry, 2020), but there is a lively debate within the social sciences as well on how to ensure greater replicability and impact of those studies (Freese / Peterson, 2017; Camerer et al., 2018; Charnley et al., 2017; Smith et al., 2019). Boosting the robustness of also social science studies is fundamental especially in the light of the current positive efforts at integrating foresight and technology assessments into the Better Regulation agenda of governments.[13] From a risk regulatory perspective, the contribution of social sciences is critical to better characterise, organise and represent the complexity of human and collective behaviour – be it in the form of perception, beliefs, or communication (Wendling, 2012; Borraz / Vergriette, 2014).

Risk Regulation 2.0: Governing Algorithmic Risk Management

Big Data is here to stay – and it affects decision-making. Computational science, machine learning and artificial intelligence are increasingly deployed to perform regulatory, adjudication and enforcement tasks.[14] So-called "algorithmic risk assessment" allows processing of potentially immense and diversified datasets at super-human speed and make highly accurate predictions. Such *algorithmic governance* is emerging in different fields – from environmental protection, social welfare, food safety, to taxation. Data-driven approaches have the potential to better monitor and anticipate problems; perfect and mainstream risk-based methods for enforcement and inspections (thereby reducing regulatory burdens); and reduce information asymmetries between consumers and service providers (thereby creating incentives to steer markets in specific directions more effectively) (Houser / Sanders, 2017).

Sensitive issues nonetheless persist. Because of the sheer volume of datasets available and the velocity of processing them, for instance, computers will almost certainly identify data patterns and correlations that may however remain spurious. In the case of biometric and health data, this may possibly lead to addressing hypothetical risks; unduly amplifying risk across society; and skewing risk communication (Lee / Yee, 2020). The governance of privacy is a further issue, as algorithmic decision-making may inadequately protect (or fully disregard) the consent by third parties to use personal data. Algorithmic decision-making risks might also be biased against vulnerable groups, by amplifying bias which could affect human decisions (Kleinberg et al., 2018; Mayson, 2019) and organised parties may moreover use information to capture the system or escape control (Bambauer / Rogers, 2018). Judicial review might also be jeopardised (Selbst / Barocas, 2018). This is why it may be opportune to strengthen the transparency principle by requiring "explainability" of machine learning algorithms so as to allow people to understand how and why a decision has been taken (Finck, 2020; Yeung, 2019). Ultimate human oversight should moreover avoid that regulatory or administrative decisions be grounded exclusively on automated processes and techniques.[15] However, both transparency and the "human in the loop" approach might be undermined due to the self-learning capability of some applications, as well as by automation bias that can lead individuals to over-relying on the output of the algorithm or by its opposite, the "algorithm aversion" bias (Dietvorst et al., 2015).

Big Data management furthermore exasperates the proliferation and fragmentation of regulatory agencies highlighted above. The need to "make sense" of disparate data sources and deploy several disciplines to interpret and act on data-driven information calls for a coherent and cohesive approach to risk regulation, which may be jeopardised by siloed policy portfolios, administrative mandates, and organisational arrangements of the individual regulators (Lewallen, 2020). Last but not least, storing and processing Big Data comes at significant environmental costs, with the current environmental footprint of the ICT sector being estimated at more than 2% of all global emissions (EC, 2020b).

In the light of these trade-offs, therefore, the distinctive feature for risk regulators to operate in the algorithmic era is not about replacing human judgment with artificial machine learning, but about incorporating and calibrating fundamentally similar (albeit more accurate and often practically more useful) processes of decision-making, as well as adhering to procedural safeguards (Citron, 2008). The imperative to meaningfully weigh the pros and cons of risk regulation decisions is arguably more important than ever.

"Humanising" Risk Regulation: Leveraging Behavioural Research

This last section of the chapter shifts the attention onto the human – not the artificial – element of risk regulation, namely the irrational and biased nature of the individual and society. Regulators must take account of that when addressing and managing risks. Established literature has proven the existence of several common heuristics and biases that play a crucial role in *risk perception*. For instance, people tend to think that an event is more likely to occur if they recall personal experiences related to it, and risks with more emotional impact are perceived as being greater. By the same token, people may lull into complacency when facing certain risks that are however not easily accessible or seem invisible. Moreover, "self-serving" and "attribution" biases lead people to systematically misinterpret data when they have some emotional stake in the outcome.[16] In addition, exponential grow bias (i.e. a lack of appreciation of risks that grow exponentially) might have led some policy-makers to postpone the legal response to the COVID-19 pandemic (Zamir / Teichman, 2021). These cognitive reactions contribute to explaining divergent risk management patterns undertaken by different countries when facing equivalent risks. The way we perceive risk and become used (indifferent) to communication must be central in risk management considerations, especially in situations of prolonged extreme uncertainty, as during the COVID-19 crisis (Chater, 2020).

Socio-psychological insights help shifting preferences and behaviours, notably by modifying the "choice architecture" – for instance, colourful alcohol-based hand sanitisers standing directly in front of doors and centrally in public areas have facilitated COVID-19 preventative measures (Lunn et al., 2020; Sunstein, 2020). These measures might be supported by checklists and images which, leveraging on the same socio-psychological insights, summarise what should be done to protect oneself and others from the disease and routinise (new) behaviours (BIT, 2020). Physical distancing might also be incentivised by forms of "RegTech", such as apps which provide information elaborated by algorithms and framed so as to make things easily approachable – for instance hinting to whether a bus or a train is full or how crowded an area is likely to be.[17]

Cognitive-based measures may also make regulation more effective by leveraging on bias (*nudging*) or helping people overcome them (*cognitive empowerment*). Cognitive-based experiments for regulation might detect the individual's limited ability to evaluate risk and probability and mis-informed decisions. When it comes to enforcement, cognitive insights can help plan more effective controls (Rangone, 2018).

CONCLUSIONS: TOWARDS "BETTER RISK REGULATION" – A HOLISTIC VISION

In the light of the diverse and dynamic nature of risk, regulatory frameworks must be shaped and run comprehensively, and agencies regulating risks feature centrally in such governance. The existence of multiple ancillary impacts and countervailing risks is a constant feature of modern government. In an extremely globalised world, the pace of technological and societal changes has skyrocketed. Regulation can no longer be conceived to be static, but truly needs to be adaptive, agile, and responsive.

No matter what tool and practice agencies introduce to deliver future-proofed risk regulation, efforts will be limited if such steps are taken in isolation, if the tools are run independently and do not fit within a more strategic, comprehensive approach to reform; and if public action is hampered by sclerotic, siloed organisational structures. A *Better Risk Regulation* for the twenty-first century requires the design of a cohesive *ecology of procedures and tools* that are conducive to the sustainable and sustained protection of health and the environment.

Agencies regulating risks are not only called upon to react to fast evolving contexts. They must also take on a more assertive role as champion and drivers for reform. The journey is not downhill, but they are not starting from scratch. Several decades of regulatory design and implementation form a robust basis upon which to share and integrate experiences. Experimenting can maximise learning, but predictability must be guaranteed. In its tragedy, the COVID-19 crisis has brought about a renewed attention to trustworthy scientific expertise and its importance to support our well-being. The pandemic has shown how risks are inter-connected and the value of – and need for – innovation as well as scientific and medical progress to preserve health security and high living standards.

It is on this basis that regulators should work, embracing a "holistic vision" of Better Risk Regulation and working on three levels of the decision-making cycle – before, during and after a decision is taken. *Upstream*, informed dialogue and participation should be enhanced within society. Innovation must be embraced, but not a-critically. Innovation means change, and with change comes risk. Not all innovation is acceptable and accepted. It is not enough to have the public opinion trust new technologies such as 5G or new genomic engineering. The public must trust the governance that manages the risk associated with those innovations and redistributes the resulting benefits. Governments earn that trust by establishing credible foresight practices and engaging with the public early in the process; by setting clear criteria for the evidence and expertise they use to underpin their decisions; and by then creating the favourable conditions to incentivise investors to create value in support of societal goals.

Better Risk Regulation should then be at work also *throughout* the legislative and regulatory process. Future-proofing decision-making means focusing on performance and outcomes; remaining technologically neutral; and maximising societal well-being. Experimentation and co-creation help as much as a deeper understanding of unintended consequences (risk–risk trade-offs) and dynamic regulatory impacts.

Finally, the *downstream* phase is also crucial, as regulatory impacts are increasingly generated by the way laws are implemented and enforced. Risk regulators play an important role in the extent to which risk management decisions are accepted and complied with. They can use innovative tools that exploit real-time data generation and analysis and tailor enforcement mechanisms, for instance by following risk-based approaches and by creating user-friendly, "advice-first" principles to inspections. Agencies can also make better and more systemic use of *ex post* evaluations, for instance crafting strategic evaluations so as to draw "horizontal" lessons that help officials understand the wider impacts of regulation on society and on innovation eco-systems.

NOTES

1.   The author acknowledges the support of the EC Erasmus + Programme for the production of this publication. However, such support does not constitute an endorsement of the contents which reflects the views of the author only, and the European Commission cannot be held responsible for any use which may be made of the information contained therein.

2. Several definitions of risk exist in accordance with the domain and discipline it refers to – financial economics, geology, epidemiology, etc. – which we cannot further investigate in this chapter.

3. https://www.weforum.org/agenda/archive/the-great-reset.

4. To compare, South Korea arguably stands up as an example of crisis preparedness (Moon, 2020).

5. On the economic analysis of regulation (including the use of Value of Statistical Life techniques) to underpin COVID-19 responses, see sources at https://www.benefitcostanalysis.org/covid -19_benefit_cost_analysis.php and https://www.theregreview.org/tag/value-of-a-statistical-life/.

6. See https://ec.europa.eu/commission/presscorner/detail/en/ip_20_1839.

7. Social innovation, instead, places emphasis on the social processes of innovation (besides its outcomes) – for example open-source methods and co-creation approaches – to make progress in areas such as working conditions, education, community development or health. Examples of social innovations include virtual volunteering, microcredit, or distance learning (Moulaert et al., 2013). However, differentiating between the types of innovation does not mean to antagonise them (WEF, 2016).

8. This understanding of the role of the State has influenced for instance the design of the EU research policy under the Horizon Europe, the EU's framework financing programme for R&I. The programme includes "missions" that are meant to mobilise resources around a targeted pressing challenge in our society. For a critique to the entrepreneurial State concept, see Mingardi (2015).

9. RRI is an approach that anticipates and assesses potential implications and societal expectations with regard to research and innovation, with the aim to foster the design of inclusive and sustainable research and innovation.

10. See for instance OECD (2009); ALLEA (2017); US NASEM (2017); and Nature (2013).

11. For an analysis of the EU institutions, see Meads / Allio (2016).

12. On the systemic issues triggered by the re-authorisation process at the EU level of glyphosate, see the Symposium on the Science and Politics of Glyphosate, *European Journal of Risk Regulation*, 11 (3) (2020), at https://www.cambridge.org/core/journals/european-journal-of-risk-regulation/issue/ 9B32A1834829BB49EBB15DAD77458278.

13. For example, see the profiled role played by foresight in the European Commission (EC, 2020, and https://ec.europa.eu/knowledge4policy/foresight_en) and the "horizon scanning" activities in the UK Government (https://www.gov.uk/government/groups/futures-and-foresight).

14. On these various activities by risk regulators, see for instance Coglianese / Lehr (2017); Pijnenburg et at. (2017); Veale / Brass (2019); Engstrom et al. (2020).

15. The latter are prohibited in European countries under the EU GDPR Regulation and by the proposed European regulation on artificial intelligence for high-risk AI.

16. A quick review of relevant contributions includes Tversky / Kahneman (1974; 1983); Finucane et al. (2000); Sunstein (2002); Pachur et al. (2012); Keller et al. (2006).

17. The apps might also allow users to rate businesses based on how much they respect the rules on mask use, for instance, or social distancing. The "wisdom of the crowd" could thereby be leveraged to identify the safest businesses and at the same time increase compliance to safe norms (Ayres et al., 2020).

REFERENCES

Aksoy, C.G. et al. (2020), *Revenge of the Experts: Will COVID-19 Renew or Diminish Public Trust in Science?*, LSE Systemic Risk Centre, at https://www.systemicrisk.ac.uk/publications/discussion -papers/revenge-experts-will-covid-19-renew-or-diminish-public-trust-science.

Alemanno, A. (2020), "Taming COVID-19 by regulation: an opportunity for self-reflection", *European Journal of Risk Regulation*, 11 (2), at https://doi.org/10.1017/err.2020.43.

All European Academies (ALLEA) (2017), *The European Code of Conduct for Research Integrity. Revised Edition*, at https://ec.europa.eu/research/participants/data/ref/h2020/other/hi/h2020 -ethics_code-of-conduct_en.pdf

Allio, L. (ed.) (2015), *Improving Risk Regulation*, EPFL-IRGC, at https://irgc.org/risk-governance/risk -regulation/improving-risk-regulation/.

Ambec, S. et al. (2011), *The Porter Hypothesis at 20: Can Environmental Regulation Enhance Innovation and Competitiveness?*, at http://www.rff.org/rff/documents/rff-dp-11-01.pdf.

Ansell, C. and P. Baur (2018), "Explaining trends in risk governance: how problem definitions underpin risk regimes", *Risk, Hazards and Crisis in Public Policy*, 9(5), at https://onlinelibrary.wiley.com/doi/abs/10.1002/rhc3.12153.

Ashner, M. et al. (2016), "Upholding science in health, safety and environmental risk assessments and regulations", *Toxicology*, 371, at https://doi.org/10.1016/j.tox.2016.09.005.

Aven, T. and F. Bouder (2020), "The COVID-19 pandemic: how can risk science help?", *Journal of Risk Research*, at https://www.tandfonline.com/doi/full/10.1080/13669877.2020.1756383.

Ayres, I. et al. (2020), "How to make COVID-19 contact tracing apps work: insights from behavioral economics", in *COVID-19 SARS-CoV-2 preprints from medRxiv and bioRxiv*, at https://www.medrxiv.org/content/10.1101/2020.09.09.20191320v1.

Baldwin, R. and J. Black (2016), "Driving priorities in risk-based regulation: what's the problem?", *Journal of Law and Society*, 43 (4), at https://doi.org/10.1111/jols.12003.

Bambauer, J. and J.E. Rogers (2018), "The algorithm game", *Notre Dame Law Review*, 94 (1), at https://scholarship.law.nd.edu/ndlr/vol94/iss1/1/.

Bar-Siman-Tov, I. (2020), "Covid-19 meets politics: the novel coronavirus as novel challenge for legislatures", *The Theory and Practice of Legislation*, 8 (1–2), at https://doi.org/10.1080/20508840.2020.1800250.

Beck, U. (1999), *World Risk Society*, Polity Press.

Behavioural Insight Team and UK Cabinet Office (BIT) (2020), *Testing the efficacy of coronavirus messaging experiment: 'How to wash your hands'*, at https://www.bi.team/blogs/bright-infographics-and-minimal-text-make-handwashing-posters-most-effective/.

Berry, C. (2020), "Frameworks for evaluation and integration of data in regulatory evaluations: the need for excellence in regulatory toxicology", *Toxicology Research and Application*, 4, at https://journals.sagepub.com/doi/full/10.1177/2397847320951377.

Black, J. (2007), "Tensions in the regulatory state", *Public Law*, Spring, at http://eprints.lse.ac.uk/23107.

Blanc, F. et al. (2020), Decisioni politiche, regolamentazione e attuazione della normativa in tempi di crisi. Cosa (in caso ci sia qualcosa) può essere appreso dalle risposte emerse durante i primi mesi del COVID-19?, Osservatorio AIR, at https://www.osservatorioair.it/decisioni-politiche-regolamentazione-e-attuazione-della-normativa-in-tempi-di-crisi-cosa-in-caso-ci-sia-qualcosa-puo-essere-appreso-dalle-risposte-emerse-durante-i-primi-mesi-del-covid-19/.

Blind, K. (2012), *The Impact of Regulation on Innovation*, NESTA, at https://media.nesta.org.uk/documents/the_impact_of_regulation_on_innovation.pdf.

Bonvillian, W.B. and R.B. Van Atta (2011), "ARPA-E and DARPA: applying the DARPA model to energy innovation", *Journal of Technology Transfer*, 36, art, 469 at https://link.springer.com/article/10.1007/s10961-011-9223-x

Borraz, O., and B. Vergriette (2014), "Opening Editorial. Symposium on the use of social sciences in risk assessment and risk management organisations in Europe and North America", *European Journal of Risk Regulation*, 5 (1), at https://www.cambridge.org/core/journals/european-journal-of-risk-regulation/article/opening-editorial/7043609602E1FB15B5A0BD6146653359.

Camerer C.F. et al. (2018), "Evaluating the replicability of social science experiments in nature and science between 2010 and 2015", *Nature Human Behaviour*, 2 (9), at https://www.nature.com/articles/s41562-018-0399-z.

Chakraborty, S. (2020), "How risk perceptions, not evidence, have driven harmful policies on COVID-19", *European Journal of Risk Regulation*, 11 (2), at https://doi.org/10.1017/err.2020.37.

Charnley, S. et al. (2017), "Evaluating the best available social science for natural resource management decision-making", *Environmental Science and Policy*, 73, at http://dx.doi.org/10.1016/j.envsci.2017.04.002.

Chater, N. (2020), "Facing up to the uncertainties of COVID-19", *Nature Human Behaviour*, 4, at https://www.nature.com/articles/s41562-020-0865-2.

Chief Scientific Advisors – SAM (2019), Scientific Advice to European Policy in a Complex World, European Commission, at https://op.europa.eu/en/publication-detail/-/publication/86c7c378-f553-11e9-8c1f-01aa75ed71a1.

Citron, D.K. (2008), "Technological due process", *Washington University Law Review*, 85 (6).

Coglianese, C. and D. Lehr (2017), "Regulating by robot", *The Georgetown Law Journal*, 105, at https:// scholarship.law.upenn.edu/faculty_scholarship/1734/.

Coglianese C. and N.A. Mahboubi (2021), "Administrative law in a time of crisis: comparing national responses to COVID-19", *Administrative Law Review*, 73 (1), at https://scholarship.law.upenn.edu/ faculty_scholarship/2300/.

Demortain, D. (2020), *The Science of Bureaucracy: Risk Decision-Making and the US Environmental Protection Agency*, The MIT Press, at https://doi.org/10.7551/mitpress/12248.001.0001.

Dietvorst, B.J., J.P. Simmons and C. Massey (2015), "Algorithm aversion: people erroneously avoid algorithms after seeing them err", *Journal of Experimental Psychology: General*, 144 (1), at https:// psycnet.apa.org/record/2014-48748-001.https://psycnet.apa.org/record/2014-48748-001.

DiMasi, J.A. et al. (2016), "Innovation in the pharmaceutical industry: new estimates of R&D costs", *Journal of Health Economics*, 47, at https://doi.org/10.1016/j.jhealeco.2016.01.012.

Douglas, M. and A. Wildavsky (1982), *Risk and Culture*, University of California Press.

Economic and Societal Impact of Research and Innovation (ESIR) Group (2020), *Protect, prepare and transform Europe: Recovery and resilience post COVID-19*, European Commission, at https:// ec.europa.eu/info/publications/protect-prepare-and-transform-europe-recovery-and-resilience-post -covid-19_en.

Engstrom, D.F. et al. (2020), *Government by Algorithm: Artificial Intelligence in Federal Administrative Agencies*, Report submitted to the Administrative Conference of the United States, at https://www-cdn .law.stanford.edu/wp-content/uploads/2020/02/ACUS-AI-Report.pdf.

European Commission (EC) (2019), *The European Green Deal*, COM(2019) 640 final, at https://ec .europa.eu/info/sites/info/files/european-green-deal-communication_en.pdf.

European Commission (EC) (2020a), *Critical Raw Materials Resilience: Charting a Path towards greater Security and Sustainability*, COM(2020) 474 final, at https://ec.europa.eu/docsroom/ documents/42849.

European Commission (EC) (2020b), *White Paper on Artificial Intelligence – A European Approach to Excellence and Trust*, COM(2020) 65 final, at https://ec.europa.eu/info/sites/info/files/commission -white-paper-artificial-intelligence-feb2020_en.pdf.

Finck, M. (2020), "Automated decision-making and administrative law", in P. Cane et al. (eds), *Oxford Handbook of Comparative Administrative Law*, Oxford University Press, forthcoming.

Finucane, M.L. et al. (2000), "The affect heuristic in judgments of risks and benefits", *Journal of Behavioral Decision Making*, 13 (1), at https://onlinelibrary.wiley.com/doi/abs/10.1002/%28SICI %291099-0771%28200001/03%2913%3A1%3C1%3A%3AAID-BDM333%3E3.0.CO%3B2-S.

Fisher, E. (2010), *Risk Regulation and Administrative Constitutionalism*, Hart Publishing.

Foucault, M. (1982), "Structuralism and post-structuralism", *Telos*, 55.

Freese, J. and D. Peterson (2017), "Replication in social science", *Annual Review of Sociology*, 43, at https://www.annualreviews.org/doi/abs/10.1146/annurev-soc-060116-053450.

Funtowicz, S.O. and J.R. Ravetz (1995), "Science for the post-normal age", in L. Westra and J. Lemons (eds), *Perspectives on Ecological Integrity*, Dordrecht: Springer.

Garnett, K. and G. van Calster (2021), "The concept of essential use: a novel approach to regulating chemicals in the European Union", *Transnational Environmental Law*, 1, at https://doi.org/10.1017/ S2047102521000042.

Gori, G.B. (2016), "An appeal for the integrity of science and public policy", *Toxicology*, 371, at https:// doi.org/10.1016/j.tox.2016.08.015.

Graham, J.D. and J.B. Wiener (eds) (1995), *Risk vs. Risk. Trade-offs in Protecting Health and the Environment*, Harvard University Press, at https://www.hup.harvard.edu/catalog.php?isbn= 9780674773073.

Jasanoff, S. (ed.) (2004), *States of Knowledge: The Co-Production of Science and the Social Order*, Routledge.

Keller, C. et al. (2006), "The role of the affect and availability heuristics in risk communication", *Risk Analysis*, 26 (3).

Kleinberg, J. et al. (2018), "Discrimination in the age of algorithms", *Journal of Legal Analysis*, 10, at https://academic.oup.com/jla/article/doi/10.1093/jla/laz001/5476086.

Lee, E.W.J. and A.Z.H. Yee (2020), "Toward data sense-making in digital health communication research: why theory matters in the age of big data", *Frontiers in Communication*, at https://doi.org/10.3389/fcomm.2020.00011.

Lewallen J. (2020), "Emerging technologies and problem definition uncertainty: the case of cybersecurity", *Regulation & Governance*, at https://onlinelibrary.wiley.com/doi/abs/10.1111/rego.12341.

Lunn, P.D. et al. (2020), "Using behavioural science to help fight the coronavirus: a rapid, narrative review", *Journal of Behavioral Public Administration,* 3 (1), at http://www.journal-bpa.org/index .php/jbpa/article/view/147.

Madhav, N. et al. (2017), "Pandemics: risks, impacts, and mitigation", in D.T. Jamison et al. (eds), *Disease Control Priorities*, 9, World Bank, at http://dcp-3.org/chapter/2601/pandemics-risks -mitigation-and-costs.

Majone, G. (1994), "The rise of the regulatory state in Europe", *Western European Politics*, 17 (3).

Mayson, S.G. (2019), "Bias in, bias out", *The Yale Law Journal*, 128 (8) https://www.yalelawjournal .org/article/bias-in-bias-out.

Mazzucato, M. (2014), *The Entrepreneurial State: Debunking Public vs. Private Sector Myths*, Anthem Press

Meads, R. and L. Allio (2016), *Scientific Evidence and the Management Of Risk. Monograph*, European Risk Forum, at https://www.eriforum.eu/uploads/2/5/7/1/25710097/erf_-_scientific_evidence_and _the_management_of_risk_002.pdf.

Meads, R. and L. Allio (2019), *Risk Management and the EU's Administrative State: Implementing Law through Science, Regulation and Guidance. Monograph*, European Risk Forum, at https:// www.eriforum.eu/uploads/2/5/7/1/25710097/erf_monograph_-_risk_management_and_the_eus _administrative_state.pdf.

Mingardi, A. (2015), "A critique of Mazzucato's entrepreneurial state", *Cato Journal*, 25 (3), at https:// www.cato.org/sites/cato.org/files/serials/files/cato-journal/2015/9/cj-v35n3-7.pdf.

Monfort, J.P. (2021), "The concept of essential use to regulate chemicals: legal considerations", *International Chemical Regulatory and Law Review*, 4 (1), at https://icrl.lexxion.eu/article/ICRL/ 2021/1/5.

Moon, M.J. (2020), "Fighting COVID-19 with agility, transparency, and participation: wicked policy problems and new governance challenges", *Public Administration Review*, 80 (4). at https:// onlinelibrary.wiley.com/doi/full/10.1111/puar.13214.

Moore, D.A. et al. (2010), "Conflict of interest and the intrusion of bias", *Judgment and Decision Making*, 5 (1), at http://sjdm.cybermango.org/journal/10/91104/jdm91104.pdf.

Moulaert, F. et al. (eds) (2013), *The International Handbook of Social Innovation. Collective Action, Social Learning and Transdisciplinary Research*, Cheltenham, UK and Northampton, MA, USA: Edward Elgar Publishing.

Mulgan, G. (2016), *Good and bad innovation: what kind of theory and practice do we need to distinguish them?*, NESTA, at https://media.nesta.org.uk/documents/good_and_bad_innovation_by_geoff _mulgan.pdf.

Nature (2013), "Announcement: reducing our irreproducibility. Editorial", *Nature*, 496, at https://www .nature.com/news/announcement-reducing-our-irreproducibility-1.12852.

OECD (2009), *Investigating Research Misconduct Allegations in International Collaborative Research Projects. A Practical Guide*, OECD Publishing, at http://www.oecd.org/science/inno/42770261.pdf.

OECD (2010), *Risk and Regulatory Policy: Improving the Governance of Risk*, OECD Publishing, at https://www.oecd.org/publications/risk-and-regulatory-policy-9789264082939-en.htm.

OECD (2019), *Regulatory Effectiveness in the Era of Digitalisation*, OECD Publishing, at https://www .oecd.org/gov/regulatory-policy/Regulatory-effectiveness-in-the-era-of-digitalisation.pdf.

OECD (2020a), *Providing Science Advice to Policy Makers During COVID-19*, OECD Publishing, at   http://www.oecd.org/coronavirus/policy-responses/providing-science-advice-to-policy-makers -during-covid-19-4eec08c5/.

OECD (2020b), *Regulatory Quality and COVID-19: Managing the Risks and Supporting the Recovery*, OECD Publishing, at https://www.oecd.org/regreform/regulatory-policy/Regulatory-Quality-and -Coronavirus%20-(COVID-19)-web.pdf.

OECD (2020c), *COVID-19 and Global Value Chains: Policy Options to Build More Resilient Production Networks*, at http://www.oecd.org/coronavirus/policy-responses/covid-19-and-global-value-chains-policy-options-to-build-more-resilient-production-networks-04934ef4/.

OECD (2021), *International Regulatory Co-operation, OECD Best Practice Principles for Regulatory Policy*, OECD Publishing, at https://www.oecd.org/gov/regulatory-policy/international-regulatory-co-operation-5b28b589-en.htm.

Pachur, T. et al. (2012), "How do people judge risks: availability heuristic, affect heuristic, or both?", *Journal of Experimental Psychology: Applied*, 18 (3), at https://www.researchgate.net/publication/224916547_How_Do_People_Judge_Risks_Availability_Heuristic_Affect_Heuristic_or_Both.

Pijnenburg, M.G.F. et al. (2017), "A roadmap for analytics in taxpayer supervision", *Electronic Journal of e-Government*, 15 (1), at https://openaccess.leidenuniv.nl/bitstream/handle/1887/48093/ejeg-volume15-issue1-article452.pdf?sequence=1.

Porter, M.E. (1990), *The Competitive Advantage of Nations*, Free Press.

Rangone, N. (2018), "Making law effective: behavioural insights into compliance", *European Journal of Risk Regulation*, 3.

Rangone, N. (2020), "Italy's complex legislative framework impairs its COVID-19 response", *The Regulatory Review. Penn Program on Regulation*, at https://www.theregreview.org/2020/06/08/rangone-italy-complex-legislative-framework-impairs-covid-19-response/.

Rothstein, H. et al. (2013), "Risk and the limit of governance: exploring varied patterns of risk-based governance across Europe", *Regulation and Governance*, 7, at https://onlinelibrary.wiley.com/doi/abs/10.1111/j.1748-5991.2012.01153.x.

Royal Netherlands Academy of Arts and Sciences (KNAW) et al. (2017), *Code for the prevention of improper influence due to conflicts of interest*, Updated version from 2012, at https://knaw.nl/shared/resources/actueel/publicaties/pdf/code-for-the-prevention-of-improper-influence-due-to-conflicts-of-interest.

Selbst, A.D. and S. Barocas (2018), "The intuitive appeal of explainable machines", *Fordham Law Review*, 87, at https://ir.lawnet.fordham.edu/cgi/viewcontent.cgi?article=5569&context=flr.

Smith, A. et al. (2019), "Communicating to and engaging with the public in regulatory science", *EFSA Journal*, 17 (S1), at https://efsa.onlinelibrary.wiley.com/doi/full/10.2903/j.efsa.2019.e170717.

Stewart, L. A. (2010), *The Impact of Regulation on Innovation in the United States: A Cross-Industry Literature Review*. Institute of Medicine Committee on Patient Safety and Health IT. Information Technology & Innovation Foundation. https://itif.org/files/2011-impact-regulation-innovation.pdf.

Šucha, V. and M. Sienkiewicz (eds) (2020), *Science for Policy Handbook*, Joint Research Centre, European Commission, at https://ec.europa.eu/jrc/communities/sites/jrccties/files/science_for_policy_handbook_fin.pdf.

Sunstein, C.R. (2002), *Risk and Reasons. Safety, Law and the Environment*, Cambridge University Press.

Sunstein, C.R. (2020), "The meaning of masks", *Journal of Behavioral Economics for Policy*, Vol. 4, COVID-19 Special Issue, at https://sabeconomics.org/wordpress/wp-content/uploads/JBEP-4-S-1.pdf.

Tversky, A. and D. Kahneman (1974), "Judgment under uncertainty: heuristics and biases", *Science*, 185, at https://www.socsci.uci.edu/~bskyrms/bio/readings/tversky_k_heuristics_biases.pdf.

Tversky, A. and D. Kahneman (1983), "Extensional versus intuitive reasoning: the conjunction fallacy in probability judgment", *Psychological Review*, 90 (4), at https://psycnet.apa.org/record/1984-03110-001.

UK Royal Society (1992), *Risk: Analysis, Perception, Management*, London.

Url, B. (2018), "Don't attack science agencies for political gain", *Nature*, 553, at https://www.nature.com/articles/d41586-018-01071-9.

US National Academy of Sciences, Engineering and Medicine (NASEM) (2003), *Policy on the Committee Composition and Balance of Conflicts of Interest*, at https://www.nationalacademies.org/about/institutional-policies-and-procedures/conflict-of-interest-policies-and-procedures.

US National Academy of Sciences, Engineering and Medicine (NASEM) (2017), *Fostering Integrity in Research*, National Academies Press, at https://doi.org/10.17226/21896.

US National Research Council (NRC) (1983), *Risk Assessment in the Federal Government: Managing the Process*, National Academies Press.

Veale, M. and I. Brass (2019), "Administration by algorithm? Public management meets public sector machine learning", in K. Yeung and M. Lodge (eds), *Algorithm Regulation*, Oxford University Press.

Vecchione, E. (2017), "Risk analysis", in C.A. Dunlop and C.M. Radaelli (eds), *Handbook of Regulatory Impact Assessment*, Cheltenham, UK and Northampton, MA, USA: Edward Elgar Publishing.

von Schomberg, R. (ed.) (2019), *International Handbook on Responsible Innovation. A Global Resource*, Cheltenham, UK and Northampton, MA, USA: Edward Elgar Publishing.

Wendling, C. (2012), "What role for social scientists in risk expertise?", *Journal of Risk Research*, 15 (5), at https://www.tandfonline.com/doi/abs/10.1080/13669877.2011.636837.

Wiener, J.B. (1998), "Managing the iatrogenic risks of risk management", *RISK: Health, Safety & Environment (1990–2002)*, at https://scholars.unh.edu/cgi/viewcontent.cgi?article=1351&context=risk.

Wiener, J.B. (2002), "Precaution in a multi-risk world", in D. Paustenbach (ed.), *Human and Ecological Risk Assessment*, John Wiley, at https://scholarship.law.duke.edu/cgi/viewcontent.cgi?article=1923&context=faculty_scholarship.

Wilsdon, J. and R. Doubleday (eds) (2015), *Future Directions for Scientific Advice in Europe*, Centre for Science and Policy, at http://www.csap.cam.ac.uk/projects/future-directions-scientific-advice-europe/.

Wittrock, C. et al. (2021), *Implementing Responsible Research and Innovation. Organisational and National Conditions*, Springer Briefs in Ethics, at https://www.springer.com/gp/book/9783030542863.

World Economic Forum (WEF) (2016), *Social Innovation. A Guide to Achieving Corporate and Societal Value*, at http://www3.weforum.org/docs/WEF_Social_Innovation_Guide.pdf.

Yeung, K. (2019), "Why worry about decision-making by machine?", in K. Yeung and M. Lodge (eds), *Algorithm Regulation*, Oxford University Press.

Young, S.D. (2009), "Bias in the research literature and conflict of interest: an issue for publishers, editors, reviewers and authors, and it is not just about the money", *Journal of Psychiatry and Neuroscience*, 34 (6), at https://www.ncbi.nlm.nih.gov/pmc/articles/PMC2783432/pdf/0340412.pdf.

Zamir, E. and D. Teichman (2021), "Mathematics, psychology, and law: the legal ramifications of the exponential growth bias", *Consumer Law eJournal*, at: https://www.semanticscholar.org/paper/Mathematics%2C-Psychology%2C-and-Law%3A-The-Legal-of-the-Zamir-Teichman/6a200c9e48 73e7096a8f4daba840f32f60f2ea75.

12. Anticorruption authorities

Fabrizio Di Mascio, Martino Maggetti and Alessandro Natalini

INTRODUCTION

Since the 1990s, states have adopted numerous international and regional treaties, agreements, and resolutions in the fight against corruption, which is considered a core inibitor of issues related to market openness, quality of public services, equality and rule of law. This profusion of legal instruments reflects a widespread concern about the harmful effects of corruption, a renewed awareness of its transnational nature, as well as a collective commitment to tackle this phenomenon and its enabling factors (De Sousa et al. 2009; Sampson 2010). Drawing on the institutional economics literature, the international community has promoted anticorruption efforts that have commonly followed the logic of principal–agent theory, which depicts corruption as occurring when public officials who have discretion over the provision of public services lack accountability. The policy implications following from this approach is that corruption is 'solvable' with policies that alter the level of discretion granted to agents as well as the degree to which principals are able to monitor and sanction their agents. Consequently, the international community has prescribed a "holistic anticorruption strategy" targeted at reducing the discretion of public officials, increasing monitoring mechanisms, promoting transparency in government, and strengthening sanctions on those who engage in corruption, so as to better align the incentives of potential agents with those of their respective principals (Persson et al. 2013; Marquette and Peiffer 2018).

In the context of the global fight against corruption, the international community has incessantly recommended the introduction of distinct anticorruption authorities (ACAs) as central pieces to national integrity systems (Johnston 1999). For the purposes of this chapter, we understand ACAs as "public bodies of a durable nature, with a specific mission to fight corruption and reducing the opportunity structures propitious for its occurence in society through preventive and/or repressive measures" (De Sousa 2010, p. 5). These agencies use their powers to expose and address undue influence over state power by private interests. They typically address a range of issues related to public integrity: criminal acts such as bribery, ethical violations such as conflicts of interest, and problems of systemic corruption such as regulatory capture or opaque procurement. In countries seeking development assistance, ACAs have been actively promoted as "best practice" by international financial institutions, which tied the agenda of economic development together with the effectiveness of government, leading to new conditions of loans (Doig 1995). In other cases, these bodies have been set up as an attempt to upgrade the country's ethical infrastructure, or simply to fulfill obligations deriving from the signing of international anti-bribery conventions (Recanatini 2011).

Most ACAs are responsible for the development and implementation of anticorruption policies at the national level; they are entrusted with the pivotal mission of translating international standards into domestic action; they constitute focal points for evaluating national compliance with international legal instruments, and can be held accountable for their states' concrete results in achieving integrity. ACAs are often regarded by international agreements as the ultimate institutional response to corruption (De Sousa 2010). For instance, the United Nations Convention against Corruption (UNCAC) mandates that member states set up specialized bodies to combat corruption through preventive and law enforcement functions. Furthermore, multilateral bodies like the Organisation for Economic Co-operation and Development (OECD), global advocacy groups like Transparency International and intergovernmental conventions, such as the Council of Europe's Criminal Law Convention on Corruption, the Inter-American Convention against Corruption, the African Union Convention on Preventing and Combating Corruption and the Arab Convention against Corruption, also recognize the usefulness of establishing separate, permanent agencies whose primary function is to provide centralized leadership in core areas of anticorruption activity. Completing the round of international agreements in 2012, the Jakarta Statement on Principles for Anti-Corruption Agencies was adopted by multilateral organizations including the United Nations Development Programme, regional anticorruption networks, and anticorruption agency officials from 30 states. It emphasizes the need for stability and permanence, financial autonomy, operational independence and visibility in the society in which ACAs operate (UNODC 2012). In other words, the principles that are promoted by the international anticorruption community call to mind the conventional recipe for regulatory reform: to grant the newly created agencies structural insulation from government (Heilbrunn 2004; De Jaegere 2012; Tomić 2019).

This chapter first tracks the worldwide proliferation of ACAs whose number has increased rapidly in the two decades between 1990 and 2010. Unsurprisingly given their ubiquity, ACAs represent a highly heterogenous group and there is still some uncertainty as to how to classify the different agencies with sometimes vastly different functions and levels of independence. Yet, little comparative work has been done to explain the diversity of ACAs institutional design and their development trajectories. Anticorruption policy experts tend to analyze ACAs without paying much attention to the political and administrative context in which these agencies are embedded. Mainstream research on independent regulatory authorities, on the other hand, has not included the anticorruption sector in their investigation of contextual factors that explain the variation in the independence of regulators (Jordana et al. 2018; Özel and Unan 2021). The second section reviews an emerging strand of research that has built on regulatory theory to investigate ACAs as bodies analogous to independent regulatory authorities. Within this emerging literature that aims to explain the diversity of the organizational forms taken by the anticorruption drive in different contexts, research questions typically involve investigating why and how governments enact reforms to curb or enhance their statutory power to shape an agency's personnel, budget and powers. This strand of research has provided insight into the structure of incentives behind anticorruption reform: as the ideal of anticorruption makes political principals a potential target for sanctions, the independence of ACAs becomes appealing to leaders only to the extent that it generates popular support, and otherwise dangerous whenever their particular interests are threatened (Pozsgai-Alvarez 2018). Diachronic examination of variations in the independence of ACAs has highlighted that the life-cycles of agencies is shaped by the interplay between the degree of political support from changing governments and agency activism. The latter factor has been taken into account by recent studies, which argue that the *de facto* autonomy of ACAs is not only a product of their legislative frameworks, but equally emanates from their leaders' ability to construct their organizational legitimacy, identity and reputation in the eyes of multiple audiences. The third section reviews these studies, which draw on the bureaucratic reputation theory to contribute novel insights into the processes of building, maintaining, and defending credibility from the viewpoint of ACAs. The concluding section sketches several paths for further research, with the goal of contributing to a more comprehensive understanding of ACAs.

THE RISE OF ANTICORRUPTION AUTHORITIES

ACAs proliferated worldwide in the 1990s and early 2000s, inspired by the achievements of pioneering offices like Singapore's Corruption Practices Investigation Bureau (established in 1952), and Hong Kong's Independent Commission against Corruption (established in 1974). The concept of specialized anticorruption bodies was initially somewhat slow to catch on, and by 1990 there were still fewer than 20 ACAs worldwide (Gemperle 2018). Because the establishment of ACAs became a popular policy among international institutions, donors and development practitioners, ACAs were initially largely concentrated in the Global South. Yet with increasing sophistication of the anticorruption debate in the 1990s and the mounting realization that corruption was by no means only a concern in developing countries, ACAs have spread in the Global North (Schöberlein 2020).

However, differences exist between countries from different regions of the world. ACAs appear to be mostly concentrated in Asia (Quah 2007), postcommunist Europe (Smilov 2010; Batory 2012; Tomić 2019) Latin America (Pozsgai-Alvarez 2021), and sub-Saharan Africa (Doig et al. 2007). In most of Western countries, under the assumption that their institutions were generally fir for purpose, and raising awareness or educating about corruption was not considered a priority, countries largely opted for building anticorruption capacities within existing law enforcement entities instead of creating new specialized institutions. In Europe, ACAs have largely been established in two types of countries: old democracies whose former anticorruption framework was deemed ineffective and was faced with substantial criticism and/or did not meet international standards (for example, France and Italy); new democracies in Eastern and Southeastern Europe that were encouraged (or required) to reform their frameworks in the absence of sufficient trust in existing institutions as part of their political transition and/or accession to the European Union (Schöberlein 2020).

In breaking down ACA's responsibilities, the OECD (2013) identifies the following four sets of functions: (a) policy development, research and coordination to assess existing anticorruption measures, reform policy, coordinate anticorruption strategies and collaborate with international stakeholders; (b) prevention of corruption in power structures by promoting integrity in public service; (c) education and awareness raising of the general public and relevant domestic stakeholders; (d) investigation (sometimes prosecutorial) of suspected cases of corruption. The extent to which a given agency will fulfil all or only some of the functions listed above depends on whether a country adopts a single-agency approach or whether different functions are spread across different bodies, and how wide a jurisdiction and mandate these agencies are equipped with.

Despite the global diffusion of anticorruption reform, there is a continued lack of clarity in terms of what exactly constitutes an ACA as a wide variety of agencies with very different mandates are lumped together in the same category, rendering comparisons even more challenging (Krambia-Kapardis 2019). It is therefore not surprising that the precise number of ACAs globally is hard to quantify as different organizations use different definitions, and there is a lack of comprehensive databases. A recent survey undertaken by the Agence Française Anticorruption, together with the OECD and GRECO, yielded responses from 171 ACAs spread across 114 countries (AFA 2020). There is no universally accepted model for shaping national integrity systems, but the centralized single-agency approach to the anticorruption mandate seems to be predominant (84 out of 114 countries). When it comes to the missions entrusted to ACAs, it is worth highlighting that a majority of respondents are tasked with designing and implementing national anticorruption strategies. The survey seems to confirm that many governments have chosen to fulfil the requirements of UNCAC, in particular of Article 5 that calls upon states parties to adopt effective, coordinated anticorruption policies, through the development of a national anticorruption strategy or action plan. The survey also shows that 63 percent of respondent ACAs are authorized to conduct investigations and/or criminal proceedings, which mainly concern natural persons. Concerning ACAs' power to sanction, it can be highlighted that less than half of the respondents (48 percent) have sanction mechanisms, and that these mechanisms are mainly administrative.

According to the OECD (2013), countries experiment with three different models: "multipurpose ACAs", commonly identified with the success stories of anticorruption commissions in Hong Kong and Singapore, which combine prosecutorial, investigative, preventive, and educational functions; "law enforcement type agencies", which focus on investigation and prosecution; and "corruption prevention institutions", whose prerogatives are limited to the coordination of anticorruption strategies and the regulation of preventive tools, such as disclosure requirements and anticorruption plans. Recent anticorruption scholarship has tended to adopt those three categories (Recanatini 2011). However, it is worth noting that individual ACAs might defy easy categorization or evolve from one category to another. Moreover, the multipurpose model is rare in Europe. What is more, European ACAs that do have both preventive and law enforcement powers have the latter mostly in select administrative matters.

As suggested by Kuris (2015), it is more helpful to draw a fundamental distinction within the OECD typology between agencies with strong law enforcement powers ("guard dogs") and those that lack them ("watchdogs"). The distinction is more of a continuum than a clear division. Each ACA is endowed with a distinct toolbox of powers to carry out its investigative and/or preventive functions, framed by its mandate, institutional position, and legal context. Conventional wisdom holds that guard dog ACAs have greater freedom to operate and greater chance of success (Meagher 2005). Guard dog ACAs may secure the conviction of high-level politicians. The exposure of networks of corruption may galvanize popular movements against corruption and usher in sweeping reforms. Conversely, watchdog ACAs rely on police and prosecutors. This makes it harder to demonstrate the value of their preventive functions to the public. However, the use of criminal investigations makes guard dog ACAs more susceptible to the influence of factors that typically account for failure of any ACA as they need strong organizational factors to sustain a pattern of harsh enforcement (Tomić 2019).

First, international organizations and domestic stakeholders often have unrealistic expectations for quick results from ACAs they have invested with powers and resources. The introduction of ACAs tend to crowd out other anticorruption efforts, and it might even have a negative impact because it detracts attention from the need for systemic reforms that ensure enabling conditions for anticorruption like freedom of the press, independence of the judiciary, fiscal transparency and administrative simplification (Mungiu-Pippidi and Dadašov 2017). Managing expectations can be a hard challenge particularly for guard dog ACAs as constituents expect to see clear achievements resulting from the use of coercive powers. One reason that ACAs struggle to meet expectations is that they face tight constraints because the use of their powers carry high stakes for those they target (Kuris 2015). ACAs without proper mechanisms of control and accountability may abuse their powers and lose legitimacy in a context characterized by the rule of law (Skidmore 1996). In particular, the public may fear a guard dog ACAs in liberal states where coercive powers are bound by restrictions and oversight mechanisms in order to protect civil liberties. Another reason is that ACAs tend to suffer from a capacity gap as they require significant investments of resources and this holds true particularly for investigations of a sophisticated crime like corruption. It should be kept in mind that it takes only a small reduction of an agency's budget to alter its investigative agenda because this will reduce the funds available for discretionary, short-term activities (e.g., investigations), as opposed to fixed expenses (Maor 2004).

Second, ACAs face two important political risks: politicization and pushback. On the one hand, governments may be tempted to pressure an ACA to act against opposition politicians (Batory 2012). On the other hand, if an ACA resists political pressure and/or its action targets government leaders, political executives may respond by stripping its powers, removing its leadership, overturning its decisions, and reducing its funding. It is nor surprising that political risks are most likely to occur in those contexts where criminal investigations of guard dog ACAs are more personally threatening to political actors (Maor 2004).

Finally, ACAs may also face difficulties interacting with other state bodies (Kuris 2015). Other justice-sector partners may see ACAs as competitors and may be resentful of the attention and resources that such specialized bodies receive. In particular, guard dog ACAs may have unclear jurisdictional boundaries, provoking a "turf war" with other law enforcement agencies. ACAs may also face difficulties interacting with partners outside the justice system. In particular, there is an inherent tension between the advisory roles that multipurpose ACAs exercise when they coach partner agencies on corruption risk reduction and the adversarial role they play when they police the same agencies for violations. In other words, public officers trying to implement preventive recommendations may worry that disclosing corruption to the multipurpose ACA may invite unwanted scrutiny and open up a criminal investigation (Kuris 2015).

If we consider the shortcomings in moving functions such as investigation and prevention into a single powerful agency, it is not surprising that multipurpose ACAs have not gained prominence in most of advanced democracies. Watchdog ACAs can respond quickly to emerging concerns and issue findings that are not required to meet the high evidentiary standards of individual culpability. Their reports can focus on systemic weaknesses in areas like transparency and management of conflicts of interest rather than the presence or absence of grounds for criminal charge. Without coercive powers, watchdog ACAs face difficulties attracting public support. Much like guard dog ACAs, they require partners inside and outside of government to act upon their findings. To achieve results, a watchdog ACA must build strong partnerships and respond strategically to specific corruption problems (Kuris 2015).

ANTICORRUPTION AUTHORITIES AND THE POLITICS OF DELEGATION

Watchdog ACAs can be considered specific instances of independent regulatory agencies, as they deal with integrity issues by enjoying the same competencies of agencies that regulate the functioning of markets (Levi-Faur 2011). Distinctive features, like a lack of investigative and prosecutorial power and a focus on issues like asset disclosure and management of conflicts of interest, mean preventive institutions resemble other regulators, as they are mainly involved with rule-making, fact-finding, monitoring, and sanctioning in administrative matters (Di Mascio et al. 2020).

These features make watchdog ACAs particularly interesting for the exploration of research arguments from the literature on independent regulatory authorities that draws on the principal–agent framework (Batory 2012; see also Chapter 15 by Maggetti and Chapter 13 by Selin in this volume). One example of the relevance of this literature is the applicability of "mainstream" explanations of why independent authorities are established through a public act of delegation (Thatcher 2002). Many, if not all, of the motivations for governments to establish independent regulatory agencies apply in the anticorruption context (Batory 2012). Political principals can constitute ACAs to help them: address information asymmetries by utilizing technical expertise; legitimize policies by choice of a valued institutional model; reduce political uncertainty by insulating the policy area from the impact of electoral volatility (i.e. decisions cannot be reversed by future politicians); enhance the credibility of commitments.

The demand for credible commitment to anticorruption policy often constitutes a crucial factor encouraging delegation of powers to ACAs, particularly under the pressure caused by high-profile corruption scandals (Batory 2012). The case of ACAs is particularly interesting because the government is not merely the "principal" who will gain credibility by creating credible policy commitments, it is also the target of regulation, meaning it could lose credibility if an independent regulator exposes possible misconduct in the public sector or, above all, in the core executive of the government itself (Maor 2004). To some extent this argument can also be applied to other, more conventional independent regulatory agencies, as it is the case for authorities whose regulatory tasks may concern some government activities, such as for antitrust authorities (see Chapter 8 by Guidi in this volume) and privacy regulators (see Chapter 9 by Schütz in this volume), and to telecom or energy regulators when a government is a main shareholder of a recently liberalized public utility (see Chapter 10 by Finger in this volume).

However, this state of affairs is magnified in the case of ACAs. On the one hand, ACAs are typically established in countries where corruption is a prominent feature of public life, meaning that pressures for credible commitment are intense. On the other hand, delegation to ACAs is extremely costly for politicians subject to electoral pressures: they would not only forego direct policy influence by insulating the area, as it happens with delegation in any policy area, but also increase political risk by becoming ACA's regulatory target (Batory 2012). Consequently, the power and independence that ACAs are granted at the outset depend – in theory – on the balance between the pressures for credibility and the political principals' incentives for using a repertoire of political control tools that minimize agency losses, which occur when ACAs target their political principals. In this sense, the use of political control tools corresponds to less statutory independence.

According to previous studies on formal independence of regulatory authorities, operationalization of political control include powers to: appoint boad members; determine budget and staff; overturn agency decisions; alter the organizational basis, powers and duties of agencies by legislation (Thatcher 2005; Gilardi and Maggetti 2011). There is considerable variation in the degree of independence ACAs are granted at the outset, which primarily reflects domestic political dynamics. As highlighted by Batory (2012, p. 649), the desire to please international organization or to flaunt anticorruption credentials to voters could well result in nothing more than symbolic action, given strong incentives to avoid the risk that the ACA will target its political principals. Unless these incentives are counterbalanced by a pressing need to send a credible signal, then the ACA created will not be endowed with either too much independence. Conversely, if a government wants to use the agency against its political opponents and has sufficient time and opportunity to do so (this is most likely at the beginning of the electoral cycle), chances are better that the ACA will in fact get substantial powers, but hardly any distance from its political principal.

However, it has been noted that the capacity of political principals to design public agencies for the long run is limited (Boin et al. 2010), as design features have time-varying effects and often generate unanticipated consequences of delegation (Wilks and Bartle 2002). This holds true in particular for those contexts where political competition generates incentives for political actors to engage in credit claiming around anticorruption. Political uncertainty, not only about who will hold power in the future but also about how this power will be exercised, can feed into expectations that anticorruption measures will not be consistently enforced, lowering resistance to ACA by reducing its perceived costs. In the longer term, if political competition persists, controlling the agency – that is, ensuring targeted compliance or systematic non-compliance – turns out to be more difficult than expected, because sustained attention to the working of anticorruption institutions only serves to further heighten the ACA's agenda status – thus requiring ever more "expensive" signals to be sent. Thus, the independence of ACA can lock in, and over time start generating costs that were not anticipated at the moment of agency design (Schnell 2018).

The inherent vulnerability of ACAs has been called the "Icarus paradox", meaning that their survival depends on the capacity of the agency leaders to identify a level of performance which provides sufficient resources to satisfy and support the evolution of an operating environment that gradually becomes less corruption-tolerant, without producing a level of political hostility that increases the degree of prevailing political resistance to combating corruption (Doig et al. 2005). More generally, the Icarus paradox implies a constant threat of falling into politically driven cycles of anticorruption reform, each iteration launched by the emergence of corruption scandals (Pozsgai-Alvarez 2021). Changes in government often mean that the cycle of support (where it exists) is interrupted, diluted or becomes conditional on a shift in focus towards investigating corruption in the previous administration (Doig et al. 2007).

Research on ACAs in Central Eastern Europe has tracked changes over time in ACAs' mandates, highlighting that their life-cycles are not simply a function of initial act of delegation as independence evolves in a "series of attacks and counterattacks," the outcomes of which are shaped by the interplay between political factors and agency activism (Batory 2012). These findings are consistent with those reported by a longitudinal analysis of ACAs in Italy, a country that exhibited a pattern of frequent and wholesale alternation in government (Di Mascio et al. 2020). By influencing the career background of political principals and their time horizons, the alternation in government has provided a variation in the incentives for political control. Findings confirm that the extent of delegation corresponds to the balance struck by Italian governments, between expected credibility gains as a principal and expected credibility losses as a target, in a context punctuated by domestic crises and scandals that acted as triggers for reforms.

Furthermore, a process of layering (Van der Heijden 2011) – understood as a process of incremental change that involves active sponsorship of amendments, additions, or revisions to an existing set of institutions – seems at work in Italy, which is characterized by the high frequency of reform activity in the anticorruption field. This suggests that, even in an unfavorable context like Italy populated by many veto players and with low discretion in implementation, institutional change is possible and even likely. Specifically, the activism of an agency leader who could use his vast reputation to catalyze and exploit pressures stemming from international organizations and from the media is key in explaining the high pace of anticorruption reforms in Italy. This is an underestimated factor, which suggests rethinking the "principal–agent" framework in the anticorruption field by including reputational concerns more systematically and more explicitly along the lines of an emerging strand of research that is reviewed in the next section.

DE FACTO INDEPENDENCE AND REPUTATIONAL ACTIVISM OF ANTICORRUPTION AGENCIES

In a broad sense, the anticorruption literature has highlighted the importance of the credibility and legitimacy of ACAs (Baniamin and Jamil 2018; Ankamah 2019). However, the literature has not adequately consolidated these disparate insights into a cogent theoretical framework until recently, when a strand of research has addressed the emerging debate in delegation scholarship over the role of *de jure* independence versus reputational activism of agency leaders in shaping *de facto* independence of ACAs (Busuioc and Lodge 2016; see also Chapter 16 by Lodge and Wegrich in this volume).

Research on ACAs in Southeast European countries has found considerable deviations between their *de jure* and *de facto* independence, which ran in both directions – from low formal to high factual, and from high statutory to low *de facto* autonomy (Tomić 2018). The study has also found cross-time reversals in *de facto* independence of ACAs, triggered by their leadership changes. These findings challenge the "structural paradigm" that has been promoted by international organizations and donors across the world, which assumes that statutory independence is a crucial determinant of an ACA's *de facto* independence. They also challenge recent research on Thailand, which has highlighted that a high level of formal independence is essential to the ACA as to safeguard it in a highly politicized environment (Prateeppornnarong 2021).

More specifically, findings show that organizational distance from the government is not a sufficient factor for autonomous agency conduct in Southeast European countries. In those contexts where corruption is systemic, opportunities for non-institutional pressures are rife, given the strong role of informal networks (Tomić 2019). Instead of organizational distance, findings show that it is the role of agency leaders, particularly their reputational management, that crucially shapes the *de facto* independence of ACAs. Political principal is not seen as the only key account holder since the management of an ACA's reputation hinges on multiple audiences for agency's account-giving such as the political sphere, civil society, media, businesses, other public bodies and external/international actors. By enhancing their own reputation among the watching audiences, agency leaders can increase the cost of a prospective principal's statutory reprisal and thus potentially pre-empt it.

Research on *de facto* independence contributes a theoretical bridge between bureaucratic reputation theory and the anticorruption literature, by studying how ACAs build and manage their reputations upon four dimensions: performative reputation, which is built through reference to achieved results; moral reputation, which is advanced by preaching ethical and widely approved values such as transparency, accountability, and integrity; procedural reputation, which denotes the ability of an ACA to appropriately follow legal dispositions despite multiple jurisdictional and judicial hurdles; technical-professional reputation, which rests on proven expertise of an ACA's staff (Tomić 2019; Bautista-Beauchesne 2021a).

To capture the reputational strategies of the ACAs in Southeast European countries, Tomić (2018) has counted how many public statements (press releases, interviewe and public comments made by agency leaders) referred to each of the four reputational dimensions, and how many statements featured an insistent tone. Insistent statements feature a degree of assertiveness, an offensive or negative connotation, an accusatory tone (towards politicians or the political class), a demanding attitude, or an aspiration to change the status quo. Non-insistent statements feature neutral or positive messages. The greatest consistency across the ACAs was in the procedural dimension, where they all demonstrated considerable focus on compliance with legal dispositions, as well as in the technical dimension, which was almost absent in the statements. The greatest variation was in the moral and performative dimensions as well as variation in tone. Findings show that emphasis on the moral and performative dimensions was combined with a highly insistent tone in the rhetorical patterns of those ACAs which displayed a high level of *de facto* independence. The latter has been measured by adopting the enforcement style as a proxy, which builds on two constituent dimensions: zealotry and stringency. High zealotry is demonstrated when an ACA shows high proactiveness, whether by launching its own initiatives or by quickly responding to others' reports of misconduct, and when in the sanctioning stage it demonstrates high punitiveness. High stringency involves harsh fines, which include criminal sanctions and drastic forms of non-criminal fines. Given the positive connotation of high zealotry in the field of anticorruption, the occurrence of non-zealous enforcement styles has been treated as an indicator of low *de facto* independence. The analysis illustrates how agency leaders can sustain a zealous enforcement style by adopting a strong rhetorical pattern to mobilize stakeholders and thus develop reputational safeguards' against the principal's statutory intervention.

Research on the case of Quebec's (Canada) ACA has found that reputation management constitutes an integral part of its bureaucratic processes, which is intertwined with the agency's *de facto* independence in a time-sensitive and non-linear manner (Bautista-Beauchesne 2021a). The research design derives narratives from the parliamentary oversight commissions' hearings, during which the director of the ACA is held accountable. To enhance the qualitative analysis, semi-structured interviews were conducted with senior agency employees and external stakeholders. A quantitative analysis of two data sources – the media and the agency's official website – subsequently complemented the main findings of the qualitative analysis. The analytic sequencing of data enabled an appreciation of three broad narrative phases, each which its specific management strategies: during the first phase, the building strategy invested resources in crafting a performative reputation; during the second phase, the proactive strategy maintained a reputation for effectiveness and increased efforts to boost agency's legitimacy in the eyes of various bureaucratic stakeholders on the technical-professional level; during the third phase, the defensive strategy increasingly managed the procedural dimension of reputation to reassure external stakeholders of ACA's adherence to legal dispositions amid contentious political debate.

In other words, reputation management is dynamic and its multiplicity has increased over time in Quebec. The performative dimension is the most prominent feature of reputation. Yet, over time this dimension is increasingly balanced with profiling the ACA as a professional agency following due procedure. These findings are consistent with previous research on regulatory agencies in other policy sectors, which has shown increasing multiplicity of reputation management over time (Christensen and Gornitzka 2019). The key difference between ACAs in Southeast European countries and Quebec concerns the focus on the moral and technical-professional dimensions of performance reputation: whereas ACAs have combined the performative and moral dimensions to enhance their reputation in Southest European countries, results show that the moral dimension remained barely managed in Quebec where the emphasis has been put on the technical-professional dimension. This might be due to the strong resentment towards corruption in new democracies, which makes likely that moral appeals will resonate with the electorate but further research is needed to better understand why different reputational dimensions are neglected in different context.

A core dimension of the interplay between bureaucratic autonomy and reputation consists in the importance of inter-agency collaboration and networks. Rather than analyzing ACAs in isolation, research on ACAs in Quebec has proposed a novel understanding of autonomy-building by accounting for the underlying reputational dimension of the broader collaborative and regulatory environment (Bautista-Beauchesne 2021b). This research has employed a collective case study research design of four anticorruption bodies, which used both qualitative (interviews and non-participant observations) and quantitative (website data) sources. Findings show that, on one hand, ACAs are faced with defending their organizational legitimacy and uniqueness, and on the other hand, they need to collaborate with other anticorruption institutions to further their performance as well as cultivate their bureaucratic reputation. This dilemma leads agency leaders to strike a delicate equilibrium between "turf protecting" tendencies and inter-agency collaboration. By successfully collaborating, ACAs can enhance their performative reputations by increasing outputs, solidify their procedural reputations by complying with increasingly complex regulations, and shore up their technical and professional reputations by devising innovative solutions to a "wicked" problem like corruption. The key challenges ACAs face while building inter-agency cooperation stem from two inherent features of the anticorruption field: first, the complexity and legal minutia surrounding corruption, which makes it difficult to determine which agency retains jurisdiction in a crowded field of anticorruption institutions; second, the instability generated by sustained policy layering in the institutional field of anticorruption, which requires adaptativeness of refining collaborative processes in response to frequent reforms that incrementally shape the anticorruption model over time.

FORESIGHT AND CONCLUSIONS

This chapter has contributed to the literature on both independent regulatory agencies and anticorruption policy, which have practically ignored each other until recently, when two emerging strands of research on delegation and reputational dynamics in the life-cycle of ACAs have addressed the call for more research on independent authories in regulatory fields like anticorruption that have seen hardly any analysis (see Chapter 14 by Koop and Jordana in this Handbook). With regard to research on delegation dynamics, it has highlighted that regulatory theory provides a useful analytical lens for the study of ACAs. The field of anticorruption is particularly interesting for studying delegation processes over time since it is exposed to contradictory pressures between agency independence and political control that also affect regulators in other policy areas (Batory 2012; Di Mascio et al. 2020). As for research on reputational dynamics, ACAs serve as critical case of sorts. The centrality of their post-delegation independence – as well as the hyper-mediatized context in which they evolve – acts as an "acid-test" for the significance of reputational dynamics (Bautista-Beauchesne 2021a). Analyzing these dynamics may not causally determine the inherent difficulties of exercising autonomy, as other intervening factors may hamper an agency's effort to build reputation in a multiplicity of forums and in the multidimensionality of its management. However, as recent research has shown, events and actions regarding an ACA's reputation have a tendency to feedback through time and they can either further or hinder its efforts to acquire necessary powers, cultivate institutional relations, build citizen trust, and ultimately, successfully implement anticorruption policies.

Against this background, further studies are needed, especially on the following four issues. First, it would be important to systematically investigate variations in *de jure* and *de facto* independence of ACAs across political systems and governance contexts. Research on the variation in the independence of ACAs might include contextual variables such as authoritarianism vs democratization (Pavón Mediano 2020; Koop and Kessler 2021), the number of veto players in the broader context of majoritarian/consensual patterns of democracy (Lijphart 1999; Tsebelis 2003), patterns of state intervention in the economy (Hopkin and Rodriguez-Pose 2007), administrative traditions (Peters 2021), the level of judicial independence (Hanretty and Koop 2013), and the level of aid assistance (Dubash and Morgan 2012). From a methodological perspective, research on cross-national variation in independence would imply a major shift from case studies, which have been the dominant method in the literature on ACAs, to quantitative and mixed-method approaches. In particular, Qualitative Comparative Analysis (QCA) is especially suitable for studies that deal with a small to medium *n*, balancing intensive and extensive investigation that allows researchers to conceive connection between variables in terms of multiple and conjunctural causation (Maggetti 2007).

Second, more research is needed to fill the gap of studies comparing performance metrics across ACAs (Choi 2011). This gap is surprising if we consider the focus of ACAs' leaders on the performative dimension of reputation. Efforts to evaluate the performance of anticorruption measures, including the establishment of ACAs, face numerous difficulties related to the complexity and hidden nature of corruption (Heywood and Rose 2014). These features make it difficult to measure changes in corruption levels and even more problematic to attribute changes to particular interventions. Given the absence of reliable measures of corruption before and after the establishment of ACAs, performance must be evaluated in relation to intermediate outcomes that are achievable in the contexts in which ACAs operate (Doig and Norris 2012). Previous studies generated indicators to benchmark ACAs but they combined performance indicators with others that are, in fact, requirements for success, such as budget and staff. Drawing on recent work by David-Barrett et al. (2020), the focus on different dimensions of capacity-building as a core part of the evaluation of ACAs can be a way of defining measurable intermediate outcomes. It is also worth highlighting that research on capacity-building may also yield practical implications relevant to the work of ACAs' leaders who manage the performance of their organizations (see Chapter 19 by Coglianese in this volume).

Third, the relational nature of ACAs' independence in a multi-level and multi-actor context deserves more attention. Initiatives like the establishment of the international Network of

Corruption Prevention Authorities (NCPA) in 2017 aim at providing a platform for practitioners around the world to exchange technical information, share good practices, and find concrete solutions for common challenges. The work on regulatory networks and the way they influence national agencies' actions is very relevant in this regard. In particular, the work on the micro-dynamics of knowledge circulation in regulatory networks is a promising avenue for research on international regulatory cooperation in the field of anticorruption (Papadopoulos 2018). This stream of research could also investigate how ACAs' leaders draw on global calls for strengthening international legal anticorruption instruments to advocate a human-rights based approach to corruption at the national level (United Nations 2020). With regard to research on the interactive dynamics between independence and multi-actor influence, interorganizational relationships in the context of "regulation inside government" (Hood et al. 1998) needs more attention, specifically regarding how ACAs' staff manages the inherent tension between the advisory roles that ACAs exercise when they coach public bureaucracies on corruption risk reduction and the adversarial role they play when they police the same bureaucracies for violations. The study of the "delegation triangle" between political principal(s), ACAs and independent regulatory authorities in other policy sectors is also particularly relevant because ACAs may represent a means to diminish information asymmetries between political principal(s) and independent regulatory authorities with regard to the regulators' compliance with rules and standards that define inappropriate conflicts of interest. Research on multi-actor dynamics may also benefit from the literature on the rise of stakeholder engagement practices in regulatory governance (Braun and Busuioc 2020). This literature has raised important questions regarding implications for regulatory legitimacy that are particularly relevant in the field of anticorruption in which responding to diverse stakeholder expectations is foundational to regulatory power and authority. It is also worth highlighting that, despite the important role that judicial actors play to supervise the legality of ACAs' actions, no research has analyzed the political role of judicial oversight over regulatory authorities in the field of anticorruption. Further research could build on comparative administrative law scholarship and administrative capacities literature to study the extent to which judicial review and the broader strategic action of judges influence ACAs' development (Mejía 2021; see also Chapter 22 by De Somer et al. and Chapter 23 by Murphy in this volume).

Finally, work on ACAs could draw on recent research that has delved into the possible negative side-effects of repetitive reforms (Wynen et al. 2017; Kleizen et al. 2018; Wynen et al. 2019). As highlighted by previous research (Di Mascio et al. 2020; Bautista-Beauchesne 2021b), ACAs typically operate in an environment of continuous reform efforts. Therefore, a greater insight about the negative effects of repetitive reforms is crucial for ACAs to remain adaptable to a turbulent environment. It is also worth investigating in more depth how ACAs' leaders contribute to repetitive reforms by acting as agenda-setters in the post-delegation stage (see Chapter 25 by Guaschino in this volume). Another factor that may well contribute to the turbulence of the environment in which ACAs operate is the populist surge in the context of the broader process of democratic backsliding (Bauer et al. 2021). On the one hand, populist parties have benefited from politicising corruption, implying that populist appeals have increased pressures for signaling political commitment to anticorruption reform. On the other hand, the rhetoric about the fight against corruption has not been matched with much action or a strong and consistent emphasis on changing patterns of governance (Peters and Pierre 2019). However, there are many varieties of populism and it would be worth to empirically study the extent to which different populist pressures shape the trajectory of ACAs across countries and over time.

REFERENCES

AFA (2020) *Global Mapping of Anti-Corruption Authorities: Analysis Report*. Paris: Agence Française Anticorruption.

Ankamah, S.S. (2019) Why do "teeth" need "voice"? The case of anti-corruption agencies in three Australian states. *Australian Journal of Public Administration*, 78(4), 481–496.

Baniamin, M.H. & Jamil, I. (2018) Dynamics of corruption and citizens' trust in anticorruption agencies in three South Asian countries. *Public Organization Review*, 18(3), 381–398.

Batory, A. (2012) Political cycles and organizational life cycles: Delegation to anticorruption agencies in Central Europe. *Governance*, 25(4), 639–660.

Bauer, M.W., Peters, B.G., Pierre, J., Yesilkagit, K. & Becker, S. (Eds.) (2021) *Democratic Backsliding and Public Administration: How Populists in Government Transform State Bureaucracies*. Cambridge: Cambridge University Press.

Bautista-Beauchesne, N. (2021a) Crafting anti-corruption agencies' bureaucratic reputation: An uphill battle. *Crime, Law & Social Change*, 75(4), 327–329.

Bautista-Beauchesne, N. (2021b) Building anti-corruption agency collaboration and reputation: Hanging together or separately hanged. *Regulation & Governance*, https://doi.org/10.1111/rego.12433

Boin, A., Kuipers, S. & Steenbergen, M. (2010) The life and death of public organizations. *Governance*, 23(3), 385–410.

Braun, C. & Busuioc, M. (2020) Stakeholder engagement as a conduit for regulatory legitimacy? *Journal of European Public Policy*, 27(11), 1599–1611.

Busuioc, M. & Lodge, M. (2016) The reputational basis of public accountability. *Governance*, 29(2), 247–263.

Choi, J.-W. (2011) Measuring the performance of an anticorruption agency: The case of the KPK in Indonesia. *International Review of Public Administration,* 16(3), 45–63.

Christensen, T. & Gornitzka, A. (2019) Reputation management in public agencies: The relevance of time, sector, audience, and task. *Administration & Society*, 51(6), 885–914.

David-Barrett, E. Murray, A., Polvi, J. & Burge, R. (2020) Evaluating anti-corruption agencies: Learning from the Caribbean. *Journal of Development Effectiveness*, 12(1), 74–88.

De Jaegere, S. (2012) Principles for anti-corruption agencies: A game changer. *Jindal Journal for Public Policy*, 1, 79–120.

De Sousa, L. (2010) Anti-corruption agencies: Between empowerment and irrelevance. *Crime, Law and Social Change*, 53(1), 5–22.

De Sousa, L., Larmour, P. & Hindess, B. (Eds.) (2009) *Governments, NGOs and Anti-corruption: The New Integrity Warriors*. Abingdon: Routledge.

Di Mascio, F., Maggetti, M. & Natalini, A. (2020) Exploring the dynamics of delegation over time: Insights from Italian anti-corruption agencies. *Policy Studies Journal*, 48(2), 367–400.

Doig, A. (1995) Good government and sustainable anti-corruption strategies: A role for independent anti-corruption agencies. *Public Administration and Development*, 15(2), 151–165.

Doig, A. & Norris, D. (2012) Improving anti-corruption agencies as organisations. *Journal of Financial Crime*, 19(3), 255–273.

Doig, A., Watt, D. & Williams, R. (2005) *Measuring the Success of Five African Anti-Corruption Commissions*. Bergen, U4 Anti-Corruption Resource Centre, Chr. Michelsen Institute.

Doig, A., Watt, D. & Williams, R. (2007) Why do developing country anti-corruption commissions fail to deal with corruption? Understanding the three dilemmas of organisational development, performance expectation, and donor and government cycles. *Public Administration and Development*, 27(3), 251–259.

Dubash, N.K. & Morgan, B. (2012) Understanding the rise of the regulatory state of the South. *Regulation & Governance*, 6(3), 261–281.

Gemperle, S.M. (2018) Comparing anti-corruption agencies: A new cross-national index. *International Review of Public Administration*, 23(3), 156–175.

Gilardi, F. & Maggetti, M. (2011) The independence of regulatory authorities. In Levi-Faur, D. (Ed.) *Handbook on the Politics of Regulation*. Cheltenham, UK and Northampton, MA, USA: Edward Elgar Publishing.

Hanretty, C. & Koop, C. (2013) Shall the law set them free? The formal and actual independence of regulatory agencies. *Regulation & Governance*, 7(2), 195–214.

Heilbrunn, J.R. (2004) Anti-corruption commissions: Panacea or real medicine to fight corruption? In Campos, J.E. & Pradhan, S. (Eds.) *The Many Faces of Corruption: Tracking Vulnerabilities at the Sector Level*. Washington, DC: World Bank Institute.

Heywood, P.M. & Rose, J. (2014) "Close but no cigar": The measurement of corruption. *Journal of Public Policy*, 34(3), 507–529.

Hood, C., James, O., Jones, G., Scott, C. & Travers, T. (Eds.) (1998) *Regulation Inside Government: Waste-Watchers, Quality Police, and Sleazebusters*. Oxford: Oxford University Press.

Hopkin, J. & Rodriguez-Pose, A. (2007) "Grabbing hand" or "helping hand"? Corruption and the economic role of the state. *Governance*, 20(2), 187–208.

Johnston, M. (1999) A brief history of anticorruption agencies. In Schedler, A., Diamond, L. & Plattner, M.F. (Eds.) *The Self-Restraining State: Power and Accountability in New Democracies*. Boulder: Lynne Rienner Publishers.

Jordana, J., Fernández-i-Marín, X. & Bianculli, A. (2018) Agency proliferation and the globalization of the regulatory state. *Regulation & Governance*, 12(4), 524–540.

Kleizen, B., Verhoest, K. & Wynen, J. (2018) Structural reform histories and perceptions of organisational autonomy: Do senior managers perceive less strategic policy autonomy when faced with frequent and intense restructuring? *Public Administration*, 96(2), 349–367.

Koop, C. & Kessler, P. (2021) Keeping control of regulation? Domestic constraints on the creation of independent authorities in emerging and developing economies. *Governance*, 34(2), 545–564.

Krambia-Kapardis, M. (2019) Disentangling anti-corruption agencies and accounting for their ineffectiveness. *Journal of Financial Crime*, 26(1), 22–35.

Kuris, G. (2015) Watchdogs or guard dogs: Do anti-corruption agencies need strong teeth? *Policy and Society*, 34(2), 125–135.

Levi-Faur, D. (2011) Regulation and regulatory governance. In Levi-Faur, D. (Ed.) *Handbook on the Politics of Regulation*. Cheltenham, UK and Northampton, MA, USA: Edward Elgar Publishing.

Lijphart, A. (1999) *Patterns of Democracy: Government Forms and Performance in Thirty-Six Countries*. New Haven: Yale University Press.

Maggetti, M. (2007) De facto independence after delegation: A fuzzy-set analysis. *Regulation & Governance*, 1(4), 271–294.

Maor, M. (2004) Feeling the heat? Anticorruption mechanisms in comparative perspective. *Governance*, 17(1), 1–28.

Marquette, H. & Peiffer, C. (2018) Grappling with the "real politics" of systemic corruption: Theoretical debates versus "real-world" functions. *Governance,* 31(3), 499–514.

Meagher, P. (2005) Anti-corruption agencies: Rhetoric versus reality. *Journal of Policy Reform*, 8(1), 69–103.

Mejía, L.E. (2021) Judicial review of regulatory decisions: Decoding the contents of appeals against agencies in Spain and United Kindgom. *Regulation & Governance*, 15(3), 760–784.

Mungiu-Pippidi, A. & Dadašov (2017) When do anticorruption laws matter? The evidence on public integrity enabling contexts. *Crime, Law, and Social Change*, 68(1), 387–402.

OECD (2013) *Specialised Anti-Corruption Institutions – Review of Models*. Paris: Organisation for Economic Co-operation and Development.

Özel, I.D. & Unan, A. (2021) Decoupling trends: Drivers of agency independence in telecommunications. *Regulation & Governance*, 15(1), 32–62.

Papadopoulos, Y. (2018) How does knowledge circulate in a regulatory network? Observing a European Platform of Regulatory Authorities meeting. *Regulation & Governance*, 12(4), 431–450.

Pavón Mediano, A. (2020) Agencies' formal independence and credible commitment in the Latin American regulatory state: A comparative analysis of 8 countries and 13 sectors. *Regulation & Governance*, 14(1), 102–120.

Persson, A., Rothstein, B. & Teorell, J. (2013) Why anticorruption reforms fail – systemic corruption as a collective action problem. *Governance*, 26(3), 449–471.

Peters, B.G. (2021) *Administrative Traditions: Understanding the Roots of Contemporary Administrative Behavior*. Oxford: Oxford University Press.

Peters, B.G. & Pierre, J. (2019) Populism and public administration: Confronting the administrative state. *Administration & Society*, 51(10), 1521–1545.

Pozsgai-Alvarez, J. (2018) The political cycle of fighting corruption: Peru's experience with its first National Anti-corruption Commission. *Stability: International Journal of Security and Development*, 7(1), 1–19.

Pozsgai-Alvarez, J. (2021) Introduction: Locating anti-corruption agencies within the politics of anti-corruption in Latin America. In Pozsgai-Alvarez, J. (Ed.) *The Politics of Anti-Corruption Agencies in Latin America*. London: Routledge.

Prateeppornnarong, D. (2021) Fighting corruption while having hands tied: A case study of Thailand's public sector anti-corruption commission. *Journal of Asian and African Studies*, 56(2), 320–334.

Quah, J.S.T. (2007), Anti-corruption agencies in four Asian countries: A comparative analysis. *International Public Management Review*, 8(2), 73–96.

Recanatini, F. (2011) Anti-corruption authorities: An effective tool to curb corruption? In Rose-Ackerman, S. & Søreide, T. (Eds.) *International Handbook on the Economics of Corruption*. Cheltenham, UK and Northampton, MA, USA: Edward Elgar Publishing.

Sampson, S. (2010) The anti-corruption industry: From movement to institution. *Global Crime*, 11(2), 261–278.

Schnell, S. (2018) Cheap talk or incredible commitment? (Mis)calculating transparency and anti-corruption. *Governance*, 31(3), 415–430.

Schöberlein, J. (2020) *Anti-corruption Agencies in Europe: Typology and Case Studies*. Berlin: Transparency International.

Skidmore, M.J. (1996) Promise and peril in combating corruption: Hong Kong's ICAC. *The Annals of the American Academy of Political and Social Science*, 547(1), 118–130.

Smilov, D. (2010) Anticorruption agencies: Expressive, constructivist and strategic uses. *Crime, Law and Social Change*, 53(1), 67–77.

Thatcher, M. (2002) Delegation to independent regulatory agencies: Pressures, functions and contextual mediation. *West European Politics*, 25(1), 125–147.

Thatcher, M. (2005) Independent regulatory agencies and elected politicians in Europe. *Governance*, 18(3), 347–373.

Tomić, S. (2018) Legal independence vs leaders' reputation: Exploring drivers of ethics commissions' conduct in new democracies. *Public Administration*, 96(3), 544–560.

Tomić, S. (2019) *Leadership, Institutions and Enforcement: Anti-Corruption Agencies in Serbia, Croatia and Macedonia*. Basingstoke: Palgrave Macmillan.

Tsebelis, G. (2003) *Veto Players: How Political Institutions Work*. Princeton: Princeton University Press.

United Nations (2020) *The UN Common Position to Address Global Corruption*. United Nations, Global Task Force on Corruption.

UNODC (2012) *Jakarta Statement on Principles for Anti-Corruption Agencies*. Jakarta, United Nations Office on Drugs and Crime.

Van der Heijden, J. (2011) Institutional Layering: A Review of the Use of the Concept. *Politics*, 31(1), 9–18.

Wilks, S. & Bartle, I. (2002) The unanticipated consequences of creating independent agencies. *West European Politics*, 25(1), 148–172.

Wynen, J., Verhoest, K. & Kleizen, B. (2017) More reforms, less innovation? The impact of structural reform histories on innovation-oriented cultures in public organisations. *Public Management Review*, 19(8), 1142–1164.

Wynen, J., Verhoest, K. & Kleizen, B. (2019) Are public organisations suffering from repetitive change injury? A panel study of the damaging effect of intense reform sequences. *Governance*, 32(4), 695–713.

PART III

CONCEPTUAL ISSUES

13. Political control of regulatory authorities

Jennifer L. Selin

INTRODUCTION

Through regulation, liberal democracies seek to deliver important services that enhance the lives of their citizens. Regulatory policy touches almost every aspect and sector of the international economy and helps ensure government production of efficient and effective outcomes. Yet, when liberal democracies establish regulatory authorities that are not directly elected by the people, politicians must balance the need for comparatively neutral, competent policy expertise with a desire for democratic accountability (e.g., Wilson 1887; Thatcher 2002).

This balance is often a matter of institutional choice. Because organizational design influences the decisions made by those within regulatory authorities, different organizational features affect regulators' willingness and capacity to respond to political direction. By carefully selecting the structural aspects and decision-making procedures of regulatory authorities, politicians can influence how regulators make policy and to whom they are responsible (e.g., Macey 1992; Fernández-i-Martin, Jordana, and Bianculli 2016; Miller and Whitford 2016; Berry and Gerson 2017).

This chapter examines foundational and emerging research on how politicians design regulatory authorities for political control. Scholarly consideration of political control is simultaneously extensive and restricted. A wealth of research from varying academic disciplines has examined the political tools that are important for control, the organizational aspects of regulatory authorities, and how regulators and politicians interact. At the same time, because these studies explore political control from different perspectives and do not always participate in sustained interchange, many aspects of control remain underdeveloped.

In this chapter, I highlight key insights from the literature and propose new avenues for research across disciplines. Existing scholarship on political control tends to reflect three features of organizational design. First, important work recognizes that regulatory personnel vary in the extent to which political considerations affect their employment. By specifying who works in regulatory authorities, politicians can influence regulatory policy. Commonly referred to as politicization, this aspect of political control includes the rules that authorize regulators to join government service and govern the terms of their careers. Yet, much of the research on political control does not consider the supply side of politicization or how politicized personnel manage regulatory authorities.

In addition to politicizing personnel, politicians can impose procedural requirements on regulatory decision-making in an attempt to enhance control. These requirements establish specific decision-making processes that make certain regulatory outcomes more or less likely. While important work has examined such procedural rules and other forms of regulatory structure, scholars tend to focus on the policies that regulators create rather than how regulatory authorities create policy.

Finally, politicians can provide for external review of regulatory outputs. These *ex post* mechanisms of political control are designed to adjust the incentive structure of regulators when making policy. Scholarship in this area is perhaps the most underdeveloped. Scholars center their examinations on the presence of review devices or on regulators' willingness and capacity to respond to review. Comparatively less research explores the capacity of politicians to implement or enforce external review or the effects of review on regulatory work environments.

Considered together, scholarship on political control suggests that the strategic manipulation of regulatory authorities' structure and personnel is multifaceted and evolves as political environments change. Yet additional research could provide important insights into the dynamics of political control and ultimately increase our understanding of the democratic accountability of regulatory authorities.

FOUNDATIONS

Regulatory authorities' critical roles in policymaking give regulators an important voice in governance. However, as these authorities and the policies delegated to them grow increasingly complex, questions emerge about the ability of democratically elected officials to control them. The creation of regulatory authorities often results from politicians' need to credibly commit not to interfere in policy functions that require time-consistent decision-making (e.g., Lewis 2004; Krause, Lewis, and Douglas 2013; Maggetti and Verhoest 2014; Miller and Whitford 2016; Di Mascio, Maggetti, and Natalini 2020). Yet, if unelected regulators have a substantial role in making policy, liberal democracy requires some causal relationship between regulatory outputs (whether it be in process, activity, or outcomes) and the preferences of officials who are directly accountable to citizens (Koop and Hanretty 2018).

Recognizing this need, elected officials manipulate the structure and personnel of regulatory authorities to influence the authorities' willingness and capacity to respond to political demands (McCubbins 1985; Hammond 1986; Hammond and Thomas 1989; Bawn 1995, 1997; Lewis 2003; Selin 2015). This manipulation varies with context, in part because the need for credible commitment does not apply uniformly across all political environments or policy domains (e.g., Dahlström and Niklasson 2013; Hustedt and Salomonsen 2014; Ennser-Jedenastik 2016b; Hollibaugh and Rothenberg 2020; Matthews 2020). Thus, the degree to which regulatory authorities operate autonomously from political control is relative, multifaceted, and evolves over time (Yesilkagit and van Thiel 2008; Boin, Kuipers, and Steenbergen 2010; Carrigan and Coglianese 2011; Dommet and Skelcher 2014; Holmgren 2018; Koop and Hanretty 2018; Di Mascio, Maggetti, and Natalini 2020).

Scholarly consideration of political control of regulatory authorities reflects three features of organizational design: the politicization of personnel, the specification of processes, and the review of regulatory outputs.

Politicization of Personnel

Scholars vary in their conception of "politicization." This likely is a function of the fact that a variety of disciplines examine regulatory personnel and do so from different perspectives (Resh 2019). Research on politicization tends to define the concept in one of two ways: the extent to which (1) the recruitment, retention, promotion, and discipline of employees is a result of political, rather than meritorious, considerations (Heclo 1977; Moe 1985; Lewis

2008; Dahlström and Niklasson 2013; Boräng et al. 2018; Ebinger, Veit and Fromm 2019; Lee 2020) and (2) policy-relevant decisions embody political deliberation (Öhberg, Christiansen, and Niklasson 2017; Cooper 2018; Richardson 2019; Shaw and Eichbaum 2020).

Personnel management

An important aspect of organizational design for control involves the rules that authorize regulators to join government service and govern the terms of their employment. In general, regulatory authorities may contain two types of employees – appointees who receive and keep their jobs based on political considerations and public servants who work under a system of merit-based rules that emphasize neutral competence. The decision to provide for the political appointment of regulatory personnel as an organizational design feature is called *formal politicization* and is intended to compensate for elected officials' commitments not to formulate policy directly (Hustedt and Salomonsen 2014; Bach, Hammerschmid, and Löffler 2020; Shaw and Eichbaum 2020). Organizations with more appointees are likely to complete tasks with politics in mind, make personnel decisions based on political views, and can generate outputs that reflect the preferences of their political principals (Moe 1985; Lewis 2008, 2012).

Like other methods of political control, the use of formal politicization fluctuates widely across political context. Regulatory authorities vary in terms of the types of appointments that politicians can make, the positions that politicians may fill with appointments, and the layers of the administrative hierarchy that may contain appointments (e.g., Maranto 2005; Lewis and Waterman 2013; Haglund 2015; Krause and O'Connell 2016; Hustedt and Salomonsen 2017; Hollibaugh and Rothenberg 2018; Moore 2018). How politicians work within the formal rules that dictate regulatory appointments also varies. While provisions that reduce the ability of politicians to use appointments can make regulatory elites less vulnerable to partisan turnover, they also raise the political stakes (Ennser-Jedenastick 2015; Hollibaugh and Rothenberg 2018). As a result, politicians become highly strategic in their use of appointments and learn over time how to sift through potential appointees to best achieve political goals (Krause and O'Connell 2016).

Researchers recognize that the presence of political appointees not only allows politicians to have a direct say in who works in a regulatory authority, but also influences the incentive structure of regulatory personnel who operate under merit systems. Referred to as *functional politicization*, political pressure can influence how even merit-based employees structure their careers and prompt an internal labor market for merit-based employees that mimics that for political appointees (Christensen, Kelmmensen, and Opstrup 2014; Doherty, Lewis, and Limbocker 2019a, 2019b; Ebinger, Veit and Fromm 2019; Shaw and Eichbaum 2020). Put another way, the formal rules that govern appointment do not tell the full story. Political appointees can, at times, operate similarly to regulators employed under merit systems and merit-based regulators can, at times, behave like appointees. For example, political links across government may protect appointed regulators from removal and merit-based executives may accommodate political principals in order to minimize conflict or protect their future professional opportunities (Christensen, Kelmmensen, and Opstrup 2014; Fernández-i-Martin, Jordana, and Bianculli 2016; Lee 2020). Furthermore, in response to decisions by appointed regulators that marginalize individuals whose preferences diverge from political officials or threaten their professional identity, merit-based employees can choose to exit the organization (Cooper 2018; Doherty, Lewis, and Limbocker 2019a). Considered in the aggregate, these decisions can lead to regulatory authorities that are more or less responsive to political control.

Internal deliberation

Efforts to make an agency more politically responsive through personnel management can also have administrative consequences. Scholars consider *administrative politicization* to be procedural if political appointees act as gatekeepers who control the flow of information and substantive if they influence the content of the organization's decision-making process (Eichbaum and Shaw 2008; Öhberg, Christiansen, and Niklasson 2017; Ebinger, Veit, and Fromm 2019; Shaw and Eichbaum 2020). Political appointees can complicate regulatory tasks by adding layers of review to regulatory decision-making, adjusting resource allocation, or generating management problems (Wood and Lewis 2017). Furthermore, regulatory officials' political connections can create in- and out-groups for decision-making (Pauls and Yackee 2016). Often, this results in gatekeeping of information or management that works to the comparative benefit of political co-partisans (Öhberg, Christiansen, and Niklasson 2017; Doherty, Lewis, and Limbocker 2019b; Dahlström, Fazekas, and Lewis 2021).

Political appointees also may adjust regulatory decision-making to encourage informal communication with key stakeholders (Haeder and Yackee 2015; Ban and You 2019). The extent to which appointees do so may, in part, reflect the regulatory environment. Regulatory authorities are highly strategic when consulting stakeholders, draw distinctions between sponsors and clients, and may broker informal relationships to benefit certain political interests over others (Waterman, Rouse, and Wright 1998; Schmidt 2002; Lee 2012; Yesilkagit and van Thiel 2012).

This is particularly likely when regulatory authorities have broad policymaking responsibilities (West 2005). Broad policy mandates give political appointees more freedom to direct regulatory policy. Regulatory authorities operate under resource constraints and are unable to accomplish all policy goals delegated to them. As a result, every choice about where to direct regulatory attention is also a choice about where *not* to direct attention (e.g., Jennings et al. 2011; Boydstun, Bevan, and Thomas 2014; Gilad 2015; Workman 2015; Carrigan 2018). Political appointees can influence both of these choices by subjecting a regulatory authority to internal and external manipulation regarding how a regulatory authority interprets its mission and implements regulatory tasks (Dommett and Skelcher 2014; González and Verhoest 2020).

Specification of Structure and Process

Of course, rather than relying on political appointees indirectly to manage deliberation within a regulatory authority, politicians can directly stipulate the legal requirements an authority must follow when making policy. In some ways, this strategy may be more efficient for politicians. Instead of expending costly resources to monitor regulatory authorities or sanction them for failure to adhere to political preferences, politicians can require authorities to follow intricate decision-making processes (McCubbins, Noll, and Weingast 1987, 1989). These procedures can channel policy to a small subset of options and therefore reduce an authority's substantive discretion (McCubbins 1985).

Specification of process tends to fall into one of two categories. First, the imposition of procedures can establish decision-making processes that enfranchise certain political interests and push the regulatory environment to reflect the preferences of the coalition that enacted the procedures. Second, and relatedly, procedures can structure decision-making in a way that makes regulation more or less likely. The two categories are not mutually exclusive (Potoski 2002; Woods 2018).

Furthermore, political principals can impose procedures across all regulatory authorities or target specific agencies for specific procedures (e.g., Jensen and McGrath 2011; Selin and Lewis 2018). Not only does the imposition of procedural mandates influence the content of regulatory policymaking, but procedures also help politicians acquire the information needed to conduct meaningful oversight and to explore the political consequences of regulatory policy decisions (e.g., McCubbins 1985; Bendor, Taylor and Van Gaalen 1987; Bawn 1995, 1997; Balla 1998; de Figueiredo, Spiller and Urbiztondo 1999).

Politicians likely choose certain procedures under different conditions and for different purposes. Like other methods of control, the effectiveness of administrative procedures varies with the details of the procedures, the complexity of subject matter, and political environment in which a regulatory authority operates (Baum and Bawn 2011; Blom-Hansen 2013). Certain procedures may be ineffective as mechanisms of control because they actually encourage regulatory authorities to cultivate expertise and analytic capacity, exacerbating information asymmetries between politicians and regulators (Woods 2018). Additionally, from a regulatory perspective, the imposition of procedures may introduce inefficiencies in the policy process (Posner 2001).

Review of Outputs

While specification of process itself can be a mechanism of control, regulatory procedures can provide opportunities for external review of outputs. These structural features allow political actors to confirm that regulatory authorities' policy decisions adhere to political preferences (Selin 2015). Even if one does not observe the use of these *ex post* review mechanisms, their mere presence may adjust incentives so that regulators are more responsive.

Yet, when compared to politicization of personnel and specification of process, there is little evidence that *ex post* mechanisms result in increased responsiveness to political preferences (e.g., Prakash 2012; Koop and Hanretty 2018). In fact, in some circumstances, *ex post* review can induce strategic behavior by regulators to propose more extreme policies than they would otherwise (Patty and Turner 2021). Furthermore, external review can provide incentives for regulators to provide ambiguous, strategically biased, inaccurate, or contradictory information about their activities (Dekker and Hansén 2004; Boräng et al. 2018).

The most successful form of *ex post* review appears to be administrative reorganization or agency termination. Facing a credible threat of reorganization or termination, regulators are more likely to respond to their external environments, receive political signals, and change deliberations within their organizations by incentivizing uniformity and formalization of processes (Corbett and Howard 2017; Wynen et al. 2020). Reorganization and termination are more likely in some circumstances than others, and often depend upon partisan environment (Lewis 2002; Bertelli and Sinclair 2015; James et al. 2016; Holmgren 2018). Additionally, regulatory authorities created with more autonomous structures are less susceptible to termination (Greasley and Hanretty 2016).

As is evident from the above discussion, regardless of design, the legal instruments that structure an organization and the way a regulatory authority operates in practice are not necessarily the same (Maggetti 2007; Hanretty and Koop 2013). Regulation involves complicated interactions negotiated within ever-changing political environments. As a result, scholars who seek to gain substantive understanding of political control must account for these contexts.

FORESIGHT

Regulatory outputs vary based on the signals regulatory authorities receive from politicians, conditional on the degree to which those authorities have been structured for political control (Arel-Bundock, Atkinson, and Potter 2015; Anderson and Potoski 2016). However, existing research tends either to conflate various strategies of control or examine them in isolation, resulting in conceptions of political control and regulatory accountability that are overlapping and underspecified (Christensen and Laegried 2007; Berry and Gersen 2017). These tensions have consequences for the conclusions scholars draw from empirical studies. Because all three forms of political control – politicization of personnel, specification of process, and review of regulatory outputs – coexist and vary in different ways at different times in different contexts, an examination of one to the exclusion of others can present a skewed picture of the extent to which politics affect regulatory authorities.

Furthermore, most research on political control relies on operationalizations that are mere proxies (Wood and Lewis 2017). Scholars measure agency features that should correlate with political influence, rather than measuring influence itself. For example, those who examine formal politicization often operationalize this concept by indicating whether agency leadership is appointed, counting the number of appointees in an agency, or constructing a ratio of the number of managers in an authority that are appointed. In the same way, those who seek to explore organizational structure or political review of outputs examine the presence of specific features.

One of the benefits of such approaches is that the data is available and concrete. However, by focusing on the concrete, these studies often have to make assumptions about how regulatory authorities operate in practice. Yet not all agency features are equal in importance, are viewed the same way by politicians, or have consistent effects across agencies. To circumvent these problems, some scholars utilize qualitative case studies or survey data to explore the relative influence of various political actors and to capture interactions that are not easily quantifiable by observational studies. While such research sheds light into regulatory operations, these studies raise questions about sample bias and generalizability. For example, qualitative case studies are, by their nature, limited to at most an examination of a handful of regulatory authorities and survey-based research only provides a snapshot of operations at the time the survey was administered. As a result, they likely obfuscate variation in political control across different contexts.

Some scholars seek to avoid these problems by focusing on whether or not outputs adhere to political preferences. This approach has resulted in a body of literature that generally considers an increase of political control for one set of political actors to result in a decrease in control for another. Yet it is not clear that political control is a zero-sum game. Combined strategies of political control can enhance regulatory responsiveness to one set of political interests without diminishing control exercised by another set of interests (Rosenbloom, Newbold, and Doughty 2018). Furthermore, these studies tend to overlook the degree of variance in outcomes under different institutional arrangements (Stephenson 2008).

Politicization of Personnel

Many scholars who study politicization oversimplify the concept by equating the presence of political appointees with the establishment of political control (Hustedt and Salomonsen 2017).

Careful consideration of the supply side of politicization as well as the management strategies politicized personnel employ would make significant contributions to our understanding of political control. Important research has established that political appointees can advance both political and policy goals (e.g., Weko 1995; Pfiffner 1996; Bertelli and Feldman 2007; Lewis 2008; Parsneau 2013; Hollibaugh, Horton, and Lewis 2014). Yet because this research tends to center around an examination of the individuals who serve in appointed positions, it ignores aspects of the political environment which produce appointments in the first place.

Regulators – politically appointed or merit-based – are part of an economic labor market. Like all markets, the regulatory labor market has a demand and supply side (Grissom, Viano, and Selin 2015). Labor demand refers to the number of positions within a regulatory authority at a given compensation level or appointment type. Labor supply encompasses the number of qualified individuals willing to take those positions. The bulk of politicization research has focused on labor demand at the expense of examining labor supply (Lewis and Waterman 2013). This omission is consequential for political control, as the number, quality, and distribution of individuals willing to work in regulatory authorities undoubtedly influences politicization.

A fruitful line of research would treat the demand for politicized labor as fixed and then consider potential regulators' decisions to join government service or to pursue other employment opportunities. Not only is the labor supply greater in some policy contexts than in others, but the political environment can lead some individuals to aggressively seek appointments or key stakeholders to play active roles in the recruitment of regulatory personnel (Maranto 2005). Relatedly, in some political contexts, politicians may feel compelled to add a specific individual to government; politicians must find a position for a particular individual rather than an optimal individual for a particular position (Hollibaugh 2017).

Understanding the nuance of labor supply is important for several reasons. First, it likely informs initial choices regarding political control. Theoretical considerations of political control tend to assume implicitly that politicization is always an option and that, in deciding whether to employ this strategy, politicians weigh the costs against the benefits of doing so. Yet, practically, the supply of potential regulators may limit politicization choices. If few individuals are willing to take regulatory positions, then formal politicization becomes a less viable option.

Of course, once regulatory positions exist, politicians may decide not to fill them. This is itself a form of politicization, as the decision whether to place an individual in an open regulatory position or to allow a vacancy to remain is strategic (Kinane 2021; Resh et al. 2021). During times of vacant or less stable leadership, uncertainty regarding an authority's policy mission resulting from a lack of management and/or conflicting directives can lead regulatory personnel to exert less effort and turnover more (O'Connell 2008; Richardson 2019; Rutherford et al. 2019). Furthermore, because it can be difficult to successfully recruit regulators when vacancies exist, regulatory authorities may defer searches for personnel (Tenpas 2018). The resource constraints and inefficiencies that result from such an environment can have real effects on regulatory work environments and outputs and, in the aggregate, influence political control (Johnasen 2013).

In addition to considering how the supply for regulatory personnel correlates with political control, scholars would benefit from increased attention to the management strategies politicized personnel employ. For example, while important research suggests that political appointees tend to have fewer years of regulatory and governmental management experience than merit-based employees in similar positions (e.g., Lewis 2007, 2008; Gallo and Lewis 2012), we have less understanding of how this lack of experience translates to daily managerial decisions or how politicized personnel evolve over time. Potentially fruitful research could examine how politicized personnel are oriented when they enter a regulatory authority and the evolution of the relationship between political appointees and merit-based regulators over time (Maranto 2005; Berman et al. 2013; Tenpas 2018).

Finally, because politicized personnel tend to be transitory, it is hard for them to build relationships with and effectively manage more permanent employees within a regulatory authority (e.g., Ingraham 1987; Ingraham, Thompson, and Eisenberg 1995; Resh 2015). Given that the effectiveness of management, combined with organizational context, influences an individual's decision to remain in an organization (Bertelli 2007; Ryu and Lee 2013), research considering the relationship between politicization and turnover in regulatory authorities would help illuminate the effects of this form of political control.

Specification of Structure and Process

While scholars have dedicated much research to the politics, presence, and effects of politicization, less research examines how politicians balance politicization of personnel with procedural rules and other forms of regulatory structure over time. Politicians respond to structural choices designed to insulate regulatory authorities by placing greater emphasis on the strategic placement of political allies in key regulatory positions (Ennser-Jedenastik 2016a). Yet because research tends to explore regulatory design, politicization of personnel, administrative procedure, or internal agency management in isolation, basic descriptive questions about structure and process remain unanswered. Two productive avenues of research include more nuanced consideration of the structural design of regulatory authorities beyond politicization or external review and these authorities' adherence to traditional regulatory processes.

With respect to structure, important scholarship demonstrates that regulatory features such as size, hierarchy, and decentralization all influence political control and agency performance (e.g., Gulick 1937; Kaufman 1960; Scholz and Wei 1986; Scholz, Twombly, and Headrick 1991; Whitford 2007). These features can affect an authority's ability to coordinate internal decisions and can slow changes in regulatory policy (e.g., Hammond and Miller 1985; Carpenter 1996; Rudalevidge 2005; Patacconi 2009). Additionally, such structural features can result in differing organizational values and preferences within a single regulatory authority (Krause 2009). The need for coordination across multiple regulatory actors at different levels or across and within sectors likely influences the ability of politicians to control regulatory outcomes (see González and Verhoest 2020).

Of particular relevance is the transfer of regulatory authority from the political center to field offices. Deconcentration of authority in large, spatially dispersed governments can serve to enhance political control in some contexts and to diminish control in others (Whitford 2002). For example, deconcentration can leverage regional political networks and tailor regulatory relationships to favor certain stakeholders (Schmidt 2002; Reuter and Robertson 2012). At the same time, deconcentration can create barriers to national political oversight (Whitford 2002). Simply, the closeness of regulatory policymaking to the political center may be more important than many other forms of control (Furlong 1998; Yesilkagit and van Thiel 2008, 2012).

In part, this may be because deconcentration affects organizational experiences and the ability of regulators to influence policy. These aspects of employment influence how regulators perceive their jobs, how much they invest in the authority, and whether they remain in the organization (Buchanan 1974; Romzek 1990; Brehm and Gates 1997; Perry and Wise 1990; Golden 2000; Bertelli 2007; Lee and Whitford 2008; Bertelli and Lewis 2013; Dull and Roberts 2009; Pitts, Marvel and Fernandez 2011). Thus, a regulatory authority's internal structures, management strategies, and staff experiences all reflect the sensitivity of the organization to politics (Ali 2019, 2020). Scholars would benefit from additional consideration of the aggregate effects of organizational design on regulatory personnel on political control.

Additionally, it is worth considering that regulatory authorities often create policy outside of conventional processes (Gluck, O'Connell, and Po 2015). The landscape of mechanisms through which regulators make policy is quite varied, flexible, and underappreciated by scholarly research (Magill 2004; Walker 2018; Potter 2019). Descriptive research that illuminates how regulatory authorities make policy could shed light into why these authorities are more or less susceptible to political control.

Relatedly, most research has explored the policies that regulators prioritize in the face of procedural controls, rather than on how regulatory authorities circumvent political control by redistributing budgetary and human resources towards processes that produce those policies (e.g., Boydstun, Bevan, and Thomas 2014; Chun and Rainey 2005; Gilad 2015; Rainey 1993). Differentiating between *de jure* and *de facto* regulatory processes is essential (Manning 2004). If regulatory authorities do not follow conventional processes, then scholars' theoretical understanding of the relationship between specification of procedures and regulatory outputs may be flawed (Hill and Brazier 1991).

Review of Outputs

One of the most underdeveloped areas of recent research in political control involves review of outputs. This may be a result of an observational equivalency problem – observing an absence of political review mechanisms does not necessarily indicate that regulatory authorities have autonomy. If political officials have an effective system of politicization and process in place, then it is possible that review techniques are unnecessary because regulatory authorities are already structured to pursue political preferences (e.g., Weingast and Moran 1983; McCubbins and Schwartz 1984; McCubbins, Noll, and Weingast 1987, 1989). A lack of observable review mechanisms could be the result of regulatory authorities doing what politicians want them to do or could indicate a desire to grant regulators autonomy (Thatcher 2005). Differentiating between these two possibilities is difficult, but theoretically important. Scholars would benefit from research that elaborates upon when politicians put review mechanisms in place and how those mechanisms influence the regulatory environment.

When considering political review, scholars tend to focus on the incentives and capacity of regulators to respond to pressure from politicians without understanding the ability of politicians to exert such pressure (Drolc and Keiser 2021). Given that institutional features such as capacity and decision rules result in systematic differences in delegation (e.g., Huber, Shipan and Pfahler 2001; Franchino 2004), those same features should influence the establishment and use of political review. For example, a lack of capacity can have consequences for politicians' abilities to analyze regulatory information, identify and interpret various policy alternatives, and to sanction regulators for poor performance (Montgomery and Nyhan 2017).

Not only should increased capacity lead to the implementation of formal review mechanisms, but it also makes the threat of sanction for failure to adhere to political preferences more credible (Selin and Milazzo 2021). Simply, some strategies are more effective when politicians are familiar with the inner workings of the regulatory process (Lewis, Bernhard, and You 2018).

This fact creates opportunities for regulatory authorities themselves. Evidence suggests that close relationships between and among regulators, politicians, and political staff facilitate information sharing about policy and process (e.g., Aberbach 1990; Carpenter and Krause 2015; Mills and Selin 2017; Workman 2015). As a result, regulatory authorities have under-appreciated power to shape political control and may even influence their own design features (Carpenter 2001; Dommett and Skelcher 2014). Participation in the policy process and consistent interaction with key stakeholders provides regulators with knowledge of the social, economic, and political context within which their organizations operate and thus can place regulators in a strong position vis-à-vis politicians (Selin 2021).

Furthermore, the opportunity for political review can change agency working environments. Consistent review can create frustration within an agency, damage morale, and even push some regulators to exit public service (Ali 2019). Returning to considerations of labor supply, one of the most attractive nonpecuniary benefits of employment within a regulatory authority is the ability to impact policy. Yet a highly political environment can significantly impact individual regulators' policymaking influence (Gailmard and Patty 2007). Subjecting a regulatory authority to review of outputs may allow political officials to keep tabs on policy decisions, but may also result in a decreased sense of efficacy among regulators. While research has explored the influence of political review on turnover, little research has explored the effects review may have on the recruitment of regulators.

In summary, there is much potential for future research in the areas of politicization of personnel, organizational structure and process, and political review of outputs. Not only would scholars benefit from additional exploration of these topics in isolation, but research on how politicians employ these combined strategies would help further understanding of regulatory authorities. Such studies would complement foundational scholarship and provide important empirical and theoretical insights into the dynamics of political control.

CONCLUSION

The need to understand political control of regulatory authorities is steadily increasing as the amount and complexity of government regulation grows. The democratic legitimacy of regulatory authorities depends on an assumption that regulatory policy reflects legitimate policy choices made by politicians who have an electoral connection to citizens. Yet politicians must balance this need for political control against the desirability of credibly committing not to interfere in the development of regulation by a cadre of experts.

Decades-worth of important research conducted across the globe has explored the dynamics of this balance. While I could not hope to capture the nuance of the valuable insights scholarship has provided on topic, this chapter's brief account suggests that while many aspects of political control are well understood, others remain underdeveloped or unexplored. Notably, quite a diverse set of devices exist to facilitate the political control of regulatory authorities. Politicians' design and use of control mechanisms varies across time and political context. Not only do the structure and incentives of politicians affect political control, but the structure and incentives of regulatory authorities and personnel have real consequences for how responsive these authorities are to the preferences of politicians.

In sum, creative thinking and sustained dialogue across and within academic disciplines and research communities will help illuminate how politicians hold regulatory authorities accountable. For those who endeavor to study political control of regulatory authorities, the future is filled with boundless possibilities (to complete the political dynamics of regulatory agencies, see also Chapter 25).

REFERENCES

Aberbach, Joel D. 1990. *Keeping a Watchful Eye: The Politics of Congressional Oversight.* Washington, DC: Brookings Institution.

Ali, Susannah Bruns. 2019. "Politics, Bureaucracy and Employee Retention: Toward an Integrated Framework of Turnover Intent." *Administration and Society* 51(9):1486–1516.

Ali, Susannah Bruns. 2020. "Does Political Turbulence Encourage Fight or Flight for Federal Employees? Examining Political Environments and Turnover Intent." *Public Personnel Management* 49(2):262–289.

Anderson, Sarah E. and Matthew Potoski. 2016. "Agency Structure and the Distribution of Federal Spending." *Journal of Public Administration Research and Theory* 26(3):461–474.

Arel-Bundock, Vincent, James Atkinson, and Rachel Augustine Potter. 2015. "The Limits of Foreign Aid Diplomacy: How Bureaucratic Design Shapes Aid Distribution." *International Studies Quarterly* 59(3):544–556.

Bach, Tobias, Gerhard Hammerschmid, and Lorez Löffler. 2020. "More Delegation, More Political Control? Politicization of Senior-Level Appointments in 18 European Countries." *Public Policy and Administration* 35(1):3–23.

Balla, Steven J. 1998. "Administrative Procedures and Political Control of the Bureaucracy." *American Political Science Review* 92(3):663–673.

Ban, Pamela and Hye Young You. 2019. "Presence and Influence in Lobbying: Evidence from Dodd–Frank." *Business and Politics* 21(2):267–295.

Baum, Jeeyang Rhee and Kathleen Bawn. 2011. "Slowing at Sunset: Administrative Procedures and the Pace of Reform in Korea." *Journal of East Asian Studies* 11(2):197–222.

Bawn, Kathleen. 1995. "Political Control Versus Expertise: Congressional Choices about Administrative Procedures." *American Political Science Review* 89(1):62–73.

Bawn, Kathleen. 1997. "Choosing Strategies to Control the Bureaucracy: Statutory Constraints, Oversight and the Committee System." *Journal of Law, Economics, and Organization* 13(1):101–126.

Bendor, Jonathan, Serge Taylor, and Roland Van Gaalen. 1987. "Politicians, Bureaucrats, and Asymmetric Information." *American Journal of Political Science* 31(4):796–828.

Berman, Evan, Don-Yun Chen, Chung-Yuang Jan, and Tong-Yi Huang. 2013. "Public Agency Leadership: The Impact of Informal Understandings with Political Appointees on Perceived Agency Innovation in Taiwan." *Public Administration* 91(2):303–324.

Berry, Christopher R. and Jacob Gersen. 2017. "Agency Design and Political Control." *Yale Law Journal* 126(4):1002–1049.

Bertelli, Anthony M. 2007. "Determinants of Bureaucratic Turnover Intention: Evidence from the Department of Treasury." *Journal of Public Administration Research and Theory* 17(2):235–258.

Bertelli, Anthony and Sven E. Feldman. 2007. "Strategic Appointments." *Journal of Public Administration Research and Theory* 17(1):19–38.

Bertelli, Anthony M. and David E. Lewis. 2013. "Policy Influence, Agency-Specific Expertise, and Exit in the Federal Service." *Journal of Public Administration Research and Theory* 23(2):223–245.

Bertelli, Anthony M. and J. Andrew Sinclair. 2015. "Mass Administrative Reorganization, Media Attention, and the Paradox of Information." *Public Administration Review* 75(6):855–866.

Blom-Hansen, Jenss. 2013. "Legislative Control of Powers Delegated to the Executive: The Case of the EU." *Governance* 26(3):425–448.

Boin, Arjen, Sanneke Kuipers, and Marco Steenbergen. 2010. "The Life and Death of Public Organizations: A Question of Institutional Design?" *Governance* 23(3):385–410.

Boräng, Frida, Agnes Cornell, Marcia Grimes, and Christian Shuster. 2018. "Cooking the Books: Bureaucratic Politicization and Policy Knowledge." *Governance* 31(1):7–26.

Boydstun, Amber E., Shaud Bevan, and Herschel F. Thomas III. 2014. "The Importance of Attention Diversity and How to Measure It." *Policy Studies Journal* 42(2):173–196.

Brehm, John and Scott Gates. 1997. *Working, Shirking, and Sabotage: Bureaucratic Response to a Democratic Public*. Ann Arbor, MI: University of Michigan Press.

Buchanan, Bruce II. 1974. "Government Managers, Business Executives, and Organizational Commitment." *Public Administration Review* 34(4):339–347.

Carpenter, Daniel P. 1996. "Adaptive Signal Processing, Hierarchy, and Budgetary Control in Federal Regulation." *American Political Science Review* 90(2):283–302.

Carpenter, Daniel. 2001. *The Forging of Bureaucratic Autonomy*. Princeton, NJ: Princeton University Press.

Carpenter, Daniel and George A. Krause. 2015. "Transactional Authority and Bureaucratic Politics." *Journal of Public Administration Research and Theory* 25(1):5–25.

Carrigan, Christopher. 2018. "Unpacking the Effects of Competing Mandates on Agency Performance." *Public Administration Review* 78(5):669–683.

Carrigan, Christopher and Cary Coglianese. 2011. "The Politics of Regulation: From New Institutionalism to New Governance." *Annual Review of Political Science* 14(2011):107–129.

Christensen, Jørgen Gronnegaard, Robert Kelmmensen, and Niels Opstrup. 2014. "Politicization and the Replacement of Top Civil Servants in Denmark." *Governance* 27(2):215–241.

Christensen, Tom and Per Laegreid. 2007. "Regulatory Agencies – The Challenges of Balancing Agency Autonomy and Political Control." *Governance* 20(3):499–520.

Chun, Young Han and Hal G. Rainey. 2005. "Goal Ambiguity and Organizational Performance in U.S. Federal Agencies." *Journal of Public Administration Research and Theory* 15(4):529–557.

Cooper, Christopher A. 2018. "Bureaucratic Identity and the Resistance of Politicization." *Administration & Society* 50(1):30–52.

Corbett, Jack and Cosmo Howard. 2017. "Why Perceived Size Matters for Agency Termination." *Public Administration* 95(1):196–213.

Dahlström, Carl, Mihály Fazekas, and David E. Lewis. 2021. "Partisan Procurement: Contracting with the United States Federal Government." *American Journal of Political Science* 65(3):652–669.

Dahlström, Carl and Birgitta Niklasson. 2013. "The Politics of Politicization in Sweden." *Public Administration* 91(4):891–907.

Dekker, Sander and Dan Hansén. 2004. "Learning under Pressure: The Effects of Politicization on Organizational Learning in Public Bureaucracies." *Journal of Public Administration Research and Theory* 14(2):211–230.

Di Mascio, Fabricio, Martinao Maggetti, and Alessandra Natalini. 2020. "Exploring the Dynamics of Delegation Over Time: Insights from Italian Anti-Corruption Agencies (2003–2016)." *Policy Studies Journal* 48(2):367–400.

Doherty, Kathleen M., David E. Lewis, and Scott Limbocker. 2019a. "Presidential Control and Turnover in Regulatory Personnel." *Administration & Society* 51(10):1606–1630.

Doherty, Kathleen M., David E. Lewis, and Scott Limbocker. 2019b. "Executive Control and Turnover in the Senior Executive Service." *Journal of Public Administration Research and Theory* 29(2):159–174.

Dommett, Katharine and Chris Skelcher. 2014. "Opening the Black Box of Administrative Reform: A Strategic-Relational Analysis of Agency Responses to Termination Threats." *International Public Management Journal* 17(4):540–563.

Drolc, Cody and Lael R. Keiser. 2021. "The Importance of Oversight and Agency Capacity in Enhancing Performance in Public Service Delivery." *Journal of Public Administration Research and Theory* 31(4): 773–789.

Dull, Matthew and Patrick S. Roberts. 2009. "Continuity, Competence, and the Succession of Senate-Confirmed Agency Appointees, 1989–2009." *Presidential Studies Quarterly* 39(3):94–127.

Ebinger, Falk, Sylvia Veit, and Nadin Fromm. 2019. "The Partisan-Professional Dichotomy Revisited: Politicization and Decision-Making of Senior Civil Servants." *Public Administration* 97(4):861–876.

Eichbaum, Chris and Richard Shaw. 2008. "Revisiting Politicization: Political Advisers and Public Servants in Westminster Systems." *Governance* 21(3):337–363.

Ennser-Jedenastik, Laurenz. 2015. "Credibility Versus Control: Agency Independence and Partisan Influence in the Regulatory State." *Comparative Political Studies* 48(7):823–853.

Ennser-Jedenastik, Laurenz. 2016a. "The Politicization of Regulatory Agencies: Between Partisan Influence and Formal Independence." *Journal of Public Administration Research and Theory* 26(3):507–518.

Ennser-Jedenanstik, Laurenz. 2016b. "Do Parties Matter in Delegation? Partisan Preferences and the Creation of Regulatory Agencies in Europe." *Regulation & Governance* 10(3):193–210.

Fernández-i-Martin, Xavier, Jacint Jordana, and Andrea C. Bianculli. 2016. "Are Regulatory Agencies Independent in Practice? Evidence from Board Members in Spain." *Regulation and Governance* 10(3):230–247.

de Figueiredo, Rui J.P., Pablo T. Spiller, and Santiago Urbiztondo. 1999. "An Informational Perspective on Administrative Procedures." *Journal of Law, Economics, and Organization* 15(11):283–305.

Franchino, Fabio. 2004. "Delegating Powers in the European Community." *British Journal of Political Science* 34(2):269–293.

Furlong, Scott R. 1998. "Political Influence on the Bureaucracy: The Bureaucracy Speaks." *Journal of Public Administration Research and Theory* 8(1):39–65.

Gailmard, Sean and John W. Patty. 2007. "Slackers and Zealots: Civil Service, Policy Discretion, and Bureaucratic Expertise." *American Journal of Political Science* 51(4):873–889.

Gallo, Nick and David E. Lewis. 2012. "The Consequences of Presidential Patronage for Federal Agency Performance." *Journal of Public Administration Research and Theory* 22(2):219–243.

Gilad, Sharon. 2015. "Political Pressures, Organizational Identity, and Attention to Tasks: Illustrations from Pre-Crisis Financial Regulation." *Public Administration* 93(3):593–608.

Gluck, Abbe R., Anne Joseph O'Connell, and Rosa Po. 2015. "Unorthodox Lawmaking, Unorthodox Rulemaking." *Columbia Law Review* 115(7):1789–1866.

Golden, Marissa Martino. 2000. *What Motivates Bureaucrats? Politics and Administration During the Reagan Years.* New York, NY: Columbia University Press.

González, Camilo Ignacio and Koen Verhoest. 2020. "*De Facto* Regulatory Decision-Making Processes in Telecommunications Regulation: Explaining Influence Relationships with Exponential Random Graph Models." *Journal of Public Policy* 40(1):144–170.

Greasley, Stephen and Chris Hanretty. 2016. "Credibility and Agency Termination Under Parliamentarism." *Journal of Public Administration Research and Theory* 26(1):159–173.

Grissom, Jason A., Samantha L. Viano, and Jennifer L. Selin. 2015. "Understanding Employee Turnover in the Public Sector: Insights from Research on Teacher Mobility." *Public Administration Review* 76(2):241–251.

Gulick, Luther. 1937. "Notes on the Theory of Organization." In Luther Gulick and L. Urwick, eds., *Papers on the Science of Administration.* Concord, NH: The Rumford Press.

Haglund, Evan T. 2015. "Striped Pants versus Fat Cats: Ambassadorial Performance of Career Diplomats and Political Appointees." *Presidential Studies Quarterly* 45(4):653–678.

Haeder, Simon F. and Susan Webb Yackee. 2015. "Influence and the Administrative Process: Lobbying the U.S. President's Office of Management and Budget." *American Political Science Review* 109(3):507–522.

Hammond, Thomas H. 1986. "Agenda Control, Organizational Structure, and Bureaucratic Politics." *American Journal of Political Science* 30(2):379–420.

Hammond, Thomas H. and Gary J. Miller. 1985. "A Social Choice Perspective on Expertise and Authority in Bureaucracy." *American Journal of Political Science* 29(1):1–28.

Hammond, Thomas H. and Paul A. Thomas. 1989. "The Impossibility of a Neutral Hierarchy." *Journal of Law, Economics, and Organization* 5(1):155–184.

Hanretty, Chris and Christel Koop. 2013. "Shall the Law Set Them Free? The Formal and Actual Independence of Regulatory Agencies." *Regulation and Governance* 7(2):195–214.

Heclo, Hugh. 1977. *A Government of Strangers: Executive Politics in Washington.* Washington, DC: Brookings Institution.

Hill, Jeffery S. and James E. Brazier. 1991. "Constraining Administrative Decisions: A Critical Examination of the Structure and Process Hypothesis." *Journal of Law, Economics, and Organization* 7(2):373–400.

Hollibaugh, Gary E., Jr. 2017. "The Incompetence Trap: The (Conditional) Irrelevance of Agency Expertise." *Journal of Public Administration Research and Theory* 27(2):217–235.

Hollibaugh, Gary E., Gabriel Horton, and David E. Lewis. 2014. "Presidents and Patronage." *American Journal of Political Science* 58(4):1024–1042.

Hollibaugh, Gary E., Jr. and Lawrence S. Rothenberg. 2018. "The Who, When, and Where of Executive Nominations: Integrating Agency Independence and Appointee Ideology." *American Journal of Political Science* 62(2):296–311.

Hollibaugh, Gary R. and Lawrence S. Rothenberg. 2020. "Appointments and Attrition: Time and Executive Disadvantage in the Appointments Process." *Journal of Public Policy* 40(3):473–491.

Holmgren, Mikael. 2018. "Partisan Politics and Institutional Choice in Public Bureaucracies: Evidence from Sweden." *Journal of Public Administration Research and Theory* 28(3):355–370.

Huber, John D., Charles R. Shipan, and Madelaine Pfahler. 2001. "Legislatures and Statutory Control of Bureaucracy." *American Journal of Political Science* 45(2):330–345.

Hustedt, Thurid and Heidi H. Salomonsen. 2014. "Ensuring Political Responsiveness: Politicization Mechanisms in Ministerial Bureaucracies." *International Review of Administrative Sciences* 80(4):746–765.

Hustedt, Thurid and Heidi H. Salomonsen. 2017. "Political Control of Coordination? The Roles of Ministerial Advisers in Government Coordination in Denmark and Sweden." *Public Administration* 95(2):393–406.

Ingraham, Patricia W. 1987. "Building Bridges or Burning Them? The President, the Appointees, and the Bureaucracy." *Public Administration Review* 47(5):425–435.

Ingraham, Patricia W., James R Thompson, and Elliot F. Eisenberg. 1995. "Political Management Strategies and Political/Career Relationships: Where Are We Now in the Federal Government?" *Public Administration Review* 55(3):263–272.

James, Oliver, Nicolai Petrovsky, Alice Moseley, and George A. Boyne. 2016. "The Politics of Agency Death: Ministers and the Survival of Government Agencies in a Parliamentary System." *British Journal of Political Science* 46(4):763–784.

Jennings, Will, Shaun Bevan, Arco Timmermans, Gerard Breeman, Sylvian Brouard, Laura Chaques-Bonafont, Chistoffer Green-Pedersen, Peter John, Peter B. Mortensen, and Anna M. Palau. 2011. "Effects of the Core Functions of Government on the Diversity of Executive Agendas." *Comparative Political Studies* 44(8):1001–1030.

Jensen, Christian B. and Robert J. McGrath. 2011. "Making Rules about Rulemaking: A Comparison of Presidential and Parliamentary Systems." *Political Research Quarterly* 64(3):656–667.

Johnasen, Morgen. 2013. "The Impact of Managerial Quality on Employee Turnover." *Public Management Review* 15(6):858–877.

Kaufman, Herbert. 1960. *The Forest Ranger: A Study in Administrative Behavior.* Baltimore, MD: Johns Hopkins.

Kinane, Christina. 2021. "Control without Confirmation: The Politics of Vacancies in Presidential Appointments." *American Political Science Review* 115(2):599–614.

Koop, Christel and Chris Hanretty. 2018. "Political Independence, Accountability, and the Quality of Regulatory Decision-Making." *Comparative Political Studies* 51(1):38–75.

Krause, George A. 2009. "Organizational Complexity and Coordination Dilemmas in U.S. Executive Politics." *Presidential Studies Quarterly* 39(1):74–88.

Krause, George A., David E. Lewis, and James W. Douglas. 2013. "Politics Can Limit Policy Opportunism in Fiscal Institutions: Evidence from Official General Fund Revenue Forecasts in American States." *Journal of Policy Analysis and Management* 32(2):271–295.

Krause, George A. and Anne Joseph O'Connell. 2016. "Experiential Learning and Presidential Management of the U.S. Federal Bureaucracy: Logic and Evidence from Agency Leadership Appointments." *American Journal of Political Science* 60(4):914–931.

Lee, Don D. 2020. "Executive Control of Bureaucracy and Presidential Cabinet Appointments in East Asian Democracies." *Regulation and Governance* 14(1):82–101.

Lee, Jongkon. 2012. "The Administrative Broker: Bureaucratic Politics in the Era of Prevalent Information." *American Review of Public Administration* 43(6):690–708.

Lee, Soo-Young and Andrew B. Whitford. 2008. "Exit, Voice, Loyalty, and Pay: Evidence from the Public Workforce." *Journal of Public Administration Research and Theory* 18(4):647–671.

Lewis, David E. 2002. "The Politics of Agency Termination: Confronting the Myth of Agency Immortality." *Journal of Politics* 64(1):89–107.

Lewis, David E. 2003. *Presidents and the Politics of Agency Design.* Stanford, CA: Stanford University Press.

Lewis, David E. 2004. "The Adverse Consequences of the Politics of Agency Design for Presidential Management in the United States: The Relative Durability of Insulated Agencies." *British Journal of Political Science* 34(3):377–404.

Lewis, David E. 2007. "Testing Pendleton's Premise: Do Political Appointees Make Worse Bureaucrats?" *Journal of Politics* 69(4):1073–1088.

Lewis, David E. 2008. *The Politics of Presidential Appointments: Political Control and Bureaucratic Performance.* Princeton, NJ: Princeton University Press.

Lewis, David E. 2012. "Presidential Politicization of the Executive Branch in the United States." In Martin Lodge and Kai Wegrich, eds., *Executive Politics in Times of Crisis.* Hampshire, UK: Palgrave Macmillan.

Lewis, David E., Patrick Bernhard, and Emily You. 2018. "President Trump as Manager: Reflections on the First Year." *Presidential Studies Quarterly* 48(3):480–501.

Lewis, David E. and Richard W. Waterman. 2013. "The Invisible Presidential Appointments: An Examination of Appointments to the Department of Labor, 2001–11." *Presidential Studies Quarterly* 43(1):35–57.

Macey, Jonathan R. 1992. "Organizational Design and Political Control of Administrative Agencies." *Journal of Law, Economics, and Organization* 8(1):93–110.

Maggetti, Martino. 2007. "De Facto Independence after Delegation: A Fuzzy-Set Analysis." *Regulation and Governance* 1(4):271–294.

Maggetti, Martino and Koen Verhoest. 2014. "Unexplored Aspects of Bureaucratic Autonomy: A State of the Field and Ways Forward." *International Review of Administrative Sciences* 80(2):239–256.

Magill, Elizabeth. 2004. "Agency Choice of Policymaking Forum." *University of Chicago Law Review* 71(4):1383–1448.

Manning, John F. 2004. "Nonlegislative Rules." *George Washington Law Review* 72(5):893–945.

Maranto, Robert. 2005. *Beyond a Government of Strangers.* Lanham, MD: Lexington Books.

Matthews, Felicity. 2020. "Parliamentary Scrutiny of Executive Patronage: The Relationship between Institutional Norms, Reputation, and Accountability." *Public Administration* 98(3):625–642.

McCubbins, Mathew D. 1985. "The Legislative Design of Regulatory Structure." *American Journal of Political Science* 29(4):721–748.

McCubbins, Mathew D., Roger G. Noll, Barry R. Weingast. 1987. "Administrative Procedures as Instruments of Political Control." *Journal of Law, Economics, and Organization* 3(2):243–277.

McCubbins, Mathew D., Roger G. Noll, Barry R. Weingast. 1989. "Structure and Process, Politics and Policy: Administrative Arrangements and the Political Control of Agencies." *Virginia Law Review* 75(1):431–482.

McCubbins, Mathew D. and Thomas Schwartz. 1984. "Congressional Oversight Overlooked: Police Patrol versus Fire Alarm." *American Journal of Political Science* 28(1):165–177.

Miller, Gary J. and Andrew B. Whitford. 2016. *Above Politics: Bureaucratic Discretion and Credible Commitment.* New York, NY: Cambridge University Press.

Mills, Russell W. and Jennifer L. Selin. 2017. "Don't Sweat the Details! Enhancing Congressional Committee Expertise through the Use of Detailees." *Legislative Studies Quarterly* 42(4):611–636.

Moe, Terry M. 1985. "The Politicized Presidency." In John E. Chubb and Paul E. Peterson, eds., *The New Direction of American Politics.* Washington, DC: The Brookings Institution.

Moore, Emily H. 2018. "Polarization, Excepted Appointments, and the Administrative Presidency." *Presidential Studies Quarterly* 48(1):72–92.

Montgomery, Jacob M. and Brendan Nyhan. 2017. "The Effects of Congressional Staff Networks in the House of Representatives." *Journal of Politics* 79(3):745–761.

O'Connell, Anne Joseph. 2008. "Vacant Offices: Delays in Staffing Top Agency Positions." *Southern California Law Review* 82(5):913–999.

Öhberg, Patrick, Peter Munk Christiansen, and Birgitta Niklasson. 2017. "Administrative Politicization or Contestability? How Political Advisers Affect Neutral Competence in Policy Processes." *Public Administration* 95(1):269–285.

Parsneau, Kevin. 2013. "Politicizing Priority Departments: Presidential Priorities and Subcabinet Experience and Loyalty." *American Politics Research* 41(3):443–470.

Patacconi, Andrew. 2009. "Coordination and Delay in Hierarchies." *RAND Journal of Economics* 40(1):190–208.

Patty, John W. and Ian R. Turner. 2021. "Ex Post Review and Expert Policymaking: When Does Oversight Reduce Accountability?" *Journal of Politics* 83(1):23–39.

Pauls, Christine Kelleher and Susan Webb Yackee. 2016. "Clerks or Kings? Partisan Alignment and Delegation to the U.S. Bureaucracy." *Journal of Public Administration Research and Theory* 26(4):693–708.

Perry, James L. and Lois Recasino Wise. 1990. "The Motivational Bases of Public Service." *Public Administration Review* 50(3):367–373.

Pfiffner, James P. 1996. *The Strategic Presidency: Hitting the Ground Running*. Lawrence, KS: University Press of Kansas.

Pitts, David W., John Marvel, and Sergio Fernandez. 2011. "So Hard to Say Goodbye? Turnover Intention among U.S. Federal Executives." *Public Administration Review* 71(5):751–760.

Posner, Eric A. 2001. "Controlling Agencies with Cost–Benefit Analysis: A Positive Political Theory Perspective." *University of Chicago Law Review* 68(4):1137–1199.

Potoski, Matthew. 2002. "Designing Bureaucratic Responsiveness: Administrative Procedures and Agency Choice in State Environmental Policy." *State Politics and Policy Quarterly* 2(1):1–23.

Potter, Rachel Augustine. 2019. *Bending the Rules: Procedural Politicking in the Bureaucracy*. Chicago, IL: University of Chicago Press.

Prakash, Saikrishna B. 2012. "Independence, Congressional Weakness, and the Importance of Appointment: The Impact of Combining Budgetary Autonomy with Removal Protection." *Harvard Law Review* 125(2012):1822–1843.

Rainey, Hal G. 1993. "A Theory of Goal Ambiguity in Public Organizations." In J.L. Perry, ed., *Research in Public Administration*, Vol. 2. Greenwich, CT: JAI Press.

Reuter, Ora John and Graeme B. Robertson. 2012. "Subnational Appointments in Authoritarian Regimes: Evidence from Russian Gubernatorial Appointments." *Journal of Politics* 74(4):1023–1037.

Resh, William G. 2015. *Rethinking the Administrative Presidency: Trust, Intellectual Capital, and Appointee-Careerist Relations in the George W. Bush Administration*. Baltimore, MD: Johns Hopkins University Press.

Resh, William G. 2019. "The Disarticulation of the Administrative State (and Public Administration." *Administration and Society* 51(3):347–370.

Resh, William G., Gary E. Hollibaugh, Jr., Patrick S. Roberts, and Matthew M. Dull. 2021. "Appointee Vacancies in U.S. Executive Branch Agencies." *Journal of Public Policy* 41(4): 1–24.

Richardson, Mark D. 2019 "Politicization and Expertise: Exit, Effort, and Investment." *Journal of Politics* 81(3):878–891.

Romzek, Barbara S. 1990. "Employee Investment and Commitment: The Ties that Bind." *Public Administration Review* 50(3):374–382.

Rosenbloom, David H., Stephanie P. Newbold, and Meghan Doughty. 2018. "Madison's Ratchet: Ambition Counteracting Ambition and the Aggregation of Political, Managerial, and Legal Controls Over Federal Administration." *American Review of Public Administration* 48(6):495–505.

Rudalevidge, Andrew. 2005. "The Structure of Leadership: Presidents, Hierarchies, and Information Flow." *Presidential Studies Quarterly* 35(2):333–360.

Rutherford, Amanda, Jeryl L. Mumpower, Ricardo A. Bello-Gomez, and Malisa Griffin. 2019. "Understanding Vacancy Time: A Theoretical Framework Informed by Cross-sector Comparison." *Perspectives on Public Management and Governance* 2(1):3–20.

Ryu, Sangyub and Young-Joo Lee. 2013. "Examining the Role of Management in Turnover." *Public Performance and Management Review* 37(1):134–153.

Schmidt, Diane E. 2002. "Politicization and Responsiveness in the Regional Offices of the NLRB." *American Review of Public Administration* 32(2):188–215.

Scholz, John T., Jim Twombly, and Barbara Headrick. 1991. "Street-Level Political Controls over Federal Bureaucracy." *American Political Science Review* 85(3):829–850.

Scholz, John T. and Feng Heng Wei. 1986. "Regulatory Structure in a Federalist System." *American Political Science Review* 80(6):1249–1270.

Selin, Jennifer L. 2015. "What Makes an Agency Independent?" *American Journal of Political Science* 59(4):971–987.

Selin, Jennifer L. 2021. "The Headless Fourth Branch: Rethinking the Assumptions of Administrative Jurisprudence." *Perspectives on Public Management and Governance* 4(2): 170–185.

Selin, Jennifer L. and David E. Lewis. 2018. *Sourcebook on United States Executive Agencies.* Washington, DC: Administrative Conference of the United States.

Selin, Jennifer L. and Caylie Milazzo. 2021. "'If Men Were Angels': The Legal Dynamics of Overseeing the Executive Branch." *Presidential Studies Quarterly* 5(2):426–449.

Shaw, Richard and Chris Eichbaum. 2020. "Bubbling Up or Cascading Down? Public Servants, Political Advisers and Politicization." *Public Administration* 98(4):840–855.

Stephenson, Matthew C. 2008. "Optimal Political Control of the Bureaucracy." *Michigan Law Review* 107(1):53–110.

Tenpas, Kathryn Dunn. 2018. "White House Staff Turnover in Year One of the Trump Administration: Context, Consequences, and Implications for Governing." *Presidential Studies Quarterly* 48(3):502–516.

Thatcher, Mark. 2002. "Delegation to Independent Regulatory Agencies: Pressures, Functions and Contextual Mediation." *West European Politics* 25(1):125–147.

Thatcher, Mark. 2005. "The Third Force? Independence Regulatory Agencies and Elected Politicians in Europe." *Governance* 18(3):347–373.

Walker, Christopher J. 2018. "Administrative Law Without Courts." *UCLA Law Review* 65(6):1620–1641.

Waterman, Richard W., Amelia Rouse, and Robert Wright. 1998. "The Venues of Influence: A New Theory of Political Control of the Bureaucracy." *Journal of Public Administration Research and Theory* 8(1):13–38.

Weingast, Barry R. and Mark J. Moran. 1983. "Bureaucratic Discretion or Congressional Control? Regulatory Policymaking by the Federal Trade Commission." *Journal of Political Economy* 91(5):765–800.

Weko, Thomas J. 1995. *The Politicizing Presidency: The White House Personnel Office, 1948–1994.* Lawrence, KS: University Press of Kansas.

West, William F. 2005. "Neutral Competence and Political Responsiveness: An Uneasy Relationship." *Policy Studies Journal* 33(2):147–160.

Whitford, Andrew. 2002. "Decentralization and Political Control of the Bureaucracy." *Journal of Theoretical Politics* 14(2):167–193.

Whitford, Andrew B. 2007. "Decentralized Policy Implementation." *Political Research Quarterly* 60(1):17–30.

Wilson, Woodrow. 1887. "The Study of Administration." *Political Science Quarterly* 2(2):197–222.

Wood, Abby K. and David E. Lewis. 2017. "Agency Performance Challenges and Agency Politicization." *Journal of Public Administration Research and Theory* 27(4):581–595.

Woods, Neal D. 2018. "Regulatory Analysis Procedures and Political Influence on Bureaucratic Policymaking." *Regulation and Governance* 12(2):299–313.

Workman, Samuel. 2015. *The Dynamics of Bureaucracy in the U.S. Government: How Congress and Federal Agencies Process Information and Solve Problems.* New York, NY: Cambridge University Press.

Wynen, Jan, Bjorn Kleizen, Koen Verhoest, Per Lægried, and Vidar Rolland. 2020. "Keeping a Watchful Eye in Times of Turmoil? How Repeated Structural Reform Leads to More Attention to Political Signals." *Public Administration* 98(3):570–590.

Yesilkagit, Jutsal and Sandra van Thiel. 2008 "Political Influence and Bureaucratic Autonomy." *Public Organization Review* 8(2):137–153.

Yesilkagit, Jutsal and Sandra van Thiel. 2012. "Autonomous Agencies and Perceptions of Stakeholder Influence in Parliamentary Democracies." *Journal of Public Administration Research and Theory* 22(1):101–119.

14. Regulatory independence and the quality of regulation

Christel Koop and Jacint Jordana[1]

INTRODUCTION

Regulatory independence can be traced back to the late nineteenth and early twentieth century, when in some countries, new public regulatory bodies were created with special protections to avoid interference from other public institutions, especially the executive. In the United States, in particular, legislators set up independent regulatory commissions (IRCs) with administrative, legislative, and judicial powers, and with commissioners appointed by Congress. In other parts of the world, state ownership remained more common for much of the twentieth century (Majone 1997), even though there are cases of early delegation to institutionally 'protected' regulatory bodies, established to overcome implementation problems. Still, it was only in the last decades of the twentieth century that the establishment of separate commissions or agencies became dominant in many policy areas, in parallel to the increased use of regulatory instruments by all types of governments. In many cases, these regulatory bodies were granted formal protections to ensure their independence from the executive. For instance, the United Kingdom (UK) created several independent regulatory offices in the 1980s, and was soon followed by other parts of Europe and Latin America, particularly in utilities sectors like telecoms and electricity.[2] By the early 2000s, most countries had at least some experience with regulatory independence, especially in areas of economic regulation (i.e., competition policy and financial and utility regulation) (e.g., Jordana et al. 2011; Koop & Kessler 2020).

Despite its prevalence as an institutional model in many sectors, the independent regulatory agency (IRA) is not uncontested. That is, its compatibility with standards of democratic governance – especially responsiveness and accountability – has always been questioned (see Jordana et al. 2015; Maggetti 2010; Koop 2015; Scott 2000). One of the arguments provided to justify independence is related to the better-quality decisions that independent regulators would produce, whether because of the stability of their preferences or the absence of requirements to balance varied social and economic interests, as compared to both legislatures and politically subordinate bureaucracies. In those sectors where they were established, their specialisation and single-purpose orientation would 'compensate' for the loss of democratic legitimacy in the delegation process, whether in terms of social or economic efficiency.

Yet, empirical research has also pointed to other motivations to establish independent regulators; in particular, blame-shifting and the desire to entrench policy ideas and eventually (private) interests so as to protect them from changes in public opinion and alterations in policy preferences after government turnover (e.g., Thatcher 2002; DeCanio 2015, Ch. 10). Moreover, the rapid expansion of the institutional model in recent decades could hardly be explained without considering the role of policy diffusion across sectors and countries. In particular, diffusion by emulation has played a key role in expanding independence as a new standard for regulatory agencies (e.g., Gilardi 2005; Jordana & Levi-Faur 2005). Hence, regulatory independence may enhance efficiency and effectiveness, but its establishment is often based on broad normative pressures within different professional and political environments rather than on outcome-related considerations.

In this chapter, we do not examine the reasons behind the creation of independent regulators; much literature has already been devoted to this question. Instead, we take regulatory independence as the starting point, and ask what it can deliver for the policy process in the sectors in which it is embedded. Answering this question is essential given that independence has been broadly proclaimed as the distinctive character of regulatory governance around the world – thus conveying beneficial properties – whilst at the same time triggering debate and contestation, whether because of weak democratic legitimacy, biased policy preferences, or simply administrative isolation. It is, therefore, important to examine whether regulatory independence actually does what it promises. In the first section we take stock of the empirical literature on the link between independence and regulatory quality or performance. After discussing the key concepts and theoretical arguments, we review studies on the impact of independence in different areas of regulation with a view to drawing some conclusions on how convincing its main justification is. In the second section we conclude by discussing what we believe are the key issues and questions that future research needs to address.

FOUNDATIONS

Key Concepts

Though regulatory independence may characterise the relationship between regulatory agencies and the regulated industry – or even society at large – it is typically meant to refer to regulators' relationship with governments and, to some extent, parliaments. This independence from politics is sometimes seen as a proxy for independence from business since politicians are regarded as particularly susceptible to business lobbying (Wilks & Bartle, 2002, p.151). Yet, ultimately, the question of the relationship between political independence and independence from regulatees is an empirical one, and there is nothing that prevents independent regulators from being directly persuaded by business lobbying. In this chapter, however, we solely focus on independence from politics.

Political independence is defined in both dichotomous and ordinal terms, depending on whether the research focus is on independent regulators as a category or on the variation in independence within that category.[3] For instance, aiming to identify what characterises the category of independent agencies, Thatcher and Stone Sweet refer to "those governmental entities that (a) possess and exercise some grant of specialised public authority, separate from that of other institutions, but (b) are neither directly elected by the people, nor directly managed by elected officials" (2002, p.2).[4] Definitions like this emphasise regulators' position outside ministerial or governmental hierarchies; indeed, this is widely seen as the category's core element (e.g., Henisz et al. 2005; Casullo et al. 2019). Moreover, in almost all cases, regulators are appointed by elected politicians in the executive and/or legislature. Defined this way, independence has become highly prominent in regulation, though not all regulatory agencies are independent (e.g., Jordana et al. 2018).

Meanwhile, studies looking at the (remaining) variation within the category of independent agencies rely on ordinal definitions. For example, Hanretty and Koop define independence as "the degree to which the day-to-day decisions of regulatory agencies are formed without the interference of politicians and/or consideration of politicians' preferences" (2012, p.199). Definitions like this allow for multi-dimensional operationalisations of independence, including items on the appointment and dismissal of key decision-makers, the budget process, and the potential overruling of regulatory decisions (Gilardi 2002; cf. Hanretty & Koop 2012; Jordana et al. 2018). What is implicit here is the assumption that independence refers to rules that protect regulators' decisions from politicians so that in the case of discrepancies, politicians cannot impose their preferences on regulators. Many of the studies measuring the intensity of (formal) independence use the indicators proposed by Gilardi (2002); indicators that were themselves inspired by the literature on central bank independence. We will discuss studies that rely on either dichotomous or ordinal definitions and operationalisations, as long as the focus is on the impact of independence from politics on the quality of regulation, broadly defined.

Before moving to the concept of quality, one more aspect of independence needs to be addressed; namely, the relationship between formal (de jure) and actual (de facto) independence. Whilst statutory provisions (formal rules) provide regulators with an important layer of protection from political interference, there is another dimension in the relation between regulators and politicians based on informal rules. Though some studies do not find a clear relationship between formal and actual independence (e.g., Maggetti 2007; Eckert 2010), many others report that statutory provisions provide agencies with a layer of protection against political interference (e.g., Boadu & Olofinbiyi 2003; Ennser-Jedenastik 2015; Hanretty & Koop 2013; Thatcher 2005). Most of the literature on the impact of independence focuses on formal provisions, but the underlying premise is that formal independence affects regulatory quality via actual independence. We make the same assumption in reviewing the empirical literature, but return to the question in the second section. In addition, we need to take into account that independence is never complete. This is not only because politicians can employ a range of informal signalling mechanisms to influence regulatory decision-making (e.g., Ferejohn & Shipan 1990), but also because regulators look for, and act upon, political signals since they are aware of the fact that their competences and independence can ultimately be revoked by means of acts of 'de-delegation' (Özel 2012).

Regulatory quality is notoriously difficult to capture, both conceptually and empirically. Conceptually, it broadly refers to the performance of regulatory actors in relation to their task and objectives. Yet, the concept has multiple dimensions, especially in the public sector. In the field of regulation, it not only refers to efficiency and effectiveness, but also to other aspects such as proportionality, consistency, due process, and transparency (Radaelli 2004, p.271). Efficiency and effectiveness tend to be associated with the *outcome* of regulation – "the effect that [regulatory] activity has on the economy, the market and the behaviour (and perceptions) of market actors" (Guidi 2015, p.1200). By contrast, features like consistency and proportionality tend to be related to the quality of regulatory decision-making. Such multidimensionality makes it especially difficult to compare regulators' performance, not least because there is sectoral variation in which indicators matter most for regulatory quality.

We should note that a third option is available: quality can, at least in principle, be measured in terms of direct *outputs*; for instance, the number of investigations and decisions. Yet, such measures are problematic in the field regulation (Koop & Hanretty 2018). On the one hand, higher levels of activity may imply that a regulator is performing its task well; that is, it monitors market behaviour well and manages to detect problematic behaviour. On the other hand, more activity may imply that a regulator has failed to do a good job in the sense that it has not adjusted regulation to make markets work smoothly. In addition, to the extent that activity measures are included in targets or performance reporting, they may lead to gaming by regulators, with non-measured and non-measurable activities being neglected. As a consequence, output measures are not prevalent, and have remained associated more with regulators' enforcement style than with performance (e.g., McAllister 2010).

Independence and Regulatory Quality: Theoretical Arguments

Since the 1990s, independence from politics has been promoted as an institutional model for regulation by international bodies such as the European Union (e.g., Directive 2009/72/EC), the Basel Committee (1997), the OECD (2014), and UNCTAD (2008). In line with this, national governments and parliaments have adopted this design in various sectors and for a variety of reasons, as discussed before. Theoretically, the model of the independent agency has been linked to better-quality regulation via two different mechanisms, generally used by international organisations and policy-makers to justify their reform proposals: an expertise-based and a credible commitment-based mechanism.

The expertise-based argument was for a long time dominant in the literature on regulatory commissions. The argument has perhaps been best theorised by Bawn (1995), who presents a model of the trade-off between political control and expertise in bureaucratic decision-making. She associates control with procedures that hamper the gathering and use of information on policy consequences, including coordination with political leaders, advisors, and politically favoured private interests. Constraints on expertise may also result from formal restrictions on the short-term hiring of external experts and consultancies. By contrast, Bawn argues, decision-making that is exempted from such procedures and restrictions will incorporate more and better information on policy consequences. This is, by extension, a claim for professional stability and expertise-based tenure in managing public affairs since it should contribute to better policy decisions and outcomes in areas with high degrees of policy uncertainty (like regulation). This does not mean that formal agency independence is necessary, but it does suggest that politicians should – one way or another – respect the stability of professional staff in public agencies beyond political changes.

In recent decades, scholars and policy-makers have come to focus more on the role of credible commitment in policy delegation in regulation. The argument here originates from the literature on central banking. Monetary policy, it is said, is an area characterised by time inconsistency: what is attractive in the short run is not necessarily beneficial for society and the economy in the long term. This means that elected officials have incentives to use monetary policy to boost the economy, especially before elections; yet, as such moves are rationally anticipated by price- and wage-setters, the net result is above-target inflation without an increase in employment and economic output (Kydland & Prescott 1977). Institutional solutions to the time inconsistency problem are available though, in particular, politicians could tie their hands by delegating monetary policy competences to an independent and time-consistent central bank (Rogoff 1985). Empirical research suggests that there is at least conditional evidence of a negative effect of central bank independence on levels of inflation (e.g., Bodea & Hicks 2015; Crowe & Meade 2008).

The credible commitment argument for monetary policy delegation has been extended broadly to the field of regulation (e.g., Majone 1996; Levy & Spiller 1996; Levine et al. 2005).

Like in monetary policy, regulatory decisions can be affected by time inconsistency problems, with politicians facing incentives to use regulatory tools for electoral purposes – for instance, by altering utilities' regulated prices – and to break commitments made by previous governments. Also, in some sectors, it is necessary to make commitments on policy stability to investors to attract long-term investments, and agency independence can contribute to make these commitments more credible. The alternative – because inconsistency is anticipated by sectoral actors – would be under-investment in the regulated industry (Levy & Spiller 1994; 1996), or the need for over-investment by the public sector. Similarly, politicians may face a dilemma regarding whether or not to prioritise (short-term) economic growth at the cost of financial stability, whilst an independent agency may pre-determine the choice, providing some level of protection to the financial stability goal (Jordana & Rosas 2014). Taking these trade-offs as a starting point, it is argued that by delegating to independent regulators with professional staff and different time horizons, politicians can commit credibly to long-term regulatory objectives and, eventually, to the provision of higher levels of policy stability.

There is an empirical relationship between the need for credible commitment and agency independence. Various empirical studies show that levels of agency independence are higher in those sectors where the rationale for credible commitment is stronger (e.g., Elgie & McMenamin 2005; Gilardi 2002; Wassum & De Francesco 2020; but see Pavón Mediano 2020). Hence, politicians may decide to set up independent agencies, and provide a particular level of independence according to the credible commitment problem they aim to address. In other words, this is a political decision to tie their hands, with long-term implications. In fact, under some conditions, the commitment can be even stronger; for example, when independent regulators are established as a consequence of international agreements (e.g., in the European Union), or included in the constitutional design of a country. What existing studies of the relationship between credible commitment and independence do not address is the question of the impact of independence. The latter is important to analyse, not only because it is at the heart of the commitment argument, but also because independence comes at the cost of a loss of democratic legitimacy. If the relationship does not hold empirically, this will raise even more serious questions about regulatory independence since it implies that output- and outcome-based justifications cannot in any way compensate for the loss of input-based legitimacy (cf. Scharpf 1999).

Independence and Quality: Empirical Findings

To what extent have theoretical arguments about the benefits of regulatory independence been confirmed in practice? In this section, we assess the findings of comparative empirical studies in different areas of regulation. However, as shown below, work on the impact of regulatory independence is unevenly distributed: areas of regulation where independence is a common standard (telecommunications, financial markets) have been extensively analysed, whilst areas where it is less common (especially social regulation) have seen hardly any analysis.

Utility Regulators

Most empirical studies on the impact of independence have centred on utility regulators. Utility sectors like telecommunications, gas and electricity, and water are characterised by economies of scale and scope, specificity of assets (and large sunk investments), and the use of services by most of the population. This means that regulation is crucial, but also that the risk of administrative expropriation after privatisation is acutely present if credible commitments are not well anchored (e.g., Levy & Spiller 1994). This raises questions of design and effectiveness of agency independence. Crucially, the argument for independence is not only made in relation to private utility companies: political insulation is also seen as highly relevant in situations where companies are still (partially) publicly owned. There is an additional argument for independence in such cases: to attract private companies when public firms operate in a market, the regulator has to remain neutral to avoid the fear of government favouring its own companies. Agency independence can guaranty such neutrality.

The sector that has received most attention is *telecommunications*. In their seminal work on institutions and regulatory credibility, Levy and Spiller (1994; 1996) analyse the determinants of the performance of telecoms companies in Argentina, Chile, Jamaica, the Philippines, and the UK. Their in-depth case studies show that performance (and investment in particular) can be traced back to "a regulatory governance structure that is adequate, given the nature of the country's institutions, to constrain arbitrary administrative action" (1994, p.241). Though the authors do not assess the individual role of regulatory independence, they do present it as one type of restraint on administrative expropriation.

More recent (and more quantitative) work has zoomed in on (formal) independence, though the main focus is often on the impact of privatisation and liberalisation. Several studies use dummy variables for regulatory independence. Wallsten (2001) finds that in Africa and Latin America, the presence of an independent regulator is associated with increased mainline penetration, payphone penetration, and connectivity capacity, but only when privatisation has taken place. Focusing on mainline penetration and Latin America only, Gutiérrez and Berg (2000) show that the presence of an independent regulator alone does have an effect. Bortolotti et al. (2002) report that agency independence leads telecoms companies to increase their output, but does not affect their profitability, efficiency, employment, capital expenditure and leverage. Ros (2003) demonstrates that independence alone is associated with higher levels of mainline penetration and operating efficiency (measured as mainlines per employee) in Latin America. Finally, looking at mobile network penetration, Li and Lyons (2012) show that independent regulators have a positive effect, though the authors' diffusion model shows that the effect weakens when mobile prices are controlled for.

Indices of regulatory independence have become more commonly used. Gutiérrez (2003) creates a regulatory governance index that includes independence, and finds that it positively affects mainline penetration and operating efficiency. Edwards and Waverman (2006) use an index of regulatory independence, and study its effect on the interconnect rates paid by entrants to incumbents in Europe. Their analysis does not show an independent effect of independence, but supports their hypothesis that independence mitigates upwards pressures on interconnect rates under (partial) public ownership of incumbent telecoms operators. Returning to the question of mainline penetration, Trillas and Montoya (2011), using both de jure and de facto indices, confirm the effect of regulatory independence in their study of Latin America and the Caribbean.

In *electricity regulation*, studies of regulatory independence have primarily focused on emerging and developing economies. Using a governance index that includes independence, Cubbin and Stern (2006) report a positive effect on per capita electricity generation (cf. Gutiérrez 2003).[5] This outcome is often seen as a proxy for investment in the sector, thus capturing the key rationale behind delegation. Estache and Rossi (2008) look at the performance of electricity distributing firms and find that the presence of an independent regulator (alone) is associated with higher labour efficiency, higher labour productivity, lower operating expenditures, fewer electricity interruptions, and better service coverage. Also, electricity losses and residential tariffs are lower under regulatory independence, but only when private firms distribute electricity. Focusing instead on electricity generating companies, Zhang et al. (2008) show that independence (an index) has a positive effect on electricity generation, electricity generating capacity, labour productivity and capital utilisation, but in all instances *only* when electricity generation is privatised.

Some studies compare areas of utility regulation, looking at both generally beneficial outcomes (e.g., investment) and outcomes which are more ambiguous (e.g., financial leverage). Bortolotti et al. (2011) assess the impact of regulatory independence on the leverage of a range of regulated utilities in Europe. They find that when utilities are privately controlled, the presence of an independent regulator is associated with higher leverage. Moreover, higher leverage leads to higher regulated prices (but not vice versa). These outcomes may contribute to investment and better-quality services, but this does not need to be the case, and leverage in particular may pose considerable risk for companies and consumers. Bortolotti et al. (2013) look at the market value of regulated utilities in the energy and telecoms sectors. Surprisingly, their analysis shows that the presence of an independent regulator (a dummy) has a negative effect on market value; however, regulatory independence interacted with public ownership has a positive effect on market value. Focusing on a range of European utilities, Cambini and Rondi (2017) assess the impact of the presence of an independent regulator on firms' investment rates. They find that independence boosts investment; yet the positive effect decreases when the government in office is distinctly right-wing. Finally, Guasch et al. (2008) analyse the renegotiation of concessions awarded in the transport and water sectors in Latin America. Concessions in these sectors have been awarded to attract private investment, but their widespread renegotiation has raised questions about the effectiveness of this model. The authors show that the presence of a regulatory body with at least some degree of independence dramatically reduces the occurrence of renegotiations of concessions.

In sum, regulatory independence in utility regulation tends to have no or a positive effect on outcomes of interest. Moreover, there do not seem to be clear differences between developed and developing economies. The associations are strongest where studies focus on outcomes that are most directly linked to private investment, although there are a variety of methodological approaches and forms of measuring key variables. In other words, they are strongest when the outcomes are closest to theoretical arguments about the effect of independence. We should note though that several studies show that the effect of independence is dependent on privatisation; moreover, endogeneity problems are not always well considered.

Competition Authorities

Though competition (or antitrust) policy is one of the areas in which independent regulators are most prevalent (Jordana et al. 2011), there are only few studies of the impact of independence. This should at least partially be attributed to the fact that competition policy is meant to benefit the economy as a whole; in particular, its competitiveness and mechanism of price formation. As these outcomes are affected by a great number of variables, establishing the role and impact of (the independence of) competition authorities is an important methodological and theoretical challenge.

Guidi (2015) nonetheless takes up the challenge, analysing the effect of independence on two outcomes: foreign investment and consumer prices (consumer price index). Using an index of formal independence that varies over time, the author finds that neither foreign investment nor consumer price changes can be traced back to agency independence.[6] Ma (2010) moves away from outcomes in the economy, focusing instead on the impact of de jure and de facto independence on the perceived effectiveness of antitrust policies. The study's cross-country analysis shows a positive association between independence and effectiveness, with the effect of de jure independence disappearing once a de facto measure is included. Finally, Koop and Hanretty (2018) use a still more proximate dependent variable; namely, perceptions of the quality of competition policy enforcement. Using this process measure, with data varying over time and across countries, they report that independence (a scale) positively affects regulatory quality. These different findings suggest that independence matters for competition policy, but that we may only observe an effect in variables that are directly affected by competition authorities (e.g., the type of decisions it produces), and no effect in variables that are only partially and indirectly affected by agency decisions (e.g., the competitiveness of economies).

Financial Market Regulators

The relationship between independence and outcomes in financial markets has also received considerable attention. Most studies look at the financial 'health' of banks, though some focus on the stability of the overall financial system; in particular, on how independence may help to prevent or moderate crisis. The effect of agency independence on the 'conduct' of financial institutions in other market activities, and on the health of non-credit institutions, has so far hardly been studied.

The findings in this field are somewhat mixed, though regulatory (or supervisory) independence tends to have either no effect or a positive effect on desired outcomes.[7] Relying on cross-country survey data on the structure of banking supervision, Barth et al. (2002) do not find a relationship between independence and capital adequacy, though some of their models suggest a weak negative association between independence and non-performing loans. However, using the same survey data, Barth et al. (2004) find no relationship either between independence and non-performing loans; moreover, independence is unrelated to bank development, interest margins, and overhead costs. Similarly, Barth et al. (2003) show the absence of a relationship between independence and the profitability of banks (in terms of returns on assets). Yet, Gaganis and Pasiouras (2013) – still using the same cross-country survey data – report a negative association between supervisory independence and bank profit efficiency.[8] Relying on a different, dichotomous measure of independence, Dincer and Eichengreen (2012) find no association with bank capitalisation, the provision of credit to the economy, and deposit rates, but do report a negative association with non-performing loans.

Some more recent studies have taken advantage of (newly collected) time-varying data on independence. Building on three waves of survey data on banking supervision, Barth et al. (2013) show that supervisory independence has a positive effect on banks' operating efficiency, especially when combined with stronger supervisory powers. Using the same survey data, Doumpos et al. (2015) report a positive effect of independence on the soundness of banks (in terms of bank z-scores). Both studies demonstrate that independence matters in its de jure and de facto forms. By contrast, Jordana and Rosas (2014) find no effect of either type of independence on non-performing loans and the onset of banking crisis, unless the number of veto players in the system is taken into consideration. That is, the authors show that independence boosts stability only when there are few veto players. The latter is associated with fewer incentives for independent regulators to shirk: with few veto players, institutional change is more feasible than in political environments highly populated by veto players. These more recent studies suggest that agency independence – whether formal or actual – plays a role in financial market regulation (and bank regulation in particular), but that some of its effects may be conditional. This should not surprise us given the multiplicity of factors driving the behaviour of financial institutions.

Social Regulation

The impact of regulatory independence has so far attracted little attention in social regulation.[9] Actually, levels of formal independence in social regulatory agencies are by far lower than in other sectors, and informal independence used to be more grounded in the role of professional evaluative commissions integrated into the agency (Jordana et al. 2018). Therefore, we cannot draw easy conclusions on the impact of agency independence in this area. Social regulation is typically seen as suffering less from credible commitment problems (Gilardi 2002; Bertelli & Whitford 2009), which means that there is less ground to justify the establishment of formal independence, particularly when well-functioning market competition is not the goal of regulation. However, as risk and rights regulation are most prominent in social regulation, this may lead us to expect a different effect of formal independence on regulatory quality. The development and use of independent expertise may be equally important for social regulators, to assess risks properly, and this opens up relevant challenges in discussing their impact on the quality of regulation. Moreover, we have observed a large expansion of the scope of social regulators in recent decades, even though not as widespread as in economic regulation (Jordana et al. 2011), meaning that the institutional landscape has been transformed in many countries and regulatory independence is also an issue in social regulation.

    There are, therefore, good reasons to study the impact of independence and its relation with professional decision-making and agency reputation. Case study research has offered some insight into this question. We mention two examples here. First, Krapohl (2004) argues that there is a credible commitment problem in food safety and pharmaceutical regulation, at least at the European level. The author shows that member states' institutional commitment is stronger in pharmaceutical than food safety regulation, which is associated with better EU regulation in the former area. Second, Nunes et al. (2007) analyse the performance of the Portuguese Regulatory Authority of Health. They point to a positive effect of the introduction of an independent regulator in a sector where some private providers operate, often in collaboration with the public health service. They associate the role of the agency with the (partial) correction of various forms of market failure, including information asymmetry, monopolisation and externalities, considering also consumer protection issues. Case studies like these offer important in-depth insight; yet, they will need to be complemented by studies analysing broader patterns.

    In social regulation, and risk regulation more generally, independence tends to be defined more in professional and scientific terms, aimed to improve the assessment of complex matters that require profound expertise. The key issue here is how to protect professionals' decision-making, and how to limit their power as well, considering broader political debates. Analysis of such configurations and their impact on the quality of regulation is a relevant avenue for future research. In addition, there are areas where competitive markets are embedded in social and risk regulation; for instance, in energy, water, medicine, and health services. In most of these areas, credible commitment issues are present in regulatory decision-making, but cannot be easily separated. Thus, hybrid regulatory decision-making becomes more and more common, and such situations have created a demand for stronger independence (comparable to the levels existing in economic regulation) in some countries and sectors.

FORESIGHT

The question of impact of regulatory independence on the quality of regulation has not (yet) attracted as much attention as the design and determinants of independence. Nonetheless, our review painted a picture of considerable interest in the question. This interest is unequally divided between disciplines, with economics (perhaps unsurprisingly) being dominant. It is also unequally divided between regulatory areas, with studies of economic regulation outpacing those of social regulation. What has thus far stood out is the similarity of the findings: most studies report some positive effect of regulatory independence on output and (economic) outcomes, even though often conditional. From a perspective of legitimacy, this is surely reassuring.

Still, our review exposed considerable gaps in the literature. In this last section, we discuss these gaps in the context of a proposed two-pronged approach to future research, including a deepening and a broadening of the research question.

Deepening the Research

Many of the studies discussed use composite measures of (formal) regulatory independence. Given the largely quantitative nature of the research, this is highly appropriate: agency independence has different components, and these are interrelated, which makes aggregation a necessity. Yet, this feature of the study of independence has opened up an empirical and theoretical gap. Empirically, it has prevented us from exploring in more detail which elements of independence do most in producing (desirable) output and outcomes. Theoretically, it has resulted in a shortage of arguments on the role of individual observed variables, be they structural separation from the core of government, long and protected terms of office, or budget and personnel selection autonomy. We suggest that future research address both gaps. We need more (formal and informal) theorising of what the constitutive variables may achieve, both individually and in conjunction. Are some more conducive to the expertise-building that is associated with better quality? Are some more capable of signalling a credible commitment? Furthermore, we need diversity in research methods to test the resulting theoretical arguments. Traditional regression models may be complemented by, for instance, structural equation modelling and in-depth qualitative case studies of the individual and combined causal mechanisms.

Regulatory quality would benefit from a similar deepening of the research. For instance, we are still not sure whether independence affects market behaviour and risk prevention directly (by boosting the reputation of the regulator) or indirectly, by impacting the nature of regulatory decisions. This gap in our knowledge is at least partially driven by the research focus on economic outcomes rather than the quality of regulatory decisions and actions. The latter are more difficult to capture, but as they can be linked to independence with a higher degree of certainty – whether in quantitative or qualitative studies – their analysis has the potential to offer considerable insight into how independence matters.

Finally, we need to rethink our approach to the (very real) issue of endogeneity. The strategies so far have been to either neglect the issue or use (highly imperfect) instruments borrowed from other subfields of political economy. Both impede the estimation of the impact of independence. Whilst no easy solutions are available, the literature would benefit from the creation of more bespoke instruments, but also from mixed methods research that includes techniques such as process tracing.

Broadening the Research Question

Whilst the avenues for future research discussed above can be seen as elaborations on existing studies, we also propose that the research agenda be expanded. We (again) suggest that advances target both sides of the equation.

First, as illustrated also by the focus of our own chapter, there is a rather sharp distinction between the literature on regulatory independence (from politics) and on the relationship between regulators and the regulated industry (Benoît 2021). Yet, close relations between regulators and regulatees – relations that are typically characterised as capture – may just as well be seen as a form of collaboration that facilitates the production of high-quality regulation. To assess such arguments empirically, more variables need to be introduced; for example, vibrant agency accountability may contribute to preventing capture, despite strong collaboration with regulatees. We know relatively little about these configurations, and even less about their effect on regulatory output and outcomes. Moreover, the presence of two separate literatures may have resulted in an incomplete or even biased picture of the impact of independence on regulatory quality. There is, therefore, every reason for studies of regulatory independence to build on both literatures and to develop new theoretical arguments on the interplay between the two dimensions of independence.

Second, studies of the effect of regulatory independence have centred on those outcomes that are closest to the (original) statutory objectives of regulators. These tend to be aggregate economic outcomes. Yet, the nascent literature on the (re)politicisation of regulation in Western democracies suggests that these are not the only outcomes that matter for citizens and politicians. In particular, in the aftermath of the global financial crisis, more attention has been paid to the winners and losers of economic liberalisation and regulation by independent agencies with narrow aggregate economic objectives (e.g., Koop & Lodge 2020). In other words, the question of distribution has been reintroduced. This may be unsurprising from the perspective of developing economies, where regulation and distribution have never been completely separated (e.g., Dubash & Morgan 2012), but it confronts the relevant regulators with a dilemma: should they seek to stick to their old objectives and methods, or should they adapt to new political expectations, and somehow internalise additional policy goals? The latter may protect them from political intervention, but may equally put their independence at risk as it will unavoidably make them more political. But wherever these political developments may lead us, there are good reasons to empirically analyse how regulatory independence has affected a wider range of outcomes – aggregate economic as well as distributive ones. To what extent, and under what conditions, are there indeed trade-offs?

CONCLUDING REMARKS

In this chapter, we have not only taken stock of the existing literature on the relationship between regulatory independence and the quality of regulation, but have also proposed avenues for future research that both deepen and broaden the agenda. The proposals are ambitious but – at least in our view – feasible. Many independent regulators have existed now for well over two decades, which means that there is a wealth of data to analyse. Moreover, the growing maturity of agencies in most countries and sectors should allow us to distinguish the effect of institutional design from the impact of variables related to their early establishment (including broader regulatory reforms and privatisations that coincided with the creation of independent regulators), from the initial reaction of the administrative landscape, and from agencies' internal adjustments in a context in which they needed to develop their own administrative and regulatory cultures. Now that the model of the independent agency is widespread – whilst the variation in the design of independence is still large – the challenge of better understanding the long-term political, economic and social impact of regulatory independence can no longer wait.

NOTES

1. The authors would like to thank Adam Rosenberg for his excellent research assistance.
2. Whilst independent economic regulators were most of all creatures of the 1980s and 1990s, many countries had already introduced social and civil rights regulators in the 1970s (Majone 1994). Also, financial market regulators and competition authorities were relatively widespread before the 1980s, though in most cases, they were not fully independent; only organisationally separated (Jordana et al. 2011).
3. In line with most literature, we treat independence and autonomy as synonyms in this chapter.
4. Thatcher and Stone Sweet use the term 'non-majoritarian institution' rather than independent agency (cf. Majone 1997), but the two terms refer to largely the same concept. The concept is much broader than 'independent regulatory agency', which (solely) refers to agencies that exercise public authority in the field of regulation. Regulation can be defined as the "intentional intervention in the activities of a target population, where the intervention is typically direct – involving binding standard-setting, monitoring, and sanctioning – and exercised by public-sector actors on the economic activities of private-sector actors" (Koop & Lodge 2017, p.105).
5. A model with regulatory independence alone also shows a positive effect, but the correlation with other variables in the index, particularly the adoption of a law, makes interpretation of that finding difficult.
6. In another outcome-focused study, Dutz and Vagliasindi (2000) show a positive association between institutional effectiveness and economy-wide enterprise mobility in transition economies. Institutional effectiveness includes de facto independence, but this is only one component, and the study does not provide results for individual components.
7. The literature in this field primarily uses the terms supervision (rather than regulation) and supervisory independence (rather than regulatory independence); given our broad definition of regulation, we treat these different terms as synonyms.
8. The main focus of their study – and of various other studies in the field – is on *central bank* independence. Central banks may be responsible for (part of) the supervision of banks, but also, they are considered to indirectly influence financial stability via monetary policy, though this influence is not necessarily positive. We do not review the literature on central bank independence, but note that authors who look at both central bank and financial supervisory independence (e.g., Gaganis & Pasiouras 2013; Doumpos et al. 2015) draw similar conclusions for both types of measures.

9. The distinction between economic and social regulation is not completely straightforward, but areas typically included in the latter category are the regulation of food and work safety, pharmaceutical products, health services, and the environment (e.g., Gilardi 2005; Jordana et al. 2011). In the case of pharmaceutical regulation, independence from the regulated sector has been studied more extensively.

REFERENCES

Barth, James R., Luis G. Dopico, Daniel E. Nolle & James A. Wilcox (2002). Bank safety and soundness and the structure of bank supervision: A cross-country analysis. *International Review of Finance* 3(3–4), 163–188.

Barth, James R., Daniel E. Nolle, Triphon Phumiwasana & Glenn Yago (2003). A cross-country analysis of the bank supervisory framework and bank performance. *Financial Markets, Institutions & Instruments* 12(2), 67–120.

Barth, James R., Gerard Caprio Jr. & Ross Levine (2004). Bank regulation and supervision: What works best? *Journal of Financial Intermediation* 13(2), 205–248.

Barth, James R., Chen Lin, Yue Ma, Jesús Seade & Frank M. Song (2013). Do bank regulation, supervision and monitoring enhance or impede bank efficiency? *Journal of Banking & Finance* 37(8), 2879–2892.

Basel Committee on Banking Supervision (1997). Core principles for effective banking supervision. Basel, CH: Bank for International Settlements.

Bawn, Kathleen (1995). Political control versus expertise: Congressional choices about administrative procedures. *American Political Science Review* 89(1), 62–73.

Benoît, Cyril (2021). Politicians, regulators, and regulatory governance: The neglected sides of the story. *Regulation & Governance* 15, 8–22.

Bertelli, Anthony M. & Andrew B. Whitford (2009). Perceiving credible commitments: How independent regulators shape elite perceptions of regulatory quality. *British Journal of Political Science* 39(3), 517–537.

Boadu, Fred O. & Tolulope Olofinbiyi (2003). Regulating the market: Competition law and policy in Kenya and Zambia. *World Competition* 26(1), 75–99.

Bodea, Cristina & Raymond Hicks (2015). Price stability and central bank independence: Discipline, credibility, and democratic institutions. *International Organization* 69(1), 35–61.

Bortolotti, Bernardo, Juliet D'Souza, Marcella Fantini & William L. Megginson (2002). Privatization and the sources of performance improvement in the global telecommunications industry. *Telecommunications Policy* 26(5–6), 243–268.

Bortolotti, Bernardo, Carlo Cambini, Laura Rondi & Yossi Spiegel (2011). Capital structure and regulation: Do ownership and regulatory independence matter? *Journal of Economics & Management Strategy* 20(2), 517–564.

Bortolotti, Bernardo, Carlo Cambini & Laura Rondi (2013). Reluctant regulation. *Journal of Comparative Economics* 41(3), 804–828.

Cambini, Carlo & Laura Rondi (2017). Independent agencies, political interference, and firm investment: Evidence from the European Union. *Economic Inquiry* 55(1), 281–304.

Casullo, Lorenzo, Alexis Durand & Filippo Cavassini (2019). The 2018 Indicators on the Governance of Sector Regulators. OECD Economics Department Working Papers 1564. Paris: Organisation for Economic Co-operation and Development.

Crowe, Christopher & Ellen Meade (2008). Central bank independence and transparency: Evolution and effectiveness. *European Journal of Political Economy* 24(4), 763–777.

Cubbin, John & Jon Stern (2006). The impact of regulatory governance and privatization on electricity industry generation capacity in developing economies. *World Bank Economic Review* 20(1), 115–141.

DeCanio, Samuel (2015). *Democracy and the Origins of the American Regulatory State*. New Haven, CT: Yale University Press.

Dincer, N. Nergiz & Barry Eichengreen (2012). The architecture and governance of financial supervision: Sources and implications. *International Finance* 15(3): 309–325.

Directive 2009/72/EC of the European Parliament and the Council of 13 July 2009 concerning common rules for the internal market in electricity and repealing Directive 2003/54/EC (2009). Official Journal L 211, 14.8.2009, pp.55–93.

Doumpos, Michael, Chrysovalantis Gaganis & Fotios Pasiouras (2015). Central bank independence, financial supervision structure and bank soundness: An empirical analysis around the crisis. *Journal of Banking & Finance* 61(S1): S69–S83.

Dubash, Navroz & Bronwen Morgan (2012). Understanding the rise of the regulatory state of the South. *Regulation and Governance* 6(3), 261–281.

Dutz, Mark A. & Maria Vagliasindi (2000). Competition policy implementation in transition economies: An empirical assessment. *European Economic Review* 44(4–6), 762–772.

Eckert, Sandra (2010). Between commitment and control: Varieties of delegation in the European postal sector. *Journal of European Public Policy* 17(8), 1231–1252.

Edwards, Geoff & Leonard Waverman (2006). The effects of public ownership and regulatory independence on regulatory outcomes. *Journal of Regulatory Economics* 29, 23–67.

Elgie, Robert & Iain McMenamin (2005). Credible commitments, political uncertainty or political complexity? Explaining variation in the independence of non-majoritarian institutions in France. *British Journal of Political Science* 35(3), 531–548.

Ennser-Jedenastik, Laurenz (2015). Credibility versus control: Agency independence and partisan influence in the regulatory state. *Comparative Political Studies* 48(7), 823–853.

Estache, Antonio & Martin A. Rossi (2008). Regulatory agencies: Impact on firm performance and social welfare. WB Policy Research Working Paper No. 4509. Washington, DC: World Bank.

Ferejohn, John & Charles Shipan (1990). Congressional influence on bureaucracy. *Journal of Law, Economics, & Organization* 6, 1–20.

Gaganis, Chrysovalantis & Fotios Pasiouras (2013). Financial supervision regimes and bank efficiency: International evidence. *Journal of Banking & Finance* 37(12), 5463–5475.

Gilardi, Fabrizio (2002). Policy credibility and delegation to independent regulatory agencies: A comparative empirical analysis. *Journal of European Public Policy* 9(6), 873–893.

Gilardi, Fabrizio (2005). The institutional foundations of regulatory capitalism: The diffusion of independent regulatory agencies in Western Europe. *Annals of the American Academy of Political and Social Science* 598, 84–101.

Guasch, J. Luis, Jean-Jacques Laffont & Stéphane Straub (2008). Renegotiation of concession contracts in Latin America: Evidence from the water and transport sectors. *International Journal of Industrial Organization* 26(2), 421–442.

Guidi, Mattia (2015). The impact of independence on regulatory outcomes: The case of EU competition policy. *Journal of Common Market Studies* 53(6), 1195–1213.

Gutiérrez, Luis H. (2003). The effect of endogenous regulation on telecommunications expansion and efficiency in Latin America. *Journal of Regulatory Economics* 23, 257–286.

Gutiérrez, Luis H. & Sanford Berg (2000). Telecommunications liberalization and regulatory governance: Lessons from Latin America. *Telecommunications Policy* 24(10), 865–884.

Hanretty, Chris & Christel Koop (2012). Measuring the formal independence of regulatory agencies. *Journal of European Public Policy* 19(2), 198–216.

Hanretty, Chris & Christel Koop (2013). Shall the law set them free? The formal and actual independence of regulatory agencies. *Regulation & Governance* 7(2), 195–214.

Henisz, Witold J., Bennet A. Zelner & Mauro F. Guillén (2005). The worldwide diffusion of market-oriented infrastructure reform, 1977–1999. *American Sociological Review* 70(6), 871–897.

Jordana, Jacint & David Levi-Faur (2005). The diffusion of regulatory capitalism in Latin America: Sectoral and national channels in the making of a new order. *Annals of the American Academy of Political and Social Science* 598, 102–124.

Jordana, Jacint, David Levi-Faur & Xavier Fernández i Marín (2011). The global diffusion of regulatory agencies: Channels of transfer and stages of diffusion. *Comparative Political Studies* 44(10), 1343–1369.

Jordana, Jacint & Guillermo Rosas (2014). When do autonomous banking regulators promote stability? *European Journal of Political Research* 53(4), 672–691.

Jordana, Jacint, Andrea C. Bianculli & Xavier Fernández i Marin (2015). When accountability meets regulation. In Andrea C. Bianculli, Xavier Fernández i Marin & Jacint Jordana (Eds) *Accountability* and *Regulatory Governance: Audiences, Controls and Responsibilities in the Politics of Regulation* (pp.1–22). Basingstoke, UK: Palgrave Macmillan.

Jordana, Jacint, Xavier Fernández i Marín & Andrea Bianculli (2018). Agency proliferation and the globalization of the regulatory state: Introducing a data set on the institutional features of regulatory agencies. *Regulation & Governance* 12(4), 524–540.

Koop, Christel (2015). Non-majoritarian institutions: A challenge for liberal democracy. In Ferdinand Müller-Rommel and Fernando Casal Bértoa (Eds) *Party Politics and Democracy in Europe: Essays in Honour of Peter Mair* (pp.227–241). London: Routledge.

Koop, Christel & Martin Lodge (2017). What is regulation? An interdisciplinary concept analysis. *Regulation & Governance* 11(1): 95–108.

Koop, Christel & Chris Hanretty (2018). Political independence, accountability, and the quality of regulatory decision-making. *Comparative Political Studies* 51(1): 38–75.

Koop, Christel & Philip Kessler (2020). Keeping control of regulation? Domestic constraints on the creation of independent authorities in emerging and developing economies. *Governance* 34(2), 545–564.

Koop, Christel & Martin Lodge (2020). British economic regulators in an age of politicisation: From the responsible to the responsive regulatory state? *Journal of European Public Policy* 27(11): 1612–1635.

Krapohl, Sebastian (2004). Credible commitment in non-independent regulatory agencies: A comparative analysis of the European agencies for foodstuffs and pharmaceuticals. *European Law Journal* 10(5), 518–538.

Kydland, Finn E. & Edward C. Prescott (1977). Rules rather than discretion: The inconsistency of optimal plans. *Journal of Political Economy* 85(3), 473–492.

Levine, Paul, Jon Stern & Francesc Trillas (2005). Utility price regulation and time inconsistency: Comparisons with monetary policy. *Oxford Economic Papers* 57(3), 447–478.

Levy, Brian & Pablo T. Spiller (1994). The institutional foundations of regulatory commitment: A comparative analysis of telecommunications regulation. *Journal of Law, Economics, & Organization* 10(2), 201–246.

Levy, Brian & Pablo T. Spiller (1996). *Regulations, Institutions, and Commitment: Comparative Studies of Telecommunications*. Cambridge, UK: Cambridge University Press.

Li, Yan & Bruce Lyons (2012). Market structure, regulation and the speed of mobile network penetration. *International Journal of Industrial Organization* 30(6), 697–707.

Ma, Tay-Cheng (2010). Competition authority independence, antitrust effectiveness, and institutions. *International Review of Law and Economics* 30(3), 226–235.

Maggetti, Martino (2007). De facto independence after delegation: A fuzzy-set analysis. *Regulation & Governance* 1(4), 271–294.

Maggetti, Martino (2010). Legitimacy and accountability of independent regulatory agencies: A critical review. *Living Reviews in Democracy* 2, 1–9.

Majone, Giandomenico (1994). The rise of the regulatory state in Europe. *West European Politics* 17(3), 77–101.

Majone, Giandomenico (1996). Temporal consistency and policy credibility: Why democracies need non-majoritarian institutions. EUI Working Paper, RSC No 96/57. Fiesole, IT: European University Institute.

Majone, Giandomenico (1997). From the positive to the regulatory state: Causes and consequences of changes in the mode of governance. *Journal of Public Policy* 17(2), 139–167.

McAllister, Lesley K. (2010). Dimensions of enforcement style: Factoring in regulatory autonomy and capacity. *Law & Policy* 32(1), 61–78.

Nunes, Rui, Guilhermina Rego & Cristina Brandão (2007). The rise of independent regulation in health care. *Health Care Analysis* 15(3), 169–177.

OECD (2014). The governance of regulators: OECD Best Practice Principles for Regulatory Policy. Paris: Organisation for Economic Co-operation and Development.

Özel, Işık (2012). The politics of de-delegation: Regulatory (in)dependence in Turkey. *Regulation & Governance*, 6(1), 119–129.

Pavón Mediano, Andrés (2020). Agencies' formal independence and credible commitment in the Latin American regulatory state: A comparative analysis of 8 countries and 13 sectors. *Regulation & Governance* 14(1), 102–120.

Radaelli, Claudio M. (2004). Getting to grips with quality in the diffusion of regulatory impact assessment in Europe. *Public Money and Management* 24(5), 271–276.

Rogoff, Kenneth (1985). The optimal degree of commitment to an intermediate monetary target. *Quarterly Journal of Economics* 100(4), 1169–1189.

Ros, Agustin J. (2003). The impact of the regulatory process and price cap regulation in Latin American telecommunications markets. *Review of Network Economics* 2(3), 270–286.

Scharpf, Fritz (1999). *Governing in Europe: Effective and Democratic?* Oxford: Oxford University Press.

Scott, Colin (2000). Accountability in the regulatory state. *Journal of Law and Society* 27(1), 38–60.

Thatcher, Mark (2002). Delegation to independent regulatory agencies: Pressures, functions and contextual mediation. *West European Politics* 25(1), 125–147.

Thatcher, Mark & Alec Stone Sweet (2002). Theory and practice of delegation to nonmajoritarian institutions. *West European Politics* 25(1), 1–22.

Thatcher, Mark (2005). The third force? Independent regulatory agencies and elected politicians in Europe. *Governance* 18(3), 347–373.

Trillas, Francesc & Miguel A. Montoya (2011). Commitment and regulatory independence in practice in Latin American and Caribbean Countries. *Competition and Regulation in Network Industries* 12(1), 27–56.

UNCTAD (2008). Independence and accountability of competition authorities. TD/B/COM.2/CLP/67. Geneva: United Nations Conference on Trade and Development.

Wallsten, Scott J. (2001). An econometric analysis of telecom competition, privatization, and regulation in Africa and Latin America. *Journal of Industrial Economics* 49(1), 1–19.

Wassum, Moritz & Fabrizio De Francesco (2020). Explaining regulatory autonomy in EU network sectors: Varieties of utility regulation? *Governance* 33(1), 41–60.

Wilks, Stephen & Ian Bartle (2002). The unanticipated consequences of creating independent competition agencies. *West European Politics* 25(1), 148–172.

Zhang, Yin-Fang, David Parker & Colin Kirkpatrick (2008). Electricity sector reform in developing countries: An econometric assessment of the effects of privatization, competition and regulation. *Journal of Regulatory Economics* 33(2), 159–178.

15. Independent regulators in the post-delegation stage

Martino Maggetti

INTRODUCTION

This chapter deals with independent regulators in the post-delegation stage, that is, after they received regulatory powers from their political principals. Much valuable scholarship has focused on the explanations for the establishment of independent regulators and their world-wide diffusion (Majone 1997; Moran 2002; Levi-Faur 2005; Braithwaite 2008; Gilardi 2008; Jordana et al. 2011; Jordana et al. 2018). Research on the role of regulators after delegation (Thatcher 2002) is also mushrooming, but it remains somehow more disparate. It centers on specific features, such as the role of accountability forums (Schillemans and Busuioc 2015), the dynamics of delegation when the government is both the principal and the regulatory target (Di Mascio et al. 2020), or the strategic communication of regulators (Maor et al. 2013; see also Chapter 18 by Maor in this volume). In other words, it lacks an explicit thread related to the post-delegation stage as an overarching analytical framework. The goal of this chapter is to take stock of this literature and reflect more systematically on the study of the post-delegation stage as a theoretical perspective for examining the role of independent regulators in practice. In this view, three main insights are put forward. First, the concept of de facto independence is presented as a way to study the actual unfolding of independence relationships, by assessing the extent to which a regulator can determine its preferences without undue influence, and then act based upon these preferences. Second, principal–agent relationships are described as constantly evolving after delegation. Unintended phenomena emerge, such as forum shirking and forum paralysis, the deployment of multidimensional agency relations, and the regulator playing the role of policy maker. Third, legitimacy challenges are discussed. Independent regulators have become socially valued and even taken-for-granted organizational models, but their legitimacy lies on shaky grounds. Political pressures – especially those exerted by popu-list political leaderships – appear to be potentially more pervasive than one would assume. In the concluding section, an agenda for further research is sketched based on these insights, with the goal of contributing to theory-building towards a more comprehensive understanding of the role of regulators in the post-delegation stage.

DE FACTO INDEPENDENCE

The degree of independence that regulatory agencies formally enjoy from elected officials constitutes the primary dimension that policy makers can control when delegating powers to regulators. As such, the study of formal independence – also called de jure independence – provides key insights of the process of delegation. In particular, it represents a crucial variable that has been used to explain the establishment and worldwide diffusion of regulators in many policy areas (Gilardi 2008; Jordana et al. 2011). Empirical research has shown, for instance, that more independence is statutorily granted to regulators when credible commitments in the time consistency of regulatory policies are particularly needed, and when governments are confronted with political uncertainty (Gilardi 2005). The formal independence of regulators varies across countries and sectors (Jordana et al. 2018) and it may evolve over time through legislative changes that follows external pressures and government strategies to reinforce their credible commitments (Coroado 2020).

However, when shifting the focus towards independence as it is deployed in the post-delegation stage, the concept of "de facto independence" appears to be more suitable. This concept connotes the extent of regulators' effective autonomy as they manage their day-to-day regulatory activities (Maggetti 2007). It enables researchers to acknowledge that agencies are embedded in a dense network of relationships, wherein they act as "intermediary organizations" (Braun 1993) mediating between the heterogeneous and conflicting interests of actors that populate regulatory regimes (Vibert 2014). De facto independence should indeed be conceived not only with reference to elected politicians (their political principal), but also with respect with other relevant external actors, in particular the representatives of the regulated industries. These external actors correspond to those that possess both the incentives and the capacity to influence and possibly capture the regulatory activity of agencies (Thatcher 2005; Carpenter and Moss 2013). Following this approach, the de facto independence of formally independent regulatory agencies can be seen as the combination of two constitutive components (Maggetti 2012) (see Figure 15.1). The first component corresponds to the (relative) self-determination of agencies' preferences. This occurs when their preferences are formed following an intraorganizational decision-making process within the boundaries of their mandate, also implying that they should not integrate a priori the interests of external actors populating regulatory regimes. The second component is the (relative) lack of restrictions

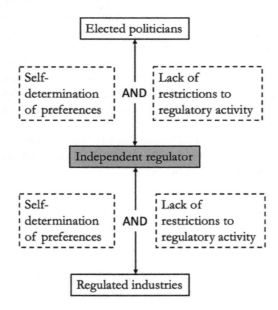

Figure 15.1   The concept of de facto independence

when enacting their regulatory activity. Conversely, there is a reduction of autonomy if external actors, once the agency's preferences are established, can still crucially manipulate the activity of regulation, so as to override the will of regulator in charge.

These insights can be operationalized with a variety of indicators of de facto independence, for example: the frequency of a revolving door between the regulator, the executive bureaucracy, and, respectively, the regulated sector; the frequency of ad hoc contacts such as meetings and exchange of expertise between the regulator and external actors; and the latter's influence on the regulator's budget (Maggetti 2012). In that regard, empirical research has confirmed that formal independence constitutes a relevant antecedent of de facto independence, but the former does not automatically translate into the latter. Evidence from 16 Western European regulators using qualitative comparative analysis (QCA) indicated that formal independence is neither sufficient to guarantee de facto independence, nor strictly necessary to elicit independence in practice (Maggetti 2007). The importance of informal networks has been underlined in an in-depth study of the Irish case, showing that non-formal networking and informal communications are widely used by regulatory agencies to support their room for maneuver in the pursuit of their mandate (MacCarthaigh 2014). More recently, an interview-based case study of the Egyptian telecoms regulatory agency has corroborated the finding that the apparent independence from government – as perceived by people in senior and strategic positions within the organization under investigation – is an important but not a sufficient factor to guarantee the de facto independence of the agency (Badran 2017).

Nonetheless, the study of independence in practice is notoriously challenging (Maggetti and Verhoest 2014). Besides being resource-intensive, it requires examining informal relations between organizations, and the behavioral implications of institutional arrangements, creating potential feasibility problems for cases where access to primary sources is difficult, and for conducting comparative research on a large number of cases. Some scholars have thereby adopted more parsimonious alternatives. An empirical investigation into the political vulnerability of 87 regulators in 17 established Western European democracies has shown that formal independence has a positive effect on the stability of the tenure of the chief executive of the agency; this effect is however smaller and less significant than that of other variables, such as the rule of law (Hanretty and Koop 2013). Conceiving de facto independence as political vulnerability allows researchers to engage in macro-comparative research more easily than when a thicker understanding is adopted. However, political vulnerability, which may be operationalized as the combination of the vulnerability of the chief executive of the agency to changes in government and of its average turnover rate as in the study mentioned above, refers to a specific dimension of de facto independence only: the ability of regulators to survive to political changes. Two additional issues shall be mentioned. First, a potential problem of observational equivalence exists: leaving office in front of political change could also be interpreted as a sign of independence, meaning that the regulator does not accept interferences from a new, pro-active political master (Trillas and Montoya 2009). Second, when the establishment of independent regulators is the result of coercive pressures exerted by international organizations, their independence can hardly be seen as the outcome of a process of strategic delegation from the government (Trillas and Montoya 2013).

Other scholars have chosen another approach, making the most of the relational nature of independence. The application of social network analysis allows researchers to adopt a more comprehensive relational approach and include other actors, namely other regulators and courts, that play a role in the regulatory regime (Ingold et al. 2013; Maggetti et al. 2013).

The findings of these pieces of research have confirmed that the relationships unfolding with actors other than elected politicians, that is, the regulatees, but also co-regulators – especially economy-wide regulatory authorities – are crucially impacting on the room for maneuver of the regulator under investigation. At the same time, it has been noted that repeated and durable interactions within networks populated by peer agencies may enhance the independence and regulatory powers of regulators (Maggetti 2014).

However, this approach also entails some limitations. On the one hand, it perceptual character makes it potentially prone to a subjectivity bias – even if perceptions can have important behavioral consequences. Perceptions of independence might nevertheless merely actually correspond to the degree of autonomy that is considered appropriate by those in office, given the institutional context; a perceptual approach is not the most suitable option for fully capturing the more structural, sometimes even unconscious, features of factual independence, which also have an impact on the political role of agencies and on their regulatory performance; finally, it is important to recognize that being independent also means to dispose from the capacity of implementing their own decisions (Maggetti 2012). On the other hand, its wider applicability comes again at the expense of a certain loss in the precision of the concept of de facto independence – trading conceptual intension with its extension (Sartori 1970). To sum up, the relevance of the de facto independence of regulators for the examination of their role in the post-delegation stage is well established. Its operationalization is however not always straightforward: a "thick" understanding is suitable for small- and medium-N research, whilst a "thin" one is more appropriate for macro-comparative research based on a large number of observations.

THE EVOLUTION OF PRINCIPAL–AGENT RELATIONSHIPS

The delegation of regulatory powers to an independent agency has been traditionally portrayed through a principal–agent framework, whereby the former – that is, the government – entrusts the latter with some specialized tasks to be executed on its behalf (Miller 2005). This structure of delegation should shield independent bodies from political interference, while allowing political principals to ensure that regulators work within the boundaries of their statutory mission as broadly defined by policy makers (Pollack 2002; Majone 2001; Thatcher and Stone Sweet 2002; Braun 2003). The principal–agent framework comes with a number of assumptions, three of which can be considered as central for the present discussion (see Table 15.1). First, it is assumed that the principal seeks to exert control over the agent so as to minimize "agency losses" due to asymmetries of information and contractual holes inherent to any principal–agent relationship, such as moral hazard, adverse selection and shirking. Second, the fulcrum of the model is structured around a vertical relation between the principal and the agent, which is supposed to shape the functioning of the regulatory regime as a whole. Third,

Table 15.1   The principal–agent model in practice

	(1)	(2)	(3)
Principal–agent expectations	Moral hazard, adverse selection and agency shirking	Vertical relation shaped by discretion vs controls	Regulator as delegate
Principal–agent relationships in practice	Forum shirking and forum paralysis	Multidimensional agency relations	Regulator as policy maker

this vertical relationship is seen as necessarily hierarchical and fully differentiated, whereby elected politicians make decisions and regulators are in charge of implementing regulatory policies through monitoring, supervision and (sometimes) the enactment of sanctions.

However, a critical review of the existing empirical literature has suggested that the unfolding of these relationships in the post-delegation stage tends to deviate from these core expectations based on the principal–agent framework (Maggetti and Papadopoulos 2018). As regards the first point, several empirical studies on independent regulators have shown that, contrary to principal–agent model prescriptions, the principal does not always strive for exerting controls and activating accountability mechanisms. The use of the existing control mechanisms – related for instance to appointment and revocation procedures – remains indeed limited (Thatcher 2002; 2005). Instead, a phenomenon of "forum shirking" or "forum drift" (Schillemans and Busuioc 2015) is frequently observed, whereby the government voluntarily relinquish its powers, and it does not perform as an active principal. Such passive attitude may stem from several factors, such as a lack of incentives, limited resources and expertise, or be a purposive strategy for allowing the government to shift the blame in the wake of a policy failure or major crisis. An example of this behavior comes from the attitude of the Swiss government towards the Swiss Financial Market Supervisory Authority (FINMA) during the 2008–2011 financial crisis (Biela et al. 2011). The government did not engage its responsibility and refrained from using its control powers, mainly because any intervention in the FINMA operations would have been interpreted as a signal of lower independence from the government.

Second, contrary to another central principal–agent assumption, the behavior of the agent also appears as crucially determined by relations with actors other than the principal: the regulatees, but also co-regulators (other domestic authorities that share regulatory competencies with a sector-specific regulator in a given jurisdiction) and peer agencies (sector-specific regulators in charge of regulating the same sector in other jurisdictions). These actors can affect the behavior of agencies, particularly through close and continual interactions in governance networks (Yesilkagit and van Thiel 2012; Bach and Ruffing 2013; Brandsma and Adriaensen 2017). Several studies have indeed shown that horizontal interorganizational relations are crucial for independent regulators, sometimes even more than vertical interactions understood as principal–agent relations. The accountability of agencies, for instance, is frequently ensured through interactions with actors that do not correspond to principals – their official accountability forums – but entertain horizontal – or "peer-to-peer" – relationships with independent regulators (Michels and Meijer 2008). A study of independent agencies in the Netherlands has shown that agencies commit themselves voluntarily to additional accountability practices – for example through disclosure and reporting – towards a variety of societal actors, such as clients, regulatees, organized interests, the media, and the public at large (Koop 2014). These findings provide more evidence on the relevant accountability forums other than the principals. Another example consists of their active engagement in regulatory communication to protect their reputation. Different external audiences are able to shape agencies attention and elicit their response when they express public claims directed towards regulatory problems, for example, about regulation considered as too lenient or excessive (Gilad et al. 2013). Therefore, chains of responsibility appear more complex than what the principal–agent theory assumes. Political principals are not necessarily the main forums controlling agencies, and, at the same time, the hierarchical relationship between agencies and their principals is only one relationship among many. In the post-delegation period, interactions between the regulator and other actors and institutions extend on different levels and become more multifaceted (Eberlein and Grande 2005; Coen and Heritier 2005).

The third point relates to the evolution of the principal–agent relation over time. After delegation, regulators progressively accumulate reputational resources and, concomitantly, more networking opportunities, which enable them to play an active role not only in regulatory implementation but also in policy creation (Carpenter 2001). Such an evolution can change the nature of the relationship between the agent and the political principal, who originally delegated regulatory powers. Including powerful agencies in lawmaking may become inescapable when elaborating a sector-specific policy or passing new legislation. For example, it has been noted that the U.S. Food and Drug Administration (FDA) has built a reputation of credibility over time that has allowed it to position itself as a protector of the public good and acquire a central role in the political process; it has thus been able to gain considerable political influence as a result of its unique regulatory expertise and frequent interactions with regulated industries (Carpenter 2010).

Furthermore, comparative studies on independent regulators in European countries have shown that agencies are not only crucial in the implementation phase, but they also actively participated in the process of policy formulation (Maggetti 2009; Bach 2012; see also Chapter 25 by Guaschino in this volume). For instance, a case study of the Flemish public sector has suggested that the theoretical distinction between policy making and operations is more nuanced than expected (Verschuere 2009). Agencies are sometimes much more involved in the preparation of policy programs and in policy decision-making than assumed, while elected politicians may in some cases play an active role in policy implementation. Finally, studies on European agencies indicated that they typically underwent a process of task expansion. They outstripped their original role as mere networking platforms and arenas for the exchange of information on "best practice" by acquiring decision-making and regulatory tasks (Egeberg et al. 2014; Borrás et al. 2007). The case of the European Food Safety Authority (EFSA) shows that EU agencies can play an active role as policy entrepreneurs at both the domestic and the international level (Groenleer and Gabbi 2013). EFSA has indeed developed a substantial role in shaping food safety policies, despite the relatively limited original scope defined by its legal framework. It achieved a central position in the international policy network in this area, through which it came to exert key influence on political institutions in the EU and towards member states.

LEGITIMACY CHALLENGES

Delegation to independent regulators may serve several functional purposes, namely to inject sector-specific expertise in the policy process and to provide long-term credibility to regulatory policies. However, it also implies a "net loss" of legitimacy for the political system (Majone 2005). This is because democratic legitimacy is an intransitive property: elected politicians can transfer their powers to the independent delegate, but not their democratic legitimacy. To counteract this loss, which might threaten the stability of the political system as a whole, additional legitimization procedures are needed (Maggetti 2010). Two solutions to this democratic deficit are usually mentioned, consisting, respectively, of the expected higher output-legitimacy of independent regulators, based on the assumption that they perform better than democratic institutions with respect to the implementation of regulatory policies; and their enhanced throughput-legitimacy, as they typically apply stricter accountability requirements than traditional bureaucracies. A third, more innovative solution relates to the aforementioned role agencies' networks could play in ensuring mutual controls and check and balances. These additional sources of legitimacy – which are supposed to work complementarily by creating a "multi-pronged" system of controls – are expected to ensure the "social sustainability" of regulatory governance (Costanza 1992; Kemp and Rotmans 2005). However, what has been left out of the door is likely to come back through the window: the lack of democratic legitimacy can hardly be fully compensated, especially in crisis moments, when output-legitimacy is under strain and throughput-legitimacy becomes devoid of substance.

In the post-delegation stage, independent regulators may experience the burden of these legitimacy challenges. On the one hand, the growing importance of independent regulators can create bureaucratic rivalries and jurisdictional conflicts with other public sector organizations that strive to protect their turf. Regulators become immersed in bureaucratic politics and their strategy of "depoliticization" can be contested. On the other hand, independent regulators may suffer from the consequences of the blame game. Blame shifting is indeed a double-edged sword. It allows policy makers to deflect criticisms towards independent regulators in crisis moments, but repeated blame attributions may jeopardize public trust in regulators and undermine their credibility overall. This way, even powerful regulators may face existential threats and be ultimately terminated, as it happened to the British Financial Services Authority that has been dismembered in the wake of the 2007–2008 financial crisis.

Notwithstanding these pending challenges, independent regulators have generally been considered as relatively uncontested, socially valued, and even taken-for-granted governance devices. As such, they have thrived across sectors and countries in the last decades (see Chapter 6 by Fernández-i-Marín, Jordana and Levi-Faur in this volume). Whilst being also influent in policy making, they have been rarely involved in partisan politics. They have been established or strengthened through regulatory reforms enacted by both left-wing and right-wing governments in OECD countries since the late 1980s (Belloc and Nicita 2011). However, this situation has evolved considerably in the wake of the rise of Western countries' populism – an elusive concept, minimally intended here as a specific political strategy grounded on the critique of the "elite" depicted as self-referential or corrupt by invoking an unmediated, organic relationship between political leadership and "the people" (Mudde 2013; Weyland 2017; Caramani 2017). Populists in government aim at structures, resources, personnel, norms, and accountability relationships, and, thereby, they can deplete policy making and democratic quality (Bauer and Becker 2020). The main focus of populist pressures so far are representative democratic institutions as they are run by elected politicians and ordinary bureaucrats (Caramani 2017). Nonetheless, populists are also inimical to independent bodies, be they courts or regulators. The underlying thread is the elimination of potentially competing sources of authority that would limit the power of populists in office (Rockman 2019). Even when they are not directly targeted, independent regulators embody the prototype of technocratic institutions that bear the burden of the anti-elite rhetoric characterizing populist political communication (Goodhart and Lastra 2018). In that respect, populist pressures can – at least potentially – modify the accountability relationships of regulators by creating emotionalized blame attributions and disciplining, producing a state of affairs where pluralism and the use of expertise in policy making are limited and restricted (Wood et al. 2021). Against this background, the scope and the room for maneuver of independent regulators, and, more extensively, their legitimacy, could become at risk.

   Little systematic empirical research exists so far on the actual impact of populist pressures on independent regulators. The case of the U.S. Environmental Protection Agency (EPA) under the Trump administration (2017–21) can nevertheless offer some hints. The Trump administration incarnated a mixture of right-wing populism and conservative ideology, pursuing a strong deregulatory agenda aiming at curtailing health and environmental protections (Pierson 2017). The effect of the pressures exerted by the presidency on this independent regulator has been considered by most scholars working on this issue as potentially huge, and likely to have long-lasting consequences. Under the Trump administration and the newly appointed agency head Scott Pruitt, EPA has undertaken quick, radical, sizeable changes in policies, priorities, and practices, so as to curb its regulatory reach (Dillon et al. 2018). Concretely, the new EPA leadership has fundamentally departed from the statutory mission to protect the health and the environment, by substantially undermining the agency's environmental regulations, shifting policy programs to favor non-renewable energy businesses and industry, undercutting its budget, reducing its work capacity, jeopardizing its internal operations, and appointing senior staff with deep ties with the regulated industries (Dillon et al. 2018). The case of the repeal of the Clean Power Plan and its replacement with the Affordable Clean Energy Rule (ACE) provides an example of this effort. By preventing EPA from promoting effective solutions to reduce power plant carbon dioxide emissions, ACE has been designed to achieve nearly no carbon dioxide emissions reductions (Goffman and Bloomer 2019). What is more, the Trump administration has entrenched EPA operations in a hyper-partisan context while limiting its scientific capacity and use of science in decision-making (Sullivan et al. 2021).
   These insights corroborate the relevance of a focus on the post-delegation stage, while offering a sobering lesson on the role of formal institutions in preserving the functions of independent regulators. As outlined above, independent regulators represent a widely diffused, socially valued, taken-for-granted organizational model for operating regulatory governance. And yet, a hostile government could override the institutional arrangements they rely on. Independent regulators may be shielded from politics in ordinary times, but they seem to be less protected when it really matters, that is, when they are under attack by a new, aggressive political master. The fact that this can occur in an established democracy based on the rule of law and with numerous institutional checks and balances such as the U.S. is quite striking. As they rely on a limited stock of legitimacy, independent regulators may actually be more fragile than how they appear on first sight. At the same time, however, it has been observed that in many other cases, populist pressures do not reshape public administration. A recent piece on the Italian case has shown that the level of administrative continuity has been significant, notwithstanding two decades of intermittent populist pressures (Di Mascio et al. 2021). The authors explain this bureaucratic resilience specifically with the absence of wide-ranging administrative reforms promoted by populists in office, which is due to the low priority assigned to these reforms, but also to the short-liveness of cabinets. In Switzerland, populist political parties have gained more electoral support in the last decades, but they have become somewhat less central in policy making, namely because their polarized stance make them less able to find political allies and forge compromises (Papadopoulos and Maggetti 2018). Further research is needed, but these diverging patterns might be determined – or at least mediated – not only by structural variables such as the political regime, institutional veto players, or the majoritarian or consensual variety of democracy, but also by the specific nature of the relationships between elected politicians and administrative actors in given contexts, including regulators. What is more, the long-term effects of these pressures, even if unsuccessful on the short term,

are still not well understood. It is still possible that such pressures might not be immediately perceptible, but they will slowly percolate into political-administrative relations, producing a gradual but ultimately transformative change over a certain amount of time.

FORESIGHT AND CONCLUSION

This chapter has briefly outlined how independent regulators take a life on their own in the post-delegation stage. They are designed to implement regulatory policies by acting as the delegate of their political principal, to whom they are formally independent according to a trustor–trustee relationship (Majone 2001). Nevertheless, over time, independent regulators tend to transform their mandate and deploy their operations in unforeseen and sometimes unintended ways. They may be reinforced in terms of powers and resources, acquire more de facto independence, and exert new functions besides their regulatory duties, such as playing an active role in lawmaking. In doing so, they can ultimately subvert the logic of the principal–agent model. However, in other circumstances, they can undertake changes that diminish their regulatory reach and put their legitimacy under strain. In particular, when a crisis reveals some severe deficiency in their regulatory approach, as it was the case for many financial regulators in the aftermath of the 2007–2008 financial crisis, or when a new political master exerts pressures that imperil their regulatory activities, their de facto independence can be curtailed and their regulatory powers can be revoked. Their formal separation from elected politicians seems to matter less than it appears at first glance.

Against this background, further studies are needed, especially on the following three issues. First, it would be important to systematically investigate variations in the de facto independence of agencies across countries and sectors and over time, in a more comprehensive way that what has been achieved so far. This is a demanding task, but it would greatly contribute to improve our understanding of regulatory governance. Determining variations of de facto independence would not only allow researchers to identify the external factors that are associated with deviations from statutory independence as initially foreseen by political "principals." It would also expose the consequences of such discrepancies on crucial variables for the regulatory process such as regulatory quality, performance and effectiveness. A pending question, for instance, is whether regulatory quality is comparatively higher when de facto independence matches de jure independence, or, conversely, whether a given level of de facto independence is consistently conducting to higher quality, irrespective of the extent to which it departs from statutory independence (for a discussion of the relation between formal independence and performance see Chapter 14 by Koop and Jordana in this volume). What is more, indicators of de facto independence could be refined to integrate even more fine-grained measures of informal relations unfolding among actors populating regulatory regimes, possibly making the most of new technologies of data analysis, for example, artificial intelligence and machine learning (which, in turn, also require regulatory oversight, see Chapter 31 by Busuioc in this volume).

Second, organizational behavior in the post-delegation stage needs more attention, specifically regarding how independent regulators interact with respect to their broader organizational environment, and, thereby, contribute to constantly reshape regulatory regimes. Their environment is populated by several actors holding key roles in regulatory regimes besides principals and the regulated industries, including peer agencies and co-regulators. The former typically correspond to international allies and partners that provide regulators with informational resources and strategic advantages through their interactions in transnational networks. The latter are more likely to cultivate rival and conflictual relations with independent regulators, as both compete for resources and for influence in the same jurisdiction. An example is the antagonism that emerges between sector-specific regulatory agencies and economy-wide antitrust regulators in areas such as telecom or financial regulation. The study of these relationships is particularly relevant because the functioning of a regulatory regime is not only determined by the vertical relation between elected politicians, the regulator, and the regulated industries. It is also influenced by the complex interactions with other actors such as co-regulators, peer agencies, tribunals, interest groups, consumer associations, and the media. These interorganizational relationships are likely to be crucially mediated by reputational concerns, and, respectively, by mutual perceptions of trustworthiness or untrustworthiness. The extent to which collaborative or conflictual relationships between different pairs of actors contribute to build or to deplete organizational reputation would deserve more consideration.

Third, independent regulators appear to be potentially more fragile than expected. In a way, this is not so surprising. Independent regulators, as any human artifact, are brought into being, blossom, then decline and perish. However, their formal independence is precisely established – and institutionalized – to ensure protection from the vagaries of the political cycle. As such they still represent a widely recognized role model for implementing regulatory governance. And yet, political pressures appear to be potentially more pervasive than one would assume. This possibly happens not only because their separation from politics is always relative and never absolute, but also because institutions come with informal norms that are critical for their maintenance and persistence. When political actors jeopardize such shared norms, institutions can no longer function properly. No institution can only work by the books. From this perspective, formal independence seems to have a largely performative function, and, in this sense, it appears as a myth and a ceremony (Meyer and Rowan 1977), which produces an effect only if it is enshrined in an organizational culture of independence matching with a political culture cherishing pluralism and the separation of powers. Against this background, it would be worth to empirically study the extent to which populist pressures create legitimacy challenges for independent regulators in democratic systems, and the scope conditions enabling or constraining these developments.

REFERENCES

Bach, T. (2012) The involvement of agencies in policy formulation: Explaining variation in policy autonomy of federal agencies in Germany. *Policy and Society*, 31, 211–222.

Bach, T. & Ruffing, E. (2013) Networking for autonomy? National agencies in European networks. *Public Administration*, 91, 712–726.

Badran, A. (2017) Revisiting regulatory independence: The relationship between the formal and de-facto independence of the Egyptian telecoms regulator. *Public Policy and Administration*, 32, 66–84.

Bauer, M. W. & Becker, S. (2020) Democratic backsliding, populism, and public administration. *Perspectives on Public Management and Governance*, 3, 19–31.

Belloc, F. & Nicita, A. (2011) The political determinants of liberalization: Do ideological cleavages still matter? *International Review of Economics*, 58, 121–145.

Biela, J., Maggetti, M. & Puppis, M. (2011) Finanzregulierer in der Krise. *Die Volkswirtschaft*, 1, 59–62.

Borrás, S., Koutalakis, C. & Wendler, F. (2007) European agencies and input legitimacy: EFSA, EMeA and EPO in the post-delegation phase. *European Integration*, 29, 583–600.

Braithwaite, J. (2008) *Regulatory Capitalism: How it Works, Ideas for Making it Work Better*, Cheltenham, UK and Northampton, MA, USA: Edward Elgar Publishing.

Brandsma, G. J. & Adriaensen, J. (2017) The principal–agent model, accountability and democratic legitimacy. In Delreux, T. & Adriaensen, J. (Eds.), *The Principal Agent Model and the European Union* (pp. 35–55). Springer.

Braun, D. (1993) Who governs intermediary agencies? Principal–agent relations in research policy-making. *Journal of Public Policy*, 13, 135–162.

Braun, D. (2003) Lasting tensions in research policy-making – a delegation problem. *Science and Public Policy*, 30, 309–321.

Caramani, D. (2017) Will vs. reason: The populist and technocratic forms of political representation and their critique to party government. *American Political Science Review*, 111, 54–67.

Carpenter, D. P. (2001) The political foundations of bureaucratic autonomy: A response to Kernell. *Studies in American Political Development*, 15, 113–122.

Carpenter, D. P. (2010) *Reputation and Power: Organizational Image and Pharmaceutical Regulation at the FDA*, Princeton University Press.

Carpenter, D. P. & Moss, D. A. (2013) *Preventing Regulatory Capture: Special Interest Influence and How to Limit It*, Cambridge University Press.

Coen, D. & Heritier, A. (2005) *Refining Regulatory Regimes: Utilities in Europe,* Cheltenham, UK and Northampton, MA, USA: Edward Elgar Publishing.

Coroado, S. (2020) Does formal independence of regulators change? Evidence from Portuguese agencies. *Governance*, 33, 61–77.

Costanza, R. (1992) *Ecological Economics: The Science and Management of Sustainability*, Columbia University Press.

Di Mascio, F., Maggetti, M. & Natalini, A. (2020) Exploring the dynamics of delegation over time: Insights from Italian anti-corruption agencies (2003–2016). *Policy Studies Journal*, 48, 367–400.

Di Mascio, F., Natalini, A. & Ongaro, E. (2021) Resilience without resistance: Public administration under mutating populisms in office in Italy. In Bauer, M. W., Peters, G. B., Pierre, J., Yesilkagit, K. & Becker, S. (Eds.), *Democratic Backsliding and Public Administration: How Populists in Government Transform State Bureaucracies* (pp. 47–75). Cambridge University Press.

Dillon, L., Sellers, C., Underhill, V., Shapiro, N., Ohayon, J. L., Sullivan, M., Brown, P., Harrison, J., Wylie, S. & Group, E. U. S. W. (2018) The Environmental Protection Agency in the early Trump administration: Prelude to regulatory capture. *American Journal of Public Health*, 108, S89–S94.

Eberlein, B. & Grande, E. (2005) Beyond delegation: Transnational regulatory regimes and the EU regulatory state. *Journal of European Public Policy*, 12, 89–112.

Egeberg, M., Trondal, J. & Vestlund, N. M. (2014) Situating EU agencies in the political-administrative space, ARENA Working Paper 6/2014.

Gilad, S., Maor, M. & Bloom, P. B.-N. (2013) Organizational reputation, the content of public allegations, and regulatory communication. *Journal of Public Administration Research and Theory*, 25(2), 451–478.

Gilardi, F. (2005) The formal independence of regulators: A comparison of 17 countries and 7 sectors. *Swiss Political Science Review*, 11, 139–167.

Gilardi, F. (2008) Delegation in the regulatory state: Independent regulatory agencies in Western Europe, Cheltenham, UK and Northampton, MA, USA: Edward Elgar Publishing.

Goffman, J. & Bloomer, L. (2019) Disempowering the EPA: How statutory interpretation of the Clean Air Act serves the Trump administration's deregulatory agenda. *Case W. Res. L. Rev.*, 70, 929.

Goodhart, C. & Lastra, R. (2018) Populism and central bank independence. *Open Economies Review*, 29, 49–68.

Groenleer, M. & Gabbi, S. (2013) Regulatory agencies of the European Union as international actors: Legal framework, development over time and strategic motives in the case of the European Food Safety Authority. *European Journal of Risk Regulation*, 4, 479–492.

Hanretty, C. & Koop, C. (2013) Shall the law set them free? The formal and actual independence of regulatory agencies. *Regulation & Governance*, 7, 195–214.

Ingold, K., Varone, F. & Stokman, F. (2013) A social network-based approach to assess de facto independence of regulatory agencies. *Journal of European Public Policy*, 20, 1464–1481.

Jordana, J., Fernández-i-Marín, X. & Bianculli, A. C. (2018) Agency proliferation and the globalization of the regulatory state: Introducing a data set on the institutional features of regulatory agencies. *Regulation & Governance*, 12, 524–540.

Jordana, J., Levi-Faur, D. & i Marín, X. F. (2011) The global diffusion of regulatory agencies. *Comparative Political Studies*, 44, 1343–1369.

Kemp, R. & Rotmans, J. (2005) The management of the co-evolution of technical, environmental and social systems. In Weber, M. & Hemmelskamp, J. (Eds.), *Towards Environmental Innovation Systems* (pp. 33–57), Springer Verlag.

Koop, C. (2014) Theorizing and explaining voluntary accountability. *Public Administration*, 92, 565–581.

Levi-Faur, D. (2005) The global diffusion of regulatory capitalism. *Annals, AAPSS*, 598, 12–32.

MacCarthaigh, M. (2014). Informal relationships and de facto independence of the regulator in the Irish telecommunications regulatory arrangement. In Aubin, D. & Verhoest, K. (Eds.), *Multi-Level Regulation in the Telecommunications Sector* (pp. 78–107), Palgrave Macmillan.

Maggetti, M. (2007) De facto independence after delegation: A fuzzy-set analysis. *Regulation & Governance*, 1, 271–294.

Maggetti, M. (2009) The role of independent regulatory agencies in policy-making: A comparative analysis. *Journal of European Public Policy*, 16, 445–465.

Maggetti, M. (2010) Legitimacy and accountability of independent regulatory agencies: A critical review. *Living Reviews in Democracy*, 2, 1–9.

Maggetti, M. (2012) *Regulation in Practice. The De Facto Independence of Regulatory Agencies*, ECPR Press.

Maggetti, M. (2014) The rewards of cooperation: The effects of membership in European regulatory networks. *European Journal of Political Research*, 53, 480–499.

Maggetti, M., Ingold, K. & Varone, F. (2013) Having your cake and eating it, too: Can regulatory agencies be both independent and accountable? *Swiss Political Science Review*, 19, 1–25.

Maggetti, M. & Papadopoulos, Y. (2018) The principal–agent framework and independent regulatory agencies. *Political Studies Review*, 16, 172–183.

Maggetti, M. & Verhoest, K. (2014) Unexplored aspects of bureaucratic autonomy: A state of the field and ways forward. *International Review of Administrative Sciences*, 88(2), 239–256.

Majone, G. (1997) Independent agencies and the delegation problem: Theoretical and normative dimensions. In Steuenberg, B. & van Vught, F. (Eds.), *Political Institutions and Public Policy* (pp. 139–156), Kluwer Academic Publishers.

Majone, G. (2001) Two logics of delegation: Agency and fiduciary relations in EU governance. *European Union Politics*, 2, 103–122.

Majone, G. (2005) Delegation of powers and the fiduciary principle. CONNEX Workshop, Paris.

Maor, M., Gilad, S. & Bloom, P. B.-N. (2013) Organizational reputation, regulatory talk, and strategic silence. *Journal of Public Administration Research and Theory*, 23, 581–608.

Meyer, J. W. & Rowan, B. (1977) Institutionalized organizations: Formal structure as myth and ceremony. *American Journal of Sociology*, 83, 340–363.

Michels, A. & Meijer, A. (2008) Safeguarding public accountability in horizontal government. *Public Management Review*, 10, 165–173.

Miller, G. J. (2005) The political evolution of principal–agent models. *Annual Review of Political Science*, 8, 203–225.

Moran, M. (2002) Review article: Understanding the regulatory state. *British Journal of Political Science*, 32, 391–413.

Papadopoulos, Y. & Maggetti, M. (2018) Policy style(s) in Switzerland. Under stress. In Howlett, M. & Tosun, J. (Eds.), *Policy Styles and Policy-Making: Exploring the Linkages* (pp. 157–179), Routledge.

Pierson, P. (2017) American hybrid: Donald Trump and the strange merger of populism and plutocracy. *The British Journal of Sociology*, 68, 105–119.

Pollack, M. A. (2002) Learning from the Americanists (again): Theory and method in the study of delegation. *West European Politics*, 25, 200–219.

Rockman, B. A. (2019) Bureaucracy between populism and technocracy. *Administration & Society*, 51, 1546–1575.

Sartori, G. (1970) Concept misformation in comparative politics. *The American Political Science Review*, 64, 1033–1053.

Schillemans, T. & Busuioc, M. (2015) Predicting public sector accountability: From agency drift to forum drift. *Journal of Public Administration Research and Theory*, 25, 191–215.

Sullivan, M., Sellers, C., Fredrickson, L., Cordner, A., Kohl, E. & Ohayon, J. L. (2021) Re-envisioning EPA and its work in the post-Trump era: Perspectives from EPA employees. *Journal of Public Health Policy*, 42, 281–297.

Thatcher, M. (2002) Regulation after delegation: Independent regulatory agencies in Europe. *Journal of European Public Policy*, 9, 954–972.

Thatcher, M. (2005) The third force? Independent regulatory agencies and elected politicians in Europe. *Governance*, 18, 347–373.

Thatcher, M. & Stone Sweet, A. (2002) Theory and practice of delegation to non-majoritarian institutions. *West European Politics*, 25, 1–22.

Trillas, F. & Montoya, M. A. (2009) The measurement of regulator independence in practice: Latin America and the Caribbean. *International Journal of Public Policy*, 4(1/2), 113–134.

Trillas, F. & Montoya, M. A. (2013) Independent regulators: Theory, evidence and reform proposals. *Info*, 15(3), 39–53.

Verschuere, B. (2009) The role of public agencies in the policy making process. *Public Policy and Administration*, 24, 23–46.

Vibert, F. (2014) *The New Regulatory Space: Reframing Democratic Governance*, Cheltenham, UK and Northampton, MA, USA: Edward Elgar Publishing.

Weyland, K. (2017). Populism: A political-strategic approach. In Rovira Kaltwasser, C., Taggart, P. A., Ochoa Espejo, P. & Ostiguy, P. (Eds.), *The Oxford Handbook of Populism* (pp. 48–72), Oxford University Press.

Wood, M., Matthews, F., Overman, S. & Schillemans, T. (2021) Enacting accountability under populist pressures: Theorizing the relationship between anti-elite rhetoric and public accountability. *Administration & Society*, 00953997211019387.

Yesilkagit, K. & van Thiel, S. (2012) Autonomous agencies and perceptions of stakeholder influence in parliamentary democracies. *Journal of Public Administration Research and Theory*, 22, 101–119.

PART IV

REPUTATION, PERFORMANCE
AND CONTROL

16. Reputation and independent regulatory agencies

Martin Lodge and Kai Wegrich[1]

INTRODUCTION

The rise of the regulatory state in the 1980s and 1990s coincides with the rise of the independent regulatory agency. Regulatory agencies were seen as an essential device to signal policy credibility and seemed to mark the rise in significance of non-majoritarian institutions in policy-making more generally. It was therefore not surprising that the emergence of regulatory agencies, especially in terms of their formal institutional design, attracted considerable interest. However, as the experience with regulatory agencies became more extensive, driven by comparative and longitudinal studies, a range of puzzles emerged: One, why was it that despite similar formal statutory arrangements, some agencies enjoyed political support and considerable discretion, whereas others were regarded as 'political footballs' and blame magnets? Second, formal statutory provisions also had little to say when it came to the 'entrepreneurial' behaviours of regulatory agencies, whether in terms of expanding or defending jurisdictional turf, or in terms of displaying reluctance to engage in certain activities. Such enthusiasm or reluctance to engage mattered, for example, in terms of areas of transboundary collaboration (Cabane and Lodge 2022) or the responses to a growing political scepticism regarding the problem-solving capacity of regulatory agencies (Koop and Lodge 2020).

Since the 2010s, and partly in response to these emerging puzzles, there has been a marked departure from an interest in formal (statutory) provisions as indicators for independence to a much broader interest in the 'de facto' behaviours of regulatory agencies, often building on ideas of 'reputation'. This chapter first discusses the move from formal to reputational accounts, then it points to the key questions that a reputational perspective has advanced, before concluding with some questions for future attention. It should be noted that the interest in 'reputation' in the context of the study of executive politics in general, and in the study of regulation more particularly, has boomed in recent years. This chapter cannot therefore aspire to offer a comprehensive account of this expanding literature, but point to some of the key issues, namely what a reputation-based perspective adds to our understanding of regulatory agencies, and, second, how to take the agenda further.

FROM MEASURING STATUTORY PROVISIONS TO REPUTATION

As noted, regulatory agencies have been regarded as a central feature of the institutional landscape of the regulatory state that is said to have emerged in the context of the public sector reforms since the 1980s. Since then, regulatory agencies, especially in the area of network industries, spread globally (Jordana et al. 2011; Jordana et al. 2018). In this section, we discuss the emergence of the interest in reputation in the context of regulatory agencies, explore the key aspects of a reputation-based account, and consider overlaps with the wider literature in executive politics.

Regulatory agencies represented as significant departure from the 'normal' state organization of a welfare state characterized by a degree of public ownership over key industries. The emergence of regulatory agencies was therefore both about separating ownership and control, as well as separating political direction from immediate control. A key motivation for the creation of regulatory agencies, which often entailed removing existing regulatory powers from ministerial departments, was to establish enhanced policy credibility: taking out political considerations from day-to-day decision-making, enabling the development of focused attention and dedicated expertise in regulatory oversight, and enhancing long-term expertise through careers within regulatory agencies. As noted by Majone (1997), those countries that could not offer private investors 'credible commitment' (see also Levy and Spiller 1994) would be 'punished' by private investors moving to those jurisdictions that offered greater commitment against 'administrative expropriation'. In other words, regulatory agencies were created in order to signal political commitment that investors were not to fear the widely diagnosed time inconsistency problem of electoral politics, that is, myopic political decision-making and policy reversals after changes in the priorities of government. Of course, constitutional features shape to what extent an agency can provide for credibility: a legislative context with few veto points allows for easy policy reversals and therefore also change to regulatory arrangements (Immergut 1990).

In view of this interest in the 'hardwiring' of organizational arrangements, the regulation literature paid considerable attention to questions of institutional design to explore independence *from* politics (questions of independence from industry were arguably of surprisingly little interest until the financial crisis). Formal independence was measured mostly in terms of how legal authority of an agency was defined. For example, aspects such as leadership appointment, tenure and dismissal, financing, organizational competence and jurisdictional exclusive authority were used to construct indicators on independence of regulatory agencies (see Gilardi 2002, Elgie and McMenamin 2005). Higher levels of independence have been associated with leadership terms of tenure that are decoupled from electoral cycles, parliamentary approval procedures for leadership appointment (rather than relying on ministerial appointment powers), clearly specified and restrictive circumstances to permit for premature regulator dismissal, budgetary independence from annual governmental budgets, and human resource autonomy.

Such indices have come under considerable criticism (see Hanretty and Koop 2012). Judgements as to what makes regulatory agencies 'more' independent from politics have changed over time; for example, whereas in the early days of the UK privatization policy boom, single person leadership (the 'Director General' model) was seen as 'gold standard', since the 2000s more collective forms of leadership (the 'board model') have been regarded as superior (i.e. being considered as a more effective shield against political influence, whilst also reducing 'cliff edge' problems in terms of different leader personalities encouraging radical shifts in agency approach). Similarly, rather than being concerned about the origins of budgetary resources (e.g., from the finance ministry and/or industry levies), the diversity and stability of income seems to matter more for the operational autonomy of regulatory agencies.

Changing views about 'what matters' for regulatory agencies' independence from politics might be said to reflect the sort of doctrinal 'hunting around' typical of public administration theory and practice (see Hood and Jackson 1991, Hood 1998, Lodge and Gill 2011, Lodge and

Wegrich 2012). However, the interest in formal provisions soon gave way to the realization that agencies' life and times in the world of regulation was not just a matter of statutory provisions, but other aspects, such as broader political-administrative traditions or types of rules of law (see Maggetti 2007, Yesilkagit and van Thiel 2008, Hanretty and Koop 2013). The interest in the relation to the broader political, administrative, legal and social environment coincided with the emergence of reputation as a factor in regulatory politics. This interest in particular related to the seminal work by Daniel Carpenter. Starting with the puzzle as to how some agencies achieved autonomy from political interference rather than others, despite sharing similar statutory provisions, Carpenter (2001) noted how leadership was essential. He showed that the skill of administrative leadership in building support networks in the political domain was critical for 'forging bureaucratic autonomy'. This work was further expanded in the study of how reputation could account for the evolution and conduct of the US Federal Drugs Administration (FDA) (Carpenter 2010). His historical account showed how the reputation of the FDA as a global model of a regulator in the field has developed over decades; formal provisions played a role, but the engagement with science and professions and in particular decisions in the context of some critical decisions proved crucial (e.g., the licensing of drugs, such as Thalidomide).

Since the publication of Carpenter's seminal work, the study of reputation and regulatory agencies has moved in multiple directions (see also Carpenter and Krause 2012). One main direction has been to explore how agencies seek to use strategic communication to enhance and/or protect their reputation (see Maor et al. 2013, Maor and Sulitzeanu-Kenan 2016, Maor 2020, Bach et al. 2019, Bach et al. 2021a, 2021b), especially also in the context of responding to different types of criticisms from their environment (see Gilad et al. 2015). Agencies are more likely to react to public criticism targeting core aspects of their organizational identity and reputation. Reputation has been utilized to account for regulatory decision-making (Demortain and Borraz 2021, Rimkuté 2018, 2020), for the dynamics of account-giving and -holding (Busuioc and Lodge 2016, 2017, Christensen and Lodge 2018) and consultation (Fink and Ruffing 2020), the willingness of agencies to cooperate (Busuioc 2016, Heims 2019, 2017, 2016), the adaptation of regulatory agencies' agendas in view of growing scepticism (Koop and Lodge 2020), and audience perceptions (see Dantas Cabral et al 2021). A 'reputation barometer' has also been developed (Overman et al. 2020).

None of these accounts suggest that formal structures and statutory provisions do not matter. Rather, formal structures represent an aspect of the kind of expectations placed on regulatory agencies. At the same time, the reputation-based literature suggests that statutory provisions cannot fully account for the numerous ways in which regulatory agencies select their focus and attention across different and often competing expectations (see also Busuioc and Lodge 2017) – an insight familiar to students of policy implementation and street-level bureaucracy since the late 1970s.

What, then, are the core ingredients of a reputation-based account for the study of regulatory agencies? The main strain of interest relates to the classic sociological study by Erving Goffman (1959) on the *Presentation of Self in Everyday Life*. The complex ideas from Goffman's work (Morawski 2014) have subsequently found much currency in organizational theory, social psychology and cognitive behavioural theory, often developing their own particular meanings and interpretations. We cannot give justice to Goffman's work in this brief chapter. However, some key aspects are central for our understanding of regulatory agencies. In his work, Goffman highlighted the centrality of human social interaction and the importance for individuals to avoid embarrassment (e.g., the avoidance of 'losing face'). In other words, crucial to this account is the interaction between the different parties present and the ways in which individuals seek to shape, if not control the impression that they make on audience(s).

Impression management is therefore central. In particular, individuals are seen as taking on 'front stage' roles in which they seek to offer a persuasive account of their self-imagined role, both in terms of appearances (e.g., dress) and approach (e.g., manner). Individuals are concerned about signaling their issue-related subject expertise, but also their presence. Most of the studies on regulatory agencies have arguably focused solely on the observable, namely the intentional communication, whilst neglecting (possibly inevitably) the importance of non-intended information to audiences (audiences' reception of appearances) and their evaluation of the credibility of the performance.

Goffman also includes the 'backstage' where actors prepare for their role (and are 'themselves'). For the study of regulatory agencies, the focus here would arguably be on the 'inside' of the organization (which, in turn, has many 'frontage' aspects for employees whose own 'backstage' might be found in their individual workspaces or private lives). Carpenter (2010), in turn highlighted linkages to social identity theory (see Ellemers et al. 2002), namely the importance that individuals attach to working for organizations associated with high social esteem and a particular identity (or mission).

Central to the impression management, according to Goffman, was a shared understanding of the situation that brought – intentionally or not – the individual together with the wider audience. To 'save face' in an embarrassing social situation (by, for example, the audience 'looking away') requires a broad shared understanding of that particular situation so as to avoid misunderstandings over what missteps can or cannot be politely ignored. Within this broader context, Goffman subsequently developed an extensive conceptual arsenal to account for the kind of strategic games individuals played in structured settings.

This is not the place to discuss in detail as to whether the literature on regulation and regulatory agencies could gain from a more detailed engagement with Goffman's work. However, even at a relative broad level, focusing on reputation as a central factor in regulatory politics offers a departure from those perspectives that view regulation as an institutional design exercise, based on quantitative text analysis of statutory provisions, or as a result of 'capture' by concentrated interests (see Carpenter 2010).

At the same time, it is noticeable how the influence of Carpenter's seminal study has shaped subsequent interest in reputation and regulatory agencies, in particular by focusing on the organizational and leadership level. In doing so, the recent literature does not pay much attention to a much earlier literature in the field of regulation, namely on enforcement (see Hawkins 1984). This (socio-legal) literature, emerging from the interest in the exercise of state power at the 'frontline', was particularly interested in the way reputation played a role in the ways that enforcement actions were taken. Inconsistencies in terms of levels of enforcement decisions could be accounted for by the way in which individual frontline inspectors sought to be consistent in view of their own role understandings and the kind of reputation they sought to maintain in view of their community (and their peers). The work of individual enforcement officers, whether police officer or safety inspector, can therefore be potentially explained through a Goffman-informed reputation lens: enforcement officials seek to maintain a reputation in view of different audiences ('to the community', 'to their peers') and therefore adapt their action in light of anticipated and perceived signals from these different constituencies.

They also develop moral norms to justify particular enforcement styles (see also in context of the welfare state, Zacka 2017).

Similarly, Hawkins noted how issuing a complaint against a particular party represented an opportunity for an agency 'for public relations work, an opportunity [...] to demonstrate its [the agency's] worth' (1984, p.97). While rarely explored in the literature on regulatory agencies and arguably relating more directly to the work on implementation and street-level bureaucracy (Wegrich 2015), the frontline experience points to the importance of reflecting further on the way in which different reputational considerations across all levels of an organization may or may not be in competition with each other.

Adding to this interest in the (acknowledged or non-acknowledged) connections to the wider literature, reputation-based accounts clearly overlap with accounts that emphasize bureaucratic politics. However, in the latter case, the importance is paid to the internal governmental processes to account for policy decisions, whereas a reputation-based account, partly because of its interest in front- and backstage activities, emphasizes the importance of the interaction with various audiences. In doing so, the focus is on a wider set of actors ('the network of audiences').

At the same time, an emphasis on how organizations seek to shape their jurisdictional boundaries to maximize their autonomy is related to the argument presented in James Q. Wilson's *Bureaucracy* (1989). For Wilson, organizations strive for autonomy to ensure their survival in light of dependence on resources provided in the political domain. They do so by carefully shielding their core mission, by fighting off any organization that seeks to compete in the areas of core interest, by being reluctant in expanding into jurisdictional areas where there is overlap, and by avoiding divided constituencies and unpopular issues outright. Wilson, too, highlights the challenges that diverse types of agencies encounter so as to be able to present a consistent 'face' to their audiences. Linking a reputational approach to such an (executive politics-related) perspective highlights further that autonomy-seeking through reputation management might be regarded as a double-edged sword: on the one hand, it promises autonomy from the meddling instincts of politics; on the other hand, it might enable agencies, by also exploiting supportive and powerful aspects of their network of audiences, from criticism and pressure for change.

A second key overlapping interest is the literature on *blame*. Goffman highlighted the importance of understanding the role-playing as part of teams and offered insights into different types of (what he called) 'games'. This argument overlaps with the literature emphasizing the importance of blame and lightning rods (Hood 2011, Weaver 1986). Pre-emptive impression management is clearly at the heart of these blame-related accounts and the central argument here is that blame magnets (regulatory agencies), presentational strategies and policy choices are designed so as to ensure that political leaders can claim reputational credit for things going well whilst avoiding being held responsible ('blamed') for things perceived to have gone wrong (e.g., fare increases, operational failures by regulated entities). A reputational perspective also highlights why in certain cases we may expect 'blame boomerangs', namely where individuals, concerned with their own reputation, re-shuffle the blame to politicians or other agencies (cf. Bach and Wegrich 2019a). Equally, it might be said that once individual agency leaders see their own reputation wrecked, they will decide not to take the bullet on their own, but to 'bring down' others with them. Regulatory agency leaders may therefore not fall on their proverbial sword following ministerial blaming but may return 'the favour' by pointing to ministerial meddling, government incompetence or lack of authority to alter policy trajectories.

Central for questions of blame is one key aspect of Goffman's work, namely the importance of a shared definition of the situation. Blame games can easily emerge when the underlying understandings that supported a shared definition of a situation are shifting. Such a shift may occur in the context of the replacement of ministers that assume different relationships with regulatory agencies (see Hood and Lodge 2006: Chapter 7). It can also reflect long-term change, such as the kind diagnosed by Michael Moran (2003) in terms of how informal 'club government' in the British elite had to give way to more codified relationships given the more heterogeneous population governing Britain. In the context of regulatory agencies, the argument is that a setting in which there is no cohesive elite or where regulatory agencies become part of increasing party polarization, blame games are more likely to occur.

In conclusion, this section has sought to explore why reputation has become a prominent concern in the study of regulatory agencies. It is important to explore some of the linkages between Goffman's seminal work and its potential application to regulatory agencies' relationships with their network of audiences. In doing so, this section has also noted some of the overlaps with complementary and long-standing literatures. The following section now turns to some of the critical questions for the study of regulatory agencies.

REPUTATION AND REGULATORY AGENCIES

In this section, we turn to those promising questions where a reputation-based study contributes to our understanding of regulatory agencies. As noted already, this is not to say that other accounts, focusing on the brute force of interest group politics or politics do not matter. This section does not aspire to provide for a literature review, but to illustrate some of the key themes that directly emerge from the key concerns as put forward by Goffman and subsequently developed by Carpenter.

First, a reputation-based account is central for developing our understanding of regulatory capacity (Lodge 2014, Lodge and Wegrich 2014). As noted by Carpenter (2010), agencies can be said to seek a reputation for competence in view of their network of audiences. He distinguishes between performative (outputs/outcomes), moral (wider contribution to some broadly shared notion of the public good), technical (subject expertise) and procedural dimensions of reputations for competence. An organizational 'ideal point' in terms of reputation would be to be well-regarded on all of these four competencies. However, regulatory agencies (and other government agencies for that matter) are unlikely to enjoy such a position for numerous reasons (Busuioc and Lodge 2017). First, the direct impact of regulatory interventions can rarely be measured (beyond highlighting some broad trends, such as reduced fatalities on building sites, fewer cases of food-borne diseases, reduced broadband prices or the level of competition on retail markets). Second, an emphasis on the careful following of procedures is unlikely to gain much traction with audiences if the result of such decision-making is seen as contradicting 'common sense' or 'moral purpose' (e.g., regulators involved in the rationing of publicly available medicine are likely to face strong challenges when their (utilitarian) cost calculations has implications for individual tragic cases). And, third, decisions as to what skills and types of expertise should be central to regulatory decision-making also involves potential conflict with wider audiences. For example, this might involve trade-offs between an emphasis on 'regulatory' versus 'scientific' expertise within regulatory agencies. More generally, this relates to wider conflicts as to the appropriate 'relational distance' between regulators and their regulated professions (see Lodge and Wegrich 2012). Fourth, conflict over regulatory agendas is likely also in view of the dynamics of the regulatory state, especially when it comes to attempts by central government 'better regulation units' to shape the decision-making of regulatory agencies through devices such as regulatory impact assessments, compliance cost assessments or the prescription of risk-based enforcement models (Black and Baldwin 2010; Baldwin 2010; Lodge and Wegrich 2012, pp.192–220).

What follows from these accounts is that regulatory capacity is linked to the ability to navigate tensions and trade-offs between demands from diverse stakeholders (or audiences). At the same time, organizational reputation and the place of individuals within such organizations is dependent on organizations being able to develop a sense of 'core mission'. Regulatory agencies, just like other public organizations, are unlikely to be able to autonomously follow the pursuit of their 'niche' (as defined by Wilson): political careers depend on the praise and criticism of regulatory agencies (e.g., the (entirely hypothetical) example of politicians seeking to please certain media barons by attacking communications regulators),[2] and there is formal and informal overlap between regulatory jurisdictions (see Koop and Lodge 2014). In other words, this world of addressing the fall-out of spats over regulatory jurisdiction as well as of managing complex networks and overlapping jurisdictions is exactly not the kind of world identified by Wilson as 'ideal' for securing organizational survival, namely the carrying out of popular tasks only without attracting political criticism and/or organizational rivalry. In sum, the challenge for regulatory agencies in developing their 'impression management' to signal their competence is to carefully select strategies that stress particular aspects of their competence rather than others so as to establish their particular, indispensable (in view of their audiences) role.

Second, reputation matters when it comes to regulatory decision-making over time. One argument is that policy reversals are the equivalent of 'losing face'. Agencies might be reluctant to correct decisions in light of criticism and emerging evidence because any 'U-turn' would imply admission of failure or wrongdoing (e.g., losing face). This suggests that role perceptions will also shape the selection of particular problem definitions and solutions, such as the need to appear 'competent' in view of certain professional perspectives. The result of such reputational considerations is that regulatory agencies might develop a preference for taking a 'principled approach' (Ansell and Boin 2019, Boin and Lodge 2021). Such an approach is characterized by the existence of a preferred lens for the analysis of problems and a reluctance to engage in alternative viewpoints or policy experimentation. One example might be the way in which central banks initially responded to the banking crises of the late 2000s, namely by emphasizing the 'moral hazard' problem. In other words, a reputation-based account highlights why organizations might be 'sticky' in their approach because their key reference points in the wider audience share that problem definition. Future research is likely to identify further the reputation-based mechanisms that lead to such 'stubbornness' with a particular attention on the way in which an agency's overall reputation might decline in the medium-to-long term as a consequence of such short-term reputation-seeking behaviour, especially as desired outcomes are not forthcoming.

The third key reputation-based contribution to the study of regulatory agencies is the emphasis on front- and backstage activities (see Gilad 2012). We already noted some concerns with the way in which front- and backstage activities need to be understood, as individuals within organizations may regard organizational decision-making as frontstage appearances. The problem for regulatory agencies therefore is how to combine potential contestation within the organization (backstage) with a unified 'face' at the front of the stage, and to what extent such frontstage appearances might lead to motivating or demotivating signals to staff within the regulatory agencies. At the same time, the notion of front- and backstage also points to a central challenge for regulatory oversight, namely how to move beyond an evaluation of frontstage appearances by regulated organizations and to move towards an understanding of the 'backstage' of regulated organizations. After all, it is in the backstage where the analysis of 'blind spots' is conducted, (Bach and Wegrich 2019b) where emerging risks become apparent and where 'normalisation of deviance' (Vaughan 1996) is prominent. How regulatory agencies develop relationships with their regulated organizations will therefore greatly depend on the way in which they and their key audiences characterize the target population of regulatory attention, leading to, for example, differences in enforcement practices ranging from high trust advisory-egalitarian approaches to low trust, surprised-based contrived randomness (Hood 1998, Lodge and Wegrich 2012).

Fourth, and related, the importance of the interaction with the network of audiences is key to a reputational approach. How, therefore, agencies seek to appeal to particular audiences, how they respond to types of criticisms and from whom, as well as how audiences perceive agency competence is central to a reputation-based research agenda. However, it also raises questions as to how regulatory agencies view their audiences, especially in terms of the extent to which they think they need to be responsive to them. In UK economic regulation, for example, it has been argued that regulatory agencies only belatedly released the extent of growing political dissatisfaction with the performance of certain sectors (e.g., rising energy prices) and equally that populist outpourings (such as the Brexit referendum) presented a rude awakening as to 'who mattered' in terms of audiences and how to communicate to or with these ('left behind') audiences. There is, at the same time, limited understanding as to 'who' identifies such growing discrepancy between internal beliefs and external perception and whether such openness to be responsive is a signal that such agencies enjoy a high or low degree of reputation or whether other factors might be more important for explaining as to why some agencies are more responsive to external criticism than others.

Finally, reputation-based accounts also highlight the importance of legitimacy and the expression of regulatory power. Control, in the context of regulation, but also more generally, is ultimately about self-regulating maintenance of and compliance with rules (e.g., Weber's acceptance of the authority of the ruler by the ruled). This requires that different parties do not regard regulatory decision-making to be deck-stacked or biased towards certain particular interests. A reputation for even-handedness is therefore central for regulatory agencies, but to what extent an agency can shape such a perception on its own is a different question.

THE WAY AHEAD

Reputation-based approaches are, at the time of writing, en vogue. This chapter highlights that much of this sustained interest builds on existing research traditions and supports our understanding of dynamics in the regulatory state. The previous section has also sought to point to some of the areas where a reputation-based approach adds distinct value to the study of regulatory dynamics. We have only provided for a limited perspective on the literature. In the following section, we point to a few avenues that deserve further attention.

One central theme is to consider the importance of coordination and how a concerns with the reputation of a single agency might accentuate system fragmentation. As noted, Goffman highlighted the importance of 'teams'. The literature on regulatory agencies has largely focused on single agencies, whether in terms of their responses to criticisms, the way they are being perceived by core audiences, or the way they seek to 'present themselves'. However, in a world of 'co-production' across levels of government and between different agencies, more attention needs to be paid to situations where reputational damage to one regulatory agency can be 'caused' by the (non)-actions of other agencies. Such an interest particularly relates to so-called transboundary crises. For example, during the financial crisis, the activities of national regulatory agencies were impacted not just by the action of 'transboundary-trading' financial institutions, but also by the (non-coordinated) actions of other national regulatory authorities (and governments). However, reputations are not just dependent on the other actions of other regulatory institutions in the absence of standard operating procedures. Any attempt at creating transboundary regulatory regimes is open to blind spots and Achilles' Heels, and the way in which regulatory agencies engage with such transboundary regimes greatly depends on whether these regimes are seen as reputation enhancing in making their own work more effective.

A second central theme is the way in which reputations are made and lost. Carpenter's initial study of the FDA might be said to look at one unique setting. It might be worth considering further the context in which regulatory agencies can build their reputation. Work on the creation of regulatory agencies in the Commonwealth Caribbean (see Lodge and Stirton 2006) highlighted that in the case of Jamaica, it was the presence of particular organizational leaders, backed by a supportive political leadership, that was essential in building a high reputation regulator, the Office of Utilities Regulation. In other low capacity settings, agencies resort to external certification through international organizations. For example, Mexican regulatory agencies have sought reputation- and capacity-building through close engagement with the OECD. Similarly, the executive leadership of Brazil during the presidency of Luiz Inácio Lula da Silva ('Lula') (2003–2011) worked with the OECD on a 'regulatory review' so as to signal its commitment to 'high quality regulation' to an international audience, but also to gain external support for a programme facing considerable domestic opposition (OECD 2008). Mexico also points to a further set of questions, namely whether having a 'high reputation' in national and international circles matters when an incoming political leadership of a country regards these regulatory agencies as part of the problem rather than the solution. In other words, it raises the question as to whether reputation in front of a *network* of audiences matters, when, possibly, it is ultimately only national political leadership that *really* matters.

Moe generally, a concern with the ways in which regulatory agencies gain and lose their reputation for competence relates to wider debates about 'trust'. One might argue that having a reputation for competence in the public view should also strengthen the public acceptance of the regulatory regime as such. Trusting the regulatory decision might therefore be a central issue when it comes to questions of the public acceptance of vaccines and such like. However, to what extent a public reputation for competence matters when the political climate turns hostile is a separate matter. Furthermore, public disquiet over certain dynamics, such as rising prices for water and energy, might have very little to do with wider perceptions of regulatory competence. Such questions also point to the growing importance of the 'internal life' of regulatory organizations: changing external demands might violate strong professional norms within a regulatory agency (for example, a competition authority's staff might find it very problematic to change its framework of analysis as to what constitutes an abuse of market dominance).

In turn, such questions point to the importance of different regulatory strategies to gain and maintain reputation (as noted above). The extent to which agency reputations are made and 'broken' by routine public communication activities (such as annual reports) is questionable. We need to therefore know more about how different audiences receive and process information that enables them to make a judgement as to an agency's reputation. An ability (and permissive environment) to link one's institution to a socially valued dynamic is likely to reinforce an agency's standing (and autonomy) whereas short-term analysis of press releases, annual reports or court rulings might best indicate temporary and gradual changes to an agency's reputation. At the same time, certain catastrophic events (in terms of suggesting that the agency's conduct has directly contributed to a socially perceived disaster) are likely to lead to calls for resignation, governance changes, organizational relabelling or jurisdictional redrawing. Such an agenda also points to the study of the 'dark side' of reputation-seeking agency behaviour. After all, agencies are seen as seeking to gain a reputation for competence from some audiences rather than others, and this might therefore lead to exclusion of certain populations and the reluctance to engage with particular issues, sources of information, or fields of knowledge. A reputation-related account therefore, as noted, also points to important implications of a 'blame avoidance' agenda. First of all, how far should an agency seek to enhance its reputation by occupying a certain issue in the absence of explicit political encouragement? Second, if such political endorsement is not forthcoming, as decisions are likely to create redistributive losers and winners, to what extent will agencies be forced to take on such decisions, thereby becoming blame-magnets? Or will regulatory agencies carefully manage their reputations so as to minimize criticism. In other words, a world in which the 'loss of face' becomes central to organizational life is also a world that is least likely to be taking any action where this might incur criticism: reputation management is therefore at best reactive to external events and largely about generating a 'blame teflon' (Hood 2011). In short, reputation management is a central impediment to active problem-solving capacity across states and systems of government.

Related, a third central theme is the understanding of networks of audiences. The public sector reform literature has highlighted the importance of 'generational change' within bureaucratic organizations (see Pusey 2018) that happens to coincide with wider political change. Recruiting particular kinds 'econocrats' to regulatory agencies with particular ways of 'seeing the world' (or, in reverse, broadening the recruitment pool) matters as this will also influence the selection of audiences they seek to particularly 'please'. Similarly, change can occur among audiences, too, for example, in the context of growing partisan polarization. How agencies respond to such qualitative changes within their networks of audiences is therefore central to our understanding of how agencies proactively seek to shape their reputation for competence.

A fourth central theme is what kind of plurality of methods needs to be explored in order to address the many important questions that arise from a reputation-based perspective, as noted above. Studying public statements in one way or another offers important insights but does not address the much wider understanding of communication present in Goffman's work. In light of the booming literature on regulatory agencies and reputation, the lack of further studies exploring in comparative perspective the development of reputational strengths and weaknesses over time therefore remains ripe for further exploration, especially in terms of taking the 'backstage' more seriously.

CONCLUSION

This chapter has not aspired to provide for a comprehensive account of the booming literature on reputation and regulatory agencies. This chapter has instead sought to go 'back to basics' and highlighted some of the key issues on which the current interest is based. It then explored some of the key questions of interest for the study of regulatory agencies and pointed to some avenues for future research. The reputation-based literature on regulatory agencies is arguably moving from 'youthful discovery' to 'middle-aged refinement' in that methodological fine-tuning and additional cases build on earlier studies and provide for a basis of incremental learning. To advance the study of regulatory agencies further, it is important to reflect on the key issues arising from Goffman's work. The challenge is therefore not necessarily only methodological sophistication, but careful reflection on core intellectual interests. Furthermore, the extent to which reputation really matters in contrast to other factors (such as short-term tactical considerations or interest group constellations) needs to be carefully considered. For some agencies, reputation might be at the heart of all concern, for other agencies, reputational concerns might be less relevant (or present highly complex trade-offs).

This is not to say that the interest in reputation for understanding the organization of (and individual behaviours in) regulatory agencies is not here to stay. As noted, a reputation-based approach points to many long-standing interests and questions in the study of organizations, and it is therefore likely that exploring the reputational implications in regulatory dynamics will remain a key part of future regulatory research. At the same time, the focus needs to move beyond the focus on single agencies. In a world of economic, administrative and political interdependence, questions as to how reputations are made, sustained and lost, are unlikely to remain within national and sectoral silos.

NOTES

1.   Martin Lodge would like to acknowledge the contribution of the ESRC-funded seminar series 'Regulation in Crisis?' for the development of this chapter, as well as collaboration with Mauricio Dussauge Laguna (CIDE) on his British Academy-funded Newton Fellowship to support joint working between LSE's Centre for Analysis of Risk and Regulation and CIDE ('Regulatory Capitalism and Development in Latin America').
2.   https://www.theguardian.com/media/2009/jul/06/ofcom-david-cameron (last accessed 3 May 2021).

REFERENCES

Ansell, C., & Boin, A. (2019). Taming deep uncertainty: The potential of pragmatist principles for understanding and improving strategic crisis management. *Administration & Society, 51*(7), 1079–1112.
Bach, T., & Wegrich, K. (2019a). The politics of blame avoidance in complex delegation structures: The public transport crisis in Berlin. *European Political Science Review, 11*(4), 415–431.

Bach, T., & Wegrich, K. (eds) (2019b). *The Blind Spots of Public Bureaucracy and the Politics of Non-coordination*. London: Palgrave Macmillan.

Bach, T., Boon, J., Boye, S., Salomonsen, H.H., Verhoest, K., & Wegrich, K. (2019) 'In the line of fire: European financial regulators before, during, and after the crisis', *Der Moderne Staat*, *12*(1), 5–29.

Bach, T., Jugl, M., Köhler, D., & Wegrich, K. (2021a). Reputational threats and democratic responsiveness of regulatory agencies. In Eriksen, E.O. (ed.), *The Accountability of Expertise: Making the Un-elected Safe for Democracy*. London & New York: Routledge, pp. 81–98.

Bach, T., Jugl, M., Köhler, D., & Wegrich, K. (2021b). Regulatory agencies, reputational threats, and communicative responses. *Regulation & Governance*. https://doi.org/10.1111/rego.12421

Baldwin, R. (2010). Better regulation: The search and the struggle. In Baldwin, R., Cave, M, & Lodge, M. (eds), *The Oxford Handbook of Regulation*. Oxford: Oxford University Press, pp.259–278.

Black, J., & Baldwin, R. (2010). Really responsive risk-based regulation. *Law & Policy*, *32*(2), 181–213.

Boin, A., & Lodge, M. (2021). Responding to the COVID-19 crisis: A principled or pragmatist approach. *Journal of European Public Policy, 28*(8), 1131–1152.

Busuioc, E. M. (2016). Friend or foe? Inter-agency cooperation, organizational reputation, and turf. *Public Administration*, *94*(1), 40–56.

Busuioc, E. M., & Lodge, M. (2016). The reputational basis of public accountability. *Governance*, *29*(2), 247–263.

Busuioc, M., & Lodge, M. (2017). Reputation and accountability relationships: Managing accountability expectations through reputation. *Public Administration Review*, *77*(1), 91–100.

Cabane, L., & Lodge, M. (2022). Banking regulation in and for crisis. In Thompson, W. (ed.), *Oxford Research Encyclopedia of Politics*. Oxford: Oxford University Press.

Carpenter, D. (2001). *The Forging of Bureaucratic Autonomy: Reputations, Networks, and Policy Innovation in Executive Agencies, 1862–1928*. Princeton, NJ: Princeton University Press.

Carpenter, D. (2010). *Reputation and Power: Organizational Image and Pharmaceutical Regulation at the FDA*. Princeton, NJ: Princeton University Press.

Carpenter, D. P., & Krause, G. A. (2012). Reputation and public administration. *Public Administration Review*, *72*(1), 26–32.

Christensen, T., & Lodge, M. (2018). Reputation management in societal security: A comparative study. *The American Review of Public Administration*, *48*(2), 119–132.

Dantas Cabral, A., Peci, A., & Van Ryzin, G. G. (2021). Representation, reputation and expectations towards bureaucracy: Experimental findings from a favela in Brazil. *Public Management Review*. https://doi.org/10.1080/14719037.2021.1906934

Demortain, D., & Borraz, O. (2021). Managing technical reputation: Regulatory agencies and evidential work in risk assessment. *Public Administration*. https://doi.org/10.1111/padm.12734

Elgie, R., & McMenamin, I. (2005). Credible commitment, political uncertainty or policy complexity? Explaining variations in the independence of non-majoritarian institutions in France. *British Journal of Political Science*, *35*(3), 531–548.

Ellemers, N., Spears, R., & Doosje, B. (2002). Self and social identity. *Annual Review of Psychology*, *53*(1), 161–186.

Fink, S., & Ruffing, E. (2020). Stakeholder consultations as reputation-building: A comparison of ACER and the German Federal Network Agency. *Journal of European Public Policy*, *27*(11), 1657–1676.

Gilad, S (2012). Attention and reputation: Linking regulators' internal and external worlds. In Lodge, M. & Wegrich, K. (eds), *Executive Politics in Times of Crisis*. London: Palgrave Macmillan, pp.157–175.

Gilad, S., Maor, M. & Bloom, P.B.N. (2015). Organisational reputation, the content of public allegations, and regulatory communication. *Journal of Public Administration Research and Theory*, 25(2), 451–478.

Gilardi, F. (2002). Policy credibility and delegation to independent regulatory agencies: A comparative empirical analysis. *Journal of European Public Policy*, *9*(6), 873–893.

Goffman, E. (1959). *The Presentation of Self in Every-day Life*. Garden City, NY: Doubleday-Anchor.

Hanretty, C., & Koop, C. (2012). Measuring the formal independence of regulatory agencies. *Journal of European Public Policy*, *19*(2), 198–216.

Hanretty, C., & Koop, C. (2013). Shall the law set them free? The formal and actual independence of regulatory agencies. *Regulation & Governance*, *7*(2), 195–214.

Hawkins, K. (1984). *Environment and Enforcement: Regulation and the Social Definition of Pollution.* Oxford: Oxford University Press.

Heims, E. (2019). Why cooperation between agencies is (sometimes) possible: Turf protection as enabler of regulatory cooperation in the European Union. In Bach, T. & Wegrich, K. (eds), *The Blind Spots of Public Bureaucracy and the Politics of Non-Coordination.* Cham: Palgrave Macmillan, pp.113–131.

Heims, E. M. (2016). Explaining coordination between national regulators in EU agencies: The role of formal and informal social organization. *Public Administration, 94*(4), 881–896.

Heims, E. M. (2017). Regulatory co-ordination in the EU: A cross-sector comparison. *Journal of European Public Policy, 24*(8), 1116–1134.

Hood, C. (1998). *The Art of the State: Culture, Rhetoric, and Public Management.* Oxford: Oxford University Press.

Hood, C. (2011). *The Blame Game: Spin, Bureaucracy, and Self-preservation in Government.* Princeton, NJ: Princeton University Press.

Hood, C., & Jackson, M. (1991). *Administrative Argument.* Aldershot, UK: Dartmouth.

Hood, C., & Lodge, M. (2006). *The Politics of Public Service Bargains.* Oxford: Oxford University Press.

Immergut, E. M. (1990). Institutions, veto points, and policy results: A comparative analysis of health care. *Journal of Public Policy, 10*(4), 391–416.

Jordana, J., Fernández-i-Marín, X., & Bianculli, A. C. (2018). Agency proliferation and the globalization of the regulatory state: Introducing a data set on the institutional features of regulatory agencies. *Regulation & Governance, 12*(4), 524–540.

Jordana, J., Levi-Faur, D., & i Marín, X. F. (2011). The global diffusion of regulatory agencies: Channels of transfer and stages of diffusion. *Comparative Political Studies, 44*(10), 1343–1369.

Koop, C., & Lodge, M. (2014). Exploring the co-ordination of economic regulation. *Journal of European Public Policy, 21*(9), 1311–1329.

Koop, C., & Lodge, M. (2020). British economic regulators in an age of politicisation: From the responsible to the responsive regulatory state?. *Journal of European Public Policy, 27*(11), 1612–1635.

Levy, B., & Spiller, P. T. (1994). The institutional foundations of regulatory commitment: A comparative analysis of telecommunications regulation. *The Journal of Law, Economics, and Organization, 10*(2), 201–246.

Lodge, M. (2014). Regulatory capacity. In Lodge, M. & Wegrich, K. (eds), *The Problem-Solving Capacity of the Modern State: Governance Challenges and Administrative Capacities.* Oxford: Oxford University Press, pp.63–85.

Lodge, M., & Stirton, L. (2006). Withering in the heat? In search of the regulatory state in the Commonwealth Caribbean. *Governance, 19*(3): 465–495.

Lodge, M., & Gill, D. (2011). Toward a new era of administrative reform? The myth of post-NPM in New Zealand. *Governance, 24*(1), 141–166.

Lodge, M. & Wegrich, K. (2012). *Managing Regulation.* Basingstoke: Palgrave Macmillan.

Lodge, M., & Wegrich, K. (2014). Administrative capacities. In Hertie School of Governance (ed.), *Governance Report 2014.* Oxford: Oxford University Press, pp.27–48.

Maggetti, M. (2007). De facto independence after delegation: A fuzzy-set analysis. *Regulation & Governance, 1*(4), 271–294.

Majone, G. (1997). From the positive to the regulatory state: Causes and consequences of changes in the mode of governance. *Journal of Public Policy, 17*(2), 139–167.

Maor, M. (2020). Strategic communication by regulatory agencies as a form of reputation management: A strategic agenda. *Public Administration, 98*(4), 1044–1055.

Maor, M., & Sulitzeanu-Kenan, R. (2016). 'Responsive change: Agency output response to reputational threats. *Journal of Public Administration Research and Theory, 26*(1), 31–44.

Maor, M., Gilad, S. & Bloom, P.B.N. (2013). Organisational reputation, regulatory talk, and strategic silence. *Journal of Public Administration Research and Theory, 23*(3), 581–608.

Moran, M. (2003). *The British Regulatory State: High Modernism and Hyper-innovation.* Oxford: Oxford University Press.

Morawski, J. (2014). Livelihoods of theory: The case of Goffman's early theory of the self. *Theory & Psychology, 24*(3), 281–304.

OECD. (2008). OECD Reviews of Regulatory Reform – Brazil: Strengthening Governance for Growth. Paris: OECD. https://www.oecd.org/gov/regulatory-policy/oecdreviewsofregulatoryreform -brazilstrengtheninggovernanceforgrowth.htm (last accessed 4 May 2021).

Overman, S., Busuioc, M., & Wood, M. (2020). A multidimensional reputation barometer for public agencies: A validated instrument. *Public Administration Review*, *80*(3), 415–425.

Pusey, M. (2018) 'Economic rationalism in Canberra 25 years on?. *Journal of Sociology*, 54(1): 12–17.

Rimkutė, D. (2018). Organizational reputation and risk regulation: The effect of reputational threats on agency scientific outputs. *Public Administration*, *96*(1), 70–83.

Rimkutė, D. (2020). Building organizational reputation in the European regulatory state: An analysis of EU agencies' communications. *Governance*, *33*(2), 385–406.

Vaughan, D. (1996). *The Challenger Launch Decision: Risky Technology, Culture, and Deviance at NASA*. Chicago: University of Chicago Press.

Weaver, R. K. (1986). The politics of blame avoidance. *Journal of Public Policy*, *6*(4), 371–398.

Wegrich, K. (2015) Jeffrey L. Pressman and Aaron Wildavsky, 'Implementation'. In Balla, S., Lodge, M. & Page, E. (eds), *Oxford Handbook of Classics in Public Policy and Public Administration*. Oxford: Oxford University Press, pp.342–358.

Wilson, J. Q. (1989). *Bureaucracy: What Government Agencies Do and Why They Do It*. New York: Basic Books.

Yesilkagit, K., & Van Thiel, S. (2008). Political influence and bureaucratic autonomy. *Public Organization Review*, *8*(2), 137–153.

Zacka, B. (2017). *When the State meets the Street*. Cambridge, MA: Harvard University Press.

17. Accountability and regulatory authorities

Sjors Overman, Thomas Schillemans and Machiel van der Heijden

INTRODUCTION

In most (Western) countries, regulatory authorities have been set up at arm's length of central governments. The justifications, logics, and rationales behind this trend have been extensively discussed elsewhere in this handbook (Parts I and II; see also, Gilardi 2008; Majone 2001; Overman 2016). This chapter looks at the accountability concerns arising from this empirical trend of '*agencification*' and the intense scholarly and political debate that has developed around the ensuing accountability regimes of independent regulatory authorities (Busuioc & Lodge 2016; Bianculli et al. 2014; Koop 2011; Schillemans & Busuioc 2015; Thatcher 2011).

A crucial starting point for this debate is the consideration that when looking at the role and functioning of regulatory authorities, straightforward conceptualizations of accountability quickly become problematic (Maggetti 2010; Nesti 2018). Given their role as *independent* regulators, particular tensions emerge for regulatory agencies in comparison to other organizations in the public sector (e.g. executive agencies). At face value, being independent or autonomous would imply the absence of accountability to others. However, as regulatory authorities are constitutive of democratic governance, *some* form of democratic accountability is clearly needed. In addition, accountability is also a potential source of legitimacy and for this reason a proficient system of accountability is required for independent regulatory authorities (Black 2008; Fernández-i-Marín et al. 2015). The increasing internationalization of their activities have added to these concerns (see Black 2008; Nesti 2018).

In the *Foundations* part of this chapter, we first reflect on the different conceptual distinctions related to accountability and relate those to independent regulatory authorities. We then look at how scholars have made sense of two crucial developments across countries and sectors: *agencification* and internationalization. We analyze how these trends have led to a re-conceptualization of accountability for regulatory authorities, after which we discuss some according lines of empirical research that have emerged. In the *Foresight* part, we first introduce new insights in the accountability of regulatory authorities and compare those to autonomous executive agencies, based on comparative international research. We then identify four lines of future research for the study of regulatory authorities and accountability that scholars could address as the literature continues to develop.

FOUNDATIONS

In broad terms, accountability refers to "the obligation for an individual or an organization to [regularly] account for his/her conduct towards another person or organization" (Bovens 2007, p. 450). Accountability is, as many other academic concepts, not settled and tamed but is subjected to ongoing theoretical and conceptual debates. Still, there are several widely used conceptualizations of accountability in the literature which revolve around a common core or a minimal conceptual consensus. This entails that accountability (1) is a *relational* concept linking those who owe an account to those to whom it is owed; (2) is a *retrospective* activity in which judgment is passed on decisions or behaviours in the past; and (3) involves the opportunity of *sanctions and rewards*. On this minimal conceptual basis, a long list of descriptive typologies have been developed that help scholars to make sense of the divergent practices and mechanisms of accountability in the public sector. These typologies have also been applied to better understand the role and functioning of regulatory authorities, for which the main foundational challenges are discussed next. We start with some of the conceptual challenges related to accountability for regulators and continue with foundational challenges, related to overarching developments in society and the role of regulators.

CONCEPTUAL CHALLENGES: WHAT'S IN A NAME?

A large part of the academic literature on accountability is conceptual, focusing on the meaning of the term rather than its empirical manifestations (see Brandsma & Schillemans 2012). Although existing empirical studies typically point to *gaps* or *deficits* in accountability systems for regulatory agencies (cf. Overman et al. 2015), the way in which to actually measure these accountability deficits is often left implicit. An important line of research is thus to develop a more systematic body of evidence that traces or maps out accountability processes empirically. First stabs at this effort have been made (see Brandsma & Schillemans 2012; Han & Perry 2019; Overman et al. 2021), but require further elaboration. This also entails a thorough conceptual understanding of the different ways in which accountability is used, as the concept refers to a family of phenomena with a common core rather than one specific phenomenon. To this end we shortly present four important further distinctions.

Accountability as an End or as a Means to an End

A major source of misunderstanding in the academic literature on accountability is about the status of the main concept: is it a descriptive variable and a means to some end or is it a normative concept with which some state of affairs is evaluated and, thus, an end in itself (Bovens 2010)?

When studied as a means to an end, accountability is typically used as an independent variable in research and shifts the analytical focus to the specific mechanisms and norms with which regulatory agencies can be held accountable. These mechanisms and norms entail, amongst other things, legal obligations, annual reports, parliamentary hearings and judicial review. In some of the literature on the accountability of regulatory authorities, the existence or effectiveness of such mechanisms is also discussed (cf. De Haan & Eiffinger 2000; Biela & Papadopoulos 2014).

In other studies, 'accountability' features as an end in itself. It is then the dependent variable and normative benchmark which is invoked to assess some state of affairs. As a normative concept, accountability draws on democratic theory (Biela & Papadopoulos 2014) or can be comparable in meaning to the responsiveness or a sense of responsibility of the focal actor. Specifically with regard to regulatory authorities, this normative perspective on accountability would imply providing sufficient insight into and transparency of decisions or explicitly taking substantive norms of democracy into account (Black 2008; Buess 2015).

In theory, both usages of accountability can be related. Accountability mechanisms should lead to accountable outcomes; thus linking both usages of the concept. In practice, however, this is not necessarily the case. One can imagine that existing accountability mechanisms do not produce the desired outcomes or, conversely, that accountable outcomes are achieved without formal accountability. The desired or accountable outcomes can for instance also result from internalized professional norms and socialization, particularly for complex governance settings (see Van Kersbergen & Van Waarden 2004).

Formal, Factual or Felt Accountability

Whether or not we can positively speak of accountability to exist will depend on one's (implicit) disciplinary perspective. From a legal perspective, the existence of formal mechanisms of accountability would suffice to draw the conclusion that there 'is' accountability (i.e., *de jure* accountability). The scholar might point at reporting requirements of a regulatory authority, Parliament's right to scrutinize its conduct, and the existence of some formal accountability documents (Fernández-i-Marín et al. 2015).

From an empirical or social science perspective on accountability, however, these formal rights and documents might not be enough to warrant such a conclusion. The social scientist would look at the factual patterns of interaction between the regulatory authority and its accountability forum in order to assess whether this indeed entails provision of information, scrutiny of conduct and the possibility of sanctions or rewards (i.e., *de facto* accountability). Accountability practices need not be formalized, but can also be institutionalized informally (Romzek et al. 2012). Core questions become whether we actually observe accountability processes and what they mean to regulators (Thomann & Sager 2017). The sociologically informed scholar could then proceed to conclude that the formal accountability requirements are dead letters that in practice do not actually lead to factual accountability (Schillemans & Busuioc 2015). Or perhaps the formal (legal) and informal dimensions are uncoupled (Hanretty & Koop 2013) and accountability may rely mostly on informal interactions rather than formal ones (Romzek et al. 2012).

The psychologically informed scholar would focus on the individual perceptions of the manager or regulatory professional in the agency. Do they hold a belief that they will be held accountable to some salient forum (Hall et al. 2017), and do they hold the belief that this forum is able to pass a meaningful and powerful judgment with actual consequences? Whether a forum is perceived as 'able', is constituted by the perception of its legitimacy, and of its expertise (Overman et al. 2021).

Ideally, formal accountability requirements and mechanisms should lead to factual accountability processes that are felt as meaningful and authoritative by the important decision-makers in regulatory authorities. In practice, however, there can be numerous disjunctions between formal, factual and felt accountability (Schillemans et al. 2021).

Regime, Dyadic or Operational Accountability

A third important distinction regards the level of analysis: whose accountability to whom is analysed? Many studies of the accountability of regulatory authorities take *the organization* as point of departure and study the dyadic accountability relations of regulatory authorities towards, for instance, central government or Parliament (Hanretty & Koop 2013). This hierarchical form of accountability is the most common and logical dyadic accountability relation to study, although it is also tricky given the autonomous nature of regulatory organizations (Gilardi 2008). Furthermore, this dyadic perspective implicitly assumes that the executive or managerial level of the organization is most important in regulatory agencies. However, regulatory authorities are also *professional* organizations (Scott 1965), in which a major part of the key work is performed by a highly skilled and trained core staff, that is, *professional* regulators.

As the individual regulatory professionals may enjoy quite some discretion in their everyday work and will take many important regulatory decisions themselves (within legal and organizational frameworks), forms of *operational accountability* (Biela & Papadopoulos 2014) are also needed. Operational accountability refers to the accountability of the individual regulatory professionals for operational regulatory decisions and their use of discretion. Particularly given the 'normal' errors of judgment to which individual regulators are also prone (Dudley & Xie 2020), these forms of operational accountability have to be effective, as to keep regulatory professionals, as all other professionals, focused and on their toes.

While operational accountability pushes the investigator to look inside the organization, the concept of *accountability regimes* (Scott 2000) invites us to do the opposite and focuses on the wider context of the organization. As we will discuss later, regulatory agencies are subjected to multiple accountability relations and standards, which by wilful design or unplanned institutional growth engross organizations in broader regimes. A regime approach captures this perspective and aims to understand how the different salient dyadic accountability relations operate in conjunction and keep the regulatory authority accountable (or not) from a more holistic whole. The sum total of accountability relationships within which an actor operates is often described as its 'accountability regime' (Scott 2000). Importantly, this regime approach allows for the outcome that autonomous bodies may not be under control by one specific principal, yet the regime as a whole still yields sufficient control (Biela & Papadopoulos 2014).

Political, Legal, Public and Professional Accountability

Finally, in the accountability regime of regulatory authorities, many different accountability forums may exist. In practice, regulatory agencies tend to operate in webs of accountability in which they are accountable to various political, legal, societal and professional account holders for different aspects of their behaviour (Thomann & Sager 2017).

Compared to other organizations in the public sector, the hierarchical political accountability of independent regulatory agencies is theoretically more limited. Due to the necessity of credible commitment, decision making powers have been delegated from the political center to the independent regulator. This results in what Levi-Faur (2005) has dubbed as the rise of a second-level indirect representative democracy, in which elected representatives select regulatory experts to carry out some of the tasks of government.

Also, the societal or horizontal forms of accountability that have increased for executive agencies are more challenging for regulators (Brummel 2021). Regulators run the risk of regulatory capture by interest groups (Braun 2012) when fostering too strong (accountability) bonds to societal stakeholders. Moreover, experimental research clearly suggests that accountability relationships to regulatees has a softening effect on regulators' judgments (Harari & Rudolph 2017).

For regulatory agencies, political and societal accountability are thus relatively less applicable than for other types of public organizations. Therefore, legal and professional accountability are theoretically more relevant to consider. Regulators often monitor and assess economic agents and can apply sanctions to enforce compliance with norms (Koop & Lodge 2017). Legal norms are, thus, at the heart of regulatory practice. As a result, legal challenges of regulatory decisions should not follow the route of democratic accountability. Rather, challenges should be incorporated in some form of legal accountability (see Scott 2000; Thatcher 2002). Also, the smaller relevance of political and societal forms of accountability increases importance of forms of professional accountability that provide feedback and assure high level quality of decisions and judgments.

Figure 17.1 summarizes the argument above with a perspective of balance in accountability regimes. It suggests that more legal and professional accountability is needed to balance the more limited possibilities for political and societal accountability for regulatory authorities. The empirical section below will underline and illustrate this logic.

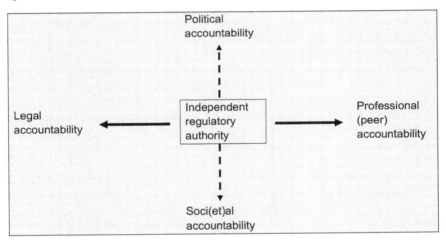

Figure 17.1   *Accountability regimes of independent regulatory authorities*

ACCOUNTABILITY FOR REGULATORS: FOUNDATIONAL CHALLENGES

In the academic literature on the accountability of regulatory agencies, the issues surrounding accountability often relate to the process of *agencification* and according autonomy of agencies, as well as to the more macro process of internationalization, which has affected regulatory authorities in many ways. Both of these developments and their implications are discussed below.

Accountability and Agencification

In recent decades, elected officials have increasingly entrusted independent authorities with regulatory competencies (see Gilardi 2005; Jordana et al. 2011). However, given that agencies are independent by design (as to ensure credible commitment to market players and other stakeholders that the rules of the game don't change over time), traditional notions of (chains of) accountability towards democratic institutions quickly become problematic (Majone 2001; Lodge 2004; Nesti 2018). In other words, for regulatory agencies to effectively fulfil their tasks, they are required to be *unresponsive* to parent ministries/political interests and act on the basis of their expert judgment (see Maggetti & Papadopoulos 2018). The need to insulate agencies from "petty politics", while still requiring them to give account for their actions in rulemaking, enforcement, and adjudication has been a challenge for both theory and practice (Everson 1995; Scott 2000).

In tackling this challenge, scholars have primarily pursued a conceptual agenda in mapping out and describing the alternative formal and informal accountability mechanism through which regulatory agencies can be held accountable (Biela & Papadopoulos 2014; Jordana et al. 2018). Given the tensions between independence and forms of vertical accountability, forms of bottom-up and horizontal accountability have been emphasized and applied to the study of regulatory authorities (Maggetti 2010). Here, the focus is less on giving account to authoritative (and democratically legitimate) principals, but more on a broader set of audiences such as organized interests, the media, and the public at large (Maggetti 2012). Regulatory agencies can be held accountable by virtue of openness and transparency in terms of rules and procedures and by requiring them to answer, explain, and justify their actions (see Scott 2000; Lodge 2004; Biela & Papadopoulos 2014). In this fashion, formal and informal accountability mechanisms can ensure that nobody controls the regulators "yet they are under control" (Majone 2001) and independence and accountability can co-exist (see Busuioc 2009; Maggetti et al. 2013).

The above-described conceptual agenda has also spawned several lines of empirical scholarship, of which one has been to map out different forms of accountability and asses the degree to which they vary across sectors and countries (see Koop 2014; Fernández-i-Marín et al. 2015; Jordana et al. 2018). In addition, scholars have looked at what potentially explains this cross-country and cross-sector variation, looking at factors such as political salience (Koop 2011) or government capacity (Yesilkagit & Christensen 2010). More recently, scholars have started to empirically assess the credible commitment claim that justifies the delegation of competences to regulatory authorities, analyzing the effects of independence and accountability on regulatory quality (Koop & Hanretty 2018; see also May 2007).

In terms of theoretical lines of research regarding regulatory agencies and accountability, scholars have also increasingly emphasized the relational nature underlying accountability, focusing on the reputational basis of public accountability and the different *audiences* that regulators have (Carpenter 2010; Busuioc & Lodge 2016). In particular, reputational considerations are theorized as an important driver for voluntary (pro-active) accountability behaviour, while also shaping the intensity of account-holding of agencies by accountability forums (Busuioc & Lodge 2016). In this fashion, the reputational approach provides a powerful theoretical framework for understanding regulatory (organizational) behaviour in accountability relationships.

Accountability and Internationalization

A second main issue for the question of regulatory authorities and their accountability, has been the increasing transnational dimension that has come to characterize their work. To regulate internationalized markets, national authorities are required to collaborate with foreign counterparts as to exchange necessary information and regulate cross-border market activity (Farrell & Newman 2016). In addition, regulatory networks have taken up an increasing role in standard-setting (Koppell 2010; Newman & Zaring 2012). Scholars have debated the likely consequences of these trends of internationalization for the question of the accountability of regulators, in which two main positions can be identified.

On the one hand, studies underline the risk of these regulatory networks becoming "agencies on the loose", in which they increasingly come to fulfil policy roles outside of public scrutiny (see Slaughter 2004; Papadopoulos 2007). Given the ambiguous and secretive nature of many transgovernmental networks, questions are frequently raised about their legitimacy and accountability (Eilstrup-Sangiovanni 2009). Moreover, the lack of hierarchy within these networks diffuses who is and can be held accountable.

On the other hand, through the concept of horizontal accountability, scholars have noted how transnational networks can also provide a potential new means by which IRAs are held accountable by their regulatory peers (Maggetti 2010; Mills & Koliba 2015). As domestic regulators become increasingly connected to foreign counterparts, reputational considerations may become increasingly important and derive accountable behaviour on behalf of regulators (see Busuioc & Rimkute 2019). Moreover, being part of a network of similarly-minded regulators, helps national agencies to better resist external influence and strengthens their position vis-à-vis regulatees (Yesilkagit & Christensen 2010). In addition, the pooling of resources through transnational networked structures enables them to fulfil their regulatory functions more effectively (Vestlund 2017).

Regarding specific forms of internationalization, the development of EU agencies has been particularly interesting to consider from an accountability perspective. The positioning of these agencies *in between* Members States and EU institutions inevitably complicates accountability relations, for instance regarding the potential "double-hattedness" of national agencies heavily involved in these structures (see Egeberg & Trondal 2017). In response, scholars have analyzed what mechanisms of accountability exist within this multi-level context, underlining the important difference between *de jure* and *de facto* accountability that need not necessarily correspond (Busuioc 2009; Buess 2015).

EMPIRICAL INSIGHTS: FELT ACCOUNTABILITY AND ACCOUNTABILITY REGIMES

As noted in the conceptual discussion provided above, the focus of the scholarly debate on public accountability has shifted from the formal-legal perspective (Bovens 2010; Strøm et al. 2003) towards informal (Romzek et al. 2012), perceptual (Overman 2021), reputational (Busuioc & Lodge 2016), and behavioural perspectives (Aleksovska et al. 2019; Schillemans 2016). These new perspectives also imply different analytical foci, presenting scholars interested in accountability and regulatory agencies with particular empirical challenges. This section presents an illustration of how these perspectives can be empirically substantiated, focusing particularly on the perceptual and behavioural perspectives towards accountability.

Felt Accountability

The perceptual and behavioural perspectives imply a focus on the individual who anticipates a future moment of accountability (Hall et al. 2017). This conceptualization of accountability has raised interest, as it uncovers the black box that links formal accountability arrangements to decisional and behavioural outcomes for individual public sector workers (Overman & Schillemans 2021).

Felt accountability denotes the set of beliefs about a future instance of accountability, and is composed of beliefs about the *anticipation* of accountability, the *legitimacy* of the account holder, and the perceived *expertise* of the account holder (Overman et al. 2021). Felt accountability appreciates the fact that individuals are known to perceive identical accountability arrangements in quite diverging ways (Tetlock 1992). This point is pivotal in the understanding of accountability from a behavioural perspective. Felt accountability, therefore, facilitates the study of individual behavioural consequences, based on accountability arrangements.

The three dimensions of felt accountability (anticipation, legitimacy and expertise) in the public sector have been measured in survey research. Data from a large scale international survey (Schillemans et al. 2021) among agency CEOs in seven Western countries was used to describe regulatory authority CEOs' perceptions of their accountability environment. A total of 496 agency CEOs in Australia, Denmark, the Netherlands, Norway, Sweden, Switzerland, and the UK responded to the survey. We use the analysis of this data to present a number of patterns in accountability perceptions among CEOs of regulatory agencies and compare them to other types of public semi-autonomous agencies.

The analysis demonstrates that felt accountability among CEOs of regulatory agencies towards their parent department is generally lower than for other types of arm's length bodies, including service providers, distributors of benefits, and research agencies.[1] We conducted a multivariate regression to analyze the difference between the regulatory authorities and other semi-autonomous agencies on the three dimensions of felt accountability (anticipation of accountability, legitimacy of the account holder, and perceived expertise of the account holder), while controlling for agency size and country. Based on this analysis, we find a lower anticipation of accountability (β=-0.207, p=0.098), lower legitimacy of the ministry as an account holder (β=-0.326, p=0.005), and lower perceived expertise of the ministry (β=-0.337, p<0.001). See Figure 17.2 for a graphical comparison. These are small but significant effects (total R^2 in the three analyses: 0.08, 0.20, and 0.11 respectively). This shows that the felt accountability of CEOs in independent regulatory authorities is generally lower on all dimensions than the felt accountability of CEOs in other semi-autonomous agencies. This underscores that the leadership of regulatory authorities do indeed, as is theoretically to be expected, feel less accountable to the politico-administrative center than other large governmental organizations.

Accountability Regimes

Furthermore, these data demonstrate that CEOs of independent regulatory authorities see their environment as politicized. We asked them whether they assess their stakeholders as

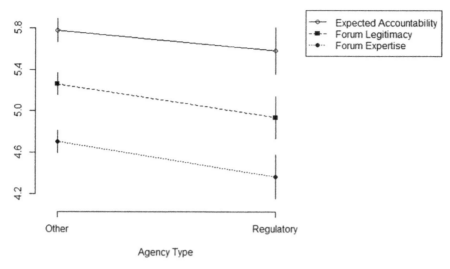

Note: Error bars represent 95% confidence intervals.

Figure 17.2   *Estimates between regulatory and other agencies for the three dimensions of felt accountability to the ministry*

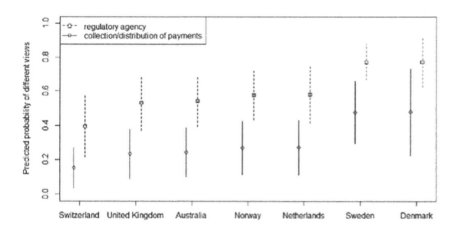

Figure 17.3   *Predicted probability for difference in views for two agency types of average size*

holding similar, or different views among each other. In comparison with executive agencies, such as distributors of benefits, CEOs of regulatory authorities perceive their stakeholders as having more different views, implying a more politicized context. Figure 17.3 demonstrates the agency CEOs' assessments of the (dis)similarity of viewpoints among various relevant stakeholders.[2] Regulatory agencies faced on average 79 per cent more conflictual regimes than other agencies.

That regulatory tasks provoke more conflictual responses can be explained by several task-specific traits. Regulation limits the decision-making autonomy of regulated entities which is naturally more contentious. Also, the outcomes of regulation are more contentious (can market failure be attributed to the regulatory authority?), leaving more room for interpretation and, thus, competing accountability expectations. Lastly, depoliticizing a task does not change the conflicts among stakeholders over task execution. These conflicts may play out at the agency level, rather than at the political level. The politicization of arm's length regulatory authorities was also confirmed in experimental research that involved stakeholders of these agencies (Alon-Barkat & Busuioc 2019).

The politicization would imply more controversy over decisions of regulators and, consequently, that legal battles are more important for regulatory authorities than for other semi-autonomous agencies, which is supported by the data: regulators consider courts more important for the execution of their tasks than other semi-autonomous agencies ($t(162.84) = 5.338$, $p < 0.001$), as are Ombudsmen ($t(138.28) = 3.656$, $p < 0.001$). And, in line with the trend towards more internationalization of regulatory authorities, we see a higher relevance of supranational bodies for regulators than for other semi-autonomous agencies ($t(143.81) = 2.463$, $p = 0.015$). All of this suggests that the accountability regime of regulators is marked more by conflict-resolving forms of accountability than those of other independent public organizations. This also suggests that the main accountability focus is on how core regulatory functions are discharged of, rather than on more general administrative or organizational issues.

RESEARCH FORESIGHTS

In this section we conclude by identifying four salient challenges for future research on accountability of regulatory agencies. Varying from the micro- to the macro-level, these challenges are (1) behavioural, (2) relational, (3) transnational, and (4) normative.

The Behavioural Challenge

The behavioural perspective on public accountability of regulatory agencies opens up a new avenue of empirical research for the time to come. The current public administration and political science literature does not have a very good understanding of what the causal effects are of accountability mechanisms on individual decision-making and behaviour, particularly for regulators. However, there is a recent surge of experimental research on the effects of accountability pressures on individual decision-making and behaviour (Aleksovska et al. 2019). One key outcome of these studies is that although accountability arrangements often have positive outcomes, they can also lead to accountability pathologies and overloads (Koppell 2005; Power 1999). Particularly the concept of "felt accountability", relating to the expectation that one will be held accountable for one's actions or decisions (Hall et al. 2017; Overman et al. 2021), is important to consider here, as well as the characteristics of and the relationship between account-givers and account-holders (Lerner & Tetlock 1999).

Research in the behavioural sciences documents that accountability has its effect on judgment and decision making by individuals (Aleksovska et al. 2019; Hall et al. 2017; Lerner & Tetlock 1999). This research focuses on important aspects of judgment and decision making, including the cognitive complexity of and biases prior to a decision (Schillemans 2016). The effects of accountability depend, among other things, on the timing of accountability, the focus of the accountability demand – that is, on the process or on the outcome of a decision, and on whether the views of the account holder are known to the account giver (ibid.). What this research does not yet document, however, is the moderating effect of the accountability environment (Hall et al. 2017). The particularities of the regulatory environment should be taken into account in the translation of this research. For instance, what is the effect of accountability conditional on the different professional roles that individuals have? It is expected that a CEO of a regulatory agency reacts differently to accountability than a street-level regulator (Thomann et al. 2018). Also, given the heuristics and biases that are likely prevalent for regulatory decision-making, organizational or institutional structures that help mitigate cognitive biases should be further explored (see Dudley & Xie 2020).

Another challenge that lies ahead is the alignment of accountability information. As witnessed in several accounts of voluntary accountability, many people are motivated to be accountable independent of a formal obligation to give an account of decisions and performance (Karsten 2015; Koop 2014). These motivations can vary from veracious to downright strategic (Busuioc & Lodge 2016). More insight is needed in the particular conditions under which an individual has a tendency to be accountable. At the same time, the substance of accountability – that is, about which topic an account is rendered – may lead to disagreement among the account holder and account giver (Busuioc & Lodge 2016; Overman 2021). It is, therefore, essential to analyse the substance of accountability in relation to the specific accountability relationship as well. This point leads us to the relational challenges for the study of accountability, which are discussed next.

The Relational Challenge

As discussed in the foundations-section of this chapter, the idea of "relational accountability" is firmly established in the standing literature that has studied regulatory agencies. However, despite important steps in theorizing about different forms of relational accountability and their potential effects, the analytical challenge of operationalizing and measuring the effects of these forms of accountability have been lagging behind. Most importantly, the empirical analysis of relational phenomena requires particular analytical methods that can account for the relational interdependence of observations (i.e., actors and organizations) and data structures. One way to do so is through social network analysis (SNA). In particular, SNA can help us map out the way in which agencies are embedded within a broader network of public authorities (e.g., government, specific ministries), regulatees, and other stakeholders representing economic interest groups (e.g., business associations, trade unions), to whom they give account of their activities through information exchange, ongoing reporting, and hearings. This helps to better assess the empirical manifestations of *ex post* accountability arrangements (see Romzek et al. 2012).

Initial steps have already been made in using SNA-methods to map out accountability relationships (see Maggetti et al. 2013). By operationalizing accountability as the *out-degrees* of an agency in its contact network, Maggetti et al. (2013) provide a straightforward measure of the extent to which agencies are *relationally* accountable (see also Ingold et al. 2013), that is, the extent to which they provide information and disclosure on their actions to external actors, how often, and to whom. Importantly, such an operationalization can measure variation in terms of the degree to which agencies engage in relational forms of account-giving, allowing us to also model relational accountability as either a dependent or independent variable.

In addition, given the importance of accountability norms, investigating the *network structures* in which such norms can develop (i.e., network embeddedness) is an important agenda for future research. Rather than merely focusing on the direct *ego-networks* of agencies (see Maggetti et al. 2013), a broader network-analytical approach focuses more on the shape of (local) networks structures by which agencies are embedded. Particular network structures give rise to institutionalized norms and according expectations about appropriate behaviour (see Powell et al. 2005). For instance, accountability pressures may be much more severe if the external actors of regulatory agencies are themselves also connected to each other (Gulati & Gargiulo 1999). In that sense, a network-analytical approach can give more empirical substantiation to "the shared norms and facilitative behaviours that foster informal accountability for collective outcomes" (see Romzek, LeRoux, & Blackmar 2012).

Lastly, network analysis can also improve our analysis of the *power dynamics* involved in transnational forms of networked interaction. Powerful actors can use transnational networks to promote policy export and shape foreign legislative agendas (Bach & Newman 2010), and this potentially raises a number of accountability concerns. Network analysis, can identify the way in which actors within a network influence each other in terms of attitudes or behavioural change (e.g., standard adoption). It this way, it provides an idea of which agencies play a prominent role in international standard-setting and processes of regulatory harmonization. For instance, through measures of centrality, network analysis can identify the actors that are able to shape the flow of information within the network and can potentially influence the adoption decisions of others to align with their own preference. Studying which actors are in structurally advantageous or disadvantageous positions can go a long way in identifying the winners and losers in processes of regulatory harmonization and helps to ascribe responsibility to actors for products of international standard setting (Van der Heijden & Schalk 2020). Exposing these power dynamics are important for questions of accountability and the concerns we should have about increased forms of transnational collaboration. This is the challenge to which we turn next.

The Transnational Challenge

The internationalization of regulation has shifted the accountability relationships in which domestic regulatory agencies find themselves and have altered the way in which rules and regulations are formulated, enforced, and implemented. Not only are domestic regulators increasingly forced into transnational collaborative structures and international policy arenas, regional and global standard setters have also entered the scene (see Koppell 2010). These empirical developments call up a wide range of analytical challenges, of which the most prominent are noted here.

First, scholarship focusing on accountability and regulation first has a descriptive challenge of mapping out the (empirical) manifestations of transnational regulation. Documenting the "networks of rule" is an important way in which accountability can be improved (see Papadopoulos 2007; Richardson 2009). This means analyzing the structures through which decisions about international standards are made (see Iborra et al. 2018), identifying which actors are involved (see Van der Heijden 2021), and, as noted above, critically analyzing whose interests are reflected in products of transnational collaboration (Drezner 2008; Van der Heijden & Schalk 2020). Such a research agenda forms the basis for discussions on who can and should be held accountable for outcomes of regulatory networks/international standard setting.

Second, we should acknowledge that peer pressure and scrutiny of foreign regulators in regulatory networks not only provide a form of accountability (e.g., towards a professional community), but are also a form of influence. Several scholars have argued that powerful actors can use transnational networks to promote policy export and shape foreign legislative agendas (Drezner 2008; Bach & Newman 2010). Peer influences are thus dictated by the more powerful peers (with particular interests). This can be problematic given that transnational regulation and international standards also lead to national adoption and thus have consequences for domestic stakeholders and audiences. In that sense, there is a hard edge to international soft law that raises a number of accountability concerns (Shaffer & Pollack 2012). On the one hand, these problems lie in the considerations that domestic stakeholders are confronted with rules and regulation flowing down from international arenas that reflect the interests of foreign governments/administrations, with whom they have accountability relationship. On the other hand, they lie in the weak visibility and secretive nature of international standard-setting, creating further problems of due process and a lack of channels for stakeholders through which to communicate concerns (see Bogason & Musso 2006; Zaring 2009).

Third, the transnational networks in which domestic agencies are increasingly required to operate are layered upon already existing domestic bureaucratic structures and accountability relationships. These developments may bring about competing accountability demands and requirements for regulatory agencies, potentially resulting in accountability overload. More studies should focus on what *internal* problems these competing accountability demands create for domestic agencies. Particularly problematic in this regard is the consideration that the organizational changes required to effectively operate in complex transnational environments may not be compatible with those needed to remain accountable in a national context (see McGuire & Agranoff 2010; Van der Heijden 2020). Insights and concepts from organizational theorists can be valuable to consider in this regard and can help answer questions about how domestic agencies can cater to the various accountability forums/demands of a transnational context, without losing the overall coordination and integration needed to remain accountable within a national context.

The Normative Challenge

Besides challenges for empirical analyzes, processes of internationalization and the development of polycentric governance arrangements (Nesti 2018) also problematize the normative underpinnings of accountability. National states are no longer the sole locus of authority. Within polycentric regulatory regimes, fragmentation, complexity, and interdependence exists between actors and state and non-state actors are both regulators and regulated (Black 2008). Given these developments, there is thus also a challenge in answering normative questions about the accountability and legitimacy of new forms of regulation that have and continue to emerge as regulatory regimes develop further (e.g. soft law standard setting, non-state actors, private regulators etc.). For regulatory governance, there are inevitable tensions between governability and accountability (Van Kersbergen & Van Waarden 2004). In other words, further checks and balances potentially render regulatory institutions incapable of governing, while a lack of checks and balances potentially result in technocratic rule and "agencies on the loose".

At the same time, we witness a displacement of the politics of regulation. Granting independence to regulators was, for a large part, inspired by a depoliticization of regulation (Majone 2001). However, the institutional separation of politics and regulation have not eradicated the differences in perspectives, opinions, and interests of the involved stakeholders. The empirical data in this chapter have demonstrated that regulators see more relevance of courts and ombudsmen. This is an indication of conflicts that are no longer settled in the political arena, but in the direct environment of the regulator (see also Alon-Barkat & Busuioc 2019). The displacement of regulatory politics also increases the relevance of regulatory regimes and, thus, to other forms of accountability, in all directions, as illustrated in Figure 17.1. These developments in the politics of regulation increase the relevance of new instruments of power, including the reputation of the regulatory authority (Busuioc & Lodge 2016; Carpenter 2010). These are not only empirical questions, but should be assessed from a normative perspective, as well.

NOTES

1. We selected 1,096 public semi-autonomous agencies at the national level in the seven mentioned countries. We selected all of the agencies that can be classified as an internally autonomous agency without legal personality or as an autonomous agency with legal personality. These were all organizations that carry out public tasks, but are not structurally a part of the parent department (Verhoest et al. 2012). The survey was completed by 496 agency heads (response rate 45%). Felt accountability was measured using the Utrecht Felt Accountability scale (Overman et al. 2021). Agency heads self-classified the main task of their organization as regulatory or one of 10 other tasks, including collection/distribution of payments (Figure 17.2). In total, 118 (20.5%) of the responses were classified as belonging to a regulatory agency.
2. Figure 17.1 contains out-of-sample predictions based on a logistic regression analysis that predicts the probability of different views among stakeholders, based on task (see note 1), country, and size in full time equivalent staff (as reported in the agency's 2018 annual report). The analysis is estimated using maximum likelihood, with a statistically significant model fit (Δ-2LL = 76.00, Δdf= 22, p < .001).

REFERENCES

Aleksovska, M., Schillemans, T., & Grimmelikhuijsen, S. (2019). Lessons from five decades of experimental and behavioral research on accountability: A systematic literature review. *Journal of Behavioral Public Administration*, 2(2).

Alon-Barkat, S, & Busuioc, M. (2019). Testing the link between agency independence and credibility: Evidence from a survey experiment with regulatory stakeholders. Paper presented at 2019 EGPA conference, Belfast.

Bach, D., & Newman, A. (2010). Transgovernmental networks and domestic policy convergence: Evidence from insider trading regulation. *International Organization*, 64, 505–528.

Bianculli, A., Jordana, J., & Fernández-i-Marín, X. (2014). *Accountability and Regulatory Governance: Audiences, Controls and Responsibilities in the Politics of Regulation*. New York: Springer.

Biela, J., & Papadopoulos, Y. (2014). The empirical assessment of agency accountability: A regime approach and an application to the German Bundesnetzagentur. *International Review of Administrative Sciences*, 80(2), 362–381.

Black, J. (2008). Constructing and contesting legitimacy and accountability in polycentric regulatory regimes. *Regulation & Governance*, 2(2), 137–164.

Bogason, P., & Musso, J. A. (2006). The democratic prospects of network governance. *The American Review of Public Administration*, 36(1), 3–18.

Bovens, M. (2007). Analysing and assessing accountability: A conceptual framework 1. *European Law Journal*, 13(4), 447–468.

Bovens, M. (2010). Two concepts of accountability: Accountability as a virtue and as a mechanism. *West European Politics*, 33(5), 946–967.

Brandsma, G. J., & Schillemans, T. (2012). The accountability cube: Measuring accountability. *Journal of Public Administration Research and Theory*, 23(4), 953–975.

Braun, C. (2012). The captive or the broker? Explaining public agency–interest group interactions. *Governance*, 25(2), 291–314.

Brummel, L. (2021). Social accountability between consensus and confrontation: Developing a theoretical framework for societal accountability relationships of public sector organizations. *Administration & Society*, 53(7), 1046–1077.

Buess, M. (2015). European Union agencies and their management boards: An assessment of accountability and democratic legitimacy. *Journal of European Public Policy*, 22(1), 94–111.

Busuioc, M. (2009). Accountability, control and independence: The case of European agencies. *European Law Journal*, 15(5), 599–615.

Busuioc, E. M., & Lodge, M. (2016). The reputational basis of public accountability. *Governance*, 29(2), 247–263.

Busuioc, M., & Rimkutė, D. (2019). The promise of bureaucratic reputation approaches for the EU regulatory state. *Journal of European Public Policy*, 1–14.

Carpenter, D. (2010). *Reputation and Power: Organizational Image and Pharmaceutical Regulation at the FDA*. Princeton, NJ: Princeton University Press.

De Haan, J., & Eijffinger, S. C. (2000). The democratic accountability of the European Central Bank: A comment on two fairy-tales. *Journal of Common Market Studies*, 38(3), 393–407.

Drezner, D. W. (2008). *All Politics is Global: Explaining International Regulatory Regimes*. Princeton, NJ: Princeton University Press.

Dudley, S. E., & Xie, D. Z. (2020). Nudging the nudger: Toward a choice architecture for regulators. *Public Administration Review*, Advance Access.

Egeberg, M., & Trondal, J. (2017). Researching European Union agencies: What have we learnt (and where do we go from here)?. *Journal of Common Market Studies*, 55(4), 675–690.

Eilstrup-Sangiovanni, M. (2009). Varieties of cooperation. Government networks in international security. In M. Kahler (Ed.), *Networked Politics: Agency, Power, and Governance* (pp. 194–227). Ithaca: Cornell University Press.

Everson, M. (1995). Independent agencies: hierarchy beaters?. *European Law Journal*, 1(2), 180–204.

Farrell, H., & Newman, A. (2016). The new interdependence approach: Theoretical development and empirical demonstration. *Review of International Political Economy*, 23(5), 713–736.

Fernández-i-Marín, X., Jordana, J., & Bianculli, A. (2015). Varieties of accountability mechanisms in regulatory agencies. In A. Bianculli, X. Fernández-i-Marín & J. Jordana (Eds.), *Accountability and Regulatory Governance* (pp. 23–50). London: Palgrave Macmillan.

Gilardi, F. (2005). The institutional foundations of regulatory capitalism: The diffusion of independent regulatory agencies in Western Europe. *The Annals of the American Academy of Political and Social Science*, 598(1), 84–101.

Gilardi, F. (2008). *Delegation in the Regulatory State: Independent Regulatory Agencies in Western Europe*. Cheltenham, UK and Northampton, MA, USA: Edward Elgar Publishing.

Gulati, R., & Gargiulo, M. (1999). Where do interorganizational networks come from? *American Journal of Sociology*, 104(5), 1439-1493.

Hall, A. T., Frink, D. D., & Buckley, R. M. (2017). An accountability account: A review and synthesis of the theoretical and empirical research on felt accountability. *Journal of Organizational Behavior*, 38(2), 204–224.

Han, Y., & Perry, J. (2019). Employee accountability: development of a multidimensional scale. *International Public Management Journal*, 1–28.

Hanretty, C., & Koop, C. (2013). Shall the law set them free? The formal and actual independence of regulatory agencies. *Regulation & Governance*, 7(2), 195–214.

Harari, M. B., & Rudolph, C. W. (2017). The effect of rater accountability on performance ratings: A meta-analytic review. *Human Resource Management Review*, 27(1), 121–133.

Iborra, S. S., Saz-Carranza, A., Fernández-i-Marín, X., & Albareda, A. (2018). The governance of goal-directed networks and network tasks: An empirical analysis of European regulatory networks. *Journal of Public Administration Research and Theory*, 28(2), 270–292.

Jordana, J., Fernández-i-Marín, X., & Bianculli, A. C. (2018). Agency proliferation and the globalization of the regulatory state: Introducing a data set on the institutional features of regulatory agencies. *Regulation & Governance*, 12(4), 524–540.

Jordana, J., Levi-Faur, D., & Fernández-i-Marín, X. F. (2011). The global diffusion of regulatory agencies: Channels of transfer and stages of diffusion. *Comparative Political Studies*, 44(10), 1343–1369.

Karsten, N. (2015). Scrutinize me, please! The drivers, manifestations and implications of accountability-seeking behaviour. *Public Administration*, 93(3), 684–699.

Koop, C. (2011). Explaining the accountability of independent agencies: The importance of political salience. *Journal of Public Policy*, 31(2), 209–234.

Koop, C. (2014). Theorizing and explaining voluntary accountability. *Public Administration*, 92(3), 565–581.

Koop, C., & Hanretty, C. (2018). Political independence, accountability, and the quality of regulatory decision-making. *Comparative Political Studies*, 51(1), 38–75.

Koop, C., & Lodge, M. (2017). What is regulation? An interdisciplinary concept analysis. *Regulation & Governance*, 11(1), 95–108.

Koppell, J.G.S. (2005). Pathologies of accountability: ICANN and the challenge of 'multiple accountabilities disorder'. *Public Administration Review*, 65(1), 94–108.

Koppell, J. G. (2010). Administration without borders. *Public Administration Review*, 70, s46–s55.

Lerner, J. S., & Tetlock, P. E. (1999). Accounting for the effects of accountability. *Psychological Bulletin*, 125(2), 255.

Levi-Faur, D. (2005). The global diffusion of regulatory capitalism. *Annals of the American Academy of Political and Social Science*, 598 (1), 12–32.

Lodge, M. (2004). Accountability and transparency in regulation: Critiques, doctrines and instruments. In J. Jordana & D. Levi-Faur (Eds.), *The Politics of Regulation: Institutions and Regulatory Reforms for the Age of Governance* (pp. 123–139). Cheltenham, UK and Northampton, MA, USA: Edward Elgar Publishing.

Maggetti, M. (2010). Legitimacy and accountability of independent regulatory agencies: A critical review. *Living Reviews in Democracy*, 2.

Maggetti, M. (2012). The media accountability of independent regulatory agencies. *European Political Science Review*, 4(3), 385–408.

Maggetti, M., Ingold, K., & Varone, F. (2013). Having your cake and eating it, too: Can regulatory agencies be both independent and accountable? *Swiss Political Science Review*, 19(1), 1–25.

Maggetti, M., & Papadopoulos, Y. (2018). The principal–agent framework and independent regulatory agencies. *Political Studies Review*, 16(3), 172–183.

Majone, G. (2001). Two logics of delegation. *European Union Politics*, 2(1), 103–122.

May, P. J. (2007). Regulatory regimes and accountability. *Regulation & Governance*, 1(1), 8–26.

McGuire, M. S., & Agranoff, R. (2010). Networking in the shadow of bureaucracy. In R. F. Durant (Ed.), *The Oxford Handbook of American Bureaucracy* (pp. 372–395). Oxford, NY: Oxford University Press.

Mills, R. W., & Koliba, C. J. (2015). The challenge of accountability in complex regulatory networks: The case of the Deepwater Horizon oil spill. *Regulation & Governance*, 9(1), 77–91.

Nesti, G. (2018). Strengthening the accountability of independent regulatory agencies: From performance back to democracy. *Comparative European Politics*, 16(3), 464–481.

Newman, A. L., & Zaring, D. (2012). Regulatory networks: Power, legitimacy, and compliance. In J. Dunoff & M. A. Pollack (Eds.), *Interdisciplinary Perspectives on International Law and International Relations* (pp. 244–265). Cambridge, MA: Cambridge University Press.

Overman, S. (2016). Great expectations of public service delegation: A systematic review. *Public Management Review*, 18(8), 1238–1262.

Overman, S. (2021). Aligning accountability arrangements for ambiguous goals: The case of museums. *Public Management Review*, 23(8), 1139–1159.

Overman, S., & Schillemans, T. (2021). Toward a public administration theory of felt accountability. *Public Administration Review*. https://doi.org/10.1111/puar.13417

Overman, S., Schillemans, T., & Grimmelikhuijsen, S. (2021). A validated measurement for felt relational accountability in the public sector: Gauging the account holder's legitimacy and expertise. *Public Management Review*, 23(12), 1748–1767.

Overman, S., Van Genugten, M., & Van Thiel, S. (2015). Accountability after structural disaggregation: Comparing agency accountability arrangements. *Public Administration*, 93(4), 1102–1120.

Papadopoulos, Y. (2007). Problems of democratic accountability in network and multilevel governance. *European Law Journal*, 13(4), 469–486.

Powell, W. W., White, D. R., Koput, K. W., & Owen-Smith, J. (2005). Network dynamics and field evolution: The growth of interorganizational collaboration in the life sciences. *American Journal of Sociology*, 110(4), 1132-1205.

Power, M. (1999). *The Audit Society: Rituals of Verification*. New York: Oxford University Press.

Richardson, A. J. (2009). Regulatory networks for accounting and auditing standards: A social network analysis of Canadian and international standard-setting. *Accounting, Organizations and Society*, 34(5), 571–588.

Romzek, B. S., LeRoux, K., & Blackmar, J. M. (2012). A preliminary theory of informal accountability among network organizational actors. *Public Administration Review*, 72(3), 442–453.

Schillemans, T. (2016). Calibrating public sector accountability: Translating experimental findings to public sector accountability. *Public Management Review*, 18(9), 1400–1420.

Schillemans, T., & Busuioc, M. (2015). Predicting public sector accountability: From agency drift to forum drift. *Journal of Public Administration Research and Theory*, 25(1): 191–215.

Schillemans, T., Overman, S., Fawcett, P., Flinders, M., Fredriksson, M., Laegreid, P., Maggetti, M., Papadopoulos, Y., Rubecksen, K., Hellebø Rykkja, L., Houlberg Salomonsen, H., Smullen, A., & Wood, M. (2021),

Scott, C. (2000). Accountability in the regulatory state. *Journal of Law and Society*, 27(1), 38–60.

Scott, W. R. (1965). Reactions to supervision in a heteronomous professional organization. *Administrative Science Quarterly*, 65–81.

Shaffer, G., & Pollack, M. A. (2012). Hard and soft law. In J. Dunoff & M. A. Pollack (Eds.), *Interdisciplinary Perspectives on International Law and International Relations* (pp. 197–222). Cambridge, MA: Cambridge University Press.

Slaughter, A.-M. (2004). *A New World Order*. Princeton, NJ: Princeton University Press.

Strøm, K., Bergman, T., & Müller, W. C. (2003). *Delegation and Accountability in Parliamentary Democracies*. Oxford, NY: Oxford University Press.

Tetlock, P. E. (1992). The impact of accountability on judgment and choice: Toward a social contingency model. *Advances in Experimental Social Psychology*, 25, 331–376.

Thatcher, M. (2002). Regulation after delegation: Independent regulatory agencies in Europe. *Journal of European Public Policy*, 9(6), 954–972.

Thatcher, M. (2011). The creation of European regulatory agencies and its limits: A comparative analysis of European delegation. *Journal of European Public Policy*, 18(6), 790–809.

Thomann, E., Hupe, P., & Sager, F. (2018). Serving many masters: Public accountability in private policy implementation. *Governance*, 31(2), 299–319.

Thomann, E., & Sager, F. (2017). Hybridity in action: Accountability dilemmas of public and for-profit food safety inspectors in Switzerland. In P. Verbruggen & H. Havinga (Eds.), *Hybridization of Food Governance* (pp. 100–120).Cheltenham, UK and Northampton, MA, USA: Edward Elgar Publishing.

Van der Heijden, M. (2020). Transnational networks and domestic agencies: Making sense of globalizing administrative patterns [Phd Dissertation]. Leiden University.

Van der Heijden, M. (2021). Agencies without borders: Explaining partner selection in the formation of transnational agreements between regulators. *Regulation & Governance*, 15(3), 725–744.

Van der Heijden, M., & Schalk, J. (2020). Network relationships and standard adoption: Diffusion effects in transnational regulatory networks. *Public Administration*, 98(3), 768–784.

Van Kersbergen, K., & Van Waarden, F. (2004). 'Governance' as a bridge between disciplines: Cross-disciplinary inspiration regarding shifts in governance and problems of governability, accountability and legitimacy. *European Journal of Political Research*, 43(2), 143–171.

Verhoest, K., Van Thiel, S., Bouckaert, G., & Lægreid, P. (2012). *Government Agencies: Practices and Lessons from 30 Countries*. New York, NJ: Palgrave Macmillan.

Vestlund, N. M. (2017). Pooling administrative resources through EU regulatory networks. *Journal of European Public Policy*, 24(1), 61–80.

Yesilkagit, K., & Christensen, J. G. (2010). Institutional design and formal autonomy: Political versus historical and cultural explanations. *Journal of Public Administration Research and Theory*, 20(1), 53–74.

Zaring, D. (2009). International institutional performance in crisis. *Chicago Journal of International Law*, 10(2), 475–504.

18. Taking stock: strategic communication by regulatory agencies as a form of reputation management

Moshe Maor

INTRODUCTION

What is strategic communication? What does it mean for regulatory agencies to pursue strategic communication as a form of reputation management? How does this sustain, create, or destroy value, or affect the chances of pursuing particular opportunities? Over the last decade, the answers to these questions have become increasingly important for scholars and practitioners seeking to understand the creation, management, and role that bureaucratic reputation plays in the life of regulatory agencies. A substantial reason for this lies in the growing complexity of risk regulation, which nowadays includes a wider array of actors, institutions, processes, and interests, in the contexts of knowledge society and blame culture that have increased agencies' concerns with reputational risk. This change is also accompanied by audience fragmentation, the proliferation of information channels and new technologies, and the shifting economic foundations of the news business, which have led to a situation in which dominant news narratives are increasingly advanced by those with power (McChesney and Pickard 2017). Yet, despite growing interest in the reputation and legitimacy of regulatory agencies, only a handful of studies have explored these questions.

This chapter takes stock of studies that focus on regulatory agencies' deliberate use of strategic communications as a form of reputation management, discussing the critiques that have recently surfaced and responding to them. To bring clarity to these issues, the chapter begins by defining the core concepts and briefly reviewing the major findings, paying particular attention to regulatory agencies' decisions regarding whether and how to communicate. It thereafter describes unanswered questions that can inspire and guide future research.

CORE CONCEPTS

A growing literature focuses on the concept of bureaucratic reputation, which is defined as "a set of symbolic beliefs about the unique or separable capacities, roles, and obligations of an organization, where these beliefs are embedded in audience networks" (Carpenter 2010a, p. 45). This definition centers on the premises that an agency's behavior is explained by (i) interactions with the broader environment, rather than merely via the relationship with political superiors (Maor 2015), and (ii) the evaluation of the organization's unique character and activities by multiple audiences (Carpenter 2010a). Evaluation of the organization's unique character and activities is based on past experiences with, and attitudes to, observations and perceptions of, the organization's ability to provide unique services capably. Reputation uniqueness, according to Carpenter (2001), refers to agencies' ability to demonstrate that they can create solutions (e.g., expertise, efficiency) and provide services (e.g., moral protection) that no other agency in the polity offers. Bureaucratic reputations derive from individuals' perceptions, which aggregate into shared understandings among members of a particular audience or multiple ones. A bureaucratic reputation is therefore a property that is attached to a specific government agency, has an independent ontological basis that audience members may share, and can be experienced, observed, measured, valued, and influenced (Fombrun 2012, p. 102). However, "[…] what audiences see is not the perfectly tuned or visible reality of the agency" (Carpenter and Krause 2012). Rather, it is an image that embeds considerable uncertainty and ambiguity (Gioia, Schultz, and Corley 2000) regarding the agency's performance, the expertise of its staff, its values, and the legality of its actions (Carpenter 2010a). "Complex public organizations are seen 'through a glass but dimly' by their manifold audiences" (Carpenter and Krause 2012, p. 27).

Understanding the behavior of a regulatory agency operating in multi-audience environment, requires a recognition of the key role of the mass media as the most important source of information for citizens about government performance (Arnold 2004). In reputational terms, the media provides: channels through which regulatory agencies signal their reputation uniqueness to their manifold audiences and observe the subsequent feedback from these and/or other audiences; informal forums for political accountability (Bovens 2007); and "audiences in their own right and [the] institutional intermediaries used by other audiences—and the agencies themselves—to make sense of agency performance" (Boon et al. 2019a, p. 173). The media also activates (and deactivates) accountability forums and induces (and suppresses) formal accountability processes (Jacobs and Schillemans 2016). In a saturated media environment, agencies identify, process, and prioritize the multiple (and potentially conflicting) expectations among various audiences concerning different dimensions of their reputations. They do so by more or less rationally choosing which dimension to stress vis-à-vis specific audiences. Maor (2015, p. 32) has referred to this process as *prioritizing* among the four dimensions of agency reputation, namely, the performative (does the agency do its job?), moral (does the agency protect the interests of its clients?), technical (does the agency have the skills and capacity required?), and procedural (does the agency follow accepted rules and norms?). Prioritizing among the four dimensions is undertaken simultaneously by all actors in the reputation game (Maor 2020).

Because strong reputations are powerful assets for agencies and are, in fact, equivalent to agency coalition building (Carpenter 2001, p. 22), many incentives exist in order to protect them. "There are other things that bureaucracies protect and 'maximize', but for many agencies […], reputation protection serves as the simplest and most powerful dynamic governing their behavior" (Carpenter 2004, p. 54). Much of the political science research on reputation has therefore been motivated by the idea that "[…] when trying to account for a regulator's behavior, *look at the audience,* and *look at the threats*" (Carpenter 2010b, p. 832; *italics in original*). Here, a reputational perspective argues that agency reputation-management strategies vary depending on the degree of reputational threats originating from the array of conflicting audience assessments concerning an agency's outputs, processes, and behavior (Carpenter 2010a; Maor, Gilad and Ben-Nun Bloom 2013). Potential sources of these threats include a gap between an agency's policy performance and reputation, weak organizational performance (e.g., a lack of coordination among the agency's subunits), and changing audience expectations regarding the agency or the sector within which it operates.

The notion of reputational risk is therefore one of the cornerstones of this body of research (e.g., Carpenter 2001, 2002, 2004, 2010a; Carpenter and Krause 2012, 2015; Gilad and Yogev 2012; Krause and Douglas 2005; Krause and Corder 2007; Maor 2007, 2010, 2011, 2015; Moffitt 2010, 2014; Moynihan 2012; Whitford 2002, 2003; Wæraas and Maor 2015; Fink and Ruffing 2020; Bartelli and Busuioc 2020; Demortain and Borraz 2021; Bustos Pérez 2021). Studies have indeed related the ramifications of reputational concerns on the way agencies approve some drugs more quickly than others (Carpenter 2002) and allocate resources across tasks (Gilad 2012), on organizational task prioritization (Gilad 2015), endogenous construction of jurisdictions (Maor 2010), the degree of an agency's legal independence (Maor 2007), the observability of decisions and errors (Maor 2011), the duration of enforcement decisions (Maor and Sulitzeanu-Kenan 2013), the agency's policy, regulatory, and scientific outputs (Krause and Douglas 2005; Maor and Sulitzeanu-Kenan 2015; Rimkuté 2018), inter-agency cooperation behavior (Busuioc 2016), regulatory enforcement (Etienne 2015; Gilad and Yogev 2012), the provision of public advice (Moffitt 2010, 2014), accountability relations and behavior (Busuioc and Lodge 2016, 2017; Christensen and Lodge 2018), and the initiation of procedures against EU member states (van der Veer 2021).

A few studies, which are at the heart of this chapter, have also demonstrated the extent and ways in which regulatory agencies manage their reputations through the strategic use of communication (e.g., Abolafia and Hatmaker 2013; Busuioc and Rimkuté 2020a; Gilad, Maor, and Ben-Nun Bloom 2015; Maor, Gilad, and Ben-Nun Bloom 2013; Moschella and Pinto 2019; Schanin 2015). In addition, reputation-based accounts have been used to explain how reputation and blame avoidance might deteriorate network performance (Moynihan 2012), and how agencies protect their reputation in times of crisis (Carpenter 2010b; Christensen and Lægreid 2015; Bækkeskov 2017; Bach et al. 2019; Moschella and Pinto 2019). The theory's assumptions have been tested with regard to agencies in the U.S. (Carpenter 2010a, 2010b; Maor 2010, 2011; Maor and Sulitzeanu-Kenan 2013; Moffitt 2010, 2014; Moschella and Pinto 2019; Abolafia and Hatmaker 2013), Australia, New Zealand and the province of British Columbia, Canada (Maor and Sulitzeanu-Kenan 2015; Maor 2007), Israel (Gilad, Maor, and Ben-Nun Bloom 2015; Schanin 2015; Gilad, Alon-Barkat, and Braverman 2016; Maor, Gilad, and Ben-Nun Bloom 2013), Ireland (O'Dwyer 2015), Germany, Belgium, Denmark, and Norway (Verhoest, Rommel, and Boon 2015; Bach et al. 2019; Boon et al. 2019b; Kolltveit, Karlsen, and Askim 2019; Kolltveit 2019), Cyprus (Capelos et al. 2016), as well as the EU (Busuioc 2016; Busuioc and Rimkuté 2020a; 2020b; Rimkuté 2018, 2020; van der Veer and Haverland 2018).

In addition, attempts to develop standardized measures of bureaucratic reputation and to gauge bureaucratic reputation in the eyes of citizens were undertaken in the context of US federal agencies (Lee and Van Ryzin 2019, 2020) and EU regulators (Overman, Busuioc, and Wood 2020). Recently, Bellodi (2022) has developed a strategy to measure bureaucratic reputation from legislative speeches in the US and the UK. Studies have also found that reputational considerations influence decision-making within regulatory agencies (Bach 2015) and that reputational signals affect the response of employees (Gilad, Ben-Nun Bloom, and Assouline 2018). The bureaucratic reputation approach therefore brings to the fore assessments by multiple audiences concerning agencies' past behavior as well as the way agencies communicate this behavior; the perception, processing, and prioritizing of this information by reputation-sensitive agencies according to the degree of reputational threats they pose; and the response of these agencies to such reputational threats. We now turn our attention to key findings regarding these responses in the media arena.

RESEARCH FINDINGS

If there is an overarching thread linking research in this area, it is comprised of the notions that a reputation-sensitive agency hears, sees, and feels the public; that in some functional areas the agency feels comfortable because it possesses a strong reputation, whereas in others it does not; and that in its response to reputational threats, an agency's external communication can broadly assume many forms. By describing communication of a reputation-sensitive agency as *strategic*, attention is centered on deliberate strategies that seek to shape an agency's reputation in different situations and contexts, with a role for choice about the organization, planning, initiation, maintenance, and termination of the agency's communication activities (for alternative definitions and approaches, see Fredriksson and Pallas 2016, p. 154; Wittington and Yakis-Douglas 2012, p. 404; Hallahan et al. 2007, p. 7; Heide et al. 2018). Strategic communication activities by regulatory agencies range from strategic silence (Maor 2016a) to regulatory talk. The former is a passive *blame-avoidance strategy* (Hood 2011; see also Hinterleitner and Sager 2015, 2017, 2019) intended to avoid attention. However, its occurrence should be carefully gauged because agencies may be subject to political pressures to keep silent. Regulatory talk ranges from an active blame-avoidance strategy (Hood et al. 2009), by engaging in problem denial, problem admission, and responsibility denial, or admission, to a deliberate *credit-claiming strategy* (Hood 2011; Highhouse, Brooks, and Gregarus 2009; Neu, Warsame, and Pedwell 1998) that is intended to communicate favorable information about the agency's activities and outputs (Gilad, Alon-Barkat, and Braverman 2016, p. 373).

Focusing on the Israeli banking regulator's responses to public expressions of opinion, research on strategic silence has established that a regulatory agency tends to keep silent on issues regarding which it generally enjoys a strong reputation, and on issues that lie outside its distinct jurisdiction, while responding to opinions about core functional areas with regards to which its reputation is weaker and areas wherein its reputation is still evolving (Maor, Gilad and Ben-Nun Bloom 2013). These findings are important because they demonstrate how an organization's assessment of the relative threat to its reputation influences its communicative strategy *across functional areas*. The choice between silence and talk emphasizes the agency's attempt to actively construct how multiple audiences, which may hold conflicting views and apply different assessment criteria, judge its performance. It also highlights the possibility that strategic silence may be employed in order to minimize the association of the regulatory agency with actual as well as potential reputational threats (Ehrmann and Fratzscher 2009; Heugens et al. 2004). Striking a fine balance between strategic silence and talk is a very complex task, as is the task of maintaining silence. It requires centralization of external communication, formulation of blackout guidelines, the creation of an incentive structure to enhance compliance with these guidelines, and the establishment of enforcement mechanisms to ensure that none of the organization's employees break these guidelines and, if required, to penalize deviant behavior (Maor 2016a). Alternatively, strategic silence may be accomplished through transformational leadership behaviors where leaders succeed in aligning employees' goals with the vision and mission of the agency.

The aforementioned variations in how agencies manage the expectations of their multi-faceted audiences across functional areas is also evidenced by Moschella and Pinto's (2019) study, which demonstrates that when concerns about policy reversibility are higher, the Federal Reserve is more likely to focus on the issues of credit easing and systemic financial regulation, where its reputation is weak or not yet established. In contrast, issues related to economic activity and inflation, regarding both of which the Federal Reserve's reputation is established, are likely to become less salient. A similar pattern of issue attention has been observed when the Federal Reserve addressed political audiences compared to other audiences.

In an attempt to further uncover the variation in how agencies manage the expectations of multiple audiences, Busuioc and Lodge (2017, p. 95) distinguished between 'core' and 'noncore' reputational concerns, and argued that the ways agencies respond to external criticism are shaped by the agency's understanding of its core reputation and associated reputational threats. This distinction has been employed in an attempt to gauge how the communication of different aspects of organizational reputation vary over time and across EU agencies (Busuioc and Rimkuté 2020a). A study of all EU agencies furthermore reveals that regulatory agencies utilize a more diverse set of reputational strategies by emphasizing the technical, procedural, and moral reputations more than non-regulatory agencies, whereas social-policy agencies foster their technical reputation more than economic-policy agencies (Rimkuté 2020).

Equally important is the question of regulatory talk, especially the determinants of this type of strategic communication. Based on the Israeli banking regulator's nuanced responses to public expressions of opinion between 1996 and 2012, Gilad, Maor, and Ben-Nun Bloom (2015) found that a regulatory agency has a greater propensity to acknowledge problems, yet mostly shifts blame to others when faced with claims that regulation is overly lenient (namely, underregulation), and to deny allegations that regulation is excessive. These findings highlight the agency's *differential* response (i.e., a choice between types of responses) to particular reputational threats.

Between strategic silence and talk, one can detect strategic communication practices associated with fine-tuning regulatory signals. Fine-tuning is defined as "the strategic practices involved in signal construction intended to shape stakeholders' estimation of any agency's ability and intentions" (Abolafia and Hatmaker 2013, p. 533). It is therefore a means to actively seek legitimacy (Suchman 1995, p. 574) and reflects "a source of deep engagement for the signaler" (Abolafia and Hatmaker 2013, p. 535). Such signals—the clarity of which varies strategically from transparency to opacity according to political and economic circumstances—were used by the Federal Reserve to influence immediate stakeholder behavior as well as to maintain a longer-term agency reputation. Abolafia and Hatmaker (2013) identify two fine-tuning practices, *expectation modulation* and *credibility filtering*. The former practice is employed by the agency in order to shape audiences' expectations about the agency's actions; the latter in an attempt to screen the signal for positive reputational effects. Both practices are part of the toolkit used by the signalers and are grounded in an agency's sense of its image and identity (Abolafia and Hatmaker 2013).

These studies not only demonstrate the interactive nature of the relations between the agency and the public but also that the agency is not acting in an ad hoc manner. Rather, the agency carefully designs its interaction with regulatees and the public at large, shaping the 'common ground' that it shares with its critics. Although it remains attuned to the public's feelings and intuitions, it selectively or differentially responds in a way that maintains its credibility.

CRITICISMS AND RESPONSE[1]

Scholars have claimed that the ways in which regulatory agencies prioritize multiple (and potentially conflicting) expectations among audiences regarding different dimensions of their reputations may be driven to a certain extent by the distinctive logic of the media (Boon et al. 2019a, p. 172). This criticism draws on the burgeoning literature concerning media logic (e.g., Altheide 2004), raising the possibility that the way the media works might interfere with the reputation signals agencies seek to communicate (Boon et al. 2019a; Boon et al. 2019b). Another challenge centers on the notion that (strategic) communication provides solely short-term, symbolic solutions to emerging threats (Grunig 1993; see also Grunig 2014; Picci 2015, p. 49; Schanin 2015).

Maor (2020) has responded to Boon et al.'s (2019a) criticism by arguing that there are clear-cut findings demonstrating that agencies design different communication strategies in line with functional areas which differ in terms of the strength of their reputations (Maor et al. 2013; Moschella and Pinto 2019); the content of allegations (Gilad et al. 2015); the agency's understanding of its core reputation and associated reputational threats over time and across (EU) agencies (Busuioc and Rimkuté 2020b); the agencies' wish to manage uncertainties in their operating environment, and not only in response to specific allegations (Moschella and Pinto 2019); and their wish to influence immediate stakeholder behavior in addition to maintaining longer-term agency reputation (Abolafia and Hatmaker 2013). These findings clearly indicate that (i) the agencies concerned are deeply engaged in crafting their communication, and (ii) actual 'prioritizing' among dimensions of an agency's reputation indeed takes place, whether intentionally or not, and whether the media try to interfere with the formulation and execution strategic communication or not.

In response to the second line of criticism, Maor (2020) has argued that some aspects of strategic communication may indeed be episodic in nature, trying to persuade audiences that specific regulatory moves are valuable, yet others may reflect a long-term effort to maintain and enhance an agency's reputation. Furthermore, "[r]eputation can shape the behavior of organizational insiders as well as external stakeholders [...]. It can influence employees' sense of self and outsiders' expectations of the organization [...]. These two aspects, the short-term and the longer-term effects of signaling, can appear separately, but are often reinforcing" (Abolafia and Hatmaker 2013, p. 535). In addition, attention should be directed at the characteristic of the message that is communicated. In this respect, strategic communication may involve *policy overreaction rhetoric*, which refers to "arguments that policymakers employ to reach and persuade the target populations of their 'all or nothing' policy commitment to achieve their policy goal, no matter what the costs are or by any means necessary" (Maor 2021, p. 188). Strategic communication may therefore involve messages primarily aimed at sending uncompromising signals regarding an agency's intentions, which are therefore likely to entail longer-term implications. A case in point is the statement made by Mario Draghi (2012) while the Eurozone was in the throes of crisis: "[W]ithin our mandate, the ECB is ready to do whatever it takes to preserve the euro. And believe me, it will be enough." Agencies' use of overreaction and underreaction rhetoric (Maor 2019, 2021), alongside other communication strategies, highlights their ability to go beyond taken-for-granted practices and symbolic constructions that limit their ability to follow a single end-means rationality.

UNANSWERED QUESTIONS

Future studies addressing the communicative dynamics of regulatory agencies may be extended to a comparison of a number of regulators operating within the same nation-state, with overall stronger and weaker reputations. It can be further applied across national settings or over time in order to analyze how variance in external circumstances (e.g., attitudes toward regulation) shapes regulators' communication strategies. And it can be further developed by analyzing the micro-foundations of reputation management. This task can be undertaken by gauging how and to what extent the reputation of the agency head shapes the agency's communication strategies (Maor 2016b). This research may be complemented by an analysis of the interaction between regulators' communication and their actual action in response to external signals.

The decision regarding whether or not to communicate is accompanied by another: how this communication should be conducted (Wittington and Yakis-Douglas 2012, p. 404). In the future, scholars should examine the manner in which reputation-sensitive agencies can achieve an equilibrium, between substantive and symbolic communication (e.g., Ashforth and Gibbs 1990); the ramifications of calculations concerning completeness, coloring, and the benefit of substantive communication (e.g., Douglas and Meijer 2016; Grimmelikhuijsen 2012); how agencies resolve issues concerning the timing, medium, frequency, content, language, and target audiences of their communications; and the justifications for alterations in communication strategy.

Research should also assess which audience segmentation strategies are selected by regulators in various times and in a range of policy sectors, and how the regulators suit regulatory messages to specific target populations. In particular, studies should highlight the employment of competing or opposing communications for divided audiences by agencies that possess exclusive jurisdiction, in contrast to instances in which agencies share regulatory authority or at least some portion thereof. The involvement of more than one agency entails a review of other agencies' audiences and inter-agency relations, and these factors should likewise be examined.

Among further issues of vital significance in cultivating a theoretical and empirical understanding of audience segmentation strategies, scholars should examine whether regulators design emotion-loaded messages for groups that are chosen according to psychological tendencies, as opposed to groups selected by behavioral profiles and socio-demographic attributes. Likewise, how can regulators balance strategic communication for groups that are chosen according to cross-sectional audience segmentation strategies in contrast to situational strategies that are centered on a particular problem or issue? How can regulators mold strategic communications for audience groups that react to a certain problem with feelings of hesitation, as opposed to doubt, anxiety, or panic? How can regulators who seek to change the behavior of audience group members appeal to their practices, attitudes, motivations, and perceptions? Here, it may be important to understand how agency audiences pass reputational judgments (Salomonsen, Boye and Boon 2021).

Examining how strategic communication is conducted may stimulate interest in the continuity and innovation in regulatory agencies' narratives; the institutionalization of strategic communication practices (e.g., Heide et al. 2018); variations in how discursive and other strategies are used to communicate and interpret meaning, together with the derived public policy implications; the significant role played by context in strategic communication (e.g., time; crisis) and in determining the range of strategic communication employed; and the relevancy of policy overreaction rhetoric in efforts to uphold a reputation. The examination of these issues should emphasize how the decisions made effect agencies' reputations and how audiences consequently allocate the resources at their disposal.

NOTE

1.   This section relies heavily on Maor (2020).

REFERENCES

Abolafia, M. Y., and Hatmaker, D. M. (2013). Fine-tuning the signal: Image and identity at the Federal Reserve. *International Public Management Journal*, 16(4), 532–556.

Altheide, D. L. (2004). Media logic and political communication. *Political Communication*, 21(3), 293–296.

Arnold, R. D. (2004). *Congress, the Press, and Political Accountability*. Princeton: Princeton University Press.

Ashforth, B. E., and Gibbs, B. W. (1990). The double-edge of organizational legitimation. *Organization Science*, 1(2), 177–194.

Bach, T. (2015). Wie "tickt" die öffentliche Verwaltung? Autonomie, Reputation und Responsivität von Regulierungsbehörden am Beispiel des Bundesinstituts für Risikobewertung. In M. Döhler, J. Franzke, and K. Wegrich (Eds.), *Der gut organizierte Staat, Festschrift für Werner Jann zum 65. Geburtstag* (pp. 162–181). Baden-Baden: Nomos.

Bach, T., Boon, J., Boye, S., Salomonsen, H. H., Verhoest, K., and Wegrich, K. (2019). In the line of fire: European financial regulators before, during, and after the crisis. dms – der moderne staat – *Zeitschrift für Public Policy, Recht und Management*, 12. Jg., Heft 1/2019, S. 5–29 https://doi.org/10.3224/dms .v12i1.03.

Bækkeskov, E. (2017). Reputation-seeking by a government agency in Europe: Direct evidence from responses to the 2009 H1N1 "Swine" influenza pandemic. *Administration & Society*, 49(2), 163–189.

Bartelli, A. M., and Busuioc, M. (2020). Reputation-sourced authority and the prospect of unchecked bureaucratic power. *Public Administration Review*. DOI: 10.1111/puar.13281.

Bellodi, L. (2022). A dynamic measure of bureaucratic reputation: New data for new theory. *American Journal of Political Science*. https://doi.org/10.1111/ajps.12695.

Boon, J., Salomonsen H. H., Verhoest, K., and Pedersen, M. Ø. (2019a). Media and bureaucratic reputation: Exploring media biases in the coverage of public agencies. In: T. Bach and K. Wegrich (Eds.), *The Blind Spots of Public Bureaucracy and the Politics of Non-coordination* (pp. 171–192). Basingstoke: Palgrave Macmillan.

Boon, J., Salomonsen, H. H., and Verhoest, K. (2019b). The effects of organisational features on media attention for public organisations. *Policy & Politics*, 47(2), 245–264.

Bovens, M. A. P. (2007). Analysing and assessing accountability: A conceptual framework. *European Law Journal*, 13(4), 447–468.

Bustos Pérez, E. O. (2021). Organizational reputation in the public administration: A systematic literature review. *Public Administration Review*. https://doi.org/10.1111/puar.13363.

Busuioc, E. M. (2016). Friend or foe? Inter-agency co-operation, organizational reputation, and turf. *Public Administration*, 94(1), 40–56.

Busuioc, E. M., and Lodge, M. (2016). The reputational basis of public accountability. *Governance*, 29(2), 247–263.

Busuioc, M., and Lodge, M. (2017). Reputation and accountability relationships: Managing accountability expectations through reputation. *Public Administration Review*, 77(1), 91–100.

Busuioc, M., and Rimkuté, D. (2020a). Meeting expectations in the EU regulatory state? Regulatory communications amid conflicting institutional demands. *Journal of European Public Policy*, 27(4), 547–568.

Busuioc, M., and Rimkuté, D. (2020b). The promise of bureaucratic reputation approaches for the EU regulatory state. *Journal of European Public Policy*, 27(8), 1256–1269.

Capelos, T., Provost, C., Parouti, M., Barnett, J., Chenoweth, J., Fife-Schaw, C., and Kelay, T. (2016). Ingredients of institutional reputations and citizen engagement with regulators. *Regulation and Governance*, 10(4), 350–367.

Carpenter, D. P. (2001). *The Forging of Bureaucratic Autonomy*. Princeton, NJ: Princeton University Press.

Carpenter, D. P. (2002). Groups, the media, agency waiting costs, and FDA drug approval. *American Journal of Political Science*, 46(3), 490–505.

Carpenter, D. P. (2004). The political economy of FDA drug review. *Health Affairs*, 23(1), 52–63.

Carpenter, D. P. (2010a). *Reputation and Power: Organizational Image and Pharmaceutical Regulation at the FDA*. Princeton, NJ: Princeton University Press.

Carpenter, D. P. (2010b). Institutional strangulation: Bureaucratic politics and financial reform in the Obama administration. *Perspectives on Politics*, 8(3), 825–846.

Carpenter, D. P., and Krause, G. A. (2012). Reputation and public administration. *Public Administration Review*, 72(1), 26–32.

Carpenter, D. P., and Krause G. A. (2015). Transactional authority and bureaucratic politics. *Journal of Public Administration Research and Theory*, 25(1), 5–25.

Christensen, T., and Lægreid, P. (2015). Reputation management in times of crisis: How the police handled the Norwegian terrorist attack in 2011. In A. Wæraas and M. Maor (Eds.), *Organizational Reputation in the Public Sector* (pp. 95–117). New York, Abingdon: Routledge.

Christensen, T., and Lodge, M. (2018). Reputation management in societal security: A comparative study. *American Review of Public Administration*, 48(2), 119–132.

Demortain, D., and Borraz, O. (2021). Managing technical reputation: Regulatory agencies and evidential work in risk assessment. *Public Administration*. https://doi.org/10.1111/padm.12734.

Douglas, S., and Meijer, A. (2016). Transparency and public value: Analyzing the transparency practices and value creation of public utilities. *International Journal of Public Administration*, 39(12), 940–951.

Draghi, M. (2012). Speech at the Global Investment Conference, July 26. https://www.ecb.europa.eu/press/key/date/2012/html/sp120726.en.html (accessed 6.4.2022).

Ehrmann, E., and Fratzscher, M. (2009). Purdah—on the rationale for central bank silence around policy meetings. *Journal of Money, Credit and Banking*, 41(2/3), 517–528.

Etienne, J. (2015). The politics of detection in business regulation. *Journal of Public Administration Research and Theory*, 25(1), 257–284.

Fink, S., and Ruffing, E. (2020). Stakeholder consultations as reputation building: A comparison of ACER and the German Federal Network Agency. *Journal of European Public Policy*, 27(11), 1657–1676.

Fombrun, C. I. (2012). The building blocks of corporate reputation: Definitions, antecedents, consequences. In T. G. Pollock and M. L. Barnett (Eds.), *The Oxford Handbook of Corporate Reputation* (pp. 94–113). Oxford: Oxford University Press.

Fredriksson, M., and Pallas, J. (2016). Diverging principles for strategic communication in government agencies. *International Journal of Strategic Communication*, 10(3), 153–164.

Gilad, S. (2012). Attention and reputation: Linking regulators' internal and external worlds. In M. Lodge and K. Wegrich (Eds.), *Executive Politics in Times of Crisis* (pp. 157–178). Basingstoke: Palgrave Macmillan.

Gilad, S. (2015). Political pressures, organizational identity and attention to tasks: Illustrations from pre-crisis financial regulation. *Public Administration*, 93(3), 593–608.

Gilad, S., Alon-Barkat, S., and Braverman, A. (2016). Large-scale social protest: A business risk and a bureaucratic opportunity. *Governance*, 29(3), 371–392.

Gilad, S., Ben-Nun Bloom, P., and Assouline, M. (2018). Bureaucrats' processing of organizational reputation signals. *Journal of Behavioral Public Administration*, 1(1), 1–11.

Gilad, S., Maor M., and Ben-Nun Bloom, P. (2015). Organizational reputation, the content of public allegations, and regulatory communication. *Journal of Public Administration Research and Theory*, 25(2), 451–478.

Gilad, S., and Yogev, T. (2012). How reputation regulates regulators: Illustrations from the regulation of retail finance. In M. Barnett and T. Pollock (Eds.), *Oxford Handbook of Corporate Regulation* (pp. 320–340). Oxford: Oxford University Press.

Gioia, D. A., Schultz, M., and Corley, K. G. (2000). Organizational identity, image, and adaptive instability. *Academy of Management Review*, 25(1), 63–81.

Grimmelikhuijsen, S. G. (2012). Transparency and Trust: An experimental study of online disclosure and trust in government. PhD dissertation, Utrecht University. https://dspace.library.uu.nl/handle/1874/218113 [accessed 6.4.2022].

Grunig, J. E. (1993). Image and substance: From symbolic to behavioral relationships. *Public Relations Review*, 19(2), 121–139.

Grunig, J. E. (2014). Replacing images, reputations, and other figments of the mind with substantive relationship. In T. M. Falconi, J. E. Grunig, E. Galli Zugaro, and J. Duarte (Eds.), *Global Stakeholder Relationships Governance: An Infrastructure* (pp. 56–82). Basingstoke: Palgrave Macmillan.

Hallahan, K., Holtzhausen, D., van Ruler, B., Verčič, D., and Sriramesh, K. (2007). Defining strategic communication. *International Journal of Strategic Communication*, 1(1), 3–35.

Heide, M., von Platen, S., Simonsson, C., and Falkheimer, J. (2018). Expanding the scope of strategic communication: Towards a holistic understanding of organizational complexity. *International Journal of Strategic Communication*, 12(4), 452–468.

Heugens P. P. M. A. R., Cees B. M. van Riel, and van den Bosch F. A. J. (2004). Reputation management capabilities as decision rules. *Journal of Management Studies*, 41(8), 1349–1377.

Highhouse, S., Brooks, M. E., and Gregarus, G. (2009). An organizational impression management perspective on the formation of corporate reputations. *Journal of Management*, 35(6), 1481–1493.

Hinterleitner, M., and Sager, F. (2015). Avoiding blame: A comprehensive framework and the Australian home insulation program fiasco. *Policy Studies Journal*, 43(1), 139–161.

Hinterleitner, M., and Sager, F. (2017). Anticipatory and reactive forms of blame avoidance: Of foxes and lions. *European Political Science Review*, 9(4), 587–606.

Hinterleitner, M., and Sager, F. (2019). Blame, reputation, and organizational responses to a politicized climate. In T. Bach and K. Wegrich (Eds.), *The Blind Spots of Public Bureaucracy and the Politics of Non-coordination* (pp. 133–150) Basingstoke: Palgrave Macmillan.

Hood, C. (2011). *The Blame Game: Spin, Bureaucracy and Self-Preservation in Government*. Princeton, NJ: Princeton University Press.

Hood, C., Jennings, W., Dixon, R., Hogwood, B., and Beeston, C. (2009). Testing times: Exploring staged responses and the impact of blame management strategies in two examination fiasco cases. *European Journal of Political Research*, 48(6), 695–722.

Jacobs, S., and Schillemans, T. (2016). Media and public accountability: Typology and exploration. *Policy & Politics*, 44(1), 23–40.

Kolltveit, K. (2019). On the minister's tight leash? Media appearance and autonomy in public agencies. *Scandinavian Journal of Public Administration*, 23(1), 41–58.

Kolltveit, K., Karlsen, R., and Askim, J. (2019). Understanding reputational concerns within government agencies. *Policy & Politics*, 47(3), 473–493.

Krause, G. A., and Corder, J. K. (2007). Explaining bureaucratic optimism: Theory and evidence from US executive agency macroeconomic forecasts. *American Political Science Review*, 101(1), 129–142.

Krause, G. A., and Douglas, J. W. (2005). Institutional design versus reputational effects on bureaucratic performance: Evidence from US government macroeconomic and fiscal projections. *Journal of Public Administration Research and Theory*, 15(2), 281–306.

Lee, D., and Van Ryzin, G. (2019). Measuring bureaucratic reputation: Scale, development and validation. *Governance*, 32(1), 177–192.

Lee, D., and Van Ryzin, G. (2020). Bureaucratic reputation in the eyes of citizens: An analysis of US federal agencies. *International Review of Administrative Sciences*, 86(1), 183–200.

Maor, M. (2007). A scientific standard and an agency's legal independence. *Public Administration*, 85(4), 961–978.

Maor, M. (2010). Organizational reputation and jurisdictional claims: The case of the U.S. Food and Drug Administration. *Governance*, 23(1), 133–159.

Maor, M. (2011). Organizational reputation and the observability of public warnings in 10 pharmaceutical markets. *Governance*, 24(3), 557–582.

Maor, M. (2015). Theorizing bureaucratic reputation. In A. Wæraas and M. Maor (Eds.), *Organizational Reputation in the Public Sector* (pp. 17–36). New York, Abingdon: Routledge.

Maor, M. (2016a). Strategic silence. In Craig E. Carroll (Ed.) *The Sage Encyclopedia of Corporate Reputation* (pp. 822–824). Thousand Oaks, CA: Sage.

Maor, M. (2016b). Missing areas in the bureaucratic reputation framework. *Politics and Governance*, 4(2), 80–90.

Maor, M. (2019). Overreaction and bubbles in politics and policy. In A. Mintz and L. Terris (Eds.) *Oxford Handbook on Behavioral Political Science*, Oxford Handbooks Online, Oxford University Press. DOI: 10.1093/oxfordhb/9780190634131.013.28

Maor, M. (2020). Strategic communication by regulatory agencies as a form of reputation management: A strategic agenda. *Public Administration*, 98(4), 1044–1055.

Maor, M. (2021). Deliberate disproportionate policy response: Towards a conceptual turn. *Journal of Public Policy*, 41(1), 185–208.

Maor, M., Gilad, S., and Ben-Nun Bloom, P. (2013). Organizational reputation, regulatory talk, and strategic silence. *Journal of Public Administration Research and Theory*, 23(3), 581–608.

Maor, M., and Sulitzeanu-Kenan, R. (2013). The effect of salient reputational threats on the pace of FDA enforcement. *Governance*, 26(1), 31–61.

Maor, M., and Sulitzeanu-Kenan, R. (2015). Responsive change: An agency output response to reputational threats. *Journal of Public Administration Research and Theory*, 26(1), 31–44.

McChesney, R. W., and Pickard, V. (2017). News media as political institutions. In K. Kenski and K. H. Jamieson (Eds.), *The Oxford Handbook of Political Communication* (pp. 263–274). Oxford: Oxford University Press.

Moffitt, S. L. (2010). Promoting agency reputation through public advice: Advisory committee use in the FDA. *Journal of Politics*, 72(3), 880–893.

Moffitt, S. (2014). *Making Policy Public: Participatory Bureaucracy in American democracy*. New York: Cambridge University Press.

Moschella, M., and Pinto, L. (2019). Central banks' communication as reputation management: How the Fed talks under uncertainty. *Public Administration*, 97(3), 513–529.

Moynihan, D. P. (2012). Extra-network organizational reputation and blame avoidance in networks: The Hurricane Katrina example. *Governance*, 25(4), 567–588.

Neu, D., Warsame, H., and Pedwell, K. (1998). Managing public impressions: Environmental disclosures in annual reports. *Accounting, Organizations and Society*, 23(3), 265–282.

O'Dwyer, C. (2015). The relationship between an Irish government department and its newly established agency: A reputational perspective. In A. Wæraas and M. Maor (Eds.), *Organizational Reputation in the Public Sector* (pp. 77–94). New York, Abingdon: Routledge.

Overman, S., Busuioc, M., and Wood, M. (2020). A multidimensional reputation barometer for public agencies: A validated instrument. *Public Administration Review*, 80(3), 415–425.

Picci, L. (2015). Actors and strategies of the bureaucratic reputation game. In A. Wæraas and M. Maor (Eds.), *Organizational Reputation in the Public Sector* (pp. 37–53). New York, Abingdon: Routledge.

Rimkuté, D. (2018). Organizational reputation and risk regulation: The effect of reputational threats on agency scientific outputs. *Public Administration*, 96(1), 70–83.

Rimkuté, D. (2020). Building organizational reputation in the European regulatory state: An analysis of EU agencies' communication. *Governance*, 33(2), 385–406.

Salomonsen, H. H., Boye, S., and Boon, J. (2021). Caught up or protected by the past? How reputational histories matter for agencies' media reputations. *Journal of Public Administration Research and Theory*, doi:10.1093/jopart/muaa056

Schanin, Y. (2015). Organizational reputation, public protest, and the strategic use of regulatory communication. In A. Wæraas and M. Maor (Eds.), *Organizational Reputation in the Public Sector* (pp. 139–160). New York, Abingdon: Routledge.

Suchman, M. (1995). Managing legitimacy: Strategic and institutional approaches. *Academy of Management Review*, 20(3), 571–610.

van der Veer, R. A. (2021). Audience heterogeneity, costly signaling and threat prioritization: Bureaucratic reputation-building in the EU. *Journal of Public Administration Research and Theory*, 31(1), 21–37.

van der Veer, R. A., and Haverland, M. (2018). Bread and butter or bread and circuses? Politicization and the European Commission in the European semester. *European Union Politics*, 19, 524–545.

Verhoest, K., Rommel, J., and Boon, J. (2014). How organizational reputation and trust may affect the autonomy of independent regulators: The case of the Flemish energy regulator. In A. Wæraas and M. Maor (Eds.), *Organizational Reputation in the Public Sector* (pp. 118–138). London: Routledge.

Wæraas, A., and Maor, M. (Eds.) (2015). *Organizational Reputation in the Public Sector*. New York: Routledge.

Whitford, A. B. (2002). Bureaucratic discretion, agency structure, and democratic responsiveness: The case of the United States attorneys. *Journal of Public Administration Research and Theory*, 12(1), 3–27.

Whitford, A. B. (2003). Adapting agencies: An essay on competition, imitation, and punishment. In G. A. Krause and K. J. Meier (Eds.), *Politics, Policy, and Organizations Frontiers in the Scientific Study of Bureaucracy* (pp. 292–308). Ann Arbor: The University of Michigan Press.

Wittington, R., and B. Yakis-Douglas. (2012). Strategic disclosure: Strategy as a Form of Reputation Management. In M. Barnett and T. Pollock (Eds.), *Oxford Handbook of Corporate Regulation* (pp. 402–419). Oxford: Oxford University Press.

19. Managing the performance of regulatory agencies

Cary Coglianese

INTRODUCTION

In recent decades, major shifts from public to private control over infrastructure and other sectors of the economy, combined with increasing demands for consumer, social, and environmental protections, have given rise to increased recognition of the importance of government regulation. As a result, in many countries virtually every aspect of economic and social life is affected by the activities of regulatory authorities.

The performance of regulatory authorities is itself affected by multiple factors, but prominent among them is the quality of their management. This chapter focuses on the management of regulatory authorities, offering a framework both for studying such management and for improving it. It defines the basic managerial challenges facing regulatory leaders and then elaborates the major steps involved in overcoming those challenges: priority-setting; rule design; public engagement; enforcement; and measurement and evaluation.

Managing regulatory authorities well ultimately demands active and vigilant efforts on the part of regulatory leaders. Not only do leaders need to be attentive and agile, but they also need to adopt a mindset that seeks to learn whether their organizations' actions are producing positive results and that strives for ongoing improvement. Further research by both academic and government analysts can promote regulatory leaders' continuous learning—a crucial ingredient in high-quality regulatory management.

REGULATORY MANAGEMENT: CHALLENGES AND DEFINITIONS

Although authorities that might be deemed "regulatory" can encompass legislatures—which also establish rules that regulate business behavior—this chapter focuses on the separate public administrative units or bodies that are dedicated to implementing legislative mandates—that is, the governmental or quasi-governmental institutions responsible for overseeing designated industries or for regulating key economic functions.

These regulatory institutions can take many forms. Some are headed by multi-member bodies, while others are headed by a single administrator. Some are closely connected with legislators or other political leaders—and perhaps are even headed by them in ministries that operate as direct extensions of a legislature. Other regulatory institutions operate at a formal arms-length relationship with the legislature, led by officials appointed for fixed time periods and who enjoy protections from ad hoc removals. Most are governmental institutions, but some are considered quasi-governmental.

No matter their structural form, regulatory institutions' missions are closely linked to regulatory law. Whether such law has been adopted by legislatures, ministries, or even by independent regulatory institutions themselves, regulation comprises a collection of rules backed up by some kind of consequences, usually civil or administrative penalties (Coglianese 2012b; Schauer 2015; Lambert 2017). Regulatory law aims to solve a variety of problems created by market activity. Some regulatory problems relate to the prices of goods and services in the economy, while others deal with the quality of or societal impacts emanating from these goods and services.

In addressing these various problems, regulatory institutions often carry out both rule-making and adjudicatory functions, the latter of which can involve the issuance of permits or licenses as well as the conducting of inspections, audits, or enforcement proceedings. In addition, many regulatory institutions engage in other activities oriented toward rule compliance and problem mitigation, including educating, disseminating information, and issuing grants, subsidies, and public recognition.

Challenges in Managing Regulatory Institutions

All regulatory institutions seek to shape the behavior of regulated individuals and entities. That behavioral change constitutes, at its essence, a core goal of all regulatory institutions and those who manage them.

But this behavioral goal presents at least three challenges for regulatory management. First, it means that the regulatory managers' success ultimately depends on the behavior of others. If just a single employee at a regulated business neglects to follow the rules (say, by failing to tighten a valve properly on a piece of dangerous equipment) and a catastrophic event occurs, this will be viewed in the public's eyes as a failure of the regulatory institution. Yet regulation and regulatory oversight can only partly affect the behavior of individuals within regulated facilities or businesses. Regulated entities are also subject to a variety of other external economic and social pressures (Gunningham, Kagan, & Thornton 2003) as well as to internal imperatives (Howard-Grenville, Nash, & Coglianese 2008).

A second challenge stems from the highly complex environments in which regulators operate. They often face competing demands from other parts of government and different segments of the public. And the regulatory entities they oversee can be highly heterogeneous. Some regulatory authorities regulate both individuals and business organizations; however, even when regulators oversee just businesses, these firms can range from small business partnerships to large multinational conglomerates. Businesses also vary in their propensity to act responsibly: some are inclined to follow the rules, while others seek to prosper outside the confines of applicable law—actively seeking to evade detection. Precisely because regulated entities themselves confront different behavioral forces and factors, the challenges associated with shaping their behavior can be highly diverse and contextual.

Finally, regulators must seek to effectuate behavioral change within a dynamic environment that reflects pressures and constraints imposed by an ever-changing set of actors, problems, and operating conditions. Regulated entities are hardly static. They typically operate within a competitive business environment where they face continual incentives to innovate for economic reasons. Advances in technology also often leave regulators struggling to keep pace (Marchant, Allenby, & Herkert 2011; Coglianese 2018). Moreover, regulated entities always have strategic reasons to try to adapt their behavior, either to evade detection by regulators or simply to achieve their goals while complying with the letter of the law but at the expense of the law's spirit (Coglianese & Nash 2017). Changing social conditions and public expectations constitute another source of dynamism confronting regulators. The rise of social media and the emergence of populism around the world, for example, have in recent years affected the operating conditions for regulatory institutions (Coglianese 2020a).

The three core challenges confronting regulators—dependency, complexity, and dynamism—make regulating a difficult endeavor. Moreover, regulators always risk either over-reacting or under-reacting to potential problems. Effective regulatory management thus will ultimately require striking a balance. Too much hesitancy may diminish a regulatory institution's performance, just as might too much eagerness to intervene in regulated entities' affairs. Regulatory managers will thus do well to inculcate an openness to adapting their regulatory strategies when needed to account both for differences across regulated entities and changes over time in relevant economic and social conditions. They will seek to optimize by making adjustments to regulatory obligations, whether through the updating of rules or the granting of waivers and exemptions when circumstances dictate (Coglianese 2020b; Coglianese, Scheffler, & Walters 2021).

The management of regulatory institutions typically demands that regulators deploy a portfolio of tactics aimed at promoting compliance. Inspection targeting may need to vary over time, and the ways that regulatory inspectors interact with regulated entities may need to vary from firm to firm and from interaction to interaction (Ayres & Braithwaite 1992; Scholz 1984). Regulators might sometimes help advance their goals through non-regulatory strategies, such as the development of educational or recognition programs that seek to diffuse best practices through an industry.

Defining Quality Regulatory Management

Given that regulatory managers must navigate many challenges, including changing conditions, pressures, and demands, they need to establish clear organizational missions and then communicate statements about these missions throughout their organizations. Although each regulatory body will define its mission in ways that are specific to the problems it seeks to address and the nature of the industry it regulates, generalizations can be made about what it means to be a high-quality or excellent regulatory organization. The OECD (2005), for example, has articulated the following seven principles to guide regulatory managers toward high-quality performance:

1. Adopt at the political level broad programs of regulatory reform that establish clear objectives and frameworks for implementation.
2. Assess impacts and review regulations systematically to ensure that they meet their intended objectives efficiently and effectively in a changing and complex economic and social environment.
3. Ensure that regulations, regulatory institutions charged with implementation, and regulatory processes are transparent and non-discriminatory.
4. Review and strengthen where necessary the scope, effectiveness, and enforcement of competition policy.

5. Design economic regulations in all sectors to stimulate competition and efficiency, and eliminate them except where clear evidence demonstrates that they are the best way to serve broad public interests.
6. Eliminate unnecessary regulatory barriers to trade and investment through continued liberalization and enhance the consideration and better integration of market openness throughout the regulatory process, thus strengthening economic efficiency and competitiveness.
7. Identify important linkages with other policy objectives and develop policies to achieve those objectives in ways that support reform.

In addition to these OECD principles, numerous other principles or attributes of successful regulation have been articulated by both academics and practitioners. Indeed, dozens of schemata exist that point to qualities that regulatory institutions should possess to perform well (Coglianese 2015; Finkel, Walters, & Corbett 2018). The proliferation of descriptors of high-quality regulation can make it difficult for regulatory managers to focus their efforts and those of others throughout their organizations, as "the longer the list of attributes grows, the more it begins to look itself like a highly detailed rule-book" (Coglianese 2015: 21). To be actionable, principles of regulatory quality should be capable of being encapsulated in a manageable framework.

One such framework is based around a metaphorical molecule—RegX, for regulatory excellence—which can provide managers with greater focus. RegX comprises three key "atoms" of regulatory quality: (1) utmost integrity; (2) empathic engagement; and (3) stellar competence (Coglianese 2015). *Integrity* reflects the regulatory institution's degree of public interest commitment: honesty; humility; public-spiritedness; respect for the law; and dedication to taking evidence and analysis seriously. *Competence* is about solving problems and delivering outcomes that are effective, efficient, and equitable. *Engagement* encompasses transparency, even-handedness in outreach, and the way in which a regulatory institution interacts with and listens to the public.

These characteristics of integrity, competence, and engagement capture well the broad range of qualities found in other schema. But by organizing these qualities into three broad categories, the RegX framework provides regulatory leaders with a clearer lodestar against which to manage their organizations. Successful regulating demands the consistent attainment of high levels of each of the three atoms, which by extension necessitates building internal organizational cultures and capacities to support the three atoms in all of a regulatory institution's actions and outcomes.

MANAGING FOR REGULATORY PERFORMANCE

Defining high-quality regulating is only the first step in managing a regulatory institution. Regulatory managers must ensure that their personnel engage in high-quality actions and deliver high-quality performance. Five broad sets of actions comprise a framework for managing regulatory institutions with these objectives in mind: (a) setting priorities, (b) designing regulations, (c) engaging the public, (d) enforcing regulations, and (e) measuring and evaluating performance.

Setting Priorities

Although regulatory problems come in many varieties, the main justifications for regulation classically fall within three main types of "market failures" (Breyer 1982)—externalities, information asymmetries, and concentrations of market power. These market failures themselves usually derive from the existence of transaction costs in private ordering (Zerbe & McCurdy 1999). Other regulatory problems do not fall within the categories of market failure but are nevertheless important. For example, regulatory institutions seek to protect civil rights, promote equity, and combat discrimination—all ways of advancing major public values, even if they do not constitute classic cases of market failure (Sunstein 1990).

Because regulatory institutions face a plethora of problems, and sources of problems, their managers need to set priorities around these problems—more than just around tasks (Sparrow 2000). They must decide how to allocate scarce individual and organizational resources: Which problems deserve more attention? Which behaviors most contribute to these problems and need regulating? Which regulated entities are the best ones to target for inspection and enforcement?

It is widely recommended that regulators become "risk-based" or "risk-informed" (Hutter 2016; Paoli & Wiles 2015). The widespread enthusiasm for risk-based regulation partly stems from the fact that the concept of "risk-based" regulation means different things to different people (Coglianese & Sapir 2017). Still, with thoughtfulness and the benefit of careful risk assessment, regulators can make better decisions about how to prioritize their use of limited regulatory resources.

Of course, risk assessment never can fully *determine* the regulator's priorities. At most, risk assessments inform regulators' decisions (Paoli & Wiles 2015). Risk assessment provides scientific or empirical answers about probabilities, hazards, and their distribution; it does not supply the policy or normative principles needed to justify particular regulatory decisions (Coglianese & Marchant 2004). Sensible priority-setting demands clarity in these principles.

One such principle could be what is sometimes called the "worst-first" principle: namely, target the biggest hazards or the biggest risks (Finkel & Golding 1994). But another principle—efficiency—will have a regulator target a mix or portfolio of risks that maximizes net benefits. This portfolio approach would entail the regulatory agency targeting smaller hazards if they have risk management costs that are correspondingly small, and it might well exclude attending to some larger hazards if they have extremely low probabilities or are impossible or disproportionately costly to manage (Kovacic 2009). From an efficiency standpoint, the key would be to balance the returns of regulating, so as to maximize overall net benefits across the suite of the regulator's activity.

Designing Regulations

Many regulatory institutions possess the authority and responsibility to create rules or to issue guidance documents. Through these actions, regulators can add necessary specificity to the law, clarify ambiguities, or close policy gaps created in legislation. The way that regulatory institutions design regulations will likely affect their performance. Careful choices about the stringency, flexibility, and other design features of a rule will be important as a regulator seeks to shape industry behavior and ultimately achieve regulatory goals (Coglianese & Bennear 2012; Carrigan & Harrington 2015).

Table 19.1   *Regulatory designs*

	Means	Ends
Micro	Micro-means	Micro-ends
	"Prescriptive"	"Performance-based"
Macro	Macro-means	Macro-ends
	"Management-based"	"General duty/liability"

Source: Coglianese (2010); National Academy of Sciences (2018).

The precise design that a regulation should take will depend on the problem the regulator seeks to solve as well as the nature of the industry being regulated. Different regulatory designs will also demand different capabilities of regulatory institutions when it comes to monitoring and enforcement (National Academy of Sciences 2018).

Regulatory designs have been described in numerous ways: command-and-control regulation, design standards, prescriptive regulation, performance standards, market-based instruments, management-based regulation, and information disclosure (Richards 2000; Goulder & Parry 2008; Richards & van Zeben 2020). These myriad types of rule designs can be simplified and grouped into four main categories based on two aspects or dimensions of regulatory design: means versus ends, and micro versus macro (Coglianese 2010; National Academy of Sciences 2018).

Means-based designs obligate regulated entities to undertake (or avoid) specified actions, while ends-based designs mandate that firms attain (or avoid) specified outputs or outcomes (Coglianese 2010). Macro versus micro designs differ based on their point of focus in the causal chain that leads to regulatory problems: micro-regulations focus on a "specific contributor or causal pathway to the ultimate problem," while macro-regulations focus the obligation on the "ultimate problem itself" (National Academy of Sciences 2018). This conceptualization is reflected in Table 19.1. Although the performance of any of the four archetypes in Table 19.1 will depend on the context within which any regulation is situated, as well as other structural features of a rule, it is possible to offer some generalizations about the advantages and disadvantages of each type.

Micro-means regulations leave regulated entities with less flexibility but can be suitable when a one-size-fits-all solution to a regulatory problem is widely available and known to be effective for most if not all regulated entities. This rule design's specificity also means that compliance may be more readily verifiable. But micro-means regulations will be less cost-effective when regulated entities are heterogeneous. Obligating all firms to adhere to the same means may even discourage the search for better or less costly solutions to a problem (Goulder & Parry 2008).

By contrast, micro-ends regulations afford regulated entities flexibility. Often referred to as performance-based regulations, they impose mandates—such as pollution limits—that regulated entities must achieve (or avoid) specified outputs at points on the causal path toward an ultimate problem (National Academy of Sciences 2018). The required outputs can be the same for all regulated entities, or they can vary, such as based on the number of permits that such an entity holds in a market-based regulatory system. Emissions trading schemes, for example, allow pollution limits to vary for each facility based on the permits they have obtained through the market-based system (Newell & Stavins 2003). Whether the limits are uniform or varied, the flexibility afforded by micro-ends regulation allows for innovation and adjustment by regulated entities. This same flexibility, though, makes monitoring vigilance important, lest regulated entities meet the letter of a required output by finding ways that create other problems or that evade the regulation's overall purpose (Coglianese 2017).

Macro-means, or management-based, regulations seek to direct the attention of regulated entities to the ultimate problem by mandating "internal planning and management practices" to induce managers to address the ultimate problem (Coglianese 2008). Firms are expected to produce plans that comply with criteria determined by regulators. An example is the widely adopted Hazard Analysis and Critical Control Points (HACCP) food safety regime, through which firms are required to create internal assessments of food safety risks and develop plans to correct potential risks that may arise. Such macro-means regulations are generally preferable when no one-size-fits-all action exists and when outputs are difficult to measure directly (Coglianese & Lazer 2003). Sometimes described as enforced or mandated self-regulation (Hutter 2001; Braithwaite 1982), macro-means regulation places the responsibility to study risks and develop responses in the hands of regulated actors. Of course, some firms, especially smaller ones, may lack the capacity for the internal analysis and planning required of macro-means regulation. In addition, macro-means regulation may be prone to the potential for "pencil whipping" or "window dressing," whereby firms simply go through the motions to comply with required management steps but do not earnestly produce meaningful results (National Academy of Sciences 2018; Gray & Silbey 2014).

A final regulatory design is that of macro-ends regulation, also sometimes referred to in terms of "general duty" requirements or *ex post* liability rules. These regulations obligate regulated entities to avoid the ultimate problem—for example, accidents or system failures—by imposing a penalty if the problem occurs. These regulations contain no explicit requirements along the causal path to a harmful event; rather, the threat of consequences after the event is intended to encourage preventive behavior. Although many regulators will include macro-ends regulations in their arsenal of tools, seldom do they rely on *ex post* liability alone.

Ultimately, the critical challenge for regulatory leaders is "choosing the right regulatory tool and understanding which one to use when and with whom" (Hutton 2015). Such decisions call for assessments of advantages and disadvantages in specific contexts. Management judgment in making these choices will be informed by various analytic tools, such as risk assessment and benefit-cost analysis (OECD 2020). Often regulatory leaders will find that, in tackling any given problem, they will need to deploy multiple regulations that collectively cut across several different archetypes, with different regulations addressing different aspects of the causal chain leading to the problem. The ultimate test of a regulator's selection and design of regulatory instruments rests with the outcomes achieved.

Engaging the Public

Members of the public who are interested in and affected by regulatory decisions should have opportunities both to learn about what the regulator is doing and to provide input. The "public" includes individuals affected by the work of the regulatory body—such as workers or consumers—as well as an array of representatives from industry, unions, advocacy groups, think tanks, media outlets, community organizations, and other governmental entities. Of course, time and resources that regulatory staff devote to engagement have their opportunity costs. Still, whenever feasible, regulators do well to start public engagement as early as possible when investigating a new problem or considering a new policy (Nash & Walters 2015).

Effective public engagement will necessitate transparency and sincerity on the part of the regulator. Information disclosed needs to be accessible, relevant, and comprehensible as well as accurate for all potential users—both those in industry as well as individuals in the public more broadly (Coglianese 2012a). Similarly, public engagement should involve meaningful listening—and even though this does not mean a regulator must always agree with what is heard, it does mean acknowledging what was heard.

Regulatory institutions should be responsive and open about their justifications for their actions, taking the time to respond to expressed concerns with sincere, well-developed, and clear explanations (Coglianese 2009). Especially when a regulator must make a decision that will be opposed or disfavored by some—as is commonly the case—the public deserves a forthright account of the reasons underlying the decision.

Transparency and public engagement can enhance public trust in a regulatory body (Coglianese, Kilmartin, & Mendelson 2009)—but only if a regulator acts fairly and listens to a full range of concerns. Although regulatory employees may well have good reason to spend more time with industry representatives during the course of their practice, regulatory managers do well to avoid giving any favor to one segment of the public over the other. Fairness will at times require taking affirmative efforts at outreach and engagement to ensure that less-advantaged groups or communities can be heard.

Not only can openness and public engagement enhance trust and legitimacy, such outreach efforts can also help produce smarter regulatory decisions. Through public engagement, regulatory officials can obtain information that can help them gather information needed to design better regulations and overall improve their performance (Coglianese, Zeckhauser, & Parson 2004).

Genuine opportunities for meaningful public engagement can also promote compliance with regulations (Malesky & Taussig 2019; Tyler 2003). Regulated entities may be more likely to comply when regulations have been designed with public input, as the rules are likely to be better understood (at least by those who participated in the process) and viewed as more legitimate.

Regulators have available to them a variety of different tools for soliciting public input: public notices, comment periods, public hearings, informal meetings and phone conversations, advisory committees, workshops, adjudicatory proceedings, negotiations, and the internet and social media (Sant'Ambrogio & Staszewski 2021). Effective regulatory management calls for selecting the public engagement tools that fit the purposes and circumstances at hand (including the capacities and needs of interested or affected individuals and groups). Having a standard, default procedure that encourages public participation—such as developing routine practices of notice and public comment solicitations—may also help embed public input into the culture of a regulatory institution.

Enforcing Regulations

Key management challenges arise as regulatory institutions develop strategies and programs to promote compliance with regulations. Some regulated individuals or entities might well be expected to comply with rules out of an intrinsic tendency toward obedience (Sommers & Bohns 2019), while others comply because they see regulatory authorities as legitimate (Malesky & Taussig 2019). Still others will need to face external pressures before they change their behavior to come into compliance with regulations—and included in this group will be the true regulatory scofflaws who actively resist complying and seek to evade detection. Compliance by other regulated entities may well depend on whether they see regulators ensuring that scofflaws are caught and face penalties (cf. Bowles 1971: 41–42).

Regulatory bodies have a variety of ways to approach their efforts to apply and enforce rules—for example, some adversarial, some more cooperative. The choices that regulatory authorities make about their enforcement strategies will affect their performance and will, by necessity, form a part of a regulatory manager's toolkit.

Regulation scholars have long urged regulatory personnel to approach enforcement flexibly (Gunningham 2016). The conventional view holds that optimal enforcement will involve a mix of cooperative and punitive actions—typically starting cooperatively, then moving to punitive measures in the face of recalcitrance (Ayres & Braithwaite 1992; Scholz 1984). It can be counterproductive for regulatory officials to take an immediately adversarial posture toward regulated firms (Bardach & Kagan 1982). But this does not mean that regulators always must be cooperative. Deterrence-oriented enforcement actions by regulators have been shown to yield behavioral change (Alm & Shimshack 2014; Gray & Shadbegian 2005; Thornton, Gunningham, & Kagan 2005; Levine, Toffel, & Johnson 2012).

The ultimate goal—as well as key challenge—of any enforcement program is to motivate behavior that achieves desired outcomes. Inspections, audits, and other enforcement-related actions by a regulatory body can together provide incentives, information, modeling, and learning. In practice, the "obligation encounter" between an inspector and a regulated entity provides for a teachable moment (Moore 1997). These encounters can obviously help a regulated entity's managers learn about applicable legal obligations, but they can also provide an opportunity for informal consultation or counseling by agency personnel about what the managers could do better to achieve the desired outcomes of the regulatory program (Hawkins 1984).

Although the goal of any enforcement program is a tall one—motivating behavior to achieve desired outcomes—the tools and resources available to a regulatory body are usually limited, at least in relation to the nature of the underlying behavior. Resource constraints mean that enforcement monitoring and obligation encounters are usually infrequent and inspections typically occur for only a limited duration. Inspectors may also only actually be able to observe or test a small subset of all the possible aspects of an operation that could be subject to regulation.

Inspections and audits are thus a sampling exercise, providing only a snapshot of a regulated entities' behavior and performance. Especially when inspections are announced in advance, they will be imperfect or noisy signals of true levels of compliance, never providing a complete picture of how a regulated entity generally behaves or operates when an inspection is not occurring. This is why priority-setting is so important: How can regulators target their resources to inspect those entities where these limited interventions can do the most good? How can regulators use the actual intervention itself—the obligation encounter—to maximal effect? And how can they also minimize any detrimental effects on outcomes (say, from backlash) from these limited interventions?

Technology can help in answering these questions and deciding what entities to target. Increasingly, regulators are finding that machine learning can help identify those entities most likely to be in serious noncompliance (Berk 2009; Hino, Benami, & Brooks 2018; Engstrom et al. 2020).

Regulatory managers also need to focus on training and management of their inspection personnel. A rote, box-checking obligation encounter can prove counterproductive, encouraging regulated entities to overinvest in box-checking at the expense of addressing potentially more important causes of regulatory problems (e.g., human factors, organizational system failures). At the end of the day, what matters are outcomes—not boxes being checked.

Measuring and Evaluating Performance

Sound regulatory management requires continual learning. Although much attention has been paid over the years to the importance of regulatory impact assessment (OECD 2020)—that is, to the analysis of options *before* adopting a new regulation—evaluation is an equally important analytical activity that should take place *after* regulations are adopted. By looking back at how well regulations are working, regulators can learn from past actions about how to make future actions better, whether by modifying existing rules, creating new ones, or changing enforcement strategies.

Evaluation or performance measurement can take several forms (Coglianese 2015). One form focuses on a regulatory institution's actions, such as the number of inspections or the size of enforcement penalties. Another form focuses on outcomes, such as the number of accidents or consumer complaints. Outcomes can be assessed based on a variety of criteria, such as:

- *Effectiveness* (delivering benefits by reducing a problem);
- *Cost-effectiveness* (achieving a specified level of problem reduction at the lowest cost);
- *Efficiency* (balancing problem reduction with costs and maximizing net benefits); and
- *Equity* (achieving a fair distribution of the benefits and costs).

To make evaluation meaningful, regulatory managers need suitable data. They need to be cautious, though, not to fall prey to the "lamppost" problem—that is, only looking where the light is. Data should be *relevant* (related to the questions asked), *reliable* (both accurate and resistant to manipulation), and *realistic* (reasonably available and intelligible to the audience for the evaluation) (Coglianese 2015).

Regulatory managers need data on both their actions as well as on outcomes. Whenever feasible, they should conduct causal or attributional evaluations to discern to what extent a causal relationship exists between the actions and outcomes (Coglianese 2016). Only attributional evaluation can give regulatory managers' high confidence that their institutional actions are in fact making a difference.

In principle, it should be possible to evaluate the causal relationship between any type of regulatory action and connect it with any type of outcome. Whether the actions involve priority setting, rule design, public engagement, or enforcement, they all can be subjected to evaluation and help managers improve their performance.

Of course, what is possible in principle is not always possible in practice. Causal attribution demands a research design or statistical strategy that supports drawing inferences about the impact of the agency action under study (Coglianese 2012b; King, Keohane, & Verba 1994). And no regulatory institution can evaluate all of its actions through the most rigorous forms of causal evaluation. But this does not mean that the regulatory manager should merely "count beans" without any regard to causation at all. Regulatory officials can learn best by taking a strategic approach to evaluation or performance measurement, developing a portfolio of data collection, evaluation plans, and research designs that help inform the most important decisions (ACUS 2017).

In seeking to learn from their experiences, regulatory managers should consider providing opportunities for external involvement in and validation of regulatory evaluations. Especially when one of the purposes of measurement aims to inform an external audience (such as a regulatory institution's overseers), it can help to seek input from the public and others outside the institution about measurement systems and study designs.

MANAGERIAL DYNAMISM AND REGULATORY VIGILANCE

The need for performance evaluation stems from a general need for ongoing learning. The series of management steps outlined above—setting priorities, designing regulations, engaging with the public, enforcing regulations, and measuring performance—may seem linear, but in fact they are iterative, disjunctive, and changing. Regulatory managers need to use what they learn from their experiences to circle back repeatedly, considering whether they need to adjust priorities, redesign regulations, engage with new or different segments of the public, make modifications to enforcement efforts, or collect new data and produce different types of research. Regulatory management, in short, needs to be dynamic and agile (National Academy of Public Administration 2020; OECD 2017).

Vigilance for a Dynamic Regulatory Environment

Although vigilance can be important for any organization, the need for it in regulation derives from the ever-changing environment within which regulatory institutions are situated. Regulatory managers need the vision and monitoring capacity to notice change as it is occurring, especially when that change involves strategic behavior by regulated firms and relevant shifts in the larger social and economic landscape.

Building a capacity for foresight and adaption demands technical expertise. The issues that regulatory organizations confront are highly complex. Managers should ensure that they foster a workforce that possesses detailed mastery of the technical aspects of the operations of the industries they oversee. Even if they cannot match industry entirely in technical knowledge, they must ensure they have the in-house capability to assess the actions and associated risks of industry operations sufficiently to be able to oversee the industry.

Yet technical skill and knowledge is not enough. Regulatory managers and their workforces also need to possess knowledge of human behavior. Regulation, after all, is fundamentally about affecting the behavior of people. The regulatory institution seldom directly fixes problems; rather, it must work with others, motivating people within businesses, shaping and steering their decisions, and ultimately eliciting a change in their behavior.

Moreover, because the problems that regulators seek to redress are ones that affect people outside of the regulated industry, regulatory managers must ensure that their personnel know how to engage professionally and empathically with members of the public, nongovernmental organizations, and other governmental institutions. As a result, regulatory managers need to build an organizational culture that fosters attentiveness to a broad range of concerns and reinforces humility, empathy, and a steadfast commitment to public service and continuous improvement.

Building a Culture of Regulatory Excellence

Regulatory management is not a task that a manager simply "accomplishes." Rather, it is an ongoing effort to strive toward consistent high attainment and continuous improvement along the three qualities of regulatory excellence: the *utmost integrity, stellar competence*, and *empathic engagement*.

Furthermore, because the path toward regulatory excellence must involve the efforts of everyone working for a regulatory institution, regulatory managers' strategic priorities need to become more than just goals for themselves; they need to become part of the day-to-day workings of all employees. The public image that an excellent regulator seeks to project—its integrity, empathy, and competence—should mirror the consistent practices and beliefs of all the people who are part of the regulatory institution. Although cultural change never comes easily or quickly (Howard-Grenville, Bertels & Boren 2015; Schein 2010), regulatory leaders will do well to set the example in their organizations and establish management practices that appropriately align employee incentives with the attainment of all three attributes of regulatory excellence.

What steps can regulatory managers take to align their organizations better with the attributes of regulatory excellence? They can follow four recommended steps, each of which provide opportunities for dialogue with elected officials and members of the public (Coglianese 2015).

1. *Self-awareness.* The first step is to gain a solid familiarity with the regulatory organization's current capacities, activities, and levels of performance. Regulatory leaders should take time to create an overall picture of their current organization.
2. *Scoping.* Regulatory managers next should ask themselves how well aligned their institutions are with the core attributes of regulatory excellence. Some aspects of their institutions will be better aligned with these values than others. Scoping is needed to inform decisions about where to place the regulator's priorities for improvement.
3. *Strategic action.* Regulatory managers next must focus on a manageable set of strategic priorities. Not every facet of an organization can be improved at once. Managers should consider prioritizing both the most important needs as well as the areas where they have opportunities for achieving demonstrable successes. They should combine strategic goals with plans for performance measurement.
4. *Assessment and continuous improvement.* Essential to any strategic plan will be subsequent efforts to determine whether improvement has been achieved, and then working to make continuous improvement.

Any distillation of cultural change into four steps, of course, risks creating the misleading impression that changing a regulatory organization's culture will be straightforward or easy. Cultural change is anything but that. Managers must remain vigilant and persistent in fostering a culture of excellence, emphasizing the importance of integrity, competence, and engagement in both words and actions.

Directions for Future Research

As evidenced by this volume and others (Baldwin, Cave, & Lodge 2012; Levi-Faur 2012; van Rooij & Sokol 2021; Rosenbloom & Schwartz 1994), it is possible to identify an abundance of academic research on regulation which can prove informative for regulatory managers.

Moreover, an extensive body of important empirical and prescriptive research on public administration and management exists which can offer helpful insight and guidance (Simon 1947; Wilson 1989; Moore 1995; Barber 2015). Yet important opportunities for future research on regulatory management still abound.

Much existing research on regulation provides prescriptive analytics to guide decisions about when to regulate and which types of instruments to use (Breyer 1982; Lambert 2017). Similarly, discrete research exists on risk analysis, benefit–cost tools, public engagement, and regulatory enforcement. But little work synthesizes across the range of tools, techniques, and knowledge required of a public regulatory manager. Indeed, with few exceptions (e.g., Sparrow 2000, 2008), academic researchers have failed to speak directly to the management questions that confront regulatory officials. Most research on public management has focused on the delivery of programs and services, not on the challenges facing regulatory authorities and the tasks of obligation management. Future scholarship is thus needed that considers more fully the distinctive managerial issues confronting regulatory leaders.

It would be helpful to have additional research on each of the steps of regulatory management provided by the framework in section 2 of this chapter. For example, when it comes to setting priorities, regulators would benefit from research about what, precisely, it means to be risk-based as well as how to choose and manage more optimal portfolios of risks, especially in the face of varying degrees of knowledge of the probabilities and consequences associated with different behaviors and business activities.

Similarly, although the challenges of regulatory design have spawned a large academic literature on instrument choice, the literature lacks research that compares, head-to-head, different regulatory designs with respect to the same problems in similar settings. Regulatory officials have even less research—virtually none—on how different *combinations of* regulatory designs fare, a surprising gap given how regulated entities are seldom subject to obligations of just a single regulatory design. The pure archetypes of regulatory designs in the academic literature are not necessarily reflective of rules (or sets of rules) applied in practice, so research would be helpful if it could pay attention to more realistic scenarios in which regulated entities are subject to a combination of rule designs.

Much academic research does exist on public engagement, both in public policymaking generally (Cairney, Heikkila, & Wood 2019) and in the context of regulatory decision-making (Sant'Ambrogio & Staszewski 2021). Still, the procedural requirements that call for transparency and public participation in various facets of a regulatory authority's operations are highly varied and could be studied further. With the emergence of new communication technologies, such as social media, regulatory managers confront still more options for seeking public input. Numerous opportunities remain for additional research on the forms and techniques of public engagement in regulatory management.

Open empirical questions also exist about the efficacy of different regulatory enforcement styles and strategies, notwithstanding an important collection of existing research studies on the efficacy of enforcement in general. When it comes to making fine-grained conclusions about specific strategies to optimize scarce enforcement resources, academic researchers have often lacked access to sufficient data. Fruitful opportunities exist for making progress through greater cooperation between regulatory practitioners and members of the research community that could unlock the value in troves of administrative data. And both researchers and managers have only started to explore the possibilities that artificial intelligence may hold for improving regulatory performance (Engstrom et al. 2020; Coglianese 2020c).

Finally, to determine whether specific regulatory management choices lead to better outcomes, there remain important opportunities for regulators to partner with independent researchers in the quest for performance measurement and evaluation. Evaluation research on both process outcomes and substantive outcomes can be helpful to guide future regulatory management decisions about priority-setting, regulatory design, public engagement, and enforcement.

CONCLUSION

Effective regulatory management, at its core, is a matter of balancing, building, and adapting. In navigating the many challenges they confront, regulatory managers must master a kind of professional multilingualism and interdisciplinary craft. They must be proficient at addressing and listening to both internal and external audiences, mastering technical knowledge of the business practices they oversee, and inculcating an understanding of human behavior and how to shape it. They must do so in complex, interconnected, and dynamic environments. And as a part of everything they do, they must hold themselves to high standards of integrity, empathy, and competence.

Successful regulatory management is thus an iterative, ongoing endeavor. The quest for regulatory excellence is just that: a quest. But it requires a commitment to undertaking one of the greatest challenges known to humanity, as it calls for working in an orderly, peaceful manner to change people's behavior when they would otherwise affirmatively prefer not to change, especially because it can be costly to do so.

Paramount to the quest for excellence in regulatory management will be an ongoing receptivity to learning and to change. Learning is essential—including learning from mistakes as well as from successes. Overall, measurement and analysis are vital for understanding problems and for solving them without creating still new problems. The academic research community can play an important role in this process by pursuing new research on each aspect of the management framework outlined in this chapter.

In the end, success in regulatory management demands active and attentive leadership, constant vigilance, rigorous data collection and research, and a commitment to the core attributes of regulatory excellence. By constantly striving to achieve the highest levels of integrity, empathy, and competence, the leaders of regulatory institutions can meet their goals and continue improving their organizations' performance.

REFERENCES

Admin. Conf. of the U.S. (ACUS). 2017. Recommendation 2017-6, Learning from Regulatory Experience, 82 Fed. Reg. 61738 (December 29, 2017).
Alm, James and Jay Shimshack. 2014. "Environmental Enforcement and Compliance: Lessons from Pollution, Safety, and Tax Settings." *Foundations and Trends in Microeconomics* 10, no. 4 (December 2014): 209–274.
Ayres, Ian and John Braithwaite. 1992. *Responsive Regulation: Transcending the Deregulation Debate.* Oxford: Oxford University Press.
Baldwin, Robert, Martin Cave, and Martin Lodge. 2012. *The Oxford Handbook of Regulation.* Oxford: Oxford University Press.

Barber, Michael. 2015. *How to Run a Government So That Citizens Benefit and Taxpayers Don't Go Crazy*. Westminster: Penguin Press UK.

Bardach, Eugene and Robert A. Kagan. 1982. *Going by the Book: The Problem of Regulatory Unreasonableness*. Philadelphia: Temple University Press.

Berk, Richard. 2009. "Forecasting Consumer Safety Violations and Violators." In *Import Safety: Regulatory Governance in the Global Economy*, edited by Cary Coglianese, Adam M. Finkel, and David Zaring, 131–150. Philadelphia: University of Pennsylvania Press.

Bowles, Chester. 1971. *Promises to Keep: My Years in Public Life, 1941–1969*. New York: Harper & Row Publishers.

Braithwaite, John. 1982. "Enforced Self-Regulation: A New Strategy for Corporate Crime Control." *Michigan Law Review* 90, no. 7 (June 1982): 1466–1507.

Breyer, Stephen. 1982. *Regulation and Its Reform*. Cambridge: Harvard University Press.

Cairney, Paul, Tanya Heikkila, and Matthew Wood. 2019. *Making Policy in a Complex World*. Cambridge: Cambridge University Press.

Carrigan, Christopher and Elise Harrington. 2015. Choices in Regulatory Program Design and Enforcement. University of Pennsylvania, Philadelphia, PA, June 2015. https://www.law.upenn.edu/live/files/4706-carriganharrington-ppr-researchpaper062015pdf.

Coglianese, Cary. 2008. "The Managerial Turn in Environmental Policy." *NYU Environmental Law Journal*, 17(54).

Coglianese, Cary. 2009. "The Transparency President? The Obama Administration and Open Government." *Governance: An International Journal of Policy, Administration, and Institutions* 22, no. 4: 529–544.

Coglianese, Cary. 2010. "Management-Based Regulation: Implications for Public Policy." In *Risk and Regulatory Policy: Improving the Governance of Risk*, OECD, 159–183. Paris: OECD Publishing.

Coglianese, Cary. 2012a. "Enhancing Public Access to Online Rulemaking Information." *Michigan Journal of Environmental & Administrative Law* 2, no. 1: 1–66.

Coglianese, Cary. 2012b. "Measuring Regulatory Performance: Evaluating the Impact of Regulation and Regulatory Policy." OECD Expert Paper no. 1, Paris, www.oecd.org/gov/regulatory-policy/1_coglianese%20web.pdf.

Coglianese, Cary. 2015. *Listening, Learning, Leading: A Framework for Regulatory Excellence*. Philadelphia: Penn Program on Regulation.

Coglianese, Cary. 2016. "The Challenge of Regulatory Excellence." In *Achieving Regulatory Excellence*, edited by Cary Coglianese: 1–19. Washington, D.C.: Brookings Institution Press.

Coglianese, Cary. 2017. "The Limits of Performance-Based Regulation." *University of Michigan Journal of Law Reform* 50, no. 3: 525–563.

Coglianese, Cary. 2018. "Optimizing Regulation for an Optimizing Economy." *Journal of Law and Public Affairs* 4, no. 1: 1–13.

Coglianese, Cary. 2020a. "Law as Scapegoat." In Maria De Benedetto, Nicola Lupo & Nicoletta Rangone, eds., *The Crisis of Confidence in Legislation*. Oxford: Hart Publishing, pp. 337–365.

Coglianese, Cary. 2020b. "Obligation Alleviation During the COVID-19 Crisis." *Regulatory Review*, https://www.theregreview.org/2020/04/20/coglianese-obligation-alleviation-during-covid-19-crisis/.

Coglianese, Cary. 2020c. *A Framework for Governmental Use of Machine Learning*. Report to the Administrative Conference of the United States.

Coglianese, Cary and Lori S. Bennear. 2012. "Flexible Approaches to Environmental Regulation." In *The Oxford Handbook of U.S. Environmental Policy*, edited by Sheldon Kamieniecki and Michael E. Kraft, 582–604. Oxford: Oxford University Press.

Coglianese, Cary, Heather Kilmartin, and Evan Mendelson. 2009. "Transparency and Public Participation in the Rulemaking Process: Recommendations for the New Administration." *George Washington Law Review* 77, no. 4: 924–972.

Coglianese, Cary and David Lazer. 2003. "Management-Based Regulation: Prescribing Private Management to Achieve Public Goals." *Law & Society Review* 31, no 4: 691–730.

Coglianese, Cary and Gary Marchant. 2004. "Shifting Sands: The Limits of Science in Setting Risk Standards." *University of Pennsylvania Law Review* 152, no. 4: 1255–1360.

Coglianese, Cary and Jennifer Nash. 2017. "The Law of the Test: Performance-Based Regulation and Diesel Emissions Control." *Yale Journal on Regulation* 34, no. 1: 33–90.

Coglianese, Cary and André Sapir. 2017."Risk and Regulatory Calibration: WTO Compliance Review of the U.S. Dolphin-Safe Tuna Labeling Regime." *World Trade Review* 16, no. 2: 327–348.

Coglianese, Cary, Gabriel Scheffler, and Daniel Walters. 2021."Unrules." *Stanford Law Review* 73: 885–967.

Coglianese, Cary, Richard Zeckhauser, and Edward A. Parson. 2004. "Seeking Truth for Power: Informational Strategy and Regulatory Policymaking." *Minnesota Law Review* 89: 277–341.

Engstrom, David Freeman, Daniel E. Ho, Catherine M. Sharkey, Mariano-Florentino Cuéllar. 2020. *Government by Algorithm: Artificial Intelligence in Federal Administrative Agencies*. Washington, D.C.: Administrative Conference of the United States.

Finkel, Adam M. and Dominic Golding. 1994. *Worst Things First?: The Debate over Risk-Based National Environmental Priorities*. Washington, D.C.: Resources for the Future.

Finkel, Adam M., Daniel E. Walters, and Angus Corbett. 2018. "Planning for Excellence: Insights from an International Review of Regulators' Strategic Plans." *Pace Environmental Law Review* 35, no. 2: 240–291.

Goulder, Lawrence H. and Ian W. H. Parry. 2008. "Instrument Choice in Environmental Policy." *Review of Environmental Economics and Policy* 2, no. 2: 152–174.

Gray, Garry C. and Susan S. Silbey. 2014. "Governing Inside the Organization: Interpreting Regulation and Compliance." *American Journal of Sociology* 120: 96–145.

Gray, Wayne B. and Ronald J. Shadbegian. 2005. "When and Why Do Plants Comply? Paper Mills in the 1980s," *Law and Policy* 27, no. 2: 238–261.

Gunningham, Neil. 2016. "Compliance, Enforcement, and Regulatory Excellence." In *Achieving Regulatory Excellence*, edited by Cary Coglianese, 188–206. Washington, D.C.: Brookings Institution Press.

Gunningham, Neil, Robert A. Kagan, and Dorothy Thornton. 2003. *Shades of Green: Business, Regulation, and Environment*. Palo Alto: Stanford University Press.

Hawkins, Keith.1984. *Environment and Enforcement: Regulation and the Social Definition of Pollution*. Oxford: Clarendon Press.

Hino, Miyuki, Elinor Benami, and Nina Brooks. 2018. "Machine Learning for Environmental Monitoring." *Nature Sustainability* 1: 583–588.

Howard-Grenville, Jennifer, Stephanie Bertels, and Brooke Boren. 2015. *What Regulators Need to Know About Organizational Culture*. Philadelphia: Penn Program on Regulation.

Howard-Grenville, Jennifer, Jennifer Nash, and Cary Coglianese. 2008. "Constructing the License to Operate: Internal Factors and Their Influence on Corporate Environmental Decisions." *Law & Policy* 30: 73–107.

Hutter, Bridget M. 2001. *Regulation and Risk: Occupational Health and Safety on the Railways*. Oxford: Oxford University Press.

Hutter, Bridget M. 2016. "A Risk Regulation Perspective on Regulatory Excellence." In *Achieving Regulatory Excellence,* edited by Cary Coglianese, 101–114. Washington, D.C.: Brookings Institution Press.

Hutton, Deirdre. 2015. *The Role of Stakeholder Relationships in Regulatory Excellence*. Penn Program on Regulation. https://www.law.upenn.edu/live/files/4727-hutton-keynote-address-penn-law-2015pdf.

King, Gary, Robert O. Keohane, and Sidney Verba. 1994. *Designing Social Inquiry: Scientific Inference in Qualitative Research*. Princeton: Princeton University Press.

Kovacic, William E. 2009. *The Federal Trade Commission at 100: Into Our 2nd Century*. Washington, D.C.: FTC. https://www.ftc.gov/sites/default/files/documents/public_statements/federal-trade-commission-100 -our-second-century/ftc100rpt.pdf.

Lambert, Thomas A. 2017. *How to Regulate: A Guide for Policymakers*. Cambridge: Cambridge University Press.

Levi-Faur, David. 2012. *Handbook on the Politics of Regulation*. Cheltenham, UK and Northampton, MA, USA: Edward Elgar Publishing.

Levine, David I., Michael W. Toffel, and Matthew Johnson. 2012. "Randomized Government Safety Inspections Reduce Worker Injuries with No Detectable Job Loss." *Science* 336, no. 6083: 907–911.

Malesky, Edmund and Markus Taussig. 2019. "Participation, Government Legitimacy, and Regulatory Compliance in Emerging Economies: A Firm-Level Field Experiment in Vietnam." *American Political Science Review* 113, no. 2: 530–551. doi:10.1017/S0003055418000849.

Marchant, Gary E., Braden R. Allenby, and Joseph R. Herkert, eds. 2011. *The Growing Gap Between Emerging Technologies and Legal-Ethical Oversight: The Pacing Problem*. London: Springer.

Moore, Mark H. 1995. *Creating Public Value: Strategic Management in Government*. Cambridge: Harvard University Press.

Moore, Mark H. 1997. "The Legitimation of Criminal Justice Policies and Practices." In *Perspectives on Crime and Justice: Lecture Series*. 1996–97, Volume 1, National Institute of Justice, 46–74. Washington, D.C.: U.S. Department of Justice, Office of Justice Programs.

Nash, Jennifer and Daniel E. Walters. 2015. *Public Engagement and Transparency in Regulation: A Field Guide to Regulatory Excellence*. Philadelphia: Penn Program on Regulation.

National Academy of Public Administration. 2020. *Building on Agile Federal Government: A Call to Action*. Washington, D.C.: Project Management Institute.

National Academy of Sciences. 2018. *Designing Safety Regulations for High-Hazard Industries*. Washington, D.C.: National Academies Press.

Newell, Richard G. and Robert N. Stavins. 2003. "Cost Heterogeneity and Potential Savings from Market-Based Policies." *Journal of Regulatory Economics* 23, no. 1: 43–59.

OECD. 2005. *OECD Guiding Principles for Regulatory Quality and Performance*. Paris: OECD Publishing. https://www.oecd.org/fr/reformereg/34976533.pdf.

OECD. 2017. *Working with Change: Systemic Approaches to Public Sector Challenges*. Paris: OECD Publishing. https://doi.org/10.1787/9789264279865-en.

OECD. 2020. *OECD Best Practice Principles for Regulatory Policy: Regulatory Impact Assessment*. Paris: OECD Publishing. https://doi.org/10.1787/7a9638cb-en.

Paoli, Greg and Anne Wiles. 2015. *Key Analytical Capabilities of a Best-in-Class Regulator*. Penn Program on Regulation. https://www.law.upenn.edu/live/files/4710-paoliwiles-ppr-researchpaper062015pdf.

Richards, Kenneth R. 2000. "Framing Environmental Policy Instrument Choice." *Duke Environmental Law and Policy Forum* 10, no. 2: 221–282.

Richards, Kenneth R. and Josephine van Zeben. 2020. *Policy Instruments in Environmental Law*. Cheltenham, UK and Northampton, MA, USA: Edward Elgar Publishing.

Rosenbloom, David H. and Richard D. Schwartz. 1994. *Handbook of Regulation and Administrative Law*. New York: M. Dekker.

Sant'Ambrogio, Michael and Glen Staszewski. 2021. "Democratizing Rule Development." *Washington University Law Review* 98, no. 3: 793–856.

Schauer, Frederick. 2015. *The Force of Law*. Cambridge: Harvard University Press.

Schein, Edgar H. 2010. *Organizational Culture and Leadership*, 4th ed. San Francisco: Jossey Bass.

Scholz, John T. 1984. "Cooperation, Deterrence, and the Ecology of Regulatory Enforcement." *Law & Society Review* 18, no. 2: 179–224.

Simon, Herbert A. 1947. *Administrative Behavior: A Study of Decision-Making Processes in Administrative Organization*. New York: Macmillan Co.

Sommers, Roseanna and Vanessa K. Bohns. 2019. "The Voluntariness of Voluntary Consent: Consent Searches and the Psychology of Compliance." *Yale Law Journal* 128, no. 7: 1962–2033.

Sparrow, Malcolm K. 2000. *The Regulatory Craft: Controlling Risks, Solving Problems, and Managing Compliance*. Washington, D.C.: Brookings Institution Press.

Sparrow, Malcolm K. 2008. *The Character of Harms: Operational Challenges in Control*. Cambridge: Cambridge University Press.

Sunstein, Cass R. 1990. *After the Rights Revolution: Reconceiving the Regulatory State*. Cambridge: Harvard University Press.

Thornton, Dorothy, Neil A. Gunningham and Robert A. Kagan. 2005. "General Deterrence and Corporate Environmental Behavior." *Law and Policy* 27, no. 2: 262–288.

Tyler, Tom R. 2003. "Procedural Justice, Legitimacy, and the Effective Rule of Law." *Crime and Justice* 30: 283–357.

van Rooij, Benjamin and S. Daniel Sokol. 2021. *The Cambridge Handbook of Compliance*. Cambridge: Cambridge University Press.

Wilson, James Q. 1989. *Bureaucracy: What Government Agencies Do and Why They Do It*. New York: Basic Books.

Zerbe, Richard O. and McCurdy, Howard E. 1999. "The Failure of Market Failure." *Journal of Policy Analysis and Management* 18, no. 4, 558–578.

20. Better regulation in the European Union[1]

Claire A. Dunlop and Claudio M. Radaelli

BETTER REGULATION IN THE EUROPEAN UNION (EU): PAST, PRESENT AND FUTURE

Calls for a strategy to improve the quality of the rules produced by the European Union (EU) date back to the early 1990s. During the last thirty years, this strategy has emerged in waves, with the labels of 'high quality legislation' and 'better regulation'. Since the early 2000s, this agenda has gradually taken its role in the EU policy process, especially at the stage of policy formulation (with the tools of consultation and impact assessment) and, in the last decade, with attempts to include other stages of policy process with tools for the retrospective review of legislation and regulatory offsetting. Better regulation is an overall commitment binding the EU institution (with the inter-institutional agreement on better law-making agreed in 2016)[2] and the Member States. The reality on the ground is that the Commission has deployed the tools of better regulation more intensively than the European Parliament and (even more so) the Council. Member States and the Commission are not always on the same page when it comes to the choice and specification of how to use the tools, and whether the political aim is to improve on regulatory quality or to reduce the quantity of rules.

For all these nuances and political differences, today, better regulation is a formally endorsed working method of the European Commission (2019a). In the near future, the challenges concern the integration of foresight, the connection between different phases of the EU policy process (what in Commission's parlance is known as 'closing the policy cycle', Mastenbroek et al. 2016), and policy coherence for sustainability (Renda 2019).

In this chapter, we outline the foundations of better regulation by reviewing the historical record tracing the main episodes. Specifically, we cover: the 1992 Edinburgh summit to the Mandelkern Report of 2001, the Prodi Commission's package on regulatory reform, impact assessment and consultation, the dialogue between the Council and the Commission on setting targets for administrative burdens, the rise of regulatory oversight first with the Impact Assessment Board (2007) and then with the Regulatory Scrutiny Board (RSB), the Juncker–Timmermans vision for better regulation and the commitment to regulatory off-setting of the von der Leyden Commission. With the foundations laid, we conclude exploring what lies ahead.

FOUNDATIONS

The EU is a political system with a comparative advantage in the production of regulatory policy (Majone 1996), with implications for both regulation in the Member States and the EU as global regulatory power (Bradford 2020). This raises the challenge of governing the EU regulatory system. The challenge has two sides: trust and effectiveness. Bad regulation implies that citizens and firms do not consider the EU institutions trustworthy. It can also negatively affect growth and corruption, provide the wrong regulatory responses to health and financial crises, and impose unnecessary burden on firms and citizens.

However, the exact specification of what 'bad' and 'good' regulation is is far from straightforward. In the abstract, we can think that good EU regulation should pass the dual tests of effectiveness and trustworthiness (see Baldwin and Cave [1999] for other academic benchmarks). In more concrete terms, the concept of regulatory quality and the so-called better regulation strategy of the EU have been the territory of ideational confrontation between the European Commission and the Member States, and between the EU institutions and different stakeholders (including business groups and civil society organizations). There has been consensus too, since it is objectively hard to 'fight' something called 'better regulation' – after all, who wants 'worse regulation'?

And so, the devil is often in the detail. Indeed, the presence of calls for, and the emergence of, strategies dedicated to better regulation since the 1990s has been the empirical manifestation of how an equilibrium between various political/economic preferences and ideas have been found, challenged and re-defined. This is because underneath the surface of ideational confrontations on this topic lies the definition of who is in control of the process of formulation, implementation, and evaluation of the EU regulatory system.

To define these variables means to define power and control in the law-making and implementation processes of the EU. Thus, better regulation is the terrain where fundamental power relations are constantly tested in concrete ways. We are thinking of power relations such as institutional balance, the right of the Commission to initiate legislation, and the regulatory discretion of Member States and independent regulators. As for the concrete ways, think of the deployment of tools in everyday policy-making: the quality of proposed regulations can be appraised in terms of different and not totally overlapping standards, such as foresight and risk assessment, cost–benefit analysis, and reduction of administrative burdens; the degree of transparency in the use of science in the *ex ante* assessments of proposed legislation can vary depending on whether one is following a hazard or risk-oriented goal; the independence of the EU-level regulatory oversight body has been the subject of intense discussions and gradual change of membership; customization when Member States transpose and implement legislation demands tight connections between the EU-level and the domestic usage of appraisal tools; the criteria deployed in the ex post evaluation of legislation cover a broad range; the interventions of the EU system of courts in topics like the publication of impact assessments for proposals that had been withdrawn by the Commission define and constrain some important choices; and; the control relationship between the Secretariat General of the Commission (SECGEN) and the Directorates General (DG) which is marked by the specific *modus operandi* of the impact assessment teams inside the bureaucratic engine of the EU.

How did the EU get to play on this political terrain of power relations and tools? It is useful to start with the major player in the formulation of proposals for EU regulation: the European Commission. Equally useful is to take the long view and go back to the 1990s. Since its origins, the Commission has been a hierarchical organization, vertically segmented into sections (the Directorates General, DGs) with slight capacities for horizontal intra-organizational regulatory management, the control of implementation structures (which limit the role of the Commission by design) across sectors and levels of governance. Further, while several Member States embarked on administrative reforms to increase their analytical and organizational capacity in the 1990s, the Commission was definitively a late-comer (on those years see Stevens and Stevens 1996; Stevens 2001). Unsurprisingly then, the early concerns for the quality of EU regulation were expressed by the Member States. This happened at the Edinburgh European Council (1992), with Germany, the Netherlands (Koopmans Report 1995) and the United Kingdom (which hosted Edinburgh) in the driving seat. Business federations were also supportive of new policies to increase the transparency of policy formulation in Brussels and for simplification of the regulatory environment (Radaelli 1999).

Edinburgh was the first agenda-setting moment for better regulation in the EU. But, it took a decade for the agenda-setting moment to become a strategy. After Edinburgh, an idea floated by the French Conseil d'Etat, taken up by the Koopmans Report and pushed (unsuccessfully) by the Dutch EU Presidency at the inter-governmental conference in 1997 was to create a body of 'guardians of the rules' (an independent review body) that would one day take the shape of a 'European Conseil d'Etat'. The spectacular resignation of the Santer Commission in 1999 strengthened the argument for a properly portfolio-structured Commission.

These events and debates were not sufficient to turn the agenda-setting moment into a single strategy in the 1990s. Instead, a patchwork approach to simplification and improvement of legislation emerged. The Commission set up a task force to do the simplification job: the Business Environment Simplification Task Force (BEST). BEST focused on the administrative and fiscal constraints on recruitment of new staff, training, access to research and technology and relations with credit and finance institutions. Instruments for the *ex ante* analysis of legislative proposals were timidly introduced in the 1990s, including checklists, rules of procedure, a legislative drafting manual, and a compendium on 'information, communication and openness'. The DGs retained high autonomy when handling the checklists, and co-ordination across services remained low. Policy evaluation remained limited to financial controls only.

A series of studies and initiatives matched simplification as goal with small and medium enterprises (SMEs) as target population. During these years the 'think small first' regulatory philosophy appeared, with the idea of thresholds below which proposed regulations would not apply, or specific derogations for SMEs (Schulte-Braucks 1997; Kellermann et al. 1998). A 'business test panel' was launched in 1998 to have participating firms assist the Commission in the assessment of the regulatory burdens. The overall impact of these initiatives on SMEs remained weak (Dannreuther 1999; Radaelli 1999). Simplification was also the conceptual foundation of the 1996 SLIM initiative (European Commission 1996). This was a pilot with limited effects (Radaelli 1999).

Taken together, the proposals, pilots and checklists failed to produce a coherent response to the challenge of governing the EU regulatory system or to increase the capacity for horizontal coordination of proposals and vertical coordination of implementation structures. The Commission reacted to the pressure of the Edinburgh summit, and the follow-up declarations and requests by the Member States, by engaging with many different instruments (the patchwork) without embracing a single template for the assessment of proposals (in particular, a regulatory impact assessment system). Neither did the Commission clarify the role of stakeholders in policy formulation. Consultation was tried in SLIM but never extended to proper, transparent, duly enforced standards of notice and comment. Finally, the SECGEN did not build capacity for overall coordination of the proposals emerging from the DGs.

After a decade, the Member States applied renewed pressure on the Brussels executive. The European Commission as an institution was recovering from the political scandal of the resignation of the Santer Commission. This new wave of calls for regulatory reform beyond the then existing efforts for simplification appeared in the so-called Mandelkern report (Mandelkern Group on Better Regulation 2001) published in November 2001. This report specifically addressed the Commission asking for a comprehensive policy on regulatory reform, including consultation, regulatory impact assessment, and the consideration of alternatives to traditional command and control regulation. Mandelkern went as far as to propose a deadline asking the Commission to 'propose by June 2002 a set of indicators of better regulation' (Mandelkern Group on Better Regulation 2001: iii and 59).

The Commission wanted to go further than a response to the Mandelkern report. Given the status and the newly found ambition of the institution under Prodi, the Brussels bureaucracy put forward its integrated approach, drawing on its own foundational principles of governance as enshrined in the White Paper on Governance (European Commission 2001) as well as on OECD good practice. The 2002 Commission Communication was the first strategic document tackling better regulation comprehensively (European Commission 2002). It included standards on consultation (then codified in the same year, 2002) to allow stakeholders to make an input in policy formulation, and to open up the policy process to evidence and expertise via regulatory impact assessment (RIA). The latter was based on a single impact assessment template to appraise policy proposals. This single template is still in use today at the Commission.

The RIA system of the Commission is original because it revolves around the three dimensions of economic, environmental and social effects of the proposals being appraised – this way the three major internal stakeholders left their imprint on the template (Allio 2007, 2008). Indeed, inside the Commission, impact assessment emerged as a compromise among the major players in EU regulation: the SECGEN and the DGs in charge of enterprise, environmental policy and social/labour market regulation (Allio 2008).

Thus, Member State pressure aside, the identification of a Commission's strategy was fundamental in refracting and re-balancing the roles and capacity of different organizational universes (DGs and Sec Gen). As Radaelli and Meuwese show (2010, p.142), the process of creating and finalizing RIAs established 'a focus for strategic and operational management within the Secretariat General' and a limitation of the silos mentality that prevailed until then. In the first decade of the 2000s, the SECGEN mutated from a *primus inter pares* with loose coordination capacity to something like a cabinet office (Radaelli and Meuwese 2010). Among other things, this explains why in the first decade of the 2000s the profile of better regulation within the SECGEN rose year-after-year, as did its capacity to steer the impact assessment steering groups inside the Commission (Radaelli and Meuwese 2010). The intention of the Commission was to lock-in these foundations of regulatory reform with a system of regulatory performance indicators. However, around 2003–2004 the Commission lost the support of the UK and the Netherlands, two countries that were most interested in experimenting with tools for the reduction of administrative burdens (Radaelli 2020).

In the Netherlands, the then Finance Minister Gerrit Zalm was championing a basic approach to measure the cost of administrative obligations – something that was miles away from the conceptual rigor (and complexity) of impact assessment. This tool is the standard cost model (SCM) (Coletti 2013, 2016). The Dutch had started using it by setting departmental *targets* for the reduction of administrative burdens. In the UK, the then Chancellor Gordon Brown became persuaded that the war on red tape was more attractive and business-friendly than a sophisticated system of regulatory indicators for the EU and its Member States. The *Less is More* Report, a report to the British Prime Minister by the Better Regulation Task Force (2005) was indicative of the new direction pursued by the Labour government.

A divide emerged: on one hand there was, the broad, governance-inspired vision of the Commission. On the other there was the Dutch and British-led de-regulatory, war on red tape vision, inspired by the desire to show that the government was doing something rele-vant for business (for these positions and added remarks on the role of Germany see Gravey 2016). A second divide emerged between the Commission and the other EU institutions. The 'better regulation' vision was supposed to bind the Council, the European Parliament and the Commission with the 2003 inter-institutional agreement on better regulation (OJ C321 31Dec 2013). This agreement was never operational on the ground however, showing that the commitment to impact assessment and evidence-based policy was not entirely shared by the EP and the Council.

Let us consider the Council first and then the EP. For the Council, better regulation was a strategy to make the Commission more accountable to the Member States and the business community through enhanced transparency, consultation and oversight of the treaty-defined right of the Commission to initiate legislation. The Member States were concerned about leaving the better regulation strategy in self-piloting mode, by this we mean entirely self-checked by the Commission. They pushed for the establishment of a regulatory oversight body, similar to the oversight bodies featuring in the Netherlands and the UK in the same period. The Commission reasoned that the introduction of an oversight body would be a good way to enhance the credibility of the better regulation strategy. But, yet again the devil in the detail, the Commission wanted this body staffed by its officers: a Commission-staffed Impact Assessment Board (IAB) appeared in 2007.

Only in 2015, was the IAB turned into a Regulatory Scrutiny Board (RSB) with three members from the Commission and three temporary agents recruited externally, and a chair from the Commission ranked at the level of Director General. Although in terms of staffing, the RSB is half-independent and half-not, de facto its behaviour has been independent (Radaelli 2018). The 2020 decision of the Commission (European Commission 2020) emphasized that the RSB does not take political instructions from the Commission, its working method is to check whether RIAs and evaluations are based on a sufficiently robust evidence base.

With the same decision, the RSB was instructed to include foresight in its mandate and to widen its operations to the scrutiny of the 'one-in, one-out' initiative (OIOO). Already an established feature of regulatory offsetting (Trnka and Thuerer 2019) in the UK (introduced in 2010) and Germany (in 2015) (see Renda 2019 Table A for a summary of OIOO[3] approaches across the then EU-28), the OIOO principle aims to bear down on the cost and volume of regulation in the economy and society. And so, where legislative proposals create new burdens – on businesses or citizens – an equivalent existing burden in the same policy area should be removed. In 2019, OIOO was adopted as part of the working methods of the von der Leyen Commission's drive to reduce red tape.

Turning to the EP, impact assessments were a new way to make the Commission account-able to parliamentary committees, and indeed in the 2010s the EP increased its capacity in critically appraising the RIAs and *ex post* legislative evaluations of the Commission – with a substantial strengthening of its research service (European Parliament Research Service [EPRS]) (Radaelli 2018). Never on the radar, at least in the 2000s, the proposition that the Council and the EP would become more accountable by taking better regulation commitments seriously. In the 2010s, the EP showed more political attention for its own RIA of amendments introduced during the legislative procedure by the MEPs and for *ex post* legislative evaluations (Radaelli 2018). However, even today the EP deploys more officers and brainpower in scru-tinizing the RIAs of the Commission rather than checking on the quality of its own appraisals of substantive amendments.

RECENT TRENDS

In May 2015 (European Commission 2015), the Juncker Commission re-calibrated better regulation by: setting the goal of closing the policy cycle, that is, making *ex post* evaluation as activity to precede any work on new proposals (the so-called 'evaluate first' principle); enhancing the flow of consultations involving stakeholders at different stages of the policy cycle; re-defining the IAB into a stronger and more independent scrutiny body (the RSB we mentioned above); finalizing a new inter-institutional agreement on better law-making (OJ L 123 vol.59, 12 May 2016); publishing a single set of methodological templates for better regulation activities (a toolbox running above 400 pages, re-adjusted in summer 2017); and finally, withdrawing proposals (Radaelli 2018 on the controversies raised by this last point). By taking the decision to embark on both systematic ex post evaluation and making evaluation the first step in the planning of new legislation, the Commission set a very high bar (Zwaan et al. 2016). The choice for consultation reveals the attempt to seek more legitimacy for policy formulation directly from stakeholders (Bozzini and Smismans 2016; Bunea 2017; Bunea and Ibenskas 2017).

As for regulatory oversight, today all RSB members work full-time, are bound to the principle of collective responsibility and enjoy a mandate that, with the 2020 additions mentioned above, is wider than that of the IAB, covering RIA, major *ex post* regulatory evaluations and fitness checks of existing legislation, and implementing and delegated acts (plus one-in-one-out and foresight as per the 2020 decision).

Some would prefer a regulatory oversight body with no Commission officials. For the Commission, instead, opinions on the quality of impact assessments of proposed initiatives should remain a component of the treaty right to initiative legislation. Inside the Berlaymont, the RSB is a fundamental component of the internal process of monitoring and learning – that is, the policy conversation among the SECGEN, the DGs, and the Commissioners (Senninger and Blom-Hansen 2020).

The Commission published a mid-term review of the better regulation agenda (European Commission 2017) and a taking-stock communication in 2019 (European Commission 2019b) supported among other things by in-house interviews (that is, carried out within the Commission) and a literature review (Listorti et al. 2019). The main achievements are the strong emphasis on consultation, the role of RIA in policy formulation, the attempts made to include *ex post* legislative evaluation into the policy cycle, and the RSB capacity to handle different types of scrutiny. On stakeholders engagement, the OECD indicators of regulatory policy and governance rank the Commission ahead of all the 27 Member States (and with a slight edge on the UK). The OECD composite indicators for RIA confirm the EU in position number 1 (OECD 2019). In both cases (consultation and RIA) the EU outperforms the OECD average by a large margin (OECD 2019).

Simplification has been carried out by the platform called REFIT[4] – whose mandate was to check that the legislation in force is still fit for purpose). The methodological robustness and timing of the *ex post* legislative evaluations provide ample room for improvement, but to be fair this is a relatively new component in the better regulation agenda in Europe, and the practice of the Commission does not lag behind the average Member State. Certainly, the quality and timing of evaluations are key to the goal of closing the policy cycle.

CHALLENGES

In terms of the better regulation horizon, we focus on the ways in which strategic challenges at the EU level play out not only in the blue skies of policy vision statements but also their coherence on the ground at particular stages of the policy process – most importantly, formulation, implementation and evaluation. This interaction between the big picture and the operational is of course where we find our perennial questions of ideational confrontation and institutional power politics.

Starting with the broad brush, the von der Leyen Commission's will have to grapple with some considerable challenges. Notable among these is how OIOO will work in practice. Despite its commitment to OIOO, up until the time of finalizing this chapter (March 2022), the Commission has lacked a robust and consistent guiding framework for its application. Critical questions found upstream in the policy-making – how burdens are defined, the limits of offsetting and what constitutes equivalence in administration costs – remain in the eye of the beholder. While the fit-for-future (F4F) expert platform (that replaces REFIT) offers a potential first step in giving these ideas concrete form, the initiative remains in its infancy. And for a platform dedicated to the future (F4F), it is odd that the main emphasis remains on burdens rather than a broader focus on dynamic efficiency and innovation.

A second big picture challenge that intersects with the ambiguity surrounding OIOO is the European Green Deal (European Commission 2019c). At its launch, Commissioner Timmermans presented the environmental ambition of the deal as akin to the medical hypocritic oath first 'do no harm'. Environmental campaigners have been keen to highlight its potential incompatibility of reducing regulatory burdens while safeguarding the environment (Green 10 2019). Just how the Commission will negotiate these tensions on the ground – fashioning new guidelines and policy formulation tools that balance sustainability issues in the least burdensome ways – remains to be seen. Think tanks close to the business community have also asked the Commission to be explicit in adopting better regulation principles in the Green Deal – indicating that so far they have not seen empirical evidence that this is the case (ERF 2020).

The realization of the 'Green Oath' also links to the EU's preferred understanding of precaution and harm and, critically, how these can be measured in a consistent and transparent way. In terms of the two flagships initiatives, the Green Deal and the Digital Single Market, there are still differences between Member States and the Commission on whether precaution or innovation is the best foundation for regulatory choice. Or, if neither innovation nor precaution should be ranked first in every case, how should they be balanced in everyday RIA, evaluations, policy appraisal?

The Competitiveness Council has endorsed the innovation principle as fundamental for the flagship initiatives of the EU but the Commission has so far preferred to consider innovation a perspective, or a means to the end of a sustainable Union – not a foundation of regulatory choice (Taffoni 2020). In these conditions, the subtle yet crucial differences of meanings (between national delegations and the Commission) on the concrete interpretation of slogans like 'regulating for innovation' (Taffoni 2020) reveal a new turn of the power struggle about who controls the EU policy process.

The absence of the UK from this struggle because of Brexit takes one pro-innovation principle and pro-deregulation voice off the table, although the UK was never alone inside the Competitiveness Council. The call for more 'regulation for innovation' in terms of sandboxes, sunset clauses, flexible pro-innovation regulatory environments is as present as before Brexit. The major impact of Brexit on better regulation will be in the domain of regulatory alignment.[5]

Considering the EP, the extent to which the EP's right of initiative is enhanced through the Better Regulation agenda is very much a 'live' issue. Upon her election as Commission President by the EP, von der Leyen confirmed her commitment to extending the EP's right with 'a legislative act in full respect of the proportionality, subsidiarity and better law-making principles' (von der Leyen 2019). That would take the EP power beyond its current role (agreed in the 2016 Interinstitutional Agreement [IIA] on Better Law-Making) where, for example, it can press the Commission to respond to requests for further evidence at any stage of the legislative process.

The nexus between innovation and regulation is also crucial for the recovery and resilience plan. The plan is not just about injecting financial resources in the ailing economy. It is about projects that will have to show how to rekindle growth via sustainable innovation. Here the main responsibility lies with the governments in the 27 Member States – it is there that the projects are initially appraised and chosen.

The pandemic has exposed the limitations of EU better regulation in terms of foresight, overall policy coherence and sustainability. There are twin challenges of inevitable economic aftermath of COVID-19 and shifting power balances in the post-Brexit EU. Both of these huge issues interact with more prosaic questions concerning the scope of EU-oriented better regulation activities in the Member States themselves. The extent to which the approaches of 27 governments align to EU level aspirations is an ongoing theme, of course. But, in a context of post-pandemic fiscal tightening and with Brexit removing one of the key cheerleaders, these questions of compliance become more significant. Previous research demonstrates that while tools such as stakeholder engagement and impact assessment have become popular both in the EU policy cycle and in domestic Better Regulation policies, underneath this process of diffusion lies a difference in the purposes and usages of the tools (Radaelli 2009). The extent to which first this variation of practice persists and second these carry consequences for an integrated approach require robust empirical research.

Arguably the most pressing challenges are to integrate foresight and the sustainable development goals in the vision and policy tools. The 2021 Communication of the Commission makes reference to these two dimensions. Questions arise about the overall coherence of the agenda portrayed in the Communication (Radaelli 2021): the flagship policy initiatives for the ecological transition, the digital economy and resilience are geared towards long-term welfare, yet OIOO is a commitment that neglects benefits (Sunstein 2020). The sustainable development goals can be operationalized in RIA by embracing and integrating the impacts on gender, distribution, poverty, environment, and health. Indeed, there are methodologies on how to integrate gender (Gains 2017; Staronova et al. 2017), social effects (Schrefler 2017; Vanclay 2020), energy (Torriti 2017), agriculture (Russel 2017), and health (Green et al. 2020) in a single RIA template – although practice has not as yet caught up with these methods.

The sustainable development goals (SDG) – we argue – should become the metrics to measure coherence and integration between the tools. The foresight dimension introduced in the RSB mandate in 2020 and reiterated by the 2021 Communication has potential. But, it should be operationalized taking on board the Agenda 2030 for sustainable development, that is, beyond the life of the present Commission. The SDGs are also promising indicators to measure the overall policy coherence[6] and the real-world progress achieved in terms of outcomes. If the causal theory behind better regulation is that robust evidence-based tools improve on the life-cycle of regulations, the capacity to manage the life-cycle should be traceable in the quality of the rules and their impact on the SDGs with the 2030 target in sight (for more information on regulatory agencies in the European context see also Chapters 3 and 9).

NOTES

1. Research for this chapter was funded by the European Research Council (ERC) project Procedural Tools for Effective Governance (PROTEGO) http://protego-erc.eu/ Grant no. 694632.
2. https://eur-lex.europa.eu/legal-content/EN/TXT/PDF/?uri=CELEX:32016Q0512(01)&from=PT accessed 29 January 2021.
3. More accurately, Renda (2019) adopts the terminology one-in X-out (OIXO) to reflect the fact that in recent years OIOO has expanded in some places to two- and three-out for any new 'in'.
4. https://ec.europa.eu/info/law/law-making-process/evaluating-and-improving-existing-laws/refit-making-eu-law-simpler-less-costly-and-future-proof_en accessed 29 January 2021.
5. The reference is to TITLE X (of the Brexit agreement) on Good Regulatory Practices and Regulatory Cooperation. https://ec.europa.eu/transparency/regdoc/rep/1/2020/EN/COM-2020-857-F1-EN-ANNEX-1-PART-1.PDF accessed 29 January 2021.
6. At the UN Environment Programme (2020) there is already work under way on indicators of policy coherence. Interestingly, this methodology refers the presence of sustainable development dimensions and goals in RIA.

REFERENCES

Allio, Lorenzo. 2007. 'Better regulation and impact assessment in the European Commission.' In Colin H. Kirkpatrick and David Parker (Eds.), *Regulatory Impact Assessment: Towards Better Regulation?* Edward Elgar Publishing.
Allio, Lorenzo. 2008. 'The Emergence of Better Regulation in the European Union.' PhD dissertation. King's College. University of London.
Baldwin, Robert, and Cave, Martin. 1999. *Understanding Regulation.* Oxford: Oxford University Press.
Better Regulation Task Force. 2005. Less is More: Reducing Burdens, Improving Outcomes. A Report to the British Prime Minister. https://www.regulation.org.uk/library/2005_less_is_more.pdf.
Bozzini, Emanuela and Smismans, Stijn. 2016 'More inclusive European governance through impact assessments?' *Comparative European Politics* 14(1): 89–106.
Bradford, Anu. 2020. *The Brussels Effect: How the European Union Rules the World.* Oxford: Oxford University Press.
Bunea, Adriana. 2017. 'Designing Stakeholder Consultation: Reinforcing or Alleviating Bias in the European Union System of Governance?' *European Journal of Political Research* 56(1): 46–69.
Bunea, Adriana and Ibenskas, Raimondas. 2017. 'Unveiling Patterns of Contestation over Better Regulation Reforms in the European Union.' *Public Administration* 95(3): 589–604.
Coletti, Paola. 2013. *Evidence for Public Policy Design.* Pivot. Palgrave Macmillan.
Coletti, Paola. 2016. 'Standard Cost Model.' In Claire A. Dunlop and Claudio M. Radaelli (Eds), *Handbook of Regulatory Impact Assessment.* Cheltenham, UK and Northampton, MA, USA: Edward Elgar Publishing.
Dannreuther, Charlie. 1999. 'Discrete Dialogues and the Legitimation of EU SME Policy.' *Journal of European Public Policy* 6(3): 436–55.
European Commission 1996. The SLIM Initiative: Communication from the Commission to the Council and the European Parliament. Brussels, 6 November 1996. COM(96) 559 Final.
European Commission. 2001. European Governance – a White Paper. Luxembourg: Office for Official Publications of the European Communities.
European Commission 2002. Action Plan for Better Regulation. COM(2002) 278. 5 June 2002.

European Commission 2015. Better Regulation for Better Results: An EU Agenda. Brussels, COM(2015) 215 Final, 19 May 2015.

European Commission 2017. Completing the Better Regulation Agenda: Better Solutions for Better Results. Brussels, COM(2017) 651 Final, 24 October 2017.

European Commission 2019a. Communication: The Working Methods of the European Commission. Brussels, 1 December 2019. https://ec.europa.eu/info/sites/info/files/working-methods.pdf.

European Commission 2019b. Communication: Better Regulation – Taking Stock and Sustaining our Commitment. Brussels. https://ec.europa.eu/info/sites/info/files/better-regulation-taking-stock_en_0 .pdf.

European Commission 2019c. The European Green Deal. Brussels, COM(2019) 640 Final.

European Commission 2020. Decision of the President of the European Commission on an Independent Regulatory Scrutiny Board. Brussels, 23 January 2020. P(2020) 2.

European Commission 2021. Better Regulation: Joining Forces to Make Better Laws. Communication from the European Commission. April 2021.

European Risk Forum (ERF). 2020. Better Regulation and the Green Deal. https://www.eriforum.eu/ uploads/2/5/7/1/25710097/erf_highlights_13_-_green_deal_and_br.pdf.

Gains, Francesca. 2017. 'Gender and RIA.' In Claire A. Dunlop and Claudio M. Radaelli (Eds), *Handbook of Regulatory Impact Assessment*. Cheltenham, UK and Northampton, MA, USA: Edward Elgar Publishing.

Gravey, Viviane. 2016. 'Does the European Union have a reverse gear? Environmental policy dismantling, 1992–2014.' PhD Dissertation, University of East Anglia. https://ueaeprints.uea.ac,uk/id/eprint/ 59419/.

Green, Liz, Gray, Benjamin J and Ashton, Kathryn. 2020. 'Using Health Impact Assessments to Implement the Sustainable Development Goals in Practice: A Case Study in Wales.' *Impact Assessment and Project Appraisal* 38(3): 214–224.

Green 10. 2019. Why the European Parliament Should Reject the Commission Proposed 'One in, one out' Principle, 13 September https://green10.org/wp-content/uploads/2019/09/Green-10-reaction-on -_one-in-one-out_-principle_13-Sept-2019.pdf.

Kellermann, A.E., Ciavarini-Azzi, G., Jacobs, S. and Deighton-Smith, R. (Eds) 1998. *Improving the Quality of Legislation in Europe*. Kluwer Law International (co-publication with T.M.C. Asser Instituut, The Hague).

Koopmans Report 1995. *The Quality of EC Legislation. Points for Consideration and Proposals*. The Hague.

Listorti, Giulia, Bastye Ferrari, E., Acs, S., Munda, G., Rosenbaum, E., Paruolo, P. and Smits, P. 2019. 'The Debate on the EU Better Regulation Agenda: A Literature Review.' In *The Debate on the EU Better Regulation Agenda: A Literature Review*, JRC Science for Policy Report.

Majone, Giandomenico. 1996. *Regulating Europe*. London: Routledge.

Mandelkern Group on Better Regulation 2001. Final Report. Brussels. https://www.smartreg.pe/ reportes/Mandelkern%20Report%20on%20Better%20Regulation%202001.pdf.

Mastenbroek, Ellen, van Voorst, Stijn and Meuwese, Anne. 2016. 'Closing the Regulatory Cycle? A Meta Evaluation of Ex-Post Legislative Evaluations by the European Commission.' *Journal of European Public Policy* 23(9): 1329–48.

OECD. 2019. *Better Regulation Practices across the EU-28*. Paris: OECD Publications.

Radaelli, Claudio M. 1999. 'Steering the Community Regulatory System: The Challenges Ahead.' *Public Administration* 77(4): 855–71.

Radaelli, Claudio M. 2009. 'Measuring Policy Learning: Regulatory Impact Assessment in Europe.' *Journal of European Public Policy* 16(8): 1145–64.

Radaelli, Claudio M. 2018. 'Halfway through the Better Regulation Strategy of the Juncker Commission: What Does the Evidence Say?' *Journal of Common Market Studies* 56(S1): 85–95.

Radaelli, Claudio M. 2020. 'Regulatory Indicators in the European Union and the Organisation for Economic Co-operation and Development: Performance Assessment, Organizational Processes, and Learning.' *Public Policy and Administration* 35: 227–46.

Radaelli, Claudio M. 2021. 'The State of Play with the Better Regulation Strategy of the European Commission.' STG Policy Papers, 2021/6, April, School of Transnational Governance, EUI, Florence. https://cadmus.eui.eu/handle/1814/70901.

Radaelli, Claudio M., and Meuwese, A.C.M. 2010. 'Hard Questions, Hard Solutions: Proceduralisation through Impact Assessment in the EU.' *West European Politics* 33: 136–53.

Renda, Andrea. 2019. Feasibility Study: Introducing 'One-In-One-Out' in the European Commission, 5 December. Brussels: Centre for European Policy Studies.

Russel, Duncan, 2017. 'Agriculture.' In Claire A. Dunlop and Claudio M. Radaelli (Eds), *Handbook of Regulatory Impact Assessment*. Cheltenham, UK and Northampton, MA, USA: Edward Elgar Publishing.

Senninger, Roman, and Blom-Hansen, Jens. 2020. 'Meet the Critics: Analyzing the EU Commission's Regulatory Scrutiny Board through Quantitative Text Analysis.' *Regulation & Governance* 15(4): 1436–53.

Schulte-Braucks, R. 1997. European Commission's Business Impact Assessment, Presentation delivered to the Conference on the Quality of European and National Legislation and the Internal Market, TMC Asser Instituut, The Hague, 23–25 April. Reprinted in Kellermann et al. 1998.

Schrefler, Lorna. 2017. 'Social Impact Assessment.' In Claire A. Dunlop and Claudio M. Radaelli (Eds), *Handbook of Regulatory Impact Assessment*. Cheltenham, UK and Northampton, MA, USA: Edward Elgar Publishing.

Staronova, Katarina, Hejzlarová, Eva and Hondlíková, Krisytyna 2017. 'Making Regulatory Impact Assessment Gender Sensitive: The Case of the Czech Republic and Slovakia.' *Transylvanian Review of Administrative Sciences* 51: 89–105.

Stevens, Anne and Stevens, Handley 1996. The Non-Management of Europe, Paper prepared for the 8th conference on the Europeanization of Public Policy, Paris, 20–21 June.

Stevens, Anne 2001. *Brussels Bureaucrats? The Administration of the European Union*. Basingstoke: Palgrave.

Sunstein, Cass 2020. On Neglecting Regulatory Benefits. https://papers.ssrn.com/sol3/papers.cfm?abstract_id=3541782.

Taffoni, Gaia. 2020. 'Regulating for Innovation? Insights from the Finnish Presidency of the Council of the European Union.' *European Journal of Risk Regulation* 11(1): 141–47.

Torriti, Jacopo. 2017. 'Energy.' In Claire A. Dunlop and Claudio M. Radaelli (Eds), *Handbook of Regulatory Impact Assessment*. Cheltenham, UK and Northampton, MA, USA: Edward Elgar Publishing.

Trnka, Daniel and Thuerer, Yola 2019. 'One-in, X-Out: Regulatory Offsetting in Selected OECD Countries.' OECD Regulatory Policy Working Papers, No. 11. Paris: OECD Publishing, Reprint.

United Nations Environment Programme. 2020. Methodology for SDG Indicator 17.14.1: Mechanisms in place to enhance policy coherence for sustainable development. New York: United Nations.

Vanclay, Frank. 2020. 'Reflections on Social Impact Assessment in the 21st Century.' *Impact Assessment and Project Appraisal* 38(2): 126–131.

von der Leyen, Ursula. 2019. Opening Statement in the European Parliament Plenary Session. 16 July 2019. https://ec.europa.eu/commission/presscorner/detail/en/SPEECH_19_4230.

Zwaan, P., van Hoorst, S. and Mastenbroek, E. 2016. 'Ex Post Legislative Evaluation in the European Union: Questioning the Usage of Evaluations as Instruments of Accountability.' *International Review of Administrative Sciences* 82(4): 674–93.

21. Better regulation in the United States

Susan Dudley and Jerry Ellig

THE U.S. CONTEXT

Three overlapping waves of regulatory reform have sought to improve regulatory outcomes in the U.S.: economic deregulation, regulatory impact analysis (RIA) of new regulations, and retrospective analysis of existing regulations. This chapter explains each of these initiatives, summarizes results to date, and identifies remaining challenges.

In the U.S. federal system, the federal government regulates goods and services that affect interstate commerce, while state governments have jurisdiction over intrastate commerce. Federal and state constitutions establish separation of powers between the legislative, executive, and judicial branches.

Many regulatory agencies are subordinate to the head of the executive branch. Some federal agencies – generally headed by multi-member commissions nominated by the president and confirmed by the Senate – have greater independence, usually because the president can only remove the commissioners for "cause" (which does not include policy disagreements). These "independent" agencies tend to be more responsive to the legislature than to the executive, so they are not as independent as independent regulators in parliamentary systems.

These institutional characteristics have several implications for U.S. regulatory policy:

- Significant statutory reforms require consent of both the legislature and the executive.
- When regulatory agencies have discretion under the law to change policies, the president can direct such policy change. However, such changes must follow the rules of the Administrative Procedure Act.
- The president's primary influence over independent agencies is the ability to nominate commissioners and designate the chair. Presidents have exerted more control over executive branch agencies through RIA requirements and executive oversight.
- Key regulatory decisions affecting intrastate commerce are under state rather than federal jurisdiction. Others, including many environmental and occupational policies, require cooperation between the federal and state governments.

ANALYTICAL CONCEPTS AND RESULTS

Economic Deregulation

The first wave of reform removed price, entry, exit, and quality of service regulations in transportation, energy, and communications industries. Safety, environmental, and antitrust regulation remained in place.

Foundational concepts

Four economic concepts provided the intellectual underpinnings for economic deregulation: market power, contestability, economic efficiency, and public choice.

A firm has market power when it can profitably raise price above marginal cost. Economic regulation ostensibly exists to prevent the exercise of market power. However, entry restrictions in potentially competitive industries create market power. Much of the case for economic deregulation rested on economic research showing that regulation indeed created market power (Green and Nader 1973).

Contestability theory identifies when *potential* competition can prevent the exercise of market power, even if the incumbent firm is a monopoly. Several deregulated markets, such as individual airline, truck, and bus routes, were thought to be highly contestable. In industries like telecommunications, natural gas, and electricity, reformers sought to promote contestability by ensuring that competitors could access facilities that involved sunk costs, such as local phone lines, pipelines, and electric wires.

Competitive or contestable markets lead to *allocative* efficiency: every unit of every resource is employed in the use that consumers value most highly. Removing restraints on competition also promoted *dynamic* efficiency. Dynamic efficiency occurs when firms discover new ways to reduce costs, improve productivity, and offer new products or services that consumers value.

Public choice theory recognizes that government decision-makers often face incentives to pursue objectives other than economic efficiency. Under the capture theory, the regulator advances the interests of the regulated industry (Stigler 1971). The economic theory of regulation posits that the regulator strikes a compromise that reflects the relative political strength of various stakeholders (Peltzman 1976). The study of rent-seeking reveals that regulation creates wealth transfers, concentrated interests expend resources to capture those wealth transfers, and those expenditures represent social waste (Buchanan, Tollison, and Tullock 1980).

Implementation

Most economic deregulation required legislation, such as the Airline Deregulation Act (1978) that phased out federal regulation of air fares and entry on individual routes, and abolished the Civil Aeronautics Board (CAB) as of 1985; the Natural Gas Policy Act (1978) and Natural Gas Wellhead Decontrol Act (1989) that removed well-head price controls; or the Motor Carrier Act (1980) that deregulated interstate trucking rates and entry on individual routes.

The communications industry also saw significant reforms via litigation. For most of the twentieth century, AT&T held a legal monopoly on long-distance telephone service. In 1969, the FCC allowed MCI to build a private network for long-distance services. MCI started offering long-distance service in competition with AT&T, and the FCC belatedly tried to protect AT&T's monopoly. In MCI v. FCC (1977), the Supreme Court held that the FCC had never explained why a long-distance monopoly was in the public interest. In 1982, the Modified Final Judgment in US v. AT&T separated AT&T into a national company that sold long-distance phone service, information services, and telecommunications equipment – all subject to competition – and seven regional holding companies that had monopolies on wireline local phone services.

Regulators were far from passive actors. CAB Chairmen John Robson (1975–77) and Alfred Kahn (1977–78), and Interstate Commerce Commission Chairmen Daniel O'Neal (1977–79) and Darius Gaskins (1980–81), advocated for deregulation and liberalized regulation of airlines, trucking, and railroads under their agencies' existing authority. Deregulation of natural gas prices at the wellhead created a glut of cheap gas. The Federal Energy Regulatory Commission (FERC) responded with Orders 436 (1985) and 636 (1992), which transformed interstate pipelines from merchants who bought and sold gas under long-term contracts to transportation companies who moved gas purchased by others.

When a federal antitrust suit broke AT&T into separate long-distance and local phone companies in 1982, the FCC devised a system of per-minute charges paid by long-distance companies to replace the implicit subsidies that existed when AT&T was an integrated company. Recognizing the inefficiencies created by these charges, the FCC gradually reduced them over the next three decades. In a series of proceedings beginning in 1966, the FCC also developed its distinction between pure communications service that can be regulated as a common carrier, and "enhanced" services that involve data processing and remain unregulated. This distinction provided the foundation for the FCC's declared policy of "unregulation" of the Internet.

Results

By 1993, deregulation-induced efficiency improvements were equivalent to a 7–9% increase in GDP produced by the deregulated industries, and consumers received most of the benefits (Winston 1993). This estimate does not include the substantial effects of additional liberalization in communications and energy since 1993. Below, we summarize the principal results from empirical studies.

Price levels

In most cases, deregulation reduced overall prices below the level that would have existed if regulation had remained in place. Deregulation saved airline passengers about $12.4 billion annually ($1993) (Morrison and Winston 1995). Between 1982 and 1996, inflation-adjusted average freight rail rates fell by 46%, and rates for individual commodities fell by 29–56%. Deregulation contributed at least one-third of this reduction (Ellig 2002). By 1985, trucking deregulation was associated with a 3% reduction in truckload rates and a 17% reduction in less-than-truckload rates. That saved shippers about $6.8 billion per year ($1977) (Winston et al. 1990). When the last price controls on natural gas were lifted in 1985, gas prices began a decade-long decline. In the nine years after the AT&T breakup, interstate long-distance rates net of federally-mandated access charges fell from 13.8 cents per minute to 7.5 cents per minute (Crandall and Waverman 1996).

The most dramatic price change, however, occurred in wireless voice communications. In 1994–95, the FCC auctioned spectrum licenses for personal communications services, enabling two additional entrants to challenge the existing cell phone duopoly in each market. Cell phone revenue per minute plummeted from more than 80 cents in 1992 to 4 cents in 2008, generating $212 billion in consumer surplus annually (Hazlett 2017).

In a few cases, deregulation produced price increases, usually due to market design flaws or other idiosyncrasies. The 1984 Cable Act, for example, pre-empted local regulation of basic cable rates but did little to eliminate cable monopolies, so basic cable rates increased. Nevertheless, because dynamic efficiencies led cable companies to add channels and sub-scribership continued to rise, Hazlett (1997) suggests that consumers were better off under unregulated monopoly than regulated monopoly. Electricity restructuring in California led to significant price spikes and utility bankruptcies because utilities were required to buy power in day-ahead spot markets vulnerable to manipulation. Price increases initially followed electricity competition in Texas, because retail prices were aligned more closely with marginal costs – primarily the cost of natural gas. After a transition period, full implementation of competition in Texas was associated with lower electric prices (Hartley, Medock, and Jankovska 2019).

Price structure

Deregulation tended to align prices more closely with costs. Thus, less-than-truckload rates fell by more than truckload rates, long-distance air fares fell by more than short-distance air fares, and natural gas prices declined more for large customers than for small customers. Electricity competition in Texas initially lowered rates for industrial customers but not for residential customers. Pricing freedom also allowed some industries to set prices that more closely reflected customers' different elasticities of demand; this was especially significant for airlines and railroads (Schmalensee et al. 2015).

Telephone deregulation involved more complicated rate changes. Long-distance competition made it difficult for regulators to subsidize local service with revenues from long-distance. As a result, regulated local telephone rates rose by 3.3% annually between 1983 and 1989 (after the AT&T breakup), then resumed falling (Crandall and Ellig 1997). As per-minute charges on long-distance fell, the associated annual welfare loss dropped from $10–17 billion ($1996) in the mid-1980s (Crandall 1991) to $2.5–7.0 billion in the mid-1990s ($1996) (Crandall and Waverman 2000) to $1.5 billion in 2002 ($2002) (Ellig 2006).

In response to the Telecommunications Act of 1996, the FCC required all elements of the local network be made available to competitors as a package at discounts much larger than the wholesale discount the FCC had previously established for leasing the local network. Some studies estimated that these discounts produced lower rates for customers, but for a service that was already cross-subsidized and sold below cost! Long-distance companies and new entrants invested in lobbying for low lease rates instead of building their own local networks. Most of these competitors collapsed after 2005, when the FCC reversed course. Competition for local phone service ultimately came from voice over Internet and wireless phones (Beard et al. 2016).

Costs and productivity

Removal of price and entry regulations increased competition, pushing prices closer to marginal cost (allocative efficiency). But much of the customer savings occurred from dynamic efficiency because deregulated firms reduced costs and improved productivity. Removal of entry restrictions on individual routes allowed airlines and trucking companies to develop "hub-and-spoke" systems that reduced costs and facilitated greater frequency of service. Interstate natural gas pipelines interconnected at "market hubs" that gave customers access to multiple suppliers and created an integrated, national market for natural gas. Deregulation increased railroad productivity by 6–7% annually from 1981 to 1988, and reduced costs per revenue ton-mile by 41–44% by 1989 (Wilson 1997).

Growth in total factor productivity in the telecommunications industry accelerated after the FCC allowed some competition in long-distance after 1970. Crandall (1991) estimated that the value of productivity improvements due to liberalization during the 1980s totaled $6.4 billion-$16.6 billion ($1988). Mergers of broadcasting stations after the Telecommunications Act of 1996 relaxed ownership restrictions reduced costs by more than $2.8 billion, increased industry revenues by almost $2 billion, and increased viewership slightly – results consistent with an overall improvement in economic efficiency (Stahl 2016).

Wasteful nonprice competition had dissipated most of the rents airlines received from pricing above cost on long-haul routes. The deregulated airlines offered lower fares combined with more crowded flights, less elaborate meals, fewer flight attendants, and in general fewer perks.

Some of the cost reductions in deregulated industries occurred because fewer rents were shared with labor, but the extent and form this change took varied by occupation and by industry. In trucking, for example, deregulation reduced the wage gap between Black and white truck drivers by creating new opportunities for Black drivers to enter the previously-regulated (and more lucrative) for-hire portion of the industry (Heywood and Peoples 1994). Reduced entry barriers and increased competition more than doubled the likelihood that a trucker would be an owner-operator instead of an employee (Peoples and Peteraf 1995).

Service quality

In some industries, the dynamic efficiency generated by deregulation improved service quality. By 1985, railroads reduced delivery times by almost 30%, and variance in delivery time declined even further. This increased shipper welfare by $2 billion to $6 billion annually (in $1977) (Winston et al. 1990). Speedier trucking service saved shippers almost $1 billion annually by 1985 (Winston et al. 1990). Deregulation allowed truckers to offer service guarantees, which made just-in-time manufacturing possible. Wellhead price regulation created widespread natural gas shortages and service curtailments in the 1970s (MacAvoy 1971); deregulation made gas service more reliable by ending these curtailments. Cable companies that face competition from other wireline cable companies or satellite TV tended to improve customer service, increase their bandwidth, offer more channels, and upgrade more quickly to digital transmission (Hazlett 2006). Removal of price regulations on cable TV is associated with price increases but also with increases in the number of available channels (Beard et al. 2001). Meanwhile, the absence of content regulation for cable TV, satellite TV, and the Internet led to an explosion of new niche video content. FCC policies that "unregulated" the Internet facilitated migration from dialup Internet service to broadband.

Arguably the most significant improvement in the quality of service occurred in wireless communications. The FCC's decision to auction spectrum for "personal communications," with no further specification of the type of service to be offered, enabled the introduction of the Blackberry in the 1990s and the iPhone in 2007, followed by millions of online apps.

Airline deregulation had a more mixed effect on service quality, but it aligned quality more closely with consumer preferences. Fare savings far outweighed the value consumers attributed to reductions in other aspects of quality, and greater flight frequency increased consumer welfare by $10.3 billion annually ($1993) (Morrison and Winston 1995).

Regulatory Impact Analysis

Since the mid-1970s, presidents have required executive branch agencies to conduct RIAs before issuing regulations with annual impacts of $100 million or more. President Clinton's executive order (E.O.) 12866 has guided executive agencies' practices since 1993.

An RIA organizes evidence about the effects of alternatives to identify whether the benefits of a proposed action are likely to justify the costs and discover which alternative is likely to be most cost-effective. The Office of Management and Budget (OMB) observes that "regulatory analysis also has an important democratic function; it promotes accountability and transparency and is a central part of open government" (OMB 2011).

Foundational concepts

OMB's guidance identifies three basic elements of a good RIA: (1) "a statement of the need for the regulatory action," (2) "a clear identification of a range of regulatory approaches," and (3) "an estimate of the benefits and costs—both quantitative and qualitative—of the proposed regulatory action and its alternatives" (OMB 2011).

Statement of Need

E.O. 12866 directs agencies to identify the problem a rule is intended to address and assess its significance. The concept of "market failure" is important here. Market economies rely on competition and price signals to allocate scarce resources to their most valued uses, to encourage innovation, and to satisfy consumer needs. Because government regulation can disrupt those signals, the first step in an RIA is an explanation of why market outcomes are less efficient than what government regulations could be expected to accomplish (Dudley et al. 2017). The order refers to "material failures of private markets," which include (1) externalities, public goods, and common property resources, (2) market power, and (3) inadequate or asymmetric information (OMB 2003). It also directs agencies to be alert for "failures of…public institutions," such as poorly defined property rights or barriers imposed by existing policies.

Even when a regulation addresses a problem other than private market failures – to improve the efficiency of government programs, protect certain rights, or achieve distributional goals – the RIA is still essential for identifying the most cost-effective way to achieve the goal.

Consideration of alternatives

A good RIA examines viable alternative approaches to achieving regulatory goals, evaluates them objectively, and presents them to decision-makers to inform policy actions. E.O. 12866 directs agencies to identify and assess available alternatives to direct regulation, such as antitrust enforcement, consumer-initiated litigation in the product liability system, or administrative compensation systems.

OMB directs agencies, when they choose to regulate, to evaluate alternative forms of regulation. In general, market-based and performance-oriented approaches are preferable to command-and-control standards, because they are likely to achieve desired goals at lower social costs (OMB 2003).

President Obama's E.O. 13563 (2011) emphasizes flexibility, encouraging agencies to consider "warnings, appropriate default rules, and disclosure requirements as well as provision of information to the public in a form that is clear and intelligible."

E.O. 12866 requires an assessment of the costs and benefits of reasonably feasible alternatives and an explanation of why the planned regulatory action is preferable. The number of alternatives explored in the RIA is a matter of judgment, but OMB encourages agencies to "explore modifications of some or all of a regulation's attributes or provisions to identify appropriate alternatives" (OMB, 2003).

Benefit–cost and cost-effectiveness analysis

E.O. 12866 directs agencies to "adopt a regulation only upon a reasoned determination that [its] benefits … justify its costs." By translating benefits and costs into monetary terms, benefit–cost analysis (BCA) allows comparisons of different regulatory options and endpoints. Comparing the incremental benefits and costs of regulatory alternatives (e.g., successively more stringent standards) can identify the alternative that maximizes net benefits (OMB 2003). For regulatory actions with the same primary endpoint, OMB guidance also finds that "cost-effectiveness analysis [CEA] can provide a rigorous way to identify options that achieve the most effective use of the resources available without requiring monetization of all of relevant benefits or costs" (OMB 2003). CEA examines the cost of achieving a unit of an outcome, such as a life-year gained.

Distributional analysis

President Biden emphasized the importance of considering distributional impacts "to ensure that regulatory initiatives appropriately benefit and do not inappropriately burden disadvantaged, vulnerable, or marginalized communities" (Biden 2021). E.O. 12866 requires agencies to consider distributive impacts and equity, directing them to minimize burdens on individuals, small businesses, small communities, and governmental entities. E.O. 13563 encourages agencies to "consider (and discuss qualitatively) values that are difficult or impossible to quantify, including equity, human dignity, fairness, and distributive impacts."

Circular A-4 requires RIAs to analyze distributive impacts separately from the BCA (OMB 2003). It thus recognizes that distributive impacts are important information, but it does not treat distribution as a benefit or a cost.

Implementation

E.O. 12866 includes procedural steps that reinforce its analytical requirements. The order applies to all "significant" executive agency regulations. U.S. agencies issue about 4,000 regulations a year, 300 of which are considered significant. About 40 of those are "economically significant" – that is, they meet the $100 million-per-year threshold.

Independent regulatory agencies are not subject to most presidential E.O.s, including E.O. 12866. However, some authorizing statutes either explicitly require economic analysis or include language that courts interpret as requiring some analysis of regulatory impacts before issuing regulations.

Centralized executive oversight

E.O. 12866 gives the Office of Information and Regulatory Affairs (OIRA) in OMB responsibility for reviewing all significant proposed and final regulations. This gatekeeper function provides an important incentive for agency compliance with the order's analytical requirements. OIRA coordinates interagency disputes on regulation, liaises with White House officials to ensure regulations are consistent with presidential policies, and reviews RIAs according to the principles in E.O. 12866 and RIA guidance, especially Circular A-4.

As an aggregator of information and perspectives across the executive branch, OIRA serves an essential coordinating function in an expansive bureaucracy made up of myriad narrow-mission entities. Its staff of about 60 career professionals with backgrounds in economics, law, public policy, statistics, and science enforces E.O. 12866 principles and provides a "dispassionate and analytical 'second opinion'" on agencies' analysis (Obama 2009). Its location in the Executive Office of the President gives the staff unusual access to political officials and adds weight to its recommendations. White House political staff rely on the expertise, institutional knowledge, and cross-cutting perspective of OIRA's career professionals.

Legislative and statutory motivations

Presidential directives have been the main impetus for regulatory analysis. Congress has required agencies to develop estimates of the costs and benefits of regulations involving large expenditures through the Unfunded Mandates Reform Act (1995) and of those likely to have a significant economic impact on a substantial number of small entities through the Regulatory Flexibility Act (1980), but these statutes' coverage is limited.

Some statutes that authorize agency regulation may contain language suggestive of RIA. For example, the Securities and Exchange Commission must, by statute, consider efficiency, competition, and capital formation when determining "whether an action is necessary or appropriate in the public interest." Recent court decisions have found some SEC regulations to be "arbitrary and capricious" because they failed to evaluate adequately a rule's economic impact (e.g., *Business Roundtable v. SEC*, 2011).

The federal courts increasingly interpret statutory language like the SEC's as requiring BCA (Noe and Graham 2020) and interpret vague statutory language as requiring some economic analysis (Mannix 2016).

Results

Executive branch agencies are more likely to conduct RIA than independent agencies not subject to presidential orders (Fraas and Lutter 2011a), suggesting the orders have had some effect. But comprehensive BCA is by no means the norm even for executive agencies. According to annual OMB reports to Congress, less than one-quarter of economically-significant regulations include monetized estimates of both benefits and costs.[1] About half (48%) are "transfer" regulations for which agencies only estimated the monetary amounts transferred between parties. For another 18%, agencies estimated only costs, while 3% only included estimated benefits and 6% estimated neither benefits nor costs.

Quality of RIAs

One way of evaluating RIA quality is to compare the benefits and costs predicted in the RIA with those actually achieved by the regulation. Relatively few such retrospective analyses exist. Studies that perform these comparisons disagree on whether benefits or costs are consistently over- or under-predicted (OMB 2005). OIRA's comparison of 47 *ex ante* and *ex post* studies of regulations found that in 11, the RIA's *ex ante* ratio of benefits to costs was accurate; in 22 cases, it was overestimated; and in 14 cases, it was underestimated (OMB 2005).

Other studies find that RIAs often fail to conform to E.O. principles and OMB guidance (Fraas and Lutter 2011b; Hahn and Dudley 2007; Ellig 2016). Some evidence suggests that agencies conduct more thorough analysis than they otherwise would because of RIA requirements and OIRA oversight (Bull and Ellig 2018; Ellig and Fike 2016). Political factors and agency ideology are associated with lower-quality analysis (Bull and Ellig 2018; Ellig and Fike 2016).

Quality of regulations

Published studies offer mixed evidence about the influence of RIAs on the quality of regulations. For example, agencies failed to explain how they used the RIA in 60% of the major regulations proposed between 2008 and 2013 (Ellig 2016). Surveying the available evidence, Hahn and Tetlock (2008) concluded that RIAs often have little influence, although they occasionally have affected marginal decisions involving large regulations. However, case studies by insiders identify numerous specific instances where well-done RIAs reduced costs, increased benefits, or introduced novel alternatives that improved regulations (e.g., Graham 2008).

Retrospective Analysis

While academics and policy practitioners agree about the value of retrospective regulatory analysis, it is much less common than *ex ante* analysis. It has generally focused on identifying burdensome or underperforming rules that might be revised or rescinded. While this is important, a life-cycle approach to retrospective review could focus attention on *ex post* evaluation of outcomes as well as costs to inform future *ex ante* analysis and improve regulatory outcomes (Dudley 2017).

Foundational concepts
Evaluation and feedback are essential for informed action and learning. Individually, we learn and modify our behavior based on experience. In business, successful firms continuously learn from market signals and experience, innovating to identify and satisfy unmet consumer needs, increase quality, improve operating efficiency, and better target potential customers. In the natural sciences, hypothesis testing is an essential feature of the experimental method, in which systematic observation, measurement, and empirical testing lead to revisions to the hypothesis and greater learning.

For public programs, retrospective analysis can be an important accountability tool, providing evidence necessary to evaluate the performance of government actions to determine how well they achieved desired outcomes (Gertler et al. 2011).

Evidence-based policy
Performance evaluation of government programs has a long history (see, e.g., Newcomer, Hatry, and Wholey 2015). The federal government's Commission on Evidence-Based Policymaking "envisions a future in which evidence is created efficiently, as a routine part of government operations, and used to construct effective public policy" (Commission on Evidence-Based Policymaking 2017, p. i). In the regulatory sphere, evidence-based policymaking implies systematic retrospective analysis of individual regulations and/or related groups of regulations. Retrospective analysis should be part of an integrated system that starts with a solid RIA to inform design of regulations, establishes clear performance metrics, plans for retrospective review, and then uses the results of that review to reassess the regulation.

Best practices for retrospective evaluation
While retrospective analysis is, by definition, done after a regulation is in effect, agencies should begin planning for the analysis when they first develop a regulation. By clearly identifying the problem the regulation is intended to address, laying out expected causal linkages between the regulatory intervention and desired outcome, and establishing a framework for empirical testing of assumptions and hypothesized outcomes, agencies can lay the groundwork for successful evaluation (Greenstone 2009). Early in the rulemaking process, governments "should describe the methods that they intend to employ to evaluate the efficacy of and impacts caused by the regulation, using data-driven experimental or quasi-experimental designs where appropriate" (Aldy 2014, p. 6).

Designing regulations from the outset in ways that allow variation in compliance (such as different compliance schedules in different regions, or small scale pilots) is essential if evaluators are to go beyond observing mere associations and gather data necessary to test hypotheses of the relationship between regulatory actions and outcomes (Greenstone 2009). Experimentation and competition among jurisdictions can be a powerful force for improving regulatory outcomes and developing a practical knowledge of what works.

In some cases, evaluation of individual rules to compare predicted costs and benefits may be appropriate. In others, examining a group of policies (including nonregulatory programs) aimed at achieving a particular outcome may be more valuable to decision makers.

Implementation

Presidents and Congress have directed agencies to analyze the effects of existing regulations; however, retrospective analysis has received much less attention and fewer resources than *ex ante* RIAs. E.O. 12866 directs each agency to "periodically review its existing significant regulations." Clinton's National Partnership for Reinventing Government directed agencies to eliminate or revise regulations that were outdated or needed reform (NPR 1995, Appendix D).

E.O. 13563 directs agencies to "consider how best to promote retrospective analysis of rules that may be outmoded, ineffective, insufficient, or excessively burdensome, and to modify, streamline, expand, or repeal them in accordance with what has been learned" and submit plans to OIRA for periodically reviewing significant regulations. Guidance implementing this order emphasized "the need for empirical assessment of the consequences of rules" (Sunstein 2011). In an attempt to "institutionalize regular assessment of significant regulations," Obama's E.O. 13610 directed agencies to "invite, on a regular basis…public suggestions about regulations in need of retrospective review and about appropriate modifications to such regulations."

An initiative that, in theory, could have incentivized retrospective evaluation was President Trump's regulatory budgeting requirements. E.O. 13771 required agencies to offset the costs of new regulations by removing existing burdens and eliminate two regulations for every new one issued. Trump also set up Regulatory Reform Task Forces within each agency to make recommendations for regulatory reforms (E.O. 13777). President Biden revoked both of these orders on his first afternoon in office (2021).

Results

Despite these directives, procedures for regulatory evaluation are not institutionalized to the extent *ex ante* RIA is. In 2005, OIRA noted that only a small fraction of major rules had been evaluated *ex post* (OMB 2005). Reviews of President Obama's initiatives reached a similar conclusion (Aldy 2014). The Clinton administration's regulatory review efforts undertaken as part of the National Partnership for Reinventing Government led to a 16,000-page reduction in the regulatory code (NPR 1995), and the number of regulatory restrictions (terms like "shall" and "must") fell by about 27,000 between 1995 and 1996 (McLaughlin and Strosko 2018). Though significant, this was a one-shot change that does not appear to have promoted retrospective analysis as an ongoing practice.

Some agencies' procedures incorporate retrospective review more than others. The National Highway Traffic Safety Administration in the Department of Transportation (DOT), in particular, publishes a regular schedule for reviewing existing regulations, and OIRA reports that its *ex post* estimates of regulatory impacts appear more accurate than other agencies' (OMB 2005). The regular data DOT collects on traffic accidents contribute to its ability to validate *ex ante* estimates (and improve future estimates). This points to the importance of committing to evaluation at the outset of a rulemaking. According to Aldy's analysis of U.S. practices, most economically-significant regulations are not designed to produce adequate data and enable causal inference of their effects (2014).

One of the greatest successes of retrospective economic analysis was the economic deregulation described in the first section of this chapter. Empirical research consistently demonstrated the consumer harms caused by existing price and entry regulations. Studies of policy reform routinely credit this research as a necessary (though not sufficient) factor in motivating change (Derthick and Quirk 1985; Robyn 1987). Research conducted in universities and think tanks was utilized by analytical offices in the federal government. This experience highlights the potential for rigorous retrospective analysis to improve public welfare.

CHALLENGES AND RECOMMENDATIONS

None of the three waves of regulatory reform described here is entirely complete. Both continue to face institutional and technical challenges.

Deregulation

Institutional
Pricing/investment in complementary infrastructure
Two of the deregulated industries – airlines and trucking – rely on complementary government-managed infrastructure that is rarely priced efficiently, and capacity is likely non-optimal. For example, Morrison and Winston (2000) estimated that limited availability of airport gates increased fares by $3.8 billion ($1998). The government has been slow to adopt new technologies that could expand runway and airspace capacity, and the U.S. lags behind many other countries in airport and air traffic control privatization.

Most highways in the U.S. are not directly priced, which leads to traffic congestion and reduces incentives to construct new capacity optimally. Winston and Shirley (1998) estimated that optimal toll pricing of highways would generate net benefits of $3.8 billion annually ($1998). The U.S. lags many other countries in granting highway concessions to leverage private capital and implement congestion pricing, but the number of new concessions, mostly funded through tolls, has accelerated in the past decade.

State or local barriers to entry
State or local governments still control entry in some segments of industries that were deregulated at the federal level. Two-thirds of the nation's electric load is in states where most customers still buy their power from monopoly utilities, even though the utilities can buy power from competitive suppliers in wholesale markets under federal jurisdiction. Similarly, some states still grant local gas utilities a monopoly over sales to some or all customer classes. Some states have enacted statewide cable franchising laws to enable competition; others leave the franchising decision to local governments.

Institutional memory

Economic deregulation has been reversed in a few cases where it appeared not to be working, such as price regulation of cable TV (deregulated in 1984, re-regulated in 1992, deregulated in 1996) and California's poorly-designed retail electricity restructuring. While there is little political impetus to reverse pro-competitive economic deregulation, this could change as policymakers and civil servants familiar with the results of deregulation in the 1980s and 1990s retire and are replaced by individuals with no firsthand knowledge of this history (Wilson and Klovers 2020).

Technical

Network economics

Most of the deregulated industries involve transportation of people, commodities, or communications signals over a network, which has several implications. First, even very large firms can consummate "end-to-end" mergers that extend the size of the network but may not eliminate much competition; most railroad, airline, and telecommunications mergers were of this type. Second, a network can simultaneously create market power and cost savings, so a complete analysis must account for the net effects on economic efficiency and consumer welfare. Third, a network firm may incur significant common costs to serve customers with different elasticities of demand, so the separate effects on multiple types of customers must be taken into account when assessing mergers or the state of competition.

Policies to control residual market power

Some markets, such as airline routes, have not been perfectly contestable. Economists disagree as to whether this is caused primarily by airlines' own business practices or by policies that discourage efficient allocation and investment in complementary infrastructure. No credible economist, however, has proposed reimposition of pre-1978 rate and route regulations as a solution.

In some cases, firms exercise significant market power over a subset of customers, and new entry is unlikely. Shippers served by a single railroad who lack intermodal competition are one example. Because railroads can tailor rates to individual shippers, high rates paid by captive shippers are unlikely to create economic inefficiency due to output restriction (Schmalensee et. al 2015). Equity concerns and political pressures, however, mean that some type of residual rate regulation will likely remain in place. The challenge is to design and implement such regulation so that it does not hamper innovation and dynamic efficiency.

Another type of residual market power exists when decision-makers choose to leave some element of the network monopolized, such as electric wires or gas pipelines. The challenges here are to design regulation that allows innovation (such as incentive regulation) and prevents the monopolist from interfering with competition (usually by requiring it to divest competitive functions), but also keeps open the possibility that technological change could introduce competition (as occurred in telephony and cable TV).

RIA

Institutional

While presidents have required RIA, most statutes are silent on whether regulations should be based on BCA, and some have been interpreted as precluding a weighing of costs against benefits (Mannix 2016). Greater congressional or judicial scrutiny will be key to improving the quality and use of analysis.

Institutional constraints within agencies can affect RIA quality. Agencies face incentives to demonstrate that the benefits of their desired actions exceed the costs. Agencies usually seek public input on regulatory analysis and alternatives toward the end of a rulemaking process, after important decisions have been made.

Technical
Frequently, agencies analyze a selected alternative, with inadequate consideration of the compelling public need for regulation or alternative approaches to achieving goals. Rather than anecdotal observations that illustrate *symptoms* of a problem, agencies should clearly articulate the underlying *cause* of those symptoms if they are to identify effective solutions.

Determining the proper scope of the analysis can be challenging, in terms of number of alternatives considered, time frame, and indirect benefits and costs. While no RIA will be comprehensive, they should select a set of viable alternatives, and be objective and balanced in selecting what benefits and costs to include (Dudley and Mannix 2018).

An RIA is only as good as the data and studies on which it relies, and obtaining reliable information is challenging, especially when addressing uncertain future problems or for new products, services, or technologies (Dudley et al. 2019).

For regulations intended to reduce human health or environmental risks, scientific risk assessments are critical inputs, yet these are rarely provided in probabilistic terms. Current approaches can lead to misaligned priorities because the degree of precaution differs across risks (Gray and Cohen 2012).

Retrospective Analysis

More rigorous retrospective evaluation could address some of the challenges with *ex ante* analysis. RIAs conducted before a regulation is in place rely on informed guesses about how the world would look absent the regulation, and how responses to regulatory requirements will alter those conditions. Better retrospective review would allow those hypotheses to be tested against actual outcomes. However, *ex post* analysis also poses challenges, both institutional and technical.

Institutional
Agencies do not have strong incentives to evaluate existing regulations. OIRA review motivates them to conduct RIAs for new regulations, but once a regulation is issued, the consequence of not conducting *ex post* analysis is that a regulation remains in place. This asymmetric incentive structure is compounded because regulated parties – motivated to prevent a potentially burdensome regulation from being implemented – may have less incentive to work to remove an existing regulation. Having invested in compliance, incumbents gain a competitive advantage and are less likely to support evaluation that may lead to changes or repeal (Dudley 2017).

In theory, a regulatory budget that makes the issuance of new regulations contingent on finding a regulatory offset could provide incentives for agencies to evaluate both the costs and effectiveness of existing programs (Dudley 2017). However, *ex post* evaluation takes time and resources, and actually changing a regulation can take years, something presidents do not have in one term.

Technical
Once a regulation is in place, it is not obvious what counterfactual would best describe the state of the world without it. Measuring opportunity costs (the value of activities or innovations foregone to achieve regulatory goals) is challenging, as is measuring regulatory benefits (e.g., changes in health outcomes that cannot reliably be attributed to the action). Understanding causal linkages from observational data may require more information on intermediary effects than agencies have.

Developing an evaluation plan when a rule is first issued and committing to gathering the data needed for evaluation might address some of these technical issues. When possible, designing regulations from the outset in ways that allow variation in compliance would provide natural experiments from which to learn. The successful economic deregulation discussed above relied on such natural experiments. Intrastate airline fares not subject to federal rate-setting authority were markedly lower than interstate fares, providing a powerful counterfactual for what interstate prices could be with more competition. Similarly, the Interstate Commerce Commission did not regulate trucking rates for agricultural products, and they were substantially lower than rates for manufactured products.

CONCLUSION

As U.S. regulation has increased over the last 50 years, so have efforts to ensure those regulations serve the public interest. The experience of three waves of regulatory reform reinforces the importance of recognizing institutional as well as technical factors that may affect outcomes. The U.S. experience suggests that significant reforms require action by the legislative, executive, and judicial branches, and may require engagement at the state, as well as federal, level. The economic deregulation of the 1970s and 1980s enjoyed bipartisan support from all branches of government and created lasting positive impacts by increasing competition, encouraging innovation, and lowering consumer prices. In contrast, *ex ante* and *ex post* RIA, largely driven by executive branch requirements, have had more mixed effects. The greatest institutional challenges to better regulation are motivating agencies to conduct impartial assessments of viable alternatives before making decisions and to revisit their regulatory decisions *ex post*.

The greatest technical challenge to better regulation is data. Designing regulations so they can later be evaluated, including allowing variations that generate natural experiments, may be critical to ensuring more evidence-based policies going forward (for more information on regulatory agencies in the U.S. context see Chapter 2).

NOTE

1. These annual OMB reports are available at https://www.whitehouse.gov/omb/information -regulatory-affairs/reports/#ORC.

REFERENCES

Aldy, J. (2014). Learning from experience: An assessment of the retrospective reviews of agency rules and the evidence for improving the design and implementation of regulatory policy. A report for the Administrative Conference of the United States. https://www.acus.gov/report/retrospective-review -report

Beard, T. R., Ekelund, R. B., Ford, G. S., & Saba, R. S. (2001). Price-quality tradeoffs and welfare effects in cable television markets. *Journal of Regulatory Economics, 20*(2), 107–123. https://doi.org/ 10.1023/A:1011124509158

Beard, T. R., Macher, J. T., Vickers, C., Schmalensee, R., & Wilson, W. W. (2016). This time it's different (?): Telecommunications unbundling and lessons for railroad regulation, *Review of Industrial Organization, 49,* 289–310. https://doi.org/10.1007/s11151-016-9517-0

Biden, J. (2021). Memorandum for the Heads of Executive Departments and Agencies: "Modernizing Regulatory Review." January 20, 2021.

Buchanan, J., Tollison, R., & Tullock, G. (1980). *Toward a theory of the rent-seeking society.* Texas A&M University.

Bull, R. T., & Ellig, J. (2018). Statutory rulemaking considerations and judicial review of regulatory impact analysis. *Administrative Law Review, 70*(4), 873–959.

Business Roundtable v. SEC, 647 F.3d 1144 (D.C. Cir. 2011).

Commission on Evidence-Based Policymaking (2017, September). *The promise of evidence-based policy making.*

Crandall, R. W. (1991). *After the breakup: U.S. telecommunications in a more competitive era.* Brookings Institution Press.

Crandall, R. W., & Ellig, J. (1997). *Economic deregulation and customer choice: Lessons for the electric industry.* Center for Market Processes, George Mason University. https://www.mercatus.org/ publications/regulation/economic-deregulation-and-customer-choice-lessons-electric-industry

Crandall, R., & Waverman, L. (1996). *Talk is cheap: The promise of regulatory reform in North American telecommunications.* Brookings Institution Press.

Crandall, R. W., & Waverman, L. (2000). *Who pays for universal service? When telephone subsidies become transparent.* Brookings Institution Press.

Derthick, M., & Quirk, P.J. (1985). *The politics of deregulation.* Brookings Institution Press.

Dudley, S. E. (2017). *Retrospective Evaluation of Chemical Regulations* [OECD Environmental Working Papers 118]. OECD. https://doi.org/10.1787/368e41d7-en

Dudley, S., Belzer, R., Blomquist, G., Brennan, T., Carrigan, C., Cordes, J., Cox, L., Fraas, A., Graham, J., Gray, G., Hammitt, J., Krutilla, K., Linquiti, P., Lutter, R., Mannix, B., Shapiro, S., Smith, A., Viscusi, W., & Zerbe, R. (2017). Consumer's guide to regulatory impact analysis: Ten tips for being an informed policymaker. *Journal of Benefit–Cost Analysis, 8*(2), 187–204. https://doi.org/10.1017/ bca.2017.11

Dudley, S., & Mannix, B. (2018). Improving regulatory benefit–cost analysis. *The Journal of Law & Politics*, XXXIV(1).

Dudley, S., Pérez, D., Mannix, B., & Carrigan, C. (2019). Dynamic benefit–cost analysis for uncertain futures. *Journal of Benefit–Cost Analysis, 10*(2), 206–225. doi:10.1017/bca.2019.13

Ellig, J. (2016). Evaluating the quality and use of regulatory impact analysis: The Mercatus Center's regulatory report card, 2008–2013. Working Paper, Mercatus Center at George Mason University, Arlington, VA, July 2016.

Ellig, J. (2002). Railroad regulation and consumer welfare. *Journal of Regulatory Economics, 21*(2), 143–167. https://doi.org/10.1023/A:1014331206366

Ellig, J. (2006). Costs and consequences of federal telecommunications regulations. *Fed. Comm. LJ, 58*(1), 37–102.

Ellig, J., & Fike, R. (2016). Regulatory process, regulatory reform, and the quality of regulatory impact analysis. *Journal of Benefit–Cost Analysis, 7*(3), 523–559. https://doi.org/10.1017/bca.2016.20

E.O.12866, 58 FR 52735 (1993).

E.O. 13563, 76 FR 3821 (2011).

E.O. 13610, 77 FR 28467 (2012).

E.O. 13771, 82 FR 9339 (2017).

E.O. 13777, 82 FR 12285 (2017).

Fraas, A., & Lutter, R. (2011a). On the economic analysis of regulations at independent regulatory commissions. *Administrative Law Review, 63*, 213–241.

Fraas, A., & Lutter, R. (2011b). The challenges of improving the economic analysis of pending regulations: The experience of OMB Circular A-4. *Annual Review of Resource Economics, 3*(1), 71–85. https://doi.org/10.1146/annurev-resource-083110-120042

Gertler, P. J., Martinez, S., Premand, P., Rawlings, L. B., & Vermeersch, C. M. J. (2011). *Impact evaluation in practice.* The World Bank.

Graham, J. D. (2008). Saving lives through administrative law and economics. *University of Pennsylvania Law Review, 157*(2), 395–540.

Gray, G., & Cohen, J. (2012). Policy: Rethink chemical risk assessments. *Nature, 489*(7414), 27–28. https://doi.org/10.1038/489027a

Green, M., & Nader, R. (1973). Economic regulation vs. competition: Uncle Sam the monopoly man. *Yale Law Journal, 82*(5), 871–889. https://doi.org/10.2307/795533

Greenstone, M. (2009). Toward a culture of persistent regulatory experimentation and evaluation. In D. Moss and J. Cisternino (Eds.), *New perspectives on regulation.* The Tobin Project.

Hahn, R. W., & Dudley, P. M. (2007). How well does the U.S. government do benefit – cost analysis? *Review of Environmental Economics and Policy, 1*(2). 192–211. https://doi.org/10.1093/reep/rem012

Hahn, R. W., & Tetlock, P. C. (2008). Has economic analysis improved regulatory decisions? *Journal of Economic Perspectives, 22*(1), 67–84. https://doi.org/10.1257/jep.22.1.67

Hartley, P. R., Medlock, K. B., & Jankovska, O. (2019). Electricity reform and retail pricing in Texas. *Energy Economics, 80*, 1–11. https://doi.org/10.1016/j.eneco.2018.12.024

Hazlett, T. W. (1997). A common property experiment with a renewable resource. *Economic Inquiry, 35*(4), 858–861. https://doi.org/10.1111/j.1465-7295.1997.tb01969.x

Hazlett, T. W. (2006). Cable Television. In Sumit K. Majumdar et al. (Eds.), *Handbook of telecommunications economics.* Elsevier Science.

Hazlett, T. W. (2017). *The political spectrum: The tumultuous liberation of wireless technology, from Herbert Hoover to the smartphone.* Yale University Press.

Heywood, J. S., & Peoples, J. H. (1994). Deregulation and the prevalence of black truck drivers. *Journal of Law & Economics, 37*(1), 133–156.

MacAvoy, P. W. (1971). The regulation-induced shortage of natural gas. *Journal of Law & Economics, 14*(1), 167–199. https://doi.org/10.1086/466707

Mannix, B. F. (2016). Benefit–cost analysis as a check on administrative discretion. *Supreme Court Economic Review, 24*(1), 155–168. https://doi.org/10.1086/696841

McLaughlin, P., & Strosko, S. (2018, September). *What can the 1990s tell us about good regulatory policy in the 21st century?* Mercatus Center at George Mason University.

Morrison, S. A., & Winston, C. (1995). *The evolution of the airline industry.* Brookings Institution Press.

Morrison, S. A., & Winston. C. (2000). The remaining role for government policy in the deregulated airline industry. In Peltzman, S., & Winston, C. (Eds.), *Deregulation of network industries: What's next?.* Brookings Institution Press, AEI-Brookings Joint Center for Regulatory Studies.

National Partnership for Reinventing Government (NPR) (1995). *1995 Report: Common sense government.* National Performance Review. https://govinfo.library.unt.edu/npr/library/nprrpt/annrpt/comsen95/index.html

Newcomer, K. E., Hatry, H. P., & Wholey, J. S. (2015). *Handbook of practical program evaluation*, 4th ed. Jossey-Bass.

Noe, P. R., & Graham, J. D. (2020). The ascendancy of the cost–benefit state? *ALR Accord, 5*(3), 85–151. http://www.administrativelawreview.org/wp-content/uploads/2020/01/Ascendancy-of-the-Cost-Benefit-State_Accord-5.3_Final.pdf

Obama, B. (2009). Memorandum on regulatory review, January 30. https://www.presidency.ucsb.edu/documents/memorandum-regulatory-review

OMB. (2003). Circular A-4, regulatory analysis.

OMB. (2005). Validating regulatory analysis: 2005 report to Congress on the benefits and costs of federal regulations.

OMB. (2011). *Regulatory Impact Analysis: A Primer* https://obamawhitehouse.archives.gov/sites/default/files/omb/inforeg/regpol/circular-a-4_regulatory-impact-analysis-a-primer.pdf

Peltzman, S. (1976). Toward a more general theory of regulation. *Journal of Law & Economics, 19*(2), 211–240. https://doi.org/10.1086/466865

Peoples, J., & Peteraf, M. (1995). Deregulation and the competitive fringe: Owner-operators in the trucking industry. *Journal of Regulatory Economics 7*, 27–42.

Robyn, D. (1987). *Braking the special interests: Trucking deregulation and the politics of policy reform.* University of Chicago Press.

Schmalensee, R. L., Boyer, K. D., Ellig, J., Gómez-Ibáñez, J. A., Goodchild, A. V., Wilson, W. W., & Wolak, F. A. (2015). *Modernizing freight rail regulation.* [Special Report 318]. Transportation Research Board.

Stahl, J. (2016). Effects of deregulation and consolidation of the broadcast television industry. *American Economic Review, 106*(8), 2185–2218. https://doi.org/10.1257/aer.20110948

Stigler, G. (1971). The theory of economic regulation. *Bell Journal of Economics and Management Science, 2*(1), 3–21. https://doi.org/10.2307/3003160

Sunstein, C. R. (2011). *Implementation of retrospective review* [Memorandum for the Heads of Executive Departments and Agencies]. Executive Office of the President. https://obamawhitehouse.archives .gov/sites/default/files/omb/assets/inforeg/implementation-of-retrospective-review-plans.pdf

Wilson, C. S., & Klovers, K. (2020). The growing nostalgia for past regulatory misadventures and the risks of repeating these mistakes with Big Tech. *Journal of Antitrust Enforcement, 8*(1), 10–29. https:// doi.org/10.1093/jaenfo/jnz029

Wilson, W. W. (1997). Cost savings and productivity in the railroad industry. *Journal of Regulatory Economics, 11*(1), 21–40. https://doi.org/10.1023/A:1007946111577

Winston, C. (1993). Economic deregulation: Days of reckoning for microeconomists. *Journal of Economic Literature, 31*(3), 1263–1289.

Winston, C., Corsi, T. M., Grimm, C. M., & Evans, C. A. (1990). *The economic effects of surface freight deregulation.* Brookings Institution Press.

Winston, C., & Shirley, C. (1998). *Alternate route: toward efficient urban transportation.* Brookings Institution Press.

22. Judicial review of agency action in Europe

Stéphanie De Somer, Ute Lettanie and Patricia Popelier

INTRODUCTION

This chapter addresses judicial review of regulatory policy-making by independent regulatory authorities (IRAs). IRAs are one type within the broader category of autonomous public bodies (APBs), that is, non-elected public bodies that make decisions with a certain degree of autonomy vis-à-vis those who are politically accountable (De Somer 2017). Most regulatory bodies are APBs, but not all of them are IRAs. IRAs have in common that (1) their decisions are insulated from any form of direct political oversight (e.g. a possibility to suspend or quash) (2) to ensure that policies are stable and based on expert opinions. IRAs can preserve continuity ('time consistency') in their policy field, because they do not depend on elected mandates. This is deemed necessary to attract investments and to foster economic initiative in general (Hawkins et al. 2005; Majone 1996). Being typically operative in complex and technical areas, IRAs, unlike elected politicians, are expected to base their policies on objective criteria instead of ideological preferences (Oliver 2010).

IRAs confront the judiciary with a dilemma. Reduced political accountability gives it a particular responsibility in holding IRAs to account. At the same time, judges may want to show deference to IRAs' technical judgements and shy away from becoming 'regulator in second instance', for which they lack legitimacy and qualifications. Depending on how deeply rooted such concerns are in a legal system's tradition of judicial review, this may result in higher or lower degrees of intensity of review and corresponding adjudication techniques. Arguably, the institutional engineering of judicial bodies and their ability to review complex evidence play an important role in this respect (Mak 2012).

This chapter examines how judicial bodies in Europe deal with this dilemma. It commences with the theoretical foundations to explain the dilemma and review modalities (section 2). It then discusses three case studies in the field of economic, financial and banking regulation, concerning national economic network regulators and the European Central Bank (ECB) (section 3), before concluding with an outlook on the way forward to address the challenges arising from the tension between IRAs' independence and judicial review (section 4).

Two arguments explain the case selection. First, the choice to discuss national economic regulators in the network industries helps us to overcome a methodological difficulty. Judicial review, as a central feature of any national system of administrative law, differs among legal systems on various levels: access to the court and standing, procedure, type of relief, standards of proof, intensity of the review, etc. In many areas of regulation, providing general statements on judicial review of the decisions of national regulatory bodies in Europe is therefore quite challenging. For national IRAs (NRAs) whose decisions fall within the scope of EU law (of which network regulators are the most notorious ones), however, the case law of the Court of Justice of the European Union (CJEU) creates some uniformity. The starting point remains that Member States enjoy procedural autonomy. In a case concerning NRAs in the telecommunications sector, the CJEU ruled that, in absence of relevant European rules, it was solely for the Member States to determine, in accordance with the principles of equivalence and effectiveness of judicial protection, the competent court, the nature of the dispute and, consequently, the detailed rules of judicial review.[1] Nevertheless, consistent with its case law in other areas (Widdershoven 2019), the CJEU is increasingly inclined to direct national courts, especially with respect to the standard and intensity of review. This enables us to define common features of judicial review of regulatory policies in the network industries in Europe. Second, including both national IRAs and an IRA established at EU-level enables us to show a wide range of review modalities. For the ECB, we will distinguish between two very different tasks that it assumes, to examine whether and the intensity of judicial review is related to the nature of the task.

THEORETICAL FOUNDATIONS

The Courts' Dilemma

Traditionally, academics use the principal–agent (PA) theory (Epstein and O'Halloran 1999; Pollack 2002) or the fiduciary theory (Majone 2001; Quintyn and Taylor 2007) to theorize delegation of public functions. Both theories have four common variables: the nature of the delegation, the contents of the contract, the delegator's control and the delegate's zone of discretion. They allow us to situate APBs on a sliding scale, with a more restricted PA relation on the left side of the scale, and a looser fiduciary relation on the right (Lettanie 2019). Time-inconsistency arguments and a need for expertise explain a tendency to attribute policy-making exclusively to IRAs and to exclude the influence of political preferences. In this vein, the contract confers wide discretionary powers to the IRAs, which brings them into a fiduciary relationship.

The sliding scale reveals two reasons why this makes legal accountability more pressing. The first has to do with the combination of two variables: the delegator's control and the delegate's zone of discretion. IRAs move to the right side, where delegator's control, including *ex ante*, ongoing and *ex post* control mechanisms, are reduced to secure political independence. At the same time, the delegate's zone of discretion, that is, its room for manoeuvre, increases. The lack of control leaves room for increasing the factual room for manoeuvre, beyond the mandate enshrined in the contract. The factual room increases in particular when the delegate assumes more discretionary powers while simultaneously the delegator makes little use of what control mechanisms remain (Thatcher and Stone Sweet 2002). In that case, the 'politics of post-delegation' (Delreux and Adriansen 2017) deviates from the politics of delegation, which means that the delegate makes farther-reaching policy decisions than initially intended in the contract.

This makes legal accountability a central point of attention. Independence protects IRAs against political intervention; it is not defined in relation to judicial authorities. Consequently, the judiciary is one of the external actors that serve as a counterweight to manage the politics of post-delegation (Spyrelli 2003-04; Prosser 2011a). The CJEU has confirmed that national administrative authorities with high degrees of independence that shield their decisions from political influence, have to comply with the law and are subject to judicial review.[2] Lavrijssen and Ottow (2011) see a particular role for the CJEU in this respect: offering more legal protection against NRAs' decisions may compensate for the fact that it was EU law in the first place that decreased the role of the political arena to control NRAs. This means that also govern-ments can use legal actions to hold NRAs to account when they cannot intervene directly.[3] In France, for instance, the *Conseil Constitutionnel* has held that the government (and any other person with an interest) can initiate judicial proceedings against the decision of an economic regulator to legitimize the conferral of broad decision-making powers to these independent authorities (Heringa 2003).[4] This also gives national governments a grip on EU regulators: as 'privileged applicants', governments can initiate an action for annulment of ECB decisions (Art. 263 TFEU)[5] as well as an action for failure to act (Art. 265 TFEU) without meeting specific requirements such as 'direct concern'.

At the same time, legal accountability is limited. Judicial bodies cannot rule on the expedi-ency or political desirability of a policy, only on its legality. The fact that IRAs are technocrat bodies also means that judicial bodies are expected to show at least some degree of deference and will typically refrain from extensively reviewing the scientific assessments made by regu-latory bodies (Donnelly 2010; Harlow and Rawlings 2009; Prosser 2011b). Judicial bodies are at risk of compromising their own credibility if they do not get this difficult balance right. This brings us to the matter of review modalities.

Review Modalities

The judiciary can modulate the standard of review by opting for substantive review, procedural review, or procedural rationality review (also called semiprocedural review: Bar-Siman-Tov 2012).

In the case of procedural review, decisions are taken in conformity with formal require-ments that are laid down in the law. Decisions that have been quashed on this basis can be adopted again, if the formal requirements are respected. The underlying idea is that procedure guides content: the outcome will probably differ if, for example, consultation requirements or voting thresholds are respected.

Substantive review means that the content of IRAs' decisions is reviewed against substan-tive requirements. Such review can be 'full' or 'marginal', referring to the intensity of review that the courts apply to the (technical) cases that they are called on to adjudicate. In the case of marginal review, courts abstain from second guessing substantive outcomes, thereby widening the IRAs' zone of discretion.

To keep this within limits, judicial bodies may turn to procedural rationality review. In that case, procedural safeguards are taken into account in substantive review, to assess whether decisions can be deemed proportional or reasonable. This way, even in the absence of a legal duty to consult, use expert advice or make impact assessments, such practices (or the absence thereof) may determine whether the content of a decision is legally sound. Again, the standards of this review may vary. Judicial bodies may simply check whether an informed, evidence-based decision was reached, or they may examine the value of the evidence that supports the decision. Considering that IRAs have a mandate based on their expertise, scru-tiny will most often remain marginal, unless judicial bodies feel confident that they have the capacity to assess the quality of scientific evidence. This links intensity of review with the type of judicial bodies.

JUDICIAL REVIEW IN PRACTICE

Selection of IRAs and Types of Court

This section examines the practice of judicial review of decisions made by NRAs in the network industries and by the ECB.

The markets that NRAs in the network industries supervise are characterized by natural monopolies. Even after liberalization, many incumbents continue to own the essential infrastructure that makes up the physical network needed to distribute goods and services to consumers. Regulation is needed to ensure access to these infrastructures and hence to enable competition (Lavrijssen and Ottow 2011). Since the network industries produce so-called 'merit goods', regulation also aims to ensure universal service. In recent years, the EU legislature has gradually introduced obligations for Member States to establish IRAs in these various sectors and to entrust them with powers that comprise rule making, adjudication and enforcement. This has been the case for the markets of energy, electronic communications and railway transport. In the area of postal services, the Member States must only ensure that the NRA is independent of the regulated parties; there is no explicit requirement for political independence.[6] Nevertheless, many national regulators for the postal market in Europe today already take the form of an IRA, often because they are also charged with regulatory tasks in one or more of the other network industries (e.g. the Belgian BIPT/IBPT and the Dutch ACM).

At the EU level, we focus on the ECB as a showcase for the difficult balance between independence and legal accountability. With its independence constitutionally anchored (Arts. 120 and 282(3) TFEU), it is often considered the most independent central bank in the world (Claeys et al. 2014). Similarly to what is the case for most IRAs, efficiency reasons and credible commitment underpin delegation of monetary policy to the ECB (Kydland and Prescott 1977). We will investigate two main tasks of the ECB: monetary policy and prudential supervision. The former is the ECB's core task. As to the latter, the ECB and the National Competent Authorities (NCAs) have formed the Single Supervisory Mechanism (SSM) since 2014.

The legality of the ECB's acts and omissions is scrutinized by the CJEU,[7] which is a general court. For the NRAs, the picture is different. The various EU Directives that entrench the missions and powers of NRAs in the network industries all address their legal accountability but use different wordings.

In the field of railway transport,[8] for instance, the legislation explicitly mentions a duty for Member States to ensure that decisions taken by the regulatory authority are subject to 'judicial review', whereas in the fields of electricity,[9] gas[10] and electronic communications[11] it speaks of 'an appeal to a body which is independent of the parties involved'. In the field of energy, the directives clarify that this body also has to be independent of 'any government'. In the field of electronic communications, the appeal body has to be independent of 'any external intervention or political pressure liable to jeopardize its independent assessment of matters coming before it'. The European Electronic Communications Code clarifies that the appeal body 'may be a court'; if it is not judicial in nature, the directive submits it to a duty to give reasons and orders that its decision shall be subject to review by a court or a tribunal.[12] The preamble of the Electricity Directive refers to 'a court or another tribunal that is empowered to conduct a judicial review'.[13]

In practice, there seems to be considerable variation in the nature of the judicial body entrusted with judicial review of network regulators' decisions. Often, specialized chambers are established within courts with a generalist mandate (the ordinary courts). Even in dualist systems, these are often sections of the civil court (e.g. the Paris Court of Appeals in France and the 'Court of Markets', i.e. a chamber of the Brussels Court of Appeal in Belgium), even though some powers may remain with the administrative courts. In the UK – no longer an EU Member State but its current domestic law is still largely inspired by the EU legislation to which it has long been subject – the Competition Appeal Tribunal (CAT) now plays the lead when it comes to appeals against the decisions of economic regulators, but the Administrative Court hears some of the cases as well (Elliot 2013).

Arguably, the type of judicial body influences the extent to which the technical assessments made by IRAs and the policies in which the result will be subject to review: a generalist court will typically be less inclined to do so than a specialized judicial body (Mejía 2020).[14] In the UK, for instance, the Administrative Court has always been reluctant to review the technical judgements made by NRAs (Rawlings 2010). Procedural rationality review is firmly established, with the courts examining if the regulator has, for instance, carried out all necessary consultations, responded to the regulated party's concerns throughout the administrative process and gave reasons for its decisions, which may also include an explanation of why the regulator itself deems its actions to be proportionate.[15] By contrast, the UK's Competition Appeal Tribunal (CAT), a tribunal composed of experts in law, economics, business and accountancy, is known to exercise a profound substantive scrutiny of (the appropriateness of) the evidence used to substantiate the decision. To the extent that regulatory decisions involve balancing various policy considerations, however, the CAT's review has, especially in recent years, been more deferential to the regulators' margin of appreciation (Mantzari 2019).

The CJEU may help to bring the two approaches closer. Its own approach to the review of complex economic assessments by the EU courts, as revealed by its judgement in the *Tetra Laval* case, is a guideline. In this judgement, the Court held that the European Commission's margin of discretion with regard to economic matters (here: in a merger case) did not mean that the EU courts must refrain from reviewing the Commission's interpretation of information of an economic nature. The courts should not only establish whether the evidence relied on is factually correct, reliable and consistent, but also 'whether that evidence contains all the information which must be taken into account in order to assess a complex situation and whether it is capable of substantiating the conclusions drawn from it'.[16] National approaches to judicial review of decisions made by IRAs are often assessed in the light of this *Tetra Laval*-standard (Lavrijssen et al. 2016 for the Netherlands; Van de Weyer 2019 for Belgium).

Intensity of Review

National economic regulators in the network industries

The European Electronic Communications Code specifies that the appeal body shall have the appropriate expertise to enable it to carry out its functions effectively and that the Member States shall ensure that the merits of the case are duly taken into account.[17] It is assumed that this provision intends to prevent that substantively valid regulatory decisions would be quashed for merely procedural reasons, not that a full review would be preferable to a marginal one (Larouche and Taton 2011). The other directives do not provide any clarification as to what is expected of the courts.

The wish for an effective and final solution explains the preference for substantive review over formal review. At the same time, there is a concern that courts would become substitutes for regulators. It has been argued that national courts hearing cases against NRAs' decisions may pursue regulatory policies, which provokes the question of whether the EU should take initiatives to ensure coherence and consistency in the case law of the national courts (Szydlo 2014).

A 2011 study carried out within the Centre on Regulation in Europe revealed a broad tendency towards the following trichotomy in judicial review of decisions made by NRAs in the sectors of energy, electronic communication and railway regulation: a full review with respect to errors of law, a broad review regarding errors of fact and a marginal review of the discretion exercised by the NRA (Larouche and Taton 2011). It is not always easy, however, to determine where the establishment of facts stops and the exercise of discretion begins. The debate at the heart of the *Tetra Laval* judgement reveals that the most delicate issue for the judiciary is how to deal with the regulatory body's assessment of (complex) economic information, that is, the way in which the body draws conclusions from factual information and hence constructs the reasons underlying its decisions. This is at the same time linked to the establishment of the facts and to the body's discretionary power, in those cases in which facts can be interpreted in multiple ways. Research reveals that the EU courts themselves have applied a rather close scrutiny to the European Commission's assessment, which may also cover the choice for a certain economic theory rather than another to appraise those facts (Lavrijssen and de Visser 2006; Renshaw and Blockx 2013).

The debates on the role of courts in reviewing the economic evidence that IRAs base their decisions upon are not yet closed. However, it seems generally accepted (and the case law of the European Court of Human Rights has played a vital role in this respect) that enforcement decisions, especially those entailing sanctions or fines, should be subject to a full review of the merits (Ottow 2015). Whether this entails a power for the court to substitute its judgement for that of the regulator (e.g. by imposing a lower fine) remains unclear and law and practice seem to go in various directions across European legal systems here.

Lavrijssen and Çapkurt (2019) emphasize the need for the regulator to demonstrate that the means chosen to attain the regulatory goals pursued are appropriate (suitable) and necessary. This may be difficult, however, since the outcomes of policies will seldom be predictable with a hundred per cent certainty.

In *Koninklijke KPN NV et al.*, the CJEU addressed the scope of the proportionality test applied to the decisions of an electronic communications regulator. A decision of the Dutch Authority for Consumers and Markets setting price caps for fixed and mobile call termination services had been challenged and the referring court wondered whether it was allowed to assess the proportionality of the obligations laid down in this decision considering the objectives set out in the (European) legislation. The CJEU ruled that the national judge may assess whether these obligations are directed at achieving these objectives, but is not entitled to require the authority to demonstrate that the obligation *actually attains* the objectives set out in the Directive. According to the Court, the adoption of regulatory obligations is based on a prospective analysis of market developments. Therefore, the proof that such measures attain the objectives set out in the Directive is 'impossible or excessively difficult to adduce'.[18]

It has been argued that the CJEU devises the proportionality test differently depending on the authority under review: it tends to be stricter towards a national authority than towards an EU institution (Haguenau-Moizard and Sanchez 2016). NRAs, however, occupy a peculiar position in this respect. Because of their independence of the national political institutions and the fact that they derive most of their powers directly or indirectly from EU law, they are 'agents of EU law' (De Somer 2018). Institutionally, they are embedded in the national administrative realm; functionally, they behave more as if they were EU bodies. Because their goal is to promote and protect the internal market, they are perceived as less prone to pursue national interests than other national administrative bodies. This may explain the CJEU's reluctance to push the proportionality test to its limits with respect to their decisions.

The *Koninklijke KPN* judgement reveals the link between the standard of review and the burden of proof. Previously, the CJEU had ruled that, given the lack of rules in EU law, Member States can establish the rules of evidence applicable, in accordance with their rules of procedure, including the allocation of the burden of proof between the NRA and the claimant. This competence, as always, has to be exercised in accordance with the Community principles of effectiveness and equivalence of judicial protection.[19] It has been noted before that the courts are prepared to demand actual proof of independent market supervisors to justify their intervention (Ottow 2015).[20] In *KPN*, the CJEU seems to set a subtle limit to this type of rationality review: the national court cannot go so far as to demand proof that the IRAs policy is effective, i.e. that the outcome envisaged will actually be achieved. This judgement does not imply that courts can no longer ask IRAs to convince them that their policies are *likely* to contribute to these outcomes, since that would compromise the suitability test as the traditional first step in the proportionality assessment. It does mean that a demand for *conclusive* evidence is beyond the courts' scope of review.

The ECB: judicial review of monetary policy

The ECB's primary task relates to monetary policy, namely maintaining price stability. In secondary order, the ECB supports the general economic policies of the EU.[21] Since its creation, the ECB has been a rules-based institution, governed by provisions determining its independence, the separation between monetary and economic policies,[22] and the prohibition of monetary financing.[23] The Masters of the Treaties presumed that as a technocrat that does not engage in political decision making, the ECB needs less democratic legitimation. Economic policy, with its redistributive consequences, is considered to be more political and therefore requires more democratic legitimation.

In the crisis case law, it was claimed that the ECB's measures could qualify as economic policy, which is the responsibility of the Member States, and therefore went beyond the ECB's monetary policy mandate. The CJEU was called to adjudicate two monetary policy measures in the light of the attribution of powers, the proportionality principle and the prohibition of monetary financing. The tension that recently arose on this matter between the CJEU and the German Constitutional Court (GCC) illustrates varying approaches to legal accountability. The CJEU's approach is characterized by a combination of marginal control and procedural rationality, whereas the GCC demands a stricter standard.

The CJEU

In the absence of a Treaty definition of monetary policy and building upon a principle established in *Pringle*,[24] the CJEU considered the objectives and instruments of monetary policy to determine to which policy field the measures belonged.[25] The Court merely looked at the objectives stated by the ECB and concluded that the contested measures belonged to the monetary policy toolbox established in Article 18 ESCB Statute.[26] Moreover, the CJEU accepted that monetary policy measures can affect the economy indirectly,[27] even if these effects are foreseeable.[28] Following this marginal standard of review, the Court disregarded the risk that the ECB actually aimed for other objectives under the vein of attaining price stability or that the economic effects would be disproportional to the monetary policy objective.

As to proportionality, the CJEU focused on the suitability and necessity limbs and did not attach much weight to the limb of proportionality *sensu stricto*. Given the ECB's broad discretion in making complex technical assessments, the CJEU advanced procedural review.[29] To this end, the Court scrutinized the ECB's statement of reasons. Even though the monetary policy reasoning is prone to controversies, 'nothing more can be required of the ESCB apart from that it use its economic expertise and the necessary technical means at its disposal to carry out that analysis with all care and accuracy'.[30] In this regard, the CJEU looked at the wording and the entire body of legal rules considering the circumstances instead of going into every relevant point of law.[31] The proportionality test boiled down to a manifest error assessment.[32] The suitability test is passed if there is no manifest error of assessment, considering the ECB's statement of reasons, that is, the crisis circumstances, practices of other central banks, and the documents presented by the ECB.[33] The necessity test is passed if the programmes do not manifestly go beyond what is necessary to reach the objectives, taking into account the context and the programmes' characteristics (volume, period, …).[34]

The CJEU also applied marginal control to assess compliance with the prohibition of monetary financing. It introduced two rules. First, the prohibition cannot be circumvented by the purchases on the secondary market that have the effect of purchases on the primary market. Second, the purchases cannot diminish the fiscal discipline of the Member States. The Court ruled that the ECB complied with these rules because various (legal) safeguards were built into the programmes.[35] It emphasized that the safeguards 'depend on both the particular features of the programme under consideration and the economic context in which the programme is adopted and implemented'.[36] This way, the CJEU avoided to get entangled in complex economic assessments and granted flexibility for future cases of judicial review.

The foregoing paragraphs demonstrate that the CJEU adheres a marginal standard of review combined with a minimal form of procedural rationality control through a duty of care. For example, the CJEU did not examine the duty of care in the cases at hand nor did it tackle adequately proportionality *sensu stricto*. Consequently, it accepted the increased scope of influence, which the ECB assumed out of necessity to save the euro(zone) in the absence of a fiscal and political union (Chang 2019). The CJEU invoked the ECB's technical expertise and its wide discretion, as enshrined in the Treaties, to withhold itself from carrying out a second assessment. This approach, however, appears to create a legally untouchable ECB in the field of monetary policy.[37]

The GCC
The GCC advocated a substantive standard of review and in doing so criticized the CJEU's review method. In *Weiss*, it stated that the CJEU's ruling disregarded the principle of proportionality, 'which also applies to the division of competences, and is no longer tenable from a methodological perspective given that it completely disregards the actual effects of the PSPP.'[38] For this reason, it held that the CJEU acted *ultra vires*: it violated the principle of conferral and its mandate under Article 19(1) TEU. According to the GCC, the ECB's independence is an exception to democratic legitimacy, and must therefore be interpreted narrowly.[39] It ruled that the ECB needed to make a clear and reasoned assessment between the

monetary objectives and the economic impact of the programme to fulfil the proportionality principle.[40] Even though the GCC's reasoning is debatable (e.g. Nicolaidis 2020), it exposes the thinness of the CJEU's marginal standard of review. Where the CJEU did not even consider the adequacy of the legal requirements in the technical context, its review comes down to a ticking-the-box exercise. Instead, the Court could, for example, have requested an impact assessment of the ECB to substantiate the duty of care (Dawson and Bobić 2019). Yet, it remains to be seen whether the CJEU will consider the GCC's remarks.

The ECB: judicial review of prudential policy

The SSM establishes close cooperation between the ECB and the NCAs of the euro area Member States with regard to prudential supervision. It contributes to the safety and soundness of credit institutions, financial stability within the euro area,[41] and an internal market for financial services. Due to its expertise in macroeconomic and financial stability matters, the ECB is qualified to perform clearly defined supervisory tasks (Recital 13 SSM Regulation), pursuant to Article 127(6) TFEU. Prudential supervision entails the application of prudential regulation, which is affected by policy considerations. The latter involves the need to balance different interests (public and private, national and supranational) in the decision-making process (Magliari 2019). Furthermore, in line with general practice,[42] the ECB and the NCAs are independent when acting in the SSM (Art. 19 SSM Regulation).

Given the SSM's lack of legal personality and its composite nature,[43] judicial review engages national as well as EU courts. In accordance with an integrationist approach (Beck 2017), the CJEU has assigned itself an important role in the review of prudential policy. The ECB has specific exclusive decision-making powers for *all* credit institutions and the NCAs assist it to carry them out (decentralized implementation).[44] In these cases, the CJEU has exclusive competence to review the ECB's decisions (Art. 263 TFEU) as well as errors of national preparatory measures that would affect the validity of the final ECB decision.[45] National courts review the NCA's preparatory measures if they are binding and leave no or limited room for ECB discretion.[46]

An increasing number of cases on the ECB's actions as a prudential supervisor have been brought before the EU courts.[47] The claims and preliminary questions cover a wide range of topics, showing that prudential supervision will remain a stable source of litigation for the years to come, especially given the large number of decisions taken by the ECB (Prek and Lefèvre 2019). Moreover, the direct adjudication by EU courts can be explained by the fact that prudential supervision entails policy considerations and affects, among others, the fundamental rights of the supervised entities or persons (e.g. effective judicial protection or right to property). The following analysis is based on the first judgements of the EU courts.[48]

The CJEU follows its settled case law and its intensity of review depends on the specific action of the ECB as prudential supervisor. In complex technical assessments, such as determining additional capital requirements[49] and the calculation of the leverage ratio,[50] the CJEU endorses procedural rationality. It examines whether the evidence relied on by the ECB contains all the necessary information, is factually accurate, reliable and consistent as well as substantiate its conclusion. It investigates whether the decision is based on materially incorrect facts, or is vitiated by an error of law, manifest error of assessment or misuse of powers.[51] The CJEU does not give any consequences to an additional hypothetical reasoning that errs in law.[52] Nonetheless, it checks the administrative proceedings to assess whether the ECB has examined all relevant aspects of the individual case in a careful and impartial way.[53] The duty to state reasons is of particular importance with regard to individual decisions because the persons concerned must have sufficient information to verify the ECB's reasoning. The overall assessment is based on the wording, the context and all the legal rules in the field concerned.[54] The context includes, *inter alia*, the Administrative Board of Review's opinion[55] if the contested decision is in conformity with the opinion.[56] The foregoing examples show that the CJEU is willing to perform a more substantive review of the ECB's discretionary choices, by addressing the reliability of the factual elements, even with regard to technical assessments, and the statement of reasons (hesitant: Zilioli 2019; Magliari 2019). With regard to the ECB's sanctioning power, the CJEU enjoys 'unlimited jurisdiction'[57] and is therefore able to alter the amount of the ECB's administrative pecuniary penalties imposed (i.e. substantive review).[58]

To conclude, the CJEU's approach towards the ECB is stricter in prudential policy cases than in monetary policy. The Court regards the ECB as an administrator acting in a more restricted legal environment. Consequently, the CJEU has better tools to assess the ECB's supervisory decisions and even reviews the ECB's technical assessments to verify whether the ECB 'correctly' exercised its administrative discretion in the case at hand.

OUTLOOK

More explicitly than in most other areas of administrative law, the courts have reflected upon the appropriate standard and intensity of their review in matters of economic and financial regulation. The consciousness with which they set the limits for their own intervention reveals awareness of their crucial role as an accountability forum for regulators that enjoy substantial political independence.

The question arises, however, if the CJEU's approach is coherent and applies the same principles to its own intervention regarding the ECB as to that of national judges reviewing the decisions of NRAs. As suggested in this contribution, the CJEU treats NRAs in the network industries as (functionally) part of the supranational administrative realm. Their independence acts as a shield against the temptation to put national interests above European ones. Logically, one would then expect that the CJEU adopts the same view with respect to the standard and intensity of review for both the ECB and the NRAs: distance (from the EU political and legal order) cannot explain variety in this respect. Our analysis for the three case studies that we selected has indeed revealed a common tendency towards a standard of review that offers a compromise between substantive and formal review, being procedural rationality review. For NRAs, *Tetra Laval* serves as a basis in this respect. Perhaps surprisingly, no references to this landmark judgement are made in any of the CJEU's major judgements on the ECB. Nonetheless, with respect to prudential policy, the CJEU has referred[59] to its judgement in *Technische Universität München*,[60] which is often seen as the case creating the basis for what the Court would later state in *Tetra Laval*.

For monetary policy, however, the Court approaches procedural rationality review with greater restraint. As others have pointed out, the Court's expectations are 'lighter' in this area: it 'does not, for example, seem to require the ECB to have considered other mechanisms to tackle deflation or to have relied on external evidence of the relation between asset purchases and prices' (Dawson and Bobić 2019: 1026). Arguably, this can be explained by the sense of urgency and political sensitivity characterizing the crisis case law: the Court was well aware of the ECB's difficult position and the potential consequences of overturning its decisions at that time. That monetary policy is characterized by a broad legal mandate, with not much in the legislation for the Court to work with in terms of requirements and conditions, is in itself not a sufficient reason to design procedural rationality review in a narrow way. On the contrary: the wider the discretionary power, the more pressing the need to gather robust evidence, to hear parties affected, to consult broadly and to give adequate reasons. The CJEU acknowledged this itself in *Technische Universität München*, where it stated that the Commission's power of appraisal as a result of the need to make complex technical evaluations meant that respect for the rights guaranteed by administrative procedures is 'of *even more* fundamental importance' (emphasis added).[61] Viewed against the sliding scale, the CJEU's deferential approach towards procedural rationality does not provide a genuine counterweight to the ECB's actions during the financial crisis. In fact, the CJEU should have demanded a more coherent and detailed account of the interests considered (Mendes 2017) and the value judgements made to reach the ECB decision.

Procedural rationality review offers a middle ground in the courts' search for performing as a credible accountability forum without assuming the role of the regulators. In order to exercise that review in a meaningful way, however, they need to be sufficiently equipped, especially to review the value and reliability of (economic) evidence. In *Weiss*, for instance, the GCC consulted experts in the oral hearing.[62] Entrusting appeals or judicial review to specialized judicial bodies or adding lay judges (experts in other disciplines than the law) to the regular courts could also help in this respect.

NOTES

1. Case C-55/06 *Arcor AG & Co. KG*, EU:C:2008:244, paras 160–170.
2. Case C-518/07 *Commission/Germany* [2010] ECR I-1885, para 42.
3. Commission Staff Working Paper 22 January 2010, Interpretative Note on Directive 2009/72/EC concerning common rules for the internal market in electricity and Directive 2009/73/EC concerning common rules for the internal market in natural gas – The Regulatory Authorities, http://ec.europa .eu/energy/gas_electricity/interpretative_notes/doc /implementation_notes/2010_01_21_the_regu-latory_authorities.pdf, 19 and 20.
4. Conseil Constitutionnel, déc. 86-217 DC du 18 septembre 1986, para 23; Conseil Constitutionnel, déc. 93-333 DC du 21 janvier 1994, para 14.
5. Art. 263 TFEU. E.g. Case T-496/11, *UK v ECB* ECLI:EU:T:2015:133.
6. Art. 22 of Directive 97/67/EC of the European Parliament and of the Council of 15 December 1997 on common rules for the development of the internal market of Community postal services and the improvement of quality of service *OJ L 15, 21.1.1998, 14–25*.
7. Art. 263 TFEU and Art. 35 Statute of the European System of Central Banks and the European Central Bank (ESCB Statute).
8. Art. 56(10) of Directive 2012/34/EU of the European Parliament and of the Council of 21 November 2012 establishing a single European railway area, *OJ L* 343, 14.12.2012, 32–77.
9. Art. 60(8) of Directive 2019/944 of the European Parliament and of the Council of 5 June 2019 on common rules for the internal market for electricity and amending Directive 2012/27/EU, *OJ L 158, 14.6.2019, 125–199*.
10. Art. 41(17) of Directive 2009/73/EC of the European Parliament and of the Council of 13 July 2009 concerning common rules for the internal market in natural gas and repealing Directive 2003/55/EC, *OJ L 211, 14.8.2009, 94–136*.
11. Art. 31(1) of Directive 2018/1972 of the European Parliament and of the Council of 11 December 2018 establishing the European Electronic Communications Code (Recast), *OJ L* 321, 17.12.2018, 36–214.
12. Ibid, Art. 31(2).

13. Preamble of the Electricity Directive, para 86.
14. See e.g. the findings in 1.
15. See e.g. *Npower Direct Ltd v the Gas and Electricity Markets Authority and the Competition Markets Authority* [2018] EWHC 3576 (Admin).
16. Case C-12/03 *Commission v Tetra Laval*, ECLI:EU:C:2005:87, para 39.
17. Art. 31(1) of Directive 2018/1972 of the European Parliament and of the Council of 11 December 2018 establishing the European Electronic Communications Code (Recast), *OJ L* 321, 17.12.2018, 36–214.
18. Case C-28/15 *Koninklijke KPN NV et.al.*, EU:C:2016:692, para 59.
19. Case C-55/06 *Arcor AG & Co. KG*, EU:C:2008:244, paras 188–191.
20. See e.g. an example from Belgium: Court of Appeal of Brussels 6 February 2013, 2012/AR/205, 2012/AR/2017 conn. 2012/AR/220.
21. Art. 127(1) TFEU.
22. Arts. 4(1) *ju.* 5 TEU; Arts. 2(1); 3(1) (c) TFEU.
23. Art. 123(1) TFEU.
24. Case C-370/12 *Thomas Pringle v Government of Ireland and Others*, ECLI:EU:C:2012:756, para 53.
25. Case C-62/14 *Gauweiler*, ECLI:EU:C:2015:400, para 46; Case C-493/17, *Weiss*, ECLI:EU:C:2018: 1000, para 53 (further: *Gauweiler* and *Weiss*).
26. *Gauweiler*, paras 53–59; *Weiss*, paras 54–70.
27. Moreover, the Masters of the Treaties did not establish an absolute separation between economic and monetary policies. *Weiss*, para 60.
28. *Weiss*, paras 62–63.
29. *Gauweiler*, paras 66–69; *Weiss*, para 30.
30. *Gauweiler*, para 77; *Weiss*, para 91. The CJEU also holds that the 'ESCB [should] examine carefully and impartially all relevant elements'; *Gauweiler*, ECLI:EU:C:2015:400, para 69; *Weiss*, para 30.
31. *Gauweiler*, paras 68–70 and 75; *Weiss*, paras 30–33.
32. Case C-62/14 *Gauweiler*, paras 74, 81, 91; Case C-493/17, *Weiss*, paras 24, 78–79, 81, 86, 91.
33. *Weiss*, paras 74–77.
34. *Gauweiler*, paras 81–90; *Weiss*, paras 79–99.
35. *Gauweiler*, para 121–122;127; *Weiss*, paras 101–144.
36. *Gauweiler*, paras 105 and 115; *Weiss*, para 108.
37. For an opposite view, see e.g. Goldmann 2016: 122.
38. GCC, 2 BvR 859/15 *Weiss*, para 119.
39. GCC, 2 BvR 2728/13 *Gauweiler*, para 59; GCC, 2 BvR 859/15 *Weiss,* para 143.
40. GCC, 2 BvR 859/15 *Weiss*, paras 165–178.
41. Art. 1 Council Regulation (EU) No 1024/2013 of 15 October 2013 conferring specific tasks on the European Central Bank concerning policies relating to the prudential supervision of credit institutions, OJ L 287 (29 October 2013) p. 63 (SSM Regulation).
42. See e.g. Core Principles for effective banking supervision, principle 2, at https://www.bis.org/basel _framework/chapter/BCP/01.htm?inforce=20190101.
43. I.e. cooperation of various jurisdictions. Moreover, the ECB can apply national law (Art. 4(3) SSM Regulation).
44. Case T-122/15 *Landeskreditbank Baden-Württemberg – Förderbank v ECB*, ECLI:EU:T:2017: 337, paras 22, 50-63 (further: CaseT-122/15 *Landeskreditbank*); Case C-450/17 *Landeskreditbank Baden-Württemberg – Förderbank v ECB*, ECLI:EU:C:2019:372, paras 37–41 (further: ; Case C-450/17 *Landeskreditbank*).
45. See e.g. Case T-281/18 *ABLV Bank v ECB,* ECLI:EU:T:2019:296, paras 30–32.
46. Case C-219/17 *Silvio Berlusconi and Finanziaria d'investimento Fininvest SpA (Fininvest) v Banca d'Italia and Istituto per la Vigilanza Sulle Assicurazioni (IVASS),* ECLI:EU:C:2018:1023, paras 45–46.
47. The European Banking Institute provides an overview of European case law relating to the European Banking Union: https://ebi-europa.eu/publications/eu-cases-or-jurisprudence/.
48. See Zilioli and Wojcik 2021, on judicial review in the European Banking Union.

49. Case T-712/15 *Crédit mutuel Arkéa v ECB*, ECLI:EU:T:2017:900, paras 178–188 (further: Case T-712/15 *Crédit mutuel Arkéa*); Case T-52/16 *Crédit Mutuel Arkéa v ECB*, ECLI:EU:T:2017:902, paras 177–187 (further: Case T-52/16 *Crédit Mutuel Arkéa*).
50. See e.g. Case T-733/16 *La Banque postale v ECB*, ECLI:EU:T:2018:477, paras 76–96 (further: *La Banque postale*), in which the CJEU annulled the challenged ECB decision because the grounds raised by the ECB to endorse its conclusion were impaired by illegality.
51. *La Banque postale*, paras 69–70; Case T-712/15 *Crédit mutuel Arkéa*, paras 178–179; Case T-52/16 *Crédit Mutuel Arkéa*, paras 176–177.
52. Case T-122/15 *Landeskreditbank*, paras 91–100.
53. *La Banque postale*, paras 69–70; Case T-712/15 *Crédit mutuel Arkéa*, para 180; Case T-52/16 *Crédit mutuel Arkéa*, para 179; Case T-122/15 *Landeskreditbank*, para 147.
54. Case T-122/15 *Landeskreditbank*, para 124; Case C-450/17 *Landeskreditbank*, para 87.
55. An optional internal review mechanism; Art. 24 SSM Regulation.
56. Case T-712/15 *Crédit mutuel Arkéa*, para 51; Case T-52/16 *Crédit mutuel Arkéa*, para 49; Case T-122/15 *Landeskreditbank*, paras 125–127; Case C-450/17 *Landeskreditbank*, paras 88–93 and 95.
57. Art. 261 TFEU *ju*. Art. 5 Council Regulation (EC) No 2532/98 of 23 November 1998 concerning the powers of the European Central Bank to impose sanctions, OJ L 318 (27 November 1998), p. 4. Article 18(7) and recital 36 SSM Regulation refer to Article 132(3) TFEU and Council Regulation 2532/98.
58. Case T-576/18 *Crédit agricole v ECB* ECLI:EU:T:2020:304, para 73.
59. See e.g. Case T-733/16 *La Banque postale*, para 70.
60. Case C-269/90 *Technische Universität München v Hauptzollamt München-Mitte* ECLI:EU:C:1991: 438.
61. Ibid, paras 13–14.
62. GCC, 2 BvR 859/15 *Weiss*, para 82.

REFERENCES

Bar-Siman-Tov, I. (2012) Semiprocedural Judicial Review. *Legisprudence* 6(3): 271–300.
Beck, G. (2017) Judicial Activism in the Court of Justice of the EU. *University of Queensland Law Journal* 36(2): 333–353.
Chang, M. (2019) The Constraints of Central Bank Independence: The European Central Bank's Unconventional Monetary Policy and Incremental Accountability in the Euro Crisis. *Journal of Contemporary European Research* 15(2): 143–161.
Claeys, G., M. Hallerberg and O. Tschekassing (2014) European Central Bank Accountability: How the Monetary Dialogue Could Be Improved. *Bruegel Policy Contribution* 3, at http://bruegel.org/2014/03/european-central-bank-accountability-how-the-monetary-dialogue-could-be-improved/.
Dawson, M. and A. Bobić (2019) Quantitative Easing at the Court of Justice – Doing Whatever it Takes to Save the Euro: *Weiss and Others*. *Common Market Law Review* 56: 1005–1040.
Delreux, T. and J. Adriansen (2017) Twenty Years of Principal–Agent Research in EU Politics: How to Cope with Complexity? *European Political Science*, 17: 258–268.
De Somer, S. (2017) *Autonomous Public Bodies and the Law: A European Perspective*. Cheltenham, UK and Northampton, MA, USA: Edward Elgar Publishing.
De Somer, S. (2018) The powers of national regulatory agencies as agents of EU law. *ERA Forum*, 18(4): 581–595.
Donnelly, C. (2010) Participation and expertise: Judicial Attitudes in Comparative Perspective. In S. Rose-Ackerman and P. Lindseth (eds), *Comparative Administrative Law*. Cheltenham, UK and Northampton, MA, USA: Edward Elgar Publishing.
Elliot, M. (2013) Ombudsmen, Tribunals, Inquiries: Re-fashioning Accountability Beyond the Courts. In N. Bamforth and P. Leyland (eds), *Accountability in the Contemporary Constitution*. Oxford: Oxford University Press.
Epstein, D. and S. O'Halloran (1999) *Delegating Powers: A Transaction Costs Politics Approach to Policy Making under Separate Powers*. Cambridge: Cambridge University Press.

Goldmann, M. (2016) Constitutional Pluralism as Mutually Assured Discretion: The Court of Justice, the German Federal Constitutional Court, and the ECB. *Maastricht Journal of European and Comparative Law* 23(1): 119–135.

Haguenau-Moizard, C. and Y. Sanchez (2016) The principle of proportionality in European law. In S. Ranchordás and B. de Waard (eds), *The Judge and the Proportionate Use of Discretion*. London: Routledge.

Harlow, C. and R. Rawlings (2009) *Law and Administration*. Cambridge: Cambridge University Press.

Hawkins, D.G. and D.A. Lake, D.L. Nielson and M.J. Tierney (2005) Delegation Under Anarchy: States, International Organizations, and Principal–Agent Theory. In D.G. Hawkins, D.A. Lake, D.L. Nielson and M.J. Tierney (eds), *Delegation and Agency in International Organizations*. Cambridge: Cambridge University Press.

Heringa, A.W. (2003) Agencies in France. Autorités Administratives Centrales Indépendantes / National Independent Administrative Authorities. In T. Zwart and L. Verhey (eds), *Agencies in European and Comparative Law*. Antwerp: Intersentia.

Kydland, F.E. and E.C. Prescott (1977) Rules Rather than Discretion: The Inconsistency of Optimal Plans. *Journal of Political Economy* 85(3): 473–492.

Larouche, P. and X. Taton (2011) *Enforcement and Judicial Review of Decisions of National Regulatory Authorities: Identification of Best Practices*. Centre on Regulation in Europe (CERRE), https://www.cerre.eu/publications/enforcement-and-judicial-review-decisions-nras 137.

Lavrijssen, S. and F. Çapkurt (2019) Who Guards the Guardians? Judicial Oversight of the Authority Consumer and Market's Energy Regulations in the Netherlands. In J. de Poorter, E. Hirsch Ballin and S. Lavrijssen (eds), *Judicial Review of Administrative Discretion in the Administrative State*. The Hague: Springer.

Lavrijssen, S. and M. de Visser (2006) Independent Administrative Authorities and the Standard of Judicial Review. *Utrecht Law Review* 2(1): 111–135.

Lavrijssen, S. and A. Ottow (2011) The Legality of Independent Regulatory Authorities. In L. Besselink, F. Pennings and S. Prechal (eds), *The Eclipse of the Legality Principle in the European Union*. Alphen aan den Rijn: Kluwer Law International.

Lavrijssen, S., J. Eijkens and F. Çapkurt (2016) Rechterlijke toetsing van energieregulering door het CBb en het recht op effectieve rechtsbescherming? *SEW, Tijdschrift voor Europees en Economisch Recht* 142–161.

Lettanie, U. (2019) The ECB's Performance Under the ESM Treaty on a Sliding Scale of Delegation. *European Law Journal* 25: 317–332.

Magliari, A. (2019) Intensity of Judicial Review of the European Central Bank's Supervisory Decisions. *Central European Public Administration Review* 17(2): 73–86.

Majone, G. (1996) *Regulating Europe*. London: Routledge.

Majone, G. (2001) Two Logics of Delegation: Agency and Fiduciary Relations in EU Governance. *European Union Politics* 2: 103–122.

Mak, E. (2012) Judicial Review of Regulatory Instruments: The Least Imperfect Alternative? *Legisprudence* 6(3): 301–319.

Mantzari, D. (2019) Judicial Scrutiny of Regulatory Decisions at the UK's Specialist Competition Appeal Tribunal. In J. de Poorter, E. Hirsch Ballin and S. Lavrijssen (eds), *Judicial Review of Administrative Discretion in the Administrative State*. The Hague: Springer.

Mejía, L.E. (2020) Judicial Review of Regulatory Decisions: Decoding the Contents of Appeals Against Agencies in Spain and the United Kingdom. *Regulation & Governance*, https://doi.org/10.1111/rego.12302.

Mendes, J. (2017) Bounded Discretion in EU Law: A Limited Judicial Paradigm in a Changing EU. *The Modern Law Review* 20(3): 443–472.

Nicolaidis, P. (2020) The Judgment of the Federal Constitutional Court of Germany on the Public Sector Asset Purchase Programme of the European Central Bank: Setting an Impossible and Contradictory Test of Proportionality. 15 May 2020, *EU Law Live,* https://eulawlive.com/op-ed-the-judgment-of-the-federal-constitutional-court-of-germany-on-the-public-sector-asset-purchase-programme-of-the-european-central-bank-setting-an-impossible-and-contradictory-test-of/.

Oliver, D. (2010) Regulation, Democracy and Democratic Oversight in the UK. In D. Oliver, T. Prosser and R. Rawlings (eds), *The Regulatory State: Constitutional Implications*. Oxford: Oxford University Press.

Ottow, A. (2015) *Market & Competition Authorities. Good Agency Principles*. Oxford: Oxford University Press.

Pollack, M.A. (2002) Learning from the Americanists (Again): Theory and Method in the Study of Delegation. *West European Politics* 25(1) 200–219.

Prek, M. and S. Lefèvre (2019) Le contentieux de la surveillance prudentielle des établissements de crédit devant le tribunal de l'Union européenne' *Journal de droit européen* 3: 99–106.

Prosser, T. (2011a) Regulation and legitimacy. In J. Jowell and D. Oliver (eds), *The Changing Constitution*. Oxford: Oxford University Press.

Prosser, T. (2011b) The Powers and Accountability of Agencies and Regulators. In D. Feldman (ed.), *English Public Law*. Oxford: Oxford University Press.

Quintyn, M. and M.W. Taylor (2007) Robust Regulators and their Political Masters. In D. Masciandaro and M. Quintyn (eds) *Designing Financial Supervisions Institutions: Independence, Accountability and Governance*. Cheltenham, UK and Northampton, MA, USA: Edward Elgar Publishing.

Rawlings, R. (2010) Changed Conditions, Old Truths: Judicial Review in a Regulatory Laboratory. In D. Oliver, T. Prosser and R. Rawlings (eds.), *The Regulatory State: Constitutional Implications*. Oxford: Oxford University Press.

Renshaw, A. and J. Blockx (2013) Judicial Review of Mergers in the EU. *The Antitrust Bulletin* 58(2–3) 495–519.

Spyrelli, C. (2003–04) Regulating the Regulators? An Assessment of Institutional Structures and Procedural Rules of National Regulatory Authorities. *International Journal of Communications Law and Policy* 1: 42–49.

Szydło, M. (2014) Judicial Review of Decisions Made by National Regulatory Authorities: Towards a More Coherent Application of EU Sector-Specific Regulation. *International Journal of Constitutional Law* 12(4) 930–953.

Thatcher, M. and A. Stone Sweet (2002) Theory and Practice of Delegation to Non-Majoritarian Institutions. *West European Politics* 25(1): 1–22.

Van de Weyer, P.-J. (2019) *De rechterlijke toetsing van bestuursrechtelijke handelingen. Een onderzoek naar de invloed van de vereiste van volle rechtsmacht in de zin van art. 6 EVRM*, unpublished doctoral thesis KU Leuven.

Widdershoven, R. (2019) The European Court of Justice and the Standard of Judicial Review. In J. de Poorter, E. Hirsch Ballin and S. Lavrijssen (eds), *Judicial Review of Administrative Discretion in the Administrative State*. The Hague: Springer.

Zilioli, C. (2019) Proportionality as the Organizing Principle of European Banking Regulation. In T. Baums, H. Remsperger, M. Sachs and V. Wieland (eds.) *Zentralbanken, Währungsunion und stabiles Finanzsystem (in the honor of Helmut Siekmann)*. Berlin: Duncker & Humblot.

Zilioli, C. and Wojcik, K.-P. (eds.) (2021) *Judicial Review in the European Banking Union*. Cheltenham, UK and Northampton, MA, USA: Edward Elgar Publishing.

23. Judicial review of agency action in the United States

Richard Murphy

INTRODUCTION

Judicial review of agency action in the United States controls and purports to help legitimate the exercise of regulatory power that the legislature delegates to agencies lodged in the executive branch. A typical agency has authority both to promulgate legislative rules as well as to enforce its enabling act and rules through adjudication. For the most part, regardless of which of these two procedural modes an agency uses to make policy, the same complex web of legal doctrines governs judicial review of agency action. Various interrelated doctrines limit access to the courts to challenge the underlying merits of agency action—for example, threshold doctrines governing subject matter jurisdiction, causes of action, reviewability, standing to sue, sovereign immunity, and timing of challenges. Other doctrines governing scope of review purport to determine the intensity of scrutiny that courts apply when reviewing agency determinations of fact, policy, or law.

Considered at a high enough level of abstraction, the doctrines governing scope of review of fact-finding and policymaking are relatively straightforward. Congress has delegated these tasks to agencies, not to courts, and agencies should also enjoy relevant expertise. Accordingly, courts generally review such agency determinations under some form of rationality review. In the context of review of significant agency policy, such review has evolved into review for 'reasoned decisionmaking' or 'hard look review.'

Doctrines governing judicial review of agency interpretations of law are considerably more complicated and a source of much controversy. Craig observes that many legal systems regard the proposition that courts should exercise independent judgment when determining legal meaning as axiomatic, and he adds that 'it would be seen as constitutional heresy to suggest otherwise' (Craig 2006, p. 436). American law might be said to start from this same baseline presumption, famously articulated in *Marbury v. Madison*, that it is the particular role of the courts 'to say what the law is.'[1] American law has also, however, long recognized that courts should apply rationality review to agency legal interpretations in some contexts.[2] This approach is now most closely associated with the *Chevron* doctrine, which, subject to many qualifications, instructs courts to apply a form of rationality review to an agency's construction of a statute that it is specially charged with administering.[3]

Important elements of current doctrines governing scope of review grew out of judicial efforts during the mid- to late-twentieth century to legitimize and ensure the rationality of agency policymaking. Accordingly, this chapter's first subpart offers an extremely brief account of this judicial transformation of American administrative law. The second subpart focuses directly on current doctrines governing scope of judicial review of agency determinations of fact, policy, and law. It takes special note of some of the controversies engendered by 'hard look' review of agency policymaking and the application of *Chevron* deference to agency statutory constructions.

JUDICIAL REVIEW AND "DEMOCRATIZATION" OF AGENCY POLICYMAKING

A certain skepticism of agency policymaking power is embedded in the United States' constitutional commitment to a strong version of separation of powers that attempts a sharp divide between legislative and executive power. Policymaking based on the value judgments of unelected bureaucrats has provoked perennial complaints of a 'democracy deficit' (Strauss 2010, p. 1351). In the early stages of the modern administrative state, its apologists sometimes addressed the problem of agency discretion by minimizing or denying its existence (Stewart 1975, p. 1675; Seidenfeld 1994, p. 92). As the growth of agency power and discretion made this type of response untenable, responses to the democracy deficit shifted away from denial and toward defending and improving the democratic bona fides of agency policymaking.

Courts participated in this 'democratization' process in two ways with marked effects on their approach to judicial review of agency action. One approach with roots in both pluralist and deliberative theories of democracy expanded opportunities for public participation in rulemaking and tightened review of agency policy decisions to ensure they are supported by reasoned, public deliberations (Stewart 1975, p. 1712; Staszewski 2012, pp. 885–92). A second approach has focused on political control of agencies by elected officials as a source of democratic legitimation for agency governance (Bressman 2003, p. 492). The *Chevron* doctrine reflects this model insofar as it justifies judicial deference to agency statutory constructions in part on the ground that agencies are answerable to elected officials.[4]

Constitutional Backdrop: The Nondelegation Doctrine and a Democracy Deficit

The U.S. Constitution provides that '[a]ll legislative Powers herein granted shall be vested in a Congress of the United States.'[5] This 'vesting clause' does not expressly bar Congress from delegating its legislative authority to other entities. It does, however, arguably reflect a premise that the legislature should be the primary locus of legitimate policymaking power.[6] In keeping with this premise, the Supreme Court has construed this clause as barring congressional delegations of legislative power to other entities.[7] Congress, however, lacks the time, expertise, and incentives to carry out all of the discretionary policymaking decisions required for reasonable governance of a complex, modern society. As Strauss notes, 'we would not think that assessing precisely what levels of arsenic make drinking water acceptably safe is appropriate for determination as a matter of political will' (Strauss 2010, p. 1354).

For nearly a century, the Supreme Court has reconciled its formalist adherence to the nondelegation doctrine with practical necessity by holding that Congress can, without violating that doctrine, grant policymaking discretion to an agency so long as Congress supplies an 'intelligible principle' that limits that discretion.[8] The Supreme Court has rejected a delegation for lacking an 'intelligible principle' on just two occasions, both in 1935 before the Court reconciled itself to the New Deal's expansion of agency governance.[9]

The nondelegation doctrine has thus existed for a century as a judicial expression of constitutional doubt regarding the legitimacy of bureaucratic rulemaking while at the same time, in practice, bowing to the demands of practical necessity. This longtime equilibrium is now under notable threat as a majority of the current Supreme Court has signaled interest in adopting a stricter nondelegation doctrine that would tighten the constitutional limits on the permissible scope of agency policymaking power.[10]

Denying the Democracy Deficit

Near the dawn of the modern administrative state, the 'traditional model of administrative law' avoided the potential democracy problem inherent in agency discretion by denying the existence of such discretion. On this view, an agency was a 'mere transmission belt for implementing legislative directives in particular cases' (Stewart 1975, p. 1675; Berle, 1917, p. 431). Under this transmission-belt model, rule by unelected bureaucrats is not undemocratic as they are simply carrying out the ministerial function of following legislative orders.

The transmission-belt model, regardless of whether it was ever accurate, could not survive contact with the New Deal of the 1930s and the powerful agencies created in response to the Great Depression (Bressman 2003, p. 471). Proponents of agency government accordingly shifted ground to the argument that agencies, even when implementing very broad statutory delegations of regulatory power, are essentially engaged in a technocratic exercise (Schiller 2007, p. 417). On this model, neutral expertise, rather than inherently contestable value judgments, provides the bases for agency policymaking (Seidenfeld 1994, p. 92).

Ultimately, this defense of administration as neutral expertise, which always had its critics (Stewart 1975, pp. 1678–79), was not sustainable given that it, too, was so plainly wrong. Factual expertise can identify the consequences of various courses of action, but it cannot determine which set of consequences to prefer as a matter of policy (Strauss 2010, p. 1359).

Democratizing Rulemaking with Interest Representation

During the 1960s and 1970s, efforts to legitimize agency rulemaking turned toward models that, rather than minimizing agency discretion, instead sought to democratize it in some fashion. Building on pluralistic conceptions of democratic governance, the 'interest representation' model sought to ensure that all interested parties can participate in agency rulemaking (Stewart 1975, p. 1712; Sunstein 1985, p. 32). This participation enables rulemaking to function as a forum for compromise among competing interests, providing a 'democratic' substitute for legislation. Broad participation also improves rulemaking as a means of gathering information from the public and thus enhancing agency expertise.

Courts transformed rulemaking to enable greater public participation by adopting extremely aggressive interpretations of the procedural requirements of the Administrative Procedure Act [APA], a foundational statute enacted in 1946 that still serves as a sort of quasi-constitution for the administrative state. On its face, the APA indicates that an agency can promulgate a legislative rule via a minimalist notice-and-comment process that merely requires the agency to provide public notice regarding the subject matter of its proposal, to grant interested persons a chance to submit written comments, and to publish the final rule along with a 'concise general statement of [its] basis and purpose.'[11] Courts, motivated in part by an impulse to enlist the public to combat the 'capture' of agencies by regulated interests (Merrill 1997, p. 1065), construed the APA's spare text as requiring disclosure of all scientific and technical information underlying a proposed rule in time for the public to offer comment before finalization.[12] Courts also interpreted the requirement that agencies accompany a final rule with a 'concise general statement of … basis and purpose' as requiring agencies to respond to all significant comments submitted by the public.[13] This requirement transformed 'concise general statements' into specific, exhaustive documents in which agencies attempt to respond to any comments that they fear a reviewing court might find significant (Beerman & Lawson 2007, p. 857).

Rulemaking as Deliberative Democracy

At about the time that courts essentially rewrote the procedural requirements for legislative rulemaking, they also tightened their scrutiny of agency policy decisions to ensure rational deliberation by agencies. The APA instructs courts to review agency actions to determine if they are 'arbitrary, capricious, an abuse of discretion, or otherwise not in accordance with law.'[14] Prior to the APA's adoption, the Supreme Court had held that arbitrariness review of an agency rule required a court merely to determine whether any reasonably conceivable set of facts could support the rule.[15] Under the 'hard look' model for arbitrariness review, courts instead examine an agency's contemporaneous rationale for its discretionary action to determine whether the agency based it on 'reasoned decisionmaking'[16] (Shapiro & Murphy 2016, pp. 341–48). Modern review thus focuses not on how an agency *might have* justified its policy choice, but instead on how an agency *did* justify its policy choice. The Supreme Court gave its definitive stamp of approval to this form of review in one of the most important American administrative law cases of the twentieth century, *Motor Vehicle Manufacturers Association of the United States, Inc. v. State Farm Mutual Automobile Insurance, Co.*, which is discussed below.[17]

Combined, judicial transformations of rulemaking procedures and arbitrariness review greatly expanded opportunities of interested persons to participate in rulemaking and obligations of agencies to respond to such participation. To their proponents, these changes shifted rulemaking toward a form of 'deliberative democracy,' that 'combine[s] accountability with a commitment to reflection and reason-giving' (Sunstein 2016, pp. 1619–24; Staszewski 2012, pp. 885–92). Critics have countered that excessive 'fetishization' of procedural controls implemented by judicial review has 'drain[ed] agencies of their legitimacy, impair[ed] their responsiveness to the public, and expose[d] them to capture' by special interests best able to manipulate those procedures (Bagley 2019, p. 400).

Presidentialism as Legitimator

Another influential model for improving the democratic bona fides of agency governance focuses not on interest representation and deliberation but instead on control by elected officials (Staszewski 2012, p. 856; Watts 2009, pp. 35–39). The 'presidentialist' variant of this model asserts that agency discretionary power should be controlled by the president for a mix of constitutional, pragmatic, and democratic reasons (Bressman & Vandenbergh 2006, pp. 54–55; Watts 2009, pp. 35–36). 'Presidentialism' has been characterized as the leading theoretical justification for agency policymaking discretion of the last several decades (Bressman 2003, p. 492; Staszewski 2012, p. 858).

In one of the most prominent works of scholarship advancing presidentialism, Justice Elena Kagan has argued that presidential control of bureaucratic discretion enhances democratic accountability both by heightening the transparency of agency action and by establishing an 'electoral link' between the public and the bureaucracy (Kagan 2001, pp. 2231–35). Regarding this electoral link, she observed, 'because the President has a national constituency, he is likely to consider, in setting the direction of administrative policy on an ongoing basis, the preferences of the general public, rather than merely parochial interests' (Kagan 2001, p. 2235).

The most aggressive practitioners of presidentialism have been, unsurprisingly, presidents. For instance, presidents of both parties have for forty years imposed centralized executive review of significant agency rules by the Office of Information and Regulatory Affairs (OIRA).[18] This review requires rules to undergo a highly formal, monetized form of cost–benefit analysis. It also, as its critics are quick to note, provides a locus for applying White House pressure to bend agency rules.

Judicial approaches to scope of review reflect a partial embrace of presidentialist and political control models. When reviewing agency policy choices for arbitrariness, courts generally demand technocratic justifications—that is, they do not accept political preferences of elected officials as justifications for the rationality of agency actions. Courts do accept and expect, however, that an agency will choose among reasonable policy choices based on the political preferences of elected officials.[19] Political control is acceptable within the limits of a zone set by rationality.

Chevron deference provides the most notable expression of presidentialism in scope-of-review doctrine. In *Chevron*, the Supreme Court explained that one reason why courts should defer to an agency's reasonable construction of its enabling act is that agencies, unlike federal judges, are answerable to the president, who is in turn 'directly accountable to the people.'[20] In light of this electoral accountability, as well as agencies' subject matter expertise, the Court deemed it 'entirely appropriate' for agencies to resolve ambiguities in statutes they administer to reflect 'the incumbent administration's views of wise policy.'[21]

DOCTRINES GOVERNING SCOPE OF REVIEW OF AGENCY ACTION

This subchapter discusses current scope-of-review doctrines that govern judicial scrutiny of agency determinations of fact, policy, and law. While it is true that these doctrines have continued to evolve over the last forty years, it is also true that their basic parameters have remained largely in place since the Supreme Court's decisions in *State Farm* and *Chevron* briefly discussed above. That said, the *Chevron* doctrine in particular has generated a great deal of criticism and commentary concerning its constitutionality, scope, and application.

Review of Fact

Courts generally review agency findings of fact to determine whether an agency reached a reasonable conclusion based on evidence available in the administrative record.[22] This deferential standard reflects both congressional delegation of fact-finding authority to agencies as well as an expectation that agencies should enjoy relevant expertise. In application, the actual intensity of rationality review naturally depends on many factors, for example, technical complexity, perceived quality of agency decision making, judicial sympathies, and so on.

Technically, some statutory provisions instruct courts to review agency findings of fact for 'substantial evidence' whereas others instruct courts to review them to determine if they are 'arbitrary.' Both of these standards are understood to require rationality review, but courts and commentators have long debated whether the former standard is somewhat more demanding on agencies than the latter. Some authorities insist that a congressional decision to require 'substantial evidence' review evidences a legislative intention for stricter review.[23] Another view insists that, as substantial evidence review merely checks for rationality, arbitrariness review cannot sensibly demand less.[24] Perhaps most sensibly, some courts sidestep this debate by conceding that substantial evidence review is stricter but adding that 'the difference between the two standards should not be exaggerated.'[25]

The distinction between substantial evidence and arbitrariness review of findings of fact grew out of a dichotomy between 'record' and 'non-record' proceedings that, thanks to judicial reform of arbitrariness review, has substantially dissolved. Under the APA, substantial evidence review applies to findings of fact determined by 'formal,' trial-type proceedings that produce a closed administrative record.[26] Substantial evidence review requires an agency to produce rational support for its factual determinations from this closed record. Arbitrariness review generally applies to factual determinations produced by 'informal' agency proceedings that, at the time of the APA's adoption, were regarded as 'non-record' proceedings.[27] In 1971's *Citizens to Preserve Overton Park v. Volpe*, the Supreme Court held that arbitrariness review of informal agency action requires an agency to produce an administrative record, and later cases have clarified that this record consists of material information that the agency considered at the time it made its decision.[28] Under this reformed understanding, an agency defending a finding of fact is generally limited to relying on materials contained in the administrative record regardless of whether substantial evidence or arbitrariness review applies. Given this convergence, continuing to distinguish between the two standards adds a small but needless complication to administrative law.

Review of Policy—*State Farm*-style Arbitrariness Review

Agency policy determinations are generally subject to review for arbitrariness.[29] As discussed above in the initial subchapter, during the 1960s and 1970s, courts aggressively interpreted this standard as requiring significant agency policy determinations to undergo review for 'reasoned decisionmaking.' This standard sometimes goes by the name, 'hard look review.'

The Supreme Court's 1983 opinion in *Motor Vehicles Manufacturers Association of the United States v. State Farm Mutual Automobile Insurance Co.* provides both the canonical description of review for reasoned decisionmaking, as well as an illuminating illustration of some of the difficulties it creates.[30] This litigation arose from a decision by the National Highway Traffic Safety Administration [NHTSA] to rescind a rule, Modified Standard 208 [MS 208], that it had adopted in 1977 during the Carter administration. This rule would have required automobile manufacturers to install passive restraints in the form of either airbags or automatic seatbelts in new motor vehicles. NHTSA estimated that installation of passive restraints could save approximately 12,000 lives per year. Early in the Reagan administration in 1981, NHTSA rescinded MS 208. To justify this decision, the agency explained that the 1977 rulemaking had assumed that manufacturers would install airbags in 60% of cars and passive belts in 40%. NHTSA had, however, determined that manufacturers would instead install passive belts rather than airbags in 99% of automobiles and that most of these belts would be easily detachable. As a result, the agency lacked a basis for predicting that MS 208 would significantly increase safety. The agency also expressed concern that, given the costs of implementing the rule and its limited benefits, MS 208 would prompt public backlash against ineffective regulation.

The Court's discussion of the parameters of arbitrariness review emphasized that the validity of an agency's policy choice depends on the agency's contemporaneous rationale for adopting it. An agency's explanation must provide a 'rational connection between the facts found and the choice made.'[31] In examining this explanation, a reviewing court's limited task is to determine 'whether the decision was based on a consideration of the relevant factors and whether there has been a clear error of judgment.'[32] The Court added that an agency's policy choice should generally fail arbitrariness review where examination of its contemporaneous rationale reveals that the agency has relied on factors which Congress has not intended it to consider, entirely failed to consider an important aspect of the problem, offered an explanation for its decision that runs counter to the evidence before the agency, or is so implausible that it could not be ascribed to a difference in view or the product of agency expertise.[33]

In short, judicial review for reasoned decisionmaking examines whether an agency's policy choice was a reasonable result of consideration of those factors that Congress intended the agency to consider in exercising its discretionary judgment.

The Court unanimously held that the rescission of MS 208 failed this standard because the agency's explanation had given no consideration to the possibility of amending the rule to eliminate the option of installing automatic seatbelts and flatly require installation of airbags. The failure to consider requiring airbags was plainly arbitrary given that the agency's own record indicated that airbags were an 'effective and cost-beneficial life-saving technology' with the potential to save on the order of 10,000 lives per year.[34]

The Court nicely illustrated that reasonableness can sometimes lie in the eye of the judicial beholder by splitting 5–4 on the issue of whether NHTSA's analysis of the safety benefits of detachable automatic seatbelts was also arbitrary. In essence, the agency concluded that it could not predict a meaningful increase in usage of seatbelts that automobile occupants could readily detach. A five-justice majority, although declining to 'upset the agency's views of the facts,' concluded that the agency's analysis did not satisfy the demands of reasoned decisionmaking because the agency had not considered the possibility that 'inertia' might lead to a substantial increase in seatbelt usage even for detachable belts.[35] Four justices thought that the agency's explanation of this point, 'while by no means a model, [was] adequate.'[36]

The Court also split 5–4 on the role that political control should play in arbitrariness review. Consistent with the 'presidentialist' model of legitimating agency policymaking, Justice Rehnquist, writing for a minority of four justices, explained:

> The agency's changed view of the standard seems to be related to the election of a new President of a different political party. … A change in administration brought about by the people casting their votes is a perfectly reasonable basis for an executive agency's reappraisal of the costs and benefits of its programs and regulations. As long as the agency remains within the bounds established by Congress, it is entitled to assess administrative records and evaluate priorities in light of the philosophy of the administration.[37]

The majority implicitly rejected this approach by focusing its analysis on the technocratic sufficiency of NHTSA's explanation and essentially ignoring Justice Rehnquist's accurate assessment of the politics of rescinding MS 208. Agencies have followed the majority's cue and generally offer technocratic justifications for their actions (Watts 2009, p. 2).

Scholarship on the proper role of politics in judicial review of agency policymaking continues to reflect the 5–4 split in *State Farm*. Watts, for instance, has argued that, to further the transparency, legitimacy, and efficacy of agency policymaking, courts conducting arbitrariness review should give weight to legitimate political influences that agencies disclose as influencing their policymaking decisions (Watts 2009, p. 84). Seidenfeld, by contrast, contends that hard look review, to serve its purpose of enabling facts and law to limit the zone of political discretion, 'must focus on the objective reasoning of the agency decision and not substitute statements of support by the President, or any other political actor, for such analysis' (Seidenfeld 2013, p. 1456).

Debate over the proper role of political preferences in arbitrariness review relates to the problem of 'secret records.' An agency's official explanation for its action is likely to focus on technocratic justifications and avoid comment on political forces that may have provided necessary motivation. The Supreme Court's response to this problem is to accept that 'unstated considerations of politics' are natural facts of bureaucratic life.[38] Reflecting this reality, 'a court may not reject an agency's stated reasons for acting simply because the agency might also have had other unstated reasons.'[39] Looking past an agency's official explanation for its decision to inquire into such unstated reasons is permissible only upon a 'strong showing of bad faith or improper behavior' by an agency.[40]

The most important criticism leveled against *State Farm*-style review for reasoned decisionmaking is that it has caused 'ossification' of rulemaking by requiring agencies to pour excessive resources into processes for developing, explaining, and defending their rules (Pierce, Jr., 2012, p. 1494; Cross 2000, pp. 1021–22; McGarity 1992, pp. 1401–03). As a result of this ossification, the process for promulgating significant rules can often drag on for years. Pierce observes, '[t]here is a veritable army of people with agency-specific substantive expertise who have expressed the view that ossification is a source of many serious problems' (Pierce, Jr. 2012, p. 1503).

Critics of the ossification charge have responded that empirical evidence that it 'is either a serious or widespread problem is mixed and relatively weak' (Yackee & Yackee 2012, p. 1421). Others observe that the costs of ossification should be balanced against the benefits that judicial review generates by improving agency decisionmaking processes—for example, by protecting against systematic biases (Seidenfeld 2002, p. 547).

Beyond ossification, some critics charge that courts use *State Farm*-style review to displace agency policymaking authority. Evidence for this charge can arguably be found in studies demonstrating that affirmance rates for agency policy decisions vary depending on whether a judge was appointed by a Democratic or Republican president and on the ideological valence of the agency action (Sunstein & Miles 2009, p. 2193). Some notable scholarship, however, minimizes the potential distorting effect of arbitrariness review by concluding that, at least at the Supreme Court level, arbitrariness review actually is highly deferential to agency policy choices (Gersen & Vermeule 2016, pp. 1362–67).

Review of law—*Chevron* deference and its discontents
As in other legal systems, the default position in American law is that courts exercise independent judgment to determine legal meaning. Courts have, however, often found reasons to defer to at least some agency constructions of law. During most of the twentieth century, courts did not seem overly concerned to develop a coherent doctrine for determining whether to apply *de novo* or deferential review to an agency's interpretation of law. This attitude

shifted after the Court's decision in 1984's *Chevron U.S.A., Inc. v. Natural Resources Defense Council, Inc.*, which, simplifying, instructed courts to apply a form of rationality review to an agency's construction of a statute it is specially charged with administering.[41] This instruction became the foundation of a substantial but arguably unsuccessful effort to rationalize this messy corner of the law.

The *Chevron* case arose out of a dispute regarding the meaning of 'stationary source' as used by the Clean Air Act Amendments of 1977, which require 'new or modified stationary sources' of pollution to undergo an expensive permitting process in 'nonattainment' states.[42] Interpreting the phrase 'stationary source' raised the issue of whether it should refer to the entirety of an industrial facility or to individual pollution-emitting components within such a facility. Adopting a facility-wide approach would allow regulated parties to avoid permitting to make changes to individual components so long as these changes did not cause the total amount of emissions emitted from a metaphorical 'bubble' encasing the entire facility to increase. During the Carter administration, the Environmental Protection Agency [EPA] adopted a rule that interpreted 'stationary source' as barring application of the bubble concept in nonattainment states. A year later, during the Reagan administration, the EPA reversed course and adopted a rule that interpreted 'stationary source' as permitting application of the bubble concept in both attainment and nonattainment states. This interpretation became the subject of the *Chevron* litigation.

The Supreme Court began its analysis by criticizing the lower court for 'adopt[ing] a static judicial definition of the term "stationary source" when it had decided that Congress itself had not commanded that definition.'[43] Instead of reading judicial preferences into an agency's enabling act, a court reviewing an agency's construction of a statute that it administers should instead ask and answer two questions:

> First, always, is the question whether Congress has directly spoken to the precise question at issue. If the intent of Congress is clear, that is the end of the matter; for the court, as well as the agency, must give effect to the unambiguously expressed intent of Congress. If, however, the court determines Congress has not directly addressed the precise question at issue, the court does not simply impose its own construction on the statute, as would be necessary in the absence of an administrative interpretation. Rather, if the statute is silent or ambiguous with respect to the specific issue, the question for the court is whether the agency's answer is based on a permissible construction of the statute.[44]

The Court offered three justifications for what came to be widely called the '*Chevron* two-step.' First, the Court characterized ambiguity in an agency's enabling act as an implicit congressional delegation of authority to the agency to resolve it.[45] Second, courts should defer to reasonable agency statutory constructions in light of agencies' greater subject-matter expertise.[46] Third, consistent with the presidentialist model for legitimating agency action, the Court explained that deference is appropriate because agencies, unlike federal judges, are accountable to the president and through the president to the public.[47]

Applying the *Chevron* framework to the EPA's interpretation of 'stationary source,' the Supreme Court concluded that the 'general terms in the text of the statute' did not 'reveal an actual intent of Congress' and that the legislative history was similarly 'unilluminating.'[48] The parties' debate over whether to interpret 'stationary source' to allow application of the bubble concept was therefore actually a 'policy battle' rather than a legal one.[49] As such, this debate was 'more properly addressed to legislators or administrators, not to judges.'[50] The Court thus acknowledged that, within a zone of reasonable construction where traditional tools of statutory construction do not yield a determinate legal answer, the project of resolving statutory ambiguity is a function of agency policymaking to which courts should extend deference. This conclusion in turn suggests that *Chevron* review should be regarded, in essence, as a form of arbitrariness review for policymaking that happens to be embedded in statutory construction (Levin 1997, p. 1276).

During the Reagan administration, conservative forces seized upon the *Chevron* doctrine as a means to enhance executive control of agency power. It is therefore all the more noteworthy that, in recent years, a strong movement has developed in conservative jurisprudential circles that condemns the *Chevron* doctrine as an unconstitutional violation of separation of powers. Justice Thomas contends that *Chevron* rips from the courts their 'ultimate interpretative authority to "say what the law is."'[51] In like vein, Justice Gorsuch (while still a lower-court judge) condemned *Chevron* for enabling 'executive bureaucracies to swallow huge amounts of core judicial and legislative power.'[52] Critics have also condemned *Chevron* as a statutory violation, contending that it ignores the APA's instruction to courts to 'decide all relevant questions of law' when reviewing agency action.[53]

A great deal of scholarly and judicial energy has been devoted to the 'step-zero' problem of determining limits on *Chevron*'s scope of applicability (Merrill & Hickman 2001). Where *Chevron* deference does not apply to an agency's construction of a statute that it administers, *Skidmore* deference generally should instead. This doctrine instructs courts to give an agency statutory construction whatever 'weight' it deserves in light of 'the thoroughness evident in its consideration, the validity of its reasoning, its consistency with earlier and later pronouncements, and all those factors which give it power to persuade.'[54] In essence, a court applying *Skidmore* deference should adopt the statutory construction that it deems best after giving due consideration to the agency's effort. 'Step-zero' doctrines that have evolved to govern the choice between *Chevron* and *Skidmore* include: (1) *Chevron* should generally apply to agency statutory constructions developed through relatively formal procedures that promote agency deliberation and public participation, such as notice-and-comment rulemaking or trial-type adjudications;[55] (2) the applicability of *Chevron* to agency statutory constructions developed through less formal means turns on a multi-factor balancing test (that usually yields a negative conclusion);[56] (3) *Chevron* does not apply to statutory constructions developed through defective procedures;[57] (4) *Chevron* does not apply to statutory constructions that agencies adopt as mere litigation positions;[58] (5) *Chevron* does not apply to an agency's construction of generally applicable statutes, such as the APA;[59] and (6) *Chevron* does not apply to 'extraordinary cases' involving 'major questions.'[60]

The last of these step-zero doctrines, the 'major questions' limitation, featured prominently in the Supreme Court's 2015 decision in *King v. Burwell*.[61] One of the most significant pieces of progressive legislation of the last several decades, the Affordable Care Act [ACA], instructed states to create insurance exchanges for the purchase of regulated health insurance products. If a state declined to do so, the ACA provided that the federal government would instead establish and operate an exchange within that state. The existence of federally created exchanges raised an interpretive problem, however, given that the ACA subsidizes the purchase of insurance with tax credits that are calculated based on premiums for insurance plans in 'an Exchange established by the State.'[62] The Internal Revenue Service [IRS] adopted a rule that construed this provision as authorizing tax credits for purchases made on either state- or federally created exchanges. Opponents of the ACA challenged the rule, contending that the statute authorized tax credits solely for purchases from the state-created exchanges. The

Supreme Court ultimately affirmed the agency's construction, but it declined to apply *Chevron* deference in its analysis. The majority opinion explained that *Chevron* deference 'is premised on the theory that a statute's ambiguity constitutes an implicit delegation from Congress to the agency to fill in the statutory gaps.'[63] This presumption was inapt in 'extraordinary cases.'[64] Congress, had it wished an agency such as the IRS to resolve an issue of such 'deep economic and political significance' as the availability of many billions of dollars in tax credits, 'surely would have done so expressly.'[65] In the absence of a clear delegation of *Chevron*-style authority to the IRS, it was a task for the courts to resolve statutory ambiguity.[66]

This 'major questions' limitation on the applicability of *Chevron* deference seems in notable tension with elements of the *Chevron* opinion itself, which counseled that agencies are better at resolving statutory ambiguity in their enabling acts than courts because agencies have greater expertise and political accountability.[67] One might think that these justifications would apply with even greater force to 'major' questions than to 'minor' ones. Regardless of the merits of the major questions limitation, however, it does provide a good illustration of how the Court has responded to criticisms of its deference doctrines by narrowing rather than overturning them.[68]

In addition to various step-zero problems, *Chevron*'s step one and step two present their own notorious difficulties. Step one instructs a court reviewing an agency's statutory construction to use the 'traditional tools of statutory construction' at its disposal to determine whether Congress has expressed a 'clear' and 'unambiguously expressed intent' that must be given effect.[69] This instruction to determine whether a statute is clear may seem straightforward enough, but one prominent scholar has observed that it 'would take a book' to dissect decades of arguments regarding how to apply step one (Manning 2014, pp. 1529–30). One problem is that different judges seem to have different intuitions concerning the strictness of the step-one inquiry (Beermann 2010, pp. 817–22). There is also disagreement regarding the set of 'traditional tools' that properly apply to step-one analysis. For instance, courts often deploy 'canons of construction' as heuristics to resolve ambiguity—for example, courts should, if they reasonably can, construe statutes to avoid raising serious constitutional questions; courts should construe statutes to avoid retroactive effect, and so on. Courts applying *Chevron* deference sometimes have invoked a canon to resolve statutory ambiguity and thus find a 'clear' meaning at step one that precludes application of *Chevron* deference (Bamberger 2008, pp. 77–80; Walker 2012). In other cases, courts have held that the existence of ambiguity signals that *Chevron* deference rather than a canon should apply (Bamberger 2008, pp. 81–84).

Step two instructs courts to affirm an agency's statutory construction that has survived step one so long as it is 'permissible' or reasonable. Step two is theoretically puzzling but, as a practical matter, usually unimportant. If an agency statutory construction survives step one, then it should, by hypothesis, provide a reasonable way of resolving statutory ambiguity in the agency's enabling act. If, however, a statutory construction must be reasonable to survive step one, then there might seem to be little point to step two. One response to this problem is to characterize *Chevron* as really only having one step, which is to check whether an agency statutory construction is reasonable.[70] Some judicial decisions, however, address this difficulty by treating step two as a variant of review for reasoned decisionmaking.[71] On this view, step two, rather than repeating the step-one task of determining whether the agency's statutory construction happens to fall within a zone of reason, instead checks whether the agency has supported its construction with reasoned decisionmaking (Levin 1997, p. 1276). On a practical level, however, these step-two metaphysics generally do not matter much given that, if a court reaches step two, an agency is extremely likely to prevail (Barnett & Walker 2017, p. 33).

The most ironic aspect of the four decades of scholastic debate over *Chevron* deference is that it is not clear that its application actually changes the outcome of judicial review in many cases. The choice between *Chevron* and *Skidmore* deference certainly governs how judges write their opinions to justify their conclusions. It is not so obvious that this choice alters the cognitive processes that actually determine judicial decisions. It could be the case that, generally speaking, where a court would be willing to affirm an agency statutory construction as 'reasonable' under *Chevron*, it would also be willing to affirm the agency statutory construction as 'persuasive' under *Skidmore*. Scholars have attempted to test whether the choice between *Chevron* and *Skidmore* materially affects outcomes by comparing affirmance rates of courts applying these standards. In part based on these studies, a consensus arguably formed that this choice had little practical impact (Zaring 2010, p. 135). More recently, an impressively extensive study found that courts of appeals affirm at a substantially higher rate when applying *Chevron* (77.4%) than when applying *Skidmore* (56%) (Barnett & Walker 2017, p. 6). The significance of this finding for the practical effects of these standards remains somewhat unclear, however, given that there is reason to expect *Chevron*-eligible interpretations, as a group, to be stronger on their merits than interpretations to which courts apply *Skidmore* (Murphy 2017, pp. 46–47).

Although the *Chevron* doctrine is an idiosyncrasy of the American legal system, the problem of determining whether courts should defer to agency statutory constructions is implicit in all legal systems. Barnett and Vinson provide a comparative exploration of how the United Kingdom, Italy, Germany, Canada, and Australia have addressed this problem, ranging from a near embrace of *Chevron* to outright rejection. (Barnett & Vinson 2020).

NOTES

1.   Marbury v. Madison, 5 U.S. 137, 177 (1803).
2.   United States v. Vowell, 9 U.S. 368, 372 (1810).
3.   Chevron, U.S.A., Inc. v. Nat. Res. Def. Council, Inc., 467 U.S. 837 (1984).
4.   *Id.* at 865.
5.   U.S. CONST., ART. I, § 1.
6.   Indus. Union Dep't, AFL-CIO v. Am. Petroleum Inst., 448 U.S. 607, 685 (1980) (Rehnquist, J., concurring).
7.   Whitman v. Am. Trucking Ass'n, 531 U.S. 457, 472 (2001) (noting that the constitutional text granting legislative authority to Congress, 'permits no delegation of those powers').
8.   J.W. Hampton, Jr., & Co. v. United States, 276 U.S. 394, 409 (1928).
9.   A.L.A. Schechter Poultry Corp. v. United States, 295 U.S. 495, 537 (1935) (striking delegation of authority to the president to approve codes of 'fair competition'); Panama Refin. Co. v. Ryan, 293 U.S. 388, 430 (1935) (striking delegation of authority to president to bar interstate transportation of 'hot oil').
10.   *See, e.g.*, Gundy v. United States, 139 S. Ct. 2116, 2141 (2019) (Gorsuch, J., dissenting); Dept. of Transp. v. Ass'n of Am. Railroads, 135 S. Ct. 1225, 1242 (2015) (Thomas, J., concurring).
11.   *See* 5 U.S.C. § 553 (setting forth the APA's default requirements for rulemaking).
12.   United States v. Nova Scotia Food Prod. Corp., 568 F.2d 240, 251 (2d Cir. 1977); Portland Cement Ass'n v. Ruckelshaus, 486 F.2d 375, 394 (D.C. Cir. 1973).
13.   *Portland Cement*, 486 F.2d at 394.
14.   5 U.S.C. § 706(2)(A).
15.   Pacific States Box & Basket Co. v. White, 296 U.S. 176, 185 (1935).

16. For a seminal discussion of the 'hard look,' see Greater Bos. Television Corp. v. FCC, 444 F.2d 841, 851–52 (D.C. Cir. 1970) (Leventhal, J.) (explaining that a court reviewing an agency's discretionary decision should intervene if the court concludes that 'the agency has not really taken a "hard look" at the salient problems' and has not based its decision on 'reasoned decision-making').
17. 463 U.S. 29, 41–43 (1983).
18. Since 1993, the primary executive order controlling this process has been Exec. Order No. 12,866, 58 Fed. Reg. 51,735 (Sept. 30, 1993).
19. F.C.C. v. Fox Television Stations, Inc., 556 U.S. 502, 515 (2009).
20. Chevron, U.S.A., Inc. v. Nat. Res. Def. Council, Inc., 467 U.S. 837, 865–66 (1984).
21. *Id.*
22. Consol. Edison Co. of N.Y. v. NLRB, 305 U.S. 197, 229 (1938) (discussing the substantial evidence standard); Const. Pipeline Co. v. N.Y. St. Dep't of Env't Conservation, 868 F.3d 87, 102 (2d Cir. 2017) (discussing arbitrariness review).
23. *In re* Gartside, 203 F.3d 1305, 1312 (Fed. Cir. 2000).
24. Ass'n of Data Processing Serv. Orgs., Inc. v. Bd. of Governors of Fed. Rsrv. Sys., 745 F.2d 677, 683–84 (D.C. Cir. 1984) (Scalia, J.).
25. Nat'l Oilseed Processors Ass'n v. OSHA, 769 F.3d 1173, 1178–79 (D.C. Cir. 2014) (internal quotations omitted).
26. *See* 5 U.S.C. § 706(2)(E) (instructing courts to apply 'substantial evidence' review to facts determined by agencies through formal, on-the-record proceedings).
27. *See id.* at § 706(2)(A) (establishing a default standard of arbitrariness review).
28. Citizens to Pres. Overton Park v. Volpe, 401 U.S. 402, 420 (1971).
29. 5 U.S.C. § 706(2)(A).
30. Motor Vehicle Mfrs. Ass'n of the U.S. v. State Farm Mut. Auto. Ins. Co., 463 U.S. 29 (1983).
31. *Id.* at 43 (quoting Burlington Truck Lines v. United States, 371 U.S. 156, 168 (1962)).
32. *Id.* (quoting Bowman Transp., Inc. v. Arkansas-Best Freight Sys., Inc., 419 U.S. 281, 285 (1974)).
33. *Id.*
34. *Id.*
35. *Id.* at 52–54.
36. *Id.* at 58 (Rehnquist, J., concurring in part and dissenting in part).
37. *Id.* at 59 (Rehnquist, J., concurring in part and dissenting in part) (footnote omitted).
38. Department of Commerce v. New York, 139 S. Ct. 2551, 2573 (2019).
39. *Id.*
40. *Id.* at 2573–74 (quoting Citizens to Preserve Overton Park v. Volpe, 401 U.S. 402, 420 (1971)).
41. Chevron, U.S.A., Inc. v. Nat. Res. Def. Council, Inc., 467 U.S. 837 (1984). A similar (and similarly controversial) doctrine instructs courts to defer under some conditions to an agency's reasonable construction of a rule that it has promulgated. Kisor v. Wilkie, 139 S. Ct. 2400 (2019).
42. *Chevron,* 467 U.S. at 839–40 (discussing permitting requirements of Clean Air Act Amendments of 1977, Pub. L. 95-95, 91 Stat. 685).
43. *Id.* at 842.
44. *Id.* at 842–43 (internal footnotes omitted).
45. *Id.* at 843.
46. *Id.* at 865.
47. *Id.* at 865.
48. *Id.* at 861–62.
49. *Id.* at 864.
50. *Id.*
51. Michigan v. EPA, 135 S. Ct. 2699, 2712 (2015) (Thomas, J., concurring) (quoting Marbury v. Madison, 5 U.S. 137, 177 (1803)).
52. Gutierrez-Brizuela v. Lynch, 834 F.3d 1142, 1149 (10th Cir. 2016) (Gorsuch, J., concurring).
53. 5 U.S.C. § 706.
54. Skidmore v. Swift & Co., 323 U.S. 134, 140 (1944).
55. United States v. Mead Corp., 533 U.S. 218, 227–30 (2001).
56. Barnhart v. Walton, 535 U.S. 212, 222 (2002).
57. Encino Motorcars, LLC v. Navarro, 136 S. Ct. 2117, 2125 (2016).

58. Bowen v. Georgetown Univ. Hosp., 488 U.S. 204, 212 (1988).
59. Collins v. Nat'l Transp. Safety Bd., 351 F.3d 1246, 1253 (D.C. Cir. 2003).
60. King v. Burwell, 576 U.S. 473, 485 (2015).
61. *Id.*
62. *Id.* at 485 (quoting 26 U.S.C. §§ 36B(b)(2)(A), (c)(2)(A)(i)).
63. *Id.* at 485 (quoting FDA v. Brown & Williamson Tobacco Corp., 529 U.S. 120, 159 (2000)).
64. *Id.*
65. *Id.* at 486 (internal quotations omitted) (quoting Util. Regul. Grp. v. EPA, 573 U.S. 302, 324 (2014)).
66. *Id.*
67. Chevron, U.S.A., Inc. v. Nat. Res. Def. Council, Inc., 467 U.S. 837, 865–66 (1984).
68. *Cf.* Kisor v. Wilkie, 139 S. Ct. 2400, 2415–18 (2019) (narrowing the applicability of *Auer* deference).
69. *Chevron*, 467 U.S. 842–43 (1984).
70. Michigan v. EPA, 576 U.S. 743, 751 (2015) (Scalia, J.).
71. Judulang v. Holder, 132 S. Ct. 476, 483 n.7 (2011) (equating step two and arbitrariness review).

REFERENCES

Bagley, Nicholas (2019). The procedure fetish. *Michigan Law Review*, 118(3), 345–401.
Bamberger, Kenneth A. (2008). Normative canons in the review of administrative policymaking. *Yale Law Journal*, 118(1), 64–125.
Barnett, Kent & Vinson, Lindsey (2020). Chevron abroad. *Notre Dame Law Review*, 96(2), 621–675.
Barnett, Kent & Walker, Christopher J. (2017). Chevron in the circuit courts. *Michigan Law Review*, 116(1), 1–73.
Berle, A.A. (1917). The expansion of American administrative law. *Harvard Law Review*, 30(5), 430–448.
Beermann, Jack M. (2010). End the failed Chevron experiment now: How Chevron has failed and why it can and should be overruled. *Connecticut Law Review*, 42(3), 779–851.
Beermann, Jack & Lawson, Gary (2007). Reprocessing Vermont Yankee. *George Washington Law Review*, 75(4), 856–901.
Bressman, Lisa Schulz (2003). Beyond accountability: Arbitrariness and legitimacy in the administrative state. *New York University Law Review*, 78(2), 461–556.
Bressman, Lisa Schulz & Vandenbergh, Michael P. (2006). Inside the administrative state: A critical look at the practice of presidential control. *Michigan Law Review*, 105(1), 47–99.
Craig, Paul (2006). *EU Administrative Law*. Oxford University Press.
Cross, Frank B. (2000). Pragmatic pathologies of judicial review of administrative rulemaking. *North Carolina Law Review*, 78(4), 1013–1069.
Gersen, J. & Vermeule, A. (2016). Thin rationality review. *Michigan Law Review*, 114(8), 1355–1412.
Kagan, Elena (2001). Presidential administration. *Harvard Law Review*, 114(8), 2245–2385.
Levin, Ronald M. (1997). The anatomy of Chevron: Step two reconsidered. *Chicago-Kent Law Review*, 72(4), 1253–1297.
Manning, John F. (2014). Chevron and legislative history. *George Washington Law Review*, 82(5), 1517–1552.
Merrill, Thomas W. (1997). Capture theory and the courts: 1967–1983. *Chicago-Kent Law Review*, 72(4), 1039–1117.
Merrill, Thomas W. & Hickman, Kristin E. (2001). Chevron's domain. *Georgia Law Journal*, 89(4), 833–921.
McGarity, Thomas O. (1992). Some thoughts on 'deossifying' the rulemaking process. *Duke Law Journal*, 41(6), 1385–1462.
Murphy, Richard W. (2017). Abandon Chevron and modernize stare decisis for the administrative state. *Alabama Law Review*, 69(1), 1–57.

Pierce, Jr., Richard J. (2012). Rulemaking ossification is real: A response to testing the ossification thesis. *George Washington Law Review*, 80(5), 1493–1503.

Schiller, Reuel E. (2007). The era of deference: Courts, expertise, and the emergence of New Deal administrative law. *Michigan Law Review*, 106(3), 417–441.

Seidenfeld, Mark (2013). The role of politics in a deliberative model of the administrative state. *George Washington Law Review*, 81(5), 1397–1457.

Seidenfeld, Mark (2002). Cognitive loafing, social conformity, and judicial review of agency rulemaking. *Cornell Law Review*, 87(2), 486–548.

Seidenfeld, Mark (1994). A syncopated Chevron: Emphasizing reasoned decisionmaking in reviewing agency interpretations of statutes. *Texas Law Review*, 73(1), 83–138.

Shapiro, Sidney A. & Murphy, Richard (2016). Arbitrariness review made reasonable: Structural and conceptual reform of the "hard look." *Notre Dame Law Review*, 92(1), 331–379.

Staszewski, Glen (2012). Political reasons, deliberative democracy, and administrative law. *Iowa Law Review*, 97(3), 885–892.

Stewart, Richard B. (1975). The reformation of American administrative law. *Harvard Law Review*, 88(8), 1669–1813.

Strauss, Peter L. (2010). Legislation that isn't—attending to rulemaking's "democracy deficit." *California Law Review*, 98(4), 1351–1370.

Sunstein, Cass. R. (2016). The most knowledgeable branch. *University of Pennsylvania Law Review*, 164(7), 1607–1648.

Sunstein, Cass. R. (1985). Interest groups in American public law. *Stanford Law Review*, 38(1), 29–87.

Sunstein, Cass. R. & Miles, Thomas J. (2009). Depoliticizing administrative law. *Duke Law Journal*, 58(8), 2193–2230.

Walker, Christopher J. (2012). Avoiding normative canons in the review of administrative interpretations: A Brand X doctrine of constitutional avoidance. *Administrative Law Review*, 64(1), 139–190.

Watts, Kathryn A. (2009). Proposing a place for politics in arbitrary and capricious review. *Yale Law Journal*, 119(1), 2–85.

Yackee, Jason Webb & Yackee, Susan Webb (2012). Testing the ossification thesis: An empirical examination of federal regulatory volume and speed, 1950–1990. *George Washington Law Review*, 80(5), 1414–1492.

Zaring, David (2010). Reasonable agencies. *Virginia Law Review*, 96(1), 135–197.

PART V

BEYOND REGULATION

24. Agency capture

Justin Rex

INTRODUCTION

Crises and disasters in regulated industries highlight the ways businesses push their regulators to weaken oversight at the expense of the broader public interest—a phenomenon often called capture (Carpenter and Moss 2014b). Despite the difficulty in defining and rigorously measuring the concept (Coglianese 2016), it is used frequently by journalists and academics in many disciplines. In this chapter I review the scholarship on capture across a variety of disciplines to untangle various definitions of both capture and related concepts like corruption and lobbying, as well as the public interest. I then review some of its main findings about the capture mechanisms, their prevalence, and their remedy. Finally, I outline several lingering issues in the literature, suggesting promising avenues on which future research can build.

FOUNDATIONS

Defining Capture and the Private and Public Interest

Scholars define capture in a variety of ways: over time, the tendency of agencies to "relate their goals and objectives to the demands of dominant interest groups in the economy" (Bernstein 1955, p. 92); "the control of agency policy decision-making by a sub-population of individuals or organizations outside of the agency" (Yackee 2014, p. 296); "…responsiveness to the desires of the industry or groups being regulated" (Barkow 2010, p. 21); the ability of the regulated industry to secure rents by using regulation to create entry barriers to a market (Stigler 1971); or "… the phenomenon whereby regulated entities wield their superior organizational capabilities to secure favorable agency outcomes at the expense of the diffuse public" (Bagley 2010, p. 2). Makkai and Braithwaite (1992) use surveys to identify three distinct motivational dimensions captured regulators display: sympathy with the issues the industry faces when under inspection, identification with, or feeling part of, the industry, and attitudes toward strong enforcement of rules. Despite a lack of agreement, two common themes run through most definitions: the key actors are regulators and regulated industries, and regulators who fail to uphold the public interest because business interests successfully pressure them to do so.

To the above, Carpenter and Moss (2014a) add the severity or intensity of capture. Strong capture is so pervasive that the public interest is better achieved through no regulation, whereas weak capture reduces attainment of the public interest, but not enough that the public would be better off without regulation, which is similar to what Makkai and Braithwaite (1992) call "situational capture". Though literature covered in this chapter discusses both forms, most identify cases of weak capture. The strong version, espoused by many economists and public choice scholars, has been heavily criticized: its key assumptions have weak empirical support and offer an incomplete understanding of how interest groups, legislators, and administrators behave (Carrigan and Coglianese 2016; Croley 2011).

We can get a better sense of capture by establishing its relationship to corruption, rent seeking, and lobbying. Corruption involves the misuse of public office for private gain by some illegal act, such as bribery, fraud, self-enrichment cronyism, or fees or tolls on the public (Tollison 2004), whereas capture relies on legal mechanisms of influence (Carpenter and Moss 2014a). They remedy for corruption is civil service reform, while capture requires additional remedies discussed below because it persists in countries despite a strong rule of law and robust civil service system (ibid).

Rent seeking involves searches for profit by getting favorable treatment from government using policies like tariffs or entry barriers (Krueger 1974; Tullock 1967). From an economic efficiency standpoint, rent seeking involves firms gaining unproductive income, or extracting rent, through artificially manipulating policy, which harms general consumer welfare (Fischer 2007). Society is worse off with rent seeking because inefficient producers spend money trying to obtain rents through lobbying, which could otherwise be put toward more productive uses (Tollison 2012). Thus, rent seeking is a type of capture. The language of rent seeking tends to be used more frequently in economics and public choice scholarship, whereas regulation and governance scholars in political science and related disciplines tend to use the language of capture.

It is important to distinguish rent seeking and capture from the mechanisms used to achieve these ends. Lobbying refers to the menu of strategies interests groups use to influence legislators using exchange (vote buying), persuasion, or subsidies (via performing legislative labor) (Hall and Deardorff 2006). Interest groups use similar tactics to influence the executive and judicial branches as well (Mayer 2007). The presence of lobbying does not in and of itself constitute capture, though some scholars argue it is a necessary condition for capture (Carpenter 2014); lobbying is an attempt to influence, but influence requires explaining a counterfactual of what agencies would have decided absent lobbying and comparing the two outcomes (Coglianese 2016).

Private interest capture also presumes a clear notion of the public interest from which regulatory decisions allegedly deviate (Carpenter 2014). For Croley, "'public interested' regulation is used in contradistinction to 'special interest' regulation, where the former refers to regulation that promotes diffuse interests while the latter describes the delivery of rents to narrow groups" (2000, p. 8). In other words, regulators do something different than what well-organized and powerful regulated interests want. Similarly, Levine and Forrence (1990) argue the general interest is the public's preferred regulatory outcome assuming no transaction costs, meaning absent any information or monitoring costs or organizational biases that typically favor business. More generally, in economics, the public interest is explicitly or implicitly associated with consumer welfare and the efficient distribution of societal resources.

Shapiro (2012) adds a temporal dimension to the notion of the public and private interest. He notes that the legislative intent in creating agencies is typically to maximize public welfare while balancing additional statutory considerations. Regulators that *consistently* favor the industry, even agencies with a dual mandate to promote an industry and protect the public, fail to meet this sense of the public interest. In other words, because the typical private interest of a regulated industry is to avoid stringent regulations (ibid), an agency consistently catering to this private interest is not upholding the public one. Pursuing the public interest does not mean agencies avoid any decisions that align with industry interests. However, consistently favoring the industry is distinct from a normal pattern of influence we would expect the industry to exert.

Scholarship on Capture

The capture literature is broad across disciplines and deep within several. The typology in Table 24.1 provides some organizational coherence to this literature using two key dimensions: the presence of industry influence, the *agents* of capture, and the scope of capture across the *targets* of capture. As Carpenter (2014) notes, a key element of establishing capture is evidence that regulated parties are intentionally influencing regulators, which is often assumed without being proven. The rows indicate whether socially undesirable industry influence is present, allowing us to distinguish findings in the literature that demonstrate industry protection without capture (Carpenter 2004) from findings of capture.

The vertical dimension has two primary targets of capture, the agency and its personnel, and elected officials, including the executive or legislature. Within the agency, low level operators, regional managers, or appointed executives can be captured (Wilson 1989), as well as the entire agency (Huntington 1952). The agent and target dimensions draw from Tirole's (1986) three-tiered principal agent theory of capture, Shapiro's (2010) concepts of political and sabotage capture, Wagner's (2010b) institutional and political capture, and Carpenter's (2014) agency and statutory capture. The two sets of actors also provide a rough approximation of capture at different points in time in the policy cycle: capture of legislatures typically happens during the policy formulation and adoption stages, while capture of agencies happens during policy implementation.

Table 24.1   Type and scope of capture

	Socially Undesirable Industry Influence	Targets of Capture	
		Agency—Policy Implementation	Elected Officials—Policy Adoption
Agents of Capture	No	Industry Influence/Exchange/Protection/ Coproduction Without Capture	Electorally Sanctioned/Unintentional Pro-Business Regulation
	Yes	Agency Capture	Elected Official/Statutory Capture

Note: Together, the typology provides four broad conceptual categories with which to organize the literature on capture mechanisms and remedies, as detailed below.

Synthesizing the Capture Literature

Protection without capture
Industry friendly regulation can occur in the absence of direct pressure, resulting from unintended consequences of regulatory decisions. Such outcomes fit under the umbrella of "protection without capture" (Carpenter 2004). For example, Carpenter (2004) finds that the FDA's drug approval decisions are guided by a concern for reputation and consumer welfare but protect older firms with quicker approvals, in part because these firms have established reputations and previous interactions with the agency. Similarly, Gilad (2008) argues UK financial regulators engage in industry exchange without capture when they devise consumer dispute resolution processes in line with industry preferences, but in a way that preserves regulatory autonomy. Further, industry influence

may be socially desirable, when agencies leverage industry expertise (Tai 2017; Thaw 2014) and coproduce knowledge (Slayton and Clark-Ginsberg 2018) to achieve the public interest.

Unintentional/electorally sanctioned pro-business regulation
Legislatures also provide industry benefits without necessarily being captured by unintentionally empowering industry when democratizing rulemaking (Wagner 2010a), balancing difficult tradeoffs in regulatory (re)design (Carrigan 2013), and jurisdictional fragmentation (Provost 2016). Alternatively, industry deference may actually be responsiveness to signals from elected officials (Gordon and Hafer 2013; Wood and Waterman 1994), "electorally sanctioned pro-business regulation" (Carpenter 2014), or "gifts" that promote broad macro-economic goals (Browne 2020). Thus, what appears like deference to the industry is actually agencies being sensitive to democratic influences consistent with hierarchical political control.

Agency capture
The potential for agency capture occurs at the personnel selection, rulemaking, and can enforcement stages of the regulatory process. Financial incentives and competing loyalties resulting from the revolving door between agency and regulated industry personnel creates the potential for capture, but research finds mixed support for this capture dynamic (Cohen 1986; Gormley 1979; Makkai and Braithwaite 1992; Shive and Forster 2016). With personnel in place, industry comments during agency rulemaking can shift rules in their favor (Yackee 2020), though not always (Yackee 2014) . With rules in place, repeated interactions between regulators and firms create political and social-psychological pressures that can push enforcement personnel to so identify with the industry they regulate them favorably in return (Kaufman 1960; Kwak 2014). Enforcement vigor can also decline as agencies age (Bernstein 1955). Similarly, others argue that regulators who oversee a single industry are more likely to be captured (Gormley 1983; Thomas et al. 2010). This dynamic is particularly pronounced when the industry is a monopoly provider (Laffont and Tirole 1991).

Elected official or statutory capture
Likewise, elected officials provide firms regulatory benefits during policy formulation. Stigler (1971) argues firms demand regulation to limit competition by lobbying elected officials to create tariffs or occupational licensing as entry barriers into a particular market that allow extant firms to capture rents. Though Stigler focused on entry barriers, firms also use threats (Dal Bó and Di Tella 2003) or resource (Fellowes and Wolf 2004) and mobilization advantages (Hall and Wayman 1990) to pressure legislatures to provide a variety of benefits, including appointing an agency head who is a former industry participant and hostile to regulation (Shapiro 2012), adopting deregulatory legislation or what Carpenter and Moss (2014a) call "corrosive capture", creating a captured agency that is set up to benefit regulated interests (Sabatier 1975), or reducing agency budgets to undermine their effectiveness (Shapiro 2012). This kind of transactional lobbying and revolving door dynamics may be more pronounced in the U.S. (Drutman 2015) than in the European Union (Coen and Vannoni 2016).

Often, business influence develops into a regular pattern in the policymaking process that includes influence over both agencies and the legislature. Iron triangle theorists argue that close connections between agencies, legislative committees, and regulated industries form elite subsystems that favor participants but exclude the broader public (Huntington 1952; Wood and Waterman 1994). A well-coordinated industry can shape public opinion to such a degree it develops deep seeded opposition to governmental regulation that envelopes the policymaking process in system-wide deep capture (Hanson and Yosifon 2003). Though industry-friendly subsystems are a frequent part of the policymaking process, public interest groups can expand the scope of conflict to other institutional venues to increase public salience and improve chances for public interest regulation (Schattschneider 1975). Further, public interest groups can overcome mobilization biases and penetrate iron triangles to expand participation to additional interests (Heclo 1978; Trumbull 2012).

Capture Across Industries

Broad conclusions about capture are difficult given the number of industries and geographies. Regulation also varies in quality over time, so captured agencies can improve (Meier and Plumlee 1978) and high quality regulators can decline (Bernstein 1955). To simplify, Gormley (1986) argues a policy domain's public salience and technical complexity drive the likelihood of capture, finding it occurs infrequently across industries. To these Meier (1985) adds agency power, agency goals, and the organization of interests, among other variables. He argues capture does occurring in licensed professions, but not banking, environmental, consumer protection, or agricultural regulation. Additional broad surveys have not found widespread capture either (Quirk 1981; Wilson 1980), though these are focused on the U.S. only.

That caveat aside, what follows are some non-exhaustive examples of capture scholarship in a few prominent industries and issues areas. Perhaps no industry has been understood through the lens of capture more than the U.S. financial industry (Baker 2010; Barth et al. 2012; Baxter 2011; Cohn 2019; Levitin 2014), though others find similar patterns in other countries (Wade and Sigurgeirsdottir 2010; Pagliari 2012), and international financial regulatory bodies (Goldbach 2015). Despite the proliferation of this narrative post-global financial crisis, just as many scholars challenge financial industry capture (Gilad 2008; Trampusch and Fastenrath 2021; Young 2012).

Environmental regulation is another area scholars worry about capture, including offshore drilling (Portman 2014), the oil and gas industry (MacLean 2016), pesticide use (Perlman 2020), solar energy (Wolff 2019), fishing (Thomas et al. 2010), mining (Briody and Prenzler 1998), public utilities (Barrett 2015; Laffont and Tirole 1991), and nuclear power (Kurokawa and Ninomiya 2018). However, numerous strategies exist to mitigate environmental regulatory capture (Carruthers and Lamoreaux 2016; Costello and Grainger 2018; Law and Long 2011; Zinn 2002). Ultimately, though generalizations are difficult, the above suggests that capture is a threat across many industries and jurisdictions.

Policy Responses

What is the appropriate policy response to capture, if any? Policymakers should respond differently depending on the scope and intensity of capture; strong/weak agency and legislative capture each require different solutions. According to public choice theorists and some economists, strong capture is prevalent and society would be better off without regulation, while weak capture scholars argue more appropriately tailored remedies to improve regulation are better than eliminating regulation altogether. Policymakers must also be careful to recognize that capture is often misdiagnosed (Carpenter 2014) and that some level of industry influence is beneficial (Makkai and Braithwaite 1992; Reiss 2011).

Protection without capture

Before fixing an allegedly captured agency, one must first establish capture occurred. In situations of protection or influence without capture, no remedy is necessary. Relatedly, policymakers should acknowledge there are inherent tradeoffs in agency design decisions; the potential for mitigating capture must be weighed against coordination problems these reforms may create (Carrigan 2013). When industry comments overwhelm agency rulemaking, Wagner (2010b) recommends critical review by independent experts while others recommend centralized executive review (Livermore and Revesz 2014). Gordon and Hafer (2013) imply an electoral rather than a policy-based remedy; because agencies are responsive to political controls, voters should elect politicians who will influence agencies to be more independent from industry. Additionally, evidence shows that political controls, like budgets and executive appointments of new agency leadership, can reverse weak enforcement (Wood and Waterman 1994).

Agency capture

Because revolving door theory has not stood up well to empirical tests (Cohen 1986; Gormley 1979), any remedies may really be a solution in search of a problem. Moreover, employing former industry workers can improve regulation by providing expertise and promoting cooperation (Makkai and Braithwaite 1992; Reiss 2011). Thus, Makkai and Braithwaite (1992) recommend letting "the revolving door spin for all its worth" (p. 72). Alternatively, scholars more skeptical of its benefits recommend employment restrictions to deter quick transitions between agency and industry (Barkow 2010).

Kaufman (1960) found that the forest service neutralizes the danger of examiner capture by rotating personnel often early in their career. Cultural capture is harder to counteract because it results from psychological traits inherent in human relationships (Kwak 2014). While recognizing the difficulty of prevention, Kwak (2014) offers a range of solutions, from employment restrictions, negotiated rulemaking, Office of Information and Regulatory Affairs rulemaking review, to strategies to "debias" regulator thinking and empower consumer advocates.

Capture of agency policymaking or entire agencies requires broader solutions. To counter the superior resources and information industry uses to pressure agencies during rulemaking and court battles, Shapiro (2010, 2012) calls for more systematic legislative oversight. More broadly, a variety of scholars suggest types of external agency review and checks and balances including, more clear legislative mandates (Bull 2016) better cost benefit analysis of agency decisions (Calabria 2016) independent commissions to review and evaluate agency decisions (Shapiro 2016), using agencies like the U.S. Office of Management and Budget to act as meta-regulator to detect capture (Whitehouse 2016), or an executive order clearly defining capture so that agencies can incorporate capture into their decision-making just as they do for things like procedural fairness (Carpenter 2016).

To counter information capture, Agrell and Gautier (2015) propose political principals compensate regulators for efficiency gains to incentivize them to obtain better information. Alternatively, Dewatripont and Tirole (1999), recommend agency hearings where multiple parties present information to a regulatory commission in addition to the industry. Bernstein (1955) presents the agency life cycle as an organic process, so it is unclear it can be reversed. However, he argues agencies can resist decline with strong leadership committed to the agency's mission, who also have the ability to maintain support from elected officials and the public (ibid). Empirical research suggests agencies are able to avoid decline (Mintz 2005), or come back to life after a period of apathy, with new appointments and strong leadership (Meier and Plumlee 1978). Alternatively, Huntington (1952) recommends agency redesign with broader jurisdiction and divided loyalties across industry sectors to counter overreliance on one sector's interests.

The OECD also sets out best practices for the governance of regulators, which directly and/ or indirectly limit the likelihood of capture. These principles include role clarity and clear objectives; preventing undue influence and maintaining trust; appropriate agency and decision making structure; accountability and transparency; stakeholder engagement; adequate funding; and independent performance evaluation (OECD 2012). In particular, independent regulators with overlapping terms and term-limits for board members can guard against the perception or possibility of capture. Additionally, regulators should avoid potential conflicts of interests using transparent and inclusive public engagement, which prevents overreliance on particular special interests.

Statutory capture
Campaign finance and lobbying reforms can limit industry's mobilization and resource advantages. Additional changes can lower mobilization costs for the public and public interest groups. Shapiro (2012) recommends professionalizing civil service to avoid overreliance on industry information. Further, agencies need increased transparency so outside groups can more easily hold captured agencies accountable, including publishing information on agency meetings and statistics on rulemaking comments, as well as developing and publishing metrics on how well the agencies meet their statutory goals. Rather than tweak regulatory agency policy or congressional oversight, Stigler (1971) recommends eliminating regulatory agencies because the social welfare loss from a captured agency is higher than any benefits regulation promises. As mentioned earlier, the empirical support for Stigler's strong version of capture is wanting and the theoretical assumptions are not well supported, so eliminating agencies should be done with caution. Hanson and Yousifon (2003) offer no easy policy remedies for deep capture, but, they argue recognizing the structural influences that shape individuals, is a good start for rethinking our dominant approach to regulation.

Some general remedies target multiple forms of capture. Barkow (2010) supports agency designs that insulate them from one sided industry pressure, including independent funding, employment restrictions, overlapping authority and consultation with other federal and state regulators, agencies having the ability to generate high quality information, and empowering public and/or consumer advocates within agency decision making. Regulatory power can also be divided across multiple agencies or combined into fewer, more powerful agencies as necessary (Moss and Carpenter 2014). Other political actors like the media and courts can provide independent scrutiny of agency decisions (Magill 2014). Lastly, agencies can diversify the experts they rely on and seek more industry independent sources of information (Moss and Carpenter 2014).

Most scholarship ignores industry as a place to remedy capture. Yet, carefully targeted antitrust enforcement can counteract capture (Mariniello et al. 2015). Antitrust enforcement has economic impacts on competition, prices, and consumer welfare, but also political effects by reducing a firm's power to influence regulators. Alternatively, industry-focused capture remedies can channel industry behavior toward the public interest, such as subsidies to clean energy firms that counteract the power of traditionally less environmentally friendly energy producers (Wansley 2015). Ultimately, remedies that target both government and industry should be part of the preventing capture toolbox.

FORESIGHT

Despite decades of research, conceptual and methodological issues in the literature remain. The following lays out several challenges and suggestions for future research.

Defining and Measuring Capture

Capture is frequently misdiagnosed (Carpenter 2014). For example, scholars and interest groups are too quick to allege capture when agencies take actions with which they do not agree (Yackee 2021) or after single instances of salient, but atypical, industry friendly decisions, forgetting that the promise of regulation does not mean the agency will refrain from making *any* decisions that the regulated industry desires (or needs) (Carpenter 2014). Consequently, crises and industry missteps are typically used as a proxy for regulatory failure and/or capture (Carrigan and Coglianese 2012). However, the promise of regulation is to manage risk, not eliminate it (ibid). Disasters and crises could be normal accidents (Perrow 1999) or the downside inherent in managing risk when it is not feasible or desirable to ban risky activity outright (Carrigan and Coglianese 2012).

Further, it is possible that what looks like a pattern of deference to the industry is really the product of the agency being responsive to public attention, Congressional legislation, or presidential appointments that indicate "electorally sanctioned pro-business regulation" (Carpenter 2014; Gordon and Hafer 2013; Wood and Waterman 1994). Any regulatory agency must balance a complex set of interests, including being responsive to its own internal demands of expertise, and external demands from policymakers, the industry, and the public (Meier 1985; Meier and Bohte 2007). Thus, scholars must be careful to delineate capture from the responsiveness we expect agencies to display.

To avoid these pitfalls, Carpenter (2014) recommends any diagnoses of capture meet at least three empirical standards. First, scholars should clearly define the public interest. He acknowledges defining the public interest is thorny territory, but scholars should provide a defensible and empirically falsifiable definition other researchers can clearly replicate or contest. Second, the industry, or other special interest, must intentionally influence regulators through some causal mechanism, such as the revolving door. Establishing clear industry intention rules out other plausible causal mechanisms for industry friendly regulation, such as policy drift or coincidence. Third, industry influence must result in a regulatory shift away from the public interest and toward the private interest.

Though rigorous empirical scholarship has historically been lacking, a variety of existing studies meet these criteria and could be used as a model for future research (Carpenter 2014). Captures scholars use most major social science methods across a variety of disciplines, including qualitative (Slayton and Clark-Ginsberg 2018), quantitative (Young 2012), and mixed methods (Makkai and Braithwaite 1992); comparative (Monnet et al. 2019), legal (Barkow 2010), and historical analysis (Novak 2014); and formal modeling (Dal Bó 2006) to name just a few.

In addition to these empirical guidelines, conceptual tools can aid accurate capture diagnoses. Understanding capture exists along a weak-strong continuum helps determine its intensity and the scope of its remedy. Capture varies across political space as well, so a conceptual typology for determining the precise location of capture, within agencies, legislatures, or executives is important for determining the causal location and appropriate remedy (Rex 2020). Together, these empirical and conceptual tools suggest ways to measure capture and tailor policy remedies to the scope and intensity of capture.

The Role of Context

Most studies focus on capture within the U.S. context. Institutional features of U.S. government make it ripe for studying the influence of interest groups given federalism, a presidential system, judicial review, individualist political culture, and the number of access and veto points as places for influence (Kingdon 1999). As an outlier in its political values, a relatively lightly regulated version of capitalism, and a more capital and business friendly environment perhaps invites more concern over undue business influence (Esping-Andersen 1990). That said, scholarship in political contexts outside the U.S. is infrequent, though the literature review above finds capture scholarship in many countries and supranational contexts. This literature suggests the dynamics of capture transcend political institutions and cultures, though they may operate differently in different contexts, but I identified no comparative studies of capture. Thus, an important question for future research is how capture varies across national contexts.

Defining the Public Interest

Rigorously defining and measuring public interest regulation is important in its own right, as a benchmark for the high-quality regulation regulators should strive to achieve. Further, defining public interest is important for capture scholarship because it provides a clear reference point for what capture is not, so we can better understand capture when it does occur. As discussed above, there is some general agreement in the regulation literature across disciplines that the public interest is the interest of the unorganized, diffuse, broad public, as opposed to narrow special/business interests (Croley 2000; Croley 2007; Tai 2017). Conceptually this provides some clarification, but operationalizing it becomes challenging. However, regulatory scholars should not be faulted for not having a clear answer to a question that has bedeviled political theorists for millennia (Ardito 2016).

Regulated industries reveal their preferences readily through advocacy. Given their power and resources, they mobilize easily around issues and push their views through lobbying, advertising, commenting on rules and court cases, and so on. But how do we determine the preferences of a relatively much less organized general public? One simple way is to ask them through surveys and using majoritarian preferences as a guide. However, surveys are not without their limitations, and deliberative polling shows that preferences change when citizens are forced to deliberate face-to-face with others, facilitated by experts with high quality information (Luskin et al. 2002).

Because of these difficulties and the vagaries of public opinion, more long term, stable cultural values and preferences can be a guide, either central values of the political culture or the embodiment of those values in longstanding and widely supported legislation (Carpenter

2014). However, both public opinion and legislation are subject to elite influence and capture (Hanson and Yosifon 2003; Lukes 2005). A third alternative is to use technocratic expertise of scholars and scientists to guide tough regulatory decisions (Carpenter 2014). Of course experts are subject to capture themselves (Zingales 2014) and the industry can manipulate expertise and science to its own ends (Perlman 2020). An alternative to substantive conceptions of the public good is a procedural one (Carpenter 2014), such as deliberative polling, citizen participation in regulatory decisions, or public debate channeled through administrative processes like rulemaking. However, supporters of this approach need to accept that fair processes do not always lead to democratic or scientifically informed outcomes.

Though scholars have not reached a satisfactory answer to this question, what is important is to acknowledge the strengths and weaknesses of varying approaches to defining the public interest and determining an appropriate and empirically grounded definition for the particular regulatory case under study.

Delineating Influence and Capture

Defining key concepts is challenging due to the difficulty of distinguishing between influence and capture. This difficulty is evident in the lack of agreement in the literature about whether information exchange is clearly *not* capture, benign capture that achieves a higher public good by improving regulation overall (Thaw 2014), or whether information is a mechanism for capture (Agrell and Gautier 2015; Perlman 2020). One way to distinguish the two is to determine whether regulators have selfish or publicly spirited intent (Levine and Forrence 1990). Another solution is to think less dichotomously, along a continuum of strong to weak capture (Carpenter and Moss 2014a), but this only begs the question of what distinguishes weaker forms of capture from legitimate industry cooperation. Instead we could move "beyond capture" to conceptualize regulation as a process of decisions involving value tradeoffs among competing notions of the public interest; instead of understanding regulation as public and private interests in conflict, the regulatory process could be understood as a variety of public and private actors coproducing knowledge together to achieve equilibrium among competing public values (Slayton and Clark-Ginsberg 2018).

Predicting and Preventing Capture

Some previous scholarship developed models for which regulatory domains are likely to be captured (Dal Bó 2006; Gormley 1986; Meier 1985; Wilson 1980). However, much of the capture literature focuses on establishing whether regulators are captured, its severity, and potential remedies. To move the literature further, future research might build on, update, or develop new theoretical expectations about capture. If capture is not the inevitable end product of regulation (Carpenter and Moss 2014a) as some theorists pessimistically assume (Bernstein 1955; Stigler 1971), then scholars should consider what conditions we might expect or not expect capture to occur. For example, what industry characteristics make capture more likely? Is an industry with competing firms (Cartwright 2019) less likely to capture regulators than a more unified and well-coordinated one like finance (Levitin 2014; Young and Pagliari 2017)? How do industry characteristics, such as coordination, technical complexity, or policy type affect the likelihood of capture?

Further, what *agency* characteristics influence the likelihood of capture? Regulatory agencies are not static actors (Quirk 1981). Agency structure (Barkow 2010) and internal agency dynamics, like expertise or strong leadership, can push agencies toward the public interest (Meier and Bohte 2007). Thus, for example, are well-structured agencies more likely to successfully resist capture? Are agencies that regulate one industry more likely to be captured? Lastly, how do industry and agency characteristics interact to influence capture? Facing a well-insulated agency, will the industry be more likely to pursue influence through elected officials? More broadly, when, where, and why industry use particular mechanisms successfully and will regulators be able to resist these efforts? Answering these questions can point to the best remedies to prevent capture or mitigate it once it occurs.

Capture Rhetoric

Despite recent scholarship to reenergize faith in the possibilities of well-designed regulatory agencies to prevent capture (Carpenter and Moss 2014b), the rhetoric of capture may cede too much ground to opponents of regulation. While on one hand capture is an implied critique of business power, it also is a stark critique of government's capacity to represent citizens' interests adequately. Thus, government failure is implicit or explicit in the capture critique, suggesting that the public sector is weak and easily susceptible to private cooptation. Moreover, labeling the problem regulatory or agency capture puts the focus on government as the source of the problem, positing greedy public servants who want campaign dollars, more lucrative private employment, or bigger agency budgets.

Alternatively what if capture was discussed as a failure to adequately achieve the public interest? Instead of weak/strong capture, regulators could be evaluated along the weak/strong public interest continuum. This language emphasizes that most agencies most of the time are achieving outcomes that are in the public interest, even if weakly so. Further, it suggests adjustments can help regulators achieve the public interest in a more meaningful, stronger sense, if problems with resources, expertise, or negative industry influence were mitigated. Lastly, the public interest language challenges the self-interest assumptions about regulators and suggests that the public interest is also a strong motivator for regulators.

Structural Power

Capture scholarship should also engage literature on the structural power of business. Lindblom (1977) argues business has a "privileged position" in capitalist democracies because it performs substantial public functions, including making decisions about investment, employment, and production. Business can also use the threat of withholding investment or exiting a jurisdiction as a veto on new regulations (Culpepper 2015). This symbiotic relationship between business and government is a basic pillar of market democracies.

Sidelining structural power stunts the capture conversation conceptually. Much of what looks like capture in the form of regulatory gifts or deregulation, may really just the normal functioning of a political-economic system in which markets, private ownership, and state inducements to incentivize private sector cooperation are a central feature. Alternatively, might this mutual dependence suggest some degree of capture is built into the system in a capitalist democracy? Either way, critics distrustful of cooperation between industry and regulators must consider the extent to which it is a feature, not a bug, of the current system.

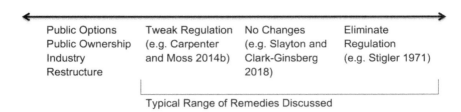

| Public Options
Public Ownership
Industry
Restructure | Tweak Regulation
(e.g. Carpenter
and Moss 2014b) | No Changes
(e.g. Slayton and
Clark-Ginsberg
2018) | Eliminate
Regulation
(e.g. Stigler 1971) |

Typical Range of Remedies Discussed

Figure 24.1   Spectrum of capture remedies

Likewise, capture skeptics who discuss the benefits of expertise sharing and coproduction, should also consider the extent to which structural capture underlays these cooperative relationships. Regardless, most capture scholarship assumes regulation in a market society as given without digging more deeply into how the structure of state-market relationships should affect the capture conversation.

Additionally, ignoring structural power narrows our understanding of capture's remedies on too narrow an ideological spectrum. Figure 24.1 represents the spectrum of capture remedies and the narrower scope of contemporary scholarship.

On one end are the more libertarian-minded thinkers skeptical of regulation because of the inevitability of capture, who argue the public is best served by eliminating regulation and relying on private market competition. In the middle are those who do not see capture so much as influence, exchange, coproduction or expertise sharing between industry and regulators. The implied solution here is one of maintaining the status quo; the public benefits from existing cooperation between sectors, so we should not limit industry's ability cooperate with regulators.

Further to the left are those who find evidence of weak capture. Their solution is typically to use technical fixes to improve regulators and their capacity to act as an independent check on business. Here is where the bulk of the conversation about remedies typically stops. The implicit assumption is that private actors should be left untouched. To use the language of structural power theory, most commonly discussed remedies to limit business influence in rulemaking, information provision, lobbying, and so on all limit firms *instrumental* power to shape regulation, but these leave untouched their sources of *structural* power, like their ability to threaten exit if regulation is not to their liking.

Limiting structural power as a way to mitigate capture is possible but requires more intrusive interventions into the market. Farrell and Newman (2015) suggest governments can extend their jurisdictional reach, for example, by moving from a state-based regulatory regime to a national one, which limits the exit threat to other states within a nation, or jurisdictions can cooperate to create national or transnational standards, as with international accounting standards. Antitrust enforcement to limit firm size and market power, public options, or state provision are additional tools. Ultimately, to limit business influence, capture scholarship must consider the extent to which we need to alter deeper structural relationships between firms and the state.

REFERENCES

Agrell, Per J, and Axel Gautier. 2015. "A Theory Of Soft Capture." *The Scandinavian Journal of Economics* 119 (3):571.

Ardito, Alissa. 2016. "Regulatory Capture, Ancient and Modern." *The Regulatory Review*: https://http://www.theregreview.org/2016/06/30/ardito-regulatory-capture-ancient-and-modern/.

Bagley, Nicolas. 2010. "Agency Hygiene." *Texas Law Review* 89:1–14.

Baker, Andrew. 2010. "Restraining Regulatory Capture? Anglo-America, Crisis Politics and Trajectories of Change in Global Financial Governance." *International Affairs* 86 (3):647–63.

Barkow, Rachel E. 2010. "Insulating Agencies: Avoiding Capture Through Institutional Design." *Texas Law Review* 89:15–79.

Barrett, Eva. 2015. "A Case Of: Who Will Tell the Emperor He Has no Clothes?—Market Liberalization, Regulatory Capture and the Need for Further Improved Electricity Market Unbundling Through a Fourth Energy Package." *The Journal of World Energy Law & Business* 9 (1):1–16.

Barth, James R., Gerard Caprio, and Ross Levine. 2012. *Guardians of Finance: Making Regulators Work for Us*. Cambridge, MA: MIT Press.

Baxter, Lawrence G. 2011. "Capture In Financial Regulation: Can We Channel It Toward The Common Good." *Cornell JL & Pub. Pol'y* 21:175.

Bernstein, Marver H. 1955. *Regulating Business By Independent Commission*. Princeton, NJ: Princeton University Press.

Briody, Michael, and Tim Prenzler. 1998. "The Enforcement of Environmental Protection Laws in Queensland: A Case of Regulatory Capture?" *Environmental and Planning Law Journal* 15 (1).

Browne, J. 2020. The regulatory gift: Politics, regulation and governance. *Regulation & Governance* 14(2): 203–18.

Bull, Reeve T. 2016. "Combatting External and Internal Regulatory Capture." *The Regulatory Review*: https://http://www.theregreview.org/2016/06/20/bull-combatting-external-internal-regulatory-capture/.

Calabria, Mark. 2016. "Preventing Regulatory Capture." *The Regulatory Review*: https://http://www.theregreview.org/2016/06/23/calabria-preventing-regulatory-capture/.

Carpenter, Daniel. 2004. "Protection without Capture: Product Approval by a Politically Responsive, Learning Regulator." *The American Political Science Review* 98 (4):613–31.

Carpenter, Daniel. 2014. "Detecting and Measuring Capture." In *Preventing Regulatory Capture: Special Interest Influence and How to Limit It*, edited by D. Carpenter and D. Moss. Cambridge, UK: Cambridge University Press.

Carpenter, Daniel. 2016. "Challenges in Measuring Regulatory Capture." *The Regulatory Review*: https://http://www.theregreview.org/2016/06/22/carpenter-challenges-measuring-regulatory-capture/.

Carpenter, Daniel, and David Moss. 2014a. "Introduction." In *Preventing Regulatory Capture: Special Interest Influence and How to Limit It*, edited by D. Carpenter and D. Moss. Cambridge, UK: Cambridge University Press.

Carpenter, Daniel, and David Moss, eds. 2014b. *Preventing Regulatory Capture: Special Interest Influence and How to Limit It*. Cambridge, UK: Cambridge University Press.

Carrigan, Christopher. 2013. "Captured by Disaster? Reinterpreting Regulatory Behavior In The Shadow Of The Gulf Oil Spill." In *Preventing Regulatory Capture: Special Interest Influence and How to Limit It*, edited by D. Carpenter and D. Moss. Cambridge, UK: Cambridge University Press.

Carrigan, Christopher, and Cary Coglianese. 2012. "Oversight in Hindsight: Assessing the U.S. Regulatory System in the Wake of Calamity." In *Regulatory Breakdown the Crisis of Confidence in U.S. Regulation*, edited by C. Coglianese. Philadelphia: University of Pennsylvania Press.

Carrigan, Christopher, and Cary Coglianese. 2016. "Capturing Regulatory Reality: Stigler's The Theory of Economic Regulation." https://papers.ssrn.com/sol3/papers.cfm?abstract_id=2805153

Carruthers, Bruce G., and Naomi R. Lamoreaux. 2016. "Regulatory Races: The Effects of Jurisdictional Competition on Regulatory Standards." *Journal of Economic Literature* 54 (1):52–97.

Cartwright, Madison. 2019. "Business Conflict and International Law: The Political Economy of Copyright in the United States." *Regulation & Governance*. https://onlinelibrary.wiley.com/doi/abs/10.1111/rego.12272.

Coen, David, and Matia Vannoni. 2016. "Sliding Doors in Brussels: A Career Path Analysis of EU Affairs Managers." *European Journal of Political Research* 55 (4):811–26.

Coglianese, Cary. 2016. "The Elusiveness of Regulatory Capture." *The Regulatory Review*: https://http://www.theregreview.org/2016/07/05/coglianese-the-elusiveness-of-regulatory-capture/.

Cohen, Jeffrey E. 1986. "The Dynamics of the 'Revolving Door' on the FCC." *American Journal of Political Science* 30 (4):689–708.

Cohn, Theodore H. 2019. "The Effects of Regulatory Capture on Banking Regulations: A Level-of-Analysis Approach." In *The Failure of Financial Regulation*, edited by Anil Hira, Norbert Gaillard, and Theodore H. Cohn. Springer. https://link.springer.com/book/10.1007/978-3-030-05680-3

Costello, Christopher, and Corbett A. Grainger. 2018. "Property Rights, Regulatory Capture, and Exploitation of Natural Resources." *Journal of the Association of Environmental and Resource Economists* 5 (2):441–79.

Croley, Steven P. 2000. "Public Interested Regulation." Florida State University Law Review 28:7.

Croley, Steven P. 2007. *Regulation And Public Interests: The Possibility Of Good Regulatory Government*. Princeton, NJ: Princeton University Press.

Croley, Steven P. 2011. "Beyond Capture: Towards a New Theory of Regulation." In *Handbook on the Politics of Regulation*, edited by D. Levi-Faur. Cheltenham, UK and Northampton, MA, USA: Edward Elgar Publishing.

Culpepper, Pepper D. 2015. "Structural Power and Political Science in the Post-crisis Era." *Business and Politics* 17 (3):391–409.

Dal Bó, Ernesto. 2006. "Regulatory Capture: A Review." *Oxford Review of Economic Policy* 22 (2):203–25.

Dal Bó, Ernesto, and Rafael Di Tella. 2003. "Capture by Threat." *Journal of Political Economy* 111 (5):1123–54.

Dewatripont, Mathias, and Jean Tirole. 1999. "Advocates." *Journal of Political Economy* 107 (1):1–39.

Drutman, Lee. 2015. *The Business of America is Lobbying: How Corporations Became Politicized and Politics Became More Corporate*. Oxford: Oxford University Press.

Esping-Andersen, Gosta. 1990. *The Three Worlds of Welfare Capitalism*. Princeton, NJ: Princeton University Press.

Farrell, Henry, and Abraham L. Newman. 2015. "Structuring power: Business and authority beyond the nation state." *Business and Politics* 17 (3):527–52.

Fellowes, Matthew C., and Patrick J. Wolf. 2004. "Funding Mechanisms and Policy Instruments: How Business Campaign Contributions Influence Congressional Votes." *Political Research Quarterly* 57 (2):315–24.

Fischer, Pius. 2007. *Rent-Seeking, Institutions and Reforms in Africa: Theory and Empirical Evidence for Tanzania*. Springer Science & Business Media.

Gilad, Sharon. 2008. "Exchange Without Capture: The UK Financial Ombudsman Service's Struggle For Accepted Domain." *Public Administration* 86 (4):907–24.

Goldbach, Roman. 2015. "Asymmetric Influence in Global Banking Regulation: Transnational Harmonization, the Competition State, and the Roots of Regulatory Failure." *Review of International Political Economy* 22 (6):1087–127.

Gordon, Sanford C., and Catherine Hafer. 2013. "Conditional Forbearance as an Alternative to Capture: Evidence from Coal Mine Safety Regulation." In *Preventing Regulatory Capture: Special Interest Influence and How to Limit It*, edited by D. Carpenter and D. Moss. New York: Cambridge University Press.

Gormley, William T., Jr. 1979. "A Test of the Revolving Door Hypothesis at the FCC." *American Journal of Political Science* 23 (4):665–83.

Gormley, William T. 1983. *The Politics of Public Utility Regulation*. Pittsburgh, PA: University of Pittsburgh Press.

Gormley, William T., Jr. 1986. "Regulatory Issue Networks in a Federal System." *Polity* 18 (4): 595–620.

Hall, Richard L., and Alan V. Deardorff. 2006. "Lobbying as Legislative Subsidy." *American Political Science Review*: 69–84.

Hall, Richard L., and Frank W. Wayman. 1990. "Buying Time: Moneyed Interests and the Mobilization of Bias in Congressional Committees." *American Political Science Review* 84 (3):797–820.

Hanson, Jon, and David Yosifon. 2003. "The Situation: An Introduction To The Situational Character, Critical Realism, Power Economics, and Deep Capture." *University of Pennsylvania Law Review*: 129–346.

Heclo, Hugh. 1978. "Issue Networks and the Executive Establishment." In *The New American Political System*, edited by A. King. Washington: American Enterprise Institute.

Huntington, Samuel P. 1952. "The Marasmus of the ICC: The Commission, the Railroads, and the Public Interest." *Yale Law Journal* 62: 467–509.

Kaufman, Herbert. 1960. *The Forest Ranger: A Study In Administrative Behavior*. Baltimore: Published for Resources for the Future by Johns Hopkins Press.

Kingdon, John W. 1999. *America the Unusual*. John W. Kingdon (copyright holder).

Krueger, Anne O. 1974. "The Political Economy of the Rent-Seeking Society." *The American Economic Review* 64 (3):291–303.

Kurokawa, Kiyoshi, and Andrea Ryoko Ninomiya. 2018. "Examining Regulatory Capture: Looking Back at the Fukushima Nuclear Power Plant Disaster, Seven Years Later." *University of Pennsylvania Asian Law Review* 13 (2):2.

Kwak, James. 2014. "Cultural Capture and the Financial Crisis." In *Preventing Regulatory Capture: Special Interest Influence and How to Limit It*, edited by D. Carpenter and D. Moss. Cambridge, UK: Cambridge University Press.

Laffont, Jean-Jacques, and Jean Tirole. 1991. "The Politics Of Government Decision-Making: A Theory of Regulatory Capture." *The Quarterly Journal of Economics* 106 (4):1089–127.

Law, Marc T., and Cheryl X. Long. 2011. "Revolving Door Laws and State Public Utility Commissioners." *Regulation & Governance* 5 (4):405–24.

Levine, Michael E, and Jennifer L Forrence. 1990. "Regulatory Capture, Public Interest, and the Public Agenda: Toward a Synthesis." *Journal of Law, Economics, & Organization* 6:167–98.

Levitin, Adam J. 2014. "The Politics of Financial Regulation and the Regulation of Financial Politics: A Review Essay." *Harvard Law Review* 127: 1991–2068.

Lindblom, Charles E. 1977. *Politics and Markets: The World's Political Economic Systems*. Basic Books.

Livermore, Michael A., and Richard L. Revesz. 2014. "Can Executive Review Help Prevent Capture?" In *Preventing Regulatory Capture: Special Interest Influence and How to Limit It*, edited by D. Carpenter and D. Moss. Cambridge, UK: Cambridge University Press.

Lukes, Steven. 2005. *Power: A Radical View*, 2nd edition. Basingstoke: Palgrave Macmillan.

Luskin, Robert C., James S. Fishkin, and Roger Jowell. 2002. "Considered Opinions: Deliberative Polling in Britain." *British Journal of Political Science* 32 (3):455–87.

MacLean, Jason. 2016. "Striking at the Root Problem of Canadian Environmental Law: Identifying and Escaping Regulatory Capture." *Journal of Environmental Law & Practice* 1:111.

Magill, M. Elizabeth. 2014. "Courts and Regulatory Capture." In *Preventing Regulatory Capture: Special Interest Influence and How to Limit It*, edited by D. Carpenter and D. A. Moss. Cambridge, UK: Cambridge University Press.

Makkai, Toni, and John Braithwaite. 1992. "In and Out of the Revolving Door: Making Sense of Regulatory Capture." *Journal of Public Policy* 12 (1):61–78.

Mariniello, Mario, Damien Neven, and Atilano Jorge Padilla. 2015. "Antitrust, Regulatory Capture and Economic Integration." International Centre for Trade and Sustainable Development. https://http://www.ictsd.org/sites/default/files/research/E15-Competition-Mariniello, Neven, Padilla-FINAL.pdf.

Mayer, Lloyd Hitoshi. 2007. "What is this Lobbying that We are so Worried About." *Yale Law & Policy Review* 26:485.

Meier, Kenneth J. 1985. *Regulation: Politics, Bureaucracy, and Economics*. New York City, NY: St. Martin's Press.

Meier, Kenneth J., and John Bohte. 2007. *Politics and the Bureaucracy: Policymaking in the Fourth Branch of Government*. Belmont, CA: Thomson-Wadsworth.

Meier, Kenneth J., and John P. Plumlee. 1978. "Regulatory Administration and Organizational Rigidity." *The Western Political Quarterly* 31 (1):80–95.

Mintz, Joel A. 2005. "Has Industry Captured the EPA: Appraising Marver Bernstein's Captive Agency Theory After Fifty Years." *Fordham Environmental Law Review* 17:1.

Monnet, Eric, Stefano Pagliari, and Shahin Vallée. 2019. "Beyond financial Repression And Regulatory Capture: The Recomposition of European Financial Ecosystems after the Crisis." LEQS Paper No. 147/2019 September 2019.

Moss, David A., and Daniel Carpenter. 2014. "Conclusion: A Focus on Evidence and Prevention." In *Preventing Regulatory Capture: Special Interest Influence and How to Limit It*, edited by D. Carpenter and D. A. Moss. Cambridge, UK: Cambridge University Press.

Novak, William. 2014. "A Revisionist History of Regulatory Capture." In *Preventing Regulatory Capture: Special Interest Influence and How to Limit It*, edited by D. Carpenter and D. Moss. Cambridge, UK: Cambridge University Press.

OECD. 2012. "The Governance of Regulators." OECD Best Practice Priciples for Regulatory Policy: https://read.oecd-ilibrary.org/governance/the-governance-of-regulators_9789264209015-en#page1.

Pagliari, Stefano. 2012. *Making Good Financial Regulation: Towards a Policy Response to Regulatory Capture*. Grosvenor House Publishing.

Perlman, Rebecca L. 2020. "For Safety or Profit? How Science Serves the Strategic Interests of Private Actors." *American Journal of Political Science* 62 (2): 293–308.

Perrow, Charles. 1999. *Normal Accidents: Living With High-Risk Technologies*. Princeton, NJ: Princeton University Press.

Portman, Michelle E. 2014. "Regulatory Capture by Default: Offshore Exploratory Drilling for Oil and Gas." *Energy Policy* 65:37–47.

Provost, Colin. 2016. "Competition and Coordination in Bank Regulation: The Financial Crisis of 2007–09." *International Journal of Public Administration* 3–9 (7):540–51.

Quirk, Paul J. 1981. Industry Influence in Federal Regulatory Agencies. Princeton, NJ: Princeton University Press.

Reiss, Dorit Rubinstein. 2011. "The Benefits of Capture." *Wake Forest Law Review* 47:569–610.

Rex, Justin. 2020. "Anatomy of agency capture: An organizational typology for diagnosing and remedying capture." *Regulation & Governance* 14 (2):271-94.

Sabatier, Paul. 1975. "Social Movements and Regulatory Agencies: Toward a More Adequate—and Less Pessimistic—Theory of 'Clientele Capture'." *Policy Sciences* 6 (3):301–42.

Schattschneider, E. E. 1975. *The Semi-Sovereign People: A Realist's View of Democracy in America*. Boston, MA: Wadsworth Publishing.

Shapiro, Sidney A. 2010. Protecting the Public Interest: Understanding the Threat of Agency Capture. Hearing of the Committee on the Judiciary, Subcommittee on Administrative Oversight and the Courts. http://www.gpo.gov/fdsys/pkg/CHRG-111shrg64724/pdf/CHRG-111shrg64724.pdf.

Shapiro, Sidney A. 2012. "The Complexity of Regulatory Capture: Diagnosis, Causality, and Remediation." *Roger Williams University Law Review* 102 (1).

Shapiro, Sidney A. 2016. "Old and New Capture." *The Regulatory Review*: https://http://www.theregreview.org/2016/06/28/shapiro-old-and-new-capture/.

Shive, Sophie A., and Margaret M. Forster. 2016. "The Revolving Door for Financial Regulators." *Review of Finance* 21 (4):1445–84.

Slayton, Rebecca, and Aaron Clark-Ginsberg. 2018. "Beyond Regulatory Capture: Coproducing Expertise for Critical Infrastructure Protection." *Regulation & Governance* 12 (1):115–30.

Stigler, George J. 1971. "The Theory of Economic Regulation." *The Bell Journal of Economics and Management Science* 2 (1): 3–21.

Tai, Laurence. 2017. "Regulatory capture and quality." *Journal of Public Policy* 37 (3):261–86.

Thaw, David. 2014. "Enlightened regulatory capture." *Washington Law Review*. 89: 329.

Thomas, Craig W., A. Bradley Soule, and Tyler Blake Davis. 2010. "Special Interest Capture of Regulatory Agencies: A Ten-Year Analysis of Voting Behavior on Regional Fishery Management Councils." *Policy Studies Journal* 38 (3):447–64.

Tirole, Jean. 1986. "Hierarchies and Bureaucracies: On The Role of Collusion in Organizations." *Journal of Law, Economics, & Organization* 2 (2):181–214.

Tollison, Robert D. 2004. "Rent seeking." In *The Encyclopedia of Public Choice*, edited by Charles K. Rowley, and Friedrich Schneider. Springer. https://link.springer.com/book/10.1007/b108558

Tollison, Robert D. 2012. "The Economic Theory of Rent Seeking." *Public Choice* 152 (1):73–82.

Trampusch, Christine, and Florian Fastenrath. (2021). "States' interests as limits to the power of finance: Regulatory reforms in early local government financialization in the US and UK." *Regulation & Governance* 15 (2):245–261.

Trumbull, Gunnar. 2012. *Strength in Numbers: The Political Power of Weak Interests*. Harvard University Press.

Tullock, Gordon. 1967. "The Welfare Costs of Tariffs, Monopolies, and Theft." *Economic Inquiry* 5 (3):224–32.

Wade, Robert Hunter, and Silla Sigurgeirsdottir. 2010. "Lessons from Iceland." *New Left Review* 65: 5–29.

Wagner, Wendy E. 2010a. "Administrative Law, Filter Failure, and Information Capture." *Duke Law Journal* 59:1321.

Wagner, Wendy E. 2010b. Protecting the Public Interest: Understanding the Threat of Agency Capture. Hearing of the Committee on the Judiciary's Subcommittee on Administrative Oversight and the Courts. http://www.gpo.gov/fdsys/pkg/CHRG-111shrg64724/pdf/CHRG-111shrg64724.pdf.

Wansley, Matthew. 2015. "Virtuous Capture." *Administrative Law Review* 67(3):419–480.

Whitehouse, Sheldon. 2016. "How Government Can Root Out Regulatory Capture." *The Regulatory Review*: https://http://www.theregreview.org/2016/06/15/whitehouse-how-government-can-root-out -regulatory-capture/.

Wilson, James Q. 1980. *The Politics of Regulation*. New York: Basic Books.

Wilson, James Q. 1989. *Bureaucracy*. New York: Basic Books.

Wolff, Jonathan. 2019. "Fighting Risk with Risk: Solar Radiation Management, Regulatory Drift, and Minimal Justice." *Critical Review of International Social and Political Philosophy* 23 (5):564–83.

Wood, B. Dan, and Richard W. Waterman. 1994. *Bureaucratic Dynamics: The Role of Bureaucracy in a Democracy*. Boulder: Westview Press.

Yackee, Susan Webb. 2014. "Reconsidering Agency Capture During Regulatory Policymaking." In *Preventing Capture: Special Interest Influence in Regulation, and How to Prevent It*, edited by D. Carpenter and D. Moss. Cambridge, UK: Cambridge University Press.

Yackee, Susan Webb. 2020. "Hidden Politics? Assessing Lobbying Success During US Agency Guidance Development." *Journal of Public Administration Research and Theory*, 30 (4):548–62.

Yackee, Susan Webb. 2021. "Regulatory Capture's Self-Serving Application." *Public Administration Review*. Early online. https://onlinelibrary.wiley.com/doi/abs/10.1111/puar.13390

Young, Kevin L. 2012. "Transnational Regulatory Capture? An Empirical Examination of the Transnational Lobbying of the Basel Committee on Banking Supervision." *Review of International Political Economy* 19 (4): 663–88.

Young, Kevin, and Stefano Pagliari. 2017. "Capital United? Business Unity in Regulatory Politics and the Special Place of Finance." *Regulation & Governance* 11 (1):3–23.

Zingales, Luigi. 2014. "Preventing economists' capture." In *Preventing Capture: Special Interest Influence in Regulation, and How to Prevent It*, edited by D. Carpenter and D. Moss. Cambridge, UK: Cambridge University Press.

Zinn, Matthew D. 2002. "Policing Environmental Regulatory Enforcement: Cooperation, Capture, and Citizen Suits." *Stanford Environmental Law Journal* 21:81.

25. Regulatory agencies and agenda-setting: state of the art and new ways forward

Edoardo Guaschino

INTRODUCTION

This chapter addresses the question of the influence of public agencies, particularly those possessing regulatory competences, in the initial stages of the policy-making process and in agenda-setting dynamics (Baumgartner and Jones 1991). The perspective according to which agenda-setting determines subsequent stages of the policy-making process rapidly became an established approach in both policy studies and the political science literature (Cobb and Elder 1983, Jones 1984, Rochefort and Cobb 1994).

Agenda-setting is usually considered to be one of the key stages of the policy-making process, encompassing the elements of value, interest, and political strategy. In this process, institutions can expand their authority by influencing decision agendas and acting as policy entrepreneurs (Jabotinsky and Cohen 2020), seeking to further their interests by promoting a given representation of public issues in political agendas.

It is well known that the establishment of regulatory agencies represents one of the main institutional transformations over the last decades. This process refers to the establishment of unelected bodies (Thatcher 2002) and thus to a separation of organizational competences (Pollitt et al. 2001, Pollitt et al. 2004, Schick 2002) which gave rise to what Thatcher (2005) called, the 'third force' in regulation. This process, which promoted a separation of administrative tasks (Christensen and Lægreid 2001) and a fragmentation of the institutional landscape, was initially intended to enhance the efficiency of the decision-making process.

The literature has approached the diffusion of regulatory agencies from different perspectives, showing that they represent a critical change in social and economic patterns (Gilardi 2005, Gilardi 2009), reflecting also the social and economic evolution of the regulatory State. In particular, a number of researchers started to explore how the decision of governments to delegate powers to non-majoritarian institutions (Thatcher and Stone Sweet 2002) and reflected their initial intentions (Coen 2005).

Overall, delegation to independent agencies has led not only to a fragmentation of the regulatory administration and breaking the executive hierarchy, but also to numerous unexpected consequences (Christensen and Yesilkagit 2006). Wilks and Bartle (2002) have been among the precursors of this perspective by looking at the unforeseen impact of independent competition agencies. In fact, it has soon become known that the diffusion of regulatory agencies has led to numerous unexpected consequences, such as an increasing role in policy-making decisions. Specifically, this literature reveals the phenomenon of non-elected institutions whose involvement extends beyond their mandate, sometimes functioning as political actors and expanding their authority into areas that are not always related to their formal prescriptions. Therefore, the question of whether agencies' influence is limited to particular stages of the policy cycle is worthy of exploration.

However, one may wonder at the significance of studying regulators as policy entrepreneurs. Although the first studies on regulatory agencies converged toward an emphasis on the democratic limits of non-majoritarian institutions and the consequential democratic deficit in their operations, new research questions have emerged in recent years. In fact, the regulatory state, characterized by both extensive delegation to external agencies and administrative fragmentation, has great implications for agenda dynamics, an understudied topic in the literature of regulatory governance and agenda-setting (Majone 2006). This chapter presents the theoretical and empirical relevance of studying agencies' involvement in policy-making with a specific focus on the agenda-setting process.

The chapter is organized in two parts. First, I review the literature of the role of agencies in the policy-making. Although an exhaustive review of the literature is beyond the scope of this chapter, I show that existing studies suggest that agencies very often act as political actors, influencing various stages of the policy process. Moreover, I argue that in order to better grasp the role of agencies in the agenda-setting process, we should focus on the concepts of policy entrepreneurs and issue definition. Then, based on the recent researches on this topic, I expose the advantages of qualitative, quantitative and mixed methods techniques in studying the role of agencies as agenda-setters and the main explanatory factors.

Second, this chapter highlights the main gaps in this research stream and offers several possible paths for further investigation, both from a theoretical and methodological standpoint. I point to the fact that conducting more extensive research on this subject is needed, specifically regarding the mechanisms through which agencies act as agenda-setters and influence policy decisions.

THE ROLE OF REGULATORY AGENCIES IN POLICY-MAKING

This literature has extensively discussed the paradox of how agency tasks have stretched over time. As a result, studies on the policy influence of both public and regulatory agencies have attracted increasing attention over the following years, especially from scholars of regulatory governance, showing that political–administrative relations are more blurry than expected (Verschuere and Bach 2012). Over time, in this framework characterized by critical management reforms, regulatory agencies have evolved beyond the initial term (Coen and Thatcher 2005). Thus, it has been found that agencies exert more leverage over the policy-making process, a role that was not explicit in their initial formal mandates.

In the following years, some authors began to decompose the policy-making process into different stages in order to determine and detail the phases in which agencies are more active, although this focus had precedents (Egeberg 1995, Elder and Page 1998, Gains 2003). It became clear that regulatory agencies systematically impact the initial stages of the policy process, particularly during the agenda-setting stage (Maggetti 2009, Painter and Yee 2012).

By looking more broadly at executive agencies, this question has increasingly attracted the attention of scholars, which have provided cross-national and cross-sectorial evidence of agencies' influence in policy-making, specifically in the policy formulation stage (Bach 2012, Handke 2010, Handke 2012, Niklasson and Pierre 2012, Verschuere and Vancoppenolle 2012). In these studies, the role of executive agencies in policy-making is usually assessed through the lens of policy autonomy. These works have the merit of providing strong empirical evidence for the unintended consequences of delegation of authority.

However, I argue that the assessment of the role of agencies in policy-making through the lens of policy autonomy can be limiting. One main reason is that autonomy, which usually refers to the relationship with parent ministries, can be challenged in the case of (independent) regulatory agencies. In fact, as Maggetti and Papadopoulos (2016) argue, the application of the principal–agent framework is indeed questionable in this case, because control mechanisms can be altered and power relations reversed. Additionally, the focus on autonomy barely helps to elucidate the 'battles' that agencies engage in order to extend their authority, produce different ideas or knowledge, and legitimize their actions. A deeper look at agenda-dynamics is more appropriate to reveal these dynamics.

Therefore, I argue that in order to increase our understanding of the role of agencies in the preliminary stages of the policy process, we should dismiss the question of policy autonomy and conceptualize the agenda-setting process as comprising elements of issue definition and policy entrepreneurship.

Agenda-Setting

Although Princen (2018) outlines very well the main insights of the agenda-setting literature, I here provide the reader with some key notions of the concept of agenda-setting which are key to understand the role of regulatory agencies as agenda-setters.

Agenda-setting can refer to all those actions that raise public issues in order to join the governmental agendas and to formulate policy solutions accordingly. To study why some issues attract attention and why other fail to do so is one of the main research objectives of agenda-setting scholars (Cobb and Elder 1971, Cobb and Elder 1972). These scholars have also examined which actors are able to promote their preferences onto decision agendas. Some key scholars have inspired the last two decades of research in this field and have been instrumental in establishing agenda-setting in the political science literature (Baumgartner and Jones 1993, Cobb, Ross and Ross 1976, Cobb and Elder 1971, Cobb and Elder 1972, Kingdon 1984).

The concept of agenda-setting is principally derived from the idea that decision-makers have limited resources, such as time or knowledge, with which to mobilize attention to all policy issues that may require a policy response (Zahariadis 2016a).

The process of agenda-setting can be defined as 'the politics of selecting issues for active consideration' (Cobb and Ross 1997, p.3). The importance of agenda-setting is without question; the agenda-setting process and, more broadly, agenda dynamics, lead to important consequences at different levels of governance, such as limited consideration to certain categories of issues, to policy sectors, or to specific demographic groups. What is more, policymakers' limited resources may lead to imbalanced policy decisions that favor particular powers, to the detriment of broader, more democratic decision-making processes.

Critical, to the literature on agenda-setting, is the role of policy entrepreneurs. In particular Kingdon (1984) significantly contributed to this concept. The next section is thus dedicated to policy entrepreneurs and issue framing as fundamental aspects to grasp the role of agencies as agenda-setters.

Policy entrepreneurship and issue definition

One of the elements common to most of the main theories on agenda-setting, is the concept of policy entrepreneur (Cohen 2016). In this literature, the descriptions of the role of policy entrepreneurs often refer to the capacity of some actors to attract the attention of decision-makers on certain issues, consequently influencing policy decisions.

It is thus well acknowledged that these actors are very influential in policy change through involving themselves in the early stages of the policy-making process. In addition, not only are policy entrepreneurs capable of raising an issue on the political agenda, but they can also ensure that a solution is adopted once a problem has emerged (Baumgartner and Jones 2009, p.29).

Thus, we observe a conscious will to link policy issues and policy solutions with the political agenda by employing strategies and tactics that may vary according to the policy sector or administrative tradition. Overall, agenda-setting dynamics and policy entrepreneurs' activities are inextricable from public and social issues. This interdependence specifically depends on how social issues are understood and constructed. In fact, the perception of social issues is far more of a product of social construction than a result of objectivity. The question of which actor has the capacity to 'construct' the issue in their own terms has gained consensus in the literatures on both social issues and agenda-setting. Thus, the determination of the identity of policy entrepreneurs within agenda dynamics is vital.

A pivotal component of policy entrepreneurship, and overall of agenda setting, is the issue definition stage (Princen 2018, Rochefort and Cobb 1994). The concept of 'framing' implies that the focus is on the actual process through which actors construct a particular interpretation of a given issue and define it in the political arena. In addition, the issue definition stage plays a critical role in the main theories on agenda-setting, such as the Multiple Stream Framework or the Punctuated Equilibrium Theory (Baumgartner and Jones 1993, Kingdon 1984). The idea behind the definition stage is that issues can face a multitude of possible definitions, and that policy solutions will result from the given representation of issues (Baumgartner and Mahoney 2008). Overall, the issue definition stage is not only at the center of agenda dynamics, but at the locus of the decision-making process in general (Stone 1989).

The literature on social and public issues has paid great attention to the role of institutions acting as entrepreneurs, focusing on the administrative 'entrepreneurs' that seek to further their interests through the construction of public issues (Carpenter 2001, Laurens 2009). Additionally, the literature offers a very wide number of studies showing that numerous and distinctive actors can behave as policy entrepreneurs (Mintrom 1997).

The agenda-setting landscape is plenty of actors who try to raise issues at the decision agendas (Anderson, DeLeo and Taylor 2020), both at the national and EU level, acting as policy entrepreneurs and agenda-setters. For example, very recently, Deters and Falkner (2021) showed that not only the European Council plays a crucial role in the agenda setting, but that other European institutions are able to play this role. Other recent works have reached similar findings, showing that agenda-setters at the EU level are numerous and somehow unexpected (Haverland, De Ruiter and Van de Walle 2018, Lubow and Schmidt 2020, Webb and Kreppel 2020).

However, even though Kingdon (1984) talks about policy entrepreneurs 'in and around governments', we do not know much about how regulatory agencies try to influence the national decision agendas. Although some studies have shown how governments do shape the legislative agenda setting (Rasch and Tsebelis 2010), the role of regulators as agenda-setters has attracted little attention in the literature. In the next section I will list the studies which have focused on this question at national level, identifying domestic (regulatory) agencies acting as agenda-setters.

The role of regulatory agencies in agenda-dynamics

If we undertake a literature review specifically on agencies' influence in the agenda-setting process, we might be disappointed by the number of contributions. In fact, minimal attention has been paid to which factors reduce agencies' discretion over political agendas (Majone 2006). While this question raises relevant implications on the democratic accountability of the policy-making process, it is probably too specific to draw a cross-sectorial and cross-national overview of this phenomenon. However, I try here to expose the existent studies which have explicitly addressed this question.

For example, Coglianese and Walters (2016) took the case of the strong involvement of the Environmental Protection Agency (EPA) in regulating climate change, to push the academic reflection further on the agenda-setting in the regulatory state.

Recently, Littoz-Monnet (2014) provided a critical contribution in this area. Littoz-Monnet's findings supply additional knowledge on agencies' influence in policy-making by observing the strategies at work during the framing stage. Then, Guaschino (2019, 2022) tried to go beyond these findings by exploring the conditions under which agencies can influence issue definitions and the national governmental agendas.

Some other authors have focused on 'regulatory entrepreneurship' and more specifically on the role of regulators as policy entrepreneurs (Jabotinsky and Cohen 2020). By looking at two regulatory reforms in Israel, they show that regulators are able to promote reforms by adopting strategies and acting as policy entrepreneurs. Similarly and very recently, Di Mascio et al. (2021) explore the role of the Italian Communications Regulatory Authority (AGCOM) in the management of disinformation during the COVID-19 crisis.

Moreover, although not strictly related to agenda-setting, it is worth mentioning that several studies have shown how American regulatory agencies, such as the Food and Drug Administration (FDA) or the Environmental Protection Agency (EPA), have played crucial roles in shaping various policy debates (Ames and McCracken 1976, Edwards 2010, Plein 1991, Roth, Dunsby and Bero 2003).

Although an exhaustive review of the existent studies goes beyond the scope of the present chapter, to my current understanding, this literature is in need of substantial renovation, as I argue in the second part of this chapter. In the next section I show how can we grasp the role of agencies as agenda-setters and what are the main explanatory factors explaining such involvement in this process.

How to Grasp the Role of Regulators as Agenda-Setters: Methods and Findings

In this section I raise several empirical questions. How can we determine whether agencies act as agenda-setters? What are the methodological approaches which are beneficial to grasp these dynamics? How can we provide a broad, systematic, and comparative overview of agencies' influence in this process? I expose here the advantages of each methodological approach and the main findings of the existent studies in this area.

Methods

Several techniques of data collection offer interesting insights to the study of the role of regulators in the agenda-setting process, in particular qualitative, quantitative and mixed methods. After mentioning the advantages of these techniques, I will show the empirical studies having adopted these techniques and the main findings.

Qualitative techniques have great merits in this area of research. For example, through the analysis of prominent documents and interviews, the researcher is able to trace back the processes leading national regulators, as in Littoz-Monnet (2014), to push their preferences on the European agenda. Although this perspective based on case studies focuses on these questions from a micro approach, it offers valuable and nuanced insights of the tactics and strategies that agencies develop over the agenda-setting process.

Researchers have also used nonparticipant observations and textual analysis to explore this phenomenon (Jabotinsky and Cohen, 2020). In fact, observation is an established technique in the studies of governance settings (Gains 2011), which is helpful to reveal inner practices, cultural beliefs and micro-dynamics of the 'meaning making' of regulators in agenda-setting. In a similar vein, workshops mixing academics and practitioners could also be useful to stimulate further theoretical reflections (Coglianese and Walters 2016).

Then, cross national or cross-sectorial differences could be observed through quantitative techniques. Comparisons between countries and policy sectors are key to understand similarities or differences of agencies' involvement in various agenda-setting processes. Although to the best of my knowledge there are no studies which address, quantitatively, the question of agencies' involvement in agenda-setting, some researches adopt quantitative techniques to explore the agencies' involvement in policy-making (Bach 2012) and policy autonomy (Verhoest et al. 2010).

Regarding mixed methods, I argue here that a mixed method approach is beneficial to the study of regulatory agencies as agenda-setters for two reasons. The first is that agenda-setting is a low visible and intractable process (Baumgartner and Jones 2009, p.39), which is difficult to grasp and to operationalize (Cairney and Zahariadis 2016). Although many studies have made significant efforts to make the process of agenda-setting an observable phenomenon, I argue that mixed methods have the merit to make the operationalization of this phenomenon particularly robust, especially through various validating techniques (Jick 1979, Moran-Ellis et al. 2006, Olsen, Haralambosm and Holborn 2004), for example by combining survey's questionnaires and follow-up interviews (Guaschino 2022). In other words, combining different techniques of data collection could be useful to strengthen the solidity of measurements of hardly visible political phenomena, like agenda-setting.

Second, a methodology that could be considered as a mixed method per se is the Qualitative Comparative Analysis (QCA) (Maggetti 2018). This methodology is not only beneficial to study agenda-setting processes (Sager and Thomann 2016), but is useful to focus on the conditions that lead agencies to act as agenda-setters. This methodology offers the possibility to develop expectations in a configurational way, a type of questioning that no others methodologies are able to offer. It will thus provide an explanation based on configuration of conditions which are necessary or sufficient for agencies to act as agenda-setters.

Findings

Although a comprehensive discussion of the empirical findings goes beyond the scope of this chapter, I provide a short illustration of the main factors explaining why agencies can act as agenda-setters by mentioning the researches who have explicitly addressed this focus. These explanatory factors that the existent literature has identified could be distinguished between the strategic behaviors of regulators, the organizational features and the administrative traditions in which they operate.

Regarding the strategic behaviours, Littoz-Monnet (2014) shows that domestic regulators can strategically frame issues and influence agendas principally when they act as 'first movers.' Although the literature had already shown that moving first is advantageous in the influence of issue definition (Héritier 2001), Littoz-Monnet's findings show that regulatory agencies can adopt this strategy to influence the EU agenda. She also shows that highly technical policy fields are favorable to agencies' influence because they can raise only technicalities of their interventions and at the same time avoid the politicization of their operations. Similarly, Di Mascio et al. (2021) show that the Italian Communications Regulatory Authority (AGCOM) have been able to take the lead in raising the issue of disinformation during the COVID-19 into the agenda. In particular they show that the regulator has been able to strategically highlight the importance of disinformation over the pandemic crisis, mobilizing evidence-base indicators and benefitting from the resonance of this issue at the European level.

In a similar vein, Jabotinsky and Cohen (2020) explain the factors leading the regulators to strategically act as policy entrepreneurs by looking at their behaviors over two regulatory reforms. In particular they showed that the factors to successfully influence and pass the reforms are: a strong expertise in the field, strong political skills, to provide concrete solutions, an already existent strong demand for reforms, excellent communication skills and a strong support of media to promote the reforms. Similarly, Painter and Yee (2012) show that various agencies with regulation or service provision as primary task, are likely to take the lead in the agenda-setting process when they prove a strong adaptability to the institutional context in Hong Kong.

Jabotinsky and Cohen (2020) suggest also that agencies may encounter several barriers when they act as policy entrepreneurs. Their activity can be limited by their relationships with politicians, advocacies by interest groups, a general lack of understanding of the reforms, the competition with other organizations and a lack of resources. Similarly, Coglianese and Walters (2016) and West and Raso (2013) take as a starting point the fact that agencies' agendas can themselves be shaped by external factors and in particular pressures from outside. In sum, the literature suggests that agencies develop strategies to exert leverage over policy agendas, also in response to the institutional context in which they operate.

Regarding the organizational factors, Guaschino (2019) posits that the agencies' high involvement in agenda-setting depends on the their age and on the number of staff members. In addition, he also looks at the institutional context, expecting that two factors would also play a critical role: the level of 'institutional competition' within each national context and membership in the EU. In a nutshell, the main results of the fuzzy-set Qualitative Comparative Analysis (fsQCA) show that the agencies that are highly involved in this process usually have a low number of staff members; they are relatively old and they operate in a low-competition institutional framework. In addition, he observes that environmental agencies are highly involved in this process when they are part of the EU. These results confirm the importance of the context in which regulators operate but also the crucial role of organizational features such the age and the size.

Finally, administrative traditions also matter. In Guaschino (2022), semi-structured interviews helped to go beyond these findings to gain additional insights on two politico-administrative contexts in which agencies operate in the agenda-setting process, highlighting which values and norms influence their roles in policy-making (Niklasson and Pierre 2012). In fact, it is thoroughly difficult to make sense of agencies' role in agenda dynamics without making sense of the administrative context in which they operate.

First, in the Italian administrative tradition, which has always been characterized by a high level of politicization, politicians have created a 'parallel administration' with the aim of bypassing regular civil service (Kickert 2005). The major reforms of the Italian public administration resulted in a lack of coordination due to high decentralization and fragmentation between different levels of governance, which is traditionally caused by a sense of belonging of local communities and results in the dismantling of the central state (Ongaro 2010). In this administrative context, the Italian Institute for Environmental Protection and Research (ISPRA) may sometimes benefit from bypassing formal channels in order to influence national agendas, although the administrative fragmentation weakens its capacity to systematically influence political agendas.

Regarding the French administrative context, regulators operate in a less politicized context, in which the administration, composed of highly qualified officials, benefits from a reputation of high esteem (Kickert 2005). In this administrative context, Guaschino (2022) shows that the French agency for food, environmental, and occupational Health and Safety (ANSES) benefits from very few 'competitors' in this area, combined with a direct and advantageous relationship with ministerial bodies. In this framework, ANSES is more capable of exerting a 'monopolistic' role in its area, benefiting from unique skills which are used to raise new issues in the agenda and its role has raised some concerns regarding its unexpected political responsibilities (Benamouzig et al. 2018).

FURTHER RESEARCH AGENDAS? THEORIES, METHODS, AND NEW WAYS FORWARD

The establishment of regulatory authorities, particularly at the national level, is a dynamic process, that is, it has ongoing and continuous consequences at many levels of governance and on the policy-making process. Shedding light on these alterations is key for further developments of this area of research. Therefore, I address four ways to advance the study of the influence of agencies in agenda dynamics. For each of the four ways, I will mention the methodological challenges with which research may be confronted.

First, further research should focus on the role of bureaucrats as entrepreneurs within the regulatory agencies. Although the literature that I employed in the present chapter looks at agencies' influence from an organizational level, more attention should be paid to the inner dynamics that lead an organization to push their preferences onto political agendas. In other words, a deeper look at staff members would be the right approach to address the following research question: why and how have some bureaucrats become able to expand organizational authority?

This question has been the object of several important studies on international organizations (Littoz-Monnet 2020, Nay 2012) while it has yet to be asked with respect to regulatory agencies. In order to detect the efforts of staff members and the agencies' abilities to influence and shape organizational preferences, it is necessary to focus on proactive entrepreneurial individuals within regulators, such as those acting as 'knowledge brokers' (Knaggård 2015).

To my knowledge, the topic is understudied, as the questions of how they self-determine, what strategies they employ, and what impact they have on agencies' authority expansion have yet to be explored. From a methodological perspective, case studies are the best way to tackle this topic. Often, this leads the researcher to employ qualitative techniques, such as interviews and participant observations. In this sense, the researcher could be confronted with difficulties in accessing the fieldwork and in selecting case studies that are generalizable.

The second way forward regards the composition of agencies' staff members. Influence in policy-making processes necessarily goes through the bureaucrats and their socio-demographic background (Genieys 2008). Does the variation of agencies' influence in policy-making change according to the socio-demographic background or the diversity of staff members? Put plainly, who are the people composing agencies' staff and how do they influence policy outputs over the decision agendas? Although some studies have focused on the biographical information of agencies' board members, both at the national (Ennser-Jedenastik 2015, Fernández-i-Marín, Jordana and Bianculli 2016) and at the EU level (Jordana, Pérez-Durán and Trivino-Salazar 2021, Pérez-Durán and Bravo-Laguna 2019), very little attention has been devoted to the profile of agencies' staff members, to my understanding.

The way socio-demographic background is reflected in agencies' policy positions could have considerable implications. For instance, it could lead to approaches to policy issues that are limited by their technical definitions and that fail to consider multiple facets of public problems. Hence, one potential output of an homogenous group of staff members could lead to a lack of holistic approaches, which is very important for the enhancement of risk regulations, for example Graham and Wiener (1995).

Although some studies have adopted a roughly similar perspective, like focusing on the social connections of agencies' boards or recruitment practices, this topic has been met with greater interest for international organizations; this is also true at the national level with respect to the consideration of different parliament compositions (Best and Cotta 2000, Cotta and Best 2007). An in-depth analysis of the influence of agencies' staff member composition on policy outputs would shed light on this understudied aspect of agencies' post-delegation settings.

From a methodological perspective, this would imply two main empirical steps: the first step, which is more descriptive, aims at mapping the social-demographic background of the staff members. The second step would be to expect a causal relationship between policy influence and bureaucrats' background, ideally from a comparative perspective. Then, one potential challenge could be that the researcher encounters very homogenous composition of staff members. This would imply a very low variation between organization, which would weaken the comparative approach. However, this issue could be anticipated by selecting very different cases to maximize the variation.

A third potential way forward examines the importance of studying how regulatory agencies turn to external knowledge to influence policy decisions over the agenda-setting process. The literature on mobilization of external knowledge has attracted great attention from scholars in international relations and on international organizations (Hall 2016, Littoz-Monnet 2017a, Littoz-Monnet 2017b). Although some scholars have explored how regulatory agencies use scientific expertise (Schrefler 2010), the question of how agencies produce knowledge has been left aside thus far.

To resort to external knowledge is problematic per se, as it gives agencies the capacity and authority to go beyond statutory prescriptions. This way, agencies justify their policy position as evidence-based in areas where they usually have little knowledge. Indeed, whether external knowledge is mobilized by non-elected institutions may raise further questioning on democratic accountability. Although I showed in the previous section that agencies use external knowledge to support their policy decisions, especially by delegating private enterprises, this topic should be tackled more systematically. In addition, regulatory agencies may expand their authority by depoliticizing strategies through a high 'technicalization' of policy issues (Littoz-Monnet 2020, Wood 2016). There is a lack of exploration of the mobilization of external knowledge by regulatory agencies and its function, considering that the knowledge could be a source of legitimization rather than a way to improve policy outputs (Boswell 2009).

This third way forward does not necessarily imply any specific methodological issue unless the researcher looks at patterns of knowledge which may shift over time. In this regard, it is worth remembering that knowledge used by organizations to enhance policy changes is not necessarily static, but it could change over time and shifting paradigms (De Francesco and Guaschino 2020). In this case, the reference to the 'most prominent documents' to support the empirical findings could be challenging, and particular attention should be given to this issue.

Finally, I consider the fourth way forward to be an extension of the previous one. It addresses the importance of studying agencies' role as 'policy advisors'. Therefore, the problem is not only whether agencies' mobilization of external knowledge is problematic for democratic accountability, but also whether the involvement of regulators as policy advisors is serviceable for supporting (and legitimizing) policy decisions.

This debate necessarily implies a deeper understanding of what constitutes an expert (Boswell 2009). In particular, it is important to gain more knowledge on whether regulators have become key actors in the 'Policy Advice Systems'(Craft and Howlett 2012, Craft and Howlett 2013).

In the present chapter we saw that in some cases, to hold great expertise in the policy field it favors the agencies' influence over regulatory reforms. Similarly, future researches should focus on whether agencies are not only central to policy-making processes, but also to the Policy Advisory Systems, which is defined as 'the wide set of organizations and individuals which previous studies identified as providing policy evidence, from scientists to political advisors' (Howlett 2019, p.242). In other words, whether regulatory agencies are used by governments as sources of policy advice is still an open question which merits great attention. This approach would also help to better contextualize the administrative traditions in which agencies' operate and which are sometimes driven by the need of responses to reputation threats (Rimkutė 2018). Moreover, attention should also be paid to the content of the advices that regulators provide. The venues and mechanisms with which knowledge and advices are developed, produced, and used can generate 'ignorance,' which is an important aspect that has recently been put forward (Henry 2017, Proctor and Schiebinger 2008). For example, Henry (2017) shows that some actors develop policies solely relying on data that are made available without any prior common, broader reflection. The production of 'ignorance' could impact the way issues are framed as well as the solutions that are taken accordingly over the decision agenda. For instance, standards, or limit values, are usually an object of sharp distinction between what is tolerated and what is not. In addition, they describe the world between what is a problem and what is not. Needless to say, this can sometimes be very problematic (Counil and Henry 2019).

Similarly, to the previous point, this approach does not imply any particular methodological concerns. However, the researcher may need to familiarize with areas and disciplines which are not directly related to the social sciences. For example, limit values are a simplistic way of categorizing what is acceptable and what is not, but they can hide technicalities to which some political scientists are not accustomed.

In conclusion, it must be mentioned that these four research avenues could also be tackled through a longitudinal perspective. In fact, agencies' role in agenda setting is not a static phenomenon as the existing literature tends to present, but rather a dynamic one that continuously evolves. Agencies' influence over decision agendas can increase or decrease over time and that could be the result of complex political dynamics.

CONCLUSION

The topic of agenda-setting had already been the subject of contributions in various handbooks (Majone 2006, Princen 2018, Zahariadis 2016b). The merit of this chapter is thus to provide a complement by bridging some features of modern regulatory states with agenda dynamics. To do so, this chapter has been structured in two main parts.

The first part highlighted the relevance of studying regulators as political actors in the decision-making process through the observation of agenda dynamics, spanning three main elements: the agenda-setting, the issue definition stage, and the role of policy entrepreneurs. This literature has extensively discussed, both empirically and theoretically, the paradox of how agencies' operations have stretched over time. In this chapter, while exploring several non-expected consequences of agencies' delegation, I draw attention to their increasing role in agenda-setting dynamics, acting as policy entrepreneurs in the agenda-setting process. This focus clarifies how institutional actors, like regulators, go beyond their formal mandates in influencing the decision agendas, but it also illuminates how they push for a given representation of issues and influence policy decisions accordingly. This process may entail strategies, tactics, and conflicts that intertwine with administrative traditions. Overall, the consideration of this aspect within studies on post-delegation settings could provide new insights about the unintended consequences of agencies' delegation.

The second part of this chapter highlighted the main ways forward in this research stream, offering four main possible ways for further investigation. In particular, it raised the importance of studying the role of bureaucrats as policy entrepreneurs within agencies, the agencies' staff composition, the agencies' mobilization of external knowledge and their role as 'policy advisors'.

Each of these four paths for further investigation address, from different theoretical perspectives, the role of agencies in policy-making. In addition, to face the issue of feasibility, for each of these four ways I addressed the potential methodological challenges the researchers may be confronted with. I also suggest that these four ways forward could also be tackled from a longitudinal perspective which could shed light on the evolution of agencies' role in agenda-setting, an unexplored question in the literature so far (to complete the political dynamics of regulatory agencies, see also Chapter 13).

REFERENCES

Ames, Charles C. and Steven C. McCracken. 1976. "Framing Regulatory Standards to Avoid Formal Adjudication: The FDA as a Case Study." *California Law Review* 64(1):14–73.

Anderson, Sarah E., Rob A. DeLeo and Kristin Taylor. 2020. "Policy Entrepreneurs, Legislators, and Agenda Setting: Information and Influence." *Policy Studies Journal* 48(3):587–611.

Bach, Tobias. 2012. "The Involvement of Agencies in Policy Formulation: Explaining Variation in Policy Autonomy of Federal Agencies in Germany." *Policy and Society* 31(3):211–22.

Baumgartner, Frank R. and Bryan D. Jones. 1991. "Agenda Dynamics and Policy Subsystems." *The Journal of Politics* 53(4):1044–74.

Baumgartner, Frank R. and Bryan D. Jones. 1993. *Agendas and Instability in American Politics*. Chicago: University of Chicago Press.

Baumgartner, Frank R. and Bryan D. Jones. 2009. *Agendas and Instability in American Politics*. Chicago: University of Chicago Press.

Baumgartner, Frank R. and Christine Mahoney. 2008. "The Two Faces of Framing: Individual-Level Framing and Collective Issue Definition in the European Union." *European Union Politics* 9(3):435–49.

Benamouzig, Daniel, Olivier Borraz, Jean-Noël Jouzel and Danielle Salomon. 2018. "L'expertise En Sciences Sociales: Une Affaire Politique? Le Cas De L'agence Nationale De Sécurité Sanitaire (Anses)." *Sociologies pratiques* 2(37):39–47.

Best, Heinrich and Maurizio Cotta. 2000. *Parliamentary Representatives in Europe, 1848–2000: Legislative Recruitment and Careers in Eleven European Countries*. Oxford: Oxford University Press.

Boswell, Christina. 2009. *The Political Uses of Expert Knowledge: Immigration Policy and Social Research*. Cambridge: Cambridge University Press.

Cairney, Paul and Nikolaos Zahariadis. 2016. "Multiple Streams Approach: A Flexible Metaphor Presents an Opportunity to Operationalize Agenda-Setting Processes," pp. 87–105 in *Handbook of Public Policy Agenda Setting*, edited by N. Zahariadis. Cheltenham, UK and Northampton, MA, USA: Edward Elgar Publishing.

Carpenter, Daniel. 2001. *The Forging of Bureaucratic Autonomy: Reputations, Networks, and Policy Innovation in Executive Agencies, 1862–1928*, Vol. 173. Princeton: Princeton University Press.

Christensen, Jørgen Grønnegaard and Kutsal Yesilkagit. 2006. "Delegation and Specialization in Regulatory Administration: A Comparative Analysis of Denmark, Sweden and the Netherlands," pp. 203–34 in *Autonomy and Regulation: Coping with Agencies in the Modern State*, edited by T. Christensen and P. Laegreid. Cheltenham, UK and Northampton, MA, USA: Edward Elgar Publishing.

Christensen, Tom and Per Lægreid. 2001. "New Public Management: The Effects of Contractualism and Devolution on Political Control." *Public Management Review* 3(1):73–94.

Cobb, R.W. and C.D. Elder. 1972. *Participation in American Politics: The Dynamics of Agenda-Building*. Boston: Allyn & Bacon.

Cobb, R.W. and C.D. Elder. 1983. *Participation in American Politics: The Dynamics of Agenda-Building*. Baltimore: Johns Hopkins University Press.

Cobb, R.W. and C.D. Elder. 1971. "The Politics of Agenda-Building: An Alternative Perspective for Modern Democratic Theory." *The Journal of Politics* 33(4):892–915.

Cobb, R., J-K. Ross and M.H. Ross. 1976. "Agenda Building as a Comparative Political Process." *American Political Science Review* 70(1):126–38.

Cobb, R.W. and M.H. Ross. 1997. "Agenda Setting and the Denial of Agenda Access: Key Concepts," pp. 3–24 in *Cultural Strategies of Agenda Denial*, edited by R.W. Cobb and J.-K. Ross. Lawrence: University Press of Kansas.

Coen, David. 2005. "Managing the Political Life Cycle of Regulation in the UK and German Telecommunication Sectors." *Annals of Public and Cooperative Economics* 76(1):59–84.

Coen, David and Mark Thatcher. 2005. "The New Governance of Markets and Non-Majoritarian Regulators." *Governance* 18(3):329–46.

Coglianese, Cary and Daniel E. Walters. 2016. "Agenda-Setting in the Regulatory State: Theory and Evidence." *Administrative Law Review* 68(1):93–118.

Cohen, Nissim. 2016. "Policy Entrepreneurs and Agenda Setting," pp. 180–99 in *Handbook of Public Policy Agenda Setting*, edited by N. Zahariadis. Cheltenham, UK and Northampton, MA, USA: Edward Elgar Publishing.

Cotta, Maurizio and Heinrich Best. 2007. *Democratic Representation in Europe: Diversity, Change, and Convergence*. Oxford: Oxford University Press.

Counil, Emilie and Emmanuel Henry. 2019. "Is It Time to Rethink the Way We Assess the Burden of Work-Related Cancer?" *Current Epidemiology Reports* 6(2):138–47.

Craft, Jonathan and Michael Howlett. 2012. "Policy Formulation, Governance Shifts and Policy Influence: Location and Content in Policy Advisory Systems." *Journal of Public Policy* 32(2):79–98.

Craft, Jonathan and Michael Howlett. 2013. "The Dual Dynamics of Policy Advisory Systems: The Impact of Externalization and Politicization on Policy Advice." *Policy and Society* 32(3):187–97.

De Francesco, Fabrizio and Edoardo Guaschino. 2020. "Reframing Knowledge: A Comparison of OECD and World Bank Discourse on Public Governance Reform." *Policy and Society* 39(1):1–16.

Deters, Henning and Gerda Falkner. 2021. "Remapping the European Agenda-Setting Landscape." *Public Administration* 99(2)290–303.

Di Mascio, Fabrizio et al. 2021. "The Role of Regulatory Agencies in Agenda-Setting Processes: Insights from the Italian Response to the COVID-19 Infodemic." *Swiss Political Science Review* 27(2): 272–82.

Edwards, Paul N. 2010. *A Vast Machine: Computer Models, Climate Data, and the Politics of Global Warming*. Boston: MIT Press.

Egeberg, Morten. 1995. "The Policy-Administration Dichotomy Revisited: The Case of Transport Infrastructure Planning in Norway." *International Review of Administrative Sciences* 61(4):565–76.

Elder, Neil C.M. and Edward C. Page. 1998. "Culture and Agency: Fragmentation and Agency Structures in Germany and Sweden." *Public Policy and Administration* 13(4):28–45.

Ennser-Jedenastik, Laurenz. 2015. "Credibility Versus Control: Agency Independence and Partisan Influence in the Regulatory State." *Comparative Political Studies* 48(7):823–53.

Fernández-i-Marín, Xavier, Jacint Jordana and Andrea C Bianculli. 2016. "Are Regulatory Agencies Independent in Practice? Evidence from Board Members in Spain." *Regulation & Governance* 10(3):230–47.

Gains, Francesca 2003. "Executive Agencies in Government: The Impact of Bureaucratic Networks on Policy Outcomes." *Journal of Public Policy* 23(1):55–79.

Gains, Francesca. 2011. "Elite Ethnographies: Potential, Pitfalls and Prospects for Getting 'up Close and Personal'." *Public Administration* 89(1):156–66.

Genieys, William. 2008. *L'élite Des Politiques De L'état*. Paris: Les Presses de Sciences Po.

Gilardi, Fabrizio. 2005. "The Institutional Foundations of Regulatory Capitalism: The Diffusion of Independent Regulatory Agencies in Western Europe." *The Annals of the American Academy of Political and Social Science* 598(1):84–101.

Gilardi, Fabrizio. 2009. *Delegation in the Regulatory State: Independent Regulatory Agencies in Western Europe*. Cheltenham, UK and Northampton, MA, USA: Edward Elgar Publishing.

Graham, John D. and Jonathan Baert Wiener. 1995. *Risk Vs. Risk*. Cambridge, MA: Harvard University Press.

Guaschino, Edoardo. 2019. "The Role of Regulatory Agencies in Framing Public Problems: An Empirical Analysis." *European Policy Analysis* 5(2): 285–316.

Guaschino, Edoardo. 2022. "Regulators as Agenda-Setters: how National Agencies Shape Public Issues." London: Routledge.

Hall, Nina. 2016. *Displacement, Development, and Climate Change: International Organizations Moving Beyond Their Mandates*. London: Routledge.

Handke, Stefan. 2010. "Yes, We Can (Control Them!)-Regulatory Agencies: Trustees or Agents?" *Goettingen Journal of International Law* 2(1):111–34.

Handke, Stefan. 2012. "A Problem of Chief and Indian—the Role of the Supervisory Authority Bafin and the Ministry of Finance in German Financial Market Policy." *Policy and Society* 31(3):237–47.

Haverland, Markus, Minou De Ruiter and Steven Van de Walle. 2018. "Agenda-Setting by the European Commission. Seeking Public Opinion?". *Journal of European Public Policy* 25(3):327–45.

Henry, Emmanuel. 2017. *Ignorance Scientifique Et Inaction Publique: Les Politiques De Santé Au Travail*. Paris: Presses de Sciences Po.

Héritier, Adrienne. 2001. "La Régulation Comme 'Patchwork'. La Coordination De La Multiplicité Des Intérêts Dans Le Processus Décisionnel Européen." *Politix* 3(55):125–47.

Howlett, Michael. 2019. "Comparing Policy Advisory Systems Beyond the OECD: Models, Dynamics and the Second-Generation Research Agenda." *Policy Studies* 40(3–4):241–59.

Jabotinsky, Hadar Y. and Nissim Cohen. 2020. "Regulatory Policy Entrepreneurship and Reforms: A Comparison of Competition and Financial Regulation." *Journal of Public Policy* 40(4):628–50.

Jick, Todd D. 1979. "Mixing Qualitative and Quantitative Methods: Triangulation in Action." *Administrative Science Quarterly* 24(4):602–11.

Jones, Charles O. 1984. *An Introduciton to the Study of Public Policy.* Monterey, CA: Brooks/Cole Publishing.

Jordana, Jacint, Ixchel Pérez-Durán and Juan Carlos Trivino-Salazar. 2021. "Drivers of Integration? EU Agency Board Members on Transboundary Crises." *Comparative European Politics* 19(1):26–48.

Kickert, W.J.M. 2005. "Distinctiveness in the Study of Public Management in Europe." *Public Management Review* 7(4):537–63.

Kingdon, J.W. 1984. *Agendas, Alternatives, and Public Policies.* Boston: Little, Brown.

Knaggård, Åsa. 2015. "The Multiple Streams Framework and the Problem Broker." *European Journal of Political Research* 54(3):450–65.

Laurens, Sylvain. 2009. *Une Politisation Feutrée. Les Hauts Fonctionnaires Et L'immigration En France.* Paris: Belin.

Littoz-Monnet, Annabelle. 2014. "The Role of Independent Regulators in Policy Making: Venue-Shopping and Framing Strategies in the EU Regulation of Old Wives Cures." *European Journal of Political Research* 53(1):1–17.

Littoz-Monnet, Annabelle. 2017a. *The Politics of Expertise in International Organizations: How International Bureaucracies Produce and Mobilize Knowledge.* Abingdon: Routledge.

Littoz-Monnet, Annabelle. 2017b. "Expert Knowledge as a Strategic Resource: International Bureaucrats and the Shaping of Bioethical Standards." *International Studies Quarterly* 61(3):584–95.

Littoz-Monnet, Annabelle. 2020. "Expanding without Much Ado. International Bureaucratic Expansion Tactics in the Case of Bioethics." *Journal of European Public Policy* 28(6):858–79.

Lubow, Alexis and Susanne K. Schmidt. 2020. "A Hidden Champion? The European Court of Justice as an Agenda-Setter in the Case of Posted Workers." *Public Administration* 99(2):321–334.

Maggetti, Martino. 2009. "The Role of Independent Regulatory Agencies in Policy-Making: A Comparative Analysis." *Journal of European Public Policy* 16(3):450–70.

Maggetti, Martino. 2018. "Mixed-Methods Designs," pp. 193–210 in *Handbuch Methoden Der Politikwissenschaft*, edited by C. Wagemann, G. A and M. Siewert. Wiesbaden: Springer VS.

Maggetti, Martino and Yannis Papadopoulos. 2016. "The Principal–Agent Framework and Independent Regulatory Agencies." *Political Studies Review* 16(3):172–83.

Majone, Giandomenico. 2006. "Agenda Setting," pp. 228–50 in *The Oxford Handbook of Public Policy*, edited by M. Moran, M. Rein and R. E. Goodin. Oxford: Oxford University Press.

Mintrom, Michael. 1997. "Policy Entrepreneurs and the Diffusion of Innovation." *American Journal of Political Science* 41(3):738–70.

Moran-Ellis, Jo, Victoria D. Alexander, Ann Cronin, Mary Dickinson, Jane Fielding, Judith Sleney and Hilary Thomas. 2006. "Triangulation and Integration: Processes, Claims and Implications." *Qualitative Research* 6(1):45–59.

Nay, Olivier. 2012. "How Do Policy Ideas Spread among International Administrations? Policy Entrepreneurs and Bureaucratic Influence in the UN Response to Aids." *Journal of Public Policy* 32(1):53–76.

Niklasson, Birgitta and Jon Pierre. 2012. "Does Agency Age Matter in Administrative Reform?: Policy Autonomy and Public Management in Swedish Agencies." *Policy and Society* 31(3):195–210.

Olsen, Wendy, Michael Haralambosm and M. Holborn. 2004. "Triangulation in Social Research: Qualitative and Quantitative Methods Can Really Be Mixed," pp. 103–18 in *Developments in Sociology*, edited by M. Haralambos and M. Holborn. Ormskirk: Causeway Press Ltd.

Ongaro, Edoardo. 2010. "The Napoleonic Administrative Tradition and Public Management Reform in France, Greece, Italy, Portugal and Spain," pp. 174–90 in *Tradition and Public Administration*, edited by M. Painter and B. G. Peters. London: Palgrave Macmillan.

Painter, Martin and Wai-Hang Yee. 2012. "Agencies and Policy in an Administrative State: The Case of Hong Kong." *Policy and Society* 31(3):223–35.

Pérez-Durán, Ixchel and Carlos Bravo-Laguna. 2019. "Representative Bureaucracy in European Union Agencies." *Journal of European Integration* 41(8):971–92.

Plein, L. Christopher. 1991. "Popularizing Biotechnology: The Influence of Issue Definition." *Science, Technology, & Human Values* 16(4):474–90.

Pollitt, Christopher, Karen Bathgate, Janice Caulfield, Amanda Smullen and Colin Talbot. 2001. "Agency Fever? Analysis of an International Policy Fashion." *Journal of Comparative Policy Analysis* 3(3):271–90.

Pollitt, Christopher, Colin Talbot, Janice Caulfield and Amanda Smullen. 2004. *Agencies: How Governments Do Things through Semi-Autonomous Organizations*. Basingstoke: Palgrave Macmillan.

Princen, Sebastiaan. 2018. "Agenda-Setting and Framing in Europe," pp. 535–51 in *The Palgrave Handbook of Public Administration and Management in Europe*, edited by E. Ongaro and S. Von Thiel: Palgrave Macmillan.

Proctor, Robert N. and Londa Schiebinger. 2008. *Agnotology: The Making and Unmaking of Ignorance*. Stanford: Stanford University Press.

Rasch, Bjorn Erik and George Tsebelis. 2010. *The Role of Governments in Legislative Agenda Setting*. New York: Routledge.

Rimkutė, Dovilė. 2018. "Organizational Reputation and Risk Regulation: The Effect of Reputational Threats on Agency Scientific Outputs." *Public Administration* 96(1):70–83.

Rochefort, David A. and Roger W. Cobb. 1994. *The Politics of Problem Definition: Shaping the Policy Agenda*. Lawrence: University Press of Kansas.

Roth, Andrew L., Joshua Dunsby and Lisa A Bero. 2003. "Framing Processes in Public Commentary on US Federal Tobacco Control Regulation." *Social Studies of Science* 33(1):7–44.

Sager, Fritz and Eva Thomann. 2016. "Multiple Streams in Member State Implementation: Politics, Problem Construction and Policy Paths in Swiss Asylum Policy." *Journal of Public Policy* 37(3):287–314.

Schick, Allen. 2002. "Agencies in Search of Principles." *OECD Journal on Budgeting* 2(1):7–26.

Schrefler, Lorna. 2010. "The Usage of Scientific Knowledge by Independent Regulatory Agencies." *Governance* 23(2):309–30.

Stone, Deborah A. 1989. "Causal Stories and the Formation of Policy Agendas." *Political Science Quarterly* 104(2):281–300.

Thatcher, Mark. 2002. "Delegation to Independent Regulatory Agencies: Pressures, Functions and Contextual Mediation." *West European Politics* 25(1):125–47.

Thatcher, Mark. 2005. "The Third Force? Independent Regulatory Agencies and Elected Politicians in Europe." *Governance* 18(3):347–73.

Thatcher, Mark and Alec Stone Sweet. 2002. "Theory and Practice of Delegation to Non-Majoritarian Institutions." *West European Politics* 25(1):1–22.

Verhoest, Koen, Paul Roness, Bram Verschuere, Kristin Rubecksen and Muiris MacCarthaigh. 2010. *Autonomy and Control of State Agencies: Comparing States and Agencies*. Basingstoke: Springer.

Verschuere, Bram and Tobias Bach. 2012. "Executive Agencies, Ministers, and Departments: Can Policy and Management Ever be Separated?" *Administration & Society* 44(2):183–206.

Verschuere, Bram and Diederik Vancoppenolle. 2012. "Policy-Making in an Era of Agencification: An Exploration of Task Divisions between Politicians, Core Departments and Public Agencies." *Policy and Society* 31(3):249–58.

Webb, Michael and Amie Kreppel. 2020. "The European Parliament's Role as an Informal EU Agenda Setter: The Influence of Own Initiative Reports." *Public Administration* 99(2):304–20.

West, William F. and Connor Raso. 2013. "Who Shapes the Rulemaking Agenda? Implications for Bureaucratic Responsiveness and Bureaucratic Control." *Journal of Public Administration Research and Theory* 23(3):495–519.

Wilks, Stephen and Ian Bartle. 2002. "The Unanticipated Consequences of Creating Independent Competition Agencies." *West European Politics* 25(1):148–72.

Wood, Matthew. 2016. "Politicisation, Depoliticisation and Anti-Politics: Towards a Multilevel Research Agenda." *Political Studies Review* 14(4):521–33.

Zahariadis, Nikolaos. 2016a. "Setting the Agenda on Agenda Setting: Definitions, Concepts, and Controversies," pp. 1–27 in *Handbook of Public Policy Agenda Setting*, edited by N. Zahariadis. Cheltenham, UK and Northampton, MA, USA: Edward Elgar Publishing.

Zahariadis, Nikolaos. 2016b. *Handbook of Public Policy Agenda Setting*. Cheltenham, UK and Northampton, MA, USA: Edward Elgar Publishing.

26. Enforcement

Miroslava Scholten

INTRODUCTION

Regulatory authorities can be delegated with rule-making and enforcement tasks. In this chapter, I focus on the latter, that is, enforcement of laws and policies, especially by agencies. I also devote attention to enforcement in an EU multi-disciplinary setting as ongoing (legislative) developments in the EU have an impact on issues relevant to (national) enforcement, including adding research and policy questions.

Enforcement is a process that aims at 'preventing or responding to the violation of a norm' in order to promote the implementation of the set laws and policies (Röben 2010, p.821). It is a process of ensuring compliance with laws with a view of ensuring core values, attainment of (policy) goals and desired social outcomes (Kagan 1989). This makes it an indispensable part of a policy cycle or a decision-taking and -implementing process, be it an EU policy on ensuring the stability of financial markets or a rule to clean common public spaces prescribed by a watchman in a student dorm as the use of a rule or norm that is not complied with is unclear.

Enforcement is a complex process and 'successful enforcement' is rather difficult to achieve. For one, its aim is not singular but twofold: it is to prevent and/or to respond to a violation of a rule or norm, and the ambiguity in determining the goal can lead to goal displacement for regulatory enforcement agencies (Huizinga and de Bree 2021). Second, it is a process of several steps – monitoring compliance (can be also called as supervision and involve education and other preventive measures), investigating possible violations and sanctioning for non-compliance (Vervaele 1999) – which is a time- and resource-consuming exercise.

Furthermore, the variety of approaches to enforcement has become so rich that it makes it difficult to determine when which approach should be used to make enforcement as successful as possible. The variety of regulatory enforcement styles depends of a great number of elements, including 'the character of the law to be enforced, the agency's task environment, and its political environment' (Kagan 1989, p.89; see also Hutter 1989; Coslovsky et al. 2011; Short 2019). It seems that adopting the 'right' style is a 'trial and error' exercise. By approach, I imply a combination of elements – strategies, styles, tasks, powers, tools and actors, who involve 'a matrix of regulators, individual targets, corporate employers, and professional intermediaries with multiple vested interests and responses through which individuals and firms attempt to steer the enforcement case' (Jordanoska 2021, p.298). Therefore, (re)designing and assessing the 'success' of enforcement will thus depend on a combination of factors related to the used approach, policy sectors' specifics, relevant legislative mandates and aims, specificity of the laws and rules, resources and even at times identification and interpretation of unwritten norms like traditions and cultures (in the EU for instance) and behaviours of the supervisees and supervisors. The lack of or non-enforcement may be furthermore attributed to a 'forbearance' strategy of a state (Dewey and Di Carlo 2021).

Designing enforcers (regulatory authorities who play a starring role in this volume) is another challenge as a number of principles need to be taken into account in law and rules are developed in practice, balancing some of such at times contradictory principles ('independent, hence unaccountable?' Scholten 2011). An additional challenge comes with the Europeanization of laws thanks to rapidly evolving EU integration. This affects how national enforcement is ought to be organized and exercised, included shared with EU counterparts.

I discuss the mentioned questions and dilemmas as follows. I start with the 'what', 'why', 'how' and 'by whom' of enforcement and in multi-disciplinary research. Then, I focus on the key issues of enforcement in a multi-jurisdictional setting of the EU. Thereafter, I turn to outlining directions for further research and practice and I conclude. My goal is twofold. First, it is to start making an overview on this topic, which is relevant for (research) issues and dilemmas, and for education purposes. Second, it is to assist further shaping of enforcement policies and theory (in the EU), which are understudied subjects and may be 'underdone' due to low political salience (in 't Veld 2021) and lacking overview of relevant factors and possible useful disciplinary connections.

ENFORCEMENT IN MULTI-DISCIPLINARY RESEARCH AND IN PRACTICE

As shown, enforcement is a contested term. Enforcement can be described as a 'process of making people obey a law or rule, or making a particular situation happen or be accepted' (Cambridge Dictionary 2021). Who can make people obey the rule? How can or should this be done? What characteristics should the rule/law and the prior rule/law-making procedure have to make it possible to try make people of obey the rule/law? The term 'enforcement' is thus a term which prompts a number of pertinent issues to be decided upon for this process to be organized and executed well, that is, achieve its aims. The aims are twofold. First, it is to prevent violation of rules and laws, including through education, explanation via soft law guidance, and so on. Second, it is to respond to violation and repair damages, at least to a certain extent. Research on the processes and issues related to enforcement is dispersed among different disciplines and literature streams. This section highlights the key issues and dilemmas of enforcement in research of different disciplines and to a certain extent in practice, which is important to study from this 'combined perspective' to understand and ensure enforcement.

Diversity of Definitions and Approaches: Enriching, Yet Confusing?

Searching for the word 'enforcement' will not yield all relevant research as a number of related terms have been used and researched. The terms of implementation of policies, compliance with rules, application and simply individual stages – monitoring or supervising, investigating, including inspecting, and sanctioning – are among the general terms, which may be related to enforcement. Additionally, specific policies, polities and sectoral or procedural laws may have more specific terms for the process of enforcement. Hence, the terminology alone, different meanings of those concepts and understandings within different disciplinary cultures and alignment of those different concepts, procedures and processes they represent for potential comparisons can be a study in its own right.

To distinguish these terms briefly, implementation of policies seems largely being used within public law and public policy domains, and includes enforcement as one of its stages;

transposition of directives, application of relevant national laws (e.g. giving licenses) and pro-cedures precede normally the enforcement as defined above (Thomann and Sager 2017; Jans et al. 2015). 'Compliance refers to a firm's effort to ensure that it and its agents adhere to legal and regulatory requirements, industry practice, and the firm's own internal policies and norms' (Root 2019, p.203) and has become an important literature stream, especially in the US (com-pliancenet.org). Some say that enforcement should be distinguished from 'compliance'; 'while the latter concerns the act of conforming to norms, for example, because of intrinsic motiva-tions of the regulated firm, enforcement comprises those activities undertaken by third parties – such as state actors, market participants and their associations, and NGOs – to achieve and compel compliance with rules' (Verbruggen 2013, p.515). It is also important to mention that specific literature streams studying enforcement approaches, may run a risk of having 'group thinking' and develop own terminology in those areas. Therefore, looking at research practice on enforcement-related issues outside of a familiar discipline can be valuable.

Researching the 'How' of Enforcement Via Stages

The next dilemma for enforcement is to find out the interrelationship between different stages of enforcement and where to put emphasis on in different policies and how. The study on reg-ulation with an outstanding volume on understanding regulation by Baldwin, Cave and Lodge (Baldwin et al. 2011), for instance, proposes the DREAM framework (detecting, responding, enforcing, assessing, modifying) in relation to enforcement of regulation and how to study and assess relevant processes. The terminology and the usage of the word enforcement may be at times confusing as it is used as more generally 'enforcing regulation' as well as one of the sub-stages of the DREAM. The idea behind these sub-stages is to list pertinent issues for policy-makers and researchers when (re)designing and evaluating policies and rules surround-ing enforcement. These include questions as to how to identify non-compliant or undesirable behaviour; how to develop and redesign relevant policies, strategies, laws, rules and tools and in what form – formal, legal solutions vs. soft law guidance; who and how should apply those rules and tools and what elements would determine the success or failure of enforcement. This emphasizes the importance of the rules and strategies in identifying the undesirable conduct, ensuring compliance and ensuring relevant powers for relevant bodies. The framework is useful and invites case-studies on its usage and relevance (in practice) and further fine-tuning.

The DREAM framework seems to offer a larger policy level perspective on the issues of enforcement, than, for instance, if one takes the three stages distinguished by Vervaele (1999): monitoring, investigating and sanctioning. This perspective is helpful (Scholten and Luchtman 2017), for instance, when analysing an enforcement authority (in comparison) by addressing the questions of what formal (and informal) powers to monitor compliance an enforcer has, when and how an investigation can take place (according to law), and what kind of sanctions the law prescribes. The (comparative) analysis could show if and if so, where enforcement powers can be unclear or lacking and propose modifications. Finally, some would also distin-guish soft enforcement means that may include processes such as monitoring, negotiations, dialogue, persuasion and even education as oppose to 'hard' interventions of investigations with dawn raids and confiscation of documents and sanctioning with high fines. In any case, distinguishing such stages is important to structure the organization of enforcement and research, also on specific instruments (inspections, information-gathering, etc).

Explaining Rationales behind Choices in Organizing Enforcement Regimes

Irrespectively of the perspective, a number of issues remain common. How to supervise effectively? Who should be monitoring? What sanctions should be prescribed to ensure enforcement?

Numerous factors to be considered (Kagan 1989). Law and economics studies (Shavell 2009; Bowles et al. 2008) offer interesting insights as to the optimality of the form of legal intervention and design of enforcement regimes. The key consideration that they offer is balancing benefits for individuals and society and costs of non-compliance and enforcement. From this perspective, if the monitoring can be done by private parties due to the availability of information about violators and if private actors can sanction or at least repair effects of non-compliance, enforcement regime may be more optimal via tort (claims for damages) and contract law. If information on (non)compliance is less accessible, it could be more optimal to employ public enforcement agencies to monitor. Furthermore, Bowles et al. argue that

> an economic approach to criminal law can contribute significantly to the debate about the appropriate scope of criminalization and about the choice of legal form. ... If private or administrative law solutions can provide the requisite degree of control, and can do so at lower cost, then there is likely to be a presumption that they represent a better approach than criminalization. (2008, p.415)

In any case, the usage of joint methods – private, administrative and/or criminal systems – seems advisable to regulate behaviour. While the usage of criminal law system is costly, the existence of a criminal punishment could have a sufficient deterrent effect to enhance compliance.

The choice of enforcement regime and legal system has been theorized and studied from the perspective of responsive regulation (Ayres and Braithwaite 1992). It has been argued there that the choice is not necessarily between deterrent or compliant enforcement approaches. It should be rather a 'pyramid' from education and warnings to civil and criminal sanctions, suspensions and revocations and from self-regulation to command and control regulation with or without discretionary punishment. Smart regulation (Gunningham and Grabosky 1998) extends the responsive regulation approach by adding the parties involved in enforcement (third parties, not only government and business) and types of interrelationships of sanctions (not escalating the ladder but also using parallel methods of going from public to self-regulatory business and other parties' sanctions). Finally, the 'really responsive regulation' takes a broader approach on the factors to consider in designing enforcement approach from not only the behaviour but also institutional and cultural settings and other factors (Baldwin and Black 2008). Addressing the questions of how to monitor and which sanctions to envisage can further go as far as employing also research from behavioural (economic) studies (Thaler and Sunstein 2003; Kahneman and Tversky 2000).

These choices are translated in different legal systems, generally speaking, systems of private and public (increasingly EU) law, which have become research and practice areas for lawyers. Private law (research) includes regulating and enforcing behaviour via contract, property and tort law (claims for damages). Public law (research) includes areas of administrative and criminal laws and has been increasingly used in enforcement of EU law and other international law obligations.

This organization of enforcement is an important issue as it has influence on the actors that would be created and delegated with the tasks to enforce laws. People making a contract among themselves, for instance, would be in charge of complying with the contract as well as enforcing its provisions if other parties to the contract do not comply, including via dispute-settlement mechanisms and private lawsuits.

In the domain of public law, public bodies, may be created to enhance compliance and impose sanctions, either by the same public body that monitored and investigated a case and/ or by another body acting on request of the investigating body. The involvement of appeal and judicial bodies is further possible but normally in relation to a decision of that public (administrative or criminal) authority to ensure the effective judicial protection and rule of law values.

Irrespective of how enforcement is organized, the study of the 'how' in law enforcement has been broad and involves various behavioural, institutional, substantive and procedural issues surrounding enforcement processes. Debates only in legal scholarship have ranged from determining behaviour that should be penalized by criminal penalties or administrative sanctions (e.g. Jansen 2013) to the scope of rights and obligations of private actors when under investigation, especially in the EU (e.g. Binder et al. 2018 ; Luchtman et al. 2017) and (national) levels of enforcement (Etienne 2015).

Enhancing Enforcement through Regulating it *Ex Ante*?

> Rules do not work when those willing to comply do not know what compliance involves and when those less willing or able to comply are not informed or stimulated in the appropriate manner. ... Effective rule use demands that those who design rules take into account the enforcement strategies that will have to be used to achieve compliance. (Baldwin, 1990, pp.336–337).

Baldwin argues that enforcement strategies are influenced by the types of mischief and hazard creators and the strategies will then in turn affect how rules should be formulated; rule-makers however are predominately busy with passing the rule – content and to a certain extent process – yet without necessarily securing compliance. The formulation of regulation, taking into account enforcement, thus seems to be crucial for rules to be effective, yet is constrained by different factors, such as the complexity and length of rule-making procedures and political pressures (see also Kagan 1989 and others on regulatory enforcement).

The time-consuming effect of making proper rules is also a concern in risk-based regulation (Black 2005), which is another type of regulation focusing on controlling specific risks, rather than compliance with rules, and 'smart enforcement' (Blanc and Faure 2018). However, as with identifying a proper enforcement strategy in the rule, it seems difficult to identify risks which may be in the way of attaining policy objectives (Baldwin et al. 2011, p.283). In both cases – compliance-orientated rules and risk-regulation, the process seems to involve making judgements, which can be questioned by various stakeholders. This leads to the question of who should be making these judgements in a democratic setting of the decision-making and if the same actor should be dealing with formulating the enforcement strategy, monitoring compliance, investigating and sanctioning.

Supervisors or Enforcement Agencies: Types, Questions, Dilemmas

It has been argued that the focus in enforcement policy design and research should be not only on enforcement but also enforcing agencies (Ottow 2015). Regulatory, supervisory or enforcement agencies play an increasing role in ensuring compliance with laws. The liberalization of markets has brought at least three types of supervisors: market authorities or market regulators for specific sectors; competition authorities ensuring competition throughout all sectors of the economy; and consumer protection agencies enforcing consumer protection law, each type having its own peculiarities in terms of aims, functions and principles to follow (ibid. 2015) and raising questions as to what extent the agency supervisor is an optimal choice and upon which conditions.

What can enforcement agencies do? Ottow shows that market authorities who regulate transport, financial sectors, utilities, and so on, have the power to give permits to operate and produce specific information about those industries. Competition authorities normally investigate anti-competitive agreements or abuses of dominant positions and hence their involvement is largely *ex post* via inspections and the imposition of sanctions. Consumer protection agencies promote consumer protection 'at the level of individual transactions' (ibid. 2015, p.31) via obliging providers to give more information, prohibiting misleading advertisement, and so on. Supervisors can have singular and multiple aims to achieve, which again is a question of debate as to how many purposes an agency should have to attain its purposes better. The different tasks that supervisors may have can be accompanied with a different set of powers and we seem to lack roadmaps and specifics which powers should be given to achieve specific aims. To use the stages of enforcement of Vervaele, for instance, the monitoring of compliance can be done via regular interactions and requesting private parties to report or have an open (online) line for receiving complaints and having the power to inspect entities. The investigation task can be done with the powers of asking for more detailed information, making ad hoc inspections (announced and unannounced), and having access to telephone and other communications. Sanctions can vary from issuing public notices to imposing periodical payments and fines.

Dilemmas and Principles of 'Good Supervision and Supervisor'

Research and practice seem to have been inconclusive as to which set of criteria is suitable to design and assess performance of supervisors. Ottow (2015) lists criteria used by the OECD, the IMF, individual countries and by supervisors in this respect; she herself distinguishes the LITER principles – legality, independence, transparency, effectiveness and responsibility – as a yardstick in this undertaking. These principles include a number of sub-elements and some of these principles may have difficult interrelationships with others, causing dilemmas and requiring a search for compromises, for instance, 'independent, hence unaccountable?' (Scholten 2011), or formulated in that fashion: Transparent, yet confidential? Effective, yet under control? Controls over supervisors are crucially important, yet they make various processes – educating, inspecting, investigating, sanctioning – time- and resource-consuming.

There is a literature stream (Kovacic 2019; Ottow 2015) from scholars–practitioners on the importance of leadership of the supervisors. A long-term development of leaders in the organization and Kovacic's analogy with the 'Formula 1' competition conditions – the owner, the car, the driver, the team, the circuit, and the weather – open additional insights into how successful enforcement could be reached. This is further interconnected with insights on setting up 'right priorities' – 'consume or invest' (Kovacic and Hyman 2016) implying the need to find a good balance between bringing 'high profile cases' and thus getting the headlines in the news, which can be beneficial for trust in and strong reputation of the supervisor, and investing in building good supervising environment which may be less 'popular' from the outside. These insights correlate with observations of Ottow on the dilemmas that need to be considered in supervisory practice. These include building trust with the sector to be overseen, yet not becoming 'too close' of a friend to lose objectivity; having a mixture of instruments to enhance cooperation for supervision, yet having possibility to sanction if necessary. Finally, as enforcement is an 'expensive' process, agencies are continuously in search of balancing efficiency – achieving results as soon as possible – and accuracy or carefulness – following all the procedural requirements and weighting interests against each other.

The 'good supervisor' is clearly not only the leadership of an agency; it is also its officials and inspectors. As van Loo (2019, pp.434–435) stipulates,

> legal scholars commonly describe agencies as engaging in ex ante rulemaking and ex post enforcement. Ongoing monitoring should be added to that standard account of agency activity and studied more closely. Those who regularly extract information from firms influence much of the administrative state's law-related activity. Any regulatory analysis that ignores regulatory monitors or groups them together with enforcement actors risks obscuring agencies' vital internal laws.

The attention on enforcement is largely devoted to courts and case-law, especially for instance in the area of EU law (see Barnard and Peers 2020), or police officers in the studies on criminal justice (van Loo 2019). Yet, the daily 'nitty-gritty' enforcement work, such as guiding the supervisees, gathering information and making inspections, and the role of street-level inspectors (Moseley and Thomann 2021; Hupe et al. 2015) seem understudied and under-accounted for *ex post* (unless a (court) investigation takes place). If we agree that success of enforcement is in attainting policy goals and protecting core values with less costs, then the success of the monitoring stage seems essential for enforcement and enforcer to be 'good' or successful (Scholten 2021).

ENFORCEMENT IN A MULTI-JURISDICTIONAL SETTING: THE CASE OF THE EU

The EU integration has influenced the dispersion of enforcement and proliferation of enforcement networks of European scale and EU enforcers. This development has brought additional questions and concerns in design and study on enforcement (Vervaele, 1999; Jans et al. 2015; Hofmann et al. 2018, 2011; Scholten, 2017) and affected national (legal) systems by Europeanizing private, administrative and criminal laws (Blanc and Faure 2018, 2020).

Ongoing debates on law-making powers of (EU) independent agencies raise questions as to what tasks and powers (and how much discretion) they can or should have (legitimacy concern). Legal scholars have become involved in addressing these issues by exploring issues of EU competences, fundamental rights and other control standards. It has showed that relying only on EU member states for compliance with EU law ('indirect enforcement', studied also under the term of implementation, see e.g. Thomann and Sager 2017) may be not enough (EU Commission, 2017) and other mechanisms, including direct enforcement by EU agencies, can be an option to explore, yet there is a lack of clarity as to when and how this option can and is allowed to be used (see Scholten 2021, contributions in the edited volume of Scholten and Luchtman 2017). The European Securities and Markets Authority (ESMA) has become, for instance, the strongest EU agency with the powers to register certain financial markets' participants (trade repositories and credit ranking agencies) and then to monitor their performance, investigate possible violations and impose fines of a different nature (van Rijsbergen and Foster 2017; van Rijsbergen and Simoncini 2020; Scholten and Ottow 2014). Yet, to what extent does the non-delegation doctrine (Meroni+) allow the proliferation of shared enforcement powers and under which conditions? The principle of national procedural autonomy (Greek Maize) and principles of conferral, subsidiarity and proportionality of EU law protect the regulatory and operational authorities of national institutions to ensure compliance with EU laws, yet there have been various 'institutional enforcement innovations' (Cacciatore and Scholten 2019) in various policy sectors showing that enforcement competences may be broadening irrespectively of the fact that the treaties are unclear or the competence has been lacking. Aiming also at inviting further debate on relevant (EU) integration theories, Scholten and Scholten (2017) suggest the idea of 'functional policy cycle spillover' to explain those developments: enforcement will move to the level of regulation if the default rule – enforcement at the national level – faces challenges.

There is an emergent literature stream on that the shift from indirect to direct administration in the EU has not been accompanied by relevant changes in the system of controls, which is inherent to the delegation standard (Scholten 2021a; Scholten and Brenninkmeijer 2020; Scholten 2019; Scholten 2017; Brandsma and Joosen 2017; Mustert and Scholten 2020; Contreras Condezo et al. 2020; Scholten and van Rijsbergen 2014). Some scholars discuss it in connection to trade-offs (e.g. Ottow 2015), such as the need to balance acceptance and trust in the supervisor (legitimacy) yet making sure it renders account to relevant parties (reporting, following other procedures). The recent developments in the EU of proliferation of 'joint enforcers' has led others to argue for the establishment of 'joint controllers' and aligned systems of controls (EU-national, national-national) to ensure the rule of law, using the non-delegation doctrine reasoning (Scholten 2021a; Scholten and Brenninkmeijer 2020; Scholten et al. 2020). Furthermore, as new forms of transnational cooperation have impacted the nation-state-orientated concepts such as the protection of fundamental rights, legality, effective judicial protection as they relate to enforcement (Karagianni and Scholten 2018; Binder et al. 2018), research has started in reconceptualization of such doctrine (Meyer 2020, contributions in the special issue of Eliantonio and Vogiatzis 2021). Further research seems relevant to address the questions as to which types of controls individual enforcement mechanisms may require and how much independence enforcement agencies, also in comparison with prosecutors and courts, may need, why and how to ensure (Kleizen and Verhoest 2020).

ENFORCEMENT AND AGENCIES: WHAT'S NEXT IN RESEARCH AND PRACTICE

Enforcement of law in theory and practice seems to have been gaining its momentum. We know that enforcement can be an essential element to ensure values and objectives, what we are still figuring out is upon which conditions which type of enforcement works best, including under novel circumstances, such as a multi-jurisdictional setting of the EU, also to include these considerations at the rule-forming stage. It is these conditions that form a central focus for further research and practice and require many (empirical, comparative and cross-sectoral) case-studies to be undertaken.

Towards Common Terminology

First, a great variety of terms are being used for the same, similar or related processes. It seems for the benefit of the study of enforcement to build up a taxonomy of various definitions, inter-relationships between different sets of criteria, stages, literature streams and other elements to advance our understandings of the relevant issues thanks to the fact that these have been studied from different perspectives.

Furthermore, it has been argued that the effectiveness in achieving compliance with laws depends on identification of relevant enforcement *ex ante*, in the rule-making procedures. Such strategies are built in part on deterrent and compliant approaches like responsive regulation and its follow-ups. These hypotheses require more studies, certainly over time, including in fields of EU law and emergent enforcement authorities. To what extent can responsive regulation be adaptive to the multi-cultural and multi-lingual environments of enforcing rules?

Questions to Address on the Intersection of Agencification and Europeanisation of Enforcement Trends

Another 'laboratory' for future research and policy is on the crossing of agencification and Europeanization of enforcement trends. The shifts of power to enforce laws from national to EU levels seems to be 'landing' predominately within EU agencies or authorities alike, for instance, within the European Public Prosecutors' Office (EPPO). This puts pressure upon the already questionable legitimacy of EU agencies. What powers can and should be given to them? How will they operate in a multi-jurisdictional case? What sanctions and remedies can be envisaged by agencies? Eleven EU agencies with decision-making powers have nine Boards of Appeal. These boards, however, have unclear status as to if they are an administrative or (quasi)judicial type of review and what the scope and intensity of review should and can be (Pander-Maat and Scholten, 2021), which can hamper trust and hence effectiveness of supervisors. Finally, agencification has led to focus on (enforcement) performance of individual agencies, their designs, powers, accountability arrangements, to name but a few (Scholten 2014; Scholten 2011). Yet, one supervisor or an agency exists within a specific policy domain. As enforcement is not a standalone process, the achieving of a bigger purpose may require studying and designing clusters of agencies (Lalikova and Scholten 2017), also to prevent having undesirable regulatory overlaps and excesses. Here, studying alignments of rule-makers and enforcers is another array to explore.

Towards Enforcement (EU) Law Enforcement Models and Roadmaps

Enforcement's twofold aim underlines the need for further case-studies, as successful enforcement is likely to be the aim which attains the first (prevention of violation), rather than the second (responding to violation) aim, yet it is still necessary to design tools and enforcers for both. I argue elsewhere (Scholten 2021) that two trends in terms of the development of EU sanctioning power are noticeable. On the one hand, the EU has a stronger influence on sanctions employed at the national level when enforcing EU law. On the other hand, there is growing understanding, as discussed above, that deterrence or sanctioning do not necessarily bring us to attaining policy goals and enforcement may be more successful, also in terms of cost and benefit analysis, when compliance is encouraged and monitoring is done well. Yet, as enforcement is sensitive to specifics of policy sectors, cultural and other traditions and rules, the study of enforcement requires a high number of case-studies, also as to what generalization can be made across sectors (see also Kagan 1989).

These 'both cases' (prevention of and responding to violation) would then differ per policy sector and can be influenced by other factors, such as the degree of internationalization or Europeanization in that area (see e.g. Scholten and Ottow 2014). Furthermore, enforcement in different policy sectors puts a different emphasis on different stages of enforcement – monitoring, investigating and sanctioning – which could be an obstacle as well as an opportunity to learn and adjust across sectors in comparative studies. For instance, there is larger emphasis on monitoring compliance and correcting potential or occurred violations by public supervisors in the financial sector where reputation damage seems a bigger sanction than paying a fine. In contrast, in the area of competition law, enforcement (research) seems largely focusing on investigation, including unannounced dawn raids, and further sanctioning. Yet, the fact that a fine is issued by a public supervisor or the fact that a court rules against a member state does not mean that enforcement has been successful. The fine can be annulled or reduced by a court, or lead to another court's ruling when the member state does not comply with the first judgement (Commission vs France, Case C-304/02). A study on the appeals against fines of the Dutch competition authority showed that a great majority of fines imposed by the supervisor were reduced or annulled by the court, which questioned to a certain extent the effectiveness of this supervisor (Kingma 2018). More empirical (legal) research is essential to see to what extent fining is an effective sanction and upon which conditions and, if not, how this could be remedied by more effective preventive, educative measures. Here, interdisciplinary research seems essential to include also insights from behavioural studies on when people and organizations are likely to abide rules and norms and from political science on how politics may influence enforcement norm-setting and further (legal) application.

Towards more Interdisciplinary Research to Enhance Enforcement and Enforcers

Interdisciplinary research seems fruitful for all kinds of issues surrounding enforcement and enforcer. Bringing insights from relevant legal, economic, political, cultural and other studies together as well as employing various doctrinal and empirical methods seems the necessary way forward in this topic and the second topic to be mentioned here. As Bowles et al. (2008, p.390) show that each discipline has its own perspective, on, for instance, the usage of criminal law:

> the legal approach tends to focus on the characteristics of harm-creating activities whilst the economics approach tends to focus on the relative merits of criminal law as a means of controlling the volume of harm produced. … We argue that the law and economics approach may be useful in predicting circumstances in which criminal law or criminal sanctions might emerge as a preferred instrument as why it is (or has been) used for controlling some activities but not others.

Almond and van Erp (2020) argue that regulatory governance and criminology could assist each other in bringing further innovation in these disciplines on the issues of criminal and regulatory law, while May and Winter (2011) discuss how different methodological approaches could contribute to studying enforcement strategies (related to the agency level) and styles (related to the inspector's level, see also Gormley 1998; de Boer 2019) and which limits different methods may have. Dewey and Di Carlo (2021, p.16) 'shed light on the non-enforcing state, that is, governments' strategic use of forbearance as a mode of regulatory governance' by 'bringing together the literature on state-centered political economy and industrial policy with sociological and political studies on law non-enforcement'.

More interdisciplinary case-studies could contribute to building up literature in the field of 'functional policy cycle spillover' (Scholten and Scholten 2017) to see to what extent regulating enforcement and creation and redesign of EU agencies with enforcement tasks has been happening or is to happen or not (Maggetti 2019). Van Kreij (2019) argues for the necessity of combining legal and political insights in studying when EU agencies or networks have been created:

> agencies, lastly, can only be delegated strong enforcement powers if substantive EU law is harmonised to a large extent. Agencies are only capable of targeting a relatively small and/or homogenous group of actors that operate across the continent, and/or whose violations and damage require a single problem and solution definition. Also, agencies are likely to be preferred if distinct national interests can impede effective enforcement, and if electoral opposition and distributional concerns are limited. (van Kreij 2019, p.10)

Further research would be valuable in terms of how existing structures in a policy field and the popularity of the agency model influence the choice of establishing of an enforcement network or agency.

This research could further feed the debate in legal scholarship, for instance, as to how we should go about the questions of competences and politics in those sectors where functional necessity does show the advantages of more centralized and direct enforcement by EU institutions and agencies. The legal debate is quite concentrated around the existing key principles of the treaties (conferral, subsidiarity and proportionality) and as defined by the case-law (Greek Maize on national enforcement and the Meroni and ESMA short-selling non-delegation doctrine), yet we witness the emergence of EU enforcers with relevant powers, which at times can be designed in a less efficient way due to the unclarities of the EU competences as to enforcement role and agencies (Scholten and Luchtman 2017; Scholten 2017). Empirical studies of law and multi-disciplinary research could help to balance (formulation of) relevant principles and laws. Would (safeguard) obligations for enforcer (like publications of fines and accountability obligations) necessarily help enforcement? Such 'classic' legal questions could benefit from insights of studies from other disciplines, like van Erp (2011), Pires (2011), de Boer et al. (2018), Versluis and Polak (2019), Zhelyazkova (2020) who notice nuances concerning transparency, accountability and performance management strategies on enforcement agencies and those who are being supervised.

More comparative studies are also welcome, to see to what extent various institutional innovations actually work and could be 'transplanted' to other policy sectors. Think about such innovations as SSM's joint supervisory teams with representatives from EU and national supervisors, novel possibility to delegate enforcement actions from national supervisors to the European Aviation Safety Agency (EASA) or a national supervisor from another member state, suggestions for new tools in light of the Digital Markets Act (European Commission 2020) to introduce gatekeepers entailing extensive *ex ante* obligations, move from ineffective enforcement of individual antitrust cases to market investigations. More empirical studies are useful to get a better understanding of implementation of EU law beyond transposition (Thomann and Sager, 2017) and application and via diversifying channels of enforcement to include also private actors, as in recent legislation on the protection of whistle-blowers

(Kafteranis 2020). Addressing these pertinent questions could bring research on (EU) law enforcement and enforcers further as well as hopefully to develop an effective EU strategy and enhance normative debates on the pertinent questions on enforcement in the twenty-first century, including effectiveness vs. controls, diversity vs. uniformity in the EU enforcement, and digital innovations (Luchtman and Scholten 2019; Nicolosi 2020; Townley 2018; Ligeti and Robinson 2021).

Finally, writing this chapter in times of a pandemic suggests that the role of crisis should be explored further concerning the emergence of more in quantity and quality (powers) supervisors, also in the EU, as well as concerning the law enforcement operation questions and dilemmas, especially on efficiency vs. carefulness, (dis)trust in supervisors and discretionary judgement (Scholten 2021a; Binder et al. 2018).

CONCLUSION

All in all, regulation leads to the necessity to enforce it. The formula of success of enforcement and enforcement agencies includes a great variety of elements – the scope and sources of legislative mandates (and powers), enforcement styles and types, 'environmental' factors, which may include cultural dimensions (in the EU for instance), technological capacities, agency leadership, and so on; these need to be balanced in the 'right' proportion in specific cases. In addition, as enforcement could be arguably better off if considered already at a designing of a rule stage, it seems important to adjust our perception the policy cycle's 'drafting of rules stage' to include determining (and studying in a cross-disciplinary way) enforcement aims, strategies, tools and institutions to be involved, while keeping in mind political, subsequent practical and other 'environmental' factors. From this perspective, uncertainty about the EU's enforcement competence could impede unnecessarily designing optimal regulatory and enforcement regimes and agencies at both national and EU levels.

BIBLIOGRAPHY

Almond, P. and van Erp, J. (2020). 'Regulation and Governance Versus Criminology: Disciplinary Divides, Intersections, and Opportunities'. *Regulation & Governance*, 14(2), pp.167–178.

Ayres, I. and Braithwaite, J. (1992). *Responsive Regulation: Transcending the Deregulation Debate* (Oxford University Press).

Baldwin, R. (1990). 'Why Rules Don't Work', *Modern Law Review*, 53, pp.321–337.

Baldwin, R. and Black, J. (2008). 'Really Responsive Regulation'. *The Modern Law Review*, 71, pp.59–94.

Baldwin, R., Cave, M. and Lodge, M. (2011). *Understanding Regulation: Theory, Strategy, and Practice* (Oxford University Press).

Barnard, C. and Peers, S. (2020). *European Union Law* (Oxford University Press).

Binder, T., Karagianni, A. and Scholten, M. (2018). 'Emergency – But What about Legal Protection in the EU'. *European Journal of Risk Regulation*, 9(1), pp.99–119.

Black, J. (2005). 'The Emergence of Risk-Based Regulation and the New Public Risk Management in the United Kingdom', *Public Law*, 2005 (Autumn), pp.512–549.

Blanc, F. and Faure, M. (2018). 'Smart Enforcement: Theory and Practice'. *European Journal of Law Reform [vii]*, 20(4), pp.78–103.

Blanc, F. and Faure, M. (2020). 'Smart Enforcement in the EU'. *Journal of Risk Research*, 23(11), pp.1405–1423.

Bowles, R., Faure, M. and Garoupa, N. (2008). 'The Scope of Criminal Law and Criminal Sanctions: An Economic View and Policy Implications'. *Journal of Law and Society*, 35, pp.389–416.

Brandsma, GJ. and Joosen, R. (2017). 'Transnational Executive Bodies: Very Effective but Hardly Accountable?' EU Law Enforcement https://eulawenforcement.com/?p=408 accessed 24 April 2021.

Cacciatore, F. and Scholten, M. (2019). 'Introduction to the Symposium on Institutional Innovations in the Enforcement of EU Law and Policies'. *European Journal of Risk Regulation*, 10, pp. 435–438.

Cambridge Dictionary, 'Enforcement' https://dictionary.cambridge.org/dictionary/english/enforcement accessed 24 April 2021.

Contreras Condezo, J.G., Kingma, A. and Scholten, M. (2020). 'Putting Dawn Raids under Control'. *Yearbook of Antitrust and Regulatory Studies*, 10, pp.145–167.

Coslovsky, S. et al. (2011). 'The Pragmatic Politics of Regulatory Enforcement' in Levi-Faur, D. (ed.), *Handbook on the Politics of Regulation* (Cheltenham, UK and Northampton, MA, USA: Edward Elgar Publishing).

de Boer, N. (2019). 'Street-Level Enforcement Style: A Multidimensional Measurement Instrument'. *International Journal of Public Administration*, 42(5), pp.380–391.

de Boer, N. et al. (2018). 'Does Disclosure of Performance Information Influence Street-Level Bureaucrats' Enforcement Style?'. *Public Administration Review*, 78(5), pp.1–11.

Dewey, M. and Di Carlo, D. (2021). 'Governing through Non-Enforcement: Regulatory Forbearance as Industrial Policy in Advanced Economies'. *Regulation & Governance*. https://onlinelibrary.wiley.com/doi/epdf/10.1111/rego.12382.

Eliantonio, M. and Vogiatzis, N. (2021). 'Judicial and Extra-judicial Challenges in the EU Multi- and Cross-level Administrative Framework'. *German Law Journal,* 22(Special issue 3), pp.315–324.

Etienne, J. (2015). 'Different Ways of Blowing the Whistle: Explaining Variations in Decentralized Enforcement in the UK and France'. *Regulation & Governance*, 9(15), pp.309–324.

European Commission (2020). 'European Commission – Competition – Public Consultations' https://ec.europa.eu/competition/consultations/2020_new_comp_tool/index_en.html accessed 24 April 2021.

EU Commission (2017). Monitoring Application of EU law: 2017 Annual Report.

Gormley, W.T. (1998). 'Regulatory Enforcement Styles'. *Political Research Quarterly*, 51(2), pp.363–383.

Gunningham, N. and Grabosky, P. (1998). *Smart Regulation* (Oxford University Press).

Hofmann, HCH. et al. (eds) (2018). *Specialized Administrative Law of the European Union: A Sectoral Review* (Oxford University Press).

Hofmann, HCH. et al. (eds) (2011). *Administrative Law and Policy of the European Union* (Oxford University Press).

Huizinga, Kees. and de Bree, M. (2021). 'Exploring the Risk of Goal Displacement in Regulatory Enforcement Agencies: A Goal-Ambiguity Approach'. *Public Performance & Management Review*.

Hupe, P., Hill, M. and Buffat, A. (eds) (2015). *Understanding Street-Level Bureaucracy* (Policy Press).

Hutter, B.M. (1989). 'Variations in Regulatory Enforcement Styles'. *Law & Policy*, 11(2), pp.153–174.

in 't Veld S. (2021). 'Mind the Gap! Why the EU Law Enforcement Gap is Growing and What We Can Do To Close It' (Webinar, 7 January 2021) https://app.livecasts.eu/mind-the-gap-why-the-eu-law-enforcement-gap-is-growing-and-what-we-can-do-to-close-it/program accessed 10 January 2021.

Jans, J., Prechal, S. and Widdershven, R. (2015). *Europeanisation of Public Law* (Europa Law Publishing).

Jansen, O. (ed.) (2013). *Administrative Sanctions in the European Union* (Intersentia).

Jordanoska, A. (2021). 'Regulatory Enforcement Against Organizational Insiders: Interactions in the Pursuit of Individual Accountability'. *Regulation and Governance*, 15, pp.298–316.

Kafteranis, D. (2020). 'Enforcing EU Law: The Case of the Whistle-Blower'. EU Law Enforcement https://eulawenforcement.com/?p=7601 accessed 24 April 2021.

Kagan, RA. (1989). 'Editor's Introduction: Understanding Regulatory Enforcement'. *Law & Policy*, 11(2), pp.89–119.

Kahneman, D. and Tversky, A. (eds) (2000). *Choices, Values, and Frames* (Cambridge University Press).

Karagianni, A. and Scholten, M. (2018). 'Accountability Gaps in the Single Supervisory Mechanism SSM Framework Research Article'. *Utrecht Journal of International and European Law*, 34, pp.185–194.

Kingma, A. (2018). 'The (in)Efficiency of ACM's Fining Practice in Terms of the Cartel Prohibition', Master thesis at Utrecht University.

Kleizen, B. and Verhoest, K. (2020). 'Opportunities and Threats of Agency Autonomy in EU Governance: Integrating Separate Debates', in Scholten, M. and Brenninkmeijer, A. (eds), *Controlling EU Agencies* (Cheltenham, UK and Northampton, MA, USA: Edward Elgar Publishing).

Kovacic, W. (2019). 'Formula for Success: A Formula One Approach to Understanding Competition Law System Performance' in *Festschrift for Eleanor Fox* (Forthcoming).

Kovacic, W. and Hyman, D. (2016). 'Consume or Invest: What Do/Should Agency Leaders Maximize? *Washington Law Review*, 21, pp.295–324.

Lalikova, LF. and Scholten, M. (2007). '"EU Agencies" Label: To What Extent Should We Treat Them All as "One"? | RENFORCE Blog' http://blog.renforce.eu/index.php/en/2017/10/17/eu-agencies -label-to-what-extent-should-we-treat-them-all-as-one-2/ accessed 24 April 2021.

Ligeti, K. and Robinson, G. (2021). 'Sword, Shield and Cloud: Toward a European System of Public-Private Orders for Electronic Evidence in Criminal Matters?' in Mitsilegas, V. and Vavoula, N. (eds), *Surveillance and Privacy in the Digital Age: European, Transatlantic and Global Perspectives* (Oxford University Press).

Luchtman, M. and Scholten, M. (2019). 'Jean Monnet Network on Enforcement of EU Law (EULEN)'. EU Law Enforcement https://eulawenforcement.com/?p=7209 accessed 24 April 2021.

Luchtman, M. et al. (2017). 'Investigatory Powers and Procedural Safeguards: Improving OLAF's Legislative Framework through a Comparison with Other EU Law Enforcement Authorities (ECN/ESMA/ECB)' (2 May 2017).

Maggetti, M. (2019). 'Interest Groups and the (Non-)Enforcement Powers of EU Agencies: The Case of Energy Regulation'. *European Journal of Risk Regulation*, 10, pp.458–484.

May, P.J. and Winter, S.C. (2011). 'Regulatory Enforcement Styles and Compliance' in Parker, C. and Lehmann, V. (eds), *Explaining Compliance: Business Responses to Regulation* (Cheltenham, UK and Northampton, MA, USA: Edward Elgar Publishing).

Meyer, F. (2020). 'Protection of Fundamental Rights in a Multi-jurisdictional Setting of the EU' in Scholten, M. and Brenninkmeijer, A. (eds), *Controlling EU Agencies: The Rule of Law in a Multi-jurisdictional Legal Order* (Cheltenham, UK and Northampton, MA, USA: Edward Elgar Publishing).

Moseley, A. and Thomann, E. (2021). 'A Behavioural Model of Heuristics and Biases in Frontline Policy Implementation'. *Policy & Politics*, 49, pp.49–67.

Mustert, L. and Scholten, M. (2020). 'Controls in the Case of the EU Civil Aviation Safety Rules' in Scholten, M. and Brenninkmeijer, A. (eds), *Controlling EU Agencies: The Rule of Law in a Multi-jurisdictional Legal Order* (Cheltenham, UK and Northampton, MA, USA: Edward Elgar Publishing).

Nicolosi, S. (2020). 'Which Enforcement Strategy for the Common European Asylum System?' EU Law Enforcement https://eulawenforcement.com/?p=7584 accessed 24 April 2021.

Ottow, A. (2012). 'Europeanization of the Supervision of Competitive Markets'. *European Public Law*, 18(1), pp.191–221.

Ottow, A. (2015). *Market and Competition Authorities: Good Agency Principles* (Oxford University Press).

Pander-Maat, E. and Scholten, M. (2021). 'The Historical Development of Boards of Appeal of EU Agencies', *forthcoming*.

Pires, RRC. (2011). 'Beyond the Fear of Discretion: Flexibility, Performance, and Accountability in the Management of Regulatory Bureaucracies'. *Regulation & Governance*, 5(1), pp.43–69.

Röben, V. (2010). 'The Enforcement Authority of International Institutions' in von Bogdandy, A. et al. (eds), *The Exercise of Public Authority by International Institutions* (Springer).

Root, V. (2019). 'The Compliance Process'. *Indiana Law Journal*, 94, pp.203–251.

Scholten, M. (2011). 'Independent, Hence Unaccountable? The Need for a Broader Debate on Accountability of the Executive'. *Review of European Administrative Law*, 4(1), pp.5–41.

Scholten, M. (2014). *The Political Accountability of EU and US Independent Regulatory Agencies* (Brill: Nijhoff Studies in European Union Law).

Scholten, M. (2017). 'Mind the Trend! Enforcement of EU Law Has Been Moving to "Brussels"'. *Journal of European Public Policy*, 24(9), pp.1348–1366.

Scholten, M. (2019). 'Shared Tasks, but Separated Controls: Building the System of Control for Shared Administration in an EU Multi-Jurisdictional Setting'. *European Journal of Risk Regulation*, pp.538–553.

Scholten, M. (2021). 'EU (Shared) Law Enforcement: Who Does What and How?' in Alberti, J., Costamagna, F. and Montaldo, S. (eds), *European Union Law Enforcement: The Evolution of Sanctioning Powers* (Routledge).

Scholten, M. (2021a). 'For EU Law Enforcement Strategy and Theory Building!', (RENFORCE Blog, 2021a) http://blog.renforce.eu/index.php/en/2021/05/09/for-eu-law-enforcement-strategy-and-theory -building/#more-1228 accessed 1 July 2021.

Scholten, M. and Brenninkmeijer, A. (eds) (2020). *Controlling EU Agencies: The Rule of Law in a Multi-jurisdictional Legal Order* (Cheltenham, UK and Northampton, MA, USA: Edward Elgar Publishing).

Scholten, M. and Luchtman, M. (2017). *Law Enforcement by EU Authorities: Implications for Political and Judicial Accountability* (Cheltenham, UK and Northampton, MA, USA: Edward Elgar Publishing).

Scholten, M., Maggetti, M. and Papadopoulos, Y. (2020). 'Towards a Comprehensive System of Controls for EU Agencies' in Scholten, M. and Brenninkmeijer, A. (eds), *Controlling EU Agencies: The Rule of Law in a Multi-jurisdictional Legal Order* (Cheltenham, UK and Northampton, MA, USA: Edward Elgar Publishing).

Scholten, M. and Ottow, A. (2014). 'Institutional Design of Enforcement in the EU: The Case of Financial Markets'. *Utrecht Law Review*, 10(5), 80–91.

Scholten, M. and Scholten, D. (2017). 'From Regulation to Enforcement in the EU Policy Cycle: A New Type of Functional Spillover?'. *Journal of Common Market Studies*, 55(4), pp.925–942.

Scholten, M. and van Rijsbergen, M. (2014). 'The Limits of Agencification in the European Union'. *German Law Journal*, 15(7), 1223–1255.

Shavell, S. (2009). *Foundations of Economic Analysis of Law* (Harvard University Press).

Short, J.L. (2019). 'The Politics of Regulatory Enforcement and Compliance: Theorizing and Operationalizing Political Influences'. *Regulation & Governance*, 15(3), pp.653–685.

Stefan, O. (2017). 'Soft Law and the Enforcement of EU Law' in Jakab, A. and Kochenov, D. (eds), *The Enforcement of EU Law and Values: Ensuring Member States' Compliance* (Oxford University Press).

Thaler, R.H. and Sunstein, C.R. (2003). 'Libertarian Paternalism'. *American Economic Review*, 93(2), pp.175–179.

Thomann, E. and Sager, F. (2017). 'Moving beyond Legal Compliance: Innovative Approaches to EU Multilevel Implementation'. *Journal of European Public Policy*, 24(9), pp. 1253–1268.

Thomann, E. and Zhelyazkova, A. (2017). 'Moving beyond (Non-)Compliance: The Customization of European Union Policies in 27 Countries'. *Journal of European Public Policy*, 24(9), pp.1269–1288.

Townley, C. (2018). *A Framework for European Competition Law: Co-ordinated Diversity* (Hart Publishing).

van Erp, J. (2011). 'Naming without Shaming: The Publication of Sanctions in the Dutch Financial Market'. *Regulation & Governance*, 5(3), pp.287–308.

van Kreij, L. (2019). 'Towards a Comprehensive Framework for Understanding EU Enforcement Regimes'. *European Journal of Risk Regulation*, 10(3), pp.439–457.

van Loo, R. (2019). 'Regulatory Monitors: Policing Firms In The Compliance Era' *Columbia Law Review*, 119(2), pp.369–444.

van Rijsbergen, M. and Foster, J. (2017). '"Rating" ESMA's Accountability: "AAA" Status' in Scholten, M. and Luchtman, M. (eds), *Law Enforcement by EU Authorities: Implications for Political and Judicial Accountability* (Cheltenham, UK and Northampton, MA, USA: Edward Elgar Publishing).

van Rijsbergen, M. and Scholten, M. (2016). 'ESMA Inspecting: The Implications for Judicial Control under Shared Enforcement'. *European Journal of Risk Regulation*, 7(3), pp.569–579.

van Rijsbergen, M. and Simoncini, M. (2020). 'Controlling ESMAs Enforcement Powers' in Scholten, M. and Brenninkmeijer, A. (eds), *Controlling EU Agencies: The Rule of Law in a Multi-jurisdictional Legal Order* (Cheltenham, UK and Northampton, MA, USA: Edward Elgar Publishing).

Verbruggen, P. (2013). 'Gorillas in the Closet? Public and Private Actors in the Enforcement of Transnational Private Regulation'. *Regulation & Governance*, 7(4), pp.512–532.

Versluis, E, and Polak, J. (2019). 'Information Disclosure by the European Union as a Tool to Improve Implementation? A Comparative Analysis of the Perception of Domestic Regulators. *European Policy Analysis*, 5(2), pp.266–284.

Vervaele, J. (1999). 'Shared Governance and Enforcement of European Law: From Comitology to a Multi-level Agency Structure?' in Joerges, C. and Vos, E. (eds), *EU Committees: Social Regulation, Law and Politics* (Hart Publishing).

Zhelyazkova, A. (2020). 'Justifying Enforcement or Avoiding Blame? The Transparency of Compliance Assessments in the European Union'. *West European Politics*, 1, pp.403–429.

Case Law

Case 68/88 Greek Maize [1989] ECR 1989 – 02965.

Case C-304/02 Commission of the European Communities v French Republic [2005] ECR 2005 I-06263.

Case 9/56 Meroni [1958] ECR 1958 – 00133.

Case C-270/12 ESMA Short-Selling [2014] ECLI:EU:C:2014:18.

27. EU regulatory agencies

Emmanuelle Mathieu

INTRODUCTION

Unlike national regulatory agencies (NRAs), European regulatory agencies (ERAs) are embedded in a supranational political regime. At the national level, the empowerment of NRAs typically results from the delegation of competences from the legislative to the administrative power. This is partly true for ERAs, who also result, to a great extent, from the delegation of competences from the member states to the European level. This means, first, that ERAs are a product of EU integration dynamics, the specificities of which need to be understood to properly grasp the agencification phenomenon in the EU. A second key implication is that ERAs result from the combination of several delegation dynamics and thus face a multiplicity of principals. As shown in the following sections, this particular context has had a considerable impact on the design and functioning of ERAs. The chapter first introduces the concept of ERA (section 1), before giving an overview of the established knowledge about ERAs (section 2) and finally presenting the more recent cutting-edge research (section 3).

ERAS: DEFINITIONS AND OVERVIEW

The definition of what is an EU regulatory agency needs some clarification. Indeed, as developed by the European Commission, the taxonomy of EU agencies, and therefore the concept of EU regulatory agency – as a subset of EU agencies – are highly confusing (Busuioc 2013). EU governance scholars have therefore developed their own categories (Wonka and Rittberger 2010, Busuioc 2013, Font and Pérez Durán 2016), which are the ones this chapter builds on.

Some agencies, called *executive agencies* are set up at the discretion of the EU commission and are entirely controlled by it (see Figure 27.1). By contrast, the creation of *EU agencies* requires a legislative act, hence the agreement of the three major EU institutions (The Commission, the Council and the EU Parliament). Both types of agencies are very different. Whereas *executive agencies* can be seen as an extension of the Commission, only *EU agencies*, enjoy legal personality and can be considered as independent. This chapter, in line with the corresponding academic literature, focusses on EU agencies and excludes executive agencies. This makes a total of 38 EU agencies.

We can then divide the population of EU agencies into EU regulatory agencies (ERAs) and non-regulatory European agencies (EAs), depending on whether they are engaged in regulatory activities or not (Wonka and Rittberger 2010, Font and Pérez Durán 2016). This distinction is based on the analysis of EU agencies' tasks. Those agencies having a direct role in the rulemaking or implementing process are qualified as regulatory. ERAs are thus either involved in the making of individual regulatory decisions (such as authorizations, product certifications, licensing, etc.), participate to the regulatory policymaking process (e.g. by providing opinions, drafting regulatory measures or adopting them), or conduct supervision,

Figure 27.1   Overview of agency types in the EU

Table 27.1   List of ERAs

Acronym	Full name	Year of creation
EMA	European medicine agency	1993
CPVO	Community plant variety office	1994
EUIPO	EU intellectual property office	1994
EFSA	European food safety authority	2002
EMSA	European maritime safety agency	2002
EASA	EU aviation safety agency	2003
ECDC	European centre for disease prevention and control	2004
ENISA	EU agency for network and information security	2004
ERA	EU agency for railways	2004
EFCA	European fisheries control agency	2005
ECHA	European chemicals agency	2006
ACER	Agency for the cooperation of energy regulation	2009
BEREC Office	Agency for support for BEREC	2009
EBA	European banking authority	2011
EIOPA	European insurance and occupational pensions authority	2011
ESMA	European securities and market authority	2011
SRB	Single resolution board	2015

inspections, or sanctioning activities in the context of regulatory implementation (in particular to ensure compliance with EU regulation). By contrast, non-regulatory EAs are typically engaged in information gathering tasks, operational tasks, network coordination and service delivery functions that are unrelated with any of the components typical of the regulatory process. Based on this classification, among the 38 EU agencies, we find 17 ERAs. These are listed in Table 27.1.

When discussing the EU agencification process, the literature identifies three waves of agencification, in the 1970s, in the 1990s and in the 2000s. Within the population of EAs, ERAs have gained importance over time. While they correspond to a minority of the EAs created throughout the 1970s and 1990s, they constitute a bit more than half of the EAs set up in the last two decades.

ESTABLISHED KNOWLEDGE

The first pieces of academic literature on ERAs tended to make general arguments about these agencies, generally complemented with illustrations from various cases. This type of contribution was then complemented with in-depth case studies, either based on a single case or a small-N comparison. The first quantitative analyses appeared a decade ago and have recently gained importance. As we shall see, the use of comparison has allowed to identify how ERAs rise, power, independence can be influenced by sector-specific characteristics, such as complexity, urgent functional needs, power-distributional sensitiveness, political salience, the type of tasks endorsed or pre-existing institutional structures.

The Rise of ERAs: Pressure and Contextual Mediation

Prior to the 1990s, the European Union market integration process relied on legislative harmonization and decentralized policy implementation by the member states. With the adoption of the single European Act, the EU placed market integration as a chief political goal, and updated its integration methods accordingly. Harmonization, or at least regulatory convergence, should be addressed at the level of policy implementation too. This required the expansion of EU regulatory capacity, that is the upload of regulatory decision-making competences and the constitution of an EU-level expert workforce to feed the production of EU implementing regulatory measures (Dehousse 1997, Chiti 2000, Mathieu 2016).

Where and how shall this new EU regulatory capacity be located and organized? The EU Commission, the EU institutional actor most engaged in the administrative side of EU policies, is the most obvious candidate to be the recipient of the expanded EU regulatory capacity. But the member states are reluctant to both further empowering the EU executive and duplicate a workforce that was already present within national ministries. Besides, following the Santer Commission scandal in 1999, the Commission lacked legitimacy (Majone 2000). The compromised solution consisted in leveraging the national expertise and decision-making capacity through the creation of network-based structures at the EU level, in the form of EU agencies (Dehousse 1997, Eberlein and Grande 2005). This institutional design allowed member states to keep some control. It was also positively seen by the Commission who realized that, given their huge legitimacy challenge, ERAs' empowerment was the only feasible way to expand EU regulatory power (Kelemen 2002). The Commission consequently started to advocate the development of EU agencies in its 2001 White Paper on European governance (European Commission 2001).

On the other end of the 'integration continuum', EU regulatory networks (ERNs) constitute an alternative to ERAs. They are a lighter and less formal way to set up EU regulatory capacity than ERAs, although potentially less effective too. The Commission and the European Parliament tend to prefer ERAs over ERNs because the former imply a stronger level of EU integration and, as a result of their more formal status, are more legitimate and accountable. But member states tend to favor ERNs that are less constraining and easier to control (Thatcher and Coen 2008, Kelemen and Tarrant 2011). The preference for ERAs vs ERNs varies across sectors. ERAs were favored over ERNs in situations with lower distributional concerns for the member states (Kelemen and Tarrant 2011) or higher functional stakes (Mathieu 2019). ERNs may also be chosen as functionally superior to ERAs, in situations requiring a high level of local knowledge or characterized by uncertainty about how to achieve policy goals (Blauberger and Rittberger 2015, Mathieu and Rangoni 2019).

Finally, time also plays a role in the creation of ERAs. The constitution of the EU regulatory capacity is an incremental process (Thatcher and Coen 2008, Ottow 2012), where the creation of ERAs can be seen as one further step, after some preliminary stages have already been reached. This observation has fostered a few studies emphasizing the path-dependent mechanisms underpinning the creation and design of ERAs. A typical pattern is the transformation of an ERN into an ERA (Levi-Faur 2011, Thatcher 2011, Ottow 2012, Mathieu 2016). This is particularly visible about ERAs' structure (Thatcher and Coen 2008, Thatcher 2011, Levi-Faur 2011, Ottow 2012). Where ERAs result from the transformation of ERNs, the network generally becomes the core regulatory decision-making organ within the new ERA – while other organs such as the directorate or management board are in charge of administrative or strategic tasks. This is also true about ERAs that are structured differently. The European Food Safety Authority (EFSA) is centered around expert panels resulting from the transformation of the former expert committees working with the Commission (Krapohl 2007).

ERAs' Power

ERAs are bodies with a low level of decision-making power compared to their national counterparts. A first limit to their empowerment is legal. In a ruling delivered in 1958, the Court of Justice of the European Union (CJEU) elaborated the so-called *Meroni* doctrine. Accordingly, it is not allowed to delegate discretionary decision-making power, involving a margin of political judgment, to a body else than those mentioned by the EU Treaties. While this interpretation of the *Meroni* doctrine has recently be questioned by legal scholars (Chiti 2009, Chamon 2011) and even relaxed by the Court in a judgment delivered in 2014 about the European Securities and Market Authority (ESMA), it did served as an important barrier to the delegation of far-reaching powers to ERAs in the past.

There are also political explanations to ERAs' limited powers. One of them is related to the multiple principals' context in which ERAs are embedded. ERAs are created through the EU legislative process that involves the Commission, the European Parliament and the Council. So each of these actors, as co-principal in the delegation to ERAs, wants to minimize the risk that other co-principals control a powerful agency, so they all have an incentive to limit ERAs' formal regulatory powers (Dehousse 2008). NRAs and their collective bodies, ERNs, can also oppose strong ERAs, which often goes hand in hand with in a loss of power for them. NRAs may also be actively engaged in lobbying their own governments and EU policymakers against the creation of powerful ERAs, as ERAs' empowerment often goes hand in hand with a loss of power for them, as for example in the telecommuncations sector (Thatcher 2011, Boeger and Corkin 2017). Interest groups may also successfully oppose the creation of ERAs with enforcement powers, as illustrated by the energy sector (Maggetti 2019).

Beyond this general tendency of weak ERAs, empirical variation across sectors has been reported. We know that, among EU agencies, those involved in regulation are the most powerful (Wonka and Rittberger 2010, Thatcher 2011). But what explains differences *across EU regulatory agencies*? One factor is the degree of complexity and uncertainty of the policy fields under consideration. Where the Commission is already well equipped in terms of regulatory power and expertise, it shall avoid delegating important powers to a potential competitor, as in telecommunications or competition policy for example (Mathieu and Rangoni 2019).

In sectors where regulatory power at the EU level is limited, creating a powerful ERA represents an important move forward in terms of regulatory integration, typically favored by the Commission and resisted by the member states. There, member states are more likely to accept the creation of a strong ERAs in case of low distributional stakes (Kelemen and Tarrant 2011) or if they anticipate significant and tangible functional gains (Mathieu 2019). In line with the functional argument, the ERAs enjoying the higher level of formal decision-making powers are those created in the wake of the financial crisis for the supervision of banks and financial markets (Dehousse 2016).

An important consequence of these barriers to the delegation of significant autonomous regulatory decision-making power is that most ERAs are in fact only 'quasi-regulatory agencies' or 'pre-decision agencies' as some scholars have put it (Busuioc 2013, Chamon 2011). In the typical EU regulatory decision-making process, the ERA prepares the substance of the regulatory measure but does not hold the formal power to adopt it. Instead, it is generally the Commission, together with comitology committees, who are in charge of the formal adoption of the regulatory measure. In general, the latter do not hold the necessary expertise to seriously ponder the scientific or technical relevance of the opinions submitted by the agency. As a consequence, the Commission's input is often limited to rubber-stamping the opinions provided by ERAs, as is particularly the case with the European Medicine Agency (EMA), but also to an important extent with other agencies, such as the European Food Safety Authority (EFSA) or the European Chemical Agency (ECHA) (Dehousse 1997, Gehring and Krapohl 2007, Groenleer 2009, Ossege 2016). These observations are consistent with Majone's early evaluation that ERAs' power would rather rest in their expertise and control of specialized information rather than in decision-making competences (Majone 1997).

The extent of ERAs' informal influence is particularly high when the agency enjoys a high level of legitimacy and a wide and unanimous political support from its principals and their constituency (Groenleer 2009, 2014). Such political support, in turn, derives from the dependence of other actors on ERAs' output, and on ERA having demonstrated their uniqueness and added-value, while sustaining good collaborative relationship with other actors (Groenleer 2009, 2014). The informal influence of ERAs is also particularly important in complex and technical areas where ERAs produce scientific opinions to prepare Commission decisions, although there, high political salience can overcome scientific considerations and lead the Commission to deviate from ERAs' scientific opinions (Ossege 2016).

ERAs' Independence

When it comes to ERAs', the concept of independence is not as straightforward as for NRAs. ERAs are embedded in the EU's particular political environment, characterized by a high level of power fragmentation. In this context, who are ERAs are supposed to be independent from? In a typical delegation perspective, ERAs should be independent from the executive, that is, from the Commission. Yet, from the Commission's viewpoint, ERAs must rather be independent from national interests, which is an equally acknowledged dimension of ERAs' independence. ERAs' independence is thus a multidimensional concept which relates to both the Commission and national interests.

A few studies have investigated the *formal* level of EU agencies' independence, found generally weak (Vos 2014), although among EAs, ERAs emerge as those enjoying the highest levels of independence (Groenleer 2009, Wonka and Rittberger 2010). Among ERAs, the highest levels of independence are found in those ERAs operating in complex and economic sectors (Wonka and Rittberger 2010) and addressing an urgent need for organizational separation of the agency from the Commission as in the case of the EFSA (Groenleer 2009).

When it comes to the *informal* dimension of ERAs' autonomy, the literature has emphasized the striking level of influence of the Commission on ERAs (Busuioc 2009, Font 2015, Egeberg et al. 2015, Ossege 2016). First, the Commission always has a seat as a member of the board of ERAs and is thus involved in ERAs' strategic decisions, such as its work program. Whereas they are in the minority on ERAs' boards, they generally manage to infer significantly more influence from this position than what their formal voting rights suggest (Busuioc 2009, Font 2015), often as a result of their power to decide on ERAs' budgets (Busuioc 2009). Besides, studies adopting an organizational approach revealed that the relationship between the Commission and ERAs tend to be particularly close and even very similar to the relations typical of a parent ministry and an administrative agency at the national level (Egeberg and Trondal 2011, Vestlund 2015, Egeberg et al. 2015). This picture should however be nuanced by the distinction between the type of ERAs' decisions considered. Whereas the Commission has a strong influence on ERAs' administrative and strategic decisions, ERAs' high level of expertise or high saliency allows them to resist the Commission's attempts to influence their regulatory decisions (Font 2015, 2018, Ossege 2016).

ERAs are also subject to national influence. This is particularly true for those ERAs that are structured around a network of NRAs in charge of the agency's regulatory decisions, as for example in the energy, telecommunications, aviation, or securities sectors. This configuration gives much room to national interests (Busuioc 2013). Examples of ERAs' permeability to national interests have been observed in several cases, such as in the aviation sector (Schout 2011) or in telecommunications (Mathieu and Rangoni 2019). National interests also influence ERAs through the participation of member states on ERAs' management boards. Although the level of involvement of national board members varies from one country to the other, their input is often guided by their perception of the national impact of ERA's activities, rather than by considerations about the agency's effectiveness (Busuioc 2012).

The de facto autonomy of ERAs is also subject to empirical variation. It was found that de facto autonomy is higher in complex and technical sectors (Groenleer 2009, Font 2015), where ERAs' expertise sustains a situation of informational asymmetry between the agency and its political principals (Groenleer 2009, Ossege 2016). Legitimacy and political support also have a considerable impact on ERAs' de facto autonomy. Among the variety of factors affecting ERAs' legitimacy and political support, the literature has emphasized expertise – or, to be more precise, stakeholders' perception of ERAs' expertise, but also the nature of ERAs' relationship with other actors, such as the Commission, national agencies or even international organizations. Sustaining inclusive and cooperative relationships fosters trust, enhances legitimacy and thus increases de facto autonomy. Hence, the key for ERAs is to achieve the right balance between positioning itself as unique and distinct from their environment while sustaining good relationship with the other actors (Groenleer 2009).

Legitimacy of ERAs: Expertise, Participation and Accountability

ERAs come with significant normative concerns, as shown by the emphasis made in the literature about their (lack of) legitimacy. To start with, being both supranational and non-majoritarian actors, ERAs lack democratic legitimacy, so their acceptance depends on alternative sources of legitimacy (Majone 1999, Curtin 2007). From an output legitimacy viewpoint, depoliticized expert-based decisions are often seen as favoring the quality and effectiveness of policies. Within the literature on ERAs, this argument is regularly criticized for being insufficient, among others because the assumption that expertise and information can be apolitical is increasingly questioned (Shapiro 1997). Besides, in socially salient and controverted issues, the expertise underpinning regulatory decisions is insufficient to generate social acceptance (Borrás et al. 2007). To palliate for these legitimacy challenges, the literature suggests alternatives, in particular stakeholders' participation and accountability.

The need to foster the participation of stakeholders to enhance ERAs' legitimacy has regularly been emphasized (Shapiro 1997, Borrás et al. 2007, Arras and Braun 2018). Yet it is only in recent years that academic research has produced detailed empirical insights on participation patterns. Stakeholders can be involved in two ways: from within, as members of ERAs' management boards or scientific committees, or as outsiders, through their participation to different types of consultations (Arras and Braun 2018, Arras and Beyers 2020). ERAs were found generally quite open to stakeholders' participation (Arras and Braun 2018, Pérez Durán 2018, Joosen 2020). Whereas the regulated industry largely dominates in both consultations and in ERAs management boards, non-business groups are also present to a non-negligible extent (Arras and Beyers 2020, Pérez Durán 2019). These features are subject to an important empirical variation. A key factor here is whether ERAs are subject to legal requirements about the institutionalization of a diverse representation of interest groups that might limit the potential bias of stakeholders' representation structures (Arras and Beyers 2020, Pérez Durán 2018, Busuioc and Jevnaker 2020).

Calls to compensate ERAs' autonomy with accountability mechanisms have always accompanied the development of EU agencies (Majone 1999, Curtin 2007). Yet, in the EU, power fragmentation and the difficulty of disentangling responsibilities for regulatory decisions make it difficult to set up clear accountability mechanisms (Crum and Curtin 2015). This is particularly true about ERAs, which are often generating input for decisions adopted by other actors, rather than adopting binding decisions themselves. This makes it generally impossible to subject ERAs to judicial accountability (Busuioc 2013), even when their opinions are systematically endorsed by the Commission – as is the case with the European Medicine Agency (EMA). Another key characteristic of ERAs' accountability structure is its complexity. ERAs are subject to a multiplicity of accountability fora: the European Commission, the Council, the European Parliament, its management board, the CJEU, the Court of Auditors and the European Ombudsman (Busuioc 2013). This results in an often incoherent accumulation of accountability mechanisms, leading to problems such as redundancies, contradictions and accountability overload (Busuioc 2013).

How accountability mechanisms are put in practice is subject to empirical variation, across both accountability fora and ERAs. For example, within the EP, the extent to which accountability mechanisms are activated varies across committees and even across individual MEPs (Busuioc 2013, Font and Pérez Durán 2016). Member states' implication in the oversight of agencies via the management board is also unequal, with only a few national board members being on top of their game – those with most organizational capacities, whereas most of them lack preparation and expertise for exercising adequately their role (Busuioc 2012, Buess 2015). Variations have also been observed across agencies, those receiving most attention being the biggest and more powerful ones, as well as those active in politically salient areas

(Font and Pérez Durán 2016, Egeberg and Trondal 2011). This highly uneven level of attention paid by accountability fora to ERAs results in important accountability gaps.

FORESIGHT

ERAs' Output: Impact and Effectiveness

ERAs have been established to facilitate the implementation of EU regulatory policies. To what extent do they live up to their mission? The few case studies on the question suggest that ERAs tend not to be very effective in the achievement of the missions for which they have been established because of their lack of power and low level of independence (Groenleer et al. 2010, Busuioc et al. 2011). This emphasis on formal competences is also underlined by research showing that the European Banking Authority (EBA), one of the most powerful ERAs, could take advantage of its formal powers to emerge as an effective leader in the management of the 2012 banking crisis (Jordana and Triviño-Salazar 2020). The level of powers enjoyed by EBA is, however, more the exception than the rule among ERAs which are generally rather characterized by a low level of formal powers. Given these limitations, under which conditions can ERAs achieve satisfying outputs?

An important mission for many ERAs is to foster regulatory convergence and compliance among the member states, that is, to have an impact at the national level. In this regard, the institutional design of ERA can be determinant. In particular, ERAs structured around a network of NRAs and involving NRAs to a large extent in their internal decision-making processes can rely on cooperative NRAs, more inclined to comply with the ERA's positions. By contrast, ERAs leaving little room for NRAs face more resistance from the latter (Ossege 2016). The quality of the cooperation between ERAs and NRAs is also affected by the delimitation of competences among them. Where the mandate and activities of the ERAs overlap with those of the national agency, they threaten NRAs' uniqueness and spur mistrust and turf-defensive reactions. By contrast, good cooperation across levels would be fostered by a European mandate that would complement that of national agencies (Busuioc 2016).

Beyond formal design, the way ERAs behave and manage their relationship with national agencies in practice also appears as important. In line with Busuioc's observation about NRAs' sensitivity about the preservation of their own space (2016), ERAs's added-value would increase when they refrain from using a hierarchical and centralized approach. Rather, a soft approach, favoring informal learning among the NRAs (Groenleer et al. 2010), and flexibility, to adapt to the wide variety of regulatory cultures and expertise characterizing the 27 NRAs (Versluis and Tarr 2013), would allow ERAs to best achieve regulatory convergence and compliance in the absence of binding decision-making powers. These findings confirm early comments on the creation of ERAs, anticipating their impact on the creation of a common professional culture, convergence of practice based on soft mechanisms such as the exchange of ideas (Dehousse 1997; Majone 1997).

While the research on ERAs' capacity to produce regulatory change at the national level can certainly be significantly expanded both empirically and theoretically, other aspects of ERAs' effectiveness could be explored. ERAs' outputs are not just meant to produce change at the national level, but also to feed into the EU regulatory process. How often are ERAs actually called to intervene in the EU policymaking process? ERAs were found to be most solicited in those areas where the commission holds a medium–high level of decision-making competences itself and in areas characterized by complexity (Migliorati 2020). Then, qualitatively, what are the changes induced by ERAs? Have ERAs been a game changer? To what extent do ERAs produce better results than their predecessors – generally ERNs? Case studies comparing the regulatory process between before and after the creation of ERAs have barely been carried out (but see Schout 2011). Regarding ERAs' input in the EU regulatory process, we know that EU agencies make a significant informational input to the Commission (Jevnaker and Saerbeck 2019) and do even enjoy a high level of informal influence on it (see section 2). Yet, we do not know much regarding ERAs' influence on other actors, such as the European Parliament or the Council (Chiti 2009). Beyond the policy implementation stage, do ERAs bring added-value to the policymaking process? Do they contribute to shape the EU political agenda? Do they try to reach political debates and if so, do they manage to have their voice heard? To what extent is their input valued and used beyond the policy implementation stage?

Another series of questions could address the feedback effect of ERAs' impact or effectiveness on their formal design. How do policymakers perceived ERAs' (lack of) effectiveness and react to their output? Do they reinforce ERAs' competences to overcome a lack of effectiveness due the agency's formal weakness (Mathieu 2016)? Do they, on the contrary, react to a lack of effectiveness by displacing ERAs and rely on other institutional solutions? ERAs' output represents an important research venue which has only partly been addressed by the literature.

ERAs on the International Scene

An emerging issue in the scholarship on ERAs is their action on the international scene. Whereas ERAs' activities are mainly focused 'inward', in relation to the implementation of EU regulatory policies within the European Union, they have developed an important activity outside of the EU too. The range of action is very wide, involving, for example, training activities, capacity building, organization of events to share know-how, exchanging information and data, developing common procedures, carrying out joint operations, participation in standard setting and in the development of best practices (Chamon et al. 2019).

This new research line sparks a wide range of new questions for both lawyers and political scientists (Hofmann et al. 2019). Lawyers are now investigating issues related to the constitutionality and legality of ERAs' international activities as well as their legal classification (Chamon and Demedts 2019, Coman-Kund 2019). Political scientists have also opened a series of new questions. One is the development of ERAs' 'actorness', the emergence of ERAs' interest and capacities to intervene on the international scene (Chatzopoulou 2019). Others have focused on the empirical variation in the extent to which ERAs interact with national administrations of neighboring countries, suggesting that policy interdependence explains the different sectoral patterns observed (Rimkutė and Shyrokykh 2017). Normative issues related to ERAs' international activities have also been identified. For example: to what extent is it legitimate that ERAs participate with international bodies engaged in the development of soft law that are later incorporated into domestic law? How can we ensure the transparency and accountability of these processes (De Bellis 2019)? And what about the impact of ERAs' international activities? Do they manage to promote the transfer of EU regulatory standards, or to contribute positively to the development of regulatory capacities in their neighboring countries? How? Under which conditions? How do ERAs' international activities relate to and contribute to the EU foreign policy and neighboring policy? Do ERAs' involvement in international fora complement, overlaps or replace that of NRAs (Egeberg and Trondal 2017)?

All these questions are calling for more empirical information, conceptual development and systematic research, crossing the study of ERAs with that on the European neighborhood policy, EU foreign policy, or with transnational and global governance. In this regard, scholars working on ERAs could gain inspiring insights from the works on EU external governance (Lavenex 2008, Lavenex and Schimmelfennig 2009).

Sociological Approaches to ERAs

The issues addressed in the literature have been mainly approached through rationalist and normative lenses. Whether emphasizing functional, political, organizational or institutional factors, authors engaged in the debates about the set up and institutional design of ERAs have generally adopted rational approaches (e.g. Dehousse 1997, Kelemen 2002, Groenleer 2009, Thatcher 2011, Mathieu 2016). The second major theoretical orientation found in this literature is a normative one, whereby authors have discussed various aspects of ERAs' legitimacy and accountability of ERAs (e.g. Majone 1997, Curtin 2007, Busuioc 2013, Borrás et al. 2007, Arras and Braun 2018, Pérez Durán 2018).

By contrast, sociological and constructivist approaches have been far less explored. Thinking about ERAs from these theoretical angles opens new perspectives. First, a sociology of ERAs is still missing. We know that ERAs generally host a network of NRAs, so we know that officials of NRAs play an important role inside. Yet ERAs are more than just networks. They also include a management board and a directorate or a secretariat that relies on a permanent staff. Who are these people, where do they come from? Which kind of background do they have? Do they mainly come from national agencies? From transnational interest groups? From the EU Commission? If we except a couple of studies on the composition of a few ERAs' management boards, focusing on the profile and characteristics of board members (Pérez Durán 2018, 2019, Pérez Durán and Bravo-Laguna 2019), the sociological composition of ERAs has remained practically unaddressed by the scholarship. More studies on this are necessary to understand ERAs from within, that is, what are ERAs made of. Additional questions could then be connected to a sociological approach of ERAs. What are the implications ERAs' social composition? To what extent do ERAs sociologically condition agencies' performance, organizational identity, relationship with other institutional actors and perceived legitimacy? This line of research could bring fascinating and new insights on ERAs' functioning and development.

In a similar vein, ERAs can be seen as socialization arenas. A few works have pointed at the impact of ERAs on the diffusion of ideas and regulatory standards among national staff participating to the work of ERAs (Dehousse 1997, Groenleer et al. 2010), but this line of research could be pushed further. More systematic empirical work could be carried out, to evaluate and map the extent to which ERAs contribute to the creation of a common professional culture within their staff, and also among the national officials and experts involved in the functioning of the agencies. Under which condition do ERAs foster the development of supranational preferences and identities? The socialization effect of ERAs is surely subject to empirical variations across agencies. What are these empirical patterns and how can they be explained? Research on ERNs has provided some insights on the impact of networks on the ideas, preferences and expertise of their members (Maggetti and Gilardi 2011, 2014,

Papadopoulos 2018). How does this work in ERAs? Does the presence of a permanent European staff and a Board within agencies accelerate this process? Does the composition of the Board, the internal structure of the ERAs or its powers condition it? Or does it depend on sector-specific characteristics?

Sociological approaches can also be mixed with rational ones to better understand the behavior of ERAs. Several recent works applied this approach, showing the different strategies used by ERAs to enhance stakeholders' perception of the quality and legitimacy of their work. This can be seen in the way ERAs engage in stakeholders' participation. ERAs carefully selecting the types of stakeholders to engage with (Arras and Beyers 2020) and the type of comments they react to, focusing on either technical or procedural comments depending on their capacities (Fink and Ruffing 2020). More generally, ERAs were found to be increasingly engaged and proactive in reputation management (Rimkutė 2018, Busuioc and Rimkutė 2019, 2020). Depending on the reputational threats and opportunities they face, they choose between silence or active communication (Rimkutė 2020a) – and in the latter case, they consciously decide to focus their communication on the technical, procedural or moral dimension of their work (Rimkutė 2020b). These works show that crossing rational, sociological and even normative approaches provide fascinating insights on the functioning of ERAs. This kind of research strategy is particularly promising.

CONCLUSION

ERAs are fascinating actors that combine the specificities of regulatory agencies and supranational bodies, while being embedded in the unique political system of the EU. On the one hand, we can often observe similarities among ERAs and NRAs. For example, as for NRAs, ERAs' independence and power tend to increase with their age and degree of institutional development, the importance of expertise, technical complexity, and agencies' legitimacy and reputation. Likewise, the constraints exerted by the EU fragmented political environment on ERAs' power and independence is in line with findings about NRAs' independence decreasing in political systems with a high number of veto players (Gilardi 2005). Another example regards the positive relationship between accountability and political saliency, which has also been observed at the level of NRAs (Koop 2011).

But ERAs also display very unique characteristics. Unlike at the national level, where the diffusion of NRAs implied a *transformation* of pre-existing national administrative systems, ERAs contribute directly to the *construction* of the EU administrative system. Being one manifestation of the EU integration process, ERAs are heavily conditioned by its dynamics. For example, the power struggle between the member states and the Commission is crucial to understand the rise of ERAs as a hybrid and compromised solution. One compelling manifestation of this struggle is the close relationship between ERAs and ERNs, whereby networks often cumulate the roles of predecessor of ERAs, institutional alternative to ERAs, and integral component of ERAs.

Research on ERAs has boomed in the last two decades. Initially very much focused on the ERAs' rise, institutional design, power, autonomy and legitimacy, the literature has recently started to explore new themes, such as ERAs' relationship with stakeholders, their reputational management strategies and international reach. This renewal in ERAs' research is a very welcome turn, which should be pursued. Now that we have a good understanding of the rationale, shape and normative features of the EU agencification phenomenon, we need to develop conceptions of ERAs as dynamic research objects, and turn our spotlight onto their evolution, actorhood, and impact.

REFERENCES

Arras, Sarah and Jan Beyers. 2020. 'Access to European Union Agencies: Usual Suspects or Balanced Interest Representation in Open and Closed Consultations?' *Journal of Common Market Studies* 58(4):836–55.

Arras, Sarah and Caelesta Braun. 2018. 'Stakeholders Wanted! Why and How European Union Agencies Involve Non-State Stakeholders'. *Journal of European Public Policy* 25(9):1257–75.

Blauberger, Michael and Berthold Rittberger. 2015. 'Conceptualizing and Theorizing EU Regulatory Networks'. *Regulation & Governance* 9(4):367–76.

Boeger, Nina and Joseph Corkin. 2017. 'Institutional Path-Dependencies in Europe's Networked Modes of Governance'. *Journal of Common Market Studies* 55(5):974–92.

Borrás, Susana, Charalampos Koutalakis, and Frank Wendler. 2007. 'European Agencies and Input Legitimacy: EFSA, EMeA and EPO in the Post-Delegation Phase'. *Journal of European Integration* 29(5):583–600.

Buess, Michael. 2015. 'Accountable and Under Control? Explaining Governments' Selection of Management Board Representatives'. *Journal of Common Market Studies* 53(3):493–508.

Busuioc, E. Madalina. 2016. 'Friend or Foe? Inter-Agency Cooperation, Organizational Reputation, and Turf'. *Public Administration* 94(1):40–56.

Busuioc, Madalina. 2009. 'Accountability, Control and Independence: The Case of European Agencies'. *European Law Journal* 15(5):599–615.

Busuioc, Madalina. 2012. 'European Agencies and Their Boards: Promises and Pitfalls of Accountability beyond Design'. *Journal of European Public Policy* 19(5):719–36.

Busuioc, Madalina. 2013. *European Agencies: Law and Practices of Accountability*. Oxford University Press.

Busuioc, Madalina, Deirdre Curtin, and Martijn Groenleer. 2011. 'Agency Growth between Autonomy and Accountability: The European Police Office as a "Living Institution"'. *Journal of European Public Policy* 18(6):848–67.

Busuioc, Madalina, and Torbjørg Jevnaker. 2020. 'EU Agencies' Stakeholder Bodies: Vehicles of Enhanced Control, Legitimacy or Bias?' *Journal of European Public Policy* 29(2):155–75.

Busuioc, Madalina and Dovilė Rimkutė. 2019. 'Meeting Expectations in the EU Regulatory State? Regulatory Communications amid Conflicting Institutional Demands'. *Journal of European Public Policy* 27(4):547–68.

Busuioc, Madalina, and Dovilė Rimkutė. 2020. 'The Promise of Bureaucratic Reputation Approaches for the EU Regulatory State'. *Journal of European Public Policy* 27(8):1256–69.

Chamon, Merijn. 2011. 'EU Agencies between Meroni and Romano or the Devil and the Deep Blue Sea'. *Common Market Law Review* 48(4):1055–75.

Chamon, Merijn and Valerie Demedts. 2019. 'Constitutional Limits to the EU Agencies' External Relations', in *The External Dimension of EU Agencies and Bodies. Law and Policy*, edited by H. Hofmann, E. Vos, and M. Chamon. Cheltenham, UK and Northampton, MA, USA: Edward Elgar Publishing.

Chamon, Merijn, Herwig Hofmann, and Ellen Vos. 2019. 'Introduction: EU Agencies Going Global', in *The External Dimension of EU Agencies and Bodies. Law and Policy*, edited by H. Hofmann, E. Vos, and M. Chamon. Cheltenham, UK and Northampton, MA, USA: Edward Elgar Publishing.

Chatzopoulou, Sevasti. 2019. 'EU Agencies – Agents of Policy Diffusion beyond the EU', in *The External Dimension of EU Agencies and Bodies. Law and Policy*, edited by H. Hofmann, E. Vos, and M. Chamon. Cheltenham, UK and Northampton, MA, USA: Edward Elgar Publishing.

Chiti, Edoardo. 2000. 'The Emergence of a Community Administration: The Case of European Agencies'. *Common Market Law Review* 37(2):309–43.

Chiti, Edoardo. 2009. 'An Important Part of the EU's Institutional Machinery: Features, Problems and Perspectives of European Agencies'. *Common Market Law Review* 46(5):1395–1442.

Coman-Kund, Florin. 2019. 'The Cooperation between the European Border and Coast Guard Agency and Third Countries According to the New Frontex Regulation: Legal and Practical Implications', in *The External Dimension of EU Agencies and Bodies. Law and Policy*, edited by H. Hofmann, E. Vos, and M. Chamon. Cheltenham, UK and Northampton, MA, USA: Edward Elgar Publishing.

Crum, Ben and Deirdre Curtin. 2015. 'The Challenge of Making European. Union Executive Power Accountable', in *The European Union: Democratic Principles and Institutional Architectures in Times of Crisis*, edited by S. Piattoni. Oxford: Oxford University Press.

Curtin, Deirdre. 2007. 'Holding (Quasi-)Autonomous EU Administrative Actors to Public Account'. *European Law Journal* 13(4):523–41.

De Bellis, Maurizia. 2019. 'Reinforcing EU Financial Bodies' Participation in Global Networks: Addressing Legitimacy Gaps?' in *The External Dimension of EU Agencies and Bodies. Law and Policy*, edited by H. Hofmann, E. Vos, and M. Chamon. Cheltenham, UK and Northampton, MA, USA: Edward Elgar Publishing.

Dehousse, Renaud. 1997. 'Regulation by Networks in the European Community: The Role of European Agencies'. *Journal of European Public Policy* 4(2):246–61.

Dehousse, Renaud. 2008. 'Delegation of Powers in the European Union: The Need for a Multi-Principals Model'. *West European Politics* 31(4):789–805.

Dehousse, Renaud. 2016. 'Why Has EU Macroeconomic Governance Become More Supranational?' *Journal of European Integration* 38(5):617–31.

Eberlein, Burkard and Edgar Grande. 2005. 'Beyond Delegation: Transnational Regulatory Regimes and the EU Regulatory State'. *Journal of European Public Policy* 12(1):89–112.

Egeberg, Morten, Maria Martens, and Jarle Trondal. 2015. 'The EU's Subordinated Agency Administration and the Rise of Executive Power at European Level', in *The Palgrave Handbook of the European Administrative System*, edited by M. W. Bauer and J. Trondal. London: Palgrave Macmillan.

Egeberg, Morten and Jarle Trondal. 2011. 'EU-Level Agencies: New Executive Centre Formation or Vehicles for National Control?' *Journal of European Public Policy* 18(6):868–87.

Egeberg, Morten and Jarle Trondal. 2017. 'Researching European Union Agencies: What Have We Learnt (and Where Do We Go from Here)?' *Journal of Common Market Studies* 55(4):675–90.

European Commission. 2001. 'European Governance – A White Paper' (2001/C 287/01). Brussels: Official Journal of the European Communities.

Fink, Simon, and Eva Ruffing. 2020. 'Stakeholder Consultations as Reputation-Building: A Comparison of ACER and the German Federal Network Agency'. *Journal of European Public Policy* 27(11):1657–76.

Font, Nuria. 2015. 'Policy Properties and Political Influence in Post-Delegation: The Case of EU Agencies'. *International Review of Administrative Sciences* 81(4):773–92.

Font, Nuria. 2018. 'Informal Rules and Institutional Balances on the Boards of EU Agencies'. *Administration & Society* 50(2):269–94.

Font, Nuria and Ixchel Pérez Durán. 2016. 'The European Parliament Oversight of EU Agencies Through Written Questions'. *Journal of European Public Policy* 23(9):1349–66.

Gehring, Thomas and Sebastian Krapohl. 2007. 'Supranational Regulatory Agencies between Independence and Control: The EMEA and the Authorization of Pharmaceuticals in the European Single Market'. *Journal of European Public Policy* 14(2):208–26.

Gilardi, Fabrizio. 2005. 'The Formal Independence of Regulators: A Comparison of 17 Countries and 7 Sectors.' *Swiss Political Science Review* 11(4):139–67.

Groenleer, Martijn. 2009. *The Autonomy of European Union Agencies: A Comparative Study of Institutional Development*. Eburon Uitgeverij B.V.

Groenleer, Martijn. 2014. 'Agency Autonomy Actually: Managerial Strategies, Legitimacy, and the Early Development of the European Union's Agencies for Drug and Food Safety Regulation'. *International Public Management Journal* 17(2):255–92.

Groenleer, Martijn, Michael Kaeding, and Esther Versluis. 2010. 'Regulatory Governance through Agencies of the European Union? The Role of the European Agencies for Maritime and Aviation

Safety in the Implementation of European Transport Legislation'. *Journal of European Public Policy* 17(8):1212–30.

Hofmann, Herwig, Ellen Vos, and Merjin Chamon. 2019. *The External Dimension of EU Agencies and Bodies: Law and Policy*. Cheltenham, UK and Northampton, MA, USA: Edward Elgar Publishing.

Jevnaker, Torbjørg, and Barbara Saerbeck. 2019. 'EU Agencies and the Energy Union: Providing Useful Information to the Commission?' *Politics and Governance* 7(1):60–69.

Joosen, Rik. 2020. 'The Tip of the Iceberg – Interest Group Behaviour in Rule Drafting and Consultations during EU Agency Rulemaking'. *Journal of European Public Policy* 27(11):1677–97.

Jordana, Jacint and Juan Carlos Triviño-Salazar. 2020. 'EU Agencies' Involvement in Transboundary Crisis Response: Supporting Efforts or Leading Coordination?' *Public Administration* 98(2):515–29.

Kelemen, Daniel R. 2002. 'The Politics of "Eurocratic" Structure and the New European Agencies'. *West European Politics* 25(4):93–118.

Kelemen, Daniel R. and Andrew D. Tarrant. 2011. 'The Political Foundations of the Eurocracy'. *West European Politics* 34(5):922–47.

Krapohl, Sebastian. 2007. 'Thalidomide, BSE and the Single Market: An Historical-institutionalist Approach to Regulatory Regimes in the European Union'. *European Journal of Political Research* 46(1):25–46.

Koop, Christel. 2011. Explaining the Accountability of Independent Agencies: The Importance of Political Salience. *Journal of Public Policy* 31(2):209–234.

Lavenex, Sandra. 2008. 'A Governance Perspective on the European Neighbourhood Policy: Integration Beyond Conditionality?' *Journal of European Public Policy* 15(6):938–55.

Lavenex, Sandra and Frank Schimmelfennig. 2009. 'EU Rules beyond EU Borders: Theorizing External Governance in European Politics'. *Journal of European Public Policy* 16(6):791–812.

Levi-Faur, David. 2011. 'Regulatory Networks and Regulatory Agencification: Towards a Single European Regulatory Space'. *Journal of European Public Policy* 18(6):810–29.

Maggetti, Martino and Fabrizio Gilardi. 2011. 'The Policy-Making Structure of European Regulatory Networks and the Domestic Adoption of Standards'. *Journal of European Public Policy* 18(6):830–47.

Maggetti, Martino and Fabrizio Gilardi. 2014. 'Network Governance and the Domestic Adoption of Soft Rules'. *Journal of European Public Policy* 21(9):1293–1310.

Maggetti, Martino. 2019. 'Interest Groups and the (Non-)Enforcement Powers of EU Agencies: The Case of Energy Regulation'. *European Journal of Risk Regulation* 10(3):458–84.

Majone, Giandomenico. 1997. 'The New European Agencies: Regulation by Information'. *Journal of European Public Policy* 4(2):262–75.

Majone, Giandomenico. 1999. 'The Regulatory State and Its Legitimacy Problems'. *West European Politics* 22(1):1–24.

Majone, Giandomenico. 2000. 'The Credibility Crisis of Community Regulation'. *Journal of Common Market Studies* 38(2):273–302.

Mathieu, Emmanuelle. 2016. *Regulatory Delegation in the European Union: Networks, Committees and Agencies*. London: Palgrave Macmillan.

Mathieu, Emmanuelle. 2019. 'Functional Stakes and EU Regulatory Governance: Temporal Patterns of Regulatory Integration in Energy and Telecommunications'. *West European Politics* 43(4):991–1010.

Mathieu, Emmanuelle and Bernardo Rangoni. 2019. 'Balancing Experimentalist and Hierarchical Governance in European Union Electricity and Telecommunications Regulation: A Matter of Degrees'. *Regulation & Governance* 13(4):577–92.

Migliorati, Marta. 2020. 'Relying on Agencies in Major European Union Legislative Measures'. *West European Politics* 43(1):159–80.

Ossege, Christoph. 2016. *European Regulatory Agencies in EU Decision-Making: Between Expertise and Influence*. London: Palgrave Macmillan.

Ottow, Annetje. 2012. 'Europeanization of the Supervision of Competitive Markets'. *European Public Law* 18(1):191–221.

Papadopoulos, Yannis. 2018. 'How Does Knowledge Circulate in a Regulatory Network? Observing a European Platform of Regulatory Authorities Meeting'. *Regulation & Governance* 12(4):431–50.

Pérez Durán, Ixchel. 2018. 'Interest Group Representation in the Formal Design of European Union Agencies'. *Regulation & Governance* 12(2):238–62.

Pérez Durán, Ixchel. 2019. 'Political and Stakeholder's Ties in European Union Agencies'. *Journal of European Public Policy* 26(1):1–22.

Pérez Durán, Ixchel and Carlos Bravo-Laguna. 2019. 'Representative Bureaucracy in European Union Agencies'. *Journal of European Integration* 41(8):971–92.

Rimkutė, Dovilė. 2018. 'Organizational Reputation and Risk Regulation: The Effect of Reputational Threats on Agency Scientific Outputs'. *Public Administration* 96(1):70–83.

Rimkutė, Dovilė and Karina Shyrokykh. 2017. 'The Role of EU Agencies in the Acquis Transfer: The Case of the European Neighbourhood Policy Countries'. *TARN Working Paper*.

Rimkutė, Dovilė. 2020a. 'Building Organizational Reputation in the European Regulatory State: An Analysis of EU Agencies' Communications'. *Governance* 33(2):385–406.

Rimkutė, Dovilė. 2020b. 'Strategic Silence or Regulatory Talk? Regulatory Agency Responses to Public Allegations amidst the Glyphosate Controversy'. *Journal of European Public Policy* 27(11):1636–56.

Schout, Adriaan. 2011. 'Assessing the Added Value of an EU Agency for Aviation Safety'. *Journal of Public Policy* 31(3):363–84.

Shapiro, Martin. 1997. 'The Problems of Independent Agencies in the United States and the European Union'. *Journal of European Public Policy* 4(2):276–77.

Thatcher, Mark. 2011. 'The Creation of European Regulatory Agencies and Its Limits: A Comparative Analysis of European Delegation'. *Journal of European Public Policy* 18(6):790–809.

Thatcher, Mark and David Coen. 2008. 'Reshaping European Regulatory Space: An Evolutionary Analysis'. *West European Politics* 31(4):806–36.

Versluis, Esther and Erika Tarr. 2013. 'Improving Compliance with European Union Law via Agencies: The Case of the European Railway Agency'. *Journal of Common Market Studies* 51(2):316–33.

Vestlund, Nina M. 2015. 'Exploring EU Commission–Agency Relationship: Partnership or Parenthood?' in *The Palgrave Handbook of the European Administrative System*, edited by M. Bauer and J. Trondal. Basingstoke: Palgrave Macmillan.

Vos, Ellen. 2014. 'EU Agencies: Features, Framework and Future', in *European Agencies in between Institutions and Member States*, edited by M. Everson, C. Monda, and E. Vos. Kluwer Law Publishing.

Wonka, Arndt and Berthold Rittberger. 2010. 'Credibility, Complexity and Uncertainty: Explaining the Institutional Independence of 29 EU Agencies'. *West European Politics* 33(4):730–52.

28. European regulatory networks: foundations and foresights

Machiel van der Heijden and Kutsal Yesilkagit

INTRODUCTION

In recent decades, the EU has seen a vast expansion of its tasks in various regulatory sectors. The European Single Market seeking to guarantee the free movement of goods, capital, services, and labour has been extended through various agreements and treaties, meaning that strictly national regulatory and market oversight no longer suffices. To establish a "level playing field" and to avoid regulatory races to the bottom, the national regulators of EU countries increasingly collaborate and exchange information at both the EU and global levels. As noted by both academics and practitioners, the harmonization of regulatory rules and the formulation of EU-wide regulatory standards has become an important pillar to the EU integration project (Donnelly 2010; Monti 2010; Bruszt & Vukov 2017).

However, important to emphasize is that the greater centralization and resources needed for meeting the demands of effectively regulating cross-border markets, are often blocked by widespread political opposition of nation-states, jealously guarding their sovereignty (Eberlein & Newman 2008). This has presented the EU with a "governance dilemma", in which a functional need for regulatory capacity is hampered by a political difficulty of obtaining it (see Keohane 2001). In response, alternative regulatory structures have emerged, in which some form of "regulation by networks" has proven to be particularly prevalent (see Eberlein & Grande 2005; Sabel & Zeitlin 2008). Essentially, such networks are perceived as a convenient solution to achieve the degree of uniformity necessary for a common market, without completely doing away with decentralized implementation and national sovereignty (Dehousse 1997).

The multi-actor and multi-level setting of the EU's regulatory governance has accordingly seen various institutional forms, such as comitology committees, specialized EU-level agencies, and European regulatory networks (ERNs) (Groenleer 2014; Egeberg & Trondal 2017). These networked structures link together actors and institutions at various levels of government in the performance of tasks, forming a common administrative order in Europe (Hofmann & Turk 2006). This European Administrative Space (EAS) has continued to develop in different phases and has been the subject of both academic and political debates (Trondal & Peters 2013). This chapter focuses on the development of ERNs that constitute an important part in how the EAS has evolved and discusses the scholarship that has studied them.

Important to note is that the formal existence of networks facilitating the collaboration between regulators are not a phenomenon particular to the European Union (EU). They exist in different regions across the world, with some networks spanning a global scale (for an overview, see Abbott & Kauffmann 2018). Many inter-governmental organizations such as the OECD, WHO and the FAO have long facilitated interaction between regulators and, increasingly, independent transgovernmental networks have taken up a role as an international standard-setter as well (see Koppell 2010). However, none of these networks are embedded by an institutional structure as heavily present as that of the EU. The interdependencies created by a deeply integrated European market and the shared (policy) competences that exist between European and national level institutions, make it so that ERNs have a unique position that warrant separate discussion. This discussion is given in the chapter below.

FOUNDATIONS: STANDING LITERATURE ON ERNS

Describing the Phenomenon: Conceptual Dimensions

The need to formulate, harmonize, and enforce international standards and rules, has facilitated the development of transgovernmental (regulatory) networks in diverse areas, such as energy, telecommunications, crime, privacy protection, human rights, international competition, and financial markets regulation (Picciotto 1997; Slaughter 2004; Raustiala 2002; Levi-Faur 2011; Newman & Zaring 2012). Backed by an implicit or explicit legislative mandate, regulatory networks are concerned with the formulation of common rules and standards in a given policy area (Lavenex & Wichmann 2009), aimed at guiding the conduct of membership organizations. Within the EU, patterns of cross-border collaboration among domestic regulatory agencies are particularly well developed and are typically described as European regulatory networks or ERNs (Newman & Zaring 2012; Mastenbroek & Martinsen 2018). Recent counts point to a population of 37 such networks, in which BEREC (telecommunications), IMPEL (environment), and the ECN (competition) are prominent examples (see Saz-Carranza et al. 2020).

Within the EU context, the creation of many ERNs was for a large part facilitated by the European Commission in the early 2000s, as to fulfil an advisory role for them on matters of regulation and to foster regulatory convergence among NRAs through voluntary coordination (Eberlein & Newman 2008). In that sense, the creation of ERNs has somewhat of a top-down, mandated nature, describing the outcome of a dual delegation that has taken place within the EU regulatory space (Coen & Thatcher 2008; see also Segato & Raab 2019). However, important to emphasize is that many ERNs also build on existing structures through which NRAs already collaborated in an informal manner (Mathieu 2016). Although some of these informal platforms were replaced by more formalized structures of ERNs, many continued to exist alongside them (see Thatcher 2011; Saz-Carranza et al. 2016). In that sense, ERNs have emerged in both a bottom-up and a top-down (or mandated) fashion (Coen & Thatcher 2008) and are characterized by various degrees of institutionalization, with some recently developing into full-fledged EU Agencies (see Levi-Faur 2011; Mathieu 2016).

The participating actors in regulatory networks are usually the task-specific regulators from various jurisdictions, responsible for market or governance oversight (Newman & Zaring 2012). In particular, these regulators specialize in rule development and enforcement. Importantly, national regulatory agencies (NRAs) have some crucial differences when compared to other national actors involved in transnational exchanges such as ministerial departments or executive agencies, particularly regarding the nature of public authority and degree of bureaucratic autonomy (Eberlein & Newman 2008). For one, their institutional design explicitly buffers them from direct political control. The government officials involved in regulatory interactions thus enjoy a large degree of formal delegation and according discretion; that is, they do not have to answer directly to a bureaucratic chain of command/political principals. In addition, many regulatory agencies have long-term leadership tenure, guaranteed budgets, and control over personnel appointments (see Yesilkagit 2012). This combination of formal independence from parent ministries, expertise, and the often proactive leadership of participating agencies has arguably facilitated the further development and flourishing of regulatory networks in general and ERNs in particular (Newman 2008; Yesilkagit 2012).

Conceptually, the interactions taking place within ERNs are transgovernmental ones. Keohane and Nye define such relations as "sets of direct interactions among sub-units of different governments that are not controlled or closely guided by the policies of the cabinets of chief executives of those governments" (1974, p.43). Based on loosely structured, peer-to-peer ties developed through frequent interaction rather than formal negotiation, these relations can form transgovernmental networks in which domestic regulators and public officials join their foreign counterparts to "share information, develop harmonized guidelines and best practice, and reduce friction resulting from globalization" (Bach & Newman 2010, p.506). Despite these rather straightforward and seemingly clear definitions, however, the phrase "transgovernmental networks" still seems to capture a strikingly wide array of contemporary cooperation (Raustiala 2002, p.5).

In terms of the institutional structure or setting of ERNs, interaction between national officials primarily occurs through the various working groups, commissions, or task forces, which carry out most of its operational work. Within the various lower-level working groups and commissions of the different networks, most of the preparatory work for the network's main decision-making bodies is done. At this level, regulatory officials engage in highly technical policy discussions, collectively writing reports, working out the technical details of proposed standards, and discussing position papers on various regulatory and policy issues. Moreover, ERNs typically have a separate secretariat that facilitates the communication structures and fulfil an administrative function, although in recent years these secretariats themselves have become increasingly powerful in terms of staff, resources, and decision-making powers. Overall, the structural complexity of ERNs and their secretariats differ significantly, depending on whether they merely have rule-setting tasks, or also endowed with member-sanctioning and rule-enforcing tasks (see Iborra et al. 2018).

Regarding this latter point, it is important to emphasize that ERNs have varying degrees of centralization and formalization, with some more aptly characterized as "agencified networks", "networked agencies", or even "full-fledged agencies" (Levi-Faur 2011). Conceptually, however, the lines between ERNs and the EU Agencies in which they have increasingly developed are thin, with the latter representing a somewhat more formalized networked organization with a separate legal personality and higher degrees of organizational and financial autonomy (Mathieu 2017). Although this arguably extends the EU's regulatory capacity even further, it should be emphasized that both EU Agencies and ERNs primarily rely on the authority and resources of the member agencies to implement and enforce agreements (Eberlein & Newman 2008; Egeberg & Trondal 2017). Both are thus concerned with decentralized implementation and some form of network governance as to achieve collective outcomes (Saz-Carranza et al. 2016; see also Chapter 27 on EU regulatory agencies in this volume).

Still, the increasing prevalence of transnational regulatory structures in the EU, in whatever form, inevitably places many national regulatory agencies (NRAs) in a difficult position. As observed by Egeberg and Trondal (2009), national regulators increasingly fulfil a dual or "double-hatted" role, in which they form part of both national and European administrative structures. As a result, they are simultaneously expected to take up a European viewpoint of regulatory needs as to ensure a smoothly regulated European single market, while also being faced with the demands of national regulatory and political concerns or interests. The double-hatted character of regulatory network participants may create contradicting demands for national agencies, potentially hampering the overall network-goal of regulatory harmonization, given the prevalence of national political interests. However, we should note that regulatory agencies are not just passive, obedient actors caught between two principals struggling over regulatory power; they may have interests and goals of their own as well (cf. Egeberg & Trondal 2009), to which we turn when discussing the bureaucratic politics literature in the remainder of this chapter.

Overall, the above provided discussion has noted some conceptual dimensions relevant to understanding the empirical phenomenon of ERNs. It should be noted that within the academic literature, scholars have only more recently started to focus more on the internal functioning of ERNs and the informal relationships by which they are characterized. For instance, through social network analysis (SNA), Vantaggiatto (2019a, 2019b) provides more of an idea of the informal patterns of interaction of which ERNs are built up (see also Papadopoulos 2018). In addition, drawing inspiration from a more general scholarship on network governance, scholars have also started to look more concretely at the (variation in) institutional structure of transnational collaboration, as well as the different modes of governance by which they are coordinated (see Eberlein & Newman 2008; Saz-Carranza et al. 2016; Iborra et al. 2018). For both of these lines of scholarship, further suggestions are provided in the foresights-part of this chapter. The next section focuses on the different theoretical perspectives scholars have used to analyze ERNs, primarily regarding the way in which they form and develop.

Understanding the Phenomenon: Competing Theoretical Perspectives

Important to note is that in studying the way in which ERNs form and develop, scholars have primarily looked at the proliferation of these forms of collaboration in general, pointing to a variety of explanatory factors at the domestic level, such as degrees of regulatory independence or market size (Bach & Newman 2014; Wilks 2007), or functional pressures at the policy or transnational levels, such as coordination problems (Coen & Thatcher 2008), issue complexity (Whytock 2005), common preferences (Bignami 2005), or high degrees of interdependence (Van Boetzelaer & Princen 2012). Different theoretical perspectives underlie these explanations, which to a large degree determine the type of explanatory factors on which scholars focus, as well as what interests are ascribed to actors involved.

First, a large part of the literature has explained the development of EU regulatory agencies and networks as a *functional* response to the need for effective European-level regulation that still preserves the prerogative of national administrative bodies (Coen & Thatcher 2008; Van Boetzelaer & Princen 2012). Through information exchange and socialization among national administrators, such networks are held to promote a level playing field by means of harmonizing rules and regulations (Eberlein & Grande 2005; Blauberger & Rittberger 2015). Arguably, this harmonization process lies at the core of European integration: by formulating and spreading shared rules, norms, and standards among participating member states, European Regulatory Networks (ERNs) – whether coordinated through European agencies or by some networked secretariat (Levi-Faur 2011) – form the heart of the EU's "harmonization-machinery". Hence, adoption and ultimately harmonization of EU policies is to a large extent a network-administrative process, working toward a desired end-state in which all national regulatory authorities have managed to adopt the supranational norms and standards. The development of ERNs are then assumed to be mainly driven by functional necessity. So for instance, the railway or energy sectors require physical interconnections between countries, creating clear cross-border problems and the need for transnational coordination. This degree of interdependence between jurisdictions would thus account for the extensive regulatory network structures that have emerged in the form of the EU railway agency (Versluis & Tarr 2013) or ACER (Mathieu et al. 2020).

Second, scholars looking from a more political perspective have focused on the influence of political interests in the creation of transnational governing structures (Keleman & Tarrant 2011). Keleman and Tarrant (2011), for instance, argue that in policy areas characterized by high distributional conflicts, the choice of regulatory institutions is often that of delegation to networks of national authorities, as to maintain a degree of member-state control. In general, from this perspective, the choice and design for bureaucratic structures within the EU are driven by political considerations, focusing primarily on power struggles between national and supranational interests. This also means that structural and institutional design are considered to be deliberative choices reflecting political interests, rather than growing out of functional necessity or growing interdependence (for a discussion, see Tarrant & Keleman 2017; Blauberger & Rittberger 2017). From this perspective, cross-sector variation is explained by the political salience of a policy sector and the degree to which distributional conflicts exist therein. This would be an explanation of why BEREC never developed into a full-fledged agency in the telecommunications sector, with national actors effectively blocking out this option (see Saz-Carranza et al. 2016).

A third approach to separate is that of scholars who have looked at the creation of ERNs through the lens of historical institutionalism (Yesikagit & Christensen 2010; Thatcher 2011). From this perspective, decisions about institutional development (i.e. the creation, development, and demise of ERNs) are strongly conditioned by the past. The mechanism of path dependency limits the available choices in terms of institutional design (Pierson 2000). Using this perspective, Mathieu (2016) argues, for instance, how the institutional structure chosen for BEREC (telecommunications) was a logical next step from earlier decisions to establish and strengthen national agencies. Similarly, Thatcher (2011) notes how the earlier strengthening of formalized ERNs have had a limiting effect on the further creation of separate EU agencies. In that sense, path dependency thus has a lot of analytical leverage for understanding the institutional development of ERNs within the broader European Administrative Space. Differences between sectors can be explained by different institutional starting positions, as Saz-Carranza et al. (2016) have shown in their comparison of ACER and BEREC. Similar explanations are provided for the way in which the European Competition Network (ECN) has developed (see Tarrant & Keleman 2017).

More recently, scholars have framed a bureaucratic politics dimension around the development and functioning of regulatory networks (see Bach et al. 2016). Concepts of organizational reputation and institutional rivalry play a prominent role in this perspective and help to better understand the actions and interests of actors and agencies involved in regulatory networks. These scholars emphasize the role of strategic motivations on behalf of administrative actors, primarily to understand the emergence and functioning of regulatory networks. Underlying such explanations is the assumption that regulatory agencies pursue their own interests across all levels of government. On the one hand, national agencies may use EU structures to achieve autonomy and legitimacy within their own domestic political and institutional structures (Heims 2016). On the other hand, EU and supranational regulatory institutions may try to control national agencies as well (see Groenleer 2014).

Overall, we can conclude that the literature studying the development of ERNs – and EU regulatory structures more generally – can be differentiated based on the theoretical perspectives they take and the according assumptions underlying them. These different assumptions also mean that scholars differ in what actors they ascribe agency in the process of network creation and whose interests are reflected therein. For instance, where Eberlein and Newman (2008) argue that the European Commission actively fosters, recruits, and incorporates transgovernmental networks in order to enhance their own policy-making capacities, Thurner and Binder (2009) conclude that (national) bureaucratic agents join transgovernmental networks because they have the strategic and political incentives to do so. Then again, several authors have emphasized important structural and institutional factors that have had an important role in network emergence, such as culture, norms and values (Legrand 2015) and processes of path dependence (Thatcher 2011). Through these different perspectives, scholars have also accounted for the variation that exists between sectors in terms of the different ways in which ERNs have developed. Arguably, the theoretical framework you use largely determines the outcome you get (e.g., different perspectives on the creation of BEREC). But factors such as degrees of interdependence, technical complexity, and political salience all seem important to consider in thinking about the creation and development of ERNs. Older work on transgovernmental networks can also be fruitfully revisited in this regard, as it contains similar theoretical discussions (Keohane & Nye 1974; Holsti & Levy 1974).

ERNs as an Independent Variable: Effects and Consequences

In general, it should be noted that the literature has been rather positive about the "new modes of governance" that have developed through these regulatory networks. Slaughter (2000, p.204) has dubbed them as the "the optimal form of organization for the Information Age" and a "blueprint for the international architecture of the 21st century". Other authors have described these networks as effective and powerful forms of governance, that is, a new way to address the problems and complexities generated by processes of globalization (Cohen & Sabel 2004; Sabel & Zeitlin 2008).

Overall, regulatory networks seem to have a dual effect on domestic policy (Bach & Newman 2010). First, several scholars have assessed the effects of TGNs on regulatory diffusion and policy convergence (Raustiala 2002; Bach & Newman 2010; Maggetti & Gilardi 2011). In particular, scholars have begun to empirically examine the patterns of relations in transgovernmental networks by shifting the analytical focus to network structure. For instance, Maggetti and Gilardi (2011) report how network centrality in the Committee of European Securities Regulators (CESR) is associated with a faster domestic adoption of soft rules (see also Van der Heijden & Schalk 2020). In a case study of energy regulation, Maggetti (2014) exposes a similar relationship and specifies the underlying causal mechanisms, pointing to a supranational logic of interaction and effective 'peer pressures' that enhance the overall level of adoption. By comparing both cases, Maggetti and Gilardi (2014) accordingly provide further explanation by relating domestic adoption to other network-level characteristics, such as the existence of review panels (cf. modes of network governance identified by Provan & Kenis 2008).

Within this literature, the process of harmonization is described as a decentralized, incremental process of interaction and emulation in which networks play an important role (Slaughter 2004). Through socialization and peer influences, networks promote norms that contribute to the effective implementation of international standards (Maggetti & Gilardi 2011). On the other hand, powerful actors can also use transnational networks to promote policy export and shape foreign legislative agendas (see Bach & Newman 2010). Concentrated regulatory power fosters convergence, as weaker and newer jurisdictions ascribe to the norms and standards set by more powerful actors (Drezner 2008).

Second, the argument has been made that networks foster the development of domestic regulatory capacity through training, information sharing, and technical assistance (Slaughter 2004; Bianculli et al. 2017). Closely related to the latter work, are studies that assess the way in which such capacity-building strengthens national regulators vis-à-vis other domestic actors, such as their parent ministries (cf. Maggetti 2007; Yesilkagit 2011; Bach & Ruffing 2013; Danielsen & Yesilkagit 2014). Building on the work of EU-integration scholars, many empirical studies have focused on how Europeanization or internationalization creates "differential empowerment of actors resulting from a redistribution of resources" at the domestic level (Börzel & Risse 2000, p.58). For regulatory agencies involved in transnational forms of collaboration, the analysis has primarily focused on how transnational networks potentially have an "autonomizing" effect on these agencies in relation to their parent ministries (see Yesilkagit 2011; Maggetti 2012). Departing from a principal–agent perspective, this "autonomizing" effect of networks is ascribed to a number of mechanisms, including acquired resources such as information and expertise (Maggetti 2007; Bach & Ruffing 2013; Vestlund 2017) agency learning (Bianculli et al. 2017), and processes of network institutionalization (Danielsen & Yesilkagit 2014).

Overall, ERNs tend to broaden the gap between national regulators and executives (see Mathieu et al. 2020), although these autonomizing effects may vary because of country-level and sector-specific characteristics (see Aubin & Verhoest 2016; Mathieu et al. 2017). Still, in terms of understanding the effects of ERNs Hobolth and Martinsen (2013) note that the mechanisms by which the reported effects are produced are not very well understood. Often, authors merely assess the effects of network membership by means of association, but fail to demonstrate how such effects manifest themselves in practice (cf. Bach & Newman 2010).

ERNs and Empirical Methods

In terms of the methods that have been used to study ERNs, the qualitative case study has been the most dominant approach. Though document analysis and qualitative interviews, scholars typically conduct a deep dive into the creation and functioning of the particular network under study (e.g., Yesilkagit 2011; Mathieu 2016). Many studies also add a comparative component to their case study design, which has led to more systematic theorizing on the differences and similarities that exist between sectors and networks (Thatcher 2011; Van Boetzelaer & Princen 2012; Saz-Carranza et al. 2016). Although large-n studies that take ERNs as their unit of analysis are not possible, survey research has been conducted by some, primarily focusing on national officials and their perceptions toward their international environment, including ERNs (e.g., Egeberg & Trondal 2009; Bach & Ruffing 2013). Moreover, medium-n like research methods such as QCA have recently been put to good use in studying the governance structures of ERNs (Saz-Carranza et al. 2020). Several scholars have also attempted quantitative approaches that account for the restricted number of cases available in the universe of regulatory networks, for example, through Bayesian statistics (Iborra et al. 2018). Social network analysis also provides a promising avenue for better understanding the development and effects of ERNs and has seen several useful applications (see Maggetti & Gilardi 2011; Vantaggiatto 2019a; Vantaggiatto et al. 2021). In that sense, the methodological toolbox of ERN research has broadened over the years, although much is still to be gained. For this, we turn to the foresight part of this chapter.

FORESIGHTS: DIRECTIONS FOR RESEARCH

Over the past decades, European regulatory networks have become part and parcel of national and European administrative systems. In recent years, several reviews and research notes have appeared that look ahead and point toward new directions for studying ERNs (see Mastenbroek & Martinsen 2018; Maggetti et al. 2020). Below, this chapter discusses several of these directions, but also adds some new ones.

Bureaucratic Politics and Reputation

One approach that takes issue with the overtly functionalist perspective on ERNs is articulated by Bach et al. (2016). They argue that much of the literature takes the presence and problem-solving capacities of European regulatory networks for granted without critically assessing the role that preferences and strategies of the regulatory actors that together make up the network. They make a case for bringing in the "administrative factor", that is, a bureaucratic politics perspective, into the analysis of European regulatory networks and to the study of transnational regulatory governance more broadly (see also Egeberg 2006).

A bureaucratic politics perspective would better unveil the "institutional rivalries" present at multiple levels of governance among the actors involved in transnational regulatory governance. Building on such a perspective would help to better understand the emergence, change and effectiveness of ERNs. In that sense, a bureaucratic politics approach is one promising way forward, as this perspective "normalizes" regulatory governance networks by applying the language and conceptual framework that public administration scholars and political scientists have been successfully applying to understand the structure and organization of national administrative systems for about four decades (see Moe 1984). Bach and his colleagues point toward fertile grounds for further research and therewith invite other scholars to develop more refined and testable propositions regarding transnational regulatory networks.

One example of a promising bureaucratic politics approach to ERNs is the application of reputation theory to European regulatory governance. Busuioc and Rimkutė (2020) argue that the concept of organizational reputation gives proper attention to the strategies and interests of regulatory actors for enhancing their own legitimacy and preferences vis-à-vis those of other institutional actors in the regulatory field. A reputational account has further merit over other principal–agency or delegation related approaches, especially within a multi-level context, in that the EU regulatory field is still evolving and in constant flux (see Schillemans & Busuioc 2015). The realm occupied by most European agencies and networks still lacks a firm basis in treaties and is shaped by the soft and hard powers of transboundary regulatory politics. It is difficult to apply the same concepts that are commonly used within national formal constitutional settings, such as delegation, to such an evolving administrative order. The key concepts thus far, such as "dual delegation" (Newman 2010), "double delegation" (Coen & Thatcher 2008), and "double hatted" agencies (Egeberg 2006) only partly capture the situation in which regulatory actors operate in a multi-level setting. In other words, these approaches only capture the (pairs of) dyadic principal–agent relationships between regulatory agencies and their national and supranational principals, respectively. Reputational theories then bear the promise of capturing not only the dyadic principal–agency models but also the interdependencies between regulatory actors and other stakeholders within an essentially networked environment.

Public Management, Network Governance, and ERNs

A second promising combination of perspectives that, we believe, opens up new venues of research on transnational regulatory networks is the development and application of theories and models from the fields of public management and network governance, in combination but also by themselves.

First, we believe scholars should more thoroughly analyze the implications that operating in ERNs have for the national agencies participating in them, and incorporating insights from scholarship of public management is a way to do so. In particular such a public management perspective allows scholars to look *inside* regulatory agencies, an analytical focus often overlooked in the current literature (for an exception, see Ruffing 2017). Currently, scholars assessing the effects of transnational networks on domestic bureaucratic structures are primarily preoccupied with the external forces "controlling" the bureaucracy, rather than studying what goes on inside bureaucracy itself (cf. Meier & Krause 2003). Quite a lot is thus known about the "politics of structural design", that is, how politicians use structure, rules, procedures, and incentives to control and influence domestic agencies, and the bargaining between political/electoral institutions to determine the fate and design of administrative agencies in light of transnationalization (see Saz-Carranza et al. 2016; Bach et al. 2016). However, relatively little is known about what happens inside these domestic agencies as they adjust to changing (transnational) environments and what they experience as they prepare to work with and within the transnational networks that have become increasingly relevant for their day-to-day operations.

Particularly important to consider in this regard, is that an increasing number of domestic officials represent agencies and ministries in complex transnational environments (see Alter & Raustiala 2018), such as ERNs. This development is potentially problematic because, for one, these officials are boundedly rational, that is, they have limited attentional capacities to cope with the complex governance settings in which they increasingly operate. This means that their actions and decisions are likely characterized by some degree of (behavioural) uncertainty (see Jones et al. 2006). Moreover, a second consideration is that the collective behaviours of these different individual officials will have to be internally managed and coordinated, as to effectively represent the domestic agency in transnational networked settings and adequately process external information originating in these environments. To do so, explicit coordination is required, given that heterogeneous transnational environments likely involve officials operating from within different units, at different managerial levels, with different sets of expertise and (strategic) interests (see Van der Heijden 2020). In addition, the transnational network activities of the agency will have to be reconciled with the need to remain accountable within a national context as well (see Groeneveld 2016; Yesilkagit 2016). How the tensions that emerge from these considerations manifest themselves in practice, can only be studied through analytical concepts that have an explicit intra-organizational dimension.

Second, a public management perspective brings attention to what public managers inside regulatory authorities and ERNs do to coordinate the multiple strategic and competitive relationships of their environment. For regulatory authorities within networked settings but also for European agencies at the core of these networks, coordination is problematic and challenging. The concepts of managerial networking or network management can be applied to such settings, as to help us think more clearly about what strategies can be employed by the director-level officials responsible for many of these processes. Although we should be careful in carelessly applying these concepts and neglecting the political context in which many of these directors operate, there is leverage in analyzing how managers operate within networked environments as to facilitate collective behaviour (Agranoff & McGuire 2003), or to tap into resources for the benefit of their agency (Meier & O'Toole 2010).

Third, from a network governance perspective, a promising path is to explore the question of "network effectiveness" for ERNs, as well as the way in which they are governed, managed, and brokered (see also Maggetti et al. 2020). In terms of network goals, the representatives of national authorities convene to exchange information, produce expertise, improve coordination, and harmonize rules in the common market (see Vestlund 2017). However, the national authorities involved typically have uneven resources and different interests. This potentially problematizes collective action at the transnational level and requires explicit (network) management and steering at the network-level to secure commitment on behalf of national agencies. Issues of network governance to minimize these tensions and ensure network effectiveness are crucial in this regard, but have not been given enough attention in the study of ERNs (for an exception, see Saz-Carranza et al. 2016).

In particular, a group of scholars have identified ERNs as a potentially interesting case of a network governed by a Network Administrative Organization (NAO) (Iborra et al. 2018), one of the modes of governance identified by Provan and Kenis (2008). This has helped to illuminate the structural complexity of the secretariats used to steer ERNs, but several other aspects remain underexplored. For one, Provan and Kenis (2008) underlined the importance of contingency theory in studying questions of network governance, meaning the appropriate modes of governance are dependent on a number of contingency factors. NAO's, the argument goes, would be most suitable in conditions of moderate density, many network participants, moderately high goal consensus, and a high need for network-level competences. For ERNs scoring differently on these contingency factors, however, other modes of governance might be more appropriate. This mismatch between contingency factors and modes of governance might then explain the ineffectiveness of particular ERNs and lines of research investigating these types of questions are further encouraged.

ERNs and Network Analysis

Another unexplored line of inquiry is about what happens inside ERNs in terms of the informal patterns of interaction between regulators of which they are built up. Recent work by Vantaggiatto (2019a; 2019b) demonstrates the potential of social network analysis (SNA) to elucidate some of these patterns and use them as an independent variable to explain a particular phenomenon. For instance, in one study she demonstrated how agencies use network ties to acquire resources and compensate for the lower staff levels with which they have to work

(Vantaggiatto 2019a; see also Vestlund 2017). Moreover, patterns of interaction can also be linked to processes of diffusion and regulatory harmonization and several scholars have used SNA to analyze the channels of influence through which such diffusion occurs (Maggetti & Gilardi 2014; Van der Heijden & Schalk 2020).

In addition, the networked patterns of interaction themselves are also interesting to explain, as regulators do not decide to join "a network" but are connected to these networks in different ways. In other words, within regulatory networks domestic agencies selectively coordinate their activities with a smaller number of agencies, for instance for the exchange of more sensitive information or to build coalitions as to influence decision-making at the network level (see Papadopoulos 2018). Policy network scholars have extensively used SNA to explore patterns of coalition building and information exchange, pointing to factors such as preference similarity or perceived influence to be important drivers of collaboration (see Henry et al. 2010; Leifeld & Schneider 2012). Given that ERNs can be considered as a type of policy network, such methods and theoretical insights can also be translated to the ERN context to better understand their functioning. So far, this has only been done sparsely (Vantaggiatto 2019b; Van der Heijden 2021).

The core questions underlying a network-analytical approach are thus whether and how networked patterns of (social) interaction matter for individual actors and communities (Kilduff & Brass 2010). Such an approach can help deepen the current understanding of transnational networks and their probable effects on domestic actors and agencies. Conceptually, it provides a more concrete conceptualization of transnational networks by further specifying the "sets of direct interactions among sub-units of different government" talked about by Keohane and Nye (1974, p.82), or the "patterns of regular and purposive relations" noted by Slaughter (2004, p.14). Analytically, it allows one to move beyond general categories of "network membership" (see Bach & Newman 2010), by providing analysis of the way in which network activity, contacts, and structural embeddedness vary between domestic agencies and what the according effects of this variation are. Moreover, these network-structural patterns can be linked to diffusion mechanism argued to play an important role in processes of regulatory harmonization (see Holzinger & Knill 2005; Van der Heijden & Schalk 2020).

External Pressures and Network Survival

Finally, we believe that future studies should pay a more substantial amount of attention to how the currently strong de-globalization tendencies will affect the functioning and perhaps survival of transgovernmental networks in general and European regulatory networks in particular. Prevailing studies have looked at the proliferation of networks, their structures, and functions. These core themes and hence the "dependent variables" of these studies put the *growth* of transnational regulatory networks and the European administrative space in general (Mastenbroek & Martinsen 2018) at the centre of their analyses. However, the context of transnational regulation is altering rapidly in fundamental ways.

Whereas the 2008 financial crisis already seriously questioned the past quality and capacities of transgovernmental (financial) regulation, the need for stronger transnational regulatory networks seemed beyond any doubt. One reaction was the upscaling of financial and monetary regulation through the establishment of the European Central Bank and European System of Central Banks. However, since 2008, we are also witnessing a sway of protectionism worldwide often in combination with the emergence of populist movements in established democracies. An early victim of protectionism have been the global trade initiatives. The Trans-Pacific Partnership (TPP) has been recalled by former President Donald Trump, while negotiations on the Transatlantic Trade and Investment Partnership (TTIP) were put on hold. In the EU, Brexit marks an unprecedented blow to the process of European integration and also has likely consequences for regulatory alignment (see Armstrong 2018). In a number of crucial policy areas, such as climate policies and international migration, the emerging populist and nationalist mood will potentially prove to be detrimental for the viability of transgovernmental networks as the smooth administrative transmission belts of information, harmonization, and enforcement of transboundary policies (Slaughter 2004). Their untransparent nature and technocratic feel, certainly won't help in this regard.

These events, albeit in different weights, have an impact on the development of transnational networks and the way they evolve. Functionalist explanations are trumped by realist politics. The demise of a multilateral order raises questions regarding the viability and perhaps future survival of the modes of transgovernmental networks as we know them today. These political dynamics and sentiments should be accounted for in the study of ERNs as well. Particularly, issues related to accountability have only scarcely received attention (Verdier 2009; Van Osch 2017; Saz-Carranza et al. 2020), although such issues may fuel discussions around the functioning and feasibility of regulatory networks in years to come (see also Chapter 17, this volume).

CONCLUSION

This chapter has summarized the literature studying ERNs and has also drawn out several lines of future research. Although some would conclude that ERNs have had their time and EU Agencies are now a more prominent phenomenon, the conceptual lines between them are thin. Both would classify as a network-like organization (albeit with different degrees of institutionalization) and can be fruitfully studied in similar ways. In conclusion, a last point to then make is not to overestimate the distinctiveness of the phenomenon under study, as it potentially hampers theorizing and possibilities for comparison. ERNs are a case of regulatory networks that exist in many different regions and also at the global level (see Newman & Zaring 2012; Abbott & Kauffmann 2018). More generally even, they are a case of inter-organizational collaboration, a phenomenon studied by a large group of scholars in the fields of organizational theory and public management. An important message of this chapter is thus that scholars interested in ERNs – or any other regulatory structure in the EU relying on collaboration – should not shut their eyes to other fields of study and research contexts characterized by similar network dynamics, albeit with different contextual factors. This contextual variation is potentially interesting to explore as to assess how it affects the nature of collaboration between regulatory agencies, as well as the outcomes they can achieve. Treating ERNs more as "as a case of" can help to engage scholars in more broad debates, while keeping enough room for contextualization to account for the nature of the EU political and institutional structure by which they are embedded.

REFERENCES

Abbott, K., & Kauffmann, C. (2018). The contribution of trans-governmental networks of regulators to international regulatory co-operation. *OECD Regulatory Policy Working Papers, No. 10*. Paris: OECD Publishing. https://doi.org/10.1787/538ff99b-en.

Agranoff, R., & McGuire, M. (2003). *Collaborative Public Management: New Strategies for Local Governments*. Washington, DC: Georgetown University Press.

Alter, K. J., & Raustiala, K. (2018). The rise of international regime complexity. *Annual Review of Law and Social Science, 14*, 329–349.

Armstrong, K. A. (2018). Regulatory alignment and divergence after Brexit. *Journal of European Public Policy, 25*(8), 1099–1117.

Aubin, D., & Verhoest, K. (Eds.) (2016). *Multi-level Regulation in the Telecommunications Sector: Adaptive Regulatory Arrangements in Belgium, Ireland, the Netherlands and Switzerland*. Dordrecht: Springer.

Bach, D., & Newman, A. (2010). Transgovernmental networks and domestic policy convergence: Evidence from insider trading regulation. *International Organization, 64*, 505–528.

Bach, D., & Newman, A. (2014). Domestic drivers of transgovernmental regulatory cooperation. *Regulation & Governance, 8*, 395–417.

Bach, T., & Ruffing, E. (2013). Networking for autonomy? National agencies in European networks. *Public Administration, 91*(3), 712–726.

Bach, T., De Francesco, F., Maggetti, M., & Ruffing, E. (2016). Transnational bureaucratic politics: An institutional rivalry perspective on EU network governance. *Public Administration, 94*(1), 9–24.

Bianculli, A. C., Jordana, J., & Juanatey, A. G. (2017). International networks as drivers of agency independence: The case of the Spanish Nuclear Safety Council. *Administration & Society, 49*(9), 1246–1271.

Bignami, F. (2005). Transgovernmental networks vs. democracy: The case of the European information privacy network. *Mich. J. Int'l L., 26*, 807.

Blauberger, M., & Rittberger, B. (2015). Conceptualizing and theorizing EU regulatory networks. *Regulation & Governance, 9*(4), 367–376.

Blauberger, M., & Rittberger, B. (2017). A rejoinder to Tarrant and Kelemen. *Regulation & Governance, 11*(2), 223–227.

Börzel, T., & Risse, T. (2000). When Europe hits home: Europeanization and domestic change. *European Integration Online Papers (EIoP), 4*(15).

Bruszt, L., & Vukov, V. (2017). Making states for the single market: European integration and the reshaping of economic states in the Southern and Eastern peripheries of Europe. *West European Politics, 40*(4), 663–687.

Busuioc, M., & Rimkutė, D. (2020). The promise of bureaucratic reputation approaches for the EU regulatory state. *Journal of European Public Policy, 27*(8), 1256–1269.

Coen, D., & Thatcher, M. (2008). Network governance and multi-level delegation: European networks of regulatory agencies. *Journal of Public Policy, 28*(1), 49–71.

Cohen, J., & Sabel, C. F. (2004). Global democracy. *NYUJ Int'l. L. & Pol., 37*, 763.

Danielsen, O. A., & Yesilkagit, K. (2014). The effects of European regulatory networks on the bureaucratic autonomy of national regulatory authorities. *Public Organization Review, 14*(3), 353–371.

Dehousse, R. (1997). Regulation by networks in the European Community: The role of European agencies. *Journal of European Public Policy, 4*(2), 246–261.

Donnelly, S. (2010). *The Regimes of European Integration: Constructing Governance of the Single Market*. Oxford, UK: Oxford University Press.

Drezner, D. (2008). *All Politics is Global: Explaining International Regulatory Regimes*. Princeton, NJ: Princeton University Press.

Eberlein, B., & Grande, E. (2005). Beyond delegation: transnational regulatory regimes and the EU regulatory state. *Journal of European Public Policy, 12*(1), 89–112.

Eberlein, B., & Newman, A. L. (2008). Escaping the international governance dilemma? Incorporated transgovernmental networks in the European Union. *Governance, 21*(1), 25–52.

Egeberg, M. (2006). *Multilevel Union Administration: The Transformation of Executive Politics in Europe*. New York, NJ: Springer.

438   *Handbook of regulatory authorities*

Egeberg, M., & Trondal, J. (2009). National agencies in the European administrative space: Government driven, commission driven or networked? *Public Administration, 87*(4), 779–790.

Egeberg, M., & Trondal, J. (2017). Researching European Union agencies: What have we learnt (and where do we go from here)? *Journal of Common Market Studies, 55*(4), 675–690.

Groeneveld, S. M. (2016). *Het Belang van Bureaucratie: Omgaan met Ambivalentie in Publiek Management*. Leiden: Leiden University Press.

Groenleer, M. L. (2014). Agency autonomy actually: Managerial strategies, legitimacy, and the early development of the European Union's agencies for drug and food safety regulation. *International Public Management Journal, 17*(2), 255–292.

Heims, E. M. (2016). Explaining coordination between national regulators in EU agencies: The role of formal and informal social organization. *Public Administration, 94*(4), 881–896.

Henry, A. D., Lubell, M., & McCoy, M. (2010). Belief systems and social capital as drivers of policy network structure: The case of California regional planning. *Journal of Public Administration Research and Theory, 21*(3), 419–444.

Hobolth, M., & Sindbjerg Martinsen, D. (2013). Transgovernmental networks in the European Union: Improving compliance effectively? *Journal of European Public Policy, 20*(10), 1406–1424.

Hofmann, H. C. H., & Turk, A. H. (2006). *EU Administrative Governance*. Cheltenham, UK and Northampton, MA, USA: Edward Elgar Publishing.

Holsti, K. J., & Levy, T. A. (1974). Bilateral institutions and transgovernmental relations between Canada and the United States. *International Organization, 28*(4), 875–901.

Holzinger, K., & Knill, C. (2005). Causes and conditions of cross-national policy convergence. *Journal of European Public Policy, 12*(5), 775–796.

Iborra, S. S., Saz-Carranza, A., Fernández-i-Marín, X., & Albareda, A. (2018). The governance of goal-directed networks and network tasks: An empirical analysis of European regulatory networks. *Journal of Public Administration Research and Theory, 28*(2), 270–292.

Jones, B. D., Boushey, G., & Workman, S. (2006). Behavioral rationality and the policy process: Toward a new model of organizational information processing. In B. G. Peters, & J. Pierre (Eds.), *Handbook of Public Policy* (pp.49–74). London: Sage Publications.

Kelemen, R. D., & Tarrant, A. D. (2011). The political foundations of the Eurocracy. *West European Politics, 34*(5), 922–947.

Keohane, R. O. (2001). Governance in a partially globalized world: "Presidential Address American Political Science Association, 2000". *American Political Science Review, 95*(1), 1–13.

Keohane, R. O., & Nye, J. S. (1974). Transgovernmental relations and international organizations. *World Politics, 27*, 39–62.

Kilduff, M., & Brass, D. J. (2010). Organizational social network research: Core ideas and key debates. *The Academy of Management Annals, 4*(1), 317–357.

Koppell, J. G. S. (2010). Administration without borders. *Public Administration Review, 70*(s1), 46–55.

Lavenex, S., & Wichmann, N. (2009). The external governance of EU internal security. *European Integration, 31*(1), 83–102.

Legrand, T. (2015). Transgovernmental policy networks in the anglosphere. *Public Administration, 93*(4), 973–991.

Leifeld, P., & Schneider, V. (2012). Information exchange in policy networks. *American Journal of Political Science, 56*(3), 731–744.

Levi-Faur, D. (2011). Regulatory networks and regulatory agencification: Towards a single European regulatory space. *Journal of European Public Policy, 18*(6), 810–829.

Maggetti, M. (2007). De facto independence after delegation: A fuzzy-set analysis. *Regulation & Governance, 1*(4), 271–294.

Maggetti, M. (2012). *Regulation in Practice: The De Facto Independence of Regulatory Agencies*. Colchester, UK: ECPR Press.

Maggetti, M. (2014). The politics of network governance in Europe: The case of energy regulation. *West European Politics, 37*(3), 497–514.

Maggetti, M., & Gilardi, F. (2011). The policy-making structure of European regulatory networks and the domestic adoption of standards. *Journal of European Public Policy, 18*(6), 830–847.

Maggetti, M., & Gilardi, F. (2014). Network governance and the domestic adoption of soft rules. *Journal of European Public Policy, 21*(9), 1293–1310.

Maggetti, M., Di Mascio, F., & Natalini, A. (2020). National regulators, regulatory networks, and European agencies: Connecting the dots. *Public Policy and Administration*, 0952076719886748.

Mastenbroek, E., & Martinsen, D. S. (2018). Filling the gap in the European administrative space: The role of administrative networks in EU implementation and enforcement. *Journal of European Public Policy, 25*(3), 422–435.

Mathieu, E. (2016). When Europeanization feeds back into EU governance: EU legislation, national regulatory agencies, and EU regulatory networks. *Public Administration, 94*(1), 25–39.

Mathieu, E. (2017). Networks, committees or agencies? The many faces of the EU regulatory space. TARN Working Paper.

Mathieu, E., Verhoest, K., & Matthys, J. (2017). Measuring multi-level regulatory governance: Organizational proliferation, coordination, and concentration of influence. *Regulation & Governance, 11*(3), 252–268.

Mathieu, E., Matthys, J., Verhoest, K., & Rommel, J. (2020). Multilevel regulatory coordination: The interplay between European Union, federal and regional regulatory agencies. *Public Policy and Administration*, 0952076719886736.

Meier, K. J. & Krause, G. A. (2003). *The Scientific Study of Bureaucracy: An Overview*. Michigan: Michigan University Press.

Meier, K. J., & O'Toole Jr, L. J. (2010). Beware of managers not bearing gifts: How management capacity augments the impact of managerial networking. *Public Administration, 88*(4), 1025–1044.

Moe, T. M. (1984). The new economics of organization. *American Journal of Political Science, 28*(4), 739–777.

Monti, M. (2010). *A new strategy for the single market. Report to the President of the European Commission José Manuel Barroso*, May, 10.

Newman, A. L. (2008). Building transnational civil liberties: Transgovernmental entrepreneurs and the European data privacy directive. *International Organization, 62*(1), 103–130.

Newman, A. L. (2010). International organization control under conditions of dual delegation: A transgovernmental politics approach. In D. D. Avant, M. Finnemore & S. K. Sell (Eds.), *Who Governs the Globe?* (pp.131–152). Cambridge, MA, USA: Cambridge University Press.

Newman, A. L., & Zaring, D. (2012). Regulatory networks: Power, legitimacy, and compliance. In J. Dunoff & M. A. Pollack (Eds.), *Interdisciplinary Perspectives on International Law and International Relations* (pp.244–265). Cambridge, MA, USA: Cambridge University Press.

Papadopoulos, Y. (2018). How does knowledge circulate in a regulatory network? Observing a European Platform of Regulatory Authorities meeting. *Regulation & Governance, 12*(4), 431–450.

Picciotto, S. (1997). Fragmented states and international rules of law. *Social & Legal Studies, 6*(2), 259–279.

Pierson, P. (2000). The limits of design: Explaining institutional origins and change. *Governance, 13*(4), 475–499.

Provan, K. G. and P. Kenis. (2008). Modes of network governance: Structure, management and effectiveness. *Journal of Public Administrative Research and Theory*, 18: 229–252.

Raustiala, K. (2002). The architecture of international cooperation: Transgovernmental networks and the future of international law. *Va. J. Int'l L., 43*, 1.

Ruffing, E. (2017). Inside regulatory bureaucracy: When Europe hits home in pharmaceuticals and chemicals. *Public Policy and Administration, 32*(1), 3–23.

Sabel, C. F., & Zeitlin, J. (2008). Learning from difference: The new architecture of experimentalist governance in the EU. *European Law Journal, 14*(3), 271–327.

Saz-Carranza, A., Albareda, A., & Federo, R. (2020). Network tasks and accountability: A configurational analysis of EU regulatory networks. *Public Administration, 98*(2), 480–497.

Saz-Carranza, A., Salvador Iborra, S., & Albareda, A. (2016). The power dynamics of mandated network administrative organizations. *Public Administration Review, 76*(3), 449–462.

Schillemans, T., & Busuioc, M. (2015). Predicting public sector accountability: From agency drift to forum drift. *Journal of Public Administration Research and Theory, 25*(1), 191–215.

Segato, F., & Raab, J. (2019). Mandated network formation. *International Journal of Public Sector Management, 32*(2), 191–206.

Slaughter, A. M. (2000). Governing the global economy through government networks. In M. Byers (Ed.), *The Role of Law in International Politics: Essays in International Relations and International Law* (pp.177–205). Oxford, UK: Oxford University Press.

Slaughter, A. M. (2004). *A New World Order*. Princeton, NJ: Princeton University Press.

Tarrant, A., & Kelemen, R. D. (2017). Reconceptualizing European Union regulatory networks: A response to Blauberger and Rittberger. *Regulation & Governance, 11*(2), 213–222.

Thatcher, M. (2011). The creation of European regulatory agencies and its limits: A comparative analysis of European delegation. *Journal of European Public Policy, 18*(6), 790–809.

Thurner, P. W., & Binder, M. (2009). European Union transgovernmental networks: The emergence of a new political space beyond the nation-state?. *European Journal of Political Research, 48*(1), 80–106.

Trondal, J., & Peters, B. G. (2013). The rise of European administrative space: Lessons learned. *Journal of European Public Policy, 20*(2), 295–307.

Van Boetzelaer, K., & Princen, S. (2012). The quest for co-ordination in European regulatory networks. *Journal of Common Market Studies, 50*(5), 819–836.

Van der Heijden, M. (2020). Transnational networks and domestic agencies: Making sense of globalizing administrative patterns [PhD Dissertation]. Leiden University.

Van der Heijden, M. (2021). Agencies without borders: Explaining partner selection in the formation of transnational agreements between regulators. *Regulation & Governance, 15*(3), 725–744.

Van der Heijden, M., & Schalk, J. (2020). Network relationships and standard adoption: Diffusion effects in transnational regulatory networks. *Public Administration, 98*(3), 768–784.

Van Osch, D. A. G. T. (2017). Accountability in the context of transgovernmental networks: A conceptual approach. TARN Working Paper Series. https://dx.doi.org/10.2139/ssrn.2962973.

Vantaggiatto, F. P. (2019a). Networking for resources: How regulators use networks to compensate for lower staff levels. *Journal of European Public Policy, 26*(10), 1540–1559.

Vantaggiato, F. P. (2019b). The drivers of regulatory networking: Policy learning between homophily and convergence. *Journal of Public Policy, 39*(3), 443–464.

Vantaggiato, F. P., Kassim, H., & Wright, K. (2021). Internal network structures as opportunity structures: Control and effectiveness in the European competition network. *Journal of European Public Policy, 28*(4), 571–590.

Verdier, P. H. (2009). Transnational regulatory networks and their limits. *The Yale Journal of International Law, 34*, 113–172.

Versluis, E., & Tarr, E. (2013). Improving compliance with European Union law via agencies: The case of the European Railway Agency. *Journal of Common Market Studies, 51*(2), 316–333.

Vestlund, N. M. (2017). Pooling administrative resources through EU regulatory networks. *Journal of European Public Policy, 24*(1), 61–80.

Whytock, C. A. (2005). A rational design theory of transgovernmentalism: The case of EU–US merger review cooperation. *BU Int'l LJ, 23*, 1.

Wilks, S. (2007). Agencies, networks, discourses and the trajectory of European competition enforcement. *European Competition Journal, 3*(2), 437–464.

Yesilkagit, K. (2011). Institutional compliance, European networks of regulation and the bureaucratic autonomy of national regulatory agencies. *Journal of European Public Policy, 18*(7), 962–979.

Yesilkagit, K. (2012). The internationalization of national bureaucracy: The impact on relationships between politicians and bureaucrats. In M. Lodge & K. Wegrich (Eds.), *Executive Politics in Times of Crisis* (pp.19–40). London: Palgrave Macmillan.

Yesilkagit, K. (2016). *Public Administration with a Focus on International Governance*. Leiden: Leiden University Press.

Yesilkagit, K., & Christensen, J. G. (2010). Institutional design and formal autonomy: Political versus historical and cultural explanations. *Journal of Public Administration Research and Theory, 20*(1), 53–74.

29. Innovation and regulatory agencies
Cristie Ford

INTRODUCTION

Innovation is a challenge to regulation, and it has ever been thus. As we grapple with the effects of a global pandemic, a climate crisis, war, and the profound and inevitable changes these will bring, we cannot lose sight of the ways in which private sector innovation will also weave its way through our responses, complicating and refracting the regulatory task and influencing both public priorities and outcomes.

Regulation – that undercelebrated and crucially important thing – operates at the front lines of policy, and reflects the normative priorities that we as societies hold dear. Many forces "regulate" in broad terms – the market regulates, the environment regulates (Lessig 1998) – although for purposes of this handbook, we are talking about actual state regulation. Regulation here refers to sustained and intentional activity by the state in attempting, through direct or indirect methods, to control, order, or influence the behaviour of others in the service of public policy priorities. It almost inevitably is a multifactorial, complicated exercise within which important but disparate priorities – growth and equality, freedom and respect, safety and privacy – must be balanced. Because they are instruments of policy and reflections of social values, regulations must at some level be accountable, transparent, demonstrably legal, and perceived as legitimate. Process therefore matters a great deal when it comes to how regulation is promulgated, and how it is given effect. There is a certain amount of sober second thought, of recourse to principle and policy, of caution, and sometimes of recourse to centralized authority, that comes inevitably with this territory.

Private sector innovation, on the other hand, is not burdened with the same range of procedural or normative concerns. (The word "innovation" can mean different things. Regulators and states can be innovators too, and they are. For our purposes, however, the word "innovation" refers to private sector innovation.[1]) The Oxford English Dictionary defines it as "the alteration of what is established by the introduction of new elements or forms" (Oxford University Press, n.d.). As opposed to an invention, which is the first creation of an idea or good, innovation is the process of applying an idea in practice. Innovations can be technological, or they can be business- or process-related.

Private sector innovation is a complicated and dynamic phenomenon that presents continual challenges for regulation. An innovation and its effects only become more complicated, dynamic, and unpredictable as the innovation diffuses. Innovation evolves in reflexive, iterative relationship to the legal environment within which it operates. Not all its impacts are socially beneficial (though sometimes we speak as if they were), and its benefits are unevenly, and sometimes unpredictably, distributed.

After reviewing some Welfare State and Regulatory State history, this chapter suggests that innovation raises three fundamental analytical problems for regulation: information and data problems, visibility problems, and legibility problems. It then sets out five regulatory priorities that will be essential to a forceful contemporary state, if it is to be resilient in the face of inno-vation, while maintaining credibility and agency in the service of public priorities.

The Only Constant is Change

Over the last 100 years, the give-and-take between private sector innovation and regulation has been a leitmotiv in policy and public law. There is no real way to understand the relationship between private sector innovation and regulation today, without understanding the postwar Welfare State regulatory approach against which more contemporary regulatory technique has defined itself over the last several decades. In its waning days in the late 1970s, the Welfare State was widely perceived to have become cumbersome and unresponsive.[2] Modern regula-tory theory developed in contraposition to that discredited model. In the process, it evolved into a model that, perhaps only semi-intentionally, actively, even excessively, celebrated private sector innovation. In its way, then, what we have come to call the Regulatory State (1990s–2008) has also become its own distinct cautionary lesson about how public sector reg-ulation should engage with private sector innovation. Today, we may wish once again to see a more forceful public actor in private spaces. To avoid the pitfalls of the past, however, any new post-pandemic regulatory model we develop will have to be capable of managing the con-stant, indeed accelerating, change that private sector innovation continues to force – without losing sight of its public obligations and normative priorities in the process.

   Innovation was not top of mind in postwar Europe and North America, when the Welfare State came to full flower (Esping-Andersen 1996; Majone 1997). Borne of hard experience with wars and economic depression, the Keynesian Welfare State's core concerns were to manage the social and natural risks – disaster, illness, economic uncertainty, poverty, old age – to which every human body was potentially vulnerable (Giddens 1990). It did so through new social programs and direct state involvement in the economy. By the late 1970s, however, in many countries including the United States and the United Kingdom, the Welfare State's credibility was under siege. By this point, public actors were being criticized for having become inaccessible, over-proceduralized; and either (or, somehow, *both*) non-transparent and unaccountable in their decision-making, and/or pathologically observant of rigid rules and procedures (McCraw 1984). By 1980, more than 60 per cent of Americans surveyed in a Gallup Poll felt that "quite a few of the people running government did not seem to know what they were doing" (Geer 2004, p. 222). The Welfare State was also facing new headwinds as a result of increasing globalization, interconnection, novel technological and transportation developments – in other words, as a function of widespread and accelerating innovation. These phenomena provoked Americans in particular to worry about their competitiveness. Forceful government interventions into the economy (e.g., interest rate caps, the use of tax-and-spend powers, state-owned utilities) came to seem too expensive and burdensome to sustain.

   Whether justified or not, by 1980 the concept of direct state involvement in the economy, the wisdom of creating state-owned enterprises to provide services that the private sector could provide, and the viability of a large public safety net had become highly unpopular. Politicians and others framed the tension as a binary contest between "public" (slow, obstructionist, out of touch) and "private" (agile, growth-oriented, full of promise) means of getting things done, with problem-solving protagonists pitted against pencil-pushing obstructionists. The need to cut "red tape" suddenly seemed urgent. The word "bureaucracy" became an epithet. Even progressive, left-of-centre administrative law scholars found themselves advocating for the "reform" of regulation (see, e.g., Breyer 1982). Enter the neoconservatives, Margaret Thatcher and Ronald Reagan chief among them.

From the time that centre-left "Third Way" advocates like Tony Blair and Bill Clinton wrested back a degree of control in the 1990s, the history of the Regulatory State has been about attempting to reflect and enact more public-oriented, socially beneficial regulation to the (often limited) extent those actors believed to be possible, while still insulating themselves politically against charges that state actors were reverting to becoming once again "bureaucratic", "command-and-control", "top-down", or even "sclerotic" (Short 2012).

The Regulatory State from the early 1990s onward was explicitly and intentionally *not* all the odious things that the late-stage Welfare State was described to be. However, it was also not fundamentally deregulatory in the way that the neoconservative 1980s reforms had been. Starting in the 1990s, regulation, theory and practice, had transformed itself. Regulation and governance had been reinvented by "an increase in delegation, proliferation of new technologies of regulation, formalization of inter-institutional and intra-institutional relations, and the proliferation of mechanisms of self-regulation in the shadow of the state" (Levi-Faur 2005, p. 13). It developed into a sophisticated, nuanced body of both practical experience and scholarship. "Flexibility" had become a watchword (Stewart 1993; Sunstein 1991). Adaptiveness, responsiveness, context-sensitivity, pragmatism, collaboration with private actors, and the ability to mete out proportionate, tit-for-tat responses became the *sine qua nons* of enlightened regulatory practice (Ayres & Braithwaite 1992; Lobel 2004). Scholars of regulation began to imagine a deeper and more ideologically agnostic regulatory "toolbox" containing new techniques for channelling and harnessing private action (Coglianese & Lazer 2003; Gunningham & Grabosky 1998). A good number of those tools were derived from economics, the belle of the late twentieth century intellectual ball (see, e.g., Becker 1983; Posner 1973). But regulation and regulatory theory also drew on critical legal studies, civic republicanism, and legal theory, to chart a coherent intellectual and practical path forward in the straitened circumstances of the post-Welfare State era (Ford 2017). While indisputably the Regulatory State had its shortcomings, it was also a significant imaginative and pragmatic achievement.

As the world become more complex, as regulatory subjects became more diverse, and as regulatory theory became more sophisticated, however, the Regulatory State project also began to bump up against some limits. At root, these limits were not so different from those the Welfare State encountered: they were about how regulation could be designed so as to safeguard public, norm- and law-driven priorities, even while achieving expected levels of growth, national competitiveness, and innovation. Relative to the postwar model, the Regulatory State had perhaps just taken hold of the other end of the stick: by this point, regulatory practice and scholarship had acknowledged that private sector actors had access to more granular and timelier information than regulators did. This suggested that private actors seemed to be in a better position than regulators to make operational, as opposed to policy, decisions. (Of course this distinction soon broke down.) This somewhat awkward regulatory situation was exacerbated by the fact that – as compared to the slower processes on which regulatory authority depends, which value certainty and justification and which aim to consider, to consult, and to deliberate – private sector innovation was moving very quickly, continually changing the "facts on the ground". Regulators seemed, then and now, to be struggling to keep up. In our highly innovative (and innovation-loving) age, then, the fundamental regulatory dilemma looks more like this: how to collaborate with and perhaps even celebrate private sector innovation, without utterly ceding the field to private actors and losing sight of the public priorities that a regulator is charged with safeguarding?

In retrospect, in the decade on either side of the millennium's turn, the importance ascribed to economic efficiency – and its kindred spirits, enthusiasm for private sector growth, unfettered competition, and innovation – may well have displaced too many other normative commitments and aspirations. Writing from a vantage point early in the year 2022 – battered by a poorly managed global pandemic and the undeniable persistence of racism and discrimination; terrified about the consequences of climate change; having suffered through years of political tumult and populist anger following the financial crisis; confronting yet another war on European soil; and having recognized once again that there is more to a person's value than the quantum of their economic productivity – it seems clear that at the height of the Regulatory State, the pendulum swung too far away from the humane, collective, and dignity-affirming priorities that animated much of the Welfare State agenda.

And yet, the problems of change, unpredictability, and uncertainty that helped to undo the Welfare State persist. If anything, they have gotten graver as the pace and scope of private sector innovation have increased. If we are to create a better state apparatus that attends to inequality, precarity, and human flourishing more comprehensively and explicitly than the Regulatory State did, these are the challenges we will have to confront.

Today, some of the greatest challenges that regulation faces stem from the speed, extent, and nature of human-driven change. In particular, private sector innovation has transformed the landscape in areas as varied as communications (social media), finance (derivatives, cryptocurrencies), retail (Amazon, e-commerce), manufacturing, health, and science (nanotechnologies, robotics, genetic engineering via CRISPR), transportation (ride-sharing, drones, global shipping and supply networks, autonomous vehicles), security (biomedical tracking, online surveillance), the platform economy (decentralized peer review, data as an asset), and more. While we are only beginning to understand these technologies' social implications, there is little sign that even a global pandemic will meaningfully limit the dynamism and complexity that private sector innovation continues to generate. On the contrary, innovation is flourishing.

So what have we learned about the relationship between innovation and regulation, over these past decades, which will be helpful as we confront these challenges? The next sections identify some of the main insights that Regulatory State and innovation scholarship developed over the last three decades. In looking ahead to creating a new, post-Regulatory State approach that also avoids the pitfalls associated with the Welfare State, these lessons will be important.

TAKING STOCK: MAIN CONCEPTS, SIGNIFICANT THEORETICAL AND EMPIRICAL ACHIEVEMENTS

One thing that we have learned is that innovation and regulation are in a reflexive relationship with one another (Orts 1995). Different innovative forms and trajectories, when combined with regulation, produce different effects. For example, sometimes, innovations are designed specifically in order to get *around* regulatory requirements (UK Financial Services Authority [FSA] 2009). In other contexts, private sector innovations can usefully be incorporated *into* public regulatory requirements, thereby improving them. The use of best practices, or best available technology standards in environmental regulation, is one such example (Flynn & Baylis 1996). In still other situations, a particular private sector innovation proceeds on a parallel track alongside a regulatory regime, or *outside* familiar regulatory boundaries. Those innovations nevertheless influence and even undermine the ground rules in the adjacent regulated space. Consider the effect that ride-sharing apps have had on the regulated taxi industry (Pollman & Barry 2017; Ranchordas 2015); and then consider the permissionless blockchain-based ride-hailing apps, like Swarm City, that are poised to undermine those very ride-sharing apps. How can a regulator even keep track, let alone make sense of the myriad ways in which private sector innovation potentially interacts with, undermines, improves, or otherwise influences regulation?

To begin with, regulation is not a monolithic thing. Regulation generally requires three main attributes: the capacity for standard-setting, the capacity for information-gathering or monitoring, and some capacity for behaviour modification (Hood et al. 2001). However, the tools one uses at each of these stages will have different effects. The form of regulation – *ex ante* compliance versus ex post enforcement, punitive versus permissive, principles-based versus rules-based, discretionary versus non-discretionary, all potentially operating at different stages or distinct scales – matters (Morgan & Yeung 2007). For example, a more principles-based structure that allows highly expert frontline regulators to move quickly, with good access to information, can be a good choice in situations characterized by a high degree of uncertainty. Yet regulatory regimes that accept fast-moving innovation as inevitable, and try to adapt themselves by becoming more flexible or by delegating more responsibility to private sector regulated actors, may unwittingly generate even more, and faster, innovation as a result (Fullenkamp & Rochon 2014). A highly rule-driven regime will provide more certainty and predictability, which can be the most important consideration in certain situations. At the same time, when it comes to innovative activity, rigid rules can create opportunities for gamesmanship and loophole behaviour.

Innovation will affect regulation no matter how it is structured. In its design, regulation constitutes the spaces in which innovation happens (Polanyi 1944). It creates loopholes, opportunities, boundaries, and incentives. Different tradeoffs will make sense in different circumstances.[3]

Private sector innovation, also, is not a monolithic phenomenon. Innovation tends to be a social process, developed through bricolage and improvisation and influenced by the tools at hand and the immediate, often idiosyncratic, challenges to be addressed (Lévi-Strauss 1962). Innovations commonly diffuse through networks and, whether or not they produce the best products or solutions, "nodes" within those networks can be especially successful at promoting uptake of their innovations. Moreover, networks are socially created and profoundly human, with all the attendant dynamics of power and human irrationality. Whether an innovation is influential may depend as much on an innovator's reputation, status, or network centrality as on the actual merits of the innovation (Lee et al. 2009). Some innovations can evolve very quickly, as was the case with deepwater oil drilling, while others can develop slowly and incrementally, like parts of the alternative energy sector.

Innovation is also environmentally and contextually contingent. Innovation looks different in different spaces, and it raises different concerns. Context matters. For example, the wholesale global financial products industry, which generated the synthetic financial innovations that underlay the financial crisis, is characterized by (a) stiff competition, plus (b) a strong first mover advantage, around (c) intangible financial products that can be engineered and re-engineered quickly and imaginatively, and (d) sold into a market that could not, because of the products' complexity, usefully distinguish between a useful product and a lemon. In this environment, the result was fast-moving innovations that generated questionable benefits for consumers or markets, but ample opportunities for rent-seeking. In other environments, different conditions will produce different effects.

It makes no sense for regulation to try to "foster innovation" in some blanket sense, without understanding the innovation in question, how it is diffusing, who benefits from its adoption, what unanticipated consequences may flow from it, and especially how it could undermine, circumvent, or otherwise neutralize existing regulatory processes and priorities. The nature of the reflexive relationship between particular regulatory structures and unique innovative environments is complex, but with concerted effort it is discoverable.

Understanding the Challenge that Innovation Presents

An innovation (whether to business process, technology, or in finding novel uses for existing products) is concerning, for regulatory purposes, because of its ability to outstrip existing regulatory structures, such that they no longer fit or work properly (Smismans & Stokes 2017). As a result, rules may stop operating as intended, perhaps because they are not broad enough to capture new behaviour or phenomena, or because activity has moved away from the formal object with which the regulation is concerned. This leaves regulators potentially focusing on the wrong things (Brummer 2015). Responding to this and similar innovation-generated problems requires that the regulator be able to recognize that its effectiveness has been compromised, to understand the particulars of how its regime has been undermined, and to respond. This is not a straightforward or easy set of tasks. However, the nature of the challenge can at least be broken down into three different kinds of regulatory analytical problems.

First, particularly fast-moving innovations can generate *information and data problems* for regulators. These were present around deep water oil drilling in the Gulf of Mexico between 1995 and 2010, for example, or with respect to the explosive growth of the over-the-counter derivatives market for credit default swaps between 2004 and 2007 (Bank for International Settlements 2018, Graph 4; National Commission on the BP Deepwater Horizon Oil Spill and Offshore Drilling 2011). The massive, and massively accelerated, shift to online living, shopping, working, banking, and communicating during the pandemic is also very likely to raise a range of information (and other) problems for regulators with respect to taxes, privacy, urban planning, consumer protection, labour and employment, accessibility of services, and more. In cases such as these, where technological or business process changes or social adoption levels are moving exceptionally quickly, a fundamental problem that regulators are likely to encounter is simply that they do not have sufficient data to make sense of fast-moving changes in real time. They may lack the data either because the phenomenon is still too new to have generated adequate longitudinal data, and/or because only the innovators themselves have access to what data exist. Those innovators may not be able to, or may not voluntarily, share it. Consider, for example, the fact that in 2010, it was British Petroleum itself that had to dream up never-before-tried responses – like the "junk shot" and the "top kill" – to the terrible and ultra-deep oil leak that followed the explosion of its Deepwater Horizon rig. The regulator was utterly unequipped to manage that disaster, for reasons that prominently included the lack of information it had on the risks that BP was running and the risks of ultra-deep oil drilling in general (National Commission on the BP Deepwater Horizon Oil Spill and Offshore Drilling 2011). Complex systems, characterized by multiple interconnections, can also create unanticipated and outsized reactions, where system effects or multiple small errors' combined effects mutually reinforce each other (Perrow 1984; Schwarcz 2008). These are also forms of information and data problems.

The second kind of problem that innovation generates for regulation is the *visibility problem*. One such example is the visibility problem that is created by incremental innovation; like the apocryphal frog in boiling water, one tends not to notice change until, seemingly suddenly, it has reached significant levels. Yet by this point, interests and practices have already accreted around it. Consider the international shipping industry. The emergence of the shipping container as a modular, multi-platform mechanism for moving goods around the world via boat, train, and truck was slow. Through the second half of the twentieth century it did not seem obvious to most observers that the container would transform the world economy, until one day it was clear that it already had (Levinson 2006). Several regulators, ports, and unions did not appreciate the significance of the transformation until it was too late to salvage their existing regulatory, business, and bargaining models.

Another kind of visibility problem arises at or near the boundaries or margins of a regulator's jurisdiction. These could be margins between particular administrative agencies, arranged "horizontally", or boundaries between states, nation states, regions, or global initiatives that are arranged "vertically" (Boeger & Joseph 2012; Langevoort 2010). Regulatory and policy boundaries, obviously, do not always map neatly onto real world phenomena. Innovation exacerbates this mapping problem, because enterprising innovators may be particularly attracted to the relatively low-visibility spaces far from any regulator's core concerns. These are areas that are not squarely within any particular regulator's expertise or jurisdiction, and where regulators' familiar analogies seem slightly off. Interest rate swaps operated for a long time in such a space, neither "fish" (securities) nor "fowl" (derivatives) (Funk & Hirschman 2014). While the U.S. Securities and Exchange Commission and its Commodity Futures and Trading Commission argued over jurisdiction and characterization, the swaps markets expanded unhindered and unregulated. The same questions around which agency has the authority to act seem now to be affecting American cybersecurity policy (Lewallen 2020). Innovative phenomena can also grow, unappreciated, outside a particular regulator's jurisdiction, only becoming visible once they have begun to have a significant impact or to wield significant power. Consider Amazon's growth: the company expanded without triggering conventional antitrust concerns, while building significant customer brand loyalty, to the point that it has now concentrated extraordinary market power and political influence (Khan 2017; Culpepper & Thelen 2019).

The third and most profound kind of problem that innovation presents for regulation is the *legibility problem*. Legibility is the ability to make sense of one's environment, to develop reasonable assumptions, and to draw appropriate analogies between the familiar and the new. Innovation, by its nature, upends categories and undermines assumptions. Consider, for example, how special purpose entities in finance, which according to the traditional legal model of the firm seem to operate on corporate law principles, actually achieve their objectives through the separate legal mechanism of contract (Bratton & Levitin 2013). Equity derivatives manage to separate the vote attached to a corporate share from the economic interest underlying it, undermining not only corporate law assumptions but also priority under bankruptcy law, and more (Hu & Black 2008). Familiar products that are characterized as "safe assets" for certain purposes may migrate into new spaces, where they substitute for other products and where they are not at all "safe" (Gelpern & Gerding 2016).

Ultimately, these problems are epistemological problems. They are questions about what we know, what we do not know, and how we know what we think we know. Sometimes, with better data, regulators can identify and measure the risks associated with a novel product or process. Addressing the information or data problem brings a degree of clarity. At other times, the uncertainty runs deeper (Knight 1921). The unknowns encompass not only questions about how external phenomena are developing, but also about how completely a regulator can rely on existing assumptions, analogies, or common wisdom about the world. These are the visibility and legibility problems. And of course, if just *seeing* developments and recognizing their significance in real time is hard, then anticipating problems is far harder.

LOOKING AHEAD: LESSONS FOR REGULATORS

Learning from the experience of the Welfare State, we can recognize that detailed, top-down, one-size-fits-all regulatory mechanisms can impose significant costs, while not necessarily achieving regulatory objectives (Bardach & Kagan 1982). This is especially true in highly dynamic environments. While we may in future want to see more of the kind of public intervention into private markets that characterized the postwar years, an unreconstructed, 1960s-style Welfare State apparatus would have no ability to manage the data and informational, visibility, and legibility problems that our fast-moving and highly innovative contemporary society produces.

More flexible Regulatory State mechanisms are better equipped to manage those kinds of problems, and its many and varied regulatory tools and strategies are a good foundation for the innovation-ready, post-pandemic, post-Regulatory State architecture that we are now going to have to construct. In order to make any new regulatory approach effective, robust, and credible, however, and to ensure that it is capable of interjecting a genuinely public-oriented and normatively engaged voice into the innovative context, it must have more capacity than some key Regulatory State actors had in the past. The paragraphs below elaborate on four crucial overarching lessons to be drawn from our recent experience: the regulator's conduct must be data-driven, the regulator must be adequately resourced, it must remain independent-minded and, ultimately, we cannot forget that there is no way to separate regulation and policy from politics.

First and above all, a nimble, data-driven regulatory approach is indispensable for dealing with the continual challenges that private sector innovation produces. The regulator must constantly be aware of the data and informational, visibility, and legibility problems that innovation creates. Because the environment will continue to change and one must be able to track that change, the regulator should be prepared to ask, continually, fundamental epistemological questions about what it knows, how it knows it, and what it does not know. This requires that regulators have access to high quality data, and that they be agile enough to respond to those data and to their own experiences of success and failure. Learning to see innovation in real time demands that regulators seek data and information, continually, to understand, for example, *who* is innovating and in response to what incentives? *What* kinds of innovations seem to be taking place? *How* are they diffusing? *Where* are the regulator's knowledge and data gaps, why do they exist, and what, if anything, can be done to fill them? (Ford 2017.)

Second, and relatedly: effective regulation, regardless of its aims, requires that regulators be adequately resourced (Ford 2010b). The prototypical Welfare State agency required a lot of "boots on the ground" to ensure compliance and impose sanctions for non-compliance. The more contemporary Regulatory State apparatus may superficially have appeared to be less resource-intensive, but regulators' ability to engage flexibly and credibly with regulated agencies actually required a great deal in the way of human resources and capacity. Meaningful enforcement is indispensable to maintaining credibility (Cortez 2014). Where things fell apart – as they did with oversight of global financial institutions in the run-up to the financial crisis, for example – under-resourcing and inattention were almost always the main part of the problem (Internal Audit Division 2008; The Financial Crisis Inquiry Commission 2011). Implementation is essential, and it is essential not only in the immediate wake of a high-salience event, but also well after the acute crisis or the political moment has passed (Baumgartner & Jones 2009).

There are no simple, all-purpose solutions for effective and legitimate regulation of innovation (Brownsword 2008). All the same, there is learning to draw on. For example: more principles-based regulation, for all its challenges, makes sense under some conditions where innovation requires that a regulator be especially responsive and attuned to street-level developments (Black et al. 2007). Rules-based regulation makes sense where certainty is important or where, for all its limitations, some sort of bright-line boundary is a useful temporary placeholder, even recognizing that it will likely generate loophole behaviour and unintended side-effects (Ford 2010a). *Ex ante* licensing regimes make sense in certain conditions, such as when the pace of innovation is making it difficult for a regulator to acquire enough data to understand the situation (Omarova 2012; Posner & Weyl 2013). Meta-regulation, or the "regulation of self-regulation," makes sense where innovators but not regulators have access to the necessary data, and where there is reason to believe that industry actors have some meaningful incentive to behave responsibly themselves (Rees 1994; Parker 2002). And virtually all contemporary regulation that tries to allocate resources effectively will involve a degree of risk assessment. Risk-based regulation can be quite effective, if adequately resourced, though again it will only be responsive to risks that it registers as significant (Black & Baldwin 2012). Only an adequately-resourced regulator will have the ability to analyze the context effectively and to use this broad range of regulatory techniques appropriately.

Learning from the experience of the Regulatory State, we recognize now that flexibility is a regulatory stance, with variable impacts depending on context – not an end unto itself. We have learned that as much as we might wish it were otherwise, the "regulatory Utopia" – within which capable, responsible private actors voluntarily engage in sincere ongoing dialogue with a flexible and outcome-oriented regulator, in the service of some hypothetical shared goal of optimized regulation – does not exist (Black 2008). Private actors have their own interests. Public sector regulators are the ones charged with speaking on behalf of broader social commitments and normative priorities. As we begin to emerge from the economic, political, social and health-related crises of the past decade, a well-resourced and skilled regulator will be in the best position to recognize the appropriate tools for the context, and to implement careful and considered responses to the circumstances that arise.

In our contemporary environment, especially where fast-moving private sector innovation continues to transform the conditions under which we operate, adequate regulatory resourcing must include access to the best possible data, awareness of the limits of that data, and the capacity to work exceptionally well with it. The regulator should understand where its data are coming from, and should make efforts to continually improve the quality, quantity, reliability and granularity of those data. To the extent possible, tools should be put in place that allow the regulator to track change and innovation not only in real time, but also across a broader span of time so as to recognize transformations in markets, practices, and attitudes. These data will form the foundation for decision-making vis-à-vis regulated actors, but also for learning about one's own regulatory technique, and for continually improving that technique based on experience. These processes must be ongoing; there is no end point. Failure of renewal is a constant challenge.

Interest in increased data and a more data-driven approach to regulation are already generating some concrete strategies, which one hopes will be implemented seriously and rigorously. The "regulatory sandboxes" proliferating in the financial sector, which in their best form establish strong incentives for private actors to share their data with regulators, are one such example. In exchange for access to a zone in which they can conduct live experiments in a controlled environment without fear of regulatory sanction, fintech players should be required in every case to provide supervising regulators with the kind of high-quality, granular, real-time data that regulators would not otherwise be able to access (Buckley et al. 2020). Better data and better analytic capacity have also given regulators themselves new and richer perspectives that can fully take into account, for example, how networks and interconnectedness operate in their sectors (Enriques et al. 2020).

Third, scepticism and independent mindedness are important characteristics in a regulator, as is a certain disinterest in whether or not one is popular. This is especially true around innovation, one of the main romantic objects of our times. Regulators should not forget that often, one of the central reasons that industry actors are pursuing an innovation may be to circumvent regulatory rules, or to unlock the competitive advantage that flows from a particularly aggressive interpretation of those rules. Regulators that are overawed by the apparent expertise that particular industry actors seem to have, as financial regulators arguably were in the run-up to the financial crisis, risk losing sight of the separate normative priorities they are charged with advancing (Desmond 2013). Just as importantly, no matter how novel the innovation, regulators should remember that "this time is [not actually] different" (Reinhart & Rogoff 2009) in terms of fundamental regulatory concerns. Regulators are as vulnerable to being swayed by the zeitgeist as anyone else. It is therefore important that they recognize the constraints that their era's popular wisdom imposes on their thinking. This also requires the ability to track change across time.

In retrospect, it may seem obvious that the structure of the postwar Welfare State was poorly-suited to manage the effects of globalization in the 1970s; or that the "light touch" financial regulatory system that began to emerge in the 1990s, combined with competitive pressures in the industry, was likely to produce an irrational and ruinous race to the bottom in terms of leverage ratios, capital adequacy, and ultimately systemic risk. Identifying these issues in real-time, however, requires a significant streak of contrariness. It may be useful to establish a role of "institutional contrarian" within regulators, whose main purpose is to challenge assumptions and to push against consensus (McDonnell & Schwarcz 2011).

In the run-up to the financial crisis, private financial industry actors deftly shaped our collective narrative around new financial products and their ability to "complete markets". Of course, this advanced their (short term) interests. Regulators, too, are in a position to behave with a certain degree of political acumen in the interest of advancing their mandate. They can and should be entitled to think strategically about how to frame issues (Smismans & Stokes 2017). For example, describing an innovation as a "radical" departure from past practice has the potential to activate political actors, in helpful or unhelpful ways. Labelling something as an unremarkable "incremental" evolution of existing practice verbally downplays the likelihood that it will have a significant potential impact, and suggests that past practice and familiar comparators should continue to apply. The fact that these terms are subjective does not undermine their usefulness to regulators in framing a phenomenon in a way that advances their regulatory objectives.

Regulating Innovation as a Deliberative, Participatory Project

The final lesson is perhaps the most important: it is that one cannot separate regulation from politics.

Political actors may be inclined to use regulatory examples to advance their own objectives. They may, for example, find it appealing to suggest that good regulatory technique, on its own, can create "simply better" outcomes along several conflicting metrics at once. In 2006, in describing the UK FSA's move to a more principles-based regulatory approach, which ultimately proved to be badly under-resourced and structurally flawed, FSA Chief Executive John Tiner argued that principles-based financial regulation produced simply "better" regulation, meaning *simultaneously* "(1) a stronger probability that statutory outcomes are secured; (2) lower cost; and (3) more stimulus to competition and innovation" (Tiner 2006). Regulators should remain mindful of the ways in which, especially around innovation, others may, for their own reasons, be inclined to present "have your cake and eat it too" solutions that undermine effective regulation.

In other respects, as well, political considerations are embedded inextricably into the regulatory task itself. There are more and less effective or suitable regulatory strategies in different situations, of course, but at the end of the day it is not possible to "bracket" or elide fundamental distributional and normative choices (Cohen 2010). Emerging technologies can intersect with and potentially challenge fundamental value concepts (Brownsword et al. 2017, pp. 15–20). Thus especially when it comes to regulating innovation, we must not let our romantic association with that term blind us to the fact that responding to private sector innovation forces us, actively or by omission, to make choices: between stability and growth; between environmental concerns and short-term capitalist goals; and between multiple, contested understandings of equity, justice, and the social good.

In the years since the financial crisis, the Regulatory State's centrist and collaborative regulatory mechanisms have attracted critique by the political right, as regulation always does, but also by a resurgent left. The critique from the left deserves to be carefully considered. In some contexts, unquestionably, 1990s- and 2000s-era regulators adopted public/private partnerships too uncritically, and progressive normative commitments fell by the wayside in the pursuit of political compromise or political advantage. In several cases the Regulatory State's moral compass, if one can speak of such a thing, did not point so much toward fairness or the public interest as toward efficiency. Those priorities are ripe for reconsideration. And some parts of Regulatory State thinking remain as important as ever. Specifically, we should not lose sight of the crucial civic republican, justice-oriented, egalitarian instincts that characterized new governance strategies – the same imperatives that now drive initiatives as disparate as human-centred design, community-based financing and empowerment, and broadly inclusive deliberative democratic initiatives (Rahman 2016; Ford 2017). We also know more than we did a generation ago about the limits of state action, and about how norms develop.

Innovation is too fast-moving now, and conditions too complex and heterogeneous to imagine that a replica of the postwar Welfare State would function well. Workable regulatory models for managing innovation will have to contend with twenty-first-century global phenomena. BigTech companies today have amassed astounding power, largely as a function of their incomparable access to data about people, and they may have spawned a new variant of capitalism in the process (Rahman & Thelen 2019; Zuboff 2019). Increasingly sophisticated computer tools, notably predictive algorithms, are generating novel challenges to regulation, the rule of law, and important social commitments including privacy and anti-discrimination efforts (Prince & Schwarcz 2020; Wachter et al. 2018; Yeung 2018). Established ways of operating have been upended by the pandemic and by the climate emergency. But given adequate resources, independent-mindedness, a data-driven mindset, and an awareness of how politics can intersect with the regulatory task, post-Regulatory State regulators can have the capacity to reconceive legacy models in their fields and to adapt to the challenges that innovation poses today (Arner et al. 2017). Thus-equipped, a regulator will be in a position to address the fundamental challenges that innovation raises – information and data problems, visibility problems, and legibility problems – and to wield the range of regulatory tools that the Regulatory State era bequeathed us, as effectively as possible.

Regulation is at the leading edge of politics and policy in ways that we do not always fully grasp. Seemingly innocuous regulatory design choices have clear and profound practical ramifications for many of our most cherished social commitments. In this time of enormous flux, private sector innovation also continues to contribute to fundamentally reordering economies and politics in ways that must be reckoned with, if we value human dignity, equitable opportunity, democracy, and justice.

NOTES

1. Note that state-driven elements of the economy, especially through the military and the space program in the United States, have catalyzed and funded many significant "private sector" innovations, both during the Welfare State years and into the present "knowledge economy" (Mowery 2010; Mazzucato, 2011). However, the state has not driven the precise development or application of such technologies, nor has it benefited from them. For purposes of understanding how innovations affect other, non-research-oriented regulatory regimes, it still makes sense to call these private sector innovations and to focus on how innovation operates in the private context.
2. Giandomenico Majone has influentially described a move from what he called the "Welfare State" – a top-down, control state that engaged directly in the economy as well as in social affairs – to a modern "Regulatory State" defined by its use of rules to intervene less directly in the economy and society. This shift is conceptually important, even if it is overdrawn. Views differ as to how cynical or, alternatively, how progressive a project it has been; about how much we can generalize across borders and subject matters; and about whether the "regulatory state" itself has gone through various stages of evolution and if so, what those stages are. Most would agree, however, that beginning around the early 1990s, in Europe and most Anglo-American jurisdictions, state action methods shifted from emphasizing direct state intervention in the economy to acting through regulation that applies to private actors in a way that is heavily enmeshed with capitalism (Levi-Faur 2005).
3. Political science and policy scholars within the interdisciplinary regulation and governance field have made recent empirical contributions to understanding how background regulatory structures also condition how a new innovation will be understood and responded to: see, e.g., special issue on "focusing on a moving target – the tentative governance of emerging science and technology", *Research Policy* volume 48 issue 5; *Regulation & Governance* special issue on "the governance of

emerging disruptive technologies", available on earlyview at https://onlinelibrary.wiley.com/doi/toc/10.1111/(ISSN)1748-5991.governance-of-emerging-disruptive-technologies.

REFERENCES

Arner, S. W., Barberis, J., & Buckley, R. P. (2017). FinTech, RegTech, and the reconceptualization of financial regulation. *Northwestern Journal of International Law & Business, 37*(3), 371–413.

Ayres, I., & Braithwaite, J. (1992). *Responsive regulation: Transcending the deregulation debate.* Oxford University Press. https://doi.org/10.1111/j.1744-1722.1994.tb00048.x

Bank for International Settlements. (2018). *Statistical release: OTC derivatives statistics at end-June 2018.* https://www.bis.org/publ/otc_hy1810.htm

Bardach, E., & Kagan, R. A. (1982). *Going by the book: The problem of regulatory unreasonableness.* Temple University Press.

Baumgartner, F. R., & Jones, B. D. (2009). *Agendas and instability in American politics* (2nd ed.). University of Chicago Press.

Becker, G. S. (1983). A theory of competition among pressure groups for political influence. *The Quarterly Journal of Economics, 98*(3), 371–400. https://doi.org/10.2307/1886017

Black, J. (2008). Forms and paradoxes of principles-based regulation. *Capital Markets Law Journal, 3*(4), 425–457. https://doi.org/10.1093/cmlj/kmn026

Black, J., & Baldwin, R. (2012). When risk-based regulation aims low: Approaches and challenges. *Regulation & Governance, 6*(1), 2–22. https://doi.org/10.1111/j.1748-5991.2011.01124.x

Black, J., Hopper, M., & Band, C. (2007). Making a success of principles-based regulation. *Law and Financial Markets Review, 1*(3), 191–206. https://doi.org/10.1080/17521440.2007.11427879

Boeger, N., & Joseph, C. (2012). How regulatory networks shaped institutional reform under the EU telecoms framework. *Cambridge Yearbook of European Legal Studies, 14*, 49–73. https://doi.org/10.5235/152888712805580462

Bratton, W. W., & Levitin, A. J. (2013). A transactional genealogy of scandal: From Michael Milken to Enron to Goldman Sachs. *Southern California Law Review, 86*(4), 783–868.

Breyer, S. G. (1982). *Regulation and its reform.* Harvard University Press.

Brownsword, R. (2008). So what does the world need now? Reflections on regulating technologies. In Brownsword, R., & Yeung, K. (Eds.), *Regulating technologies: Legal futures, regulatory frames and technological fixes* (pp. 23–48). Hart Publishing. https://doi.org/10.5040/9781472564559.ch-002

Brownsword, R., Scotford, E., & Yeung, K. (2017). Law, regulation, and technology: The field, frame, and focal questions. In Brownsword, R., Scotford, E., & Yeung, K. (Eds.), *The Oxford handbook of law, regulation and technology* (pp. 3–38). Oxford University Press. https://doi.org/10.1093/oxfordhb/9780199680832.013.1

Brummer, C. (2015). Disruptive technology and securities regulation. *Fordham Law Review, 84*(3), 977–1052.

Buckley, R. P., Arner, D., Veidt, R., & Zetzsche, D. (2020). Building fintech ecosystems: Regulatory sandboxes, innovation hubs and beyond. *Washington University Journal of Law and Policy, 61*, 55–98.

Coglianese, C., & Lazer, D. (2003). Management-based regulation: Prescribing private management to achieve public goals. *Law & Society Review, 37*(4), 691–730. https://doi.org/10.1046/j.0023-9216.2003.03703001.x

Cohen, A. J. (2010). Governance legalism: Hayek and Sabel on reason and rules, organization and law. *Wisconsin Law Review, 2010*(2), 357–388.

Cortez, N. (2014). Regulating disruptive innovation. *Berkeley Technology Law Journal, 29*(1), 175–228.

Culpepper, P. D., & Thelen, K. (2019). Are we all Amazon Primed? Consumers and the politics of platform power. *Comparative Political Studies, 53*(2), 288–318. https://doi.org/10.1177/0010414019852687

Desmond, M. (2013). Is democratic regulation of high finance possible? *The Annals of the American Academy of Political and Social Science, 649*(1), 180–184. https://doi.org/10.1177/0002716213485332

Enriques, L., Romano, A., & Wetzer, T. (2020). Network-sensitive financial regulation. *The Journal of Corporation Law, 45*(2), 351–397.

Esping-Andersen, G. (1996). After the golden age? Welfare state dilemmas in a global economy. In Esping-Andersen, G. (Ed.), *Welfare states in transition: National adaptations in global economies* (pp. 1–31). SAGE Publications. http://doi.org/10.4135/9781446216941

Flynn, A., & Baylis, R. (1996). Pollution regulation and ecological modernization: The formulation and implementation of best available techniques not entailing excessive costs. *International Planning Studies, 1*(3), 311–329. https://doi.org/10.1080/13563479608721660

Ford, C. (2010a). New governance in the teeth of human frailty: Lessons from financial regulation. *Wisconsin Law Review, 2010*(2), 441–489.

Ford, C. (2010b). Principles-based securities regulation in the wake of the global financial crisis. *McGill Law Journal, 55*(2), 257–307. https://doi.org/10.7202/045086ar

Ford, C. (2017). *Innovation and the state: Finance, regulation, and justice.* Cambridge University Press. https://doi.org/10.1017/9781139583473

Fullenkamp, C., & Rochon, C. (2014). Reconsidering bank capital regulation: A new combination of rules, regulators, and market discipline. *IMF Working Paper, 14*(160), 1–36.

Funk, R. J., & Hirschman, D. (2014). Derivatives and deregulation: Financial innovation and the demise of Glass-Steagall. *Administrative Science Quarterly, 59*(4), 669–704. https://doi.org/10.1177/0001839214554830

Geer, J. G. (Ed.) (2004). *Public opinion and polling around the world: A historical encyclopedia.* ABC-CLIO.

Gelpern, A., & Gerding, E. F. (2016). Inside safe assets. *Yale Journal on Regulation, 33*(2), 363–421.

Giddens, A. (1990). *The consequences of modernity.* Stanford University Press.

Gunningham, N., & Grabosky, P. M. (1998). *Smart regulation: Designing environmental policy.* Oxford University Press. http://doi.org/10.22459/RT.02.2017.08

Hood, C., Rothstein, H., & Baldwin, R. (2001). *The government of risk: Understanding risk regulation regimes.* Oxford University Press.

Hu, H.T., & Black, B. (2008). Equity and debt decoupling and empty voting II: Importance and extensions. *University of Pennsylvania Law Review, 156*(3), 625–739.

Internal Audit Division. (2008). *The supervision of Northern Rock: A lessons learned review* [Report]. UK Financial Services Authority. https://www.fca.org.uk/publication/corporate/fsa-nr-report.pdf

Khan, L. M. (2017). Amazon's antitrust paradox. *The Yale Law Journal, 126*(3), 710–805.

Knight, F. H. (1921). *Risk, uncertainty and profit.* Houghton Mifflin Company.

Langevoort, D. C. (2010). Global securities regulation after the financial crisis. *Journal of International Economic Law, 13*(3), 799–815. https://doi.org/10.1093/jiel/jgq032

Lee, R., Clark, G. L., Pollard, J., & Leyshon, A. (2009). The remit of financial geography—before and after the crisis. *Journal of Economic Geography, 9*(5), 723–747. https://doi.org/10.1093/jeg/lbp035

Lessig, L. (1998). The new Chicago school. *The Journal of Legal Studies, 27*(S2), 661–691. https://doi.org/10.1086/468039

Levi-Faur, D. (2005). The global diffusion of regulatory capitalism. *The Annals of the American Academy of Political and Social Science, 598*(1), 12–32. https://doi.org/10.1177/0002716204272371

Lévi-Strauss, C. (1962). *The savage mind.* Librarie Plon.

Levinson, M. (2006). *The box: How the shipping container made the world smaller and the world economy bigger.* Princeton University Press.

Lewallen, J. (2020). Emerging technologies and problem definition uncertainty: The case of cybersecurity. *Regulation & Governance*, early view available at doi:10.1111/rego.12341.

Lobel, O. (2004). The renew deal: The fall of regulation and the rise of governance in contemporary legal thought. *Minnesota Law Review, 89*(2), 342–470.

Majone, G. (1997). From the positive to the regulatory state: Causes and consequences of changes in the mode of governance. *Journal of Public Policy, 17*(2), 139–167. https://doi.org/10.1017/S0143814X00003524

Mazzucato, Mariana (2011). *The entrepreneurial state.* London: Demos.

McCraw, T. K. (1984). *Prophets of regulation: Charles Francis Adams, Louis D. Brandeis, James M. Landis, Alfred E. Kahn.* Belknap Press of Harvard University Press.

McDonnell, B. H., & Schwarcz, D. (2011). Regulatory contrarians. *North Carolina Law Review, 89*(5), 1629–1682.

Morgan, B., & Yeung, K. (2007). *An introduction to law and regulation: Text and materials*. Cambridge University Press. https://doi.org/10.1017/CBO9780511801112

Mowery, D. C. (2010). Military R&D and innovation. In Hall, B. H., & Rosenberg, N. (Eds.), *Handbook of the Economics of Innovation: Vol. 2*, (pp. 1219–1256). Elsevier Science & Technology Books. https://doi.org/10.1016/S0169-7218(10)02013-7

National Commission on the BP Deepwater Horizon Oil Spill and Offshore Drilling. (2011). *Deep water: The gulf oil disaster and the future of offshore drilling*. https://www.govinfo.gov/content/pkg/GPO -OILCOMMISSION/pdf/GPO-OILCOMMISSION.pdf

Omarova, S. T. (2012). License to deal: Mandatory approval of complex financial products. *Washington University Law Review, 90*(1), 63–140.

Orts, E. (1995). Reflexive environmental law. *Northwestern University Law Review, 89*(4), 1227–1340.

Oxford University Press. (n.d.). Innovation. In *OED Online*. Retrieved 21 October 2020, from https:// www-oed-com.ezproxy.library.ubc.ca/view/Entry/96311?redirectedFrom=innovation&

Parker, C. (2002). *The open corporation: Effective self-regulation and democracy*. Cambridge University Press. https://doi.org/10.1017/CBO9780511550034

Perrow, C. (1984). *Normal accidents: Living with high-risk technologies*. Basic Books.

Polanyi, K. (1944). *The great transformation: The political and economic origins of our time*. Beacon Press.

Pollman, E., & Barry, J. M. (2017). Regulatory entrepreneurship. *Southern California Law Review, 90*(3), 383–448.

Posner, E. A., & Weyl, E. G. (2013). An FDA for financial innovation: Applying the insurable interest doctrine to twenty-first-century financial markets. *Northwestern University Law Review, 107*(3), 1307–1357.

Posner, R. A. (1973). *Economic analysis of law*. Little, Brown and Company.

Prince, A. E. R., & Schwarcz, D. (2020). Proxy discrimination in the age of artificial intelligence and big data. *Iowa Law Review, 105*(3), 1257–1318.

Rahman, K. S. (2016). *Democracy against domination*. Oxford University Press.

Rahman, K. S., & Thelen, K. (2019). The rise of the platform business model and the transformation of twenty-first-century capitalism. *Politics & Society, 47*(2), 177–204. https://doi.org/10.1177/ 0032329219838932

Ranchordas, S. (2015). Does sharing mean caring? Regulating innovation in the sharing economy. *Minnesota Journal of Law, Science & Technology, 16*(1), 413–475.

Rees, J. V. (1994). *Hostages of each other: The transformation of nuclear safety since Three Mile Island*. University of Chicago Press.

Reinhart, C. M., & Rogoff, K. S. (2009). *This time is different: Eight centuries of financial folly*. Princeton University Press.

Schwarcz, S. L. (2008). Systemic risk. *The Georgetown Law Journal, 97*(1), 193–249.

Short, J. L. (2012). The paranoid style in regulatory reform. *The Hastings Law Journal. 63*(3), 633–694.

Smismans, S. & Stokes, E. (2017). Innovation types and regulation: The regulatory framing of nano-technology as "Incremental" or "Radical" innovation. *European Journal of Risk Regulation, 8*(2), 364–386. https://doi.org/10.1017/err.2017.9

Stewart, R. B. (1993). Environmental regulation and international competitiveness. *The Yale Law Journal, 102*(8), 2039–2106. https://doi.org/10.2307/796859

Sunstein, C. R. (1991). Administrative substance. *Duke Law Journal, 1991*(3), 607–646. https://doi.org/ 10.2307/1372706

The Financial Crisis Inquiry Commission. (2011). *Final report of the national commission on the causes of the financial and economic crisis in the United States*. https://www.govinfo.gov/content/pkg/GPO -FCIC/pdf/GPO-FCIC.pdf

Tiner, J. (2006, May 9). *Better regulation: Objective or oxymoron* [Remarks]. SII Annual Conference.

UK Financial Services Authority. (2009). *The Turner review: A regulatory response to the global banking crisis*. http://www.actuaries.org/CTTEES_TFRISKCRISIS/Documents/turner_review.pdf

Wachter, S., Mittelstadt, B., & Russell, C. (2018). Counterfactual explanations without opening the black box: Automated decisions and the GDPR. *Harvard Journal of Law & Technology, 31*(2), 841–887.

Yeung, K. (2018). Algorithmic regulation: A critical interrogation. *Regulation & Governance, 12*(4), 505–523. https://doi.org/10.1111/rego.12158

Zuboff, S. (2019). *The age of surveillance capitalism: The fight for a human future at the new frontier of power* (1st ed.). PublicAffairs.

30. Behavioural insights and regulatory authorities
Kai Wegrich and Martin Lodge[1]

INTRODUCTION

The rise of behavioural insights as a major policy trend has been widely documented. Emerging from various disciplines' interest in human cognition, the fascination with 'Nudge' (and all its variants) has been a global phenomenon attracting interest across the worlds of research and practice. The field of regulation, with its emphasis on dealing with market failures arising from 'poor' consumer choice, offers an ideal and fertile area both in terms of being receptive to behavioural insights-related ideas as well as providing advances for the wider field of behavioural economics.

This chapter focuses in particular on the field of economic regulation (Baldwin, Cave and Lodge 2012, 443–503) – the kind of sectors traditionally associated with pipes, wires and cables (and, in this chapter, we include consumer-related finance), and where the promotion of user choice has arguably been one of the central themes in regulatory policy since the 1990s. More generally, regulation should be assumed to be at the heartland of the Nudge-movement (Thaler and Sunstein 2008), given that some of its key protagonist have long-standing academic standing in this particular field (e.g. Cass Sunstein).

We focus in particular on examples from the UK, mostly because the UK is widely said to have been at the forefront of the 'Nudge' boom in executive government (John 2018) (as exemplified by the establishment of the 'Behavioural Insights Team' in central government (it was subsequently part- and then fully-'privatised')),[2] but also as economic regulators recognised 'behavioural insights' in their work programmes since the early to mid-2010s. Other jurisdictions that have made some effort to use behavioural insights for economic regulation include the EU (Baggio et al. 2021) and the US.

Focusing on the field of economic regulation means concentrating on issues of customer 'choice'. After all, a focus on reducing transaction costs, whether in terms of enabling 'better' choices or reducing administrative 'paperwork' cost and limiting other 'administrative burdens' (Herd and Moynihan 2018) has been at the heart of behavioural insights-related work. In the field of economic regulation, regulatory agencies' behavioural insights are about forcing companies to alter choice architectures (Costa et al. 2016),[3] it is therefore about indirect measures and less about the direct intervention by the state into citizen's daily lives (as would be the case, for example, if we were discussing tax authorities' compliance work). By focusing on economic regulation, we thereby leave aside the considerable attention being paid to behavioural insights in related areas, such as consumer protection and nutrition, with their emphasis on labels ('disclosure'). At the same time, the field of economic regulation is arguably the most 'econocrat'[4]-heavy area in regulation (in the sense of offices being staffed by economics-trained staff using economics-informed methodologies), thereby likely being particularly open to new intellectual fashions in the academic field of economics.

Despite this concentration on one country and area of regulation, this chapter seeks to encourage some broader reflections on the ways in which behavioural insights have been accommodated within the area of regulatory authorities and to point to pathways for future interest. As such, the incorporation of a new 'fashion' in the day-to-day practices of institutions is an important area for research, as it tells us about ways in which organisations update their standard operating procedures and resist change. Focusing on the literature on institutional adaptation more generally, this chapter may therefore also be seen as exploring how regulatory authorities have adapted to changes in political and academic currents. In particular, two rival expectations are at the core of this chapter:

1. Given the intellectual fashion moving towards 'behavioural economics', regulatory authorities, given their core interest in economic analysis, enthusiastically endorsed the behavioural insights agenda;
2. Given the institutional origins of regulatory agencies in an age where approaches were informed by a dominant concern regarding 'regulatory failure' as much as 'market failure' (Lodge and Wegrich 2012), any ideas that would potentially lead to further interventions and value choices, would be treated with resistance and scepticism.

This chapter suggests that while the adoption of behavioural insights by economic regulators has some institutional isomorphic aspects of 'appearing appropriate' in view of wider public sector trends (DiMaggio and Powell 1983, Lodge 2005), the actual utilisation of behavioural insights has progressed on a cautious basis (thereby supporting point 2 above), but in doing so has advanced our understandings of consumer choice. These advances have highlighted the complexity and side-effects of regulatory interventions rather than offered straightforward insights into how to promote engaged consumers on the market place of regulated services (see Sieber 1981; Hood 1998 and Wildavsky 1979 on unintended effects of interventions and 'policies as their own cause').

THE RELEVANCE OF BEHAVIOURAL INSIGHTS FOR ECONOMIC REGULATION

The rise of 'Nudge' and its emphasis on 'bounded rationality' (Simon 1945; Kahneman 2003) has been well-documented. The academic literature has focused on debates as to the feasibility of an approach that seeks to offer 'libertarian paternalism' (Thaler and Sunstein 2008; Sunstein 2014; White 2013; Gigerenzer 2015; Le Grand and New 2015), it has noted the rise of nudge units/consultancies in central government (such as the 'BI Unit' in the UK in 2010) (John 2014; beyond the UK: Feitsma 2018, 2019; Straßheim 2021; Mukherjee and Giest 2020), the interest of international organisations in promoting behavioural insights as a policy tool (see OECD 2017), the concern with the behavioural biases of 'nudgers' (Lodge and Wegrich 2016), the ethical implications of manipulating citizen choice (Schmidt and Engelen 2020; Sunstein 2016), and a considerable literature has explored the effectiveness of different behavioural insights-inspired interventions (noting a wide range of findings, see Hummel and Maedche 2019; cf. Tor 2020 on effectiveness and normative desirability of nudges).

The literature has also given rise to a range of 'nudge variants', ranging from prompts to encourage 'think' (level 2-type reflective thinking) (John et al. 2009), 'shoves', 'boosts' and 'budges' (Oliver 2015, Hertwig & Grüne-Yanoff 2017). We do not seek to explore the intellectual currents that might exist, but simply note here that the UK experience is characterised by regulatory experimentation informed by one particular school of behavioural insights, namely that inspired by Kahneman and Tversky (Tversky and Kahneman 1974).

At its core, behavioural insights draws attention to behavioural biases by consumers (citizen) and choice architectures. Such themes are therefore central to concerns in economic regulation. After all, the promotion of competition through encouraging consumer choice has been central to economic regulation since the early days of regulatory reform. In the following paragraphs, we highlight three key aspects. One is the emerging questions in the field of economic regulation that made an interest in behavioural insights more likely, the second is to highlight the behavioural insights agenda that provided an 'attractive' platform for answering these 'open questions', and the third is to point to some likely expectations that arise from this demand for and supply of behavioural insights for the field of economic regulation. The subsequent section then points to key insights that have emerged from select studies of usage of behavioural insights by regulators in the UK.

Turning to the 'demand' for 'new' answers and methodologies, the field of economic regulation, especially in the UK, was, by the early 2010s, one of intellectual exhaustion (cf. Baldwin et al. 2010; Lodge 2016). The long-held assumption that consumers would act 'rationally', namely proactively engage in the market place to seek out economically beneficial deals, had been widely disappointed. Large swathes of consumers remained 'inactive' even with the knowledge that they might be economically better off by switching and that the act of switching was unlikely to cause service disruption (cf. Jilke et al. 2016). The effect of what might be diagnosed as 'default bias' in the language of behavioural insights was therefore twofold – one was to encourage intellectual 'puzzling' as to why standard recipes (namely 'more information') did not seem to provide for desired responses, and, second, greater attention was also being paid to the benefits and costs to different sets of consumers, namely those that actively engaged in the market place of utility services, and those that remained inactive.

Related, there was also an increasing disquiet regarding the perception of the outcomes of regulatory decision-making, largely driven by political concerns (the rise of what one may call populist politics) and by the Brexit referendum (in the sense of creating a growing awareness that existing institutional arrangements had led to a perception among large parts of the population that they were 'left behind') (Koop and Lodge 2020). These changes in the political environment encouraged a greater interest in the notion of 'vulnerability' that went beyond the statutory provisions that required some regulators to pay particular attention to certain groups in society (the infirm, the young, the disabled).[5] Rather, in view with the awareness of observed market outcomes, it raised attention to questions as to how regulated markets were working for some rather than others. In turn, behavioural insights, with its views on studying human decision-making, provided a legitimate economics-based agenda that appealed to economic regulators. The tools of behavioural insights, in particular the emphasis on experimentation (and, if possible, randomised controlled trials) also provided considerable appeal to regulators in need of justifying their regulatory (non-) interventions.

Third, and again related, the rise of data science within regulators meant that there was, especially in the area of financial regulation, the opportunity to analyse customer behaviour in ways that previously might have been more challenging. More generally, the preferred methodologies of behavioural insights, namely 'randomised controlled trials' (RCT), had a clear appeal to economists in regulatory agencies.

Fourth, and finally, the rise of 'platform businesses' (Rahman and Thelen 2019; Culpepper and Thelen 2020) also encouraged a greater interest in consumer choice by regulatory authorities. On the one hand, the rise of (price) comparison websites may be said to enhance the ease of customer choice. On the other hand, however, the (regulatory) concern was that comparison on price alone was not necessarily leading customers to 'better' products, given that other information regarding service quality was more difficult to obtain or display. Similarly, the rise of travel booking platforms gave rise to an increasing regulatory interest in the ways in which users were 'nudged' to make potentially sub-optimal choices.[6]

It was, therefore, not surprising that behavioural insights were found to be an attractive avenue for the pursuit of regulatory strategies, as some central ideas of behavioural insights, especially ideas regarding 'thinking fast and slow' (Kahneman 2011), seemed to relate to customer choice experiences in terms of both enhancing default options and supporting reflective processes. At the same time, there was also some degree of reluctance regarding the ideas of behavioural insights. The competition-orientation of regulatory authorities in the UK in the early ages went hand-in-hand with a view that regulatory interventions should be 'light touch'. Intervening so as to enable a normative commitment towards 'better' consumer choice was widely seen as potentially inviting 'regulatory failure' and also incurring potential legitimacy problems: by intervening in choice architectures, unelected regulators might be seen as displaying normative biases towards one set of the population rather than others, a redistributive decision domain supposedly reserved for elected politicians. Nevertheless, given the political salience of many of the 'unanswered questions' of economic regulation, it was not surprising that economic regulation in the UK witnessed an increase in behavioural insights-related work, with some regulators establishing dedicated units, whilst others relying on more informal internal networks.

LEARNING FROM BEHAVIOURAL INSIGHTS

Looking across a decade or so of experience with behavioural insights, the rest of this chapter considers the ways in which the engagement of regulatory agencies with behavioural insights has generated particular insights or debates that are of wider significance for the study of economic regulation and behavioural insights. We therefore do not seek to provide exhaustive accounts of different policy trajectories or examples of nudges used by regulators. Instead, we introduce different episodes as brief 'vignettes' that point at (potentially) more general implications of the usage of behavioural insights by economic regulators.

Most of these vignettes point to the problem encountered by economic regulators across sectors, namely that a large number of customers are not actively engaged in market choices, thereby 'losing' money at the expense of a much smaller set of 'highly engaged' customers. This experience (which could be characterised as a 'loyalty penalty') stands in contrast to the widely held 'ideal world' of regulated markets in which well-informed citizens actively switch products on the basis of 'value for money' and where regulated companies compete to attract and maintain customers. At the same time, this concern also points to one important development, namely that economic regulators were proactively pursuing a behavioural insights-oriented research agenda instead of, for example, merely mimicking existing proposals and interventions. In doing so, behavioural insights-related work became part of the analytical work of economic regulators, moving beyond the worlds of 'appearing fashionable' by shallow adaptation (as, we argue, the below vignettes suggest).

In the following, we focus on a range of key insights into the application of behavioural insights in the context of UK economic regulation. The account is far from exhaustive but gives insights into the ways in which behavioural insights have informed regulatory practice (Myers 2019). The section is not intended to suggest inherent limited effectiveness, but rather to illustrate that behavioural insights as a tool for regulatory analysis offers enhanced insights into the complexity of consumer choice rather than providing 'solutions' to regulatory problems. In fact, in some cases, these insights have offered justification for pursuing more heavy-handed, direct regulatory interventions than those associated with 'Nudge'. In the following we focus on four major insights – regarding the boundaries of 'libertarian paternalism', the exploration of critical concepts, the search for effective remedies ('what works') and the need to deal with consumer-harm incurring commercial nudges.

The Boundaries of Libertarian Paternalism

One of the central themes occupying debates in the behavioural insights-movement is the importance attached to so-called choice architectures. The notion of 'choice architecture' highlights how consumer (non-) choice is strongly influenced by the ways in which choices are being presented. It is therefore not surprising that in the area of regulation, 'choice architectures' are seen as central, as decision-making is said to be influenced by the 'default option' and other biases (for example, opting for greater data bundles at the same price rather than opting for reduced data bundles at lower cost).

As noted already, one of the central themes in UK economic regulation has been the concern with limited consumer choice, even where financial gains might be achievable by making use of available choice options (such as switching providers). This concern relates directly to the dominant theme of behavioural insights, namely 'libertarian paternalism', the idea that choice should be paramount, but placed in a context in which consumers' biases would not lead to sub-optimal choices. In other words, in a market where 'shopping around' was beneficial for the individual customers (in view of cost savings), the diagnosed problem was that these cost savings were cross-subsided by the large number of non-engaged customers who, because of their non-action, were paying higher charges. One central question therefore was whether and how choice architectures may be altered so as to encourage more market-engaged (e.g. switching) customers (and whether such interventions were effective and overall desirable) (CMA 2018, 2020).

Debates in the energy sector regarding lack of active consumer engagement in the market highlighted the contested policy implications of what 'libertarian paternalism' might mean. In 2012, the energy regulator, Ofgem, published a policy review that suggested, based on considerable customer research, that customers were discouraged from engaging with energy markets by tariff complexity. Ofgem proposed, with Conservative/Liberal Democrat coalition government support, that all energy tariffs should be reduced to a set of four standardised type of tariffs (Ofgem 2012; *The Times* 2012). These measures represented a departure from previous initiatives that were largely oriented towards reducing 'search' and 'switching costs', such as by encouraging price comparison websites and reducing the administrative burden of switching suppliers.

These proposals were made following the failure of a voluntary agreement between regulators and regulated companies to reduce tariff complexity which had, in fact, led to companies offering even more complexity in tariff choice. The reduction to four standardised tariffs (or products) was, in turn, condemned as overly paternalistic; for example, by the 'godfather' of UK economic regulation, Stephen Littlechild (2012). It was argued that the measures were too paternalistic by reducing choice (and thereby limiting incentives for innovation for regulated companies) and in downplaying individuals' capacity to choose wisely in the first place.

Subsequently, the UK competition authority, the CMA, similarly criticised these measures, suggesting the need for a more behavioural insights-related approach, informed by evidence based on randomised controlled trials (see CMA (2016) and the response of Ofgem to the CMA's report, Ofgem 2016). While the CMA report highlighted the rise of behavioural insights as a way of criticising previous initiatives and measures, the broader argument for regulatory agencies was not necessarily one of appropriate methodological choices alone. Rather, it highlighted the challenges involved in defining how 'paternalistic' a regulator should be in restricting choice as part of a choice architecture. In other words, the episode highlighted the inherent tension in 'libertarian paternalism' when applied to practice: the enabling of an 'opt-in' or 'opt out' through altering the choice architecture will inevitably incur trade-offs as to the degree of choice on the one hand, and the degree of ease on the other. Indeed, as discussed also below, regulatory authorities continued to wrestle with the ethical dilemma whether it was in their remit to 'prod' consumers into engaging with markets when evidence suggested that customers rather did not want to be engaged.

Advancing Conceptual Understandings: The 'Waterbed Effect'

The so-called waterbed effect (Schiff 2008) relates to compensatory indirect responses to direct interventions. It is therefore related to phenomena such as the 'toothpaste tube effect' (if you squeeze the paste in one place, it bulges in another with potentially problematic net overall change, see Hood and Rothstein 2001). In the world of economic regulation, the 'waterbed effect' might appear on both the supply and demand side (Rochet and Tirole 2006). On the 'supply side', a regulatory intervention on one part of a regulated firm's activities (such as mandatory price reductions) might encourage compensatory responses elsewhere (e.g. price increases). Observations regarding the 'waterbed' effect on the supply side highlights regulatory firms' responses to changes to regulatory services and goods, by changing unregulated goods or services. For example, research showed that the impact of regulatory interventions regarding the reduction of wholesale mobile termination rates was accompanied by higher prices elsewhere (see the discussion of various studies in Ofcom 2017). Examples of supply-side waterbed effects also include 'counter nudges' by regulated firms where regulatory efforts to encourage 'opt ins' were met by companies' efforts to exploit default options to ensure customers were, by default, 'opted out' (see also below).

More significantly in the context of behavioural insights is the way in which consumers respond to regulatory interventions in choice architectures. On this 'demand side', customers might also respond to regulatory interventions, thereby nullifying intended policy outcomes.

One key example with important implications for regulatory practice in general, and insights into the 'waterbed effect' in particular, emerged from research conducted by the UK's Financial Conduct Authority. The main concern was related to credit card repayments and the issue that a quarter of customers were only using contractual minimum repayment options. They did so even though less costly ways of taking on debts existed. The profile of customers that relied on making only low levels of repayment and thereby incurred high-interest carrying debt varied between those in financial difficulties and those who had 'drifted' into this particular repayment pattern. In either case, this behaviour resulted in considerable profits arising to firms. In terms of behavioural insights, this kind of costly behaviour could be explained by, first, a bias towards the present ('consume now, pay later') and, second, by overconfidence in that it would be possible to pay off more debt in the future.

In response to the observed consumer behaviour, the FCA, in 2018, conducted experiments with credit card companies that involved the 'nudging' that would make customers increase their direct minimum payment. The result was that adding information on the costs of repeated minimum repayments led to hardly any reduction in an individual's overall credit card debt, even though the Nudge had the desired effect (Adams et al. 2018). The overall 'non-effect' was a result of a waterbed effect. in that customers adjusted their overall behaviour. In short, customers have two ways of credit card repayment – either by direct debit or by paying off an amount 'manually'. It was found that removing the 'minimum repayment' option (i.e. changing the 'default option') from the direct debit set-up made customers increase their direct debit amount they wished to pay every month. In other words, the 'nudge' (the removal of a costly choice option) had the desired effect in reducing the amount that would attract very high interest rate repayments.

However, this effect was offset by compensating behaviour (the 'waterbed effect') in that individuals reduced the amount of manual repayments per month (and some individuals did not set up a direct debit repayment arrangement at all). In other words, without focusing on the wider consequences of a 'nudge', regulatory authorities would have missed this 'waterbed effect'. The FCA therefore had to search for regulatory interventions that went beyond addressing default choices, namely requiring credit card firms to directly engage with customers in persistent debt so as to reduce their repayment arrangements (FCA 2018).

'What Works'

Behavioural insights is said to be an 'inductive approach' to policy-making, as defined by the OECD.[7] One of the key claims by the behavioural insights movement is therefore to be interested in 'what works'. Research by economic regulators revealed a considerable degree of difference when it came to the effectiveness of applying certain behavioural insights. In some areas, such as energy consumption, the use of 'social norms', was revealed to have a limited but noticeable effect. As reported by Allcott and Rogers (2014), customers in the US that received information regarding their own energy consumption relative to their neighbours and the 'most efficient' neighbours were shown to respond by reducing their own consumption. The study also noted a decline in effect over time.

Returning to the issue of increasing enhanced customer engagement with choice in the market place (and the concern with 'default'), the UK energy regulator Ofgem (2019) sought to increase customer awareness that default tariffs were potentially far more costly than the switch to other tariffs (and/or providers). This programme involved ten large-scale trials that were enabled through the introduction of specific regulatory powers to force energy suppliers to cooperate.[8] The trials found that single letters to disengaged customers that pointed to three alternative tariffs had a limited effect in encouraging customer choice (switching increased by 4 per cent, Ofgem 2019: 8).[9] In contrast, a series of letters that pointed customers to one exclusive tariff and switching support through a third party proved more effective, encouraging a switching rate increase by 25 per cent. One insight from this research was the variety of customer behaviour, with some customers engaging when 'nudged', whilst others required safeguards to encourage them to switch (such as positive consumer watchdog ratings). Eventually, none of this extensive research mattered as the UK central government decided on an alternative mechanism to address concern with a 'loyalty penalty', namely a price-cap.

In the area of financial regulation, the FCA (2015a) conducted extensive research, involving a randomised control trial, into why customers were not availing themselves of higher interest-rate accounts. Again, the diagnosed problem was that customers had opened up accounts some time ago but lost out to those that had opened accounts more recently. The research suggested that the use of nudges to make people choose higher interest accounts within the same firm had only limited effects, even if switching was far from time-consuming. Findings from this behavioural insights-based research led to the imposition of more direct regulation, namely by requiring firms to prominently display interest rate information, to enable consumers to manage their accounts in one place, and to facilitate switching (FCA 2015b).

These examples suggest that it was far from easy to diagnose 'what works' when it came to behavioural insights in the area of economic regulation. The research offered insights to economic regulators into the varied motives and capacities of consumers that stood in the way of more extensive engagement on the market place. At the same time, it provided justification to regulators to move towards more direct regulatory tools rather than rely on behavioural insights alone.

Addressing Commercial Nudges

Learning more about the way in which companies and websites exploit behavioural insights to lure customers into potentially costly choices ('sludge', Sunstein 2020). One example includes the ways in which certain companies offer an attractive headline price without making the cost of add-ons explicit before the final booking stages. This led, for example, the UK competition authority (CMA, and its predecessor the Office of Fair Trading) to take action against certain airlines' booking systems.[10] A further key area of interest has been hotel booking websites. In this area, the CMA investigated how booking websites 'rushed' potential buyers into making potentially suboptimal choices, such as by displaying misleading discount rates, by utilising pressure selling techniques in terms of indicating considerable customer interest in a particular offering, pointing to limited availability for particular packages, or failing to be transparent regarding hidden charges. This also included a concern with rankings, especially as to whether website rankings reflected (hidden) commission rates paid by hotels rather than a tailored service by the website for the individual customer (research revealed that most viewers did not make it to the second page of offerings). Following the research and the launching of enforcement actions, hotel booking websites (and related businesses) committed themselves to the CMA's principles to ensure that they complied with consumer law, again, a rather direct regulatory intervention.[11]

CONCLUSION

The reader may wonder how an illustration of the UK experience in utilising behavioural insights can inform a discussion directed towards a broader audience, seeking a general overview and outlook into the interaction between independent regulatory agencies and behavioural insights. In this chapter, we have argued that the (select) empirical examples highlight regulatory agencies' serious engagement with behavioural insights. This engagement went beyond appearing 'fashionable', but explored, with considerable research intensity, the complexity of consumer choice, and, frequently, established findings that went against the grain of behavioural insights-oriented tools. The methods of behavioural insights might, provocatively put, highlight the limits of policy tools advocated by behavioural insights.

Behavioural insights – such as addressing defaults on choice architectures or phrasing communication in personalised ways – can be successful. However, as the discussion has illustrated, such attempts are far from universally successful and there continued to be no broader theoretical understanding as to why some interventions seem to have a stronger impact than others. Indeed, utilising behavioural insights-oriented research (through trials) has either led the way to a greater understanding of the variety of consumer behaviours. The extensive efforts have also not shielded regulators from direct political intervention in view of dissatisfaction with a lack of action (such as in the case of outright bans and price caps). This is not to say that behavioural insights are going out of fashion, but rather that serious engagement with such a research agenda has highlighted the limitations of the Nudge in shaping customer engagement on the market place.

The observed patterns therefore suggest that behavioural insights are likely to remain central to the activities of economic regulators whilst losing their appeal as novel and 'modern' regulatory interventions. In other words, the case of behavioural insights and (economic) regulatory agencies seems to suggest, on the one hand, a process in which a new intellectual fashion is adapted and adopted by an econocracy that initially might have been regarded as at best reluctant to endorse this 'new' intellectual toolkit. However, once it was taken on, the use of behavioural insights became a central aspect and offered differentiated insights through iterative processes into the effects of regulatory interventions that went far beyond the headline grabbing projects typically communicated by central government nudge units.

On the other hand, the trialling of behavioural insights has also highlighted their limitations; especially in a political and societal setting that was increasingly dissatisfied with regulatory outcomes for consumers. This led to the preference for more interventionist mechanisms. Paradoxically, the adoption of regulatory interventions that were supposed to be 'low cost' paved the way for a fashion for far more intrusive regulatory interventions. The rationale of applying behavioural insights changes through its usage in practice. Rather than being a tool that provides alternative interventions and clear-cut answers to 'what works'-type questions, behavioural insights have turned into a tool for the exploration of unintended side-effects of interventions (including those caused by initial nudges). In short, the experience of UK economic regulation points to a decoupling of behavioural insights from the Nudge agenda. Moreover, the experience also suggests that the hope of a 'short cut' to finding answers to 'what works' questions actually leads to a detour: RCTs can seldom settle the question as to what works, but can be used as a starting point for a wider engagement.

What, then, should a future research agenda into the use of behavioural insights and regulatory agencies look like? One response would be to contribute to greater understanding of various behavioural insights by conducting experiments and supporting regulatory agencies in the design of controlled trials. One central concern here would be to move towards an agenda that explored the limits of behavioural insights. For example, what are, if any, the long-term qualitative changes of behavioural insights-inspired regulatory intervention? Similarly, is there an agenda for behavioural insights in regulation that goes beyond questions of individual choice and transactional relationships?

A second agenda would be to explore more systematically not just the organisation of behavioural insights within regulatory agencies (are behavioural units free-standing or have they been 'mainstreamed' into existing units), but also their practice, such as the ways in which issues are selected, methods explored and conclusions drawn. This chapter has largely drawn from cross-sectoral experience in economic regulation in one jurisdiction. Applications in other areas of regulation – such as in food safety, environmental protection or workplace safety – are likely to offer further insights into the varied responses to behavioural insight-inspired interventions. A further cross-sectoral issue is how the behavioural insights agenda, now in conjunction with the fascination with 'data science', shapes the self-image and role understanding of econocrats in government. The BI agenda could be seen as a way of widening the professional background of economic regulators but could also lead to a reinforcement of econocrats' privileged position in government. Cross-national studies comparing countries with varying strength of the economic profession in government could provide insights into such developments.

Finally, there is also a research agenda that draws on the conclusions from this chapter, namely one that explores the consequences of behavioural insights for regulatory agencies and their interventions. Such an agenda would explore the broader context that has given rise to the appeal of behavioural insights in regulation, but also advance our understanding of the trade-offs, side-effects and broader unintended consequences of regulatory interventions.

NOTES

1.   Martin Lodge acknowledges support under the RECONNECT project. This project is financially supported by the NORFACE Joint Research Programme on Democratic Governance in a Turbulent Age and co-funded by AEI, ESRC, NWO and RCN, and the European Commission through Horizon 2020 under grant agreement No 822166. He also is indebted to Geoffrey Myers.
2.   www.bi.team (last accessed: 25 April 2021).
3.   For a recent policy document of the EU Commission emphasising consumer rights for 'informed choice', see https://ec.europa.eu/commission/presscorner/detail/en/ip_20_2069.
4.   See Self (1975) on 'econocrats' (bureaucrats with a background in economics) in the policy process. See also Christensen (2017).
5.   In 2019, the competition regulator (UK Competition and Markets Authority, CMA) published a report on 'consumer vulnerability' (CMA 2019).
6.   For a seminal study and review, see https://www.gov.uk/cma-cases/online-hotel-booking/.
7.   https://www.oecd.org/gov/regulatory-policy/behavioural-insights.htm (last accessed 28 April 2021).
8.   This research also responded to the CMA's earlier criticism that Ofgem should make greater use of behavioural insights related research (as noted earlier). In response, Ofgem created not only its own behavioural insights unit that was committed to this line of research. It also introduced a new license condition that required energy suppliers to participate in trials.
9.   In additional work, letters sent encouraged an increase in switching from 1 per cent in the control group to 2.4 per cent of those receiving a letter from Ofgem and to 3.4 per cent if the letter was branded by the energy supplier. The heightened impact of a supplier branded letter was witnessed across trials.
10. For credit card surcharges, see https://www.gov.uk/cma-cases/airlines-payment-card-surcharges -investigation, and also for other 'add ons', see https://www.pinsentmasons.com/out-law/news/ ryanair-agrees-website-clarifications-with-oft.

11. For background into this case, see https://www.gov.uk/cma-cases/online-hotel-booking and the Parker Aranha (2019).

REFERENCES

Adams, P., Guttman-Kenney, B. Hayes, L., & Hunt, S. (2018). Helping credit card users repay their debt: A summary of experimental research. Financial Conduct Authority, Research Note, July 2018. https://www.fca.org.uk/publication/research/research-note-helping-credit-card-users-repay-their-debt -summary-experimental-research.pdf (last accessed 27 April 2021).
Allcott, H., & Rogers, T. (2014). The short-run and long-run effects of behavioral interventions: Experimental evidence from energy conservation. *American Economic Review, 104*(10), 3003–37.
Baggio, M., Ciriolo, E., Marandola, G., & van Bavel, R. (2021). The evolution of behaviourally informed policy-making in the EU. *Journal of European Public Policy, 28*(5), 658–676. DOI: 10.1080/13501763.2021.1912145
Baldwin, R., Cave, M., & Lodge, M. (2012). *Understanding regulation: theory, strategy, and practice.* Oxford: Oxford University Press.
Baldwin, R., Cave, M., & Lodge, M. (2010). Introduction: The field and the developing agenda. In: *The Oxford handbook of regulation.* Edited by Baldwin, R., Cave, M., & Lodge, M., pp. 3–16. Oxford: Oxford University Press.
Christensen, J. (2017). *The power of economists within the state.* Stanford CA: Stanford University Press.
CMA (Consumer and Market Authority) (2020). Loyalty penalty update -progress two years on from the CMA's super-complaint investigation. https://assets.publishing.service.gov.uk/media/5fc52 bdcd3bf7f7f591e141e/Loyalty_penalty_Dec_2020__-.pdf (last accessed 27 April 2021).
CMA (2019). Consumer vulnerability: challenges and potential solutions. February 2019, https://assets .publishing.service.gov.uk/government/uploads/system/uploads/attachment_data/file/782542/CMA -Vulnerable_People_Accessible.pdf (last accessed 26 April 2021).
CMA (2018). Tackling the loyalty penalty: Response to a super-complaint made by Citizens Advice on 28 September 2018. https://assets.publishing.service.gov.uk/media/5c194665e5274a4685bfbafa/ response_to_super_complaint_pdf.pdf (last accessed 27 April 2021).
CMA. (2016). Energy market investigation. Final report. 24 June 2016. https://assets.publishing .service.gov.uk/media/5773de34e5274a0da3000113/final-report-energy-market-investigation.pdf (last accessed 27 April 2021).
Costa, E., King, K., Dutta, R., & Algate, F. (2016). Applying behavioural insights to regulated markets. *The Behavioural Insights team for Citizens Advice.* http://www.behaviouralinsights.co.uk/wp-content/ uploads/2016/05/Applying-behavioural-insights-to-regulated-markets-final.pdf (last accessed 27 April 2021).
Culpepper, P. D., & Thelen, K. (2020). Are we all Amazon primed? Consumers and the politics of plat-form power. *Comparative Political Studies, 53*(2), 288–318.
DiMaggio, P. J., & Powell, W. W. (1983). The iron cage revisited: Institutional isomorphism and collec-tive rationality in organizational fields. *American Sociological Review, 48*, 147–160.
FCA. (2015a). Cash savings market study report: Part I: Final findings, Part II: Proposed remedies. Financial Service Authority, January 2015. https://www.fca.org.uk/publication/market-studies/cash -savings-market-study-final-findings.pdf (last accessed 27 April 2021).
FCA. (2015b). PS15/27: Cash savings remedies: Feedback and Policy Statement to CP15/24 and next steps. https://www.fca.org.uk/publications/policy-statements/ps15-27-cash-savings-remedies -feedback-and-policy-statement-cp15-24 (last accessed 28 April 2021).
FCA. (2018). PS18/4: Credit card market study: Persistent debt and earlier intervention - feedback to CP17/43 and final rules. https://www.fca.org.uk/publications/policy-statements/ps18-04-credit-card -market-study (last accessed 28 April 2021).
Feitsma, J. N. P. (2018). The behavioural state: Critical observations on technocracy and psychocracy. *Policy Sciences, 51*(3), 387–410.
Feitsma, J. (2019). Brokering behaviour change: The work of behavioural insights experts in govern-ment. *Policy & Politics, 47*(1), 37–56.

Gigerenzer, G. (2015). On the supposed evidence for libertarian paternalism. *Review of Philosophy and Psychology*, *6*(3), 361–383.

Herd, P., & Moynihan, D.P. (2018). *Administrative Burdens*. New York: Russel Sage.

Hertwig, R., & Grüne-Yanoff, T. (2017), Nudging and boosting: Steering or empowering good decisions. *Perspectives on Psychological Science*, *12*(6), 973–986.

Hood, C. (1998). *The art of the state: Culture, rhetoric, and public management*. Oxford: Oxford University Press.

Hood, C., & Rothstein, H. (2001). Risk regulation under pressure: problem solving or blame shifting? *Administration & Society*, *33*(1): 21–53.

Hummel, D., & Maedche, A. (2019). How effective is nudging? A quantitative review on the effect sizes and limits of empirical nudging studies. *Journal of Behavioral and Experimental Economics*, *80*, 47–58.

Jilke, S., Van Ryzin, G. G., & Van de Walle, S. (2016). Responses to decline in marketized public services: An experimental evaluation of choice overload. *Journal of Public Administration Research and Theory*, *26*(3), 421–432.

John, P. (2018). *How far to nudge*. Cheltenham, UK and Northampton, MA, USA: Edward Elgar Publishing.

John, P. (2014). Policy entrepreneurship in UK central government: The behavioural insights team and the use of randomized controlled trials. *Public Policy and Administration*, *29*(3), 257–267.

John, P., Smith, G., & Stoker, G. (2009). Nudge nudge, think think: Two strategies for changing civic behaviour. *The Political Quarterly*, *80*(3), 361–370.

Kahneman, D. (2011). *Thinking, fast and slow*. New York, NY: Farrar, Straus and Giroux.

Kahneman, D. (2003). Maps of bounded rationality: Psychology for behavioral economics. *American Economic Review*, *93*(5), 1449–1475.

Koop, C., & Lodge, M. (2020) 'British economic regulators in an age of politicisation: From the responsible to the responsive regulatory state?' *Journal of European Public Policy*, *27*(11), 1612–1635.

Le Grand, J., & New, B. (2015). *Government paternalism: Nanny state or helpful friend?*. Princeton: Princeton University Press.

Littlechild, S. (2012). Want a simpler energy deal? You'll need some bottle. EPRG Group. https://www.eprg.group.cam.ac.uk/wp-content/uploads/2013/10/Times-9-Nov-2012-Want-a-simpler-energy-deal.pdf (last accessed 27 April 2012).

Lodge, M. (2016). Regulation scholarship in crisis. *Centre for Analysis of Risk and Regulation Discussion Paper Series*, (84), 1–7.

Lodge, M. (2005). The importance of being modern: international benchmarking and national regulatory innovation. *Journal of European Public Policy*, *12*(4), 649–667

Lodge, M., & Wegrich, K. (2016). The rationality paradox of nudge: Rational tools of government in a world of bounded rationality. *Law & Policy*, *38*(3), 250–267.

Lodge, M., & Wegrich, K. (2012). *Managing regulation*. London: Palgrave.

Mukherjee, I., & Giest, S. (2020). Behavioural Insights Teams (BITs) and policy change: An exploration of Impact, location, and temporality of policy advice. *Administration & Society*, *52*(10), 1538–1561.

Myers, G, (2019). Behavioural interventions and iterative policy-making. In: *Risk & Regulation*, *37* (Summer 2019): 21–22 https://www.lse.ac.uk/accounting/assets/CARR/documents/R-R/2019-Summer/190701-riskregulation-06.pdf (last accessed: 27 April 2021).

OECD (2017). *Behavioral insights and public policy. Lessons from around the world*. Paris: OECD.

Ofcom (2017). Annex 6. Various empirical studies. Consultation on Mobile Call Termination. https://www.ofcom.org.uk/__data/assets/pdf_file/0032/46589/annex6.pdf (last accessed 27 April 2021).

Ofgem (2012). The retail market review. Updated domestic proposals, 26 October 2012. https://www.ofgem.gov.uk/ofgem-publications/39457/retail-market-review-updated-domestic-proposals.pdf (last accessed 27 April 2021).

Ofgem. (2016). Letter to Roger Witcomb, Competition & Markets Authority, 3 August 2016. https://www.ofgem.gov.uk/ofgem-publications/102095 (last accessed 27 April 2021).

Ofgem (2019). Insights from Ofgem's consumer engagement trials: What works in increasing engagement in energy tariff choices? https://www.ofgem.gov.uk/ofgem-publications/156422 (last accessed 28 April 2021).

Oliver, A. (2015). Nudging, shoving, and budging: Behavioural economic-informed policy. *Public Administration*, 93(3), 700–714.

Parker Aranha, C. (2019). Accommodation booking sites: How to comply with consumer law. Blog. Competition and Market Authority, 26 February 2019. https://competitionandmarkets.blog.gov .uk/2019/02/26/accommodation-booking-sites-how-to-comply-with-consumer-law/ (last accessed 27 April 2021).

Rahman, K. S., & Thelen, K. (2019). The rise of the platform business model and the transformation of twenty-first-century capitalism. *Politics & Society*, 47(2), 177–204.

Rochet, J.C., & Tirole, J. (2006). Two-sided markets: A progress report. *RAND Journal of Economics*, 37, 645–667.

Schiff, A. (2008). The waterbed effect and price regulation. *Review of Network Economics*, 7(3), 392–414.

Schmidt, A. T., & Engelen, B. (2020). The ethics of nudging: An overview. *Philosophy Compass*, 15(4), e12658.

Self, P. (1975). *Econocrats & the policy process: The politics & philosophy of cost–benefit analysis*. London: Macmillan.

Sieber, S. (1981). *Fatal remedies: The ironies of social intervention*. New York: Plenum.

Simon, H. A. (1945). *Administrative behavior: A study of decision-making processes in administrative organization*. New York: Free Press.

Strassheim, H. (2021). Who are behavioural public policy experts and how are they organised globally?. *Policy & Politics*, 49(1), 69–86.

Sunstein, C. R. (2020). Sludge audits. *Behavioural Public Policy*, 1–20.

Sunstein, C. R. (2016). *The ethics of influence: Government in the age of behavioral science*. New York: Cambridge University Press.

Sunstein, C. R. (2014). *Why nudge?: The politics of libertarian paternalism*. New Haven: Yale University Press.

Thaler, R. H., & Sunstein, C. R. (2008). *Nudge: Improving decisions about health, wealth, and happiness*. New Haven: Yale University Press.

The Times. (2012). Cheaper energy but savvy switchers will lose out, 2 November 2012. https://www .thetimes.co.uk/article/cheaper-energy-but-savvy-switchers-will-lose-out-3ts3g5xwd6b (last access 27 April 2012).

Tor, A. (2020). Nudges that should fail?. *Behavioural Public Policy*, 4(3), 316–342.

Tversky, A., & Kahneman, D. (1974). Judgment under uncertainty: Heuristics and biases. *Science* 185, 1124–1131.

White, M. (2013). *The manipulation of choice: Ethics and libertarian paternalism*. Basingstoke: Palgrave Macmillan.

Wildavsky, A. (1979). *The art and craft of policy analysis*. London: Macmillan.

31. AI algorithmic oversight: new frontiers in regulation

Madalina Busuioc[1]

INTRODUCTION

The rise of artificial intelligence (AI) is transforming our societies, permeating an ever-expanding array of domains ranging from finance, to employment or healthcare. AI is prognosticated to be a key driver of economic growth in years to come (European Commission 2018). Importantly, the reliance on the technology is also increasingly spilling over from private into public domains. AI is becoming a "game changer" for public bureaucracies and our public institutions, with public power increasingly exercised algorithmically. Public regulators, among others, increasingly rely on machine learning techniques in the discharge of regulatory tasks (Yeung 2018; Yeung & Lodge 2019) – for instance, in prioritising regulatory targets for regulatory attention and/or enforcement, in areas as varied as environmental protection, securities or food safety. Algorithmic enforcement tools are being relied upon by public regulators, among others, to identify misconduct, to detect fraud in reporting, to prioritise sites or regulatees for inspection, in an effort to optimise the use of limited resources at their disposal (Engstrom et al. 2020; Coglianese & Lehr 2017). But the use of AI in government stretches well beyond the field of regulation, making significant inroads into the coercive and (re)distributive powers of the state itself (Pasquale 2011; Engstrom et al. 2020). Algorithmic outputs are used by police to predict crime in the context of predictive policing technologies; for teacher appraisals and to inform school reforms; and by public authorities to allocate grants, entitlements and benefits (AI Now Institute 2018; Eubanks 2018; Ferguson 2017; Veale & Brass 2019; Young, Bullock & Lecy 2019; Busuioc 2021; Calo & Citron 2021). A recent study in the US context, mapping the use of AI by federal agencies (Engstrom et al. 2020), finds that half of all agencies canvassed have experimented with the use of artificial intelligence, testimony to the ubiquity of AI tools in the public sector.

While these developments, when adequately harnessed, undeniably come with exciting and significant promise, AI deployment simultaneously requires careful consideration. The consequences thereof, when gone awry, can be serious especially so when relied upon in high-stakes decision-making scenarios. For instance, the reliance in enforcement by tax authorities in the Netherlands on an AI algorithmic system resulted in state-sanctioned discrimination. The "learning algorithm", deployed by tax authorities as a decisional aid in benefits assessment decisions, used nationality as a predictive feature, with ensuing bureaucratic decisions amounting to structural discrimination (Dutch Data Protection Authority 2020; Parlementaire Ondervragingscommissie Kinderopvangtoeslag 2020). The scandal ('toeslagenaffaire') disproportionately affected citizens with a migration background, with mostly dual nationality families wrongly accused of fraud, and having to repay as much as tens of thousands of euros. Acute financial pressures, resulting bankruptcies, lasting mental health issues and broken families were among the costs borne by wrongly accused citizens (Geiger 2021). The scandal led to the fall of the Dutch government in early 2021 and is an illustrative example of the serious real-life implications that can arise from the reliance on under-performing, unvetted algorithmic systems.

Similar problems arise in a variety of other key areas: In specific jurisdictions, predictive policing systems trained on "dirty data" have been found to replicate bias embedded in training data sets, sending police to the same overpoliced neighbourhoods (Richardson, Schultz & Crawford 2019; Ferguson 2017, 2020), effectively automating historical bias and discrimination. Failures of facial recognition systems to accurately identify minorities and darker skinned people (Buolamwini & Gebru 2018; Medium 2019) are by now well-documented and become ever more problematic when such systems are relied upon in law enforcement or in education for instance, for student proctoring. These examples underscore the crucial relevance of meaningful checks and safeguards on AI development and deployment, especially given the transformative power of AI technologies and the often high-stakes nature of their deployment in both public and private contexts (O'Neil 2016; Ferguson 2017; Eubanks 2018). The current chapter highlights some important challenges for regulation in this area, brought on by the specificities of artificial intelligence technologies. It explores the potential advantages and disadvantages of different modes of intervention in governing the development and deployment of artificial intelligence systems. Simultaneously, it sets out to flag critical aspects for consideration by regulators in this respect, speaking also to recent draft regulatory efforts in the EU.

CHALLENGES FOR REGULATORY OVERSIGHT: INFORMATION IMBALANCES COMPOUNDED

While the need for oversight in this context is pressing, artificial intelligence systems raise important challenges of regulation as well as difficult challenges as to how to devise legal rules that can keep-up with agile technological developments and intelligent learning systems. The speed of change in this area is unprecedented: much of the technological advances we are seeing have taken place over the past decade, galvanised by the pace of digitalisation and growth in computing power. The greater availability of data and rise in computing power have allowed for the training of ever larger neural nets, leading to the leaps in AI performance we are currently witnessing across fields from computer vision to natural language processing (NLP). Beyond the head-spinning pace of innovation in this area, challenges of regulation become especially emphasised given technological specificities of these systems.

Artificial intelligence essentially refers to a set of tools that display (or can even surpass) human-level performance on given tasks traditionally associated with human intelligence. The biggest subset of AI is machine learning (ML). ML algorithms learn from data – they derive (and modify) the rules that govern their behaviour – essentially how to classify new, yet-unseen inputs from seeing lots and lots of examples. The patterns are discovered by the machine, linking inputs to outputs. By churning through large amounts of data, the algorithm learns relevant features that contribute to the particular outcome, identifying patterns that often escape the human mind.

This is a key ingredient to the success of such algorithms but is also simultaneously behind some of the recurrent failings pertaining to issues of bias we are seeing across social domains. Precisely because such algorithms are so good at discovering patterns, they can at the same time insidiously learn unwanted patterns present in the data: for instance, systemic (historical) biases embedded in training datasets, or overt as well as subtle biases embedded in human language patterns (Bender et al. 2021). Algorithms can thus come to propagate and automate human bias, disparities, and discrimination. And in this context, these behaviours, now encoded in mathematical code, can be especially difficult to spot and correct, given algorithm architectural complexity, the sheer size of the parameter space and the complexity of feature interactions.

While this will vary depending on the respective algorithm, machine learning models such as neural networks (or "deep learning") can be extremely complex in their operation: hundreds of layers deep, thousands of features and millions (and even billions) of weights that contribute to one predictive outcome (Busuioc 2021). The inbuilt ability of such algorithms to learn on their own and associated opacity constitute a *distinctive informational problem* that differentiates them from both earlier algorithmic counterparts relied upon in the past as well as from *traditional forms of expertise*, where experts, when asked, can articulate the reasons behind their decisions and recommendations.

These specificities of complex AI algorithms – opaqueness and convoluted decisional pathways – raise the prospect that they can compound bias when relied upon in social domains, demanding pressing regulatory attention. While some commentators have argued that algorithmic biases are at least preferable to human bias – algorithmic bias will be easier, the argument goes, to spot and/or correct through technical interventions compared to debiasing humans, such claims are at best tenuous. While we know how to deal with "old-fashioned" human bias as exemplified by a biased judge or bureaucrat – requirements of transparency, reason-giving, opportunities for appeal and so on are precisely in place to prevent arbitrary, capricious decision-making – by contrast, with algorithmic decision-making, these same biases are now obscured in layers of code. Human bias gets re-packaged in complex layers of mathematical code and computations, and gains the facade of objectivity, rendering it particularly difficult (not less so) to spot and challenge – especially in the case of complex, black-box algorithms.

And while algorithms are trained, tested and validated – as such, in principle creating technical opportunities to spot and "fix" bias – biases arising in implementation in real-life deployment will be especially hard to diagnose for systems used for predictive purposes in social circumstances (e.g. to predict fraud, crime, recidivism). In such cases, the "ground truth" (e.g. whether someone is a future criminal or not) is *unknown* or *as-of-yet-undetermined*. This is fundamentally different from cases where the ground truth is *known* (or verifiable by other means) such as image recognition (this is the correct label or not) or medical diagnosis (the disease is present or not). Cases where the ground truth is known allow us to establish, when challenged, if the algorithm is demonstrably erroneous in real-life implementation. By contrast, a black-box algorithmic model for recidivism that is validated as having high accuracy, and performs well on training and testing data, could still make a lot of errors in real-life circumstances if predicting on cases that are very different from what it was trained on, yet these cases will be hard to identify and prove as such. With the ground truth unknown (and the counter-factual lacking), failures will likely only be spotted much too late, when systemic level evidence reveals an accumulation of negative predictions disproportionately affecting members of specific groups.

The traditional information asymmetries characteristic of any supervisory system become compounded in the case of AI not only due to the speed of technological pace but also by virtue of the opaqueness and technical complexity of models driving current innovation, and current applications in high-stakes social domains. What is more, given resources and capacity shortages in the public sector – with efficiency savings themselves often driving the wide adoption of AI in the public sector – public regulators stand to find themselves at unprecedented knowledge and computational (model and data) literacy disadvantages.

WHY INDUSTRY REGULATION IS NOT A VIABLE ALTERNATIVE

In this context, industry self-regulation has been purported as a possible alternative – "a retreat from regulation", "drawing us away from law, or even traditional models of command and control or co-regulation and governance, towards soft self-regulation and codes of practice" (Black & Murray 2019, p. 6). After all, an important selling point of self- and co-regulatory modes is the fact that they can harness expertise and resource advantages held by private actors (Baldwin, Cave & Lodge 2012). A growing flurry of private sector regulatory initiatives have emerged ranging from the set-up of industry self-regulation and oversight boards, ethics bodies and other industry-initiated entities that produce best practice guidelines as well as the rise of public-private networks and partnerships in the field of AI. National strategies on leveraging AI for innovation centre on multi-actor collaborations and institutionalise partnerships between public and private actors, research institutes and users in areas ranging from healthcare to smart cities (Mikhaylov, Esteve & Campion 2018), while industry and non-industry collaborations increasingly play a role in the adoption of guidelines and best practices on AI (e.g. the Partnership on AI).

For all its advantages, the shortcomings of self-regulatory approaches however, are well-established and are best summarised by "the motivation problem": even when industry actors have superior information and expertise advantages to devise regulatory solutions, they do not necessarily have the incentives to do so – to self-regulate in ways consistent with public regulatory goals rather than with their own private individual interests (Baldwin, Cave & Lodge 2012; Lodge & Wegrich 2012). Propitious circumstances can serve to align private actors' interests with public goals but these are unlikely to be present in the context of AI.

In principle, "[a]ny industry shares some degree of collective interest in ensuring that each member of the industry acts responsibly lest the irresponsibility of one company lead to draconian regulatory costs placed on the others" (Coglianese & Medelson 2010, p. 160). Visible failures, crises and disasters, even when linked to abuse or negligence by specific actors, can take a toll on an industry as a whole: "[A]n unfortunate event can be thought of as analogous to a stone dropped in a pond. The ripples spread outward, encompassing first the directly affected victims, then the responsible company or agency, and, in the extreme, reaching other companies, agencies and industries" (Slovic 1987, p. 283) – think for instance, of the impact of the Fukushima disaster for the nuclear power industry or of the financial crisis for the financial sector (and even for regulators). Failures can thus have spill-over effects beyond the direct impact and can cause secondary and tertiary impacts that extract large costs from an industry such as: negative market impacts, public opposition, investor flight or demands for alternative technologies (ibid.). The anticipation of such repercussions is then expected to have a pre-emptive, restraining effect on unruly corporate behaviour. These inter-dependencies in regulation can in theory be harnessed for effective self-regulation: The desire to ward off such impacts and to avoid stricter public regulation could act as a powerful industry motivator towards self-regulation, stimulating an alignment between corporate and social goals.

The success of self-regulatory efforts however, depends on the presence of a precarious combination of auspicious conditions ranging from the presence of effective monitoring mechanisms, governmental threats and incentives, non-governmental pressures and so on (Baldwin, Cave & Lodge 2012). The characteristics of the regulated industry, too, shape incentives to self-regulate in important ways: small, homogeneous industries are said to be characterised by tighter interdependencies and as such, to share more of a common interest to meaningfully self-regulate, rendering it easier to rein in "rogue" firms acting in bad faith (Coglianese & Mendelson 2010). By contrast, firms in large, heterogenous industries will have difficulties to convincingly self-regulate and temper unruly corporate behaviour (ibid.).

In this respect, AI is a heterogeneous field characterised by the presence of big market actors but also a myriad of small-scale vendors (see for instance, facial recognition or predictive policing). While large firms, by virtue of their public visibility, will face some level of public pressures and reputational pushback from consumers, stakeholders or employees on bad practices, such pressures will be absent for smaller, less visible, vendors. At the same time, while large corporate actors are more sensitive to their corporate image, they, too, severely lack incentives to meaningfully self-regulate, given that this area, in addition to the tremendous profits at stake, strikes at the heart of Big Tech business models and firm competitiveness. Reputational concerns, rather, lead to symbolic efforts: "ethics washing" (Black & Murray 2019) and other such performative action, aimed at propping up corporate images and getting ahead of public regulatory efforts:

> As the industry's feeding frenzy on machine learning has gathered pace, so too has the proliferation of ethics boards, panels and oversight bodies established by the same companies. (…) The result is a kind of ethics theatre akin to the security theatre enacted in airports in the years when people were actually permitted to fly. And the reason this farcical charade goes on is that tech companies see it as a pre-emptive strike to ward off what they really fear – regulation by law. (Naughton 2021)

The discrepancy between corporate "talk" and action in this area could not be more evident: Google's AI ethics board lasted less than a week before disbanding following backlash over its composition; Amazon has been publicly calling for the regulation of facial recognition (and even adopted rules for responsible use thereof for policy-makers to consider), while at the same time selling its facial recognition system (Rekognition) to law enforcement departments throughout the US despite serious and well-documented issues of racial bias with the technology (Raji & Buolamwini 2019; Snow 2018; Medium 2019), and extensive pushback from shareholders, employees, researchers and civil advocacy groups alike. More recently, Google fired the co-leads of its AI ethics team, two prominent AI researchers ("Google had now fully decapitated its own Ethical AI research group", Wired 2021, p. 117) in connection with a critical paper they co-authored. The paper, which Google tried to have retracted, raised significant concerns about the risks of large language models – core to the company's business model and key to its competitive advantage. The scandal more broadly, also raised serious questions about industry research on AI ethics as well as on the pressing need for disclosure of corporate funding for academic research in this area (ibid.).

These examples speak to a serious misalignment that can arise between corporate and public interest goals and highlight the dangers of excessive trust in self-regulatory efforts as a substitute for public regulation in this area. Industry abuses abound: from predictive policing systems built on "dirty data" (Richardson, Schultz & Crawford 2019), to biased models in criminal justice, welfare or education (see O'Neil 2016; Eubanks 2018; Rudin 2019;

Broussard 2020), underscoring the pressing need for public regulation in this area: "the stakes are too high, the harms too widespread, the incentives too enticing, for the public to accept the tech industry's attempts at self-regulation" (Benjamin 2019, p. 15).

THE NEED FOR PUBLIC REGULATION: SOME KEY INGREDIENTS

Industry efforts thus cannot convincingly substitute for formal commands and public regulation of artificial intelligence. Regulatory efforts however, have significantly fallen behind practice. Powerful technologies have been deployed in a vacuum of regulation with little oversight. Significant gaps in oversight have emerged also when the user is the government itself: for instance, a recent report by the Netherlands Court of Audit revealed that while the Dutch government makes widespread use of algorithms, ministries lack overview of algorithm use under their purview (Netherlands Court of Audit 2020). Deficits in oversight range from systemic overview to system functioning: "in many cases no action is taken to limit ethical risks such as biases in the selected data" (ibid., p. 31). Governmental actors have been less than diligent users of AI: London Metropolitan Police originally trialled its facial recognition system in 2017 without any checks for racial bias (Margetts & Dorobantu 2019). An academic study by the University of Essex into the use of the facial recognition by the force across six trials found that four out of five people (81%) were wrongly flagged by the system as potential suspects (Fussey & Murray 2019). There is thus an important role to play for public regulation both *outside* and *within* government.

A critical element to public regulatory interventions in this area will be, first and foremost, to mitigate the considerable *information challenges* at stake through standard-setting aimed at redressing informational shortcomings. If regulators are to keep up with technological developments, adequately regulate AI systems to address risk and enforce rule compliance, the first step will be to attempt to reduce the considerable information disadvantage they find themselves at. These pertain to information challenges stemming both from the reliance on specific AI technologies (that are especially opaque in their operation and as such, limit opportunities for oversight) as well as those arising vis-à-vis private providers in this context.

With respect to the former aspect, what we are increasingly seeing is that AI models deployed, also in high-stakes scenarios, are "black-boxes" (Pasquale 2015), be it in a technical sense, or in a legal or proprietary sense (Rudin 2019). *Technical black-boxes* refers to models such as neural networks (or deep learning) currently driving the technological revolution in AI. By virtue of their ability to challenge human comprehension, black-box models have been flagged as the genuine "wicked problems" when it comes to algorithmic risks and the regulation of AI technologies (Andrews 2019). Such models "do not explain their predictions in a way that humans can understand" (Rudin 2019, p. 206). In other words, we do not know (and also model developers do not know) what *causes* specific outputs. The path of computations leading to a decision is opaque, rendering it especially difficult to spot when such models misperform – for developers, users and regulators alike. Given their technical complexity, such models are also considerably harder to debug or investigate for bias compared to "inherently interpretable" AI models of equivalent performance (i.e. simpler and transparent AI algorithms), computer scientists note: "It can be much easier to detect and debate possible bias or unfairness with an interpretable model than with a black box. (…) an overly complicated black box model may be flawed but we do not know it, because it is difficult to troubleshoot" (Rudin 2019, p. 208).

This becomes especially problematic when such models are applied for predictive purposes in high-stakes social circumstances (i.e. predictive policing, criminal justice) – where the ground truth is unknown and the counter-factual lacking, as noted above. Compare this situation with your classic AI image classifier example: classifying photos of "cat"/ "non-cat" – where the ground truth is directly known, evident or observable. By contrast, AI model failures (such as flawed risk predictions due to bias) arising in real-life deployments, say, of a black-box recidivism algorithm will not be directly evident: the ground truth – whether someone will actually recidivate or not – is unknown/as-of-yet undetermined, and a complicated decisional pathway will further obscure error. This highlights the need for prioritising simpler ML models in their stead – where it is directly evident (and open to investigation) how the different variables interact to produce specific outputs, if algorithms are relied upon in such high-stakes scenarios.

Relatedly, and important to highlight in this context, the reliance on technical black-box models removes opportunities for meaningful human oversight. Human-mediated decision-making (keeping humans in the decisional loop) is one of the key checks on algorithmic decision-making (see EU GDPR). To the extent that models relied upon are technical black-boxes, where decisional pathways are inscrutable, human decision-makers will not be able to act as effective decisional mediators. Human oversight then risks becoming an exercise in "rubberstamping", where effectively the human mediator has little insight into system functioning (or malfunctioning), depriving it of meaningful control. Relatedly, this also speaks to broader concerns that have been raised with the risk of "automation bias" (Parasuraman & Riley 1997; Skitka, Mosier & Burdick 1999, 2000) – the prospect that AI algorithms could give rise to undue deference or overreliance in decision-making (see Edwards & Veale 2017; Peeters 2020; Finck 2020; Busuioc 2021; Calo & Citron 2021) – as well as more broadly, concerns raised as to the understudied effects that AI inputs actually have on bureaucratic decision-makers and human agents, especially so when relied upon in high-stakes administrative and regulatory contexts (see further, Alon-Barkat & Busuioc 2022).

Simultaneously, exacerbating information challenges even further, in addition to the growing popularity of *technical black-boxes*, routinely so-called *legal black-boxes* are being deployed, that is, proprietary corporate models, subject to trade secret protections and therefore shaded from scrutiny. These models, too, are black-boxes because here too, as with technically complex models, the logic behind decisions is inscrutable. Examples abound, also in high-stakes public sector decision-making: The System Risk Indication or "SyRI", an algorithm used in the Netherlands to assess fraud, and which was disproportionately applied in disadvantaged neighbourhoods, was a secret algorithm – with its basic functioning undisclosed even to the court during proceedings. The algorithm was struck down by the court, among others, due to transparency concerns.[2] The COMPAS algorithm, used in the US in criminal justice (for bailing and sentencing), infamously flagged by *ProPublica* for "machine bias" (Angwin et al. 2016) is a proprietary third-party system, still in use. While not an ML model, the algorithm is a "black-box" by virtue of its proprietary nature. Despite being used in a highly consequential public domain, COMPAS is subject to trade secret protections precluding an assessment of the extent to which it may be unfair: "COMPAS may still be biased, but we can't tell" (Corbett-Davies et al. 2016). The example is indicative of a broader trend where public sector actors rely on algorithmic systems managed by external suppliers to implement consequential public tasks, often subject to secrecy provisions as to the algorithmic systems' set-up and functioning. In doing so, public bodies are effectively abdicating consequential public tasks to private providers with little or no oversight of system functioning (see Finck 2020; Busuioc 2021).

Reliance on proprietary models entails that algorithm set-up, methodology and functioning will remain undisclosed to the public bodies, to those adversely affected by decisions informed by it and/or to citizens, exacerbating information asymmetries vis-à-vis private providers and removing opportunities for meaningful oversight. Computer science scholars (see Rudin 2019) have demonstrated that non-proprietary alternatives of equivalent performance exist and/or can be developed for many high-stakes applications: for instance, simpler, transparent (ML) recidivism models (with two and respectively, three features) have been shown to perform as well as the proprietary COMPAS algorithm (Rudin 2019; Dressel & Farid 2018), which instead draws on 137 features. In other words, unduly complex black-box algorithms are being relied upon, also in high-stakes scenarios, even when inherently interpretable (and non-proprietary models) of equivalent performance exist or can be developed.[3] The absence of safeguards on this ensures that AI models are adopted which preclude scrutiny of their functioning. The reliance on such models will jeopardise meaningful information-gathering, compromising regulatory ability to exercise oversight of algorithm operation and functioning, especially problematic in high-stakes (public or private) contexts. For instance, the same report by the Netherlands Court of Audit noted the little insight public bodies have as to the quality of algorithms they rely on when these are managed by external providers:

> Ministries that have outsourced the development and management of algorithms *have only a limited knowledge of these algorithms*. (…) the *responsible minister does not have any information on the quality of the algorithm* in question nor on the documents underlying compliance with the relevant standards, and refers to the supplier instead. (p. 42, emphasis added)

Consequently, regulatory solutions that can address some of these disbalances to help *sustain* meaningful oversight are direly needed: namely, technical requirements giving preference to simpler, inherently interpretable AI models (over black-box alternatives of equivalent performance) in high-stakes domains; explanation requirements, when black-box models are shown to be necessary (significantly outperform humans and benefits outweigh costs) and interpretable models cannot be developed, with clear standards as to what such an explanation should entail coupled with open access to underlying models; and last but not least, requirements on private providers to forgo proprietary protections when selling into the public sector. This last aspect will become critical to public administrators' ability not only to exercise meaningful control of third-party systems they rely on in their decision-making but also to them being able to comply with their duty to give reasons for administrative decision-making when third-party algorithmic systems are used in this context. It will become equally critical also to any meaningful regulatory efforts to oversee such uses.

REGULATORY EFFORTS: THE EU DRAFT AI REGULATION

In the EU, public regulation initiatives are currently taking shape, in the form of an AI regulation (in draft form at the time of writing) regulating the development, placement on the market and use of artificial intelligence systems (COM(2021) 206 final, see European Commission

2021). However, despite efforts at expanding transparency in this context, the new draft regulation falls significantly short in terms of mitigating informational disbalances. The proposed regulation adopts a risk-based approach – regulating "high-risk" AI systems[4] – and has been criticised for important shortcomings, not least among these, that the regulation of the high-risk systems centres on conformity assessment with a range of essential requirements based largely on a system of internal checks, that is, self-assessment by providers (Veale & Zuiderveen Borgesius 2021; Smuha et al. 2021). As a result: "there are 'almost no situations' in which such industry AI self-assessments will require approval by an independent technical organization, and even then, such organizations are usually private sector certification firms accredited by Member States".

A post-marketing enforcement system is envisaged with each Member State to designate a competent national authority (so-called "market surveillance authorities", MSAs) from among existing regulators, rather than envisaging the set-up of specialised, purpose-specific regulators responsible for monitoring and enforcement. Such authorities are then likely to be under-specialised (given by contrast the high technical complexity of the regulatory domain), in addition to being severely understaffed and overburdened: despite the span of their enforcement responsibilities, it has been noted that the European Commission estimates "the entire enforcement of the Draft AI Act will only take between 1 and 25 extra full-time staff at Member State level" (Veale & Zuiderveen Borgesius 2021, p. 111), raising serious concerns as to regulatory capacity.

These market supervisory authorities are to rely on provider notification of incidents and malfunctioning and there is no mechanism provided for individuals adversely affected to lodge a complaint with market surveillance authorities. This is a significant omission both from an individual rights perspective – particularly important given the serious assymmetries of power at play between those affected by AI systems and organisations that develop and deploy them – but also from an accountability and regulatory perspective, as the enforcement system lacks much-needed "fire alarms" providing independent feedback on system (mal)functioning. Such a set-up exacerbates a heavy dependence on providers truthfully reporting on their model's malfunctioning and stands to exacerbate already significant informational deficits. The adoption of a self-assessment system (with compliance largely a matter of internal controls), coupled with potential severe shortcomings in enforcement and regulatory capacity suggests that the challenges highlighted above as to industry incentives to meaningfully self-constrain will become manifest.

Transparency and Human Oversight Requirements – Some Critical Shortcomings

The draft regulation's requirements on transparency – while containing some important innovations such as the creation of a EU-wide registration database for stand-alone high-risk systems – are overall ambiguous and in need of further clarification. Providers are to ensure that the operation of high-risk AI systems they develop are "sufficiently transparent" to allow for user interpretation of output and appropriate use, ensuring an "appropriate type and degree of transparency" (see Article 13 more broadly). Beyond the fact that these requirements pertain to obligations of providers towards users of AI systems rather than towards those (adversely) affected by these systems (Smuha et al. 2021), the provisions also remain overly underspecified. With conformity a matter of provider self-assessment, what exactly "sufficiently transparent" for interpretation or an "appropriate type and degree of transparency" entails, becomes a matter of provider perspective and judgement. Welcome transparency developments – such as requirements that information on input data used and other relevant information as to training, validation, test data and so on is to be provided – are watered-down by stipulations that these requirements need to be met only "when appropriate". Moreover, while providers are mandated to build high-risk AI systems for "human oversight" (see Article 14) (and the tendency for "automation bias" is explicitly mentioned in this connection), the regulation leaves the measures to be put in place to facilitate interpretation at provider discretion, and "as appropriate to the circumstances".

This will likely perpetuate *sub-optimal transparency practices* and opaque systems accompanied by poor (or incomplete) model explanations that are not faithful renditions of system functioning. The draft regulation gives leeway to providers as to the choice of technical measures to facilitate interpretation, opening the door to providers to "stack the deck" in their favour and provide little insight as to actual system functioning. For instance, explanation techniques of black-boxes that have received a lot of press – such as counterfactual explanation models[5] (Wachter, Mittelstad & Russell 2018) – can grant "unchecked power" to providers, leaving them wide open for abuse (Barocas, Selbst & Raghavan 2020). Feature-highlighting techniques such as counterfactuals allow for multiple explanations and give considerable discretion to providers to choose which features to disclose to the user: "while designed to restore power to decision subjects, partial explanations grant a new kind of power to the decision maker, to use for good or to abuse as desired" (ibid., p. 86). A multitude of explanations for the same output are possible with such techniques as "[b]y design, they do not provide an exhaustive inventory of all features the model considers" (ibid., p. 82). Such models leave a lot of leeway to the decision-maker which features to disclose in the explanation, opening up opportunities for gaming by providers to self-serving ends: "The key point here is that left to their own devices, decision makers are afforded a remarkable degree of power to pursue their own welfare through these choices" (ibid., p. 87).

Relatedly, an often overlooked aspect with respect to explanation models of black-boxes more generally (often advanced as a solution to overcoming black-box transparency problems) is that they represent "approximations" of underlying models rather than faithful renditions of their logic (Rudin 2019). Such techniques essentially interface a model that is not explainable in human terms with a post-hoc explanation model (e.g. extract a simple algorithm such as a decision tree to explain a black-box), with the explanation model often using entirely different features than the original black-box model (Ribeiro, Singh & Guestrin 2016). In other words, they are different models altogether. While post hoc explanation techniques can be valuable for designers and system engineers "as part of the knowledge discovery process" (Rudin 2019, p. 207), to obtain "forensic information" about a model's behaviour and to investigate systematic errors and biases, such models only approximate how a model arrived at its decision. As leading computer scientists have noted: "Calling these 'summaries of predictions', 'summary statistics' or 'trends' rather than 'explanations' would be less misleading (…) Explanations often do not make sense or do not provide enough detail to understand what the black box is doing" (Rudin 2019, p. 208). And reiterated: "Explainable ML methods provide explanations that are not faithful to what the original model computes. (…) This leads to the danger that any explanation model for a black box model can be an inaccurate representation of the original model" (ibid., p. 207). There is a real risk that explanations provide partial or misleading descriptions of model functioning (Rudin, Wang & Coker 2020), rendering them of limited use as tools of oversight from a legal and regulatory perspective.

These concerns are also echoed by work on "misleading explanations" showing how user trust can be manipulated through unreliable explanations: "explanations generated using existing techniques can actually *mislead* the decision maker into trusting a problematic black box" (Lakkaraju & Bastani 2020, p. 79). Recent computer science work also illustrates how explanation models can be manipulated, further speaking to the vulnerabilities and shortcomings of such methods (Slack et al. 2021). Giving preference to inherently interpretable ML models instead – simpler ML models of equal performance that are transparent from the outset and where it is clear how the variables are jointly related – would allow to bypass critical transparency concerns raised by black-box models and post-hoc explanation models thereof (see Rudin 2019).

Given drawbacks of various techniques for unpacking black-box models, leaving the technical measures to be put in place to afford interpretation and human oversight up to the providers of AI systems, as the draft regulation does, is highly problematic. If model functioning is not actually transparent, diagnosing failure becomes next to impossible. For instance, the draft regulation explicitly envisages a role for users in flagging system risks and mis-performance: Users of AI systems are to monitor and play a key role in flagging malfunctioning systems to providers. If transparency standards adopted by providers fall short, users will not be able to exercise these monitoring roles. The absence of robust legal standards as to what measures are required to afford meaningful interpretation of system outputs is a serious shortcoming that will detract from effective regulatory action in this area.

Leaving these crucial aspects at provider discretion is especially problematic given the current state of knowledge and uncertainty in this area. The influence that AI algorithms have on human decision-makers is poorly understood, and various studies have raised the prospect that human overseers (decisional mediators) could be prone to important cognitive biases in this respect such as "automation bias", as discussed above. Recent research raises the prospect of *additional cognitive biases* that can arise in human processing of AI algorithmic outputs: for instance, that human decision-makers are inclined to give more weight and defer to algorithmic recommendations that align with decision-makers' worldviews, with what they already believe to be true that is, when predictions conform with pre-existing beliefs and stereotypes (Alon-Barkat & Busuioc 2022). This could invertedly lead them to make decisions that are harmful and can compound (rather than mitigate) bias. In a recent empirical study on the use of AI algorithms as decisional aides, Alon-Barkat & Busuioc (2022), diagnose a tendency among human decision-makers to follow AI algorithmic advice *selectively*, in a biased manner, when this advice matches pre-existing stereotypical beliefs of decision subjects. Namely, decision-makers adhere to the algorithmic advice (rather than resist it) precisely when predictions are aligned with prevalent societal stereotypes. These experimental findings are consistent with patterns observed in real-life settings for example, in the Dutch childcare benefits scandal, mentioned above, ethnic minority citizens (of Moroccan, Turkish and Dutch Antilles origin) were disproportionately impacted (*Financial Times* 2021): erroneous algorithmic predictions aligned with prevalent stereotypes, with bureaucratic decision-makers unlikely to override such predictions (see further Alon-Barkat & Busuioc 2022).

These patterns belie the "promise of neutrality" that has propelled the use of AI in the public sector, as a way to overcome human biases and limitations, and speak to important implicit biases and blindspots in our ability to oversee and diagnose malfunctioning AI systems. These patterns also correspond to findings from studies on the use of algorithmic risk scores in pre-trial criminal justice decisions in the US context, which similarly find patterns of "disparate interactions" indicative of biased processing of algorithmic advice (Green & Chen 2019a, 2019b; see also Stevenson 2018). Broad requirements to build AI for "human oversight" brush over these knotty, yet critical issues. A much deeper understanding of our (cognitive) limits in overseeing AI is required, including investigations as to effective debiasing interventions, and what effective human oversight measures might look like – before we can take comfort in human oversight being the effective safeguard we need it to be in this context.

CONCLUSION AND WAYS FORWARD

As AI permeates our public and private lives, including highly consequential aspects thereof, regulation becomes critical to ensure we can take full advantage of the promise of artificial intelligence technologies, while managing the risks associated with these technologies' deployment and ensure responsible use. The present chapter highlighted some of the unique regulatory challenges posed by artificial intelligence and reflected on some of the advantages and disadvantages of different modes of intervention. On this basis, we highlight the critical need for *public* regulation in this area and flag the need to redress information asymmetries as a key ingredient to effective regulatory interventions. In this regard, we highlight in particular: the need to move away from black-box models in high-stakes decision-making, and to adopt clear standards to give preference to inherently interpretable ML models in high-stakes decision-making (see further Rudin 2019), and for unambiguous explanation requirements in cases where black-boxes are demonstrably necessary (outperform humans and benefits outweigh risks) and interpretable models cannot be developed – coupled with the disclosure of underlying black-box models.

Critical to addressing informational disbalances is also that regulators, on a par with other professions undergoing similar transformations, expand their expertise skillset into machine learning and computational methods. Computational journalists are already playing an important part for instance, in auditing and reverse engineering algorithms to investigate issues of bias from models in criminal justice (e.g. ProPublica, Angwin et al. 2016) to the operation of Facebook's personalisation algorithms (e.g. The Markup, Mattu et al. 2021), acting as critical fire alarms in this respect. Regulators, too, will need to "roll up their sleeves" and "sink their teeth" into complex technical details (from algorithm operation, explanation techniques to work on fairness) if they are to keep up with, and meaningfully oversee, a technology that is advancing in leaps and bounds. For all its promise, at the same time, the deployment of unvetted, sub-optimal AI systems can compound, replicate and automate bias in social domains as recent scandals (such as the Dutch childcare benefits scandal) acutely illustrate, and requires pressing regulatory attention. There is a real risk that, in the absence of adequate regulation, digital encounters will increase "administrative burdens" (Herd & Moynihan 2019), and amplify discrimination for minority groups and already disadvantaged and vulnerable citizens (Alon-Barkat & Busuioc 2022; Cobbe 2020; Ranchordas 2022).

Relatedly, a critical aspect in particular with respect to which we need to remedy our knowledge deficits in this context pertains to human-AI interactions – that is, to better understanding the influence that artificial intelligence algorithms have on human decision-makers, and the biases that might arise in this interaction. This becomes especially salient as human intervention is one of the key checks we have on algorithmic failures. Having a human decision-maker in-the-loop is rightfully seen as a much-needed check on algorithmic inaccuracies and issues of bias – in this context therefore, understanding how human overseers interact with AI, and where our cognitive limits may fail us as effective overseers, becomes critical and pertains directly to the effectiveness of our existing safeguards. Recent empirical work (Alon-Barkat & Busuioc 2022) finds that human decision-makers are not always effective decisional mediators in this context, a concern that becomes especially problematic when algorithmic bias meets human bias. These findings speak to the pressing relevance of investigating human-AI interactions in administrative and regulatory contexts – we need to first better understand our inherent limitations vis-à-vis AI to be able to devise effective oversight measures thereof.

More broadly, of high relevance in relation to redressing information and knowledge deficits in this area, is also the need for *independent* research to flagging ongoing risks – especially so given the high level of uncertainty surrounding the technology and its impact. Yet, much AI ethics, bias and fairness research is inhouse to the industry or industry-funded, and increasingly, public research councils, too, are pushing for industry collaborations as a criterion for academic research funding. This places independent research on these aspects in serious jeopardy, with industry as gatekeepers on critical research on the technology's downsides. Given strong incentives running the opposite direction, this will impair the production of critical knowledge as to the negative social impacts of the technology's use.

Information is the lifeblood of regulation (Coglianese, Zeckhauser & Parson 2004) and this is no less true in this context. Yet, information disadvantages in this area, as we have seen, loom especially large. Public regulators have a key role to play in this area in opening up the information valves – this will become a crucial pre-requisite to any meaningful regulatory efforts in this area. Alternatively, regulatory oversight in the age of automation risks becoming a rudimentary facsimile of itself, with dire implications for our collective rights as citizens and for the health of our public institutions. This calls for critical involvement and active stewardship of this process from regulation scholars and practitioners alike.

NOTES

1.   This is an open access work distributed under the Creative Commons Attribution-NonCommercial-NoDerivatives 4.0 Unported (https://creativecommons.org/licenses/by-nc-nd/4.0/). Users can redistribute the work for non-commercial purposes, as long as it is passed along unchanged and in whole, as detailed in the License. Edward Elgar Publishing Ltd must be clearly credited as the rights holder for publication of the original work. Any translation or adaptation of the original content requires the written authorisation of Edward Elgar Publishing Ltd. This book chapter is part of a project that has received funding from the European Research Council (ERC) under the European Union's Horizon 2020 research and innovation programme (grant agreement 716439).
2.   Rb (District Court) Den Haag 5 February 2020, ECLI:NL:RBDHA:2020:865.
3.   While justifications put forward by private providers pertain to intellectual property protections and risks of gaming, it has been pointed out that overly complex proprietary models are instead preferred and purposefully developed by providers as they are lucrative, while simpler, transparent alternatives of equivalent performance are harder to monetise (see Rudin 2019, 210). Gaming, too, is not a convincing concern e.g. many characteristics cannot actually be gamed but are rather immutable (gender, past record, family history etc.). It is rather systems based on poor proxies that are more likely to give rise to gaming e.g. measuring water usage as an indicator of welfare benefits fraud (system precursor of the SyRI welfare fraud system in the Netherlands). See: CHRGJ NYU School of Law (2019).
4.   The draft regulation prohibits AI systems posing "unacceptable risk" (subject to exceptions) and focuses on regulating "high-risk" systems, while imposing some specific transparency requirements on those posing "limited risk", and leaving "minimal risk" systems – "the vast majority of AI

systems", according to the European Commission (Press Release 2021) – virtually untouched. For an overview of the draft regulation, see e.g. Smuha et al. 2021; Veale & Zuiderveen Borgesius 2021.
5.   Counterfactual explanation techniques highlight the least amount of input required to change the output to result in a prediction in the opposite prediction. Essentially, they identify "features that, if minimally changed, would alter the output of the model" (Barocas et al. 2020, p. 81).

REFERENCES

AI Now Institute (2018) Automated Decision Systems: Examples of Government Use Cases". https://ainowinstitute.org/nycadschart.pdf.

Alon-Barkat, Saar and Madalina Busuioc (2022) "Human–AI Interactions in Public Sector Decision-Making: 'Automation Bias' and 'Selective Adherence' to Algorithmic Advice" *Journal of Public Administration Research and Theory*. https://doi.org/10.1093/jopart/muac007.

Andrews, Leighton (2019) "Public Administration, Public Leadership and the Construction of Public Value in the Age of the Algorithm and 'Big Data'" *Public Administration* 97 (2): 296–310.

Angwin, Julia, Jeff Larson, Surya Mattu and Lauren Kirchner (2016) "Machine Bias" ProPublica, 23 May. https://www.propublica.org/article/machine-bias-risk-assessments-in-criminal-sentencing.

Baldwin, Robert, Martin Cave and Martin Lodge (2012) *Understanding Regulation: Theory, Strategy and Practice*. Oxford: Oxford University Press.

Barocas, Solon, Andrew D. Selbst and Manish Raghavan (2020) "The Hidden Assumptions behind Counterfactual Explanations and Principal Reasons" FAT* '20, 27–30 January 2020, Barcelona. https://doi.org/10.1145/3351095.3372830.

Bender, Emily M., Timnit Gebru, Angelina McMillan-Major, and Shmargaret Shmitchell. (2021) "On the Dangers of Stochastic Parrots: Can Language Models Be Too Big?" In Conference on Fairness, Accountability, and Transparency (FAccT '21), 3–10 March 2021. https://doi.org/10.1145/3442188.3445922.

Benjamin, Ruha (2019) *Race After Technology: Abolitionist Tools for the New Jim Code*. Cambridge: Polity Press.

Black, Julia and Andrew D. Murray (2019) "Regulating AI and Machine Learning: Setting the Regulatory Agenda" *European Journal of Law and Technology* 10 (3). ISSN 2042-115X.

Broussard, Meredith (2020) "When Algorithms Give Real Students Imaginary Grades". *The New York Times*, 8 September. https://www.nytimes.com/2020/09/08/opinion/international-baccalaureate-algorithm-grades.html.

Buolamwini, Joy and Timnit Gebru (2018) "Gender Shades: Intersectional Accuracy Disparities in Commercial Gender Classification" *Proceedings of Machine Learning Research* 81: 1–15.

Busuioc, Madalina (2021) "Accountable Artificial Intelligence: Holding Algorithms to Account" *Public Administration Review* 81 (5): 825–836.

Calo, Ryan and Danielle K. Citron (2021) "The Automated Administrative State: A Crisis of Legitimacy" *Emory Law Journal* 70 (4): 797.

Center for Human Rights and Global Justice (CHRGJ) NYU School of Law (2019) "Profiling the Poor in the Dutch Welfare State" https://chrgj.org/2019/11/01/profiling-the-poor-in-the-dutch-welfare-state/.

Cobbe, Jennifer (2020) "Confronting the Algorithmic State". https://adminlawblog.org/2020/09/24/jennifer-cobbe-confronting-the-algorithmic-state/.

Coglianese, Cary, Richard Zeckhauser and Edward A. Parson (2004) "Seeking Truth for Power: Informational Strategy and Regulatory Policy Making" Faculty Scholarship at Penn Law 107, https://scholarship.law.upenn.edu/faculty_scholarship/107.

Coglianese, Cary and Evan Mendelson (2010) "Meta-regulation and Self-regulation". In *The Oxford Handbook of Regulation*, edited by Robert Baldwin, Martin Cave and Martin Lodge. Oxford: Oxford University Press.

Coglianese, Cary and David Lehr (2017) "Regulating by Robot: Administrative Decision Making in the Machine-Learning Era" *Georgetown Law Journal* 105 (1147): 1205–13.

Corbett-Davies, Sam, Emma Pierson, Avi Feller and Sharad Goel (2016) "A Computer Program Used for Bail and Sentencing Decisions Was Labeled Biased against Blacks. It's Actually Not

That Clear". *Washington Post*, 17 October. https://www.washingtonpost.com/news/monkey-cage/wp/2016/10/17/canan-algorithm-be-racist-our-analysis-is-more-cautious-than-propublicas/?utm_term=.0b00af731baa.

Dressel, Julia and Hani Farid (2018) "The Accuracy, Fairness, and Limits of Predicting Recidivism" *Science Advances* 4 (1): eaao5580. DOI: 10.1126/sciadv.aao5580.

Dutch Data Protection Authority (AutoriteitPersoonsgegevens) (2020) "Belastingdienst/Toeslagen: De vewerking van de nationaliteit van aanvragers kinderopvangtoeslag" https://autoriteitpersoonsgegevens.nl/sites/default/files/atoms/files/onderzoek_belastingdienst_kinderopvangtoeslag.pdf.

Edwards, Lilian, and Michael Veale (2017) "Slave to the Algorithm? Why a 'Right to an Explanation' is Probably Not the Remedy You Are Looking For" *Duke Law & Technology Review* 18: 18–84.

Engstrom, David F., Daniel E. Ho, Catherine M. Sharkey and Mariano-Florentino Cuellar (2020) Government by Algorithm: Artificial Intelligence in Federal Administrative Agencies. Washington D.C.: Administrative Conference of the United States. https://www-cdn.law.stanford.edu/wp-content/uploads/2020/02/ACUS-AI-Report.pdf.

Eubanks, Virginia (2018) *Automating Inequality: How High-tech Tools Profile, Police, and Punish the Poor*. New York: St. Martin's Press.

European Commission (2018) "Coordinated Plan on Artificial Intelligence" COM(2018) 795 final. Brussels, 12 July 2018.

European Commission (2021) "Proposal for a Regulation of the European Parliament and of the Council Laying Down Harmonised Rules on Artificial Intelligence (Artificial Intelligence Act) and Amending Certain Union Legislative Acts" COM(2021) 206 final.

European Commission Press Release (2021) "Europe fit for the Digital Age: Commission Proposes New Rules and Actions for Excellence and Trust in Artificial Intelligence". Press Release, 21 April. https://ec.europa.eu/commission/presscorner/detail/en/ip_21_1682.

Ferguson, Andrew Guthrie (2017) *The Rise of Big Data Policing: Surveillance, Race, and the Future of Law Enforcement*. New York: NYU Press.

Ferguson, Andrew Guthrie (2020) "High-Tech Surveillance Amplifies Police Bias and Overreach" The Conversation, 12 June. https://theconversation.com/high-tech-surveillanceamplifies-police-bias-and-overreach-140225.

Financial Times (2021) "Scandals Tarnish Dutch Reputation for Clean Government", 24 June. https://www.ft.com/content/9996a65e-0996-4a08-aa65-041be685deae?shareType=nongift.

Finck, Michele (2020) "Automated Decision-Making and Transparency in Administrative Law". In *The Oxford Handbook on Comparative Administrative Law*, edited by Peter Cane et al. Oxford: Oxford University Press.

Fussey, Peter and Daragh Murray (2019) "Independent Report on the London Metropolitan Police Service's Trial of Live Facial Recognition Technology". Project Report: University of Essex Human Rights Centre.

Geiger, Gabriel (2021) "How a Discriminatory Algorithm Wrongly Accused Thousands of Families of Fraud." Vice, 1 March 2021. https://www.vice.com/en/article/jgq35d/how-a-discriminatory-algorithm-wrongly-accused-thousands-of-families-of-fraud.

Green, Ben and Yiling Chen (2019a) "Disparate Interactions: An Algorithm-in-the-Loop Analysis of Fairness in Risk Assessments". Proceedings of the Conference on Fairness, Accountability, and Transparency' – FAT* '19, 90–99. New York: ACM Press. DOI:10.1145/3287560.3287563.

Green, Ben and Yiling Chen (2019b) "The Principles and Limits of Algorithm-in-the-Loop Decision Making". Proceedings of the ACM on Human–Computer Interaction, 3(CSCW), 1–24. DOI: 10.1145/3359152.

Herd, Pamela and Donald P. Moynihan (2019) *Administrative Burden: Policymaking by Other Means*. New York: Russell Sage Foundation.

Kaminski, Margot (2021) "The Law of AI", JOTWELL (25 October 2021) (reviewing Michael Veale and Frederik Zuiderveen Borgesius, Demistifying the Draft EU Artificial Intelligence Act, *Computer Law Review Int'l* 22 (4): 97–112), https://cyber.jotwell.com/the-law-of-ai/.

Lakkaraju, Himabindu and Osbert Bastani (2020) "'How Do I Fool You?': Manipulating User Trust via Misleading Black Box Explanations". In Proceedings of the 2020 AAAI/ACM Conference on AI, Ethics, and Society (AIES '20), 7–8 February 2020, New York. https://doi.org/10.1145/3375627.3375833.

Lodge, Martin and Kai Wegrich (2012) *Managing Regulation: Regulatory Analysis, Politics and Policy*. Basingstoke: Palgrave Macmillan.

Margetts, Helen and Cosmina Dorobantu (2019) "Rethink Government with AI" *Nature* 568 (7751): 163–165.

Mattu, Surya, Angie Waller, Jon Keegan and Micha Gorelick (2021) "How We Built a Facebook Feed Viewer". The Markup, 11 March. https://themarkup.org/show-your-work/2021/03/11/how-we-built-a-facebook-feed-viewer.

Medium (2019) "On Recent Research Auditing Commercial Facial Analysis Technology". Concerned Researchers. Medium, 26 March. https://medium.com/@bu64dcjrytwitb8/on-recent-research-auditing-commercial-facial-analysis-technology-19148bda1832.

Mikhaylov Slava J., Esteve Marc and Averill Campion (2018) "Artificial Intelligence for the Public Sector: Opportunities and Challenges of Cross-Sector Collaboration" *Philosophical Transactions of the Royal Society A* 376: 20170357.

Naughton, John (2021) "Google Might Ask Questions About AI Ethics, but it Doesn't Want Answers" *The Guardian*, 13 March. https://www.theguardian.com/commentisfree/2021/mar/13/google-questions-about-artificial-intelligence-ethics-doesnt-want-answers-gebru-mitchell-parrots-language.

Netherlands Court of Audit (2020) Understanding Algorithms. https://english.rekenkamer.nl/publications/reports/2021/01/26/understanding-algorithms.

O'Neil, Cathy (2016) *Weapons of Math Destruction: How Big Data Increases Inequality and Threatens Democracy*. New York: Crown Books.

Parasuraman, Raja, and Victor Riley (1997) "Humans and Automation: Use, Misuse, Disuse, Abuse." *Human Factors* 39 (2): 230–253.

Parlementaire Ondervragingscommissie Kinderopvangtoeslag (2020) "Ongekend Onrecht". https://www.tweedekamer.nl/sites/default/files/atoms/files/20201217_eindverslag_parlementaire_ondervraging scommissie_kinderopvangtoeslag.pdf.

Pasquale, Frank (2011) "Restoring Transparency to Automated Authority" *Journal of Telecommunications & High Technology Law* 9: 235–236.

Pasquale, Frank (2015) *The Black Box Society: The Secret Algorithms That Control Money and Information*. Cambridge, MA and London: Harvard University Press.

Peeters, Rik (2020) "The Agency of Algorithms: Understanding Human-Algorithm Interaction In Administrative Decision-Making" *Information Polity* 25 (4): 507–522.

Ranchordas, Sofia (2022) "Empathy in the Digital Administrative State" *Duke Law Journal* 71, 1341–1389.

Raji, Deborah I. and Joy Buolamwini (2019) "Actionable Auditing: Investigating the Impact of Publicly Naming Biased Performance Results of Commercial AI Products" AIES' 19: Proceedings of the 2019 AAAI/ACM Conference on AI, Ethics, and Society. https://www.aies-conference.com/2019/wp-content/uploads/2019/01/AIES-19_paper_223.pdf.

Ribeiro, Marco T., Samee Singh and Carlos Guestrin (2016) "Why Should I Trust You?": Explaining the Predictions of Any Classifier. KDD 2016 Proceedings of the 22nd ACM SIGKDD International Conference on Knowledge Discovery and Data Mining: 1135–1144.

Richardson, Rashida, Jason Schultz and Kate Crawford (2019) "Dirty Data, Bad Predictions: How Civil Rights Violations Impact Police Data, Predictive Policing Systems, and Justice" *New York University Law Review* Online 94: 192–233.

Rudin, Cynthia (2019) "Stop Explaining Black Box Machine Learning Models for High Stakes Decisions and Use Interpretable Models Instead" *Nature Machine Intelligence* 1 (5): 206–215.

Rudin, Cynthia, Caroline Wang and Beau Coker (2020) "The Age of Secrecy and Unfairness in Recidivism Prediction" *Harvard Data Science Review* 2 (1). https://doi.org/10.1162/99608f92.6ed64b30.

Skitka, Linda J., Kathleen Mosier and Mark D. Burdick (1999) "Does Automation Bias Decision-Making?" *International Journal of Human-Computer Studies* 51 (5): 991–1006.

Skitka, Linda J., Kathleen Mosier and Mark D. Burdick (2000) "Accountability and Automation Bias." *International Journal of Human-Computer Studies* 52 (4): 701–717.

Slack, Dylan Z., Sophie Hilgard, Himabindu Lakkaraju and Sameer Singh (2021) "Counterfactual Explanations Can Be Manipulated", 35th Conference on Neural Information Processing Systems (NeurIPS 2021). arXiv:2106.02666.

Slovic, Paul (1987) "Perception of Risk" *Science* 236 (4799): 280–285. DOI: 10.1126/science.3563507.

Snow, Jacob (2018) "Amazon's Face Recognition Falsely Matched 28 Members of Congress with Mugshots." ACLU, 26 July. https://www.aclu.org/blog/privacy-technology/surveillance-technologies/amazons-face-recognition-falselymatched-28.

Smuha, Nathalie, Emma Ahmed-Rengers, Adam Harkens, Wenlong Li, James MacLaren, Riccardo Piselli and Karen Yeung (2021) "How the EU Can Achieve Legally Trustworthy AI: A Response to the European Commission's Proposal for an Artificial Intelligence Act". Leads Lab @University of Birmingham (5 August 2021). https://ssrn.com/abstract=3899991.

Stevenson, Megan (2018) "Assessing Risk Assessment in Action." *Minnesota Law Review* 103: 303–384.

Veale, Michael and Irina Brass (2019) "Administration by Algorithm? Public Management Meets Public Sector Machine Learning". In *Algorithmic Regulation*, edited by Karen Yeung and Martin Lodge. Oxford: Oxford University Press.

Veale, Michael and Frederik Zuiderveen Borgesius (2021) "Demystifying the Draft EU Artificial Intelligence Act" *Computer Law Review International* 22 (4): 97–112.

Wachter, Sandra, Brent Mittelstad and Chris Russell (2018) "Counterfactual Explanations without Opening the Black Box: Automated Decisions and the GDPR" *Harvard Journal of Law & Technology* 31 (2): 841.

Wired (2021) "What Really Happened When Google Ousted Timnit Gebru". Wired, 6 August. https://www.wired.com/story/google-timnit-gebru-ai-what-really-happened/.

Yeung, Karen (2018) "Algorithmic Regulation: A Critical Interrogation" *Regulation & Governance* 12 (4): 505–523.

Yeung, Karen and Martin Lodge (2019) "Algorithmic Regulation: An Introduction". In *Algorithmic Regulation*, edited by Karen Yeung and Martin Lodge. Oxford: Oxford University Press.

Young, Matthew M., Justin B. Bullock, and Jesse D. Lecy (2019) "Artificial Discretion as a Tool of Governance: A Framework for Understanding the Impact of Artificial Intelligence on Public Administration" *Perspectives on Public Management and Governance* 2 (4): 301–313.

32. Expertise and regulatory agencies
Dovilė Rimkutė

INTRODUCTION[1]

Expertise is considered to be the raison d'être of regulatory agencies operating at various levels of government. Unlike political institutions that are expected to be responsive to their constituencies, regulatory agencies are founded to exclusively rely on reliable sources of expertise and technical knowledge in their regulatory day-to-day activities, as illustrated in the quote provided by the director of the European Food Safety Authority (EFSA), Dr. Bernhard Url, in response to grave public allegations concerning EFSA's regulatory role: "It is the role of politicians to represent the values, needs and expectations of their constituents through democratic processes. This is outside the responsibility of organizations such as EFSA, which were created to advise EU policymakers on scientific matters" (Url 2018, p. 381).

One of the rationales for the creation of independent regulatory agencies – that produce or contribute to expertise-based regulatory policy-making – is to assure that the ever-rising need for credible policy solutions is provided by specialized expertise bodies working at arm's length from their political superiors (Majone 1996). To that end, regulatory agencies are instituted to draw on high-quality data and scientific knowledge to elucidate regulatory challenges that range from food safety, pharmaceuticals, and chemicals to financial or security-related issues. Regulatory agencies' outputs are devised to provide an analytical means for assessing scientific knowledge regarding potential hazards and risks to humans, animals, and the environment. This, in turn, implies that regulatory agencies' duties are primarily a highly technical quest predominantly entrenched in the use of scientific knowledge and technical data to arrive at regulatory outputs that later inform (political) regulatory decisions.

The mainstream literature on expertise and regulatory agencies has emphasized technocratic expertise and performative conduct as the key criteria for regulatory agency legitimacy (see, for instance, Majone 1998). Expertise-based conduct – that is the core basis for credible and efficient regulatory solutions – is deemed to be the key means through which regulatory agencies justify their organizational liabilities, enhance their regulatory authority and legitimacy: "policies […] are basically legitimated by results, and hence may be delegated to such [non-majoritarian] institutions" (Majone, 1998 p. 28).

However, an increasing body of empirical studies has found that regulatory agencies' scientific or technical activities – that is, the ways in which scientific knowledge and technical data is used by regulatory agencies – can vary considerably. In other words, expertise can have many functions in regulatory policy-making (Hertin et al. 2009; Radaelli 2009; Rimkutė 2015; Schrefler 2010; Weiss 1979). Recent scholarship has observed that although regulatory agencies are keen on emphasizing the technical and performative character of their activities to justify their regulatory processes and results vis-à-vis relevant stakeholders, expertise as 'the be-all-and-end-all' criterion for regulatory agencies' legitimacy does not always hold as regulatory agencies may also draw on diverse strategies to justify their organizational conduct (Busuioc & Rimkutė 2020a, 2020b; Rimkutė 2018, 2020a, 2020b). That is to say, regulatory agencies' legitimacy is regarded as an outcome of effective handling not only of technical conduct, but also of performative aptitudes, legal-procedural appropriateness, and moral standing (Carpenter, 2010b; Carpenter & Krause 2012; Rimkutė 2018). This more differentiated understanding of regulatory agencies' behavior – drawing on bureaucratic reputation theory – has opened multiple avenues to study agency behavior when it comes to their technical conduct and other organizational liabilities that agencies rely on to respond to multifaceted stakeholders observing, assessing, and judging their regulatory processes and outputs.

Scholarship on expertise and regulatory agencies is long-established and received much scholarly attention. However, its potential could be unlocked by exploring diverse theoretical perspectives to explain why regulatory agencies behave differently in terms of their technical conduct as well as diversifying analytical tools to explain varied agency behavior patterns which could, in turn, bring new empirical insights into the field. This chapter aims to review the extant scholarship on expertise and regulatory agencies and put forward propositions on how the field could be advanced by focusing on new research avenues that draw on more differentiated understanding of regulatory agency behavior concerning its technical conduct.

This chapter is structured as follows. First, expertise as a key rationale for regulatory agency creation is introduced and discussed. Following the functionalist argument, the core scholarly contributions linking expertise to creditable commitment, regulatory autotomy, and legitimacy arguments are introduced. Second, the chapter then moves on to introducing a strand of literature concerning the role of expertise in regulatory policy-making and how expertise is actually used by regulatory agencies. Third, after identifying the prevailing conceptual, theoretical, and empirical gaps in the literature, the chapter discusses how the scholarship on expertise and regulatory agencies could be brought forward by tailoring new theoretical accounts to explain agency technical conduct.

RATIONALE FOR REGULATORY AGENCY CREATION: EXPERTISE AS A KEY LOGIC

Regulatory agencies constitute a large share of the global phenomenon called the 'rise of unelected' (Vibert 2007). Although political institutions have multiple choices regarding how regulations could be prepared and executed (e.g., regulatory agencies, quasi-regulatory bodies, regulatory networks), increasingly they have opted for the delegation of regulatory tasks to independent agencies (Elgie & McMenamin 2005; Gilardi 2008; Levi-Faur 2011; Rimkutė 2021). Political systems operating at national, supranational, and international levels have experienced a so-called 'phenomenon of agencification', that is, extensive delegation of (regulatory) powers to non-majoritarian institutions working at arm's length from their political superiors. In recent decades across various political systems worldwide, regulatory agencies were instituted to contribute to policy- and decision-making *by providing technical expertise-based solutions* to emerging regulatory challenges that modern societies face. For example, in the period between 1975 and 2020, EU lawmakers have established 46 agencies including regulatory bodies working on diverse regulatory domains (for detailed discussion see Rimkutė 2021). Similar agencification patterns have been observed at national-level political systems (see, for instance, Gilardi 2008).

One of the mainstream rationales for the independent regulatory agency creation is the increasing need for high quality expert advice to address grave issues that contemporary societies are facing (e.g., recent financial and migration crises, global pandemic). This reasoning is rooted in the functionalist argument. The reference to the functional argumentation or functionalism entails that "institutional choices are explained in terms of the functions that a given institution is expected to perform, and the effects on policy outcomes it is expected to produce" (Pollack, 2006, p. 167). Scholars following the functionalist reasoning have argued that the prompt and extensive processes of delegating regulatory tasks to independent agencies can be explained by the functional need to generate unbiased expertise-based solutions in order to attain credible policy commitments (Majone 1996, 1999). Following this line of argumentation, the increased powers of regulatory agencies have been associated with regulatory crises (Boin et al. 2014). A standard response to crises has often been to strengthen 'credible' and 'expertise-based' regulation, whether it is related to food safety (e.g., establishment of the European Food Safety Authority), the financial crisis (e.g., creation of the unprecedentedly powerful European Supervisory Authorities (ESAs): the European Banking Authority (EBA), the European Securities and Markets Authority (ESMA), and the European Insurance and Occupational Pensions Authority (EIOPA)), or the migration crisis (creation of the European Asylum Support Office (EASO) and the significant expansion of responsibilities, budget, and powers of the already existing agency dealing with border security issues, i.e., Frontex).

More specifically, with the delegation of regulatory responsibilities to independent agencies, political actors limit their own choice to opt for political intervention. Such a decision is made to send strong signals to private and public stakeholders about political institutions' commitment to regulatory stability. In the case of nondelegation, or when political institutions are in charge of regulatory matters, the possibility of regulatory inconsistencies increases because a change in political majorities may lead to an overhaul of regulatory decisions. This is the case because political uncertainty is a direct outcome of the democratic process. Furthermore, a crucial defining characteristic of democracy is government *pro tempore* (Linz 1998). Political decision-making processes are marked by the high levels of responsiveness to prevailing external demands as well as a focus on short-term gains. This results in policy outcomes that are marked by time inconsistency issues and may be skewed to policy outputs favoring particularistic interests rather than pareto efficient solutions. As a result, credible commitments are difficult to achieve provided they remain a core responsibility of majoritarian institutions. To that end, to enhance the credibility of long-term policy commitments, political institutions delegate regulatory tasks to independent authorities and provide them with institutional designs allowing them to conduct these tasks.

In order to ensure the attainment of credible commitment, regulatory agencies are delegated with a certain degree of independence and autonomy so that they can freely exercise their mandates to provide *independent expertise-based regulatory solutions*. The anticipated effect of instituting independent regulatory agencies is the supply of *impartial expertise and a credible commitment* in order to achieve unbiased and predictable regulatory outputs and outcomes. Independence from their creators and autonomy serve to insulate agencies' experts from 'undue' political influence by majoritarian actors in regulatory policy-making. And *vice versa* impartial expertise in regulatory policy-making is argued to be a key prerequisite for bureaucratic autonomy and independence from political institutions.

Empirical contributions in the field have found support for the claim that agencies with regulatory tasks tend to be more independent compared to their nonregulatory counterparts (Wonka & Rittberger 2010). As it has been argued, this is the case because there is a need to signal strong commitment to credible solutions, that is, strong commitment to expertise-based regulation rather than favoring short-term electoral motivations (Gilardi 2005; Majone 1996). As a result, expertise and independence have been regarded as the two cornerstones of regulatory institutions (Maggetti 2007, 2009; Ossege 2016). In other words, regulatory agencies are provided with protection from 'political interference' in order to assure long-term policy consistency that could not be achieved if political actors were in charge. It seems that such a logic has been respected by the formal institutional justification surrounding agency creation in national and supranational political systems, as embodied by the European Commission defending the decision to create EU agencies that function independently from EU institutions: "The independence of their [agencies'] technical and/or scientific assessments is, in fact, their real raison d'être. The main advantage of using the agencies is that their decisions are based on purely technical evaluations of very high quality and are not influenced by political or contingent considerations" (European Commission, 2002, p. 5).

Against this backdrop, regulatory agencies are expected to contribute to or generate regulations that are exclusively based on expertise that is independent from external influences. To that end, according to the functionalist argumentation, the legitimacy of regulatory agencies is argued to predominantly rest on their role as an independent expertise bodies delivering outputs that are rooted in scientific knowledge and technical data. As a result, *expertise forms the central point of reference to the legitimacy of regulatory agencies*: "Regulation depends so heavily on scientific, engineering and economic knowledge [...] expertise has always been an important source of legitimization of regulatory agencies" (Majone, 1997, p. 157). As opposed to majoritarian-institutions that derive their legitimacy drawing on democratic legitimacy sources, non-majoritarian institutions draw on "non-democratic" justifications to legitimize their existence (Majone, 1996).

More specifically, regulatory agencies are expected to follow the consequentialist take of political rule in which they legitimize themselves by proving their pledge to the efficiency and effectiveness of their regulatory undertakings. By relying on *output-oriented* sources of legitimacy (or also referred to as "performance-based"/"results-oriented" legitimacy) (Scharpf 1999), regulatory agencies shape their regulatory power and authority by delivering outputs that are expected to translate into effective regulatory outcomes that are deemed to directly originate from the use of reliable evidence. Following this line of reasoning, the legitimacy of regulatory agencies is dependent on their appropriate use of expertise and the strength of their technical rationale to justify regulatory policy- and decision-making (Majone 1996; Vibert 2007). In other words, "[t]he positive evaluation of regulatory performance is presented as the first alternative source of legitimacy" (Maggetti 2010, p. 2).

However, granting regulatory powers to regulatory agencies functioning at arm's length from majoritarian institutions fosters a democratic legitimacy problem for issues that cannot be addressed with reference to expertise and technical knowledge to justify regulatory decisions. The processes of agencification and the rise of the regulatory state, as a significant body of literature argues, have created an issue of "democratic deficit" (see, for instance, Eriksen & Fossum 2004; Majone 1999). The arguments of functionalist literature have sparked an intense normative debate arguing that the extensive delegation of regulatory tasks to regulatory agencies should be normatively justified on the basis of legitimacy standards that are in line with democratic standards (see, for example, Follesdal & Hix 2006; Holst & Molander 2019). The core values of representative democracy are argued to become less important due to the growing role of regulatory agencies that rely on expert-based regulatory policy-making (Papadopoulos 2003). To that end, there was a quest to address the "democratic deficit" issue in regulatory policy-making that tends to rely on technocratic justification to defend its legitimacy.

Against this backdrop, an increasing body of literature has argued that the normative debates regarding the legitimation standards that regulatory agencies should draw on could benefit from empirical studies on whether, how, and under what conditions independent regulatory agencies use expert knowledge and technical information. Increasingly scholarship focusing on expertise and regulatory agencies argued that the long-established literature stream leaves many research gaps (Schrefler 2010; Wonka & Rittberger 2010). While it puts forward a compelling argument explaining why expertise is the key rationale for delegating extensive powers to regulatory agencies, it does not address a very critical question – that is, *how do regulatory agencies actually cope with their primary duty to provide sound and reliable expert advice?* It does not inform us how regulatory agencies use expertise and scientific knowledge to apprise regulatory policy- or decision-making. This knowledge gap is considerable given that the prompt developments of 'agencification' are often justified by referring to the need for credible regulatory solutions that are directly derived from available expert knowledge and technical data.

A new generation of scholarship focusing on expertise and regulatory agencies has attempted to go beyond normative debates, that is, should regulatory agencies draw on technocratic or democratic legitimation sources when justifying their contribution (see, for instance, Mathieu 2016; Ossege 2016; Rimkutė 2020a; Schrefler 2010; Wood 2018). These scholars have broadened our theoretical and empirical understanding on how regulatory agencies legitimize their regulatory power and authority with reference to the provision of expertise. They have attempted to unravel the following questions: What is the role of expertise in regulatory agencies' day-to-day activities? How do regulatory agencies use scientific expertise? How do they communicate about their technical conduct and respective activities?

To that end, the scholarship in the field responded to the quest to address the prevailing research gaps by providing conceptual, theoretical, and empirical contributions on regulatory agencies' expertise-based conduct. Scholars have started to explore the role of expertise in regulatory policy-making in order to explain agencies' de facto activities when it comes to their technical conduct. In the remainder, the chapter further addresses and elaborates on this body of literature.

EXPERTISE AND REGULATORY AGENCIES: DE FACTO TECHNICAL CONDUCT OF REGULATORY AGENCIES

The contribution of the "unelected" to policy processes has been increasingly contested (Gornitzka & Holst 2015; Vibert 2007). A considerable body of literature suggested that one can witness not only the "expertization" or "scientization" of regulatory politics, but also the "politicization" of so-called scientific activities or evidence-based policy/decision-making (Fischer 2009; Jasanoff 1990; Radaelli 1999). Consequently, scholars in the field have identified a need to study how regulation is carried out in everyday regulatory practices. Boswell, for instance, argued: "there is a striking lack of research on the utilisation of expert knowledge in public policy" (Boswell, 2009, p. 165). Endeavors to examine how regulators use scientific knowledge and technical expertise in their day-to-day regulatory activities have been scarce due to the limitations in the theorization and conceptualization of diverse scientific knowledge utilization modes, that is, scientific practices (Schrefler 2010). To that end, scholarship attempted to bring the field forward by closing prevailing conceptual, theoretical, and empirical gaps.

Scholars focusing on the technical side of regulation suggested that the use of expertise in regulatory policy-making and the increasing reliance on scientific (risk) assessments can be explicated not only by its analytical role, but also by its importance as a symbol of rational policy-/decision-making (Rothstein et al. 2013). That is, although regulatory agencies are expected to offer a technical foundation for regulatory policy-making, at times agencies' scientific outputs are considered as relevant regardless of their actual scientific, technical, or methodological contribution.

Scholars have detected that regulatory agencies' scientific activities – that is, the ways in which scientific knowledge and technical data is used in regulatory policy-making – can vary considerably. Expertise can have many roles and functions in regulatory policy-making (Boswell 2008, 2009; Hertin et al. 2009; Radaelli 1995, 2009; Rimkutė 2015; Rimkutė & Haverland 2015; Schrefler 2010; Weiss 1979). To give an example, science-based risk assessments produced by regulatory agencies are often inconsistent. Agencies simultaneously working on the same base of evidence recurrently arrive at conflicting conclusions. To illustrate, an EU-level agency, the European Food Safety Authority (EFSA), concluded that bisphenol A (a chemical used in plastics) poses no health risk, whereas the French agency, the French Agency for Food, Environmental and Occupational Health & Safety (ANSES), claimed that exposure of pregnant women to bisphenol A poses a risk to the fetus and also identified bisphenol A risks to infants. Consequently, bisphenol A is restricted in France but not in other EU member states (for further elaborations, see Fox et al. 2011; Rimkutė 2018). Another example is that the regulatory agencies of the United States, Canada, Australia, Japan, and the EU have conducted independent risk assessments of glyphosate and concluded that glyphosate is unlikely to pose a carcinogenic threat and customarily authorized glyphosate with specific warnings regarding conditions for safe use. However, the International Agency for Research on Cancer (IARC) – an independent cancer center of the World Health Organization – announced that most glyphosate is genotoxic, carcinogenic to animals, and 'probably cancerogenic' for humans (see more detailed discussion in Rimkutė 2020b). Similar scientific divergences resulting in substantial differences in regulatory measures to protect consumers have been reported in fields as diverse as food safety, chemicals, medicines, and environmental protection (see, for example, Bazzan & Migliorati 2020; Lodge & Wegrich 2011; Vos 2017).

Against this backdrop, scholars working on expertise in regulatory policy-making focus on exploring the role of expertise in regulatory policy-making, that is, how expertise, evidence and scientific knowledge are used by regulatory agencies and what explains the substantial inconsistencies in scientific conclusions across regulatory agencies (see, for instance, Boswell 2008; Rimkutė 2015, 2020b; Schrefler 2010). Scholarship in the field has discovered that evidence in regulatory policy-making can be used in many ways depending on the conditions under which regulatory agencies have to deliver their scientific outputs. For example, agencies can use science not only to search for the best evidence-based solution but also for substantiating the predefined policy preferences in order to respond to prevalent external criticism.

To elaborate, in her seminal work on expertise, evidence, and research utilization, Carol H. Weiss (1979) has identified different types of knowledge use that policy makers can employ in policy-making. Weiss (1979) has argued that the use of expert knowledge, evidence and research in policy-making does not always respect "the following sequence of events: basic research → applied research → development → application" (Weiss, 1979, p. 427). Weiss argued that knowledge in policy-making can have different roles ranging from the actual use of knowledge to inform policies to more symbolic roles: the knowledge-driven model, the problem-solving model, the interactive model, the political model, the tactical model, and the enlightenment model. Scholars working on the role of expertise in regulatory policy-making have adapted the typology to explore how expertise is used by regulatory agencies (see, for instance, Jennings & Hall 2012; Mantzari & Vantaggiato 2020; Radaelli 1995, 2009; Rimkutė 2015; Rimkutė & Haverland 2015; Schrefler 2010, 2013; Zarkin 2021).

This literature stream has advanced the field by suggesting that the role of expertise goes beyond a simple dichotomy of use and non-use of expertise by regulatory agencies. Expertise in regulatory policy-making has multiple roles. For instance, expertise can be used to solve existing regulatory policy issues (problem-solving mode of expertise use). However, regulatory agencies can also engage in the strategic use of expertise: (1) expertise can be used to enhance one's regulatory power, influence, or/and to strengthen status and reputation (political use of expertise); (2) expertise can be used to justify predefined preferences (substantiating use of expertise). Furthermore, (3) expertise can be utilized to emulate or imitate the most important actors/institutions (symbolic use of expertise) (for more elaborations see Boswell 2008; Schrefler 2010).

While this typology has significantly advanced the field by introducing the idea that expertise can be used by regulatory agencies in different ways, it suffers from insufficient conceptual clarity (e.g., the knowledge utilization modes are not analytically mutually exclusive) and a lack of comprehensive theorization (e.g., under what conditions do agencies engage in different expertise use practices?). That is, scholarship on the role of experts and expertise in general "has revealed significant theoretical weaknesses and barriers to empirical study that have not been seriously addressed within the respective literatures" (Christensen, 2020, p. 13). Furthermore, the major contributions in the field exclusively rely on qualitative methodologies, that is, single or comparative case study research designs relying on interview data or primary document analysis (Boswell 2008, 2009; Mantzari & Vantaggiato 2020; Rimkutė 2015; Schrefler 2010; Zarkin 2021) with a very limited use of quantitative methodologies (a couple of examples include: Costa et al. 2019; Jennings & Hall 2012; Rimkutė & Haverland 2015). The above-mentioned conceptual, theoretical, and empirical limitations call for considerations of how the field could be brought forward by addressing the core gaps in the extant literature.

AVENUES FOR FUTURE RESEARCH ON EXPERTISE AND REGULATORY AGENCIES

This section, first, invites scholarship on expertise and regulatory agencies to explore the potential of a relatively new theoretical perspective – bureaucratic reputation theory (Carpenter 2010b) – to fill the prevailing conceptual, theoretical, and empirical gaps in the literate on expertise in regulatory policy-making. Second, it suggests how the field could be brought forward by incorporating insights from the broader literature on expert knowledge and policy-making (Christensen 2020). Third, it invites scholars in the field to address the urgent need to discuss and study the effects of the rise of populism and democratic backsliding on democracy–technocracy relationships in general and the role of expertise in regulatory politics in particular.

Novel Theoretical Avenues: Bureaucratic Reputation and Technical Agency Conduct

The use of a bureaucratic reputation perspective to explain technical agency conduct has been scarce regardless of its high potential to provide novel conceptual, theoretical, and empirical insights into our understanding of the use of expertise by regulatory agencies. A bureaucratic reputation account puts forward, first, a compelling argument regarding differentiated agency behavior that complements and further enhances mainstream arguments about expertise as a key prerequisite for regulatory legitimacy. Second, it provides well-defined and analytically mutually exclusive concepts to study agency technical conduct and, in so doing, opens many future research avenues on expertise used by regulatory agencies. Third, it offers coherent theoretical explanations regarding causal mechanisms leading to differentiated agency behavior that enables scholars working in the field to address relevant theoretical gaps. Last but not least, it offers analytical tools and reliable measures to empirically explore the technical aspects of regulatory agency conduct.

More specifically, an organizational reputation account offers a more differentiated understanding of regulatory agency behavior patterns and provides solid conceptual and analytical tools to study how regulatory agencies carry out their core mandates to provide credible solutions to emerging regulatory issues (Busuioc & Rimkutė 2020b). It enriches the literature on expertise by arguing that regulatory agencies can engage in diverse strategies to enhance their legitimacy. While functional literature argues that the ways in which regulatory agencies legitimize themselves are set in stone (i.e., regulatory agencies can legitimize themselves by delivering effective results-based outputs that are directly derived from reliable sources of evidence), reputational scholarships put forward a more nuanced argumentation stating that the legitimation sources on which agencies can draw to justify their conduct or even their existence are multidimensional. That this, regulatory agencies can engage in various reputation-balancing activities to establish, maintain, or enhance their legitimacy.

This suggests that the available array of reputation-balancing strategies creates some degree of latitude for agencies in handling their organizational legitimacy. That is to say, regulatory agencies' legitimacy is regarded as a consequence of the effective management not only of technical conduct, but also performative excellence, legal-procedural appropriateness, and moral image (Carpenter 2010b; Carpenter & Krause 2012; Rimkutė 2018). Agencies can concurrently engage in diverse reputation–advancement strategies. They can choose to emphasize diverse organizational liabilities (i.e., technical, performative, procedural, moral) when carrying out and communicating about their core technical tasks (Carpenter & Krause 2012). The successful handling of organizational reputation involves finding effective ways to respond to the most vital external expectations by emphasizing the "right" organizational liability or striking the "right" balance between technical, procedural, performative, and moral organizational conduct.

More specifically, regulatory agencies may choose to legitimize their regulatory activities and processes by sending strong professional and technical signals by emphasizing the technical, scientific, or professional features of their tasks, that is, by highlighting reputational aspects such as methodological expertise, scientific precision, and analytical capacity (Carpenter 2010b; Carpenter & Krause 2012). Regulatory agencies may also choose to empha-

Table 32.1   *Summary of organizational reputation dimensions*

Reputation dimensions	Agency focus	Agency signals to external audiences
Technical	Scientific/technical conduct	Professionalism and adherence to 'scientific gold' standard
Performative	Effectiveness and efficiency	Successful goal attainment
Legal-procedural	Due process	Adherence to legal procedures
Moral	Moral and ethical implications	Commitment to moral aspects of its organizational conduct

Source: Adapted from: Carpenter (2010b) and Carpenter and Krause (2012).

size the performative dimension of their organizational conduct, that is, the agency's duty to effectively realize its core mandate and "execute charges on its responsibility in a manner that is interpreted as competent and perhaps efficient" (Carpenter 2010b). Furthermore, Carpenter argued that procedural organizational conduct may also, at times, be emphasized by regulatory agencies. Procedural reputation "relates to the justness of the processes by which its behavior is generated" (Carpenter, 2010b, p. 47). Last but not least, agencies may choose to pay special attention to its moral reputation and focus on the following questions: Does it protect the interests of consumers? Does it "exhibit compassion for those adversely affected by its decisions or those in its environment who are less fortunate or more constrained? Is it flexible with respect to human needs?" (Carpenter, 2010b, p. 46). See Table 32.1.

In short, rather than contrasting the technocratic and democratic justifications to defend regulatory agency legitimacy, the reputational account integrates a broader range of legitimation strategies that regulatory agencies can draw on to rationalize their regulatory responsibilities (Busuioc & Rimkutė 2020b). It argues that technical expertise – regarded as the key criterion for legitimation within the mainstream literature stream – is merely one of the available ways for regulatory agencies to legitimize their regulatory outputs, processes, outcomes or even their right to exist.

Furthermore, reputational literature puts forward an argument that the multidimensional legitimacy profile of regulatory agencies is affected by the vigorous interface with their audiences (or stakeholders). The legitimacy criteria of regulatory agencies are "dependent on agency success in coalition-building and engendering support from its environment" (Busuioc & Rimkutė, 2020b, p. 1266). A bureaucratic reputation account suggests that the legitimacy principles are in "the eyes of the beholders", including a wide variety of formal and informal stakeholders possessing diverse expectations that often are conflicting with each other.

The above-mentioned theoretical claims provide not only a more differentiated understanding into the legitimation means of regulatory agency conduct, but also offer a comprehensive and lucid theoretical framework as well as concepts and analytical tools for scholars working on expertise and regulatory agencies to further theorize when and under what conditions agencies engage in different technical/scientific practices. Bureaucratic reputation literature suggests that regulatory agency outputs may incorporate a wide variety of outcomes ranging from purely expertise-based to more reputation-induced deliverables. This is the case, as reputational literature argues, because the environment in which agencies perform may affect how agencies use expertise by posing a wide set of reputational threats that agencies have to actively handle to prevent organizational failures that would lead to disempowerment and even de-legitimatization of the agency (Carpenter 2010b).

More specifically, in order to explain agency behavior (e.g., how expertise is used by regulatory agencies), one should examine the context in which agencies perform as well as identify relevant actors and threats that they pose to regulatory agencies: "when trying to account for a regulator's behavior, *look at the audience*, and *look at the threats*" (Carpenter, 2010a, p. 832). A positive reputation can be earned among various constellations of formal (e.g., political superiors) and informal (e.g., civil society, media) stakeholders. Whether a regulatory agency is regarded as contributing to credible commitment will depend on the alliances of stakeholders and their preferences regarding a certain regulatory result (Busuioc & Rimkutė 2020b). To that end, as reputational literature argues, regulatory agencies will do their utmost to address the expectations of the most relevant audiences, on which their legitimacy, regulatory power, and autonomy depend the most.

Reputation literature suggests that agencies have to carefully manage external expectations. This may require careful management of external claims among conflicting formal and informal audiences by, for example, the strategic use of available expertise to shape regulatory agency's image and actively manage audience expectations. Unsuccessful management of expectations of relevant stakeholders can lead to controversy, loss of regulatory power, and decreased legitimacy of regulatory processes, outputs, and outcomes (Busuioc & Rimkutė 2020b). And vice versa, successful attempts to build a strong reputation can result in a powerful organizational reputation that "can be deployed to tie the hands of legitimate political principals, to deflect oversight of agency action, and to disguise—at least for some time— regulatory failures" (Bertelli & Busuioc, 2020, p. 8).

As a result, the behavior of regulatory agencies is affected by their initial reputational standing and vulnerabilities. For example, recent studies argued and provided empirical evidence that agencies that possess a strong bureaucratic reputation enjoy more latitude in choosing how to respond to grave public allegations concerning their scientific conduct (Gilad et al. 2015; Maor et al. 2013; Rimkutė 2020b). On the contrary, agencies with a weak or fledgling reputation were found to be more liable for responsiveness to external expectations and demands.

Last but not least, bureaucratic reputation literature provides analytical tools and measures to empirically examine how expertise is used and how regulators communicate about their technical processes, outputs, and outcomes. The scholarship of bureaucratic reputation has employed various research methods ranging from comparative case studies, surveys, automated text analysis, and machine learning techniques to explore agency behavior (including technical conduct) and stakeholders' assessment of it (see, for instance, Busuioc & Rimkutė 2020a; Lee & Ryzin 2019; Müller & Braun 2021; Overman et al. 2020; Rimkutė 2018, 2020b; Rimkutė & De Vos 2020). Tailoring these analytical tools to explore technical agency conduct could enhance the field that is exclusively based on single or comparative case study designs (e.g., Schrefler 2010).

To summarize, a reputational perspective has a high potential to bring the scholarship focusing on expertise forward by proposing alternative explanations that could be examined against the long-established claims regarding the use of expertise by regulatory agencies. It suggests comprehensive expectations regarding agency technical behavior. Namely, a reputational account provides conceptual and analytical tools to unravel what regulatory politics entail, which stakeholders are relevant in regulatory politics and why, which reputation-balancing strategies regulatory agencies draw on to establish, maintain, or enhance their legitimacy (Busuioc & Rimkutė 2020a). This, in turn, provides a rich theoretical background for scholarship focusing on technical agency conduct to tailor bureaucratic reputation arguments to explore how regulatory agencies use expertise and why their technical conduct varies across time, domains, and regulatory regimes.

Towards a New Research Agenda: The Influence of Experts and Expert Knowledge

Scholarship on expert knowledge and policy-making has introduced a promising research agenda focusing on the question of the influence of experts and the administrative foundations of expert influence (Christensen 2020; Christensen & Yesilkagit 2019). More specifically, first, this literature stream suggests focusing on capturing the role of experts or expert knowledge in policy-making and provides theoretical explanations regarding the varying role of expert knowledge in policy-making. It suggests focusing on the influence of expert knowledge and expertise rather than the use of expert knowledge. Such an approach would enable "a 'normalization' of research on expertise and policy-making, seeing experts as one type of actor among others providing input in the political system rather than granting them a special status as providers of neutral and apolitical evidence" (Christensen, 2020, p. 2). Second, scholarship on expert knowledge and policy-making suggests that in order to explain the influence of experts and expert knowledge on policy-making one needs to pay more attention to how the organizational arrangements of expert knowledge within public administrations affects expert influence (see, for example, Christensen & Hesstvedt 2019; Hesstvedt & Christensen 2021). While this research agenda is discussed in the field of advisory/expert commission politics, it has a high potential to provide new insights into regulatory politics and expertise.

Regulatory Agencies Amidst the Rise of Populism and Democratic Backsliding

In recent years, long-established democratic systems have experienced significant changes in their democratic outlook as a result of the rise of populism and democratic backsliding. Political scientists have extensively discussed these new dynamics and warned that the effects of populism on democracy is burgeoning (Norris & Inglehart 2019). In a similar vein, public administration scholars have focused our attention on the implications of these changes on the functioning of bureaucrats that are expected to rely on neutral bureaucratic competencies, however, at the same time engage in bureaucratic responsiveness to their political superiors. In particular, scholars focusing on the technical character of non-majoritarian institutions have emphasized that the rise of populism and democratic backlisting bring new dynamics to bureaucratic politics, that is, the challenge to rely on expertise and specialized knowledge in view of political failure (Bauer & Becker 2020; Caramani 2017; Meier et al. 2019). These new tendencies have significant implications for the technical character of the (European) regulatory state in general and the use of expertise by regulatory agencies in particular. However, research on how the rise of populism and democratic backsliding affect the technical nature of regulatory agency activities has been scarce. This chapter therefore invites scholarship on expertise and agencies to consider the implications of political failure on the technical outlook of regulatory agencies: what are the implications of changing political and administrative relations on the role of expertise in regulatory politics? How is the use of expertise by regulatory authority affected by the increased demands for responsiveness to multifaceted external actors (e.g., political principals, private interest groups, the general public)? Can regulatory agencies legitimize their processes, output, and outcomes by exclusively drawing on the "results-oriented" legitimation sources?

CONCLUSION

Scholarship on expertise and regulatory agencies has been led by the long-established function-alist argument, emphasizing the need for expertise that is independent from external influences in order to achieve credible policy commitments. The swift processes of "agencification" and the growing role of regulatory agencies worldwide were deemed to be driven by the need to address regulatory challenges using independent expertise-based advice. To achieve this goal, regulatory agencies were created to draw on high-quality data and scientific knowledge to inform regulatory policies that range from food safety, pharmaceuticals, chemicals to financial and security. The provision of impartial expertise in regulatory policy-making therefore is argued to be the fundamental prerequisite for bureaucratic legitimacy. As a result, the legiti-macy of regulatory agencies is argued to be dependent on the appropriate use of expertise and the strength of the technical rationale justifying regulatory policy-/decision-making.

While the functionalist literature puts forward a compelling argument explaining why expertise is the key motive for delegating extensive powers to regulatory agencies, it does not address the very critical question of how regulatory agencies actually cope with their primary duty to provide sound and reliable expert advice. This chapter explored how a bureaucratic reputation account could bring scholarship focusing on expertise and regulatory agencies forward by providing (1) a differentiated understanding of regulatory agency legitimation sources, (2) well-defined and analytically mutually exclusive concepts to study agency tech-nical conduct, (3) theoretical arguments explaining differentiated agency behavior, and (4) analytical tools and reliable measures of technical agency conduct.

Furthermore, the chapter suggested future scholarship to consider a multi-disciplinary research agenda that suggests focusing on the influence of experts and expert knowledge in regulatory policy-making as well as the administrative foundations of expert influence. In addition, it drew attention on the urgent need to address the challenges that regulatory agencies face to provide neutral bureaucratic competencies and expertise amidst the rise of populism and democratic backsliding.

NOTE

1.   This chapter is part of a project funded by the Dutch Research Council (NWO), Innovational Research Incentives Scheme Veni SSH. Grant/Award Number: VI.Veni.191R.078.

REFERENCES

Bauer, M. W., & Becker, S. (2020). Democratic Backsliding, Populism, and Public Administration. *Perspectives on Public Management and Governance*, *3*(1), 19–31. https://doi.org/10.1093/ppmgov/gvz026

Bazzan, G., & Migliorati, M. (2020). Expertise, Politics and Public Opinion at the Crossroads of the European Commission's Decision-making: The Case of Glyphosate. *International Review of Public Policy*, *2*(2:1), 68–89. https://doi.org/10.4000/irpp.849

Bertelli, A. M., & Busuioc, M. (2020). Reputation-Sourced Authority and the Prospect of Unchecked Bureaucratic Power. *Public Administration Review*, *81*(1), 38–48. https://doi.org/10.1111/puar.13281

Boin, A., Busuioc, M., & Groenleer, M. (2014). Building European Union Capacity to Manage Transboundary Crises: Network or Lead-Agency Model? *Regulation & Governance*, 8(4), 418–436. https://doi.org/10.1111/rego.12035

Boswell, C. (2008). The Political Functions of Expert Knowledge: Knowledge and Legitimation in European Union Immigration Policy. *Journal of European Public Policy*, 15(4), 471–488. https://doi.org/10.1080/13501760801996634

Boswell, C. (2009). Knowledge, Legitimation and the Politics of Risk: The Functions of Research in Public Debates on Migration. *Political Studies*, 57(1), 165–186. https://doi.org/10.1111/j.1467-9248.2008.00729.x

Busuioc, M., & Rimkutė, D. (2020a). Meeting Expectations in the EU Regulatory State? Regulatory Communications amid Conflicting Institutional Demands. *Journal of European Public Policy*, 27(4), 547–568. https://doi.org/10.1080/13501763.2019.1603248

Busuioc, M., & Rimkutė, D. (2020b). The Promise of Bureaucratic Reputation Approaches for the EU Regulatory State. *Journal of European Public Policy*, 27(8), 1256–1269. https://doi.org/10.1080/13501763.2019.1679227

Caramani, D. (2017). Will vs. Reason: The Populist and Technocratic Forms of Political Representation and Their Critique to Party Government. *American Political Science Review*, 111(1), 54–67. https://doi.org/10.1017/S0003055416000538

Carpenter, D. (2010a). Institutional Strangulation: Bureaucratic Politics and Financial Reform in the Obama Administration. *Perspectives on Politics*, 8(3), 825–846.

Carpenter, D. (2010b). *Reputation and Power: Organizational Image and Pharmaceutical Regulation at the FDA* (1st edition). Princeton University Press.

Carpenter, D., & Krause, G. A. (2012). Reputation and Public Administration. *Public Administration Review*, 72(1), 26–32. https://doi.org/10.1111/j.1540-6210.2011.02506.x

Christensen, J. (2020). Expert Knowledge And Policymaking: A Multi-Disciplinary Research Agenda. *Policy & Politics*. https://doi.org/10.1332/030557320X15898190680037

Christensen, J., & Hesstvedt, S. (2019). Expertisation or Greater Representation? Evidence from Norwegian Advisory Commissions. *European Politics and Society*, 20(1), 83–100. https://doi.org/10.1080/23745118.2018.1515861

Christensen, J., & Yesilkagit, K. (2019). International Public Administrations: A Critique. *Journal of European Public Policy*, 26(6), 946–961. https://doi.org/10.1080/13501763.2018.1508245

Costa, M., Desmarais, B. A., & Hird, J. A. (2019). Public Comments' Influence on Science Use in U.S. Rulemaking: The Case of EPA's National Emission Standards. *The American Review of Public Administration*, 49(1), 36–50. https://doi.org/10.1177/0275074018795287

Elgie, R., & McMenamin, I. (2005). Credible Commitment, Political Uncertainty or Policy Complexity? Explaining Variations in the Independence of Non-majoritarian Institutions in France. *British Journal of Political Science*, 35(3), 531–548. https://doi.org/10.1017/S0007123405000281

Eriksen, E. O., & Fossum, J. E. (2004). Europe in Search of Legitimacy: Strategies of Legitimation Assessed. *International Political Science Review*, 25(4), 435–459. https://doi.org/10.1177/0192512104045089

European Commission (2002). "Communication from the Commission: The Operating Framework for the European Regulatory Agencies" COM(2002) 718 final, 11 December, Brussels: Commission of the European Communities.

Fischer, F. (2009). *Democracy and Expertise: Reorienting Policy Inquiry*. Oxford University Press.

Follesdal, A., & Hix, S. (2006). Why There is a Democratic Deficit in the EU: A Response to Majone and Moravcsik. *Journal of Common Market Studies*, 44(3), 533–562. https://doi.org/10.1111/j.1468-5965.2006.00650.x

Fox, T., Versluis, E., & Asselt, M. B. A. van. (2011). Regulating the Use of Bisphenol A in Baby and Children's Products in the European Union: Current Developments and Scenarios for the Regulatory Future. *European Journal of Risk Regulation*, 2(1), 21–35. https://doi.org/10.1017/S1867299X00000593

Gilad, S., Maor, M., & Bloom, P. B.-N. (2015). Organizational Reputation, the Content of Public Allegations, and Regulatory Communication. *Journal of Public Administration Research and Theory*, 25(2), 451–478. https://doi.org/10.1093/jopart/mut041

Gilardi, F. (2005). The Institutional Foundations of Regulatory Capitalism: The Diffusion of Independent Regulatory Agencies in Western Europe. *The ANNALS of the American Academy of Political and Social Science, 598*(1), 84–101. https://doi.org/10.1177/0002716204271833

Gilardi, F. (2008). *Delegation in the Regulatory State: Independent Regulatory Agencies in Western Europe*. Cheltenham, UK and Northampton, MA, USA: Edward Elgar Publishing.

Gornitzka, Å., & Holst, C. (2015). The Expert–Executive Nexus in the EU: An Introduction. *Politics and Governance, 3*(1), 1–12. https://doi.org/10.17645/pag.v3i1.271

Hertin, J., Turnpenny, J., Jordan, A., Nilsson, M., Russel, D., & Nykvist, B. (2009). Rationalising the Policy Mess? Ex Ante Policy Assessment and the Utilisation of Knowledge in the Policy Process. *Environment and Planning A: Economy and Space, 41*(5), 1185–1200. https://doi.org/10.1068/a40266

Hesstvedt, S., & Christensen, J. (2021). Political and Administrative Control of Expert Groups: A Mixed-Methods Study. *Governance*, early view. https://doi.org/10.1111/gove.12599

Holst, C., & Molander, A. (2019). Epistemic Democracy and the Role of Experts. *Contemporary Political Theory, 18*(4), 541–561. https://doi.org/10.1057/s41296-018-00299-4

Jasanoff, S. (1990). American Exceptionalism and the Political Acknowledgment of Risk. *Daedalus, 119*(4), 61–81.

Jennings, E. T., & Hall, J. L. (2012). Evidence-Based Practice and the Use of Information in State Agency Decision Making. *Journal of Public Administration Research and Theory, 22*(2), 245–266. https://doi.org/10.1093/jopart/mur040

Lee, D., & Ryzin, G. G. V. (2019). Measuring Bureaucratic Reputation: Scale Development and Validation. *Governance, 32*(1), 177–192. https://doi.org/10.1111/gove.12371

Levi-Faur, D. (2011). Regulatory Networks and Regulatory Agencification: Towards a Single European Regulatory Space. *Journal of European Public Policy, 18*(6), 810–829. https://doi.org/10.1080/13501763.2011.593309

Linz, J. J. (1998). Democracy's Time Constraints: *International Political Science Review, 19*(1), 19–37. https://doi.org/10.1177/019251298019001002

Lodge, M., & Wegrich, K. (2011). Governance as Contested Logics of Control: Europeanized Meat Inspection Regimes in Denmark and Germany. *Journal of European Public Policy, 18*(1), 90–105. https://doi.org/10.1080/13501763.2011.520880

Maggetti, M. (2007). De Facto Independence after Delegation: A Fuzzy-Set Analysis. *Regulation & Governance, 1*(4), 271–294. https://doi.org/10.1111/j.1748-5991.2007.00023.x

Maggetti, M. (2009). The Role of Independent Regulatory Agencies in Policy-making: A Comparative Analysis. *Journal of European Public Policy, 16*(3), 450–470. https://doi.org/10.1080/13501760802662854

Maggetti, M. (2010). Legitimacy and Accountability of Independent Regulatory Agencies: A Critical Review. *Living Reviews in Democracy*, 1–9.

Majone, G. (1996). *Regulating Europe*. Routledge. https://doi.org/10.4324/9780203439197

Majone, G. (1997). From the Positive to the Regulatory State: Causes and Consequences of Changes in the Mode of Governance. *Journal of Public Policy, 17*(2), 139–167. https://www.jstor.org/stable/4007608

Majone, G. (1998). Europe's 'Democratic Deficit': The Question of Standards. *European Law Journal, 4*(1), 5–28. https://doi.org/10.1111/1468-0386.00040

Majone, G. (1999). The Regulatory State and its Legitimacy Problems. *West European Politics, 22*(1), 1–24. https://doi.org/10.1080/01402389908425284

Mantzari, D., & Vantaggiato, F. P. (2020). The Paradox of Regulatory Discretion. *Law & Policy, 42*(4), 382–403. https://doi.org/10.1111/lapo.12158

Maor, M., Gilad, S., & Bloom, P. B.-N. (2013). Organizational Reputation, Regulatory Talk, and Strategic Silence. *Journal of Public Administration Research and Theory, 23*(3), 581–608. https://doi.org/10.1093/jopart/mus047

Mathieu, E. (2016). *Regulatory Delegation in the European Union: Networks, Committees and Agencies*. Palgrave Macmillan UK. https://doi.org/10.1057/978-1-137-57835-8

Meier, K. J., Compton, M., Polga-Hecimovich, J., Song, M., & Wimpy, C. (2019). Bureaucracy and the Failure of Politics: Challenges to Democratic Governance. *Administration & Society, 51*(10), 1576–1605. https://doi.org/10.1177/0095399719874759

Müller, M., & Braun, C. (2021). Guiding or Following the Crowd? Strategic Communication as Reputational and Regulatory Strategy. *Journal of Public Administration Research and Theory*, *31*(4), 670–686. https://doi.org/10.1093/jopart/muab008

Norris, P., & Inglehart, R. (2019). *Cultural Backlash: Trump, Brexit, and Authoritarian Populism*. Cambridge University Press. https://doi.org/10.1017/9781108595841

Ossege, C. (2016). *European Regulatory Agencies in EU Decision-Making: Between Expertise and Influence*. Palgrave Macmillan UK. https://doi.org/10.1057/9781137517906

Overman, S., Busuioc, M., & Wood, M. (2020). A Multidimensional Reputation Barometer for Public Agencies: A Validated Instrument. *Public Administration Review*, *80*(3), 415–425. https://doi.org/10.1111/puar.13158

Papadopoulos, Y. (2003). Cooperative Forms of Governance: Problems of Democratic Accountability in Complex Environments. *European Journal of Political Research*, *42*(4), 473–501. https://doi.org/10.1111/1475-6765.00093

Pollack, M. A. (2006). Delegation and Discretion in the European Union. In D. L. Nielson, D. G. Hawkins, D. A. Lake, & M. J. Tierney (Eds.), *Delegation and Agency in International Organizations* (pp. 165–196). Cambridge University Press. https://doi.org/10.1017/CBO9780511491368.007

Radaelli, C. M. (1995). The Role of Knowledge in the Policy Process. *Journal of European Public Policy*, *2*(2), 159–183. https://doi.org/10.1080/13501769508406981

Radaelli, C. M. (1999). The Public Policy of the European Union: Whither Politics of Expertise? *Journal of European Public Policy*, *6*(5), 757–774. https://doi.org/10.1080/135017699343360

Radaelli, C. M. (2009). Measuring Policy Learning: Regulatory Impact Assessment in Europe. *Journal of European Public Policy*, *16*(8), 1145–1164. https://doi.org/10.1080/13501760903332647

Rimkutė, D. (2015). Explaining Differences in Scientific Expertise Use: The Politics of Pesticides. *Politics and Governance*, *3*(1), 114–127. https://doi.org/10.17645/pag.v3i1.82

Rimkutė, D. (2018). Organizational Reputation and Risk Regulation: The Effect of Reputational Threats on Agency Scientific Outputs. *Public Administration*, *96*(1), 70–83. https://doi.org/10.1111/padm.12389

Rimkutė, D. (2020a). Building Organizational Reputation in the European Regulatory State: An Analysis of EU Agencies' Communications. *Governance*, *33*(2), 385–406. https://doi.org/10.1111/gove.12438

Rimkutė, D. (2020b). Strategic Silence or Regulatory Talk? Regulatory Agency Responses to Public Allegations Amidst the Glyphosate Controversy. *Journal of European Public Policy*, *27*(11), 1636–1656. https://doi.org/10.1080/13501763.2020.1817130

Rimkutė, D. (2021). EU Agencies. In D. Hodson, U. Puetter, S. Saurugger, & J. Petersen (Eds), *The Institutions of the European Union* (5th edition, pp. 203–223). Oxford University Press.

Rimkutė, D., & De Vos, H. (2020). *Organizational reputation and strategic communication: An analysis of agency communications using machine-learning techniques*. ECPR General Conference, Innsbruck.

Rimkutė, D., & Haverland, M. (2015). How does the European Commission use Scientific Expertise? Results from a Survey of Scientific Members of the Commission's Expert Committees. *Comparative European Politics*, *13*(4), 430–449. https://doi.org/10.1057/cep.2013.32

Rothstein, H., Borraz, O., & Huber, M. (2013). Risk and the Limits of Governance: Exploring Varied Patterns of Risk-Based Governance across Europe. *Regulation & Governance*, *7*(2), 215–235. https://doi.org/10.1111/j.1748-5991.2012.01153.x

Scharpf, F. W. (1999). *Governing in Europe: Effective and Democratic?* Oxford University Press. https://cadmus.eui.eu//handle/1814/21979

Schrefler, L. (2010). The Usage of Scientific Knowledge by Independent Regulatory Agencies. *Governance*, *23*(2), 309–330. https://doi.org/10.1111/j.1468-0491.2010.01481.x

Schrefler, L. (2013). *Economic Knowledge in Regulation: The Use of Expertise by Independent Agencies*. ECPR Press.

Url, B. (2018). Don't Attack Science Agencies for Political Gain. *Nature*, *553*(7689), 381. https://doi.org/10.1038/d41586-018-01071-9

Vibert, F. (2007). *The Rise of the Unelected: Democracy and the New Separation of Powers*. Cambridge University Press. https://doi.org/10.1017/CBO9780511491160

Vos, E. (2017). Three Decades of EU Risk Regulation Research. *European Journal of Risk Regulation*, *8*(1), 47–51. https://doi.org/10.1017/err.2016.7

Weiss, C. H. (1979). The Many Meanings of Research Utilization. *Public Administration Review*, *39*(5), 426–431. https://doi.org/10.2307/3109916

Wonka, A., & Rittberger, B. (2010). Credibility, Complexity and Uncertainty: Explaining the Institutional Independence of 29 EU Agencies. *West European Politics*, *33*(4), 730–752. https://doi.org/10.1080/01402381003794597

Wood, M. (2018). Mapping EU Agencies as Political Entrepreneurs. *European Journal of Political Research*, *57*(2), 404–426. https://doi.org/10.1111/1475-6765.12232

Zarkin, M. (2021). Knowledge Utilization in the Regulatory State: An Empirical Examination of Schrefler's Typology. *Policy Studies*, *42*(1), 24–41. https://doi.org/10.1080/01442872.2020.1772220

Index

1&1 142

Abdel Gawad, S. 62
Abolafia, M. Y. 277
accountability 5, 27, 38, 55, 66, 72, 88, 99–100,
    119, 130, 163, 181, 185, 211, 227, 231,
    233, 255–68, 274–5, 319, 322, 331–4,
    349–50, 395, 399, 415–17, 433, 441–2
Administrative Procedure Act 16, 314, 348–9,
    351, 355
administrative procedures 62, 65, 197, 200, 341
Adolph, C. 100
Affordable Care Act 355–6
Affordable Clean Energy Rule 234, 429
Afghanistan 91
African Union Convention on Preventing and
    Combating Corruption 178
AGCOM 383
Agence Française Anticorruption 180
Agence Nationale de Réglementation des
    Télécommunications 64
Agência Nacional de Energia Elétrica 1, 16
agencification 3, 43, 45, 56, 72, 79–87, 91–2,
    255, 259–60, 402, 410–11, 421, 427, 488,
    490–91, 498
Agency for the Cooperation of Energy Regulators
    30
Agenda 2030 161, 310
agenda-setting 3, 5, 7, 135, 188, 305, 379–89
Agrell, Per J. 367
Airline Deregulation Act 315
Aldy, J. 324
Algeria 64, 66, 72, 91
algorithmic governance 168
algorithms 3, 6, 159, 168–9, 452, 471–2, 475–7,
    480–81
Allcot, H. 463
Allio, Lorenzo 4
Almond, P. 403
Alon-Barkat, Saar 480
Alphabet see Google
Amazon 115, 121, 128, 139, 141, 444, 447, 474
Andres, L. 52, 55
Angola 91
ANSES 386, 492
anticorruption 4, 177–89
antitrust 3, 12, 113, 118–19, 121–2, 143, 148–9,
    182, 217–18, 236, 314–16, 319, 368, 373,
    404, 447

see also competition law
Apple 115, 121, 128, 318
Arab Convention against Corruption 178
arbitrariness review 349, 351–3, 355
Argentina 45, 47–9, 53, 91, 216
artificial intelligence 3, 6, 168, 235, 297, 470–82
Association of Southeast Asian Nations 79
AT&T 148, 150, 315–17
audiences 102, 105, 166, 178, 184, 231, 243–50,
    260, 267, 273–80, 294–5, 298, 464, 495–6
austerity 106
Australia 91, 262–3, 275, 357, 492
Austria 91, 115–16, 135–42
Austrian Post 142
automatization 156–7
autonomy 2, 21–2, 30, 35, 38, 45–8, 53, 55, 80,
    85–90, 96–7, 99, 103, 113, 116, 130,
    134–5, 148, 178, 184, 186–7, 201, 220,
    228–30, 242–3, 245, 247, 250, 259, 264,
    305, 331, 364, 380–81, 384, 401, 415–16,
    420, 426–7, 430, 489, 496
Autorità Nazionale Anticorruzione 1
Autorité de Régulation des Communications
    Électroniques et des Postes 1
Aydin, U. 52

Bach, D. 432
Badran, Ahmed 4, 61, 67
Baldwin, Robert 2, 396
Bangladesh 91
Bank of England 97, 100, 104
Banque de France 97
Barkow, Rachel E. 18–19, 368
Barnett, Kent 357
Barth, James R. 218
Bartle, Ian 379
Basel Committee 214
Batory, A. 182–3
Bawn, Kathleen 214
Beecher, Janice 150
behavioural insights 5, 457–66
Belgium 91, 115, 136–41, 275, 334–5
Bellodi, L. 275
Bennett, C. 129
Ben-Nun Bloom, P. 277
BEREC 30, 37, 411, 426, 429–30
Berg, Sanford 52, 216
Bernstein, Marver H. 13, 367
better regulation 167, 247, 451

in the EU 303–11
in the US 314–27
Better Regulation Task Force 306
Bianculli, Andrea 79
biases 37, 51, 98, 104, 137, 140, 162, 167–9,
    197–8, 212, 221, 230, 248, 265, 353, 363,
    366–7, 416, 458–61, 463, 471–2, 474–6,
    479–82, 489
Biden, Joe 320, 323
big data 3, 161, 168
Big Tech 128, 137, 143, 452, 474
    see also individual companies
Bignami, F. 129–31, 139, 143
Binder, M. 430
black boxes 262, 472, 475–81
Blair, Tony 443
blame 6, 97–9, 104, 106, 211, 231, 233, 241,
    245–6, 250, 273, 275–9
Blue Global Media 141
Bolivia 45, 49–50, 91
Boon, J. 278
Bortolotti, Bernardo 216–17
Bowles, R. 397, 403
Bradsma, G. 32
Braithwaite, John 362, 367
Brazil 1, 45–50, 54, 90–91, 155, 249
Bretton Woods system 113
Brexit 248, 309–10, 459
bribery 177, 363
British Airways 139, 142
British Petroleum 446
British Telecommunications 38
Brown, Gordon 306
Brunei 91
Buccirossi, Paolo 119
Bulgaria 91, 136–41
Bundeskartellamt 113
Bundesverfassungsgericht 132
bureaucratic politics 233, 245, 428–9, 432, 497
bureaucratic reputation 179, 184, 186, 273–5,
    488, 493–6, 498
Burkina Faso 91
Business Environment Simplification Task Force
    305
business models 165, 474
Business Roundtable v. SEC 15
Busuioc, Madalina 5, 277, 417, 432, 480

Cable Act 316
Cadman, R. 37
Cambini, Carlo 217
Cambodia 91
Cambridge Analytica 128, 140
Cameroon 91
Canada 91, 129, 185–6, 275, 357, 492

capitalism 33–5, 38, 43, 78, 117, 372
Çapkurt, F. 336
capture *see* regulatory capture
Carpenter, Daniel P. 3, 243–4, 246, 249, 362,
    364–5, 369, 495
Carrigan, Christopher 4
Carter, Jimmy 78, 351, 354
Cave, Martin 2, 396
central banks 1, 4, 44, 46, 48, 79, 81, 83–5, 89,
    91–2, 96–107, 116, 123, 213–14, 247, 331,
    334, 338, 435
Centre on Regulation in Europe 336
Chad 91
Chevron doctrine 346–7, 350, 353–7
Chicago School 121–2
Chile 43–7, 49, 51, 54–5, 91, 216
China 90–91, 147, 151, 155, 164
Civil Aeronautics Board 315
civil servants 32, 46, 135, 325
CJUE 106
Clayton Act 114
Clean Air Amendments Act 354
Clean Power Plan 234
climate change 6, 63, 107, 157–8, 234, 441, 452
Clinton, Bill 318, 323, 443
CMS 139
Coen, David 4, 37
coercive isomorphism 51, 68–9
Coglianese, Cary 5, 383, 385
cognitive behavioural theory 243
cognitive-based regulation 163, 169
Cohen, Nissim 385
Cold War 132, 148, 151
Colombia 44–7, 49, 52–3, 90–91
colonialism 44, 56, 147, 152
Committee of European Securities Regulators 29,
    430
Commodity Futures Trading Commission 15, 17,
    447
COMPAS 475–6
Competition and Markets Authority 462, 464
Competition Appeal Tribunal 335
competition authorities 1, 4, 36–8, 113–23,
    217–18, 250, 334, 339, 399, 403, 462
competition law 3, 30, 36–8, 45, 66, 107–23, 143,
    211, 217–18, 403, 413
    see also antitrust; redistribution
Competitiveness Council 309
compliance 2, 131, 133–4, 162, 177, 183, 185,
    188, 247–8, 259, 276, 286–7, 290, 292–3,
    310, 320, 323, 326–7, 338, 394–403, 411,
    417, 445, 449, 457, 475, 477–8
Congo 90–91
Conseil Constitutionnel 333
Conseil d'Etat 305

consultation 61, 69–70, 243, 293, 303, 305–8, 333, 335, 368, 416
Consumer Financial Protection Bureau 15–17
consumer groups 37, 63
consumer price index 119, 218
Consumer Product Safety Commission 14, 17
consumer protection 116, 154, 219, 366, 399, 446, 457
contingency theory 434
cooperation 7, 30, 32, 70, 106, 119–20, 129, 133, 186, 188, 275, 297, 314, 339, 367, 371–3, 400–401, 411, 417, 427
coordinated market economies 34, 117
Corruption Practices Investigation Bureau 179–80
Costa Rica 49, 91
cost–benefit analysis 21, 162, 164, 297, 304, 319–21, 325, 350, 367
cost-effectiveness 162, 290, 294, 318–20
Cote d'Ivoire 91
Council of Europe 131, 178
Court of Justice of the European Union 33, 36–7, 331–2, 334–41, 413, 416
courts 33–4, 36, 132, 142–3, 321, 334–5, 337–40, 348–9, 356, 403, 475, 477
   see also judicial review
   Court of Justice of the European Union 36–7, 331–2, 334–41, 413, 416
   European Court of Human Rights 336
   European Court of Justice 29, 39, 100, 134–5, 138
   Supreme Court 12–13, 15–16, 150, 315, 347–57
COVID-19 pandemic 6, 93, 107, 113–14, 121–2, 128, 142, 161, 163–4, 166, 169–70, 310, 383, 385, 441, 444, 446, 452, 489
Crandall, R. 317
Criminal Law Convention on Corruption 178
Croatia 136–8, 141
Croley, Steven P. 363
Cuba 48–50, 91
Cubbin, John 216
Cyprus 91, 136–8, 140–41
Czechia 91, 116, 136–8, 140

data protection 3–4, 6, 79, 81, 84, 92, 128–44, 476
Data Protection Convention 132
Datla, Kirti 19
David-Barrett, E. 187
de Boer, N. 404
de Cabanes, Antoine 4
De Francesco, Fabrizio 35
De Somer, Stéphanie 5
decarbonization 156–8

decentralization 27, 30, 84–5, 120, 149, 155–7, 200, 339, 386, 412, 425, 427, 431, 444
Deepwater Horizon 446
democratic deficit 2, 99, 232, 380, 490–91
Demortain, D. 162
Denmark 91, 116, 136–8, 140–41, 262–3, 275
Department of Justice 12, 120
Department of the Interior 11
Department of the Treasury 11, 16
Department of Transportation 323–4
deregulation 10, 14–15, 22, 93, 101, 234, 309, 314–18, 324–5, 327, 365, 372, 443
Deters, Henning 382
Deutsche Wohnen 142
Devins, Neal 22
Dewatripont, Mathias 367
Dewey, M. 403–4
Di Carlo, D. 403
Di Mascio, Fabrizio 4, 383, 385
Dierx, Adriaan 118
Digital Markets Act 404
digitalization 3, 6, 146, 156, 158–9, 165–6, 471
   see also Big Tech
dignity 320, 444, 452
DiMaggio, P. 68
Dincer, N. Nergiz 218
Dodd–Frank Act 15, 105
Dominican Republic 49, 91
double delegation 30, 433
double-hatted agencies 261, 427–8, 433
Doumpos, Michael 218
Draghi, Mario 278
DREAM framework 396
dual delegation 426, 433
Dubash, N. K. 33, 54
Dudley, Susan 5, 14
Dunlop, Claire A. 5
Dusk, M. 63

Eberlein, B. 32, 430
economic growth 27, 100, 106–7, 118, 215, 470
economic regulation 3, 5, 14, 30, 33, 38, 46–8, 50, 64, 114, 117, 155, 211, 219–20, 248, 288, 315, 331, 333, 335, 457–66
Ecuador 44, 49, 52, 91
Edwards, Geoff 216
effectiveness 13, 32, 37–8, 54, 70–71, 118–19, 123, 128, 130, 135, 162–4, 166, 177, 185, 197, 200, 212–13, 216–18, 235, 256, 287, 294, 303–4, 326, 332, 337, 365, 399, 402–3, 405, 415–18, 432, 434, 446, 458, 461, 463, 482, 490, 495
Egeberg, M. 427
Egypt 61–5, 67–71, 229

Egyptian Water/Wastewater Regulatory Agency 65
Eichengreen, Barry 218
Eisner, A. 61
El Salvador 45, 49, 91
Elgie, R. 99
Ellig, Jerry 5, 14
El-Nawawy, M. 64
emissions trading schemes 290
empathy 288, 295–6, 298
endogeneity 35, 65, 82, 217, 221, 275
enforcement 394–405
entrepreneurship 165, 232, 241, 379–86, 389
entry barriers 318, 362–3, 365
environmental issues 6, 14, 63, 107, 157–8, 234, 354, 383, 441, 452
Environmental Protection Agency 234, 354, 383
Equifax 141
ERRADA 61–2
Estache, Antonio 52, 55, 216–17
Estonia 91, 136–8, 140–41
EU Charter of Fundamental Rights 133
European Administrative Space 425, 429
European agencies 27, 29–30, 36–7, 43–4, 47–8, 65, 67, 82–3, 146–9, 151–6, 229, 232, 261, 277–8, 303–11, 331–41, 386–7, 410–21, 428, 432
    see also European Union; *individual agencies*; *individual countries*
European Agency for the Evaluation of Medicinal Products 30
European Asylum Support Office 489
European Aviation Safety Authority 30, 404, 411
European Banking Agency 30
European Banking Authority 30, 104, 411, 417, 489
European Central Bank 97–9, 101–7, 278, 331–4, 337–41
European Centre for Disease Prevention and Control 411
European Chemicals Agency 411, 414
European Coal and Steel Community 113
European Commission 27–34, 36, 113–14, 119–21, 123, 132, 152–5, 157–8, 303–10, 335–6, 410, 412–16, 419, 426, 430, 478, 490
European Competition Network 119–20, 426, 429
European Court of Human Rights 336
European Court of Justice 29, 39, 100, 134–5, 138
European Data Protection Board 130, 133, 136, 138–40, 142
European Economic Community 113
European Electronic Communications Code 334–5

European Fisheries Control Agency 411
European Food Safety Authority 30, 167, 232, 411, 413–14, 487, 489, 492
European Insurance and Occupational Pensions Authority 411, 489
European Maritime Safety Agency 411
European Medicine Agency 411, 414, 416
European Parliament 30, 33, 36–7, 104–5, 154, 303, 307, 310, 410, 412, 416, 418
European Public Prosecutors' Office 402
European Railway Traffic Management System 156, 429
European Regulator Group for Electricity and Gas 29
European Regulatory Networks 27–32, 37–9, 412–13, 418–20, 425–36
European Securities and Market Authority 30, 400, 411, 413, 489
European single market 27–8, 30–33, 38, 425, 428
European Supervisory Authorities 489
European System of Central Banks 435
European System Risk Board 103
European Union 3, 5–6, 27–39, 82, 98–9, 103, 114–15, 117–18, 120–21, 150–55, 157, 159, 164, 214, 219, 261, 275, 277–8, 331–40, 365, 382, 385, 387, 394, 400–405, 410–21, 425–32, 436, 457, 471, 487–90, 492
    better regulation in 303–11
    Brexit 248, 309–10, 459
    draft AI regulation 477–81
    EU law 29, 331–2, 337, 397, 400–405, 488
    General Data Protection Regulation *see* GDPR
Europeanization 38–9, 152, 402–3
Eurozone 101, 103, 105, 278
evidence-based practice 62, 163, 307, 310, 322, 327, 333, 387, 462, 491–2
executive branch agencies 10–11, 15–16, 19, 21–2
Executive Office of the President 11
executive politics 241–2, 245
experiments 45, 169–70, 180, 247, 258–9, 264, 306, 322–3, 327, 450, 459, 463, 465, 470, 480
expertise 487–98

Facebook 128, 141, 158
Fair Credit Reporting Act 131
Falkner, Gerda 382
Farrell, Henry 373
Febrizio, Mark 4
Federal Communications Commission 15, 17, 20, 150, 315–18

Federal Data Protection Act 131
Federal Energy Regulatory Commission 150, 316
Federal Housing Finance Agency 15–17
Federal Reserve 16–17, 100–101, 103–5, 277
Federal Reserve Act 105
Federal Trade Commission 12–13, 16–17, 19,
 113, 120, 131, 141
Fernández-i-Marín, Xavier 4, 79, 115
Financial Conduct Authority 462–4
Financial Services Authority 233, 451
Financial Stability Oversight Council 105
financialization 100–102, 106
Finger, Matthias 4
Finland 91, 136–8, 140–41
FINMA 231
fit-for-future platform 309
Flaherty, D. 129, 134
Fontan, Clément 4
Food and Agriculture Organization 425
Food and Drug Administration 1, 232, 243, 249,
 364, 383
food safety 2, 46–7, 79, 81, 84, 89, 92, 117,
 167–8, 219, 232, 291, 466, 470, 487, 489,
 492, 498
for-cause removal protections 16, 18
Ford, Cristie 5
Forder, J. 96
Forrence, Jennifer L. 363
France 1, 34, 66, 91, 98, 116, 129, 132, 136–42,
 147, 163–4, 179, 305, 333, 335, 386, 492
functionalists 28, 31–2, 38, 100, 432, 436,
 488–90, 498

Gaganis, Chrysovalantis 218
Gaskins, Darius 315
Gautier, Axel 367
GDPR 128–44, 475–6
General Data Protection Regulation *see* GDPR
Germany 34, 91, 105–6, 113, 129–33, 135–42,
 147, 163, 275, 305, 307, 337–40, 357
Ghana 91
Gilad, Sharon 277, 364
Gilardi, Fabrizio 45, 117, 213, 430
Global Financial Crisis 6, 15, 97, 102–7, 113–14,
 121–3, 218, 221, 231, 233, 235, 242, 249,
 304, 341, 366, 414, 435, 444–5, 449–51,
 473, 489
globalization 45, 68, 78–9, 82, 92, 146, 151, 155,
 169, 427, 430, 435, 450
Goffman, Erving 243–6, 249–50
Gómez Álvarez, S. 52
González, C. I. 52–3
González Becerra, Camilo 4
Goodhart, C. 100
Google 115, 121, 128, 139, 141–2, 158–9, 474

Gordon, Sanford C. 367
Gormley, William T. 366
Graham, John D. 387
Grande, E. 32
Great Depression 12, 348
GRECO 180
Greece 91, 136–8, 140–41
Green, J. 106
Green Deal 309
Greenleaf, G. 129
Guardiancich, Igor 117
Guasch, J. Luis 217
Guaschino, Edoardo 5, 383, 385–6
Guatemala 45, 49, 91
Guidi, Mattia 4, 38, 117, 119, 218
Gutiérrez, Luis H. 52, 55, 216

H&M 139
Hafer, Catherine 367
Hahn, Robert W. 21, 321
Haiti 49, 90–91
Hancké, Bob 33
Hanretty, Chris 119, 212–13, 218
Hansen, B. 32
Hanson, Jon 368
harmonization 29, 31–2, 38, 135, 139, 152,
 154–5, 266, 404, 412, 425–8, 431, 434–6
Hatmaker, D. M. 277
Hawkins, K. 245
Hazard Analysis and Critical Control Points 290
Hazlett, T. W. 316
health and safety 3, 63–4, 81, 386
Henisz, W. 68
Henry, Emmanuel 388
Hessian Data Protection Act 131
Hobolth, M. 431
Honduras 45, 49
Hong Kong 91, 179–80
Hoover, Herbert 12
Housing and Economic Recovery Act 15
human rights 132, 188, 426
Humphrey, William E. 12
Humphrey's Executor v. United States 12–13,
 16, 19
Hungary 91, 136–8, 140–41
Huntington, Samuel 13, 368
Hyman, David A. 123

Iceland 91
Ilzkovitz, Fabienne 118
impact assessment 5, 62–3, 71, 247, 294, 303–8,
 310, 314, 318–23, 325–6, 333, 339
Impact Assessment Board 303, 307–8
IMPEL 426
impression management 244–5, 247

see also reputation
independence 211–22, 241
    alternative methods for evaluating 18–19
    of central banks 96–107, 213–14
    consequences of competition authorities'
        118–19
    de facto 227–30
    definition of 212–13
    in the GDPR 134–5
Independent Commission against Corruption
    179–80
independent commissions 12–14, 16, 20–21,
    179–80, 367
independent regulatory agencies *see* regulatory
    agencies
India 1, 87, 91, 147, 155
Indonesia 91
Infitah 64
inflation 97–100, 102, 105–6, 116, 214, 277, 316
information asymmetry 6, 289
innovation 6, 82, 118, 165–6, 170, 309–10,
    441–52, 471
Instituto Federal de Telecomunicaciones 47
intensity 80–82, 88, 213, 260, 331–3, 335,
        339–40, 346, 350, 362, 366, 370, 402, 465
Inter-American Convention against Corruption
    178
interest groups 13, 18, 33, 53, 236, 246, 251, 258,
        265, 291, 362–3, 366, 368–70, 385, 413,
        416, 419, 497
interest rates 102, 106, 442, 447, 463–4
Internal Revenue Service 355–6
International Agency for Research on Cancer 492
International Competition Network 113, 119–21
International Monetary Fund 51, 68–9, 98, 101,
    399
Interstate Commerce Act (1887) 12, 16
Interstate Commerce Commission 2, 12–17, 315,
    325
Iran 91
Iraq 91
Ireland 91, 115, 121, 136–42, 275
Ismail, M. 64
isomorphism 51, 67–9
ISPRA 386
Israel 90–91, 275–7
Italy 1, 91, 98, 116, 129, 136–41, 147, 155, 164,
        179, 184, 357, 383, 386
Itissalat Al Maghrib 64

Jabotinsky, Hadar Y. 385
Jakarta Statement on Principles for
        Anti-Corruption Agencies 178
Jamaica 216, 249
Japan 90–91, 115, 492

Jordan 62–4, 68–70, 72
Jordana, Jacint 4–5, 33, 44, 48, 79, 115, 218–19
Jóri, András 135
judicial deference 347
judicial review 5, 138, 141–2, 168, 188, 256,
        331–41, 346–57, 370
Juncker Commission 308
Juncker–Timmermans vision 303, 309

Kagan, Elena 349–50
Kahn, Alfred 315
Kahneman, D. 459
Kalaitzake, M. 102
Kaufman, Herbert 367
Kazakhstan 91
Keleman, R. D. 429
Kemmerer, E. W. 44–5, 51
Kemmerer Mission 44–5, 51
Kenis, P. 434
Kenya 91
Keohane, R. O. 427, 435
Kessler, P. 115
Keynesianism 442
Kingdon, J. W. 381–2
Koninklijke KPN case 336–7
Koop, Christel 5, 115, 119, 212–13, 218
Koopmans Report 305
Kovacic, William E. 123, 399
Krapohl, Sebastian 219
Kraus, Bruce 20
Kudrna, Zdenek 38
Kuris, G. 180
Kuwait 91
Kwak, James 367

Laos 91
Lasheen, W. 64
Latin America 1, 3–4, 43–56, 79, 82–3, 90, 147,
        179, 211, 216–17
    see also individual countries
Latvia 91, 136–8, 140–41
Lavery, S. 106
Lavrijssen, S. 332, 336
law-making 232, 235, 303–4, 308, 310, 395, 400
Lebanon 61–3, 68–70
legibility problem 447
legitimacy challenges 7, 227, 232–6, 412, 416
Lehman Brothers 101
Lehmkuhl, Dirk 120
Lettanie, Ute 5
Levi-Faur, David 2, 4, 33, 115, 258
Levine, Michael E. 363
Levy, Brian 216
Lewis, David E. 22
Li, Yan 216

liberal market economies 34–6, 117
liberalization 2–3, 27–30, 33, 43–5, 50, 52, 60,
    66–8, 113, 117, 122, 146, 148, 151–2, 156,
    182, 216, 221, 236, 288, 315–17, 334, 398
libertarian paternalism 458, 461–2
Lindblom, Charles E. 372
LITER principles 399
Lithuania 91, 136–8, 140–41
Littlechild, Stephen 462
Littoz-Monnet, Annabelle 383–5
Livermore, Michael A. 21
lobbying 212, 317, 362–3, 365, 368, 370, 373,
    413
Lodge, Martin 2, 5, 277, 396
Lombardi, D. 104
Lula de Silva, Luiz Inácio 249
Luxembourg 91, 115, 121, 136–42
Lyons, Bruce 216

Ma, Tay-Cheng 118, 218
Maastricht Treaty 99, 151
machine learning 90, 168, 235, 293, 470–72,
    474–5, 477, 481, 496
Madagascar 91
Maggetti, Martino 4–5, 53, 265–6, 430
Majone, Giandacome 31, 54, 56, 66, 96, 242, 414
Makkai, Toni 362, 367
Malaysia 91
Mali 91
Malta 91, 136–8, 140–41
managerial autonomy 87–90
Mandelkern Report 305–6
Maor, Moshe 5, 277–8
market failures 128, 219, 264, 289, 319, 457–8
market power 117, 289, 315, 319, 325, 373, 447
market surveillance authorities 478
Marriot International 142
Martinez-Gallardo, C. 51
Martinsen, D. S. 431
Mathieu, Emmanuelle 5, 429
Mauritania 63
May, P. J. 403
MCI 315
McNamara, K. 98
Meade, E. 100
Meier, Kenneth J. 366
Meroni doctrine 413
Meuwese, A.C.M. 306
Mexico 44–5, 47, 49, 52, 54, 91, 249
Microsoft 115, 128
Middle East 4, 60–73
    see also individual countries
migration crisis 489
Moe, M. 67

monetary policy 97–106, 116, 214–15, 334,
    337–8, 340–41
monopolies 36, 64, 97, 113, 128, 147–9, 151–60,
    219, 315–16, 325, 334
Monopolies and Restrictive Practices
    Commission 113
Montoya, Miguel A. 53, 216
moral hazard 101, 230, 247
Moran, Michael 246
Morgan, B. 54
Morocco 61–4, 66, 69, 72, 91
Morrison, S. A. 324
Moschella, M. 104, 277
Moss, David 362, 365
Motor Carrier Act 315
Motor Vehicle Air Pollution Control Act (1965)
    14
multilevel governance 27
Multiple Stream Framework 382
Murillo, M. 51, 53
Murphy, Richard 5
Myanmar 90–91

Natalini, Alessandro 4
National Association of Regulatory Utilities
    Commissioners 150
National Competition Authorities *see* competition
    authorities
National Highway Traffic Safety Administration
    351–2
National Regulatory Agencies 27–39, 331–7, 340,
    410, 413–14, 417, 419–20, 426–7, 429–30
    see also individual countries
national sovereignty 31, 425
Natural Gas Policy Act 315
Natural Gas Wellhead Decontrol Act 315
natural language processing 471
neoliberalism 45, 93, 152
Nepal 91
Netherlands 90–91, 116, 136–41, 147, 231,
    262–3, 305–7, 334, 336, 470–71, 475, 477,
    480–81
network governance 36, 427–8, 430, 433–4
network industries 4, 146–60, 241, 331–2, 334–5,
    340
    see also utilities
Network of Corruption Prevention Authorities
    187–9
New Deal 12, 16, 347–8
new governance 21, 32, 451
new Keynesian macroeconomics 98, 102–3
New Zealand 91, 275
Newman, Abraham L. 373, 430
Nicaragua 45, 91
Niger 90–91

Nigeria 91
North Korea 91
Norway 91, 262–3, 275
Nuclear Regulatory Commission 14
nudge 5, 457–8, 460–65
Nunes, Rui 219
Nye, J. S. 427, 435

Obama, Barack 319, 323
Office of Information and Regulatory Affairs 11,
    19–21, 320–21, 323, 325–6, 350, 367
Office of Management and Budget 11, 318–21,
    367
Ofgem 461, 463
O'Neal, Daniel 315
'one-in, one out' initiatives 307, 309–10
Open Door Policy 64
Organisation for Economic Co-operation and
    Development 79, 115, 119–20, 131, 178,
    180, 214, 233, 249, 287–8, 306, 308, 368,
    399, 425, 463
organizational reputation 96, 185–6, 236, 247,
    277, 429, 432, 494–6
Ottow, A. 332, 399
Overman, Sjors 5
oversight 5–6, 11–12, 19–21, 46, 54, 100, 103,
    105, 149, 168, 181, 185, 188, 197, 200,
    235, 242, 248, 286, 303–4, 307–8, 314,
    320–21, 331, 362, 367–8, 416, 425–6, 449,
    470–82, 496

Pakistan 91
Panama 45, 49, 91
Paperwork Reduction Act (1995) 10–11, 16
Paraguay 91
Pardow, D. G. 51, 54
Parker, D. 55
Pasiouras, Fotios 218
paternalism 458, 461–2
Pavón Mediano, Andrés 4, 33, 53
Peci, A. 54
pensions 45–7, 54, 78–9, 81, 84, 89, 92
performance management 285–98
Peru 44–5, 47–9, 52, 55, 91
PHAEDRA/PHAEDRA II 129–30
Philippines 91, 216
Pierce, Jr., Richard J. 353
Pinochet, Augusto 45
Pinto, L. 277
Pires, R. R. C. 404
platformization 146, 158–60
Polak, J. 404
Poland 91, 136–41
policy entrepreneurs 232, 379–83, 385, 389
political choice approach 27, 33–4

political control 1, 45, 54, 104–5, 182–3, 187,
    193–203, 214, 347, 350, 352, 365, 367,
    426
political independence 48–50, 56, 78, 80, 85,
    87–90, 212, 332, 334, 340
political oversight 11, 100, 200, 331
    see also oversight
political uncertainty 66–7, 116–18, 182–3, 228,
    489
politicization 5, 7, 43, 98, 129, 181, 193–202,
    221, 264, 268, 385–6, 491
Pollack, M. A. 96
Popelier, Patricia 5
populism 6, 44, 53, 55–6, 188–9, 227, 233–4,
    236, 248, 287, 435–6, 444, 459, 493–4,
    497–8
Portugal 81, 91, 136–8, 140–41, 147, 219
Post, A. 53
post-delegation stage 187–8, 227–36, 332, 387,
    389
Potter, Rachel Augustine 22
poverty 54–5, 159, 310, 442
Powell, W. 68
presidentialism 349–50, 352
price controls 14, 316–17
Princen, Sebastiaan 381
principal–agent theory 28, 33–4, 72, 99, 177, 182,
    184, 227, 230–32, 235, 332, 364, 381, 431,
    433
prioritizing 29, 32, 121, 201, 215, 274–5, 278,
    289, 296, 470, 476
privacy 128–9, 131, 142, 168, 182, 426, 441, 446,
    452
    see also data protection
Privacy Act 131
privatization 2–3, 31, 33, 43–5, 50–51, 55, 64,
    68–9, 78, 114, 122, 148, 152, 165, 216–17,
    222, 242, 342, 457
procedural rationality 333, 335, 337–41
Prodi Commission 303, 306
professionalism 78–9
professionalization 38, 43, 368
property rights 62, 67, 319
Provan, K. G. 434
Pruitt, Scott 234
public accountability 80, 88–90, 260–61, 264
public interest 13, 18, 60, 65–6, 69, 72, 96,
    154–5, 288, 315, 321, 327, 362–3, 365–6,
    368–72, 451, 474
public opinion 170, 211, 365, 370–71
public utilities 3, 149, 366
public–private partnerships 61
Punctuated Equilibrium Theory 382

Qatar 64

qualitative comparative analysis 187, 229, 384–5
quality of regulation 211–22

R&D 165
racism 444, 474
Radaelli, Claudio M. 5, 306
randomized controlled trials 459, 462, 465
Rangone, Nicoletta 4
Raso, Connor 20, 385
rationalism 32–3, 50, 162, 419
Reagan, Ronald 78, 351, 354–5, 443
redistribution 43–4, 53–6, 170, 201, 250, 337, 431, 460
REFIT 308–9
RegTech 163, 169
regulatory agencies 1–7
    see also individual organizations
    and accountability 255–68
        see also accountability
    and agenda-setting 3, 5, 7, 135, 188, 305, 379–89
    anticorruption authorities 177–89
        see also anticorruption
    behavioural insights 5, 457–66
    data protection authorities 3–4, 6, 79, 81, 84, 92, 128–44, 476
    and democracy 84–6
    enforcement tasks 394–405
    in Europe *see* European agencies; European Regulatory Networks
    expertise 487–98
    in individual countries *see* National Regulatory Agencies; *individual countries*
    judicial review of agency action 331–41
    in Latin America 43–56
    in the Middle East 60–73
    network services 146–60
    performance management 285–98
    political control of 193–203
    in the post-delegation stage 227–36, 387
    quality of regulation 211–22
    and reputation 241–51, 273–80
        see also reputation
    risk regulation 3, 14, 45, 88, 161–70, 219–20, 273, 387, 398
    strategic communication by 5, 227, 243, 273–80
    tracking differences and similarities 78–93
    traditional characteristics of 15–18
regulatory analysis 15, 18–21, 321–2, 326, 400, 461
regulatory authorities *see* regulatory agencies

regulatory capture 10, 13–14, 22, 53, 71, 101, 116, 153–4, 177, 221, 244, 258, 315, 362–73
regulatory compact 149–50
regulatory enforcement 275, 297, 394, 398
regulatory excellence 288, 296, 298
Regulatory Flexibility Act 321
regulatory governance 2–3, 6, 27–31, 51–5, 60–61, 66, 69–70, 79, 81, 84, 90–91, 156–9, 188, 212, 216, 233–6, 267, 380, 403–4, 425, 432
regulatory impact 5, 20, 54, 62–3, 71, 73, 165, 170, 247, 294, 305–10, 314, 318–23, 325–7
    see also impact assessment
regulatory management 71, 285–8, 292, 294–8, 304
regulatory networks 5–6, 35, 93, 188, 261, 267, 488
    see also European Regulatory Networks
regulatory outcomes 21, 71, 130, 139, 193, 200, 314, 322–3, 465, 490
regulatory outputs 22, 36–8, 123, 143, 193–4, 198, 201, 221, 487, 489, 495
regulatory reforms 27, 45, 60–73, 78, 178, 222, 233, 287, 303, 305–6, 314, 323–4, 327, 383, 385, 388, 459
regulatory science 166–7
Regulatory Scrutiny Board 303, 307–8
regulatory state 2, 14, 28, 31, 43–8, 50, 60, 66–7, 70, 79, 93, 96, 122, 163, 241, 247–8, 379–80, 383, 389, 441–4, 448–9, 451–2, 490, 497
RegX 288
rent-seeking 315, 363, 446
reputation 6, 96, 102–4, 178–9, 184–7, 241–51, 273–80, 429, 432–3, 496
Revesz, Richard L. 19
Rex, Justin 5
Richardson, J. 130
ride-hailing apps 141, 159, 445
Righettini, M. S. 129–30, 139
Rimkutė, Dovilė 5, 432
risk assessment 7, 14, 162, 167–8, 289, 291, 304, 326, 449, 492
risk regulation 3, 14, 45, 88, 161–70, 219–20, 273, 387, 398
Robson, John 315
Rogers, T. 463
Romania 91, 136–8, 140–41
Rondi, Laura 217
Ros, Agustin J. 55, 216
Rosas, Guillermo 218–19
Rossi, Martin A. 216–17

rule of law 66, 177, 181, 229, 234, 363, 398, 401, 452
rulemaking 10–13, 23, 27, 182, 260, 286, 322, 324, 326, 334, 347–9, 351, 353, 355, 365, 367–8, 371, 373, 394, 398, 400, 402, 410
Russia 90, 147

Sabel, Charles F. 120
Sadat, Anwar 64
Salamon, L. M. 61
sanctions 2, 7, 48, 115, 120, 122, 130–31, 142, 177–8, 180, 182, 185, 196, 201–2, 222, 231, 256–7, 259, 336, 340, 364–5, 369, 394–403, 411, 427, 449–50, 470
Santer Commission 305, 412
Saudi Arabia 70, 91
Schillemans, Thomas 5
Scholten, D. 401
Scholten, Miroslava 5, 401
Schütz, Philip 41, 129
scientific knowledge 162, 167, 487, 490–92, 498
scientization 102–3
sector-specific regulation 1, 38, 131, 151–60, 231, 236
Securities and Exchange Commission 12, 16–17, 19, 141, 321, 447
Seidenfeld, Mark 353
Seila Law LLC v. Consumer Financial Protection Bureau 15
self-interest 32, 372
self-regulation 122, 130–31, 248, 291, 397, 443, 449, 473–5
Selin, Jennifer L. 5, 19
Senegal 91
Shapiro, Sidney A. 363–4, 367–8
Sherman Act 12, 113
Shipan, Charles R. 22
shirking 99, 227, 230–31
Shirley, C. 324
Simitis, S. 130–32
Singapore 91, 179–80
single market *see* European single market
Single Resolution Board 411
Single Supervisory Mechanism 103–4, 334, 404
Skidmore case 355, 357
Skype 158
Slaughter, A. M. 430
Slovakia 81, 91, 136–8, 140–41
Slovenia 91, 136–8
small and medium enterprises 305
Snowden revelations 128
Sobral, F. 54
social media 165–6, 287, 292, 297, 444
    see also individual platforms

social network analysis 229, 265–6, 428, 432, 434–5
social regulation 3–4, 14, 45, 50, 63, 117, 215, 219–20
South Africa 91
South Korea 90–91
sovereignty 31, 425
Spain 91, 116, 136–41, 147
Spence, David B. 22
Spiller, Pablo T. 66, 216
Sri Lanka 91
state aid 114, 121
State Farm case 349–53
state-led economies 34–5
state-owned enterprises 34, 113, 147–8, 152–3
Stern, Jon 216
Stigler, George 13–14, 365, 368
Stone Sweet, Alex 212
strategic communication 5, 227, 243, 273–80
strategic silence 276–7
Strauss, Peter L. 347
Sudan 91
superintendencias 44, 46
supervision 28–9, 43, 47–8, 80, 84, 103, 135, 137, 218, 231, 334, 339, 394, 399–400, 410–11, 414
supervisory authorities 11, 73, 128–43, 478, 489
Supreme Court 12–13, 15–16, 150, 315, 347–57
Sustainable Development Goals 310–11
Swarm City 445
Sweden 91, 129, 131–2, 136–41, 262–3
Swiss National Bank 104
Switzerland 91, 148, 231, 234, 262–3
Syria 91

Taiwan 91
Tanzania 91
Tarrant, Andrew 4, 37, 429
technical reputation 277
technocratic governance 28, 151, 233, 268, 348, 350, 352–3, 371, 436, 491, 495
Telecom Egypt 64
Telecom Italia 139
Telecom Regulatory Authority of India 1
Telecommunications Act 317
Telecommunications Corporation (Jordan) 64
Telecommunications Regulatory Authority (Egypt) 64
Telecommunications Regulatory Commission (Jordan) 64
Tetlock, Paul C. 21, 321
Tetra Laval case 335–6, 340
Thailand 184
Thatcher, Margaret 443
Thatcher, Mark 35, 212, 379, 429

think tanks 291, 309, 324
thinking fast and slow 460
Thurner, P. W. 430
time inconsistency 98–9, 116, 123, 214–15, 242,
    332, 489
Tiner, John 451
Tirole, Jean 364, 367
toeslagenaffaire 470–71, 480–81
Tomić, S. 185
'too big to fail' 101
Trademark and Designs Office 30
Transatlantic Trade and Investment Partnership
    436
transgovernmental networks 261, 425–7, 430,
    435–6
transnational networks 236, 261, 266–7, 431, 433,
    435–6
Trans-Pacific Partnership 436
transparency 23, 32, 55, 62, 66, 130, 162, 168,
    180, 185, 213, 257, 292, 297, 307, 319,
    349, 368, 399, 436, 441–2, 477–81
Transparency International 178
Treaty of Lisbon 29, 133
Treaty of Rome 151
Trillas, Francesc 53, 216
Trondal, J. 427
Trump, Donald 234, 323, 436
trustworthiness 166–7, 170, 236, 303–4
Tunisia 64, 66, 72, 91
Turkey 52, 90–91, 155
Tversky, A. 459

Uber 141, 159
Uganda 90
Ukraine 91
Unfunded Mandates Reform Act 321
unintended consequences 170, 364, 380, 389, 466
United Arab Emirates 63–4, 91
United Kingdom 34, 78, 81, 90–91, 113, 116,
    128–9, 132, 136–41, 147, 155, 163, 211,
    216, 233, 242, 246, 248, 262–3, 305–7,
    309–10, 335, 357, 364, 442, 451, 457–65
United Nations Conference on Trade and
    Development 119, 214
United Nations Convention Against Corruption
    178, 180
United Nations Development Programme 178
United States 1–5, 10–23, 43–5, 78, 91, 100,
    105, 113, 115, 120–22, 128–32, 140–43,
    146–56, 159, 211, 232, 234, 243, 275,
    314–27, 346–57, 365, 370, 396, 442, 447,
    457, 470, 474–5, 480, 492
United States Postal Service 148
Url, Bernhard 487
Urueña, R. 55

Uruguay 46–7, 49, 87, 91
US Agency for International Development 64–5
US National Research Council 162
utilities 2–3, 29–30, 44–8, 50–53, 55–6, 65, 83–4,
    88, 117, 134, 146–55, 182, 211, 215–17,
    249, 316–17, 324, 366, 399, 442
    see also network industries
Uzbekistan 91

van der Heijden, Machiel 5
Van Doorslaer, H. 106
van Erp, J. 403–4
van Kreij, L. 404
van Loo, R. 399
Vantaggiatto, F. P. 428, 434
Venezuela 43, 45, 47, 49, 52–3, 91
Verhoest, K. 53
Vermeiren, M. 106
Versluis, E. 404
Vervaele, J. 396, 399
veto players 35, 51, 92, 99, 117, 184, 187, 219,
    234, 242, 420
Vietnam 91
Vinson, Lindsey 357
visibility problem 447
Voigt, Stefan 118–19
von der Leyden Commission 303, 307, 309–10
Vranaki, A. 130

Wagner, Wendy E. 364, 367
Wallsten, Scott J. 216
Walters, Daniel E. 383, 385
Washington Consensus 51
Wassum, Moritz 35
Water Quality Act (1965) 14
Watts, Kathryn A. 353
Waverman, Leonard 216
Wavre, V. 64
Wegrich, Kai 5
Weiss, Carol H. 492–3
welfare state 113, 242, 245, 441–4, 448–52
West, William F. 385
WhatsApp 133, 139–42, 158
wicked problems 186, 475
Wiener, Jonathan Baert 387
Wilks, Stephen 379
Wilson, J. Q. 245, 247
Winston, C. 324
Winter, S. C. 403
World Bank 51, 66, 68–9, 72, 150
World Health Organization 425, 492
Wren-Lewis, L. 52

Yellen, Janet 100
Yemen 90–91

Yesilkagit, Kutsal 5
Yosifon, David 368

Zalm, Gerrit 306
Zambia 91

zealotry 185
Zeitlin, Jonathan 120
Zhang, Yin-Fang 217
Zhelyazkova, A. 404
Zimbabwe 91